Agricultural Development in the Third World

Agricultural Development in the Third World

SECOND EDITION

Edited by
Carl K. Eicher & John M. Staatz

THE JOHNS HOPKINS UNIVERSITY PRESS

Baltimore and London

© 1984, 1990 The Johns Hopkins University Press
All rights reserved
Printed in the United States of America

The Johns Hopkins University Press
701 West 40th Street
Baltimore, Maryland 21211
The Johns Hopkins Press Ltd., London

The paper used in this book meets the minimum requirements of
American National Standard for Information Sciences—
Permanence of Paper for Printed Library Materials,
ANSI Z39.48-1984.

Library of Congress Cataloging-in-Publication Data

Agricultural development in the Third World / edited by
    Carl K. Eicher and John M. Staatz.—2nd ed.
p.   cm.—(The Johns Hopkins studies in development)
    Includes bibliographical references.
ISBN 0-8018-3999-8 (alk. paper).—ISBN 0-8018-4000-7
    (pbk.: alk. paper)
1. Agriculture—Economic aspects—Developing countries.
2. Agriculture—Developing countries.   I. Eicher, Carl K.
    II. Staatz, John M.   III. Series.
        HD1417.A4483   1990
    338.1′09172′4—dc20   90-31729   CIP

Contents

Part IV
TRANSFORMING AGRICULTURE AND THE RURAL ECONOMY

Preface

The first edition of this book was published in 1984; it grew out of a graduate-level course on the economics of agricultural development that we teach at Michigan State University. In course preparation we had been struck by the cumulative knowledge that economists and agricultural scientists had gained during the previous twenty-five years about the complexity and diversity of agriculture in the Third World, its interrelationships with other sectors, and its potential roles in the structural transformation of Third World economies. As a result of this new knowledge, many of the economic growth models of the 1960s seemed remarkably unsophisticated.

Despite this increased knowledge, students in both industrial and Third World countries had not had a text that pulled together different views about what had been learned theoretically and empirically about the agricultural development process since the early 1970s. Although single-author texts are invaluable in developing and testing models of agricultural development, by their very nature they cannot reflect the diversity of opinion about alternative policies and strategies to further the development of agriculture in the Third World. This book includes articles and original essays by leading scholars on the theory and practice of agricultural development.

This second edition includes twenty new chapters while retaining twelve key contributions from the first edition, providing a perspective on the role of agriculture in economic development in the early 1990s. The essays address the two basic questions about Third World agriculture: what are the strategic roles of agriculture in national development strategies, and how can the agrarian transformation be accelerated? The articles thus focus on how agriculture interacts with the rest of the economy as well as on the mechanisms of agricultural growth itself.

Guided by favorable feedback from teachers and students, we have retained the five hallmarks of the first edition: (1) an introductory chapter that provides a framework for the book and traces the evolution of the field of agricultural development from the 1950s through the 1980s, (2) introductory comments for each section to help the reader focus on the key issues in each chapter and to serve as a guide to the broader literature, (3) a treatment of both the theory and the practice of agricultural development, (4) analysis of both macro- and microeconomic aspects of agriculture and the food system, and (5) a blend of recent empirical findings and policy analysis.

This new edition has been extensively revised to reflect the increasing diversity of Third World agriculture and the new directions in development policy and analysis that are emerging in the 1990s. This edition puts much greater emphasis, for example, on the role of and effect on agriculture of macroeconomic policies and structural adjustment and on the increasing importance of food security as a central component of development strategies. The second edition also includes contributions that fill some notable gaps in the first edition, such as the role of women in development and agricultural development strategies in centrally planned economies. The latter seem particularly germane given the momentous changes in Eastern Europe and the Soviet Union.

This book is designed to be used as a text in beginning graduate courses in international agricultural development and as a supplementary text in general economic development courses. Space constraints prevented our addressing specifically a larger number of topics in agricultural development. For example, there are no articles dealing exclusively with such topics as agricultural extension, marketing, agricultural planning, rural labor markets, nutrition or biotechnology. We have, however, included extensive references in chapter 1 and in the introductions to parts II–IV to the vast literature on agricultural development.

We are grateful to the authors of the chapters on women and agricultural development (chapter 17), the Soviet Union (chapter 29), and China (chapter 30) for preparing original essays and to those who revised unpublished papers and updated published essays. We want to thank numerous colleagues and students at Michigan State University and other universities, foundations, and international development agencies for their counsel on this edition. Our ideas on food security have been greatly affected by work that we and our colleagues at Michigan State and at several African research institutions have been conducting since 1984, under the USAID-funded Food Security in Africa Cooperative Agreement. Our task in compiling the new edition has been immensely facilitated by the efficient library service of Daniel Karanja and Lisa Schwartz and the adept typing of Sherry Rich, Eleanor Noonan, and Beryl Watters. We are also grateful to the staff at the Johns Hopkins University Press, including Anne Whitmore, for her skillful copyediting, and Anders Richter and Henry Tom, for guiding the book through publication.

I
Overview

1

Agricultural Development Ideas in Historical Perspective

JOHN M. STAATZ and CARL K. EICHER

Although economists have been concerned with growth and development since at least the time of the mercantilists, development economics has existed as a separate branch of economics only since about 1950. The history of the field can be divided roughly into three periods: the economic-growth-and-modernization era of the 1950s and 1960s, when development was defined largely in terms of growth in average per capita output; the growth-with-equity period since around 1970, when the concern of most development economists broadened to include income distribution, employment, and nutrition; and the economic growth and policy reform period of the 1980s. The prevailing view of agriculture's role in development changed profoundly during these three periods.[1]

In this chapter we will outline the changing view of agriculture in economic development since 1950 and place the readings in this volume in historical perspective. In the first section we will briefly discuss the evolution of agricultural development theory and practice during the growth-and-modernization era of the fifties and sixties. We will examine the relatively passive role assigned to agriculture in the economic growth models of the 1950s, the increasing recognition of the interdependence between agricultural and industrial growth during the 1960s, the lessons learned from the agricultural development experience of the 1950s and 1960s, and the contribution of radical and dependency scholars to an improved understanding of the process of agricultural and rural development. In the next section we will discuss the increased emphasis given to agricultural and rural development during the growth-with-equity period that began around 1970. During this period there was a sharp increase in microeconomic research on agricultural production and marketing, intersectoral linkages, rural factor markets, migration, and rural small-scale industry and a policy shift to integrated rural development and basic needs programs. Beginning in the early 1980s, the focus of agricultural development shifted to an analysis of the impact of structural adjustment on agri-

JOHN M. STAATZ is associate professor and CARL K. EICHER is professor of agricultural economics, Michigan State University.

3

culture, food policy analysis, food security, and market reform. Finally, we will outline the plan of this volume, placing the readings in the context of the theoretical and policy debates discussed in the first two sections.

THE ROLE OF AGRICULTURE IN DEVELOPMENT ECONOMICS, 1950–69

WESTERN DEVELOPMENT ECONOMISTS' PERSPECTIVES ON AGRICULTURE

Most Western development economists of the 1950s did not view agriculture as an important contributor to economic growth.[2] As I. M. D. Little comments in his survey of development economics, "It is fairly obvious from reading their works that the leading development economists of the 1950s knew little about tropical agriculture or rural life. They had no time for rural rides and there was no considerable body of empirical grassroots literature on which they could draw" (Little 1982, 106). Development was often equated with the structural transformation of the economy, that is, with the decline in agriculture's relative share of the national product and of the labor force. The role of development economics was seen as facilitating that transformation by discovering ways to transfer resources, especially labor, from traditional agriculture to industry, the presumed engine of growth. Agriculture itself was often treated as a "black box from which people, and food to feed them, and perhaps capital could be released" (ibid., 105).

Development economics throughout the 1950s and 1960s was strongly influenced by W. Arthur Lewis's 1954 article "Economic Development with Unlimited Supplies of Labour." Seldom has a single article been so instrumental in shaping the work of an entire subdiscipline of economics. In the article, Lewis presented a general equilibrium model of expansion in an economy with two sectors—a modern capitalist exchange sector and an indigenous noncapitalist sector, which was dominated by subsistence farming.[3] The distinguishing characteristics of the capitalist sector were its use of reproducible capital, its hiring of labor, and its sale of output for profit. "Capitalist" enterprises could be owned privately or by the state. The subsistence sector was pictured as the "self-employment sector," which did not hire labor or use reproducible capital. Lewis's model focused on how the transfer of labor from the subsistence sector (where the marginal productivity of a laborer approached zero as a limiting case) to the capitalist sector facilitated capitalist expansion through reinvestment of profits. The labor supply facing the capitalist sector was " 'unlimited' in the sense that when the capitalist sector offers additional employment opportunities at the existing wage rate, the numbers willing to work at the existing wage rate will be greater than the demand: the supply curve of labor is infinitely elastic at the ruling wage" (Meier 1976, 158). In Lewis's model, expansion in the capitalist sector continued until earnings in the two sectors were equated, at which point a dual-sector model was no longer relevant; growth proceeded as in a one-sector neoclassical model. Lewis's analysis was later extended by Ranis and Fei (1961, 1963, 1964) and Jorgenson (1961).

Lewis pointed out that the capitalist sector did not need to be industry (it could be mining or plantations) and that the noncapitalist sector could include handicrafts. Most analysts, however, equated the capitalist sector with industry and the noncapitalist sector with traditional agriculture and argued that "surplus" labor and other resources should be transferred from agriculture to industry in order to promote growth.[4] Many development economists conlcuded that since economic growth facilitated the structural transformation of the economy in the *long run,* the rapid transfer of resources (especially "surplus" labor) from agriculture to industry was an appropriate *short-run* economic development strategy.[5] But Johnston observed that "this preoccupation with 'surplus labor' often seems to have encouraged neglect of the agricultural sector as well as a tendency to assume too readily that a surplus can and should be extracted from agriculture, while neglecting the difficult requirements that must be met if agriculture is to play a positive role in facilitating overall economic growth" (Johnston 1970, 378). The propensity of development economists to give relatively little attention to agriculture's potential "positive role in facilitating overall economic growth" was based in part on the empirical observation that agriculture's share of the economy inevitably declines during the course of development for at least two reasons. First, the income elasticity of demand for unprocessed food is less than unity and declines with higher incomes; hence, the demand for raw agricultural products grows more slowly than consumption in general. Second, increasing labor productivity in agriculture means that the same farm output can be produced with fewer workers, implying a transfer of labor to other sectors of the economy.[6] Because agriculture's share of the economy was assumed to be declining, many economists downplayed the need to invest in the agricultural sector in the short run.

The relative neglect of agriculture in the 1950s was reinforced by two other developments. In 1949, Raul Prebisch and Hans Singer independently formulated the thesis that there is a secular tendency for the terms of trade to turn against countries that export primary products and import manufactures.[7] From this they concluded that the scope for growth through agricultural and other primary exports was very limited. Prebisch and his colleagues at the United Nations Economic Commission for Latin America (ECLA) therefore advocated that priority be given to import substitution of manufactured goods rather than to production of agricultural exports.[8] The "secular-decline hypothesis" became an article of faith for some development economists and planners, and thus the tendency to downplay agriculture's potential role in development was reinforced.

The second important event affecting development economists' view of agriculture was the publication of Albert Hirschman's influential book *The Strategy of Economic Development* (1958). In this book, Hirschman introduced the concept of linkages as a tool for investigating how, during the course of development, investment in one type of economic activity induced subsequent investment in other income-generating activities. Hirschman defined the linkage effects of a given product line as the "investment-generating forces that are set in motion, through input-output relations, when productive facilities that supply inputs to that line or utilize its output are inadequate or non-existent. Backward linkages lead to new investment in input-supplying facilities and forward linkages to investment in output-using facilities" (Hirschman 1977, 72). Hirschman argued that government investment should be concentrated in activities where the linkage effects were greatest, since this would maximize indigenous investment in related, or "linked," industries. Hirschman asserted that "agriculture certainly stands convicted on the count of its lack of direct stimulus to the setting up of new activities through linkage effects—the superiority of manufacturing in this respect is crushing" (Hirschman 1958, 109–10). Therefore, Hirschman argued, investment in industry would generally lead to more rapid and more broadly based economic growth than would investment in agriculture. Hirschman's analysis thus reinforced ECLA's policy recommendation that priority be given to import substitution of manufactures.

Ironically, Lewis's two-sector growth model, which led many development economists to focus heavily on the role of industry in economic development, in the early 1960s led others to stress the interdependence between agricultural and industrial growth. In an article comparing a Lewis-type "classical" model with a neoclassical growth model, Jorgenson (1961) argued that growth in nonfarm employment depended on the rate of growth of the agricultural surplus. Jorgenson's analysis and similar analyses by Ranis and Fei (1961, 1963, 1964) and Enke (1962a, 1962b) showed that food shortages could choke off growth in the nonfarm sector by making its labor supply less than infinitely elastic. These authors therefore concluded that in order to avoid falling into a low-level equilibrium trap, in the early stages of development a country probably needed to make some net investment in agriculture to accelerate the growth of its agricultural surplus.

Many agricultural economists found it "shocking . . . that general economists such as Jorgenson and Enke . . . felt it necessary to argue the case for *some* investment in agriculture" (Johnston 1970, 378). In a seminal article entitled "The Role of Agriculture in Economic Development" (1961), Johnston and Mellor drew on insights from the Lewis model to stress the importance of agriculture as a motive force in economic growth. They argued that far from playing a passive role in development, agriculture could make five important contributions to the structural transformation of Third World economies: it could provide labor, capital, foreign exchange, and food to a growing industrial sector and could supply a market for domestically produced industrial goods. They argued further that the nature of the interrelationships between agriculture and industry at various stages of development had important implications for the types of agricultural and industrialization strategies that would be most likely to succeed.

Johnston and Mellor's article and William H. Nicholls's influential article "The Place of Agriculture in Economic Development" (1964) were instrumental in encouraging economists to view agriculture as a potential positive force in development, and they helped to stimulate debate on the interdependence of agricultural and industrial growth. This in turn led to a growing interest in the empirical measurement of intersectoral resource transfers during the course of development.[9]

The work of neoclassical agricultural economists during the 1960s stressed not only the interdependence of agriculture and industry and the potentially important role that agriculture could play in economic development but also the importance of understanding the process of agricultural growth per se if that potential was to be exploited.[10] The need for a better understanding of the process of agricultural growth was further emphasized by some of the agricultural development experiences of the 1950s and early 1960s.

THE INFLUENCE OF THE AGRICULTURAL DEVELOPMENT PROGRAMS OF THE 1950S AND 1960S ON WESTERN DEVELOPMENT THOUGHT

Debates among Western economists about the role of agriculture in development did not take place in a vacuum; they were strongly influenced by the rural development experiences of Third World nations. Indeed, an important characteristic of the literature on agricultural development since the 1950s has been its movement from a priori theorizing towards empirical research.

Despite the emphasis that development economists placed on industrialization during the 1950s, governments of many low-income countries and donor agencies undertook a number of activities aimed at increasing agricultural output and rural incomes. The experience gained in these efforts was important in developing a better understanding of intersectoral relationships and the constraints on agricultural growth.

During the 1950s the approach of European and North American agricultural economists to development was colored by the historical experiences of their own countries and by their training in the then-current theories of development economics. For example, most Western agricultural economists working on problems of Third World agriculture during this period believed that the problem of rural surplus labor could be resolved by transferring "excess" rural workers to urban industry.[11] It was also widely assumed that Western agricultural advisers could directly transfer agricultural technology and models of agricultural extension from high-income countries to the Third World, that community development programs could help rural people overcome the shackles of traditional farming and inequitable land tenure systems, and that food aid could serve humanitarian needs and provide jobs for rural people.

Agricultural development efforts of the 1950s placed heavy emphasis on the direct transfer of agricultural technology from high-income countries to the Third World and the promotion of the American model of agricultural extension. These efforts were based on what Vernon Ruttan calls the "diffusion model" of agricultural development (see chapter 4). The diffusion model assumed that Third World farmers could substantially increase their agricultural productivity by allocating existing resources more efficiently and by adopting agricultural practices and technologies from the industrial countries.

Like the diffusion model, the community development effort of the 1950s and early 1960s (Holdcroft, 1984) assumed that small farmers were often poor decision makers who required outside assistance in planning local development projects (Stevens 1977b, 5). Community development grew out of the Cold War atmosphere of the 1950s, when Western foreign assistance programs were searching for a non-revolutionary approach to rural change. Community development advocates assumed that villagers, meeting with community development specialists, would express their "felt needs" and unite to design and implement self-help programs aimed at promoting rural development. The community development effort also implicitly assumed that rural development could be achieved through the direct transfer of Western agricultural technologies and social institutions, such as local democracy, to the rural areas of the Third World.[12]

The failure of many agricultural extension programs to achieve rapid increases in agricultural output and the inability of community development projects to solve the basic food problem in many countries (particularly India in the mid-1950s) led to a reevaluation of the diffusion model of agricultural development. Two elements were critical in this reappraisal. First, it became apparent that in many countries there were important structural barriers in rural development, such as highly concentrated political power and asset ownership. The research by economists such as Warriner (1955), Ladejinsky (see Walinsky 1977), Carroll (1961), Raup (1967), and Barraclough (1973) on land tenure and land reform in Asia, North Africa, and Latin America documented how institutional barriers inhibited the expansion of agricultural output. These authors argued that in some countries basic institutional reforms were prerequisites to effective agricultural extension and community development.[13]

The second element leading to a reevaluation of the diffusion model was research by scholars such as Jones (1960), Krishna (1967), and Behrman (1968) that documented the responsiveness of Third World farmers and consumers to economic incentives and helped to demolish the myth of the "tradition-bound peasant." The findings of these studies suggested that if farmers were not responsive to agricultural extension efforts, perhaps it was because extension workers had few profitable innovations to extend. This viewpoint was advanced most forcefully in T. W. Schultz's highly influential book *Transforming Traditional Agriculture* (1964).

As Ruttan points out in chapter 4, Schultz's book was iconoclastic at the time. Schultz argued that Third World farmers and herders, far from being irrational and fatalistic, were calculating economic agents who carefully weighed the marginal costs and benefits associated with different agricultural techniques. Through a long process of experimentation, these farmers had learned how to allocate efficiently the factors of production available to them, given existing technology. This implied that "no appreciable increase in agricultural production is to be had by reallocating the factors at the disposal of farmers who are bound by traditional agriculture. . . . An outside expert, however skilled he may be in farm management, will not discover any major inefficiency in the allocation of factors" (39).

Schultz's argument that despite low levels of per capita output, traditional agriculture was characterized by allocative efficiency became known as the "efficient-but-poor hypothesis."[14] Citing evidence from Guatemala (Tax [1953] 1963) and India (summarized in Hopper 1965) to support this hypothesis, Schultz argued that major increases in per capita agricultural output in the Third World would come about only if farmers were provided new, more productive factors of production (that is, new agricultural technologies) and the new skills needed to exploit them. The cause of rural poverty, in other words, lay in the lack of profitable technical packages for Third World farmers and the lack of investment in human capital needed to cope with rapidly changing agricultural technologies. Schultz later attributed the low levels of investment in agricultural research and rural education in most Third World countries to national policies that undervalued agriculture (Schultz 1978, 1981).

Transforming Traditional Agriculture called for a major shift from agricultural extension towards investment in agricultural research and human capital. The book, which appeared five years after the establishment of the International Rice Research Institute (IRRI) in the Philippines and one year after the establishment of the International Center for Maize and Wheat Improvement (CIMMYT) in Mexico, reinforced the increasing emphasis being given to agricultural research by the Rockefeller and Ford foundations and other donors in the 1960s. As a result of IRRI's and CIMMYT's success in developing high-yielding dwarf varieties of rice and wheat, which were rapidly adopted in many areas of the Third World during the 1960s, the "Green Revolution," or high-payoff input model, replaced the diffusion/community development model as the dominant agricultural development model for field practitioners.[15]

The appearance of the high-yielding grain varieties had important effects on the theory as well as on the practice of agricultural development. Several authors, such as Ohkawa (1964), Mellor (1966), and Ohkawa and Johnston (1969), noted that the new grain/fertilizer technologies were highly divisible and scale-neutral, allowing them to be incorporated into existing systems of small-scale agriculture. Therefore, these authors argued, intensification of agricultural production based on high-yielding cereal varieties offered the opportunity to provide productive employment for the rapidly growing rural labor force while at the same time it produced the wage goods needed for an expanding industrial labor force. The high-yielding varieties, it was argued, made it possible to achieve both employment and output objectives.[16]

The early enthusiasm for the Green Revolution was met by a barrage of criticism by Frankel (1971), Griffin (1974), and others. These authors argued that the new varieties often benefited mainly landlords and larger farmers in ecologically favored areas, while they frequently impoverished small farmers and tenants, particularly those in upland areas, by inducing lower grain prices and evictions from the land as landlords found it profitable to farm the land themselves using mechanization (see Hayami, chapter 26).

Although some authors, such as Lester Brown (1970), did tend to oversell the accomplishments of the Green Revolution, in Asia the impact of the new varieties was substantial. They have had a smaller effect in Latin America, however, where a high percentage of small farmers live in poor natural resource zones (Piñeiro, Trigo, and Fiorentino 1979), and they have had little impact in sub-Saharan Africa (see Eicher, chapter 31). Overall, high-yielding wheat and rice varieties accounted for about 40 to 50 million tons of additional grain each year in the Third World (Lipton 1989).

In chapters 25 and 26, Scobie, Posada, and Hayami evaluate some of the income-distribution effects of the new varieties. These authors find that *within* villages there has been little difference between small farmers' and large farmers' rates of adoption of the modern varieties. Farmers in upland areas, however, may have been hurt relative to farmers in irrigated areas because the new varieties are more suited to irrigated conditions. Low-income consumers, who spend a high proportion of their income on foodgrains, have been major beneficiaries of the larger harvests and lower prices made possible by the Green Revolution. One of the important lessons of the last few decades is that with rising population pressure on land throughout the Third World, technological change must be included as a central component in both the theory and the practice of agricultural and rural development.

RADICAL POLITICAL ECONOMY AND DEPENDENCY PERSPECTIVES ON AGRICULTURE

Western development economics was challenged in the 1960s and 1970s by the emergence and rapid growth of radical political economy and dependency models of development and underdevelopment. The radical political economy models have their roots in the writings of Lenin on imperialism and Kautsky on agriculture and in the post–World War II writings of Paul Baran and other Marxist economists. Baran, in an important article entitled "On the Political Economy of Backwardness" (1952), argued that in most low-income countries it would be impossible to bring about broad-based capitalist development without violent changes in social and political institutions. Although Baran was clearly ahead of his time in identifying institutional and structural barriers to development and the need to put effective demand at the center of development programs, he tended, as did many of the Western development economists he was criticizing, to see small-scale agriculture as incapable of making major contributions to economic growth. For example, Baran accepted the view that the marginal product of labor often approached zero in agriculture and that therefore "there is no way of employing it [labor] usefully in agriculture." Farmers "could only be provided with opportunities for productive work by transfer to industry." Baran, like many economists of the time, believed that "very few improvements that would be necessary in order to increase productivity can be carried out within the narrow confines of small-peasant holdings" and that therefore farm consolidation was necessary.

Marxist analysis of agricultural and rural development was further advanced in the 1950s and 1960s by several Latin American scholars, who often blended

Marxian analyses with dependency theory.[17] The dependency interpretation of underdevelopment was first proposed in the 1950s by the Economic Commission for Latin America, under the leadership of Raul Prebisch. The basic hypothesis of this perspective is that underdevelopment is not a stage of development but the result of the expansion of the world capitalist system. Underdevelopment, in other words, is not simply the lack of development; it is a condition of impoverishment brought about by the integration of Third World economies into the world capitalist system. Although a number of different views of dependency have been put forward by scholars such as Sunkel (1973), Furtado (1973), Frank (1966), Galtung (1971), and others, the following definition of dependency by Dos Santos has been widely cited: "By dependency we mean a situation in which the economy of certain countries is conditioned by the development and expansion of another economy to which the former is subjected" (1970, 231).[18]

Dependency theorists implicitly argued that trade was often a zero-sum game—that low-income countries ("the periphery") were pauperized through both a process of unequal exchange with the industrialized world ("the center") and repatriation of profits from foreign-owned businesses. Capitalist growth in the periphery was not self-sustaining; it was stunted by policies favoring import substitution of luxury goods and export of agroindustrial products, often produced on large estates. These policies limited the internal market for consumer goods (including food and other agricultural products) and led to impoverishment of the mass of small farmers. Meaningful reform was blocked by an alliance of the landed elite, local bourgeoisie, and multinational firms, all of which benefited from the dependency relationship.

Various theories of unequal exchange played important roles in dependency theory. Marxist economists, such as Emmanuel (1972), argued that unequal exchange between industrialized and Third World countries resulted from the maintenance of precapitalist relations of production in the Third World, which depressed wage rates, and the use of monopoly power by industrialized nations to turn the terms of trade against the Third World. Changes in the social relations of production in low-income countries and the organization of cartels by Third World exporters were therefore necessary to obtain countervailing power in international markets. Many non-Marxist economists, such as Singer and Prebisch, believed that unequal exchange was a logical consequence of the demand characteristics of the primary products exported by Third World countries and the noncompetitive labor markets in high-income countries, which tended to raise the price of manufactures. In these authors' view, import substitution and a shift to exports of manufactures represented ways of combatting unequal exchange. In contrast, Lewis (1978) developed a theory of unequal exchange based on a simple two-country, three-good Ricardian trade model in which food is produced in both countries and serves as the numeraire to establish the commodity terms of trade between countries. Lewis used this model to argue that unequal exchange resulted from the failure of Third World countries to invest adequately in domestic food production. If low-income countries attempted to shift from exporting primary products to exporting manufactures without improving domestic food production, they would simply "exchange one dependence for another" (70).

In the 1960s, dependency theory was imported into Africa from Latin America. Since the mid-1960s Samir Amin has provided leadership in developing a Marxist version of dependency theory. In *Accumulation on a World Scale* (1974) and *Unequal Development* (1976) Amin presents an analytical framework of underdevelopment in Africa based on surplus extraction and the domination of the world capitalist system. Amin has provided valuable insights into the development process, but his prescriptions for African agriculture have vacillated over time. During the 1960s Amin favored animal traction, promoted industrial crops, and argued that traditional social values were a serious constraint on development at the village level. He also argued that the transition to privately owned small farms was a precondition for socialism (Amin 1965, 210–11, 231). By the early 1970s Amin had reversed himself and recommended the collectivization of agricultural production, and he abandoned his support for animal traction and industrial crops (Amin 1971, 231; 1973, 56).

These criticisms notwithstanding, the radical scholars made several important contributions to the understanding of agriculture and rural development. First, they helped demolish the myth of "a typical underdeveloped country" by stressing that each country's economic development had to be understood in the context of that country's historical experience. For example, they argued that Schultz's concept of "traditional agriculture"—a situation where farmers have settled into a low-level equilibrium after years of facing static technology and factor prices—abstracted from the historical process of integration of individual Third World economies into the world capitalist system and therefore was not a very useful analytical concept. Second, in arguing that rural poverty in the Third World resulted from the functioning of the global capitalist economy, the radical writers focused attention on the relationships between villagers and the wider economic system. Unlike Schultz, who attributed rural poverty to the lack of productive agricultural technologies and human capital, radical scholars stressed the importance of the linkages and exchange arrangements that tied villages to the rest of the economy. Third, the radical economists directly attacked what Hirschman (1981a, 3) has called the "mutual benefit claim" of development economics—the assertion that economic relations between high- and low-income countries (and among groups within low-income countries) could be shaped in a way to yield benefits for all. In disputing this claim, the radical scholars stressed that economic development was more than just a technocratic matter of determining how best to raise per capita GNP. Development involved restructuring institutional and political relationships, and the radicals urged neoclassical economists to include these political considerations explicitly in their analyses. In de Janvry's words, "Economic policy without political economy is a useless and utopian exercise" (1981, 263).

Both the radical analyses and the Western dual-sector models of the 1960s suffered from some of the same shortcomings—abstract theorizing, inadequate attention to the need for technical change in agriculture, lack of attention to the biological and location-specific nature of agricultural production processes, and lack of a solid micro foundation based on empirical research at the farm and village level. Recognition of some of these shortcomings was an important element leading to a reevaluation of the goals and approaches of development economics and of the role of agriculture in reaching those goals in the period following 1970.

THE GROWTH-WITH-EQUITY ERA SINCE 1970

THE BROADENING OF DEVELOPMENT GOALS

Around 1970 mainstream Western development economics began to give greater attention to employment and the distribution of real income, broadly defined. This shift in emphasis came about for at least three reasons. The first was ideological, a response to the radical critique of Western development economics, especially the critique of the "mutual benefit claim" discussed above. The goal of economic growth for Third World countries was seriously questioned by this critique, and some development economists may have felt the need to redefine the goals of development more broadly in order to preserve the legitimacy of their subdiscipline.

Second, from the 1960s onwards it became apparent that rapid economic growth in some countries, such as Pakistan, Nigeria, and Iran, had deleterious, and in some cases disastrous, side effects. Hirschman (1981a, 20–21) argues that development economists were forced to reevaluate the goals of their profession because

the series of political disasters that struck a number of Third World countries from the sixties on . . . were clearly *somehow* connected with the stresses and strains accompanying development and "modernization." These development disasters, ranging from civil wars to the establishment of murderous authoritarian regimes, could not but give pause to a group of social scientists who, after all, had taken up the cultivation of development economics in the wake of World War II not as narrow specialists, but impelled by the vision of a better world. As liberals, most of them presumed that "all good things go together" and took it for granted that if only a good job could be done in raising the national income of the countries concerned, a number of beneficial effects would follow in the social, political, and cultural realms.

When it turned out instead that the promotion of economic growth entailed not infrequently a sequence of events involving serious retrogression in those other areas, including the wholesale loss of civil and human rights, the easy self-confidence that our subdiscipline exuded in its early stages was impaired.

The third reason for the reevaluation of development goals was a growing awareness among development economists that even in countries where rapid economic growth had not contributed to social turmoil, the benefits of economic growth often were not trickling down to the poor and that frequently the income gap between rich and poor was widening (see, for example, Fishlow 1972; Nugent and Yotopoulos 1979; and Streeten 1979). Even where the incomes of the poor were rising, often they were rising so slowly that the poor would not be able to afford decent diets or housing for at least another generation.

Rather than simply waiting for increases in average per capita incomes to "solve" the problems of poverty and malnutrition, economists, political leaders in the Third World, and the leaders of major donor agencies argued in the early 1970s that greater explicit attention needed to be paid to employment, income distribution, and "basic needs," such as nutrition and housing. For example, Robert McNamara, then president of the World Bank, called on the Bank to redirect its activities towards helping people in the bottom 40 percent of the income distribution in low-income countries (McNamara 1973).

These growth-with-equity concerns stimulated a number of important theoretical and policy debates during the 1970s. The first debate concerned the interactions between income distribution and rates of economic growth. A number of economists during the 1970s included income distribution explicitly in their frameworks of analysis, and several examined the interdependence between income growth, income distribution, and other development goals, such as literacy and health.[19] These analyses focused on changes not only in the *size* distribution of income during the course of development (for example, Chenery et al. 1974; Adelman and Morris 1973) but in the *functional* distribution as well. For example, attention was given to the impact of economic growth on small farmers (Stevens 1977a; Fei, Ranis, and Kuo 1979) and on women (Boserup 1970; Tinker and Bramsen 1976; Spencer 1976).

A second debate centered on employment generation and the possible existence of employment-output trade-offs in industry and agriculture. Although Dovring (1959) had shown that the absolute number of people engaged in agriculture in developing countries would probably continue to grow for several decades, most economists during the 1960s still assumed that urban industry would absorb most of the new entrants to the labor force. By 1970, however, it had become apparent that urban industry in most countries could not expand quickly enough in the short run to provide employment for the expanding rural labor force. Hence, the concern of development planners shifted to finding ways to hold people in the countryside (Eicher et al. 1970).

The concern about creating rural jobs raised a number of questions in both agriculture and industry about the relative output and employment-generation capacities of large and small enterprises. In agriculture, debate centered on how much emphasis should be given to improving small farms as opposed to creating larger and more capital-intensive farms, ranches, and plantations. Empirical evidence from the late 1960s and early 1970s revealed that the economies of size in tropical agriculture were more limited than previously believed and that the improvement of small farms often resulted in greater output *and* employment per hectare than did large-scale farming. In industry, the small-versus-large debate led to a number of empirical studies of rural small-scale enterprises (these are reviewed by Chuta and Liedholm in chapter 19). In both agriculture and industry the concern with possible employment-output trade-offs also stimulated research on the choice of appropriate production techniques (see chapters 18 and 19 and the introduction to part IV of this volume).

During the 1970s economists and planners also began to give explicit consideration to the impact of development programs on nutrition. Empirical studies revealed that increases in average per capita income did not always lead to improved nutrition and that at times malnutrition actually increased with growing incomes (Berg 1973; Reutlinger and Selowsky 1976). Therefore, many analysts argued that nutrition projects, targeted to the poor and malnourished, were needed to supplement other development activities.[20]

IMPLICATIONS FOR AGRICULTURE

The change in orientation of development economics in the early 1970s implied a much greater role for agriculture in development programs. Because the majority of the poor in most Third World countries live in rural areas and because food prices are a major determinant of the real income of both the rural and the urban poor, the low productivity of Third World agriculture was seen as a major cause of poverty. Furthermore, because urban industry had generally provided few jobs for the rapidly growing labor force, development planners increasingly concentrated on ways to create productive employment in rural areas, if only as a holding action until the rate of population growth declined and urban industry could create more jobs. (Nonetheless, investment policies in many countries continued to favor urban areas [see Lipton 1977].) The need to create productive rural employment was underlined by a growing awareness of the increasing landlessness in many parts of the Third World, particularly South Asia (Singh 1988),[21] Latin America (de Janvry 1981), and a few countries in Africa (Ghai and Radwan 1983).

It soon became apparent that if agriculture were to play a more important role in development programs, policy makers would need a more detailed understanding of rural economies than that provided by the simple two-sector models of the 1950s and early 1960s. In the late 1960s and early 1970s there was a rapid expansion of micro-level research on agricultural production and marketing, farmer decision making, the performance of rural factor markets, and rural nonfarm employment.[22] This micro-level research documented the complexity of many Third World farming and marketing systems and complemented the macro-level work begun in the 1950s on modeling agricultural growth and intersectoral relationships.

RESEARCH FINDINGS OF THE 1970s

Modeling Agricultural Growth

As policy makers looked to agriculture to provide more employment and wage goods for the rapidly expanding labor force, attempts to model the process of agricultural growth assumed increased importance. Hayami and Ruttan's induced innovation model of agricultural development (discussed in the introduction to part II of this book and in chapters 4 and 5) was a major contribution of the 1970s. Hayami and Ruttan argued that there are multiple technological paths to agricultural growth, each embodying a different mix of factors of production, and that changes in relative factor prices can guide a country's researchers to select the most "efficient" path. This implied that countries with different factor endowments would have different efficient growth paths and that the wholesale importation of agricultural technology from industrialized countries to the Third World could lead to highly inefficient patterns of growth. Hayami and Ruttan argued that relative factor prices not only affected technological development but also often played an important role in guiding the design of social institutions.[23]

Other major efforts to model the process of agricultural growth included detailed agricultural sector analyses (such as Thorbecke and Stoutjesdijk 1971; and Mantesch et al. 1971); the work of Mellor and Johnston and Kilby, discussed below; and the attempt by some radical scholars, notably de Janvry (1981), to move from a purely global, abstract explanation of rural poverty to a neo-Marxist analysis on a micro level.

Intersectoral Relationships

The 1970s also witnessed a great expansion in the theoretical and empirical research begun by economists in the 1960s on the interdependence between agricultural and nonagricultural growth. Particularly noteworthy was the work of Mellor and of Johnston and Kilby (1975).[24] Mellor argued that it was possible to design employment-oriented strategies of development based on the potential growth linkages inherent in the new high-yielding grain varieties.[25] Mellor's analysis drew heavily on empirical evidence from India. Unlike the many authors who mainly stressed how the new varieties could increase total food supplies, Mellor emphasized that the new varieties could also raise the incomes of foodgrain producers, thereby generating increased effective demand for a wide variety of labor-intensive products. Indeed, Mellor saw most of the potential growth in employment that could result from the new varieties as lying outside the foodgrain sector itself, in sectors producing labor-intensive goods such as dairy products, fruit, other consumer products, and agricultural inputs. This expanded employment was made possible by the simultaneous increase in effective demand for these products and the increased supply of inexpensive wage goods in the form of foodgrains. Much of Mellor's analysis focused on the types of agricultural and industrial policies needed to exploit these growth linkages of the new grain varieties.

Johnston and Kilby analyzed "the reciprocal interactions between agricultural development and the expansion of manufacturing and other nonfarm sectors" (1975, xv). In particular, they focused on the factors affecting the rates of labor transfer between sectors and the level and composition of intersectoral commodity flows. Drawing on empirical evidence from England, the United States, Japan, Taiwan, Mexico, and the Soviet Union, Johnston and Kilby argued that the size distribution of farms was a critical determinant of the demand for industrial products in a developing economy. They showed that broad-based agricultural growth was more effective than estate production in stimulating the demand for industrial products and hence speeding the structural transformation of the economy. Johnston and Kilby's analysis strongly supported the view that concentrating agricultural development efforts on the mass of small farmers in low-income countries, rather than promoting a bimodal structure of small and large farms, would lead to faster growth rates of both aggregate economic output and employment.

Factor Markets and Employment Generation

Concern for creating jobs stimulated research during the 1970s on rural labor markets and employment. Krishna (1973) addressed the basic methodological problem of defining under- and unemployment in rural economies. Noting that most unemployment studies use definitions appropriate to industrial economies, Krishna identified four different criteria commonly used to classify people as under- or unemployed: (1) a time criterion, according to which a person is under-employed if he or she is gainfully occupied for less time than some full-employment standard; (2) an income criterion, by which an individual is under- or unemployed if he or she earns less than some desirable minimum; (3) a willingness criterion, which defines a person as under- or unemployed if he or she is willing to work longer hours at the prevailing wage; and (4) a productivity criterion, which defines a worker as unemployed if the worker's marginal product is zero. Krishna showed that different policy measures were appropriate for dealing with each type of underemployment.

During the 1970s several economists, particularly those associated with the International Labour Office (ILO), spoke of dethroning GNP as the target and indicator of development and replacing growth strategies with employment-oriented approaches (see, for example, Seers 1970). During the first half of the 1970s the ILO dispatched missions to Colombia, Sri Lanka, Kenya, the Philippines, and Sudan to draw up programs to expand employment (International Labour Office 1970, 1971, 1972, 1974, 1976b). The ILO missions "studied just about everything—population, education, income distribution, appropriate technology, multinationals" (Little 1982, 214), but they frequently lacked the detailed information needed to evaluate where and to what degree output-employment trade-offs existed in these countries. The impact of the ILO studies was further limited because research during the 1970s demonstrated that because 60–80 percent of the poor in most Third World countries were employed in some fashion, the critical policy issue was not one of creating jobs per se but one of increasing the productivity of workers already employed in small-scale agriculture and nonfarm enterprises. The ILO studies were, nonetheless, important in stimulating research on labor markets and on the impact of factor-price distortions on output and employment.

A large number of studies during the 1970s evaluating the performance of labor markets in low-income countries generally found that at peak periods of the agricultural cycle there was little unemployment in rural areas, while at other periods of the year there were labor surpluses. The studies also documented that earlier researchers frequently had overestimated the size of these surpluses because they had failed to take account of the considerable time devoted to rural nonfarm enterprises and to walking to and from fields. Studies also confirmed that labor markets in most countries were generally competitive, with wage rates, particularly in rural areas, following seasonal patterns of labor demand (see Berry and Sabot 1978).

The labor-market research also documented that when labor was misallocated, in many situations the missallocation was due not only to imperfections in labor markets but to poorly functioning markets for other factors of production as well. Overvalued exchange rates and subsidized credit, for example, often encouraged excessive substitution of capital for labor in low-wage economies. Concern about the impact of such factor-price distortions on output and employment stimulated research on the choice of technique in agricultural production and processing (see Timmer, chapter 18, and Byerlee et al. 1983) and on the functioning of rural financial markets in low-income countries (see Adams and Vogel, chapter 21).

In the late 1960s and early 1970s the concern for employment generation led to questions about the productivity and labor-absorption capacity of large farms and ranches versus those of small farms. A large number of scholars (for example, Dorner and Kanel 1971; Barraclough 1973; Berry 1975; and Berry and Cline 1979) documented the strong economic case for land reform in many Third World countries because of the higher employment and land productivity potential of small family farms. The higher land productivity was due largely to greater use of labor (mainly family labor) per unit of land. Although there was widespread agreement among these scholars that land reform was an attractive policy instrument for raising farm output, increasing rural employment, and improving the equality of income distribution, political support for land reform waned during the 1970s (as discussed by Binswanger and Elgin in chapter 20).

Rural-to-Urban Migration

Rural-to-urban migration was a major area of research during the 1960s and 1970s because the rate of rural-to-urban migration in most Third World countries far outstripped the rate of growth of urban employment. This led to rising levels of open urban unemployment. The concern of policy makers therefore quickly shifted from trying to transfer surplus labor from agriculture to industry to trying to reduce "excessive" rates of urbanization.

Research by economists on migration in the Third World was sparked by Michael Todaro's attempt in the late 1960s to explain the apparently paradoxical phenomenon of accelerating rural-to-urban migration in the context of continuously rising urban unemployment in Kenya. Todaro (1969) proposed a model (later extended by Harris and Todaro 1970) in which a potential migrant's decision to migrate is motivated primarily by the difference between his or her *expected* (rather than the actual) urban income and the prevailing rural wage. The Harris-Todaro model implied that attempts to reduce urban unemployment by creating more urban jobs could paradoxically result in more urban unemployment rather than less. By leading potential migrants to believe that their chances of getting an urban job had increased, urban employment programs induced greater rural-to-urban migration. Harris and Todaro therefore argued that urban unemployment could best be addressed by reducing the incentives to migrate to the cities, for example, by raising rural incomes via a broad range of agricultural and rural development programs.[26]

The second approach to studying migration was spearheaded by several radical political economists who focused on the social, as opposed to the private, benefits and costs of migration. Samir Amin, for example, argued that although rural-to-urban migration might be privately profitable for the migrant, it imposed important social costs on the sending area, including the loss of future village leadership and the instability of rural families. Amin argued that these costs exceeded possible gains to the area from wage remittances to the home villages.

Although the net welfare impact of migration is obviously an important question, many of the studies by radical scholars lacked empirical data to support their conclusions. In a balanced and constructive assessment of both neoclassical and radical political economy studies of migration in southern Africa, Knight and Lenta (1980) conclude that there is not a clear picture of the net welfare impact of migration in the countries supplying labor to the mines in South Africa.

Product Market Performance

Rapid income growth and urbanization put increasing pressure on markets for agricultural products, particularly food, during the 1960s and 1970s. In response, economists undertook a number of studies to evaluate the performance of agricultural product markets and suggest improvements.[27] These studies generally found little support for allegations of widespread collusion and extraction of monopoly profits by private merchants in Third World countries. They did, however, document how insufficient infrastructure and the lack of reliable public information systems and other public goods often reduced market efficiency and lowered farmers' incentives to specialize for market production. The studies were often critical of state monopolies in the domestic food trade, citing the frequent high costs of state marketing agencies. The studies identified important roles for the state in providing public goods (better information systems, standardized weights and measures, and so on) to facilitate private trading, price stabilization, and regulation of international trade.[28] More recently, there has been discussion of ways the state can ensure adequate food supplies to the poor without disrupting normal market channels (see Timmer, chapter 12).

Farming Systems Research and Farmer Decision Making

During the late 1960s and the 1970s economists increasingly investigated the factors that influenced farmers' decisions concerning whether to adopt new crop varieties and farming practices. This work eventually led to the development of farming systems research (FSR), described in chapter 23. Farming systems research attempts to incorporate farmers' constraints and objectives into agricultural research by involving farmers in problem identification, on-farm agronomic trials, and extension.

Interest in farming systems research and the new household economics also led to efforts to model the farm household as both a production and a consumption unit. Inspired by Chayanov's work on the behavior of Russian peasants in the early 1900s, the farm-household models stressed the need to understand how government policies could simultaneously affect both the production and the consumption decisions of small farmers. For example, these models showed that marketed surplus of a crop might, in some circumstances, actually decline as the crop's price was increased (even if production of the crop rose) because the price increase would raise farm family income, some of which would be spent on the good whose price had risen.[29]

Summary: Research in the 1970s

The results of microeconomic research during the 1970s contributed to an accumulation of knowledge about the behavior of farmers; constraints on the expansion of farm and nonfarm production, income, and employment; the linkages between agricultural research and extension institutions; and the complexity and location-specific nature of the agricultural development process. One of the major accomplishments of the 1970s was a large increase in knowledge about agricultural development in sub-Saharan Africa, an area often ignored by development economists during the 1950s and early 1960s (see Eicher and Baker 1982). But the increased orientation to micro-level research resulted in relatively less attention being paid to macroeconomic research on food policy and the role that agriculture can play in the structural transformation of Third World economies.

DEVELOPMENT PROGRAMS OF THE 1970s: INTEGRATED RURAL DEVELOPMENT AND BASIC NEEDS

Reacting to some of the disappointments of the Green Revolution and the agricultural growth–oriented programs of the 1960s, many donors and Third World governments endorsed integrated rural development and basic needs projects in the 1970s. Integrated rural development (IRD) attempts to combine in one project elements to increase agricultural production and ones to improve health, education, sanitation, and a variety of other social services. Like the community development (CD) projects of the 1950s, IRD projects of the 1970s sometimes expanded social services faster than they expanded the economic base to support them, and they often proved to be extraordinarily complex and difficult to implement and replicate over broader areas. By 1980 many donors had retreated from IRD projects or had redesigned these projects to give greater emphasis to agricultural production.[30] The rise and decline of IRD (1973–80) was in some ways very similar to the fate of CD in the 1950s.

In the mid-1970s the basic needs approach was popularized by the ILO (1976a) and subsequently spearheaded by the World Bank. The approach holds that development projects should give priority to increasing the welfare of the poor directly, through projects to improve nutrition, education, housing, and so on, rather than focus mainly on increasing aggregate growth rates.[31] The basic needs advocates supported their case by citing impressive gains in life span, literacy, and nutrition in Cuba, Sri Lanka, and the People's Republic of China, countries that had emphasized basic needs. Although investments in health, nutrition, education, and housing can contribute importantly to the welfare of the poor and to the rate of economic growth, the experience with the basic needs approach suggests that low-income countries also need to emphasize building the economic base to finance these investments. By the early 1980s many economists were once again giving greater emphasis to economic growth. This shift in emphasis did not imply a rejection of the growth-with-equity philosophy of the 1970s. Rather, it reflected increasing recognition of the impossibility of achieving a decent living standard for the bulk of the rapidly growing populations in poor countries simply by redistributing existing assets. This recognition led the World Bank and other donors to shift to a more growth-oriented strategy in the early 1980s.

DEVELOPMENT THEMES IN THE 1980s: MACROECONOMIC REFORM, FOOD SECURITY, INCOME GENERATION, AND SUSTAINABLE AGRICULTURE

The 1980s witnessed a major swing in development economics towards economic growth, policy reform, and market liberalization. This swing from microeconomics to macroeconomics is illustrated by several of the standard texts of the 1970s and 1980s. "Projects, the Cutting Edge of Development" is the title of the opening chapter of Gittinger's influential 1972 text, *Economic Analysis of Agricultural Projects*. A decade later "macropolicies" were identified as the cutting edge of development in *Food Policy Analysis* (1983) by Timmer, Falcon, and Pearson.[32]

Accompanying the shift from micro to macro in the early 1980s was a period of intense debate and reflection on the purpose and, indeed, the future of development. Most of the dozen or more essays on the future of the subdiscipline were written in response to Hirschman's (1981) reflective essay on development economics that "begins so cheerfully but turns out to be really an obituary of development economics—no longer the envy of other social sciences" (Sen 1983). But after numerous conferences and essays on the future of development economics, a new realism emerged that recognized the complexity, the difficulty, and the long time-frame of development. This realism is captured by Amartya Sen (1988, 23):

> The different problems underlying the concept of development have become clearer over the years on the basis of conceptual discussions as well as from insights emerging from empirical work. Insofar as these problems have become clear, something of substance has in fact been achieved, and the demise of the brashness which characterized the initiation of development economics need not be seem entirely as a loss. A clearer recognition of the difficulties and problems is certainly a step in the direction of enhancing our ability to tackle them.

Macro policy reform was the dominant development theme of the 1980s. In the late 1970s and early 1980s Latin American countries were forced to tackle some of the complex issues of adjustment and growth.[33] In Africa, macro policy reform was strongly advocated in the World Bank's report, *Accelerated Development in Sub-Saharan Africa* (1981). The first structural adjustment program in Africa was launched in Ghana in 1983. By 1989, adjustment programs were underway in 32 of the 45 countries in sub-Saharan Africa.

In Asia, agricultural development proceeded more rapidly than expected and, with some qualifications, can be considered a major success story of the 1980s. India achieved self-sufficiency in grain production in the mid-1980s, and Indonesia, formerly the largest rice importer in the world, had surplus rice production in 1984 and 1985 (Vyas and James 1988). In China agricultural policy reforms were launched in 1978 and grain production expanded rapidly until 1985; then leveled off and has remained constant through 1989.

A major analytic advance in the way economists viewed policy was the development in the early 1980s of the food policy analysis approach. Summarized in the influential book *Food Policy Analysis* (1983), by Timmer, Falcon, and Pearson, this approach synthesized work in a number of areas, outlining how to trace the effects of macroeconomic adjustments as well as sectoral level policies on food production, income generation, and the consumption patterns of the poor. The food policy approach had two distinguishing characteristics that set it apart from the production incentives school led by Professor T. W. Schultz and the basic needs school headed by Frances Streeten at the World Bank and popularized in the book *Food First*, by Lappé and Collins. The production incentives school emphasized the need to "get prices right" (which usually meant raising agricultural prices), in order to increase farmers' incentives to produce. The basic needs approach stressed the need to keep food prices low in order to ensure that the poor could afford an adequate diet. The food policy approach recognized that the production concerns of the production incentives school and the consumption concerns of the basic needs school were both legitimate, and it showed how they were linked through food prices. Food policy analysis hence forms a bridge between the two approaches. The second distinguishing feature of food policy analysis was that it recognized, more explicitly than had earlier agricultural policy work, that policy formation takes place in an open economy where the financial and commodity markets are increasingly integrated. Therefore, there is a need to link food and agricultural policy with macro policies, such as the exchange rate and interest rates, in a world economy framework. Also, because international commodity markets have become more unstable with the move to floating exchange rates, more attention has to be paid to strategies for dealing with risk in agricultural commodity markets.

In the mid-1980s policy makers in many countries became increasingly concerned about food security. Despite the achievement of national food self-sufficiency in several major Asian countries such as India and Indonesia, it was apparent that a large percentage of people neither had the access to resources (e.g., land, credit) nor the purchasing power to secure their food needs. Thus, the pioneering work of Reutlinger and Selowsky (1976), followed by Sen's *Poverty and Famines* (1981), set the stage for moving beyond the belief that national food self-sufficiency could solve problems of famine and malnutrition (World Bank 1986). Both these works, as well as many that followed them, stressed that food security involved assuring both an adequate supply of food (through own production and trade) and access by the population to that supply. The poor could gain access to the food by producing it themselves, through earning sufficient income to buy food through the market, or through grants, such as free rations or food stamps. Research and empirical experience during the 1980s demonstrated that focusing on only one side of the "food security equation" (i.e., either the supply side or the access side) failed to alleviate food insecurity.

Food security has both a transitory and a chronic dimension. Transitory food insecurity refers to short-term inability to secure adequate food due to temporary shortfalls in either production or real income, as typified by a famine. Chronic food insecurity refers to a long-term problem of inadequate food intake due to low productivity and incomes. A major challenge for food security analysts is to devise short-term measures to deal with these various dimensions of food insecurity that will not have deleterious long-run effects. For example, how can food aid be used for short-term relief without undermining the long-term development of the domestic food system? (See Singer, chapter 14.)

During the 1980s, rural income and employment generation continued as important themes, for three reasons. First, the achievement of national food self-sufficiency in many countries was unable to ensure that all families could secure their food needs. Second, it became increasingly obvious that, as in the 1970s, because of population growth and industrial stagnation, the bulk of the increments to the rural labor force in many countries would have to find employment in farming and rural nonfarm activities. Third, while such countries as Sri Lanka, China, and Brazil had reaped short-term benefits from food subsidies and food transfer programs, it became apparent that most countries could not finance such measures over the long term. Hence, there obviously was a long-term need to help the rural poor increase production and/or income to secure their own food needs. This explains why increasing domestic effective demand for food through rural income and employment generation emerged as strategic issues in the 1980s.

Acid rain, pollution, environmental degradation, and sustainable agriculture also emerged as central issues in the 1980s, especially following the release of the influential Bruntland Report, *Our Common Future*.[34] Concerns about sustainability were raised at several levels: local, subnational, national, and global. Increasing population pressure on fragile environments led to worries that existing farming systems in many parts of the world were no longer sustainable at the local level, that is, that continuing current practices would lead to a downward spiral in agricultural productivity and an increase in rural poverty. At the regional (subnational) level, analysts and activists raised concerns about the externalities generated by modern agricultural practices—for example, the impact of pesticide runoff and siltation from dams on local fisheries, and the destruction of wildlife habitat caused by agricultural expansion. At the national level, additional concerns were raised about the economic capacity of many countries to afford high-input agriculture given their shortages of foreign exchange.[35] At the global level, the 1980s saw increasing consternation about the "greenhouse effect"—the increase in global temperature associated with the build-up of carbon dioxide and other gases in the atmosphere—as well as concerns about acid rain and worldwide pesticide contamination. Since the cutting and burning of tropical rainforests for conversion into agricultural land is believed to be a major contributor to global warming, there were increasing calls for the development and adoption of less destructive farming systems. As Ruttan points out in chapter 24, a key challenge is to develop technologies that respond to these concerns while still assuring rapid enough growth to meet increasing world demand for food.

The 1980s also witnessed the decline of the dependency approach to analyzing problems of underdevelopment. In part, the decline resulted from the "overselling" of the approach. Some dependency analysts in the 1970s argued that dependency precluded any economic growth or development in the Third World, a view clearly contradicted by the evidence in many countries, both in Latin America and Southeast Asia (Cardoso 1977). Many economists also argued that dependency analysis understated the constraints imposed on growth by the internal economic policies of Third World countries, concentrating almost exclusively on the external constraints imposed by the high-income countries (de Janvry 1981, 40–41). The approach also seemed to offer few concrete policy prescriptions short of socialist revolution.

Nonetheless, the dependency approach did raise important issues about the relationships between political and economic forces in development, views also raised by Marxist and institutional economists. Economic reform in the USSR, Eastern Europe, and China brought Marxist orthodoxy, as practiced in these countries, into increasing disrepute during the 1980s. It is important to distinguish, however, between the Marxist analyses of economists, sociologists, and anthropologists, who attempt to link changes in the economic structure with the class structure of society, and the practices and policies of the governments of socialist bloc. The abandonment of these policies because of the poor performance of the Eastern Bloc economies (see chapters 29 and 30) does not negate the usefulness of more open-ended types of Marxist analysis. Indeed, at least some economists (e.g., Bardhan, 1988) argued in the 1980s that there are three valid, complementary, and at times competitive approaches to analyzing development: neoclassical, Marxist, and structural-institutional. Although there was a neoclassical resurgence in the early 1980s, based on the success of market-driven economies like those of South Korea, Taiwan, Hong Kong, and Singapore, there were enough failures and setbacks in other market-driven economies in the 1980s to make the case for drawing on all three approaches for insights in the 1990s.

EMPIRICAL EVIDENCE FROM THE 1980s

A large body of empirical evidence accumulated during the 1980s on macroeconomic policy reforms and the performance of various economies. But a perspective derived from the growth experience of the nineteenth century also provides insights applicable to current Third World problems. In a twenty-year investigation of the growth and development experience of 23 countries over the period 1850 to 1914, Morris and Adelman (1988) report that no single theory of causation can account for the many directions economic development followed in these countries. Contrary to neoclassical theory, for instance, comparable resources and export opportunities did not assure countries similar patterns and paces of growth. In fact, the authors found that "diversity in growth patterns, diversity in institutions and diversity in applicable theories" were the hallmarks of the development process during the nineteenth century (Morris and Adelman 1988). The lesson from this analysis is that simple analytic models are inadequate to understand Third World development. In particular, there is a need to incorporate institutional and cultural variables more fully into analyses of the development process (Hayami and Ruttan 1985, 110–14; Stevens and Jabara 1988).

The performance of agriculture in Third World economies varied widely during the 1980s. In chapter 28, de Janvry and Sadoulet report that massive currency devaluation allowed agriculture to play a leading role in the economic growth of a number of Latin American countries during the 1980s. But de Janvry and Sadoulet, along with Valdés (1986) and the FAO (1988), point out that some of these countries were blessed with favorable domestic and international demand (e.g., Chile's fruit and vegetable exports to the United States), available technology, and responsive agricultural institutions to induce the required supply response. By contrast, many African countries, such as the Côte d'Ivoire, faced sluggish world demand for cocoa and cotton, while many others, such as Zaire, Senegal and Tanzania, were unable to break structural constraints on the supply side, such as lack of technology, roads, and vehicles (Lipumba 1988). The differing responses to structural adjustment in low-income African countries and in some of the middle-income economies of Latin America can be illuminated by referring to Timmer's four stages of the agricultural transformation (chapter 2). Most African economies are in the first stage of development, where massive investments are needed in training and rural infrastructural development, while most Latin American countries passed through this stage some 25 to 50 years ago.[36] The relatively satisfactory agricultural development experience in Asia and Latin America in the 1980s stands in contrast to the uneven progress with macroeconomic reforms in the Soviet Union (see chapter 29, by Brooks), in China (see chapter 30, by Lin, Yao, and Wen), and in Africa (see Lele 1989, and chapters 31 and 32, by Eicher and Lele, respectively), where institutional, and in some cases technological, barriers to supply response have been much stronger.

Many policy makers and scholars have been increasingly concerned since the mid-1980s about the possible harmful effects of structural adjustment on the poor. Several UNICEF-sponsored studies reported severe hardship being inflicted on the poor during structural adjustment programs in the 1980s (UNICEF 1984; Cornia, Jolly, and Stewart 1987, 1988). But a word of caution is in order. Behrman and Deolalikar (1988) report that although these studies "have attempted to evaluate the impact of macroeconomic adjustment policies, specifically on health and nutrition, these studies do not formalize explicitly the links between recession and/or economic adjustment and the health and nutrition of the children." Preston (1986), in a review of several of these UNICEF-sponsored studies, questions the quality of secondary data and the negative conclusions of these studies. Yet, as many of the policy reforms call for sharp short-run increases in food prices, the concern about the programs' impact on the poor is certainly legitimate.

Mellor (chapter 6) and Timmer (chapter 12) discuss conceptual and policy issues related to food security. Food security can be analyzed at four levels: international, regional, national (and subnational, as in provinces and districts), and household. In the early 1980s, researchers focused on international food security issues, such as international grain reserves and later regional grain reserves (e.g., in the Sahel and in Southern Africa). But in the mid-1980s, researchers shifted to national and household food security issues, especially in Africa, because of the worldwide publicity during the 1985 famine, when an estimated one million people died in Ethiopia alone. Amartya Sen's *Poverty and Famines* (1981) was one of the most influential books published by an economist in the 1980s. Sen developed an entitlement approach to analyzing the causes of four famines in Asia and Africa in historical perspective.[37]

During the later half of the 1980s, numerous studies of national food security were carried out to help answer the key policy question, What combination of policies, technological changes, and institutional reforms is required to achieve food availability and access to food for nations and for families? Many of these studies pointed to a lack of micro data on the food security status of families at different seasons of the year and the almost complete absence of data with which to generate a social profile of the poor and malnourished (Eicher and Staatz 1986; Weber et al. 1988).

The need for primary data to further food security policy analysis is particularly acute for Africa. In Africa, policy makers, scholars, and donors have commonly assumed (on the basis of secondary data) that most African farm households were net food sellers and that increasing official farm-level prices would lead to higher food output and improved rural welfare. But recent research results revealed that from 15 to 73 percent of the rural households in the major grain-producing areas of Mali, Somalia, Senegal, Rwanda, and Zimbabwe were net buyers of staple grains and only 22 to 48 percent were net sellers of these grains in recent years (Weber et al. 1988, 1046). Hence, raising grain prices in these countries would hurt, at least in the short run, a large number of rural households. From this new evidence it follows that policies to improve food security must correspondingly be tailored to local food security profiles.

In Asia, the analysis of rural poverty is sharply divided into the neoclassical and Marxist approaches. Neoclassical economists such as Hayami (1988) and Hayami and Kikuchi (1985) argue that the combination of population pressure and a limited land area reduces the average size of owned holdings allocated to heirs. The Marxist economists Bhaduri (1983), Elster (1985), and Mkandawire and Bourenane (1987) argue that technological change leads to the commercialization of agriculture and an increase in the use of purchased inputs and hired labor; and as the commercialization process uncoils, they argue, ownership becomes more concentrated. In reality, however, large farms have not inexorably gained control over farm production in Asia and Africa. The degree of concentration in land holding depends on the institutional setting within which new agricultural technologies are introduced. For example, with inputs provided and the social barriers to producing cash crops like coffee and tea removed, smallholders in Kenya have increased their share of national production from 4 percent in 1965 to 49 percent in 1985 (Lele and Agarwal 1989). Similarly, smallholders' market share of cotton and maize production in Zimbabwe rose dramatically following independence in 1980. In other countries and regions, however, such as the Sudan, Somalia, and the Punjab and other states in India, access to modern inputs has been biased toward owners of large farms, leading to an increasing share of land being cultivated by those farms.

Overall, inequality is increasing in Asia and in Africa (see chapter 31, by Eicher). Since land reform is probably a "dead topic" for the 1990s (see Binswanger and Elgin, chapter 20), one of the central challenges of the 1990s is how to design agrarian structures to accommodate rapid population growth and generate productive employment until population growth slows and/or industrialization generates more jobs. In trying to create such structures, it is critical to look beyond agriculture. Special attention needs to be paid to developing well-functioning labor markets, to avoid trapping people in low-productivity occupations if better opportunities exist elsewhere in the economy. Strengthening off-farm rural employment, small-scale manufacturing, agricultural input and output marketing, and processing are other key elements in building a more dynamic and integrated rural economy.

LESSONS AND INSIGHTS FOR THE 1990s

By the end of the 1980s, development thinking had come nearly full circle. In the 1950s and 1960s economists had developed simple two-sector models to analyze the role of agriculture in relation to industry. During the 1970s, analysts developed an increasingly detailed theoretical and empirical understanding of the rural economy. A huge amount of empirical work on the microeconomics of the rural economy took place during the 1970s and 1980s. During the 1980s, however, many economists realized that, in their quest for a better micro-level understanding of the rural economy, some had lost sight of how agriculture related to the broader macroeconomy. Hence, the 1980s, with its emphasis on macroeconomic adjustment, witnessed a renewed concern about how agriculture contributed to overall economic growth. The challenge remains to integrate the macroeconomic concerns of the 1980s and 1990s with the improved microeconomic understanding gained in the 1970s and 1980s.

The excitement generated by privatization, structural adjustment, and farming systems research during the 1980s is becoming muted. This was to be expected; similar bursts of energy and passion had surrounded previous fads in development, such as the "Big-Push" thesis of the 1950s, dual-sector models in the 1960s, and integrated rural development in the 1970s.

We believe that food/population pressure will reemerge as a critical issue in Asia in the 1990s, especially in light of the prognosis that biotechnology will not play an important role in food production in Asia until the twenty-first century (Byerlee, chapter 27, and Lipton 1989). Likewise, moderate rates of population growth in Asia and Latin America will lead to a reduction in average farm size, while rapid population growth will press hard on Africa's natural resource base over the next 20 to 30 years. Finally, because political instability will continue to undermine economic progress in much of Africa for the next several decades, the policy prescription of simply "getting prices right" seems woefully inadequate for the challenges ahead.

The main lesson from the agricultural development experience of the 1980s is that macroeconomic policies can be powerful stimuli to agricultural growth and to the national economy. But for macroeconomic and agricultural policies to succeed requires sufficient domestic and international effective demand, public investments in research and rural infrastructure, and a political environment conducive to mobilizing the energy and capability of the *majority* of rural people. While political stability in countries such as Chile and South Africa can produce impressive rates of agricultural growth for a minority of commercial farmers, the evidence is clear that the success of policies to deal with rural poverty and food insecurity will be "a function of the extent to which 'countervailing power' is available to the poor through the presence of social action groups and politically viable opposition parties" (Bhagwati 1984).

Despite this evidence, many economists and agricultural economists working on agricultural development issues in the Third World are concentrating on the purely economic and technocratic issues and leaving the political arrangements and the tough institutional issues to political scientists and sociologists.[38] To grapple with the issues of power and politics that surround agrarian change in the Third World, agricultural economists need to broaden their analyses to take into account other influences on food and agricultural policies: political factors (Bates, chapter 8; Sen 1984, 1988), institutional change (Bromley 1989; Howell 1988; Roling 1988), transactions costs and market failures (Bell 1988; Stiglitz 1989).

The research results and development experiences of the past four decades suggest that in order to attain more rapid, broad-based agricultural growth and rural development, the following components will have to be emphasized in the coming decade: strengthening the institutional base for smallholder agriculture (research, training, and extension), administration, policy analysis, and training; reaccentuating analysis of agricultural development issues in a broader macroeconomic framework; and reevaluation of the roles of international trade, food aid, and agricultural specialization in an increasingly interdependent world food economy (Stevens and Jabara 1988). One of the clearest lessons of the past four decades is that agricultural and rural development require strong local institutions and well-trained individuals. International research centers and expatriate advisers are at best complements to, not substitutes for, national research systems and local policy analysis capability.

THE PLAN OF THIS BOOK

This book draws on the agricultural and rural development literature produced during the 1970s and 1980s. Our selection of articles was guided by three convictions. First, we believe that agricultural and economic development should be viewed as a long-term historical process. Second, analysts and policy makers need to understand the growing interdependence between agriculture and the rest of the economy. Third, although agricultural development issues are often best understood in a general equilibrium framework, we believe that framework needs to be built upon a firm microeconomic data base. Careful empirical studies of farmer, merchant, and consumer behavior are needed in order to understand how rural economies function, how they are likely to react to policy interventions, and how they interact with other sectors of the economy. The contribution of empirical research to policy analysis is a major theme of this book.

Part II of the book places the agricultural and rural development literature in historical perspective by discussing models of agricultural growth that historically have been used in research and in development programs. Part III examines the questions of agricultural growth and food and agricultural policies by addressing major policy issues that have both important economy-wide consequences and significant effects on other development goals. This type of broad analysis, however, needs to be built upon a firm understanding of how rural economies function. Part IV provides some of that foundation by presenting a series of articles that analyze the forces that influence factor availability and use in agriculture, the links between agriculture and rural small-scale industry, and the generation and impact of technical change in agriculture.

Part V presents case studies of economic policy reforms in Latin America, the Soviet Union, the People's Republic of China, and sub-Saharan Africa. The articles pull together many of the elements discussed earlier in the book, such as price policy, intersectoral resource flows, and technological change in agriculture.

NOTES

Larry Lev, Carl Liedholm, Michael Morris, and Robert Stevens offered insightful comments on an earlier draft of this paper. Johnston (1970) extensively reviewed the literature of the 1950s and 1960s on the role of agriculture in development.

1. Development economics began to emerge as a subdiscipline of economics in the post–World War II period with the work of Nurkse, Mandelbaum, Rosenstein-Rodan, Singer, Prebisch, and others. The first major text on economic development was W. Arthur Lewis's influential *The Theory of Economic Growth* (1955). Lewis's emphasis on economic growth set the tone for work in development economics during the "growth era" of the 1950s and 1960s. In the introduction Lewis wrote, "The subject matter of this book is growth of output per head of population . . . and not distribution" (p. 9). Lewis did, however, include an appendix entitled "Is Economic Growth Desirable?" For reviews of the history of development economics see Hirschman 1981a; Streeten 1979; Reynolds 1977, chap. 2; and Little 1982.

2. This section draws heavily on Johnston's excellent review of the literature through 1970 on the role of agriculture in economic development, and on Stern 1989.

3. For an excellent summary of the Lewis model see Meier 1976, 157–63; see also Lewis 1972. For an analysis of Lewis's model on development economics see Gersowitz et al. 1982.

4. Lewis's statement that the marginal productivity of laborers in the noncapitalist sector approached zero as a limiting case stimulated a large number of efforts to measure the extent of surplus labor in agriculture. For a review of these efforts see Kao, Anschel, and Eicher 1964. For a critique of the concept of surplus labor in agriculture see Shultz 1964, chap. 4.

5. Nicholls (1964) was one of the first critics of the rapid transfer of surplus labor as a short-run strategy. See also Mellor 1984.

6. See Timmer, chapter 2 of this volume.

7. For a summary of this thesis see Prebisch 1959. For critical reviews see Kravis 1970; and Little 1982, chap. 4.

8. In recent years Prebisch has modified his views about import substitution (see Prebisch 1981). For a contrasting view of the potential role of agricultural exports in fostering economic growth see Myint's discussion of the "vent for surplus" model of growth in chapter 13 of this volume.

9. See Mellor 1984.

10. The literature of the 1960s on agricultural development is captured in the volumes edited by Eicher and Witt (1964), Southworth and Johnston (1967), and Wharton (1969).

11. See the first U.N. report on development problems in the Third World, *Measures for the Economic Development of Underdeveloped Countries* (1951), which focused heavily on ways of dealing with rural surplus labor.

12. Community development's emphasis on providing social services presaged the basic needs approach to development of the late 1970s, described later in this chapter.

13. See chapter 20 of this volume for a further discussion of land reform.

14. For a critical appraisal see Shapiro 1977.

15. See Ruttan's discussion of the high-payoff input model in chapter 4.

16. These arguments were most fully developed by Mellor and by Johnston and Kilby in the 1970s. See the discussion of these authors' work in the second section of this chapter.

17. French scholars also made important contributions to the Marxist analysis of agricultural development during the 1960s and 1970s (see Petit 1982).

18. For critiques of the dependency school of thought in Latin America see Cardoso and Faletto 1979; and de Janvry 1981.

19. A standard reference is the influential book *Redistribution with Growth,* by Chenery et al. (1974). See also Seers 1970; and Adelman 1975.

20. For a summary of this literature see Pinstrup-Andersen, Berg, and Forman 1984, and Berg 1987.

21. Singh (1988) estimates that about one-fifth of all rural households in South Asia (India, Pakistan, and Bangladesh) are either landless or nearly landless.

22. See, for example, the volume edited by Stevens (1977a); and Jones 1972.

23. See chapter 4; and Hayami and Ruttan 1971, 1985. For attempts to test the induced innovation hypothesis empirically see Binswanger and Ruttan 1978.

24. See also the volume edited by Reynolds (1975).

25. Mellor's views are articulated in *The New Economics of Growth: A Strategy for India and the Developing World* (1976). See also Mellor and Lele 1973; and two of Mellor's contributions to this volume, chapters 3 and 10.

26. The major extensions of the Harris-Todaro model and empirical tests of it are summarized in Todaro 1980.

27. Many of these studies are reviewed by Lele (1977) and Riley and Staatz (1981).

28. For a critical review of some of these studies see Harriss 1979.

29. For a summary of the literature on family/farm modeling see the volume edited by Singh, Squire, and Strauss (1986); and Moock 1986.

30. For reviews of IRD see Ruttan 1975; and World Bank 1988.

31. The basic needs approach is not simply a call for increased social welfare spending, however; it is also based on recognition of the importance of investment in human capital in economic growth and of

the synergism of nutrition, health, and family planning decisions. For an excellent discussion of basic needs projects and their relationships to rural development see Johnston and Clark 1982, chap. 4. The World Bank's experience with basic needs is summarized by Streeten (1981).

32. In chapter 12 of this volume, Timmer argues that "macro price policy is the cutting edge of development: projects and programs are the cutting edge of reducing nutritional inequities."

33. For details see Valdés 1986; FAO 1988; and chapter 28, by de Janvry and Sadoulet.

34. For more information see Lynam and Herdt (1989); Mellor 1988; Pingali et al. 1987; Boserup 1965, 1981; and Ruttan, chapter 24 in this volume.

35. This concern contains an implicit assumption that many of the "modern" technologies are uneconomic, that is, that they don't generate enough output that, when valued in terms of foreign exchange, could pay for the imported inputs.

36. See Mosher 1966 for insights into the policy actions required for countries at an early stage of development (Timmer's Stage I).

37. Sen defines entitlement as "the set of alternative commodity bundles that a person can command in a society using the totality of rights and opportunities that he or she faces" (Sen 1983). Also see Sen 1988; and Sen's chapter (12) in this volume.

38. See Sen 1984 and 1988 for a discussion of how political arrangements affect peoples' capability and entitlements.

REFERENCES

Adelman, Irma. 1975. "Development Economics—A Reassessment of Goals." *American Economic Review* 55(2): 302–9.

Adelman, Irma, and Cynthia Taft Morris. 1973. *Economic Growth and Social Equity in Developing Countries.* Stanford: Stanford University Press.

Amin, Samir. 1965. *Trois éxperiences Africaines de développement: le Mali, la Guinée et le Ghana.* Paris: Presses Universitaires de France.

———. 1971. *L'Afrique de l'ouest bloquée: l'économie politique de la colonisation (1880–1970).* Paris: Les Editions de Minuit.

———. 1973. "Transitional Phases in Sub-Saharan Africa." *Monthly Review* 25(5): 52–57.

———. 1974. *Accumulation on a World Scale: A Critique of the Theory of Underdevelopment.* New York: Monthly Review Press.

———. 1976. *Unequal Development: An Essay on the Social Formations of Peripheral Capitalism.* New York: Monthly Review Press.

Baran, Paul A. 1952. "On the Political Economy of Backwardness." *Manchester School of Economic and Social Studies* 20:66–84.

Bardhan, Pranab. 1988. "Alternative Approaches to Development." In *Handbook of Development Economics,* edited by Hollis Chenery and T. N. Srinivasan, vol. 1, 39–71. Amsterdam: North Holland.

Barraclough, Solon. 1973. *Agrarian Structure in Latin America.* Lexington, Mass.: Lexington Books.

Behrman, Jere R. 1968. *Supply Response in Underdeveloped Agriculture.* Amsterdam: North-Holland Publishing Co.

Behrman, Jere R., and Anil B. Deolalikar. 1988. "Health and Nutrition." In *Handbook of Development Economics,* edited by Hollis Chenery and T. N. Srinivasan, vol. 1, 631–711. Amsterdam: North Holland.

Bell, Clive. 1988. "Credit Markets and Interlinked Transactions." In *Handbook of Development Economics,* edited by Hollis Chenery and T. N. Srinivasan, vol. 1, 763–830. Amsterdam: North Holland.

Berg, Alan. 1973. *The Nutrition Factor: Its Role in National Development.* Washington, D.C.: Brookings Institution.

———. 1987. *Malnutrition: What Can Be Done?* Baltimore: Johns Hopkins University Press.

Berry, A., and R. H. Sabot. 1978. "Labour Market Performance in Developing Countries: A Survey." *World Development* 6:1199–1242.

Berry, R. Albert. 1975. "Special Problems of Policy Making in a Technologically Heterogeneous Agriculture: Colombia." In *Agriculture in Development Theory*, edited by Lloyd G. Reynolds. New Haven: Yale University Press.

Berry, R. Albert, and William F. Cline. 1979. *Agrarian Structure and Productivity in Developing Countries*. Baltimore: Johns Hopkins University Press.

Bhaduri, A. 1983. *The Economic Structure of Backward Production*. London: Academic Press.

Bhagwati, Jagdish. 1984. "Development Economics: What Have We Learned?" *Asian Development Review* 2(1): 23–38.

Binswanger, Hans P., and Vernon W. Ruttan. 1978. *Induced Innovation: Technology, Institutions, and Development*. Baltimore: Johns Hopkins University Press.

Boserup, Ester. 1965. *The Conditions of Agricultural Growth: The Economics of Agrarian Change and Population Pressure*. Baltimore: Johns Hopkins University Press.

————. 1970. *Women's Role in Economic Development*. New York: St. Martin's Press.

————. 1981. *Population and Technical Change: A Study of Long-Term Trends*. Chicago: University of Chicago Press.

Bromley, Daniel. 1989. *Economic Interests and Institutions: The Conceptual Foundations of Public Policy*. Cambridge: Cambridge University Press.

Brown, Lester R. 1970. *Seeds of Change*. New York: Praeger.

Byerlee, Derek, Carl K. Eicher, Carl Liedholm, and Dunstan S. C. Spencer. 1983. "Employment-Output Conflicts, Factor Price Distortions and Choice of Technique: Empirical Results from Sierra Leone." *Economic Development and Cultural Change* 31(2): 315–36.

Cardoso, Fernando H. 1977. "The Consumption of Dependency Theory in the United States." *Latin American Research Review* 12(3): 7–24.

Cardoso, F. H., and E. Faletto. 1979. *Dependency and Development in Latin America*. Berkeley and Los Angeles: University of California Press.

Carroll, Thomas F. 1961. "The Land Reform Issue in Latin America." In *Latin American Issues: Essays and Comments*, edited by Albert O. Hirschman. New York: Twentieth Century Fund.

Chayanov, A. V. 1966. *The Theory of Peasant Economy*, edited by D. Thorner, B. Kerblay, and R. Smith. Homewood, Ill.: Richard D. Irwin.

Chenery, H. B., M. S. Ahluwalia, C. L. G. Bell, J. H. Duloy, and R. Jolly, eds. 1974. *Redistribution with Growth*. London: Oxford University Press.

Cornia, Giovanni Andrea, Richard Jolly, and Frances Stewart, eds. 1987. *Adjustment with a Human Face*. Vol. 1, *Protecting the Vulnerable and Promoting Growth*, and vol. 2, *Ten Country Case Studies*. Oxford: Clarendon Press.

de Janvry, Alain. 1981. *The Agrarian Question and Reformism in Latin America*. Baltimore: Johns Hopkins University Press.

Dorner, Peter, and Donald Kanel. 1971. "The Economic Case for Land Reform: Employment, Income Distribution and Productivity." In *Land Reform in Latin America*, edited by Peter Dorner, 41–56. Land Economics Monograph, no. 3. Madison: University of Wisconsin Land Tenure Center.

Dos Santos, T. 1970. "The Structure of Dependence." *American Economic Review* 40(2): 231–36.

Dovring, Folke. 1959. "The Share of Agriculture in a Growing Population." *Monthly Bulletin of Agricultural Economics and Statistics* 8 (August–September): 1–11. Reprinted in *Agriculture in Economic Development*, edited by Carl K. Eicher and Lawrence W. Witt, 78–98. New York: McGraw-Hill, 1964.

Eicher, Carl K., and Doyle C. Baker. 1982. *Research on Agricultural Development in Sub-Saharan Africa: A Critical Survey*. MSU International Development Paper, no. 1. East Lansing: Michigan State University, Department of Agricultural Economics.

Eicher, Carl K., and John M. Staatz. 1986. "Food Security Policy in Sub-Saharan Africa." In *Agriculture in a Turbulent World Economy*, edited by A. Maunder and U. Renborg, 215–29. Brookfield, Vt.: Gower.

Eicher, Carl K., and Lawrence W. Witt, eds. 1964. *Agriculture in Economic Development*. New York: McGraw-Hill.

Eicher, C. K., T. Zalla, J. Kocher, and F. Winch. 1970. *Employment Generation in African Agriculture*. East Lansing: Michigan State University, Institute of International Agriculture.

Elster, J. 1985. *Making Sense of Marx*. Cambridge: Cambridge University Press.

Emmanuel, A. 1972. *Unequal Exchange: A Study of the Imperialism of Trade*. New York: Monthly Review Press.

Enke, Stephen. 1962a. "Industrialization through Greater Productivity in Agriculture." *Review of Economics and Statistics* 44 (February): 88–91.

———. 1962b. "Economic Development with Limited and Unlimited Supplies of Labor." *Oxford Economic Papers* 14 (June): 158–72.

FAO. 1988. *Potentials for Agricultural and Rural Development in Latin America and the Caribbean: Main Report*. Rome: Food and Agriculture Organization of the United Nations.

Fei, John C. H., Gustav Ranis, and Shirley W. Y. Kuo. 1979. *Growth with Equity: The Taiwan Case*. New York: Oxford University Press for the World Bank.

Fishlow, A. 1972. "Brazilian Size Distribution of Income." *American Economic Review, Proceedings* 62 (May): 391–402.

Frank, A. G. 1966. "The Development of Underdevelopment." *Monthly Review* 18(4): 17–31.

Frankel, Francine R. 1971. *India's Green Revolution: Economic Gains and Political Costs*. Princeton: Princeton University Press.

Furtado, Celso. 1973. "The Concept of External Dependence in the Study of Underdevelopment." In *The Political Economy of Development and Underdevelopment*, edited by Charles Wilber, 118–27. New York: Random House.

Galtung, J. 1971. "A Structural Theory of Imperialism." *Journal of Peace Research* 2:81–116.

Gersowitz, Mark, Carlos F. Diaz-Alejandro, Gustav Ranis, and Mark R. Rosenzweig, eds. 1982. *The Theory and Practice of Economic Development: Essays in Honor of Sir W. Arthur Lewis*. Boston: George Allen and Unwin.

Ghai, Dharam, and Samir Radwan, eds. 1983. *Agrarian Policies and Rural Poverty in Africa*. Geneva: International Labour Office.

Gittinger, J. Price. 1972. *Economic Analysis of Agricultural Projects*. Baltimore: Johns Hopkins University Press for the World Bank.

Griffin, Keith. 1974. *The Political Economy of Agrarian Change: An Essay on the Green Revolution*. Cambridge: Harvard University Press.

Harris, John R., and Michael P. Todaro. 1970. "Migration, Unemployment and Development: A Two-Sector Analysis." *American Economic Review* 60(1): 126–42.

Harriss, Barbara. 1979. "There Is a Method in My Madness: Or Is It Vice Versa? Measuring Agricultural Market Performance." *Food Research Institute Studies* 17(2): 197–218.

Hayami, Yujiro. 1988. "Asian Development: A View from the Paddy Fields." *Asian Development Review* 6(1): 50–63.

Hayami, Yujiro, and Masao Kikuchi. 1985. "Direction of Agrarian Change: A View from Villages in the Philippines." In *Agricultural Change and Rural Poverty: Variations on a Theme by Dharm Narain*, edited by John W. Mellor and Gunvant M. Desai, 132–48. Baltimore: Johns Hopkins University Press.

Hayami, Yujiro, and Vernon W. Ruttan. 1971. *Agricultural Development: An International Perspective*. Baltimore: Johns Hopkins Press. (Second edition, 1985).

Hirschman, Albert O. 1958. *The Strategy of Economic Development*. New Haven: Yale University Press.

———. 1977. "A Generalized Linkage Approach to Development, with Special Reference to Staples." *Economic Development and Cultural Change* 25 (supp.): 67–98.

———. 1981a. "The Rise and Decline of Development Economics." In *Essays in Trespassing: Economics to Politics and Beyond*. New York: Cambridge University Press.

———. 1981b. *Essays in Trespassing: Economics to Politics and Beyond*. New York: Cambridge University Press.

Holdcroft, Lane E. 1984. "The Rise and Fall of Community Development, 1950–65: A Critical Assessment." In *Agricultural Development in the Third World,* edited by Carl K. Eicher and John M. Staatz, 46–58. Baltimore: Johns Hopkins University Press.

Hopper, W. David. 1965. "Allocation Efficiency in a Traditional Indian Agriculture." *Journal of Farm Economics* 47(3): 611–24.

Howell, John, ed. 1988. *Training and Visit Extension in Practice.* London: Overseas Development Council.

International Labour Office. 1970. *Towards Full Employment: A Programme for Colombia.* Geneva.

———. 1971. *Matching Employment Opportunities and Expectations: A Programme of Action for Ceylon.* Geneva.

———. 1972. *Employment, Incomes and Equality: A Strategy for Increasing Productive Employment in Kenya.* Geneva.

———. 1974. *Sharing in Development: A Programme of Employment, Equity and Growth for the Philippines.* Geneva.

———. 1976a. *Employment, Growth and Basic Needs: A One-World Problem.* Geneva.

———. 1976b. *Growth, Employment and Equity: A Comprehensive Strategy for the Sudan.* Geneva.

Johnston, Bruce F. 1970. "Agriculture and Structural Transformation in Developing Countries: A Survey of Research." *Journal of Economic Literature* 3(2): 369–404.

Johnston, Bruce F., and William C. Clark. 1982. *Redesigning Rural Development: A Strategic Perspective.* Baltimore: Johns Hopkins University Press.

Johnston, Bruce F., and Peter Kilby. 1975. *Agriculture and Structural Transformation: Economic Strategies in Late-Developing Countries.* New York: Oxford University Press.

Johnston, Bruce F., and John W. Mellor. 1961. "The Role of Agriculture in Economic Development." *American Economic Review* 51(4): 566–93.

Jones, W. O. 1960. "Economic Man in Africa." *Food Research Institute Studies* 1:107–34.

———. 1972. *Marketing Staple Foods in Tropical Africa.* Ithaca: Cornell University Press.

Jorgenson, D. W. 1961. "The Development of a Dual Economy." *Economic Journal* 72 (June): 309–34.

Kao, Charles H. C., Kurt R. Anschel, and Carl K. Eicher. 1964. "Disguised Unemployment in Agriculture: A Survey." In *Agriculture in Economic Development,* edited by Carl K. Eicher and Lawrence W. Witt, 129–44. New York: McGraw-Hill.

Knight, J. B., and G. Lenta. 1980. "Has Capitalism Underdeveloped the Labour Reserves of South Africa?" *Oxford Bulletin of Economics and Statistics* 42(3): 157–201.

Kravis, I. B. 1970. "Trade as a Handmaiden of Growth: Similarities between the Nineteenth and Twentieth Centuries." *Economic Journal* 80(320): 850–72.

Krishna, Raj. 1967. "Agricultural Price Policy and Economic Development." In *Agricultural Development and Economic Growth,* edited by Herman M. Southworth and Bruce F. Johnston, 497–540. Ithaca: Cornell University Press.

———. 1973. "Unemployment in India." *Indian Journal of Agricultural Economics* 28(1): 1–23.

Lele, Uma. 1975. *The Design of Rural Development: Lessons from Africa.* Baltimore: Johns Hopkins University Press for the World Bank.

———. 1977. "Considerations Related to Optimum Pricing and Marketing Strategies in Rural Development." In *Decision Making and Agriculture,* edited by T. Dams and K. Hunt. Lincoln: University of Nebraska Press.

Lele, Uma, and M. Agarwal. 1989. *Smallholder and Large-Scale Agriculture in Africa: Are There Trade-Offs between Growth and Equity?* MADIA Project, Washington, D.C.: World Bank.

Lewis, W. Arthur. 1954. "Economic Development with Unlimited Supplies of Labour." *Manchester School of Economic and Social Studies* 22(2): 139–91.

———. 1955. *The Theory of Economic Growth.* London: George Allen and Unwin.

———. 1972. "Reflections on Unlimited Labor." In *International Economics and Development: Essays in Honor of Raul Prebisch,* edited by Luis Eugenio Di Marco, 75–96. New York: Academic Press.

———. 1978. *The Evolution of the International Economic Order.* Princeton: Princeton University Press.

Lipton, Michael. 1977. *Why Poor People Stay Poor: A Study of Urban Bias in World Development.* London: Temple-Smith.

Lipton, Michael, with Richard Longhurst. 1989. *New Seeds and Poor People.* Baltimore: Johns Hopkins University Press.

Lipumba, Nguyuru. 1988. "Policy Reforms for Economic Development in Tanzania." In *Africa's Development Challenges and the World Bank: Hard Questions and Costly Choices,* edited by Stephen Cummins, 53–72. Boulder, Colo.: Lynne Rienner.

Little, I. M. D. 1982. *Economic Development: Theory, Policy and International Relations.* New York: Basic Books.

Lynam, John K., and Robert W. Herdt. 1989. "Sense and Sustainability: Sustainability as an Objective in International Agricultural Research." *Agricultural Economics* 3:381–98.

McNamara, Robert S. 1973. *Address to the Board of Governors. Nairobi, Kenya, September 24, 1972.* Washington, D.C.: International Bank for Reconstruction and Development.

Mantesch, Thomas J., et al. 1971. *A Generalized Simulation Approach to Agricultural Sector Analysis with Special Reference to Nigeria.* East Lansing: Michigan State University.

Meier, Gerald. 1976. *Leading Issues in Economic Development.* 3d ed. New York: Oxford University Press.

Mellor, John. W. 1966. *The Economics of Agricultural Development.* Ithaca: Cornell University Press.

——. 1976. *The New Economics of Growth: A Strategy for India and the Developing World.* Ithaca: Cornell University Press.

——. 1984. "Agricultural Development and the Intersectoral Transfer of Resources." In *Agricultural Development in the Third World,* edited by Carl K. Eicher and John M. Staatz, 136–46. Baltimore: Johns Hopkins University Press.

——. 1988. "The Intertwining of Environmental Problems and Poverty." *Environment* 30, no. 9 (November): 8–30.

Mellor, John W., and Uma Lele. 1973. "Growth Linkages of the New Foodgrain Technologies." *Indian Journal of Agricultural Economics* 28(1): 35–55.

Mkandawire, Thandika, and Naceur Bourenane, eds. 1987. *The State and Agriculture in Africa.* London: CODESIRA Book Series.

Moock, Joyce, ed. 1986. *Understanding Africa's Rural Households and Farming Systems.* Boulder, Colo.: Westview Press.

Morris, Cynthia Taft, and Irma Adelman. 1988. *Comparative Patterns of Economic Development, 1850–1914.* Baltimore: Johns Hopkins University Press.

Mosher, Arthur. 1966. *Getting Agriculture Moving: Essentials for Development and Modernization.* New York: Praeger.

Nicholls, William H. 1964. "The Place of Agriculture in Economic Development." In *Agriculture in Economic Development,* edited by Carl K. Eicher and Lawrence W. Witt, 11–44. New York: McGraw-Hill.

Nugent, Jeffrey B., and Pan A. Yotopoulos. 1979. "What Has Orthodox Development Economics Learned from Recent Experience?" *World Development* 7:541–54.

Ohkawa, Kazushi. 1964. "Concurrent Growth of Agriculture with Industry: A Study of the Japanese Case." In *International Explorations of Agricultural Economics,* edited by Roger N. Dixey, 201–12. Ames: Iowa State University Press.

Ohkawa, Kazushi, and Bruce F. Johnston. 1969. "The Transferability of the Japanese Pattern of Modernizing Traditional Agriculture." In *The Role of Agriculture in Economic Development,* edited by Erik Thorbecke, 277–303. New York: National Bureau of Economic Research.

Petit, Michel. 1982. "Is There a French School of Agricultural Economics?" *Journal of Agricultural Economics* 33(3): 325–37.

Piñeiro, Martin, Eduardo Trigo, and Raul Fiorentino. 1979. "Technical Change in Latin American Agriculture: A Conceptual Framework for Its Evaluation." *Food Policy* 4(3): 169–77.

Pingali, Prabhu, Y. Bigot, and H. P. Binswanger. 1987. *Agricultural Mechanization and the Evolution of Farming Systems in Sub-Saharan Africa.* Baltimore: Johns Hopkins University Press.

Pinstrup-Andersen, Per, Alan Berg, and Martin Forman, eds. 1984. *International Agricultural Re-*

search and Human Nutrition. Washington, D.C.: International Food Policy Research Institute/ ACC-SCN.

Prebisch, Raul. 1959. "Commercial Policy in the Underdeveloped Countries." *American Economic Review* 64 (May): 251–73.

———. 1981. "The Latin American Periphery in the Global System of Capitalism." *CEPAL Review* April: 143–50. Reprinted in *International Economic Policies and Their Theoretical Foundations: A Source Book,* edited by John M. Letiche. New York: Academic Press, 1982.

Preston, S. H. 1986. Review of *The Impact of World Recession on Children,* edited by Richard Jolly and Giovanni Andrea Cornia. *Journal of Development Economics* 21:374–376.

Ranis, Gustav, and John C. H. Fei. 1961. "A Theory of Economic Development." *American Economic Review* 51(4): 533–65.

———. 1963. "Innovation, Capital Accumulation, and Economic Development." *American Economic Review* 53(3): 283–313.

———. 1964. *Development of the Labor Surplus Economy: Theory and Policy.* Homewood, Ill.: Richard D. Irwin.

Raup, Philip M. 1967. "Land Reform and Agricultural Development." In *Agricultural Development and Economic Growth,* edited by Herman M. Southworth and Bruce F. Johnston, 267–314. Ithaca: Cornell University Press.

Reutlinger, Shlomo, and Marcelo Selowsky. 1976. *Malnutrition and Poverty: Magnitude and Policy Options.* World Bank Staff Occasional Paper, no. 23. Baltimore: Johns Hopkins University Press for the World Bank.

Reynolds, Lloyd G. 1977. *Image and Reality in Economic Development.* New Haven: Yale University Press.

———. ed. 1975. *Agriculture in Development Theory.* New Haven: Yale University Press.

Riley, Harold, and John Staatz. 1981. "Food System Organization Problems in Developing Countries." *A/D/C Report,* no. 23. New York: Agricultural Development Council.

Roling, N. G. 1988. *Extension Science: Information Systems in Agricultural Development.* Cambridge: Cambridge University Press.

Ruttan, Vernon W. 1975. "Integrated Rural Development: A Skeptical Perspective." *International Development Review* 17(4): 9–16.

Schultz, Theodore W. 1964. *Transforming Traditional Agriculture.* New Haven: Yale University Press.

———. 1978. "On the Economics and Politics of Agriculture." In *Distortions of Agricultural Incentives,* edited by Theodore W. Schultz, 3–23. Bloomington: Indiana University Press.

———. 1981. *Investing in People: The Economics of Population Quality.* Berkeley and Los Angeles: University of California Press.

Seers, Dudley. 1970. *The Meaning of Development.* ADC Reprint. New York: Agricultural Development Council.

Sen, Amartya. 1981. *Poverty and Famines.* Oxford: Clarendon Press.

———. 1983. "Development: Which Way Now?" *Economic Journal* 93 (December) 745–62.

———. 1984. *Resources, Values and Development.* Cambridge: Harvard University Press.

———. 1988. "The Concept of Development." In *Handbook of Development Economics,* edited by Hollis Chenery and T. N. Srinivasan, vol. 1, 9–26. Amsterdam: North Holland.

Shapiro, Kenneth H. 1977. "Efficiency Differentials in Peasant Agriculture and Their Implications for Development Policies." *Contributed Papers Read at the 16th International Conference of Agricultural Economists,* 87–98. Oxford: University of Oxford Institute of Agricultural Economics for the International Association of Agricultural Economists.

Singh, Inderjit J. 1988. *Land and Labor in South Asia.* Washington, D.C.: World Bank.

Singh, I. J., L. Squire, and J. Strauss, eds. 1986. *Agricultural Household Models: Extensions, Applications and Policy.* Washington, D.C.: World Bank.

Southworth, Herman M., and Bruce F. Johnston, eds. 1967. *Agricultural Development and Economic Growth.* Ithaca: Cornell University Press.

Spencer, Dunstan S. C. 1976. "African Women in Agricultural Development: A Case Study in Sierra

Leone." Occasional Paper, no. 9. Washington, D.C.: Overseas Liaison Committee, American Council on Education.

Stern, Nicholas. 1989. "The Economics of Development: A Survey." *Economic Journal* 99 (September): 597–685.

Stevens, Robert D., ed. 1977a. *Tradition and Dynamics in Small-Farm Agriculture*. Ames: Iowa State University Press.

———. 1977b. "Transformation of Traditional Agriculture: Theory and Empirical Findings." In *Tradition and Dynamics in Small-Farm Agriculture*, edited by Robert D. Stevens. Ames: Iowa State University Press.

Stevens, Robert D., and Cathy L. Jabara. 1988. *Agricultural Development Principles: Economic Theory and Empirical Evidence*. Baltimore: Johns Hopkins University Press.

Stiglitz, Joseph. 1989. "Markets, Market Failures and Development." *American Economic Review* 79(2): 197–203.

Streeten, Paul. 1979. "Development Ideas in Historical Perspective." In *Toward a New Strategy for Development*, 21–52. Rothko Chapel Colloquium, New York: Pergamon Press. A shorter version of this paper was published in *Economic Growth and Resources*, edited by Irma Adelman, vol. 4, 56–67. New York: St. Martin's Press, 1979.

Streeten, Paul, with Shadid Burke, Mahbub Haq, Norman Hicks, and Frances Stewart. 1981. *First Things First: Meeting Basic Needs in Developing Countries*. New York: Oxford University Press.

Sunkel, O. 1973. "Transnational Capitalism and National Disintegration in Latin America." *Social and Economic Studies* 22:132–76.

Tax, Sol. [1953] 1963. *Penny Capitalism*. Smithsonian Institution, Institute of Social Anthropology Publication no. 16. [Washington, D.C.: U.S. Government Printing Office.] Chicago: University of Chicago Press.

Thorbecke, E., and E. Stoutjesdijk. 1971. *Employment and Output—A Methodology Applied to Peru and Guatemala*. Development Center Studies, Employment Series, no. 2. Paris: Development Center of Organization for Economic Cooperation and Development.

Timmer, C. Peter, Walter P. Falcon, and Scott R. Pearson. 1983. *Food Policy Analysis*. Baltimore: Johns Hopkins University Press.

Tinker, Irene, and Michele Bo Bramsen, eds. 1976. *Women and World Development*. Washington, D.C.: Overseas Development Council.

Todaro, M. P. 1969. "A Model of Labor Migration and Urban Unemployment in Less Developed Countries." *American Economic Review* 59:138–48.

———. 1980. "International Migration in Developing Countries: A Survey." In *Population and Economic Change in Developing Countries*, edited by R. A. Easterlin, 361–402. Chicago: University of Chicago Press.

UNICEF, 1984. "The Impact of World Recession on Children: A UNICEF Special Study." *The State of the World's Children, 1984*. Oxford: Oxford University Press.

United Nations, Department of Economic and Social Affairs. 1951. *Measures for the Economic Development of Underdeveloped Countries*. New York.

Valdés, Alberto. 1986. "Impact of Trade and Macroeconomic Policies on Agricultural Growth: The South American Experience." In *Economic and Social Progress in Latin America, 1986*, 161–83. Washington, D.C.: Inter-American Bank.

Vyas, Vijay, and William E. James. 1988. "Agricultural Development in Asia: Performance, Issues and Policy Options." In *Challenge of Asian Developing Countries: Issues and Analyses*, edited by S. Ichimura, 133–68. Tokyo: Asian Productivity Organization.

Walinsky, Louis J., ed. 1977. *The Selected Papers of Wolf Ladejinsky: Agrarian Reform as Unfinished Business*. New York: Oxford University Press for the World Bank.

Warriner, Doreen. 1955. "Land Reform in Economic Development." National Bank of Egypt Fiftieth Anniversary Commemoration Lectures, Cairo. Reprinted in *Agriculture in Economic Development*, edited by Carl K. Eicher and Lawrence W. Witt, 272–98. New York: McGraw-Hill, 1964.

Weber, Michael, John M. Staatz, John S. Holtzman, Eric W. Crawford, and Richard H. Bernsten. 1988.

38   *John M. Staatz and Carl K. Eicher*

"Informing Food Security Decisions in Africa: Empirical Analysis and Policy Dialogue." *American Journal of Agricultural Economics* 70, no. 5 (December): 1045–54.

Wharton, Clifton R., ed. 1969. *Subsistence Agriculture and Economic Development.* Chicago: Aldine Publishing Co.

World Bank. 1981. *Accelerated Development in Sub-Saharan Africa: An Agenda for Action.* Washington, D.C.: World Bank.

———. 1986. *Poverty and Hunger: Issues and Options for Food Security in Developing Countries.* Washington, D.C.: World Bank.

———. 1988. *Rural Development: World Bank Experience, 1965–86.* Washington, D.C.: World Bank.

World Commission on Environment and Development. 1987. *Our Common Future.* Oxford: Oxford University Press.

II

Historical and Theoretical Perspectives

Introduction

Economists traditionally have analyzed agricultural development in terms of its relationship to the growth of the overall economy. The physiocrats, for example, viewed agriculture as the engine of economic growth, arguing that agriculture was the only activity capable of generating a surplus large enough to stimulate growth in other sectors of the economy. The classical economists, on the other hand, believed that diminishing marginal returns to agricultural land would eventually lead to overall economic stagnation, or the "steady state."[1]

When development economists in the early 1950s turned their attention to agriculture in the Third World, they initially focused on the contribution of agriculture to overall economic growth instead of analyzing the process of agricultural growth per se. Two-sector models, such as those of Lewis (1954), Ranis and Fei (1961), and Jorgenson (1961), stressed intersectoral resource transfers—particularly of labor—from the traditional ("agricultural") sector to the modern ("industrial") sector. Most development economists of the 1950s viewed traditional agriculture as a passive sector that would decline in importance as industrial growth absorbed an increasing share of production and employment.

In the early 1960s, Johnston and Mellor (1961) and several other agricultural economists stressed the fundamental role that agriculture could potentially play in economic development and the importance of understanding the process of agricultural growth per se if that potential was to be exploited. There were numerous attempts in the fifties and sixties to develop increasingly sophisticated specifications of the agricultural sector in economic growth models and to model more carefully the dynamics of growth within the agricultural sector itself.[2]

The four chapters in part II present historical and theoretical perspectives on agricultural development. In chapter 2, Peter Timmer describes the agricultural transformation, "a remarkably uniform process" that is characterized by a declining share of agriculture in a country's labor force and total output as per capita incomes increase. Timmer depicts the agricultural transformation as moving through four phases, with different policy approaches associated with each phase:

1. The early stage of development, characterized by a high percentage (70 to 90 percent) of the labor force in agriculture. In this stage, public investment is needed in research and infrastructure to lay the foundation for agriculture to become a key contributor to economic growth. This is the stage in which the major policy emphasis is on "getting agriculture moving" (Mosher 1966).

2. The stage during which agriculture begins to make major contributions to the growth of other sectors of the economy (Johnston and Mellor 1961). The growth strategy during this stage emphasizes new technology to generate an agricultural surplus and the development of improved factor markets, institutions, and policies to mobilize the agricultural surplus for industrial development without destroying the incentives that sustain agricultural growth.
3. The stage of increased integration of agriculture into the rest of the economy through the development of more efficient input and output markets to link the rural and urban economies.
4. The stage of agriculture in industrial societies, where the share of the labor force in farming falls below 20 percent, the share of food in urban expenditures drops to about 30 percent, and subsidies become common vehicles for maintaining a farm production structure characterized by political influence and overproduction. Although the percentage of the population and GNP based in farming is low in this stage, it usually remains high for the food system more broadly defined. The integration of agriculture with the rest of the economy, which is a central feature of development, leads to the transfer off the farm of many tasks, such as output processing and the production of agricultural inputs. This process of specialization can proceed very far, to the point where only 10 to 15 percent of the value added in food in many industrial countries originates on the farm.

Timmer contends that agriculture's declining share of national output during the structural transformation is partially responsible for the widespread misunderstanding in many Third World countries that agriculture is unimportant, that is, that it does not require public investment and a favorable policy environment. But he shows that the combination of agricultural growth and relative decline is not a paradox but a normal and desirable process and that continuing public and private investments in agriculture are essential to the transformation process.

Agriculture's relative decline in a nation's structural transformation is caused by two well-documented but not widely understood mechanisms. First, Engel's law holds that a less-than-unitary income elasticity for the products of the agricultural sector guarantees that the gross value of sales by farmers will grow less rapidly than the gross domestic product. Second, technical change in agriculture leads to growing agricultural productivity, measured in terms of output per laborer or per hectare, leading to increased supply of farm products. The combination of slow growth in demand for farm products and increased supply leads to falling agricultural prices, which puts pressure on farmers to move out of agriculture. This explains why the proportion of the total population in farming in the United States, for example, has steadily declined, from 40 percent in 1900 to 17 percent in 1940 and 2 percent in 1990.

One of the most important of the questions that flow from Timmer's analysis concerns the role of population growth in speeding or delaying the agrarian transformation. Asia currently faces the challenge of initiating three crucial transitions simultaneously: the demographic transition, the agrarian transition, and the transition towards an industrial society (Chakravarty 1988). Integrating population growth more closely into an analysis of an agricultural transformation is a first step in responding to that challenge. The analysis of Boserup (1981), who argues that demographic pressure has been a driving force throughout history in inducing technological change and diffusion both in agriculture and in industry, lends important insights in this area.

In light of rapid population growth and the persistence of rural poverty in many Third World countries, agricultural growth by itself will not solve the problem of rural poverty. There is a need to analyze how agricultural growth stimulates or impedes growth in other sectors of the economy through intersectoral linkages. In chapter 3, Mellor presents a strategy for broad-based employment and income growth built upon a foundation of agricultural innovation. The engine of growth in this strategy is continuous and institutionalized technological change in agriculture, usually in the basic staples. Mellor argues that such technological change, combined with the proper set of policies, can lead to rapid, employment-oriented growth in the nonagricultural as well as agricultural sectors. A key variable in Mellor's strategy is how the initial adopters of improved agricultural technologies use their increased incomes. If they re-spend a high proportion of increments to income on labor-intensive agricultural and nonagricultural goods, their action generates increased demand for labor. The increased labor demand leads to higher employment in agriculture, industry, and services, so long as capital is not kept artificially cheap so as to induce premature mechanization. Higher employment, in turn, boosts the demand for basic staples, which helps maintain farm prices in the face of the expanded supply. Hence, given appropriate investments in research and policy, the growth of output and employment in the agricultural and nonagricultural sectors can reinforce each other.

The articles by Timmer and Mellor examine the links between agricultural growth and growth in the rest of the economy. The following two articles, by Ruttan and by Hayami and Ruttan, focus on the mechanisms of growth within the agricultural sector itself. In chapter 4, Ruttan outlines six models of agricultural development that are useful in understanding agricultural change in the Third World: the frontier or resource exploitation model, the conservation model, the urban-industrial impact model, the diffusion model, the high-payoff input model, and the induced innovation model. The frontier (area expansion) and conservation models will still be relevant in many countries in the 1990s. In these countries (Indonesia, Malaysia, Zaire, and Brazil are examples) public investments in transportation and rural infrastructure rather than yield-increasing innovations will be strategic factors for increasing output. For instance, until recently Thailand's agricultural boom was fueled by investments in tractors and roads and modest levels of scientific and technological inputs. Yet concerns that this strategy has led to the destruction of tropical rainforests and the possible consequence of global warming raise serious questions about whether continued area expansion truly represents a "cheap" way of expanding agricultural output.[3]

Growing environmental concern has led to revived interest in the conservation model, which in recent years has gone under the name sustainable agriculture. The challenge facing the conservation model is to develop technologies that can generate rates of agricultural growth of 4–5 percent per year, to meet the increasing demand for agricultural products due to population and income growth, rather than 0.5 to 1.0 percent per year, the historical growth rate for this model.

The diffusion model served as the intellectual justification for the heavy emphasis by foreign assistance planners on agricultural extension during the 1950s, and it had a close affinity with the community development (CD) effort of that time.[4] Because the agricultural extension programs and community development efforts of the 1950s often failed to accelerate food production, the diffusion model was deemphasized during the 1960s, and increasing attention was given to agricultural research.

T. W. Schultz's high-payoff input or Green Revolution model was instrumental in convincing international donors and policy makers to devote more resources to the development of new inputs for Third World farmers, such as high-yielding, fertilizer-responsive grain varieties. The model stresses agricultural research and human capital formation, and it became the dominant agricultural development strategy of the 1960s and the 1970s. But the high-payoff input model provides an incomplete explanation of why agricultural growth does or does not occur in a given country. Both technical and institutional change are exogenous to the model. Although technical change is the engine of agricultural growth in the high-payoff input model, the model itself does not predict whether or what types of technical change will occur in a given country's agriculture.

In chapter 5, Ruttan and Hayami present an induced innovation model of agricultural development, in which technical and institutional change are endogenous.[5] Central to the induced innovation model are the notions that countries can pursue alternative paths of technical change and productivity growth in agriculture and that changes in relative factor prices, reflecting changes in relative factor scarcities, can play a determining role in guiding the search for new agricultural technologies and institutions. For example, because of the differences in relative factor prices, reflecting different worker-land ratios, Japan and the United States followed different technological paths. Ruttan and Hayami note that "the classical problem of resource allocation, which was rejected as an adequate basis for agricultural productivity and output growth in the high-payoff input model, is, in this context, treated as central to the agricultural development process. Under conditions of static technology, improvements in resource allocation represent a weak source of economic growth. The efficient allocation of resources to open up new sources of growth is, however, essential to the agricultural development process."[6]

For the induced innovation mechanism to guide technological change along an efficient path, a number of conditions must be met: changes in factor prices must reflect changes in relative factor scarcities, researchers in both the private and public sectors must adjust their research programs in response to changes in factor prices, and so on. Beckford (1984) questions whether these conditions are met in most low-income countries. He further argues that the Ruttan-Hayami model deals with agricultural growth rather than development, because it pays little attention to who benefits from the increase in agricultural output. Since Hayami and Ruttan first outlined their induced innovation model in 1970, the model's emphasis on continuous technical change as central to long-term agricultural growth has been reaffirmed by a large number of tests of the model.[7] A strategic implication of the model is that different nations can pursue different technological paths in response to differences or changes in relative resource endowments and factor prices over time.

More controversial is Hayami and Ruttan's concept of induced *institutional* innovation, which posits that the evolution of economic institutions as well as technology is guided by relative factor prices. The theory states that as relative prices change, incentives are created for certain groups in society to push for institutional changes that would allow the groups to benefit from the changing factor prices. For example, growth in the labor force may lead to pressures to change the institutions governing remuneration of agricultural labor from a fixed share of the harvest to a daily wage. The theory then focuses on the factors affecting the supply of and demand for such institutional innovations (Hayami and Ruttan 1985, 73–114). The concept that economic forces determine the structure of economic institutions is not new; Marx argued the same point in the nineteenth century. What is controversial is the view that relative factor prices, themselves a product of the existing institutional environment, can guide society in the design of "efficient" institutions.

By the late 1980s, the increased emphasis on structural adjustment shifted much of the focus in agricultural development theory and practice back to the role of agriculture in the broader economy. A challenge for the 1990s is to meld that perspective with the more detailed knowledge of the mechanisms of agricultural growth developed during the 1960s and 1970s. Understanding both the mechanisms of agricultural growth and the links between agriculture and the rest of the economy will be crucial in developing strategies that stimulate and use agricultural growth as a tool for alleviating poverty throughout the economy.

NOTES

1. Ricardo argued that the corn yield per acre (taken as a proxy for agricultural productivity) ultimately determined the rate of return to capital invested in all sectors of the economy. Diminishing marginal returns in agriculture therefore led to falling profit rates and economic stagnation. For a discussion of the physiocrats' and classical economists' views of agriculture see Deane 1978.

2. See the volume edited by Reynolds (1975).

3. The problem of possible global warming resulting from the cutting of rainforests for agricultural expansion represents a classic case of an international externality. Although area expansion may appear to be the cheapest way in the short run of expanding agricultural output for the farmers and countries involved, such actions may impose serious long-run costs on the rest of the world's inhabitants. The problem arises because there are no international institutions in place that align the private and social costs facing these farmers (e.g., a system to tax the rest of the world to compensate the farmers for the higher private costs of production from engaging in less environmentally destructive forms of agriculture).

4. Several ingredients of CD programs—local initiative, participation, matching grants—were common to integrated rural development (IRD) projects of the 1970s. The rise and decline of IRD is discussed by Ruttan (1975) and Holdcroft (1984).

5. For more details on the induced innovation model see Hayami and Ruttan 1971, 1985; Binswanger and Ruttan 1978; and Ruttan and Thirtle 1989.

6. See Raj Krishna's comments on the limitations of the induced innovation model's explanation of technical change in agriculture (chapter 9 in this volume).

7. For a summary see Thirtle and Ruttan 1987. Also see Ruttan and Thirtle 1989 for a discussion of induced technical change and African agriculture.

REFERENCES

Beckford, George. 1984. "Induced Innovation Model of Agricultural Development: Comment." In *Agricultural Development in the Third World*, edited by Carl K. Eicher and John M. Staatz, 75–81. Baltimore: Johns Hopkins University Press.

Binswanger, Hans P., and Vernon W. Ruttan. 1978. *Induced Innovation: Technology, Institutions, and Development*. Baltimore: Johns Hopkins University Press.

Boserup, Ester. 1981. *Population and Technical Change*. Chicago: University of Chicago Press.

Chakravarty, Sukhamoy. 1988. "Development Economics in South Asia." *Asian Development Review* 6(1): 22–49.

Deane, Phyllis. 1978. *The Evolution of Economic Ideas*. New York: Cambridge University Press.

Hayami, Yujiro, and Vernon W. Ruttan. 1971 and 1985. *Agricultural Development: An International Perspective*. Baltimore: Johns Hopkins University Press.

Holdcroft, Lane. 1984. "The Rise and Fall of Community Development, 1950–65: A Critical Assessment." In *Agricultural Development in the Third World*, edited by Carl K. Eicher and John M. Staatz, 46–58. Baltimore: Johns Hopkins University Press.

Johnston, Bruce F., and John W. Mellor. 1961. "The Role of Agriculture in Economic Development." *American Economic Review* 51(4): 566–93.

Jorgenson, D. W. 1961. "The Development of a Dual Economy." *Economic Journal* 71 (June): 309–34.

Lewis, W. Arthur. 1954. "Economic Development with Unlimited Supplies of Labour." *Manchester School of Economic and Social Studies* 22(2): 139–91.

Mosher, Arthur T. 1966. *Getting Agriculture Moving: Essentials for Development and Modernization*. New York: Praeger.

Ranis, Gustav, and John C. H. Fei. 1961. "A Theory of Economic Development." *American Economic Review* 51(4): 533–46.

Reynolds, Lloyd G., ed. 1975. *Agriculture in Development Theory*. New Haven: Yale University Press.

Ruttan, Vernon W. 1975. "Integrated Rural Development: A Skeptical Perspective." *International Development Review* 4:9–16.

Ruttan, Vernon, and Colin Thirtle. 1989. "Induced Technical and Institutional Change in African Agriculture." *Journal of International Development* 1(1): 1–45.

Schultz, Theodore W. 1964. *Transforming Traditional Agriculture*. New Haven: Yale University Press.

Thirtle, Colin, and Vernon W. Ruttan. 1987. *The Role of Demand and Supply in the Generation and Diffusion of Technical Change*. London: Harvard Academic Publishers.

2

The Agricultural Transformation

C. PETER TIMMER

The agricultural transformation has been a remarkably uniform process when viewed from outside the agricultural sector itself. As documented by Clark (1940), Kuznets (1966), Chenery and Syrquin (1975), the share of agriculture in a country's labor force and total output declines in both cross-section and time-series samples as incomes per capita increase. The declining importance of agriculture is uniform and pervasive, a tendency obviously driven by powerful forces inherent in the development process, whether in socialist or capitalist countries, Asian, Latin American, or African, currently developed or still poor.

It is at least slightly puzzling, then, that a second uniform and pervasive aspect of the development process also involves agriculture—the apparent requirement that rapid agricultural growth accompany or precede general economic growth. The logic of the classical model of economic growth requires it:

> Now if the capitalist sector produces no food, its expansion increases the demand for food, raises the price of food in terms of capitalist products, and so reduces profits. This is one of the senses in which industrialization is dependent upon agricultural improvement; it is not profitable to produce a growing volume of manufactures unless agricultural production is growing simultaneously. This is also why industrial and agrarian revolutions *always* go together, and why economies in which agriculture is stagnant do not show industrial development (Lewis 1954, 433, emphasis added).

The historical record to which Lewis alludes supports the strong link between agricultural and industrial growth, at least in market-oriented economies. The English model is often held up as the case in point:

> Consider what happened in the original home of industrial development, in England in the eighteenth century. Everyone knows that the spectacular industrial revolution would not have been possible without the agricultural revolution that preceded it. And what was this agricultural revolution? It was based on the introduction of the turnip. The lowly

C. Peter Timmer is Thomas D. Cabot Professor of Development Studies, At-Large, Harvard University.

Reprinted from *Handbook of Development Economics,* volume 1, edited by H. Chenery and T. N. Srinivasan. Copyright © 1988 by Elsevier Science Publishers B. V., Amsterdam. Reprinted with omissions and minor editorial revisions by permission of Elsevier Science Publishers B. V. and the author.

turnip made possible a change in crop rotation which did not require much capital, but which brought about a tremendous rise in agricultural productivity. As a result, more food could be grown with much less manpower. Manpower was released for capital construction. The growth of industry would not have been possible without the turnip and other improvements in agriculture (Nurkse 1953, 52–53).

Despite a significantly different view in the current literature about the impact of the English agricultural revolution on labor productivity, the key importance of the increase in agricultural output has not been challenged (Timmer 1969; Hayami and Ruttan 1985). Nor is this importance restricted to the lessons from the currently developed countries. In surveying the statistical link between agricultural and overall economic growth in currently less developed countries, the World Bank reached the following conclusions:

> The continuing importance of agriculture in the economies of the developing countries is reflected in the association between the growth of agriculture and of the economy as a whole. Among countries where the agricultural share of GDP was greater than 20 percent in 1970, agricultural growth in the 1970s exceeded 3 percent a year in 17 of the 23 countries whose GDP growth was above 5 percent a year. During the same period, 11 of the 17 countries with GDP growth below 3 percent a year managed agricultural growth of only 1 percent or less. Agricultural and GDP growth differed by less than two percentage points in 11 of 15 countries experiencing moderate growth. There have been exceptions, of course, but they prove the rule: fast GDP growth and sluggish agriculture was a feature of some of the oil- or mineral-based economies such as Algeria, Ecuador, Morocco, and Nigeria.
>
> The parallels between agricultural and GDP growth suggest that the factors which affect agricultural performance may be linked to economy-wide social and economic policies. . . . Expanding agricultural production through technological change and trade creates important demands for the ouputs of other sectors, notably fertilizer, transportation, commercial services, and construction. At the same time, agricultural households are often the basic market for a wide range of consumer goods that loom large in the early stages of industrial development—textiles and clothing, processed foods, kerosene and vegetable oils, aluminum holloware, radios, bicycles, and construction materials for home improvements (World Bank 1982, 44–45).

The need for rapid agricultural growth and for the decline in the agricultural sector's share of output and the labor force are not contradictory, of course, but the apparent paradox gave rise to a widespread misperception that agriculture is unimportant—that it does not require resources or a favorable policy environment—*because* its relative share of the economy declines.

So long as market forces provide the primary direction to the sectoral allocation of resources, how academics perceive this process is irrelevant to the process itself. When government planners intercede, however, they do so within a framework of objectives and constraints, and this framework is ultimately conditioned by the prevailing academic understanding of how economic growth proceeds. The mainstream paradigm of the 1950s suggested that agriculture could and should be squeezed on behalf of the more dynamic sectors of the economy. This strategy could be successful if agriculture was already growing rapidly (as in Western Europe and Japan) or if it started with a large surplus relative to the subsistence needs of the rural population (as in the USSR). But if the agricultural sector started with traditional technology and yields and living standards near subsistence, the "squeeze agriculture" paradigm created economic stagnation, not growth. In those cases, major attention was needed to induce an agricultural transformation if the industrial revolution was to have any real hope of success.

Upon closer examination, it is not paradoxical that agricultural growth leads to agricultural decline. At least two mechanisms, now relatively well understood and documented, account for this process of structural transformation.[1] Engel's Law alone, in a closed economy with constant prices, explains a declining share for agriculture (and low farm incomes unless some farmers leave agriculture), no matter how fast the sector grows. Because growth is led by demand patterns in market economies, a less-than-unitary income elasticity for the products of the agricultural sector guarantees that gross value of sales by farmers will grow less rapidly than gross domestic product. As Lewis implies in the previous quotation, if agricultural output fails to grow rapidly enough, rising prices might actually garner farmers a higher share of consumers' expenditures. But this reflects *lower* real incomes, not the result of economic growth.

If the terms of trade are not to rise in favor of agriculture, farm productivity must rise — an agricultural revolution is needed. The second factor that explains the joint agricultural growth and relative decline is seen in the rapid growth in agricultural productivity, measured by output per laborer or output per hectare, in all the successfully developed countries. Technical change in agriculture in all of the OECD (Organization for Economic Cooperation and Development) countries proceeded at such a pace that the long-run terms of trade declined for farm products. Lower prices thus exacerbated the sluggish demand growth due to low income elasticities; the combination put pressure on agricultural resources to move out of farming and into the more rapidly growing sectors of the economy. Such intersectoral movements of resources have been painful in all societies that have undergone successful structural transformation, and all societies have found mechanisms to cushion the adjustment process.

The paradox over the agricultural transformation occurs at this point. Just as countries learn how to institutionalize the process of rapid technical change in agriculture, its product no longer has high social value. The resulting low incomes for farmers create powerful political pressures to slow the process of structural change, and the seemingly inevitable result is massive distortion of the price structure (Johnson 1973; Anderson and Hayami 1986; World Bank 1986). Nearly all rich countries protect their agricultural sectors from international competition, and countries no farther along in the development process than Malaysia, Indonesia, Zimbabwe, and Mexico protect key food-producing sectors during periods of depressed world prices.

THE PROCESS OF AGRICULTURAL TRANSFORMATION

From both historical and contemporary cross-section perspectives, the agricultural transformation seems to evolve through at least four phases that are roughly definable. The process starts when agricultural productivity per worker rises. This increased productivity creates a surplus, which in the second phase can be tapped directly, through taxation and factor flows, or indirectly, through government intervention into the rural-urban terms of trade. This surplus can be utilized to develop the nonagricultural sector, and this phase has been the focus of most dual economy models of development. For resources to flow out of agriculture, rural factor and product markets must become better integrated with those in the rest of the economy. The progressive integration of the agricultural sector into the macro economy, via improved infrastructure and market-equilibrium linkages, represents a third phase in agricultural development. When this phase is successful, the fourth phase is barely noticeable; the role of agriculture in industrialized economies is little different from the role of the steel, housing, or insurance sectors. But when the integration is not successfully accomplished—and most countries have found it extremely difficult for political reasons—governments encounter serious problems of resource allocation and even problems beyond their borders because of pervasive attempts by high-income countries to protect their farmers from foreign competition. Managing agricultural protection and its impact on world commodity markets thus provides a continuing focus for agricultural policy makers even when the agricultural transformation is "complete."

EVOLVING STAGES

The four phases in the agricultural transformation call for different policy approaches, as shown in figure 1. In the earliest stage of development the concern must be for "getting agriculture moving," to use Arthur Mosher's vivid phrase (Mosher 1966). A significant share of a country's investable resources may well be extracted from agriculture at this stage, but this is because the rest of the economy is so small. Direct or indirect taxation of agriculture is the only significant source of government revenue.

Building a dynamic agriculture requires that some of these resources be devoted to the agricultural sector itself. As the section on agricultural development policy at the end of this chapter explains, these resources need to be allocated to public investment in research and infrastructure as well as to favorable price incentives to farmers to adopt new technology as it becomes available. As these investments *in* agriculture begin to pay off, the second phase emerges in which the agricultural sector becomes a key contributor to the overall growth process through a combination of factors outlined by Johnston and Mellor (1961).

As the empirical literature on structural patterns of growth emphasizes, there is a substantial disequilibrium between agriculture and industry at this early stage of the development process (Kuznets 1966; Chenery and Taylor 1968; Chenery and Syrquin 1975). Indeed, differences in labor productivity and measured income (as

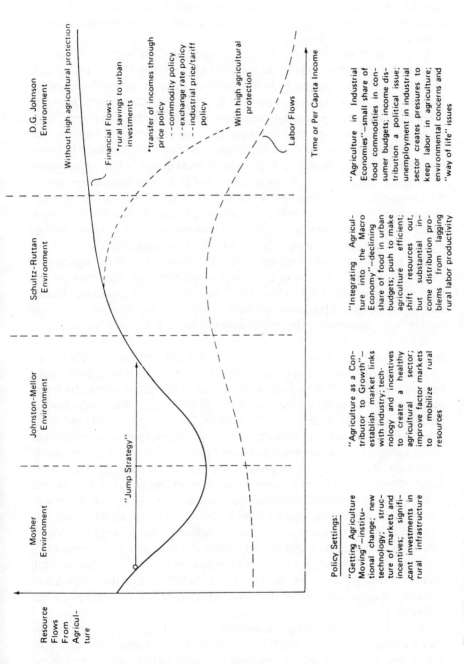

Fig.1. Changing Environments for Agriculture's Contribution to Economic Growth

opposed to psychic income) between the rural and urban sectors persist to the present in rich countries, although the gap is narrowing and now depends on agricultural prices for any given year.[2]

The process of narrowing the gap gives rise to the third environment for agriculture, in which is it integrated into the rest of the economy through the development of more efficient labor and credit markets that link the urban and rural economies. This integration is a component of the contribution process; the improved functioning of factor markets merely speeds the process of extracting labor and capital from those uses in agriculture with low returns for those in industry or services with higher productivity. The improved markets have welfare consequences as well, because they lessen the burden on individuals trapped in low-income occupations. The gain has costs, however. As agriculture is integrated into the macro economy, it becomes much more vulnerable to fluctuations in macro prices and level of aggregate activity and trade (Schuh 1976) and much less susceptible to management by traditional instruments for the agricultural sector, such as extension activities and specific programs for commodity development and marketing.

This vulnerability and complexity create the fourth phase in the agricultural transformation, the treatment of agriculture in industrialized economies. As the share of the labor force in agriculture falls below about 20 percent and the share of food expenditures in urban household budgets drops to about 30 percent, low-cost food is not as important to the overall economy nor is it as expensive in relative terms to increase in price (Anderson 1983). A host of political problems arise if low farm incomes, induced by rapid technical change and low farm-gate prices, are allowed to push resources out of agriculture. Farmers do not want to leave, especially if they must sell their farms under duress at low prices; and urban-based unions do not want to see them coming to the cities in search of industrial jobs. A nostalgic memory of farming as a "way of life" leads many second- and third-generation farm migrants living in cities to lend political support to higher incomes for agriculture, even at the expense of higher grocery bills (which may be barely noticeable). By this stage of the process, the share of the farm-gate price of the commodity in the consumer's market basket is small, because of processing and marketing costs. Commodity price supports become the primary vehicle for supporting farm incomes, and the subsidies have devastating effects on resource allocation. Farmers invest heavily in land and machinery when farm prices are high, only to produce surpluses that are impossible to sell profitably (Johnson 1985; Cochrane 1979). Eventually, the budgetary and distortionary costs of this approach become so high that even the European Community, Japan, or the United States must face choices over how to rationalize agricultural returns with their social profitability.

The economic environments for agriculture created by these four phases are shown schematically in figure 1. The financial and labor resource flows out of agriculture over time (or as incomes increase in a cross-section sample) are impressionistic. Whether the trough between the "Mosher environment" and the "Johnston-Mellor environment" in figure 1 drops into negative ground or always remains positive presumably depends on alternative sources of financial resources at this stage in development. Urban or overseas remittances, petroleum revenues, or foreign assistance might temporarily fill the gap left by a declining relative contribution from agriculture.[3] But as agricultural productivity begins to rise, labor and financial flows to the rest of the economy increase. The "Schultz-Ruttan environment" begins as the absolute population in agriculture starts to decline, and the "D. G. Johnson environment" begins as the agricultural labor force drops to a fairly small proportion of the overall labor force. Whether financial resources continue to flow out of agriculture at this stage in the process depends almost entirely on government price policy and its resulting impact on farm investment. Policies to cushion the impact on farmers of successful structural change need not inevitably rely on price interventions that impede the adjustment process, but price supports have been the most popular in the United States, Western Europe, and Japan, for plausible political reasons (Anderson and Hayami 1986).

Agriculture and Economic Development

This overview of the agricultural transformation raises two basic issues to be discussed in this chapter: the contribution or role of agriculture in economic development and the conditions or factors that lead to the modernization of the agricultural sector itself. Obviously, many other important topics are not treated here. One is the changing control over resources in the rural sector, which determines who gains and who loses during the agricultural transformation. Only the structuralist and radical political economy literature deals directly with the distribution of income and power in rural areas as an integral component of agricultural development. A major theme of "neo-neoclassical analysis" since the mid-1970s, however, has been the incorporation of such issues into rational actor models of rural household decision making. While much of the dynamic and macroeconomic perspective of the radical models is lost in the household models, much is gained in the form of testable hypotheses about the impact of new technology or pricing policies on the structure of rural markets and distribution of output in the short run.

The historical record after the Second World War suggests that many countries saw an opportunity to pursue a "jump strategy" and move directly from the early stages of the Mosher environment (see figure 1) to the later stages of the Johnston-Mellor environment, thus bypassing the necessity to invest in agricultural development.

Bairoch describes some of the difficulties inherent in a jump strategy as follows:

> . . . the most significant comparison . . . is that between the levels of productivity in the under-developed countries and the western countries at the period when the latter began to industrialize. . . . The present average level of agricultural productivity in African and Asian countries (between them representing four-fifths of the Third World population) is 45 percent below that reached by the developed countries at the start of the industrial revolution. In fact it is at the same level as that of the European countries before their agricultural revolution.
>
> Now, most under-developed countries wish, consciously or unconsciously, to by-pass

this stage just when other structural conditions of development are making a "take off" more difficult than it was when most European countries and the United States were imitating England's example. What makes the failure to admit or even to recognize this problem all the more serious is that the problem itself is intractable. Leaving aside mental attitudes, landownership and political considerations, it cannot be stressed too forcibly that an increase in the area cultivated per agricultural worker is one of the essential conditions of an increase in productivity. But in view of the population explosion it is impossible to assume, even on most hopeful assumption, that the reduction in cultivated area per worker will be anything but slight (Bairoch 1975, 42).

A jump strategy sees the extraction of resources from agriculture for economic development as being in conflict with the investment of public and private resources in its modernization. This has been especially true in countries with systems of planned resource allocations designed to force the pace of economic development. As more and more countries adopted the paradigm of central planning to direct these resource allocations, the separate issues of contribution and modernization became key analytical issues as well. Unfortunately, the economics profession was ill-equipped to address them because all previous examples of agricultural modernization had taken place within more or less market-oriented settings (except in the Soviet Union, where agricultural modernization remains quite incomplete). The behavior of backward agricultural systems under the new planning context became a topic of much theorizing and debate, but only in the 1960s and 1970s did the empirical record become both long and varied enough to draw reasonably firm conclusions.

It is worth summarizing briefly what the empirical record showed by 1960 when the results of Kuznets's decade-long study of the quantitative aspects of modern economic growth started to be widely available. The historical record began as early as the late eighteenth century in the United Kingdom and in 1839 in the United States and as late as 1880 in Japan and 1925 in the USSR. For all countries for all time periods observed, the share of agriculture in the total labor force declined, sometimes sharply, as in Sweden, the United States, and Japan, and sometimes more gradually, as in the United Kingdom, Belgium, Italy, and Australia. The share of agriculture in national output showed slightly more mixed patterns than those of the labor force. The share was nearly stable or even rose slightly over some periods in the United Kingdom, France, the United States, and Australia. The more general tendency of the share in output to decline is clear, but the share of the labor force always declined more rapidly. The obvious result was that labor productivity in agriculture rose more rapidly than in the economy as a whole when measured over the long periods of time required for sustained economic growth to cause substantial changes in the structure of an economy. Although agricultural productivity per worker was nearly always less than the level of national productivity, its faster rise meant that the gap tended to narrow.

Three clear exceptions to this trend in Kuznets's data are Italy, Japan, and the USSR, all of which are latecomers to the process of sustained growth and are countries in which state intervention into the industrialization process was much more active than in the early developers. The failure of agricultural productivity per worker to rise as fast as national productivity in these three countries might thus be seen as an early signal that the patterns in the less developed countries seeking to start down the path of modern economic growth might be significantly different from the historical path followed by the Western countries and documented by Kuznets. Hayami (1986) shows that the recent productivity record for the rapidly growing East Asian economies confirms a strongly different pattern from that in North America and Western Europe. Even the more slowing growing developing countries (Philippines and India) have a mild reversal of the "traditional" pattern in which growth in labor productivity in agriculture exceeds that of labor productivity in manufacturing.

This "premature" growth in manufacturing productivity (or, alternatively, the neglect of efforts needed to raise agricultural productivity) is especially troubling in historical perspective, as the quote from Bairoch indicated. Table 1 reproduces Bairoch's historical comparisons of "net agricultural production by male labor employed in agriculture expressed in 'direct' calories." Only Italy in 1840 had a lower productivity level than that of Africa and Asia in modern times. The gap in agricultural productivity on average between European countries beginning their in-

TABLE 1
COMPARISONS BETWEEN LEVELS OF AGRICULTURAL PRODUCTIVITY

Country and Stage of Development	Period	Index Number of Agricultural Productivity
Developed Countries		
Recent position		
France	1968/72	100.0
United States	1968/72	330.0
Position before or during "take-off"		
France	1810	7.0
Great Britain	1810	14.0
Sweden	1810	6.5
Belgium	1840	10.0
Germany	1840	7.5
Italy	1840	4.0
Russia	1840	7.0
Switzerland	1840	8.0
United States	1840	21.5
Spain	1860	11.0
Less Developed Countries		
Recent position		
Africa	1960/64–1968/72	4.7
Latin America[a]	1960/64–1968/72	9.8
Asia	1960/64–1968/72	4.8
Middle East	1960/64–1968/72	8.6
Total for all less developed countries	1960/64–1968/72	5.5

SOURCE: Bairoch 1975.
[a]Excluding Argentina.

dustrial revolutions and Africa and Asia is, as Bairoch already noted, about 45 percent. "A gap of about 45 percent is sufficiently wide for us to be able to assert that agricultural conditions in the currently developed countries before the beginning of the industrial revolution must have been very different from those of the under-developed countries of Asia and Africa today" (Bairoch 1975, 40–41).

THE ROLE OF THE AGRICULTURAL SECTOR

The debate over the role of agriculture in the process of economic development extends at least as far back as the physiocrats in the eighteenth century. The biblical advice to store during seven good years to be ready for seven lean years certainly reflects a concern for agricultural planning. Clark (1940) and Kuznets (1966) provided the general facts about the role of agriculture during the growth process available to economists and planners at the beginning of the drive for economic growth in the less developed countries. These facts formed the basis for the prevailing neoclassical view that agriculture was a declining sector, a "black box" in Little's phrase (1982), which contributed labor, food, and perhaps capital to the essential modernization efforts in industry. No policy efforts on behalf of agriculture's own modernization were needed because the sector declined naturally. Most interpretations of the Lewis model (1954), especially the Fei-Ranis versions (1964), which became the main teaching paradigms, ignored the factors needed to modernize traditional agricultural sectors so that they could play positive contributory roles in the development of the rest of the economy. The structuralist views of Prebisch (1950) about declining terms of trade for traditional products and the importance Hirschman (1958) attached to linkages to "modern" economic activities further diminished any apparent rationale for actively investing in the modernization of agriculture itself. As Hirschman wrote in 1958, "agriculture certainly stands convicted on the count of its lack of direct stimulus to the setting up of new activities through linkage effects—the superiority of manufacturing in this respect is crushing" (Hirschman 1958, 109–10).

A final reason for the neglect of agriculture has recently been clarified by Sah and Stiglitz (1984). The Soviet debate in the early 1920s over industrialization policy revolved around whether turning the terms of trade against agriculture (the "price scissors") would speed the rate of accumulation for investment by the state. Preobrazhensky (1965) argued successfully that it could. Sah and Stiglitz show the precise conditions under which he was right and the welfare consequences that flowed from implementing such a policy. Although the conditions that must hold for their analysis to be valid are very stringent, a robust result is that the agricultural terms of trade should be lowered only if the state has a low rate of time discount, that is, it favors investment over current consumption. Forced-pace industrialization campaigns in such circumstances then rely on the state's capacity to extract surpluses from agriculture even in the face of stagnant or falling agricultural production.

It is easy to see why agriculture was neglected as a source of growth in early strategies of economic development. The historical record shows that it always declines in relative importance in growing economies. It is the home of traditional people, ways, and living standards—the antithesis of what nation builders in developing countries envisioned for their societies. Moreover, agriculture was thought to provide the only source of productivity that could be tapped to fuel the drive for modernization. Surplus labor, surplus savings, and surplus expenditures to buy the products of urban industry, and even surplus foreign exchange to buy the machines to make them, could be had from an uncomplaining agricultural sector. Nothing more was needed to generate these resources than the promise of jobs in the cities and a shared nationalistic pride in the growing power of the state. Despite how simplistic these promises sound in the mid-1982s, the success of the Soviet approach caused them to be very appealing when first uttered by such charismatic leaders of the developing world as Sukarno, Nkrumah, Nasser, and Nehru. The unique features of agriculture as a sector were simply not widely understood in the 1950s. Nor was it accepted that the development of a modern agriculture was necessary as a concomitant to development of the rest of the economy.

Some of these factors began to be recognized by the 1960s, and a more positive emphasis was placed on "role" rather than the more forced concept of "contribution" of agriculture. The classic article by Johnston and Mellor (1961) listed five roles for agriculture in economic development:

1. increase the supply of food for domestic consumption;
2. release labor for industrial employment;
3. enlarge the size of the market for industrial output;
4. increase the supply of domestic savings; and
5. earn foreign exchange.

Although the second, fourth, and fifth roles are certainly consistent with the earlier "extractive" views of agriculture, Johnston and Mellor insisted that all five roles are equally important. Agriculture in the process of development is to provide increased food supplies and higher rural incomes to enlarge markets for urban output, as well as to provide resources to expand that urban ouput.

It is our contention that "balanced growth" is needed in the sense of simultaneous efforts to promote agricultural and industrial development. We recognize that there are severe limitations on the capacity of an underdeveloped country to do everything at once. But it is precisely this consideration which underscores the importance of developing agriculture in such a way as to both minimize its demand on resources most needed for industrial development and maximize its net contribution required for general growth (Johnston and Mellor 1961, 590–91).

Others, especially Nicholls (1963), Schultz (1953), and Jorgenson (1961), also emphasized this interdependence between a country's agriculture and its industry. Myint (1975) stressed a curious inconsistency between the "closed economy" model implicit in this domestic interdependence and the fifth role, earning foreign exchange, which obviously implies the country is open to international trade. This trade perspective returns in the 1970s and 1980s to dominate thinking about appropriate development strategies, but it was largely ignored in the 1960s, perhaps because of the dominance of the "Indian model" in development thinking, in which sheer size keeps the importance of foreign trade quite small, even apart from the "inward looking" strategy being pursued.

Despite the early insistence by agricultural economists that the agricultural sector must be viewed as part of the overall economy and that the emphasis be placed on the sector's interdependence with the industrial and service sectors rather than on its forced contributions to them, the notion of agriculture as a resource reservoir has persisted in general development models. Reynolds emphasized an important but usually overlooked distinction between static and dynamic views of the resource transfers:

> In most development models, modern industry is the cutting edge of economic growth, while agriculture plays the role of a resource reservoir which can be drawn on for supplies of food, labor, and finance to fuel the growth or urban activities. It is argued that this is both a logical necessity and a matter of historical experience, illustrated by the case of Japan.
>
> In commenting on this view, I must emphasize a distinction that is often not clearly drawn: (1) It is one thing to assert that, in an economy where agricultural output is not rising, the agricultural sector contains potential surpluses of labor time, food output, and saving capacity requiring only appropriate public policies for their release. This we may term the static view of resource transfer. (2) It is quite a different thing to assert that, in an economy where agricultural output is being raised by a combination of investment and technical progress, part of the increment in farm output and income is available for transfer to non-agriculture. This we may term the dynamic view of resource transfer. The model-building implications of this approach are different, and its policy implications are decidedly different (Reynolds 1975, 14–15).

The welfare consequences of the two views are also sharply different. Forced extraction of resources from a stagnant agricultural sector almost always creates widespread rural poverty, sometimes famine. Market linkages that connect a dynamic agricultural sector to rapidly growing industrial and service sectors offer an opportunity for rural inhabitants to choose in which sector they wish to participate. There are certainly losers in this process: high-cost producers in unfavorable ecological settings who cannot compete with low-cost producers in favored locales who have access to new technology; or newly landless laborers who have lost their tenancy access to land when commercial relationships replace patron-client relationships. But new technology and market linkages create more opportunities than they destroy if both the agricultural and nonagricultural sectors are growing. An emphasis on finding the policy environment that creates such mutual growth is needed. For agriculture, that environment must call forth rapid technical change. Experience since the mid-1960s has demonstrated how to do that, but the key has been to understand why the agricultural sector is different from the industrial and service sectors (Hayami and Ruttan 1985; Timmer, Falcon, and Pearson 1983).

WHY AGRICULTURE IS DIFFERENT

The early purposeful neglect of agriculture can in part be attributed to development economists who were remote from any real understanding of what makes the agricultural sector quite different from either manufacturing or services (Little 1982). In developing countries, the agricultural sector is different from other productive sectors of an economy, particularly in its large contribution to national income and the large numbers of participants in the sector. Both the agricultural transformation itself and the contribution of agriculture to the rest of the economy depend on three important features discussed here: the peculiarities of the agricultural production function, the importance of home consumption of output for the sector, and the role of the agricultural sector as a resource reservoir. These features are more evident in traditional societies, and their distinctiveness erodes during the process of economic modernization. The design of agricultural policy, in both poor and rich countries, is complicated by these features, but a recognition of them is essential to a full understanding of the contribution agriculture might realistically be asked to make to a country's development effort.[4]

DECISION MAKING IN AGRICULTURE

In both private and collective agricultures, decision making is conditioned primarily by the nature of incentives to work rather than by the pace and design of the work itself, and these incentives are difficult to structure in an efficient manner unless the cultivator owns the land. In situations where ownership and operation are separate, a host of complicated contractual arrangements that strive for second-best efficiency outcomes have evolved in different settings.

Farming is an undertaking that involves many decisions. What crops to plant, what inputs to use, when to plow, to seed, to cultivate, to irrigate, to harvest, how much to keep for home consumption, how much to sell and how much to store for later sale are the farming decisions that occupy the daily routine of most agricultural producers. What is unique about agriculture is that literally millions of individuals and households are making these decisions themselves. Changing agricultural production decisions to increase food output is an entirely different process from changing decisions about how much steel or cement to produce. In most countries a dozen or so individuals could take direct action which would lead to a 10 percent increase in steel output in a year or so, and their decisions would be decisive.

Nowhere, not even in socialist countries, can a similar small group of individuals decide to raise food production by 10 percent. A small group of planners, or the president and the cabinet, can decide they *want* food production to rise by 10 percent. They can tell the food logistics agency, the ministry of agriculture, the newspapers, and agricultural extension agents that they want food production to rise by 10 percent. But they cannot increase food production 10 percent by themselves. They must also convince the millions of farmers in their country to want to increase food production by 10 percent and make it in their self-interest to do so.

The vast number of agricultural decision makers implies that there are simply too many to reach directly with either pleas for cooperation or police power. Farmers must see the benefits of higher output for themselves because there are too many opportunities to let high yields slip beneath the hoe or in a late fertilizer application, even under the watchful eyes of a guardian. Farming is a subtle combination of skilled craft and brute force. The brute force alone will not achieve high yields.

CHARACTERISTICS OF AGRICULTURAL PRODUCTION FUNCTIONS

Several unique features of agricultural production functions contribute to the decision-intensity of farming, to the productivity of the family farm, and to the search for reasonably efficient substitutes for direct landownership where the family farm is not prevalent. Seasonality and geographical dispersion are important.

SEASONALITY

Two features of seasonality are important in designing agricultural policy. First, seasonal aspects of agricultural production frequently constrain yields because of input bottlenecks. Labor (and its supervision) is most often the constraining factor, but fertilizer, seeds, credit, or irrigation water supplies must also be available in highly specific time periods. When fertilizer reaches the village godown a month after the proper application time, it might as well not have arrived at all. Government authorities responsible for the management of agricultural input supply distribution are frequently unaware of or insensitive to the extreme importance of timely input availability. Suppliers whose incomes depend on providing inputs to farmers when and where needed are much more responsive to shifts in weather, cropping patterns, and new technologies than are agencies trying to allocate inputs within the guidelines of five-year plans and supplies available from a planned industrial sector. Modern agriculture that uses industrial inputs as the basis for high yields is a dynamic enterprise quite unlike factories. Input and output markets must function efficiently, reacting to weather changes, alterations in cropping patterns, and technical change if production is to grow rapidly. Centrally planned allocations of industrial products to the agricultural sector are almost never in the right place at the right time, nor are they even the right products.

Second, there are often very high private economic returns to eliminating seasonal bottlenecks in production. When these private returns are at least partly generated by higher and more stable yields of agricultural products, society is also likely to gain. But if the private gains come from displacing hired labor that has few alternative production opportunities, the social gains might be small or even negative. The seasonal dimensions to agricultural production complicate the planning process considerably. Most agricultural data are published on an annual basis, and there is an inevitable tendency to think about the sector in terms of the same annual growth performance criteria that are used to evaluate the steel or cotton textile industries. Such an annual approach hides two important roles for government analysis and intervention: in the appropriate provision of inputs when and where they are needed, and in the full analysis of the social impact on agricultural production of private investments to reduce seasonal bottlenecks.

GEOGRAPHICAL DISPERSION

Agriculture is the only major sector that uses the land surface as an essential input into its production function. In combination, seasonality and geographical dispersion create the need for a marketing system that can store the product from a short harvest period to the much longer period of desired consumption and can move the commodity from the farm where it was grown to the many households where it will be consumed. Both of these functions require that the commodity change hands and that exchange of ownership take place. This transaction can happen only when both parties agree on the terms of the exchange or the price for the commodity at the point of sale. In socialist economies the terms of exchange are often set by the state. But all other marketing services must still be provided if the food grown by farmers is to be eaten by consumers. This necessary growth of marketing services is an often overlooked component of the agricultural transformation.

THE FARM HOUSEHOLD AS PRODUCER AND CONSUMER

Most farm households still retain some or most of their farm production for home consumption, and this role of home consumption is a further distinguishing feature of the agricultural sector. Few steelworkers or even textile workers take their products home for household use. Only under highly restrictive and unrealistic assumptions about the completeness of markets and access of all farm households to them can production and consumption decisions be analyzed separately (Singh, Squire, and Strauss 1986). In rural areas of developing countries, the need to make connected production and consumption decisions within a single household obviously complicates life for the farm household; the value of additional time spent in food preparation or tending the children must be balanced against the productivity of an additional hour weeding the rice, driving the ducks, or tending the home garden. Where it exists, the opportunity to spend some of that time working for cash on a neighbor's farm or in a rural wage-labor market places a lower bound on the value of household-farm time, and the value of leisure ultimately places a limit on the willingness to work, especially at low-productivity tasks. For households with inadequate land to grow surplus crops for sale and with limited outside employment opportunities, however, the marginal value of leisure time might be low indeed, possibly near zero. Even tiny increments to output can be valuable for very poor households.

WHAT DIFFERENCE DOES THE DIFFERENCE MAKE?

Two important implications flow from the distinctive characteristics of agriculture relative to industry, and both are treated extensively in sections that follow.

First, if agricultural decision making is in fact based on rational assessments of highly heterogeneous environments, substantial knowledge of micro environments is necessary to understand the impact of policy interventions or technical change on the agricultural sector. Designing new technology and fostering its widespread adoption is primarily a public sector activity because of the relatively small scale of individual farmers, but the success of any given technical innovation depends on the private decisions of those same multitudinous farmers. Understanding the source, dynamics, and impact of technical change in agriculture is thus a major part of understanding the agricultural transformation, a process vastly complicated by the smallness of scale, geographic dispersion, and heterogeneity of the environment, both economic and ecological, that is characteristic of agriculture in developing countries.

The second important implication of agriculture's distinctiveness is how it conditions the role of public policy, particularly that other than the design and implementation of research leading to technical change. The vision dies hard of agriculture as a resource reservoir to be tapped indiscriminately, without reinvestment or adverse consequences for growth, on behalf of the urban economy. Although a few countries have a record of sustained progress in agriculture and concomitant overall economic growth, the list is short. Only eight countries listed in the *World Development Report 1986* have growth rates for agricultural GDP of 3 percent per year or greater for both the 1965–73 and 1973–84 periods, along with growth rates for total GDP of 4 percent per year or greater for the same two periods: Kenya, Pakistan, Indonesia, the Ivory Coast, the Philippines, Thailand, Brazil, and Mexico. Sri Lanka and Turkey came close; Malaysia would probably have been included had data been available for the earlier period. Because population growth in several of these countries is near or more than 3 percent per year, even these excellent aggregate performances leave the rate of growth per capita at levels that permit a doubling of incomes in a quarter of a century at best.

It has obviously been difficult to find the right mix of policies to sustain agricultural growth. Much of the reason traces to a failure of policy makers to understand the characteristics of agriculture that make policy design so complicated. They face yet another paradox: the essentially private-sector nature of agricultural decision making at the same time that the environment for that decision making is heavily dependent on sound government interventions into agricultural research, rural infrastructure, and market relationships. The distinctive characteristics of agriculture argue that governments intervene into agricultural decision making at great risk, for they can easily cause farmers to withdraw from making investments and producing for the market, which are essential to mobilizing resources for overall economic growth. And yet, intervene they must. The environment for transforming agriculture is a public good created by wise but active public intervention.

It is easy to get the mix wrong, even to have the elements backward. Some governments have tried to dictate farm-level decisions on inputs and outputs while totally ignoring both the investments in research and infrastructure needed to create a healthy agriculture and the pricing environment that will mobilize peasants on behalf of higher productivity.

AGRICULTURAL DEVELOPMENT STRATEGY

ALTERNATIVE STRATEGIES FOR MAINTAINING THE TRANSFORMATION PROCESS

Several lessons have been learned since the mid-1960s about the functioning of the agricultural sector and its potential role in the development process. The agricultural sector has been seen in a general-equilibrium perspective, and the importance of macroeconomic policy for agricultural performance has been recognized. Rapid economic growth has been considered necessary to deal with the human welfare concerns that stem from poverty and hunger, and such growth is feasible because of the potential for technical change. Market-oriented systems with private incentives have shown superior performance in achieving this growth. Policy analysis has tended to concentrate on one of three dimensions of government intervention into the agricultural growth process: (1) stimulating traditional agriculture into growth; (2) maintaining the transformation process and the contribution of agriculture to overall economic growth; and protecting the welfare of farmers from their own high productivity during the final and painful stages of structural change in industrialized societies. Here we discuss the second of these dimensions, maintaining the transformation process.

The agricultural sector is a means to an end—not an end in itself. Three sharply different paths for appropriate policies toward agriculture are open if the goal is to speed the overall process of development. The first path has parallels to the philosophy of the 1950s, in which benign neglect of agricultural policy was thought to be sufficient for stimulating the process of economic growth. This perspective grows out of the recognition of the role of well-functioning markets and decision makers operating in a world of "rational expectations." In this view, most policy is irrelevant to farmers in more than a very transitory sense, and this is especially true of price policy:

> One lesson that we should be able to learn from observation of the world is that the absolute incomes earned by farm families in various countries have no relationship to farm prices. Even stronger, the relative incomes of farm families have no relationship to farm prices, except as benefits of higher prices have been capitalized into the value of land and land has been acquired by gift or inheritance (Johnson 1985, 43).

In this world, agricultural incomes are determined by employment opportunities outside agriculture, the agricultural sector *must* decline in proportional output terms and absolutely in the labor force, and the long-run decline in basic agricultural commodity prices due to technical change simply emphasizes that society is best served by getting resources out of agriculture as rapidly as possible. Although the clearest case for this view of the world is in the OECD countries, a host of middle-income countries, and even some quite poor countries, are also facing the problem of declining real incomes in the agricultural sector under the impact of rapid technical change domestically and lower world prices for the resulting output. This perspective is obviously consistent with the view that open economies will show better performance than those with substantial trade barriers.

A sharply different path has been sketched by Mellor and Johnston (1984). Building on their earlier stress on balanced growth (Johnston and Mellor 1961), they call for an "interrelated rural development strategy" that improves nutrition in one dimension while it fosters the broader growth process in the other. The approach calls for a major role of government in strategic design and program implementation, a role that is in marked contrast with the free-market approach sketched out previously:

> We have, therefore, emphasized that improvements in nutrition [one of Mellor and Johnston's key objectives for agricultural development] require a *set of interacting forces:* accelerated growth in agriculture; wage goods production; a strategy of development that structures demand towards high employment content goods and services; increased employment; and increased effective demand for food on the part of the poor. Agricultural growth not only satisfies the need for food to meet nutritional requirements (which is the other side of the wage-goods coin), but fosters a favorable employment-oriented demand structure as well. Agriculture's role in generating a structure of demand, favorable to rapid growth in employment, is central (Mellor and Johnston 1984, 567–68, emphasis added).

Mellor and Johnston go on to summarize their earlier argument that agriculture can play this multiplicity of roles only if a unimodal development strategy is followed, that is, one in which a broad base of smallholders are the central focus of agricultural research and extension services and the recipient of the bulk of receipts from agricultural sales. The authors see the dualism inherent in bimodal strategies—those placing modernization efforts primarily on large, "progressive" farms while neglecting the "backward" smallholders—as the major obstacle to putting their set of interacting forces in motion:

> The most common barrier to the interrelated strategy indicated is pronounced dualism in capital allocations—too much to industry and the unproductive elements of the private sector rather than to agriculture, and to capital-intensive elements within those, as well as to large-scale and therefore capital-intensive allocations within agriculture. The outcome of the strategy will depend upon national-level decisions about macroeconomic policies, exchange rates, interest rates, and investment allocations among sectors and regions, not just within agriculture itself. Indeed, the whole strategy fails if it is viewed simply as the responsibility of agriculture ministries (Mellor and Johnston 1984, 568).

This interrelated strategy must be directed by government planners; there is relatively little concern or role for the private sector, other than small farmers. The analysis leading to the strategy remains heavily influenced by closed economy considerations, and little attention is given to either domestic marketing activities or their relationship to international markets.

Three key elements are suggested as essential to meeting all objectives of agricultural development:

1. massive investment in human capital through nutrition, health, and family planning services in the countryside;
2. creation of the complex rural organizational structures seen in Japan and Taiwan that provide services to small farmers while also serving as a voice for their interests; and
3. investment in rapid technical change appropriate to these small farmers in order to raise agricultural output and rural incomes simultaneously.

Notably missing in this list of key elements is significant concern for the structure of incentives for agriculture relative to industry's or for the country's tradables relative to those of foreign competitors. Although it is realized that the macroeconomic setting is no doubt important to agriculture, it remains outside the scope of appropriate strategy for agricultural development. Not surprisingly, given the argument in Johnston and Clark (1982), the intellectual foundation for this strategy lies in rural development, not in a vision of agriculture linked to the macro economy and world markets by powerful market mechanisms. It is this latter vision which provides the third potential path for agricultural development strategy for the 1990s.

The third approach contrasts with both the "free market" and "interrelated rural development strategy" approaches. It calls for government policy interventions into outcomes in domestic markets but uses markets and the private marketing sector as the vehicle for those policy interventions. This "price and marketing policy" approach recognizes widespread *market failures* in agriculture as well as extensive *government failures* in implementation of direct economic functions. The strategic dilemma is how to cope with segmented rural capital and labor markets, poorly functioning land markets, the welfare consequences of sharp instability of prices in commodity markets, the pervasive lack of information about current and future events in most rural economies, and the sheer absence of many important markets, especially for future contingencies involving yield or price risks.

One powerful lesson emerged from the postwar development record: direct government interventions through state-owned enterprises to correct market failures frequently make matters worse by inhibiting whatever market responses were possible in the initial circumstances, without providing greater output or more efficient utilization of resources. The agricultural sector in particular is vulnerable to well-intended but poorly conceived and managed parastatal organizations that attempt a wide array of direct economic activities, including monopoly control of input supplies, capital-intensive state farms, and mandated control over crop marketing and processing. As Bates (1981) has demonstrated, these direct controls and agencies have a strong political economy rationale for a government that tries to reward its supporters and centralize power and resources in the hands of the state. (See also Lipton 1977.)

The answer to the dilemma over making matters worse, in the "price and market policy" approach, is to gain a much clearer understanding of the necessary interaction between the public and private sectors. Government intervention into agriculture for political reasons has an ancient history. One major claim of monarchs to the throne was their capacity to keep food prices cheap and stable, as Kaplan (1984) made clear and as several modern governments have discovered, to their demise. Political objectives for the performance of agriculture—its capacity to feed the population regularly and cheaply or its ability to provide fair incomes to farmers caught in the painful pressures of successful structural transformation—are inevitable and, in some long-run sense, highly desirable.

The "price and marketing policy" path argues that these objectives are best served by making carefully designed interventions into the prices determined in markets, not by leaving markets alone or by striving to reach the objectives through direct activities by the government (Timmer 1986). If the "free market" approach incurs heavy political costs as markets relentlessly redistribute incomes to the winners in the course of economic development, and the "interrelated rural development strategy" incurs heavy managerial and administrative costs as the government plays an active and direct economic role, the "price and marketing policy" approach incurs heavy analytical costs.

These analytical costs come from the need to understand each country's path of structural change, the workings of factor and commodity markets, and the potential impact of macro and commodity price interventions on these markets and ultimately on the structural path itself. It requires that government intervention be based on an empirical understanding of economic responses to a change in policy and the political repercussions from them. There is an important role for models in illuminating where to look for these responses, but the models themselves cannot provide the answers. This is especially true as attempts are made to build into the models the response of policy itself to changes in the economic environment (see Roe, Shane, and Vo 1986). Such endogenous policy models might reveal some of the historical factors that accounted for policy shifts, but they seldom provide a sense of when the degrees of freedom for policy initiative are about to expand. Frequently, this is in times of crisis. Policy makers often embark on bold experiments in such times, and the payoff would be very high if sufficient analytical understanding already existed in order for them to anticipate the response to a policy change.

All three strategic approaches recognize the importance of government investments in agricultural research and rural infrastructure. Even here, however, there are likely to be significant differences in emphasis. The free-market approach is likely to put a relatively greater share into research, the rural development strategy into human capital investments, and the price and marketing approach into rural infrastructure that lowers marketing costs. Investments in all three areas are obviously desirable. The issue is at the margin: where are scarce resources to be invested? In addition, different countries have different starting points and different needs, so no single strategic approach makes sense for all countries. But it is difficult to see how countries can develop their rural sectors without relatively efficient marketing systems and adequate financial incentives for their farmers. Accordingly, significant elements of the price and marketing approach seem destined to be incorporated into all successful agricultural development strategies, even if they emphasize the free market or rural development approaches in other dimensions.

NOTES

I would like to thank Larry Westphal, Pranab K. Bardhan, David Dapice, and Scott Pearson for serious and critical readings of the first draft. As always, my deepest debt is to my wife and editor, Carol, for her patience and persistence in helping me make my manuscripts readable and for her mastery of the wonderful new technology that permits me to lose half the manuscript with the push of a button and for her to get it back after considerable effort and anguish.

1. For a very useful summary of the literature that documents the agricultural transformation process itself and also attempts to explain it in terms of the prevailing models of economic development, see Johnston 1970.
2. The structural rigidities in the economy that give rise to this substantial disequilibrium obviously mean that neoclassical models based solely on perfect markets and rational actors will fail to predict accurately the impact of government interventions. However, purely structural models that assume an absence of market response might be equally far from the mark. A messy amalgam of structural rigidities, imperfect markets, and decision makers interested in their own, though vaguely defined, welfare seems to characterize the actual starting point from which government interventions must be evaluated.
3. It is also important to distinguish subsectors within agriculture. An export crop subsector producing rubber or coffee might continue to provide financial resources to the rest of the economy, some of which could be returned to the foodcrop subsector in order to foster its development. Much of the discussion in this chapter is concerned with modernizing the foodcrop subsector while recognizing the important role played by the other agricultural subsectors.
4. An effort to formalize the impact of agriculture's distinct features, especially the behavioral and material determinants of production relations, is in Binswanger and Rosenzweig 1986.

REFERENCES

Anderson, K. 1983. "Growth of Agricultural Protection in East Asia." *Food Policy* 8:327–36.
Anderson, K., and Y. Hayami, with associates. 1986. *The Political Economy of Agricultural Protection: East Asia in International Perspective*. London: Allen and Unwin.
Bairoch, P. 1975. *The Economic Development of the Third World since 1900*. Berkeley: University of California Press.
Bardhan, P. K. 1984. *Land, Labor, and Rural Poverty*. Cambridge: Cambridge University Press.
Bates, R. H. 1981. *Markets and States in Tropical Africa: The Political Basis of Agricultural Policies*. Berkeley: University of California Press.
Binswanger, H. P., and M. R. Rosenzweig. 1986. "Behavioral and Material Determinants of Production Relations in Agriculture." *The Journal of Development Studies* 22:503–39.
Chenery, H. B., and M. Syrquin. 1975. *Patterns of Development, 1950–1970*. London: Oxford University Press.
Chenery, H. B., and L. Taylor. 1968. "Development Patterns among Countries and Over Time." *Review of Economics and Statistics* 50:391–416.
Clark, C. 1940; 1957. *The Conditions of Economic Progress*, 3rd ed. London: Macmillan.

Cochrane, W. W. 1979. *The Development of American Agriculture: A Historical Analysis.* Minneapolis: University of Minnesota Press.

Fei, J. C. H., and G. Ranis. 1964. *Development of the Labor Surplus Economy: Theory and Policy.* Homewood, Ill.: Irwin.

Hayami, Y. 1986. "Agricultural Protectionism in the Industrialized World: The Case of Japan." Prepared for a conference held at the East-West Center, Honolulu, February 17-21.

Hayami, Y., and V. Ruttan. 1985. *Agricultural Development: An International Perspective,* revised and expanded ed. Baltimore: Johns Hopkins University Press.

Hirschman, A. O. 1958. *The Strategy of Economic Development.* New Haven: Yale University Press.

Johnson, D. G. 1973. *World Agriculture in Disarray.* New York: St. Martin's Press.

Johnson, D. G. 1985. "World Commodity Market Situation and Outlook." In *U.S. Agricultural Policy: The 1985 Farm Legislation,* edited by B. L. Gardner. Washington, D.C.: American Enterprise Institute for Public Policy Research.

Johnston, B. F. 1970. "Agriculture and Structural Transformation in Development Countries: A Survey of Research." *Journal of Economic Literature* 3:369-404.

Johnston, B. F., and W. C. Clark. 1982. *Redesigning Rural Development: A Strategic Perspective.* Baltimore: Johns Hopkins University Press.

Johnston, B. F., and J. W. Mellor. 1961. "The Role of Agriculture in Economic Development." *American Economic Review* 51:566-93.

Jorgenson, D. W. 1961. "The Development of a Dual Economy." *Economic Journal* 71:309-34.

Kaplan, S. L. 1984. *Provisioning Paris: Merchants and Millers in the Grain and Flour Trade during the Eighteenth Century.* Ithaca: Cornell University Press.

Kuznets, S. 1966. *Modern Economic Growth.* New Haven: Yale University Press.

Lewis, W. A. 1954. "Economic Development with Unlimited Supplies of Labor." *Manchester School of Economic and Social Studies* 22:139-91.

Lipton, M. 1977. *Why Poor People Stay Poor: Urban Bias in World Development.* Cambridge: Harvard University Press.

Little, I. M. D. 1982. *Economic Development: Theory, Policy, and International Relations.* New York: Basic Books.

Mellor, J. W., and B. F. Johnston. 1984. "The World Food Equation: Interrelations among Development, Employment, and Food Consumption." *Journal of Economic Literature* 22:531-74.

Mosher, A. T. 1966. *Getting Agriculture Moving: Essentials for Development and Modernization.* New York: Praeger.

Myint, H. 1975. "Agriculture and Economic Development in the Open Economy." In *Agriculture in Development Theory,* edited by L. G. Reynolds. New Haven: Yale University Press.

Nicholls, W. H. 1963. "An 'Agricultural Surplus' as a Factor in Economic Development." *Journal of Political Economy* 71:1-29.

Nurkse, R. 1953. *Problems of Capital Formation in Underdeveloped Countries.* New York: Oxford University Press.

Prebish, R. 1950. *The Economic Development of Latin America and Its Principal Problems.* Lake Success, N.Y.: United Nations Department of Economic Affairs.

Preobrazhensky, E. 1965. *The New Economics.* Oxford: Clarendon Press.

Reynolds, L. G., ed. 1975. *Agriculture in Development Theory.* New Haven: Yale University Press.

Roe, T., M. Shane, and D. H. Vo. 1986. "Price Responsiveness of World Grain Markets: The Influence of Government Intervention on Import Price Elasticity." Technical Bulletin no. 1720. Washington, D.C.: International Economics Division, Economic Research Service, U.S. Department of Agriculture.

Sah, R. K., and J. E. Stiglitz. 1984. "The Economics of Price Scissors." *American Economic Review* 74:125-38.

Schuh, G. E. 1976. "The New Macroeconomics of Agriculture." *American Journal of Agricultural Economics* 58:802-11.

Schultz, T. W. 1953. *The Economic Organization of Agriculture.* New York: McGraw-Hill.

Singh, I. J., L. Squire, and J. Strauss. 1986. *Agricultural Household Models: Extensions, Applications, and Policy.* Baltimore: Johns Hopkins University Press for the World Bank.

Timmer, C. P. 1969. "The Turnip, the New Husbandry, and the English Agricultural Revolution." *The Quarterly Jounal of Economics* 83:375–95.

Timmer, C. P. 1986. *Getting Prices Right: The Scope and Limits of Agricultural Price Policy.* Ithaca: Cornell University Press.

Timmer, C. P., W. P. Falcon, and S. R. Pearson. 1983. *Food Policy Analysis.* Baltimore: Johns Hopkins University Press for the World Bank.

World Bank. 1982. *World Development Report 1982.* New York: Oxford University Press.

World Bank. 1986. *World Development Report 1986.* New York: Oxford University Press.

3

Agriculture on the Road to Industrialization

JOHN W. MELLOR

Economic development is a process by which an economy is transformed from one that is dominantly rural and agricultural to one that is dominantly urban, industrial, and service-oriented in composition. The objectives of the process can be usefully categorized as increased societal wealth, equity, and stability. But because these objectives require a diversification of the economy away from agriculture (no high-income, equitable, stable nations have agriculture as their dominant activity), the process is one of major structural transformation.

If economic development is a process of transforming an economy from producing mainly agricultural to producing mainly industrial and service outputs, what is the nature of a constructive role for the initially dominant agricultural sector? What is the scope for synthesizing an agricultural role into the mainstream of development thought? More specifically, what is the dynamic relation between agriculture and industry in an optimal growth strategy?

Given agriculture's initial importance, it is not surprising that it has received the explicit attention of eminent economists and has been the subject of intensive analysis by generalists and specialists alike. Yet, in view of the contemporary expansion of knowledge about how to develop agriculture, it is surprising that the principal, broad conceptualizations in development economics have not articulated a central place for agriculture. This has held true through wide-ranging shifts in development-strategy styles—from emphasis on direct allocation of resources to growth in the capital stock, to import displacement, to basic human needs, to export-led growth. In fact, each of these development fashions has had its own strong arguments for not emphasizing agriculture in either capital allocations or public policy. For countries following these mainstream strategies, occasional

JOHN W. MELLOR is director of the International Food Policy Research Institute, Washington, D.C.
Reprinted from *Development Strategies Reconsidered,* edited by John P. Lewis and Valeriana Kallab, Transaction Books, New Brunswick, N.J., for the Overseas Development Council. Copyright © 1986 by the Overseas Development Council, Washington, D.C. Published by permission of the Overseas Development Council and the author.

crises of domestic food supplies, foreign-exchange constraints in association with sudden, large food imports, or threatened cutoffs in large-scale food aid have prompted flurries of attention for agriculture. But such spurts of concern all too often have generated only such short-term palliatives as higher prices for food producers; they have not produced sustained long-run development efforts that build agriculture as part of a larger strategy.

There are, of course, numerous examples of development *practice* that have indeed given agriculture a central place. Notable are the post-Meiji restoration period in Japan as well as the developmental thrusts in Taiwan, Thailand, Ivory Coast, Malaysia, the Punjabs of India and Pakistan, and to some extent other parts of South Asia. It is ironic that, perhaps because of the critical importance of trade expansion in an agriculture-based strategy, several of these successes are perceived as examples of export-led growth rather than as a successful agriculture-based strategy.

The intellectual neglect of agriculture's role in development no doubt is rooted in an underlying view of agriculture as initially backward; development promoters have wanted to move directly to building those sectors that carry the image of modernization. An urban-based intelligentsia (including development economists), a related caste-like separation of largely micro-oriented agricultural economists and largely macro-oriented development economists, and urban-based political systems all combine to provide an intellectual basis and political pressure for directing resources to the urban sector.

In decrying this neglect, however, it is important to recognize that there is an intellectual case for downplaying agriculture in the development process. To make the contrary case, three substantial questions must be answered affirmatively:

1. Can agricultural production be increased by means of advances in resource productivity?
2. Can effective demand for agricultural commodities expand apace with accelerated agricultural growth?
3. Can a dynamic agriculture provide an effective demand "pull" for growth in other sectors?

The following discussion will show why these are the vital questions, why it is not unreasonable to think that the answer to each may be "no," and what the contrary bases are for the affirmative answer that in turn defines a central role for agriculture in a dynamic process of economic transformation and growth. This exploration will make clear the essential connection between agricultural growth and employment growth—and hence the need always to speak of an agriculture- and employment-based strategy, not of one or the other independently.

The strategy described here has two key distinguishing features aside from the emphases on agriculture and employment. First, continuous, institutionalized technological change provides the basic engine of cumulative growth. Second, growth in domestic demand provides the basic markets both for the increasing agricultural output and for the activities that create rapid growth in employment. Trade is important—but mainly to serve the purpose of restraining growth in capital-intensiveness.

Before discussing the main elements of an agriculture- and employment-based strategy, common failings of alternative strategies will be noted briefly, as well as which of those failings an agriculture-based strategy might or might not meet. A sketch of the debate as to the efficacy of agricultural and nonagriculture-based strategies follows.

DEVELOPMENT FAILINGS AND AGRICULTURE'S POTENTIAL

Robert McNamara's presidential address to the 1973 World Bank annual meeting epitomized a widespread and growing view that the ascendant development strategies of the 1950s and 1960s had an unacceptably small impact on poverty. That the expression of such concern had subsided so much by the late 1970s owed less to a diminution of the reality of the problem and more to the realization that the various direct attacks on poverty meanwhile ventured were no more successful than earlier efforts in mitigating the problem.

Failure to make a dent in the poverty problem was associated with four related phenomena:

1. Food supplies per capita rose little or not at all, and hence the diets, nutritional status, and related well-being of the poor could not be enhanced.
2. Employment growth rates seemed to lag even behind population growth rates, so that the poor could not obtain income to command more food or other basic wants.
3. Growth and basic services were often available only in a small number of immense urban concentrations, with high overhead costs and little impact on the population dispersed over the rest of the country.
4. Overall growth rates were themselves much slower and less well sustained than expected.

The first three are directly related to the lack of poverty abatement. The last, even if it was not a direct cause, certainly reinforced equity-related failings. Clearly, an agricultural emphasis strikes at one of the root causes of poverty: inadequate food supplies. Accelerated agricultural growth also provides a substantial direct increase in employment, because of the large aggregate size of the sector and the nature of its technology. An agriculture, as a broadly diffused activity, spreads economic activity and employment beyond the megalopolis.

One should be clear, however, as to what accelerated agricultural growth cannot do *directly*. First, it cannot provide high overall growth rates in output or employment. For the staple foods sector, growth of 3–4 percent is considered very rapid, and 4–5 percent for the agricultural sector as a whole is extraordinarily rapid.[1] The constraint of limited land area, the biological nature of agricultural production, and the dispersed, variable production system explain the common experience of such low ceilings on growth rates. Similarly, it is doing well indeed to experience a 0.6 percent growth rate in agricultural employment for each percentage point in the output growth rate.[2] Thus the agricultural sector can at best provide employment for its own population growth, and it is likely to fall far short of that. And agricultural growth alone obviously cannot supply the broadening of consumption patterns beyond food that all people desire.

These limitations explain why an agriculture-based strategy must have major *indirect* effects on growth and employment in other sectors if it is to be seen as central to development strategy. These indirect effects must come from the expenditure of increased agricultural income on nonagricultural goods and services, in turn creating not only additional output in those sectors but also additional employment. To be consistent with an agriculture- and employment-oriented strategy, one must ask of those activities that they be large in aggregate, employment-intensive, and broadly distributed geographically.

From these foundations, we can skip ahead of the story to outline what a development strategy must look like if agriculture and employment are to play a central role. First, the agricultural production growth rate must be accelerated; this must normally derive from technological change. Second, the expenditure pattern from the net additions to income arising from the accelerated growth must create demand for a wide range of goods and services with a high employment content, much of the production of which must be broadly diffused in rural areas (e.g., in major market towns). Third, increased food marketing will somewhat depress food prices,[3] thereby encouraging employment in other sectors by making labor somewhat cheaper relative to the goods and services it produces.

HISTORICAL SKETCH OF THE AGRICULTURE VERSUS INDUSTRY DEBATE

INDUSTRIAL ORIENTATION

With G. S. Fel'dman's writing as the theoretical base, the Soviet Union's practice in the 1920s was to equate industrialization with modernization. The arguments constantly recurred in subsequent development literature. Capital and labor were believed to be more productive in industry. Industry was seen as having major economies of scale and external economies, while agriculture was subject to diminishing returns. Industrial "externalities," including industry's modernizing force, promoting new modes of economic behavior and new forms of social organization, were all seen as supportive of growth. Given the diminishing returns in agriculture, if under-employed labor could be mobilized out of agriculture with no loss of production, the argument for industry was compelling. In this context, it is fitting that Paul Rosenstein-Rodan's piece on economic development, published in 1943, was entitled "Problems of Industrialization of Eastern and South-Eastern Europe."[4]

A major force in the development literature of the 1950s and 1960s and in the practice of both India and China[5] grew out of the conceptualization by Fel'dman, as further developed by P. C. Mahalanobis, and related to the concepts of Roy Harrod and Evsey Domar.[6] Increase in the capital stock was the source of growth. It followed, in the view of Fel'dman and Mahalanobis, that this resource should be directly allocated to capital-goods production, and not to consumer-goods, including agricultural production. In practice, industrialization became highly capital-intensive, with little employment growth and consequently little growth in demand for food; hence there was little upward pressure on food prices, even though agriculture was doing poorly. The strategy, since it was inward-looking, spawned a whole generation of closed-economy growth models showing how capital should be deployed among subsectors. The push was always on industry.

A substantial ancillary literature dealt with the balance of growth and the issue of whether or not capital intensity could be reduced by choice of technology. The answer, in the confines of an inward-looking strategy, was that it could not. A. K. Sen provided the definitive rationalization of that conclusion, basing it on the inevitable need for more food to underpin the increased wages from employment growth and diminishing returns (increasing capital intensity) in agriculture.[7] The proponents of this capital-intensive strategy realized that equity and poverty abatement would be postponed by the strategy, although they hoped that relatively inexpensive efforts in agriculture and cottage industries (e.g., community development in India) would mitigate the problem.

The import-substitution strategy popularized for Latin America by Raul Prebisch[8] was driven by the view that primary-commodity prices, particularly including those of agricultural commodities, would inevitably trend downward relative to the prices of manufactured goods. It followed that a developing country should shift out of agriculture and into industry as quickly as possible. The market would come from displacement of previously imported goods. In practice, however, as implementation of the strategy progressed, more and more capital-intensive imports were displaced by domestic production. Thus as expansion proceeded, capital intensity increased, employment growth slowed, income distribution became more skewed, and the growth rate decelerated.

By the mid-1960s, concern was growing that development was moving too slowly, and the poor were not participating significantly in such growth as was occurring. At the same time, agricultural research was demonstrating the capacity to provide major new technology to increase agricultural productivity—the Green Revolution. Why did the concurrence of these breakthroughs and the concern for poverty reduction of that time not bring a sharp swing in development strategy toward an agriculture- and employment-based strategy of growth?

The Green Revolution is based on new technology and rapid growth in fertilizer use, increased commercialization of agriculture, and a complex set of national-level institutions run by a large and rapidly growing number of highly trained people. The sharp rise in energy prices led to a wish to deemphasize the use of fertilizer and even of irrigation based on energy-using pumps. Western environmental concerns also were on the ascent and did not favor fertilizer. Mounting attention to equity problems strengthened interest in dependency theorists, who in turn also had a negative view of fertilizer as an instrument of Western multinationals. Concurrently, anti-elitism favored primary over higher education, turning foreign aid away from advanced training of the scientists and technicians essential to the success of the Green Revolution. Concern with poverty reduction, energy depletion, environment, dependency, and elitism all seemed associated with each other. All this was reinforced by a literature decrying the then reputed negative effect of the Green Revolution in further skewing the rural income distribution; it was said (incorrectly, it is now clear) that only the larger farmers benefited from the new technology[9] and that they would use their new wealth to buy out small farmers and tenants.

The combined impact of these forces retarded response to the essential requirements of the Green Revolution and spawned a "basic human needs" approach that emphasized social welfare functions and agricultural production only in highly complex regional projects. The integrated rural development projects that resulted not only were not integrated into national support structures for agricultural growth; they tended to raid the latter for personnel. Almost universally, the integrated rural development projects failed due to excessive complexity and a lack of central support services.[10] (Local institutions are, of course, central to the Green Revolution, but they are effective only when serviced by national-level support structures, including research.) The basic-needs approach had a major influence on foreign assistance in the 1970s, particularly in the least developed countries, which include the bulk of Africa and a few Asian countries, such as Nepal.

Asian countries that had benefited from earlier foreign assistance emphasizing large-scale, high-level technical training and well-developed agricultural research systems were able to pursue the Green Revolution effectively and even to restrain foreign aid from single-minded pursuit of the new directions of the 1970s. In that context, the basic-needs strategy could be used to deal with "second-generation" problems in the context of the other requisites of a successful Green Revolution. It is notable, however, that where—as in India and the Philippines—the Green Revolution was not associated with an employment orientation; it served substantially to displace food imports and build food stocks rather than as the base for a new development strategy. The basic-needs strategists, while often vigorously and specifically attacking the Green Revolution, were generally silent about strategies giving priority to capital-intensive industry and import-substitution. There was urgent need to change those strategies to provide the essential employment complement to the Green Revolution.

The failings of the capital-intensive strategies, dependent as they were on market interference, also prompted a trend quite separate from the equity-oriented basic-needs strategy: a renewed interest in a market-oriented strategy commonly emphasizing export promotion. With the gradual demise of the basic-needs orientation in the early 1980s, the strategy of export-led growth or export promotion became the new fashion. Of all the post–World War II strategies, this was the one least deleterious to agriculture. It argued against overvalued currencies, which discriminate so strongly against agriculture. It argued generally for prices favorable to agriculture, supported commercialization of agriculture (including import of key inputs), and fostered better domestic markets for agricultural output by favoring employment-intensive industries—with beneficial effects on employment for the poor and hence greater expenditure on food. In practice, however, the export-promotion strategy looks explicitly to markets abroad—rather than to the broad-based domestic markets that accelerated agricultural growth can provide. This, combined with an anti-governmental bias, works against support for large public investments in the key areas of research, education, rural roads, and rural electrification that are so critical to an agriculture- and employment-based growth strategy. In practice, the export-promotion strategy also emphasizes trade to allow economies of scale, thereby favoring more capital-intensive industries relative to relying more on vigorous domestic markets.[11]

AGRICULTURAL ORIENTATION

Although a clear agriculture- and employment-based strategy has not been ascendant, agriculture has never lacked for a good word from an eminent economist. During the postwar renaissance of concern for the macroeconomics of growth, Nicholas Kaldor stated:

> Economic development will, of course, invariably involve industrialization . . . this can be expected to follow, almost automatically, upon the growth of the food surpluses of the agricultural sector. . . . Once this is recognized, the efforts of under-developed countries could be concentrated—far more than they are at present—in tackling the problem of how to raise productivity on the land, as a prior condition of economic development.[12]

It is, however, clear from succeeding lines in Kaldor's piece that he had little grasp of what was involved in the modernization of agriculture and least of all as to what was required to provide a stream of land-augmenting technological changes—although his intuition as to the importance of agriculture and the importance of education to agricultural growth were both correct. Perhaps Kaldor was also facile in his perception of the near-automaticity of agriculture's growth converting into industrial growth. Our knowledge of these processes has improved immensely since 1954, although its scant diffusion to macroeconomists still prejudices thought about development.

Paralleling the broad orientation of development economics away from agriculture was an evolution of knowledge about how to develop agriculture. Farmers were presented as economically rational responders to prices and technology;[13] understanding of the need for radically improved technology was articulated in economic terms,[14] and the nature of a range of complementary agricultural growth requirements was set forth.[15] Myriad empirically based analyses have filled in the picture. More important, the scientific groundwork for the Green Revolution was laid by the activities of the Rockefeller Foundation in Mexico and India and by the

Ford and Rockefeller foundations in establishing the International Rice Research Institute, the precursor of and role model for the Consultative Group on International Agricultural Research. The result was the bursting of the Green Revolution in Asia in the late 1960s and a clear appreciation of the requisites of accelerated agricultural growth.

Compared with the immense gains in our understanding of the agricultural development process per se, the relationships between agriculture and the rest of a developing economy remain less fully explored. While there have been many contributions on the subject, the empirical data underlying the relationships asserted are much less complete than is the case with the microeconomics of agriculture— and hence the policies implied remain more speculative.

Nevertheless, four major threads of the analysis can be defined. First, the critical role of food as a wage good (the object of consumption from the increased income of employment) was elegantly defined in W. Arthur Lewis's classic paper.[16] Second, the need for productivity increase in agriculture and the role of technology was laid out by Johnston and Mellor.[17] Third, the resource transfers from agriculture that so facilitate growth of the nonagricultural sector were delineated from the Japanese experience by Kazushi Ohkawa, Bruce Johnston, and S. Ishikawa,[18] and meticulously documented for Taiwan by T. H. Lee.[19] Fourth, the critical role of agriculture in stimulating growth in the non-agricultural sector has been explored with respect to both consumption goods[20] and producer goods.[21]

AN AGRICULTURE- AND EMPLOYMENT-BASED STRATEGY OF ECONOMIC GROWTH

An agriculture- and employment-based strategy of economic growth has three basic elements. First, the pace of agricultural growth must be accelerated despite the limitations of fixed land area. Technological change solves a major, special problem of agricultural growth and allows low-income countries to use the most powerful element of growth. Second, domestic demand for agricultural output must grow rapidly despite inelastic demand. This can occur only through accelerated growth in employment (more precisely, increased demand for labor), which is facilitated by the indirect effects of agricultural growth itself. Third, the demand for goods and services produced by low capital-intensity processes must increase. This, too, is facilitated by the technology-based increase in agricultural income. As we proceed, we will see that these three elements continually interact in the strategy.

TECHNOLOGICAL CHANGE IN AGRICULTURE

One of the most important theoretical and empirical findings in analysis of Western economic growth is the identification of technological change as a major source of growth. Hence it is initially surprising that in the various ascendant macroeconomic theories of economic growth for developing countries, technological change has not been assigned a central role.

On a second thought, however, the neglect is understandable: These ascendant theories have been preoccupied with growth in the initially minuscule industrial sector, where the first concern necessarily has been to expand the capital stock as the basis of growth. Only if the dominant agricultural sector is to be central to growth can technological change play an immediate, major role. It happens that, because of Ricardian diminishing returns, technological change is in any case essential to agricultural growth. The land area for agriculture being generally limited, increased output is traditionally obtained via declining increments in output per unit of input as input intensity increases. The result is rising costs, which must be offset by rising prices if incentives are to prevail. It is apparent that cumulatively increasing relative food prices are not socially acceptable. Thus it is essential that the incentive to produce more in the face of constantly rising costs be met by technological change rather than by price increases. Continuous, cumulative technological change is the proven effect of institutionalized agricultural research systems.

The rudiments of getting agriculture moving through technological change have been fully understood for a long time.[22] Development of a technology system (including research) and technically competent extension are primary. The nature of agricultural technology is such that rapid growth of sophisticated input delivery systems is essential. For this latter, and for effective multipliers of other sectors, a highly developed infrastructure of roads is required. Underlying the total process is rapid growth in the number of highly trained people and of the institutional structure within which they can work effectively.

In all of these elements, the public sector must play a key role in physical investment and institution building. The essential financial and organizational requirements of governments are so immense that every effort must be made to maximize activities in the private sector and to concentrate public-sector attention on only those essential agricultural support activities not taken up by the private sector. Agriculture, with its small-scale orientation, is more in need of public-sector support than industry. The sharp turn-around in Asian agriculture—resulting in a 30 percent increase in growth rates in basic food-staple production from the 1960s to the 1970s—impressively demonstrates the results of turning the public sector's attention to the requisites of technological change in agriculture.

The urgency of moving the agricultural sector is underlined by its role as a supplier of food as essential backing to employment growth. It is generally understood that developing countries have a large pool of extremely low-productivity if not idle labor. In effect, this provides a highly elastic labor supply. If jobs become available, labor is ready to march into them. What has not been fully recognized is that the supply of labor is a function of two independent markets: a labor market and a food market.[23] Increased employment provides the labor class with added income, 60 to 80 percent of which is spent on food. If the food supply is not expanded, increased employment will cause the price of food to rise, squeezing the real incomes of laborers back nearly to the previous level, reducing the incentive to work, placing upward pressures on wages, and reducing employment. Thus, accelerated growth in employment must be accompanied by accelerated growth in food supplies.[24] Three arguments have been used against the need to emphasize domestic food production in this context.

First, the labor-surplus arguments take the position that labor is already maintained and idle in the rural sector; hence, until there is a "turning point" at which labor is fully absorbed, food supply is available for labor transferred to other occupations.[25] This argument neglects the theoretically and empirically verifiable fact that increased employment, even in the face of surplus agricultural labor, results in increased wage payments in the hands of people with high marginal propensity to spend on food. A related argument is that employment can grow only very slowly, because of the capital constraint. The striking contrary evidence is that developing countries that have done well in agriculture expand employment rapidly enough to have to increase food imports.[26] We will, however, return to this argument later.

Second, there is a widespread belief that the aggregate supply of food is elastic with respect to price. If such is the case, higher food prices induced by increased purchasing power in the hands of the poor will readily bring forth the needed increased supply of food. The theoretical and empirical evidence is clear on this point: Under essentially all conditions, the aggregate supply of food is only slightly responsive to price.[27] Most simply, this is due to Ricardian diminishing returns. It is possible to accelerate the growth rate of food production sharply, but only through the processes of technological change. With existing technology, the aggregate supply response to higher prices is comparatively limited.

Third, it is believed that the supply of food from imports is highly elastic. Up to a point, this assumption is probably correct. Certainly Singapore and Hong Kong have been able to expand employment rapidly and to meet the consequent increased demand for food with imports. It is less certain that supplies would be adequate if the bulk of the developing countries succeeded in a rapid employment growth strategy without increasing domestic food production. But the possibility of importing food to meet the demands of increased employment strengthens the argument that generating demand and resources for growth of other sectors must be an important part of the argument for an emphasis on agriculture.

ADEQUATE EFFECTIVE DEMAND FOR FOOD

There is an important theoretical problem in realizing the full potential of accelerated technological change in agriculture. The demand for food tends to be inelastic. If food production increases rapidly without increased employment, prices will tend to fall sharply and eventually cause reduced production. The way to deal with the problem is through accelerated growth in employment, which under the low-income conditions of developing countries is efficiently translated into increased demand for food. The correct response to increased food production is no more through constantly decreasing prices than the way to meet the need for increased production is through constantly increasing prices. The correct response to the former is employment; to the latter, it is technological change.

Prices, it must be emphasized, are not so much problems as indicators of problems. If food prices are rising, this indicates that the supply is not being increased rapidly enough through technological change. One should, in such circumstances, redouble efforts in the technological change arena. While waiting for those redoubled efforts to succeed, food would have to be imported, to prevent employment being held back by rapidly rising food prices.

Conversely, declining food prices mean that the success in technological change is moving ahead of the employment strategy. Governments may come under substantial pressure from organized farm interests to maintain agricultural prices as technology moves ahead, even though demand is not keeping pace. The result will be either subsidized exports or, more likely, rapid growth in domestic stocks. India's record in the early and mid-1980s has been a prime example: stocks were built up to four times the level that would be justified by optimal stocking policies. This is an example of a country achieving modest success in technological change and doing badly on employment growth. One should in those circumstances examine the allocation of capital and of demand structures to see what can be done on the employment side.

Just as the preceding discussion emphasized the need to meet food requirements by domestic production, so this discussion stresses growth in domestic income, not exports, for generating effective demand for growing supplies of food. If one is exporting staple foods, this means that one has a more-than-adequate supply of food to provide for the growth in demand from the existing rate of growth of employment. In a low-income, low-employment economy, one should obviously be striving for policies that increase domestic employment as a way of fully taking up food supplies.

DEMAND STIMULUS TO NONAGRICULTURAL EMPLOYMENT

The role of agriculture in providing effective demand for production from the nonagricultural sector has received little emphasis in the literature and has been poorly understood. In the most extreme phase of its evolution, this view was: "Agriculture stands convicted on the count of its lack of direct stimulus to the setting up of new activities through linkage effects—the superiority of manufacturing in this respect is crushing."[28] This position overlooked that technological change in agriculture can increase net national income and thereby generate added demand for consumer goods. The neglect of this aspect was reinforced by capital-centered growth theory, which tended to view consumption and the production of consumption goods as antithetical to growth. This bias was aggravated by excessive emphasis on "modern" consumer and capital goods to the neglect of services and more traditionally produced consumer goods. A more careful review of early Western development history, despite the weak technological base of its agricultural growth, would have helped avoid this misreading.[29]

A central problem of contemporary development practice is illuminated by a quote from Sir John Hicks that has roots in a long history of his own work: "That it is possible for a 'developing country,' by choice of techniques that are too capital-intensive, to expand employment in its modern sector less rapidly than it might have done is nowadays familiar."[30]

The failures in economic development to which Hicks refers have been associated with a poor record in agricultural growth and failure to connect success in agriculture to driving the rest of the economy. These failures have been associated with a marked dualism in capital investment—a small portion of the labor force operating with high capital intensity and a large portion with low capital intensity. The result, as Hicks would lead one to expect, is generally low productivity of both capital and labor. That dualism exhibits itself partly in low allocations of capital to agriculture, occasional instances of investment in state farms and other capital-intensive elements within agriculture, and a widespread tendency to place the bulk of additional capital in large-scale, capital-intensive industries with few additional employees, leaving little capital for the dominant remainder of the labor force.[31]

Agricultural development offers a potential for rapid growth in domestic demand for labor-intensive goods and services. Incremental consumption patterns of peasant farmers have a large rural-services component, and a large share of other goods consumed is also produced relatively labor-intensively.

It is essential to note two needs if the favorable demand effects of agricultural growth are to be achieved. First, the increments to demand must come from volume-increasing and unit-cost–decreasing technological change. Raising prices is not likely to help. Although the income transfer from urban to rural people arising from higher agricultural prices may provide some modest, net restructuring of demand favorable to employment, only a major, continuous increase in net national income from new technology can be expected to provide a continuous aggregate effect. Second, the infrastructure of communications essential to growth of rural industry and services must be in place. Highly developed infrastructure is essential to agricultural production growth, favorable consumption incentives, and to the complex, interactive system of region-based urban centers that are so essential to a high-employment content in an agriculture-based growth strategy.

Capital stock must grow rapidly if employment is to do the same. In an agriculture-led strategy, however, market mechanisms should work well to raise the savings rate. Much of the capital needed for agricultural growth can be generated in agriculture itself in response to technology-induced high rates of return. The non-agricultural supply response to increased demand may well be highly elastic. If capital proves to be a constraint, higher prices will result, transferring resources from newly prospering agriculture to those activities. The critical investment bottlenecks are more likely to be in the public sector, with government at the local or national level not gathering or allocating adequate resources for the massive rural infrastructure that is essential to agricultural and employment growth. The 20 to 30 percent savings rates that characterize so many contemporary developing countries are inadequate to the task only because the capital intensity of many productive processes is excessive and because too small a share of the savings is invested in infrastructure. Agricultural linkages can contribute to reducing that intensity and to spreading capital more thinly.

POLICY ISSUES

Pursuit of an agriculture- and employment-based strategy of growth requires quite different public-sector policies than those comprising alternative strategies. Discussion of key policy requirements serves to bring out distinguishing characteristics of the strategy as well as to indicate what policy shifts are needed if it is to succeed.

TRADE

An agriculture- and employment-based development strategy requires an open trading regime. That point must be made explicitly because of the emphasis on meeting the demand for wage goods arising from employment growth from domestic food production and on providing domestic demand for the increased food production. Those inward-looking emphases are a product of comparative advantage, reinforced by the high transfer costs typical of developing countries, and do not require protection.

The high employment-growth leg of the strategy requires that capital be spread thinly over a rapidly growing labor force. There is little scope to restrain rising capital-labor ratios in a closed economy. Although particular goods and services may have low capital-labor ratios, they always seem to have component parts that have very high capital-labor ratios (e.g., fertilizer for agriculture, and steel, aluminum, and petrochemicals for otherwise labor-intensive manufactured goods). Thus, while agricultural growth generates direct demand for a final product that is efficiently produced by labor-intensive processes, there must be rapid growth in imports of capital-intensive intermediate goods and services. Clearly, accelerated growth of such imports must be matched by accelerated growth of exports. The latter should be goods and services with relatively high employment content. This fits obviously with standard trade theory. The need to foster such exports will further restrain increases in aggregate capital-labor ratios. The rapid growth in domestic markets for labor-intensive manufactures would itself be favorable to low-cost production and therefore to their external competitiveness. Taiwan's rapid success in exports in the late 1950s was based on prior development of domestic demand.[32] A somewhat undervalued exchange rate facilitates full pricing of agricultural commodities; encourages restraint in using inputs that are capital-intensively produced, because they will be imported and thus more highly priced; and provides some additional incentive to export the more labor-intensive commodities, helping to overcome the various institutional hurdles to exports that inevitably exist in developing countries. This is, of course, the opposite of the exchange-rate policy that is consistent with the capital-intensive approaches.

If employment does move ahead of the capacity to produce domestic food staples, one should obviously take advantage of that opportunity and import food to support the more rapid growth rate of employment. If, on the other hand, food is being exported, one should examine carefully whether trade policies are restraining the imports of capital-intensive goods and services and the export of labor-intensive goods and services, or whether infrastructure investment is inadequate for rapid growth in domestic employment.

POVERTY REDUCTION

The agriculture-employment strategy is innately favorable to reducing poverty. Thus, it is important to mobilize resources for its vigorous pursuit. The strategy increases the supply of less expensive food and increases the demand for labor. These are the two essentials for removing poverty through growth. Wherever poverty is massive, a shift to such a strategy of growth should be the first priority of poverty alleviation. In the context of such a strategy, special attention is properly given to removing frictions that are especially deleterious to the poor. Thus, attention may be needed to provide infrastructure for remote areas; credit for small, labor-intensive processes; and technical assistance in production and marketing of vegetables and other less capital-intensive, small-scale activities.

In the longer run, the new agriculture- and employment-based strategy does bring a problem of regional disparities. Agriculture will move more rapidly in some regions than others simply because of the accident of technological breakthrough. Even over the long term, there may be some regions with physical resources for which it will be impossible to come up with improved technologies. The first-round effect of widening regional disparities through differential progress in agriculture will be strongly reinforced by the favorable local multiplier effects of accelerated agriculture growth. Historically, migration has proved the most common means of dealing with this problem. With potential for migration, it makes little sense to invest in technology at low rates of return in areas that have very little capacity for its development while at the same time starving areas that could provide faster growth of such an equity-oriented type. On the other hand, the social problems of migration need to be recognized and alternative measures sought.

There is also, of course, a residual problem of equity for persons who are handicapped by their circumstances. Income transfers are necessary for meeting such a problem. Far more pervasive is the problem of poverty during the transition while an agriculture-employment growth strategy is getting under way. Since shifting to such a strategy is so very favorable to poverty reduction, dealing with the interim and transitional problems by redistribution of resources is apt to be costly to later reductions in poverty. Large-scale rural public works may be redistributive and assist the growth strategy itself. Urban food subsidies may serve to stabilize the urban labor force. If nonfungible foreign food aid is used to support such efforts, the cost in terms of less growth and reduction of poverty in the future may be close to nil.

THE ROLE OF GOVERNMENT

The role of government is critical to an agriculture- and employment-oriented strategy. Because agriculture is a small-scale sector, there has to be substantial public-sector investment in the support for that sector in the form of, for example, transportation, power, communication, research, education, and input supply systems. Because these burdens are so heavy, government needs constantly to seek ways of transferring these activities to the private sector. Thus, activities such as marketing, which the private sector performs fairly well, should remain as much as possible in that sector. Input distribution should be moved into the private sector as quickly as the latter can take it up.

Since agricultural development is diffused over a wide geographic area, the infrastructure requirements are massive. And since the process is one of rural modernization, development of small- and medium-scale industry, and upgrading of consumption patterns, the needs for rural electrification and communications are critical. Thus, while a heavy-industry–oriented strategy requires large-scale, public-sector investment in major urban areas, a more rural-oriented strategy still requires considerable investment of this type of service market towns. This will sorely strain the capacity of government to raise capital resources; there will be a tension between the needs for private incentives and the need for public revenues. Governments will need to make tough budgetary choices that will allow scope for little beyond the investments in infrastructure, education, and technological change in agriculture that are the centerpieces of the strategy. The agriculture-employment strategy founders because governments do not recognize its large resource requirements and, therefore, the need to drop activities that may be appropriate only for alternative strategies. This explains why, for example, India and the Philippines have combined success in agriculture so inefficiently with employment growth, as compared with, for example, Taiwan or Thailand.

PRICE POLICY AND TECHNOLOGICAL CHANGE

As pointed out earlier, prices are indicators of, not solutions for, the problems of agricultural production and employment. The answer to the problem of agricultural production is technological change. When the latter has been inadequate, rising prices will indicate a problem and, one hopes, induce corrections. However, because the processes of technological change entail substantial lags between investment and results, prices are an extremely inefficient way to send signals. It is much better to analyze the need, as has been done here, and to act before the price changes indicate a problem. Of course, grossly overvalued exchange rates or other interventions may provide price relations unfavorable even to a technologically dynamic agriculture. However, such policies are probably an essential element of an alternative strategy and will change only as that whole strategy, particularly its capital allocations, changes.

A more serious price problem may arise from a highly dynamic agriculture. Technology may increase agricultural production in specific subregions much more rapidly than effective demand can be created in those regions, which in turn may be isolated by poor infrastructure. In such circumstances, it may be desirable for government to serve as buyer of last resort, build stocks, and transport basic agricultural staples to other regions. Governments must be very careful, however, not to spend massively on building stocks of food, as has been happening in India in recent years, instead of spending to accelerate technological change in agriculture and to provide the infrastructure that is so essential to increasing employment.

The role of agriculture as a stimulator of nonagricultural growth probably means that some of the benefits of lower costs of production in agriculture will be used to stimulate production in other sectors by a swing in the terms of trade in favor of the nonagricultural sector. Indeed, some market-induced depression of agricultural prices in response to lower costs seems an inevitable part of the process.[33]

FOREIGN ASSISTANCE

The critical role of foreign trade in supporting an agriculture-employment–based strategy of development requires that the industrial countries keep their markets open for relatively labor-intensive goods and services from developing countries—so that those countries will have the foreign exchange for purchasing the capital-intensive goods and services they need for a high-employment strategy.

In initiating the strategy, foreign aid has a tremendously important role to play in accelerating the growth of education—particularly higher education, which is so essential to the agriculture- and employment-based growth strategy. Vast numbers of trained people are critical to developing and running agricultural research systems, extension systems, and input supply systems. The details of public policy for an agriculture-employment strategy require constant development and analysis of data, and fine adjustments, which in turn require trained people. Decades of effort can be saved by major commitments of developed countries to expand education through foreign training and technical assistance.

It should also be noted that, although Japan and Taiwan moved into technological change in agriculture after they had already built a very substantial infrastructure in irrigation and transport systems, present-day developing countries may have to make these investments concurrently. Foreign assistance can help with these heavy investments.

Foreign assistance also can contribute to financing imports òf capital-intensive goods and services during the early stages of the strategy, when exports may still lag; and food aid can help provide infrastructure, facilitating a stable political environment through food for work and food subsidies.

Foreign assistance may have a powerful role to play in aiding the transition from an inappropriate capital-oriented strategy or an import-displacement one into the more appropriate agriculture- and employment-based strategy. There will be substantial equity problems in the transition. Because the alternative strategies are so inequitable in the short run, they are usually accompanied by food subsidies and other elements to redress the inequities. Foreign assistance can help with the sorting out of these matters, but it must take care to do so in a way that facilitates a genuine transition to the new strategy instead of delaying it.

Today, Africa faces special problems substantially because of unusually inappropriate national and foreign assistance strategies applied in the 1970s. African countries are particularly short of the trained personnel for an agriculture- and employment-oriented strategy of development. They have traditionally had some of the worst infrastructure situations of any of the developing countries, and they suffer from a high degree of instability in principal export commodities. Comparatively massive foreign assistance is needed in the realms of training, investment in infrastructure, and stabilization of export earnings.

LOOKING AHEAD

In most Asian countries, the Green Revolution has demonstrated both the potential and the basic requisites of accelerated growth in agriculture. Unfortunately, the role of investment in rural infrastructure has been inadequately understood, slowing the selective spread of technology to new areas to maintain high growth rates. Similarly, the dynamics of agricultural growth, calling for gradual diversification beyond initially dominant cereals, has not been sufficiently understood to favor continued expansion of research capacities and the dynamic development of complex marketing systems for perishables. Far more important, however, has been the very laggard response of employment growth in countries such as India and the Philippines compared with that in Taiwan and Thailand. The employment record in India and the Philippines, both of which have done moderately well in agriculture, is puzzling. The answer probably lies with a strong import displacement and a capital-intensive development strategy that has left both economies poorly structured to benefit from accelerated growth in agriculture. That problem requires considerable attention. Major past, inappropriate investments may have to be written off and a new start made.

In Africa, the situation is at once conceptually simpler and in practice more difficult. The basic act of moving the agricultural sector has not yet been put together. Training, national institution building, and giving development priority to the needs of the most responsive regions and commodities must be pursued vigorously. A complete reorientation of foreign assistance as well as of national policies is needed.[34] Given the gross inadequacies of trained personnel, institutions, and rural infrastructure, the task will be difficult and lengthy. Obviously, complex political compromises will be needed, but an urgent effort must be mobilized if measurable progress is to be made.

Once an economy gets moving, the nonagricultural sectors will rapidly increase in relative importance and take on a life of their own. Institutions must be developed to foster technological improvement in those activities. As the economy diversifies, so must the capacity to support and foster that diversification. The demands for trained personnel and institutional capacity will burgeon. But these longer-term needs must not be allowed to diminish the here-and-now priorities for agriculture and employment growth upon which the economy's postagricultural prospects so largely depend. Africa, in particular, has suffered from such a lack of priority on the part of national policies and donor-country assistance alike.

NOTES

1. For calculations of a high potential, see John W. Mellor, *The New Economics of Growth: A Strategy for India and the Developing World* (Ithaca: Cornell University Press, 1976).

2. See, for example, C. H. Hanumantha Rao, *Technological Change and Distribution of Gains in Indian Agriculture* (Delhi: Macmillan Company of India, 1975).

3. Uma Lele and John W. Mellor, "Technological Change, Distributive Bias and Labor Transfer in a Two Sector Economy," *Oxford Economic Papers,* vol. 33, no. 3 (November 1981): 426–41.

4. Paul N. Rosenstein-Rodan, "Problems of Industrialization of Eastern and South-Eastern Europe," *Economic Journal* 53 (June–September, 1943).

5. P. C. Mahalanobis, "Some Observations on the Process of Growth of National Income," *Sankhya* (Calcutta: September 1953): 307–12; and Anthony M. Tang and Bruce Stone, *Food Production in the Peoples Republic of China* (Washington, D.C.: International Food Policy Research Institute, Research Report no. 15, 1980).

6. A review of these concepts in the context of agricultural growth is found in John W. Mellor, "Models of Economic Growth and Land-Augmenting Technological Change in Foodgrain Production," in *Agricultural Policy in Developing Countries,* ed. Nural Islam (London: Macmillan, 1974), 3–30.

7. Amartya K. Sen, *Choices of Technique: An Aspect of the Theory of Planned Development* (New York: Augustus M. Kelly, 1968).

8. Raul Prebisch, *The Economic Development of Latin America and Its Principal Problems* (New York: United Nations Economic Commission for Latin America, 1950).

9. For this view, see Keith Griffith, *The Political Economy of Agrarian Change* (London: Macmillan, 1979); and for the contrary evidence, see John W. Mellor and Gunvant M. Desai, eds., *Agricultural Change and Rural Poverty: Variations on a Theme by Dharm Narain* (Baltimore: Johns Hopkins University Press, 1985).

10. Uma Lele, *The Design of Rural Development: Lessons from Africa* (Baltimore: Johns Hopkins University Press, 1975, 1979).

11. Bela Balassa, "The Policy Experience of Twelve Less Developed Countries, 1973–1979," in *Comparative Development Perspectives,* ed. Gustav Ranis. (Boulder, Colo.: Westview Press, 1984).

12. Nicholas Kaldor, *Essays on Economic Growth and Stability* (London: Duckworth, 1960), p. 242.

13. T. W. Schultz, *Transforming Traditional Agriculture* (New Haven: Yale University Press, 1964).

14. John W. Mellor and Robert W. Herdt, "The Contrasting Response of Rice to Nitrogen: India and the United States," *Journal of Farm Economics* 46, no. 1 (February 1964): 150–60.

15. Bruce F. Johnston and John W. Mellor, "The Role of Agriculture in Economic Development," *American Economic Review* 51, no. 4 (September 1961): 566–93.

16. W. Arthur Lewis, "Economic Development with Unlimited Supplies," *The Manchester School,* vol. 2 (May 1954).

17. Johnston and Mellor, "The Role of Agriculture in Economic Development"; and John W. Mellor, *The Economics of Agricultural Development* (Ithaca: Cornell University Press, 1966).

18. Kazushi Ohkawa, *Differential Structure and Agriculture: Essays on Dualistic Growth* (Tokyo: Institute of Economic Research, Hitotsubashi University, 1972); Bruce F. Johnston, "Agricultural Productivity and Economic Development in Japan," *Journal of Political Economy* 59 (December 1951): 498–513; Shigeru Ishikawa, *Conditions for Agricultural Development in Developing Asian Countries* (Tokyo: Committee for the Translation of Economic Studies, 1964).

19. T. H. Lee, *Intersectoral Capital Flows in the Economic Development of Taiwan, 1895–1960* (Ithaca: Cornell University Press, 1971).

20. John W. Mellor and Uma Lele, "Growth Linkages of the New Foodgrain Technologies," *Indian Journal of Agricultural Economics* 28, no. 1 (January–March 1973): 35–55.

21. Bruce F. Johnston and Peter Kilby, *Agriculture and Structural Transformation: Economic Strategies in Late-Developing Countries* (New York: Oxford University Press, 1975).

22. John W. Mellor, *The Economics of Agricultural Development* (Ithaca: Cornell University Press, 1966).

23. Lele and Mellor, "Technological Change," 426–41.

24. Ibid.

25. Gustav Ranis and John C. H. Fei, "A Theory of Economic Development," *American Economic Review* 51, no. 4 (September 1961): 533–46.

26. Kenneth L. Bachman and Leonardo Paulino, *Rapid Food Production, Growth in Selected De-*

veloping Countries: A Comparative Analysis of Underlying Trends, 1961–76, IFPRI Research Report no. 11 (Washington, D.C.: International Food Policy Research Institute, 1979).

27. For a careful example of a difficult genre, see Robert Herdt, "A Disaggregate Approach to Aggregate Supply," *American Journal of Agricultural Economics* 52, no. 4 (November 1970): 512–20.

28. Albert O. Hirschman, *The Strategy of Economic Development* (New Haven: Yale University Press, 1958).

29. Mancur Olson, *The Rise and Decline of Nations: Economic Growth, Stagflation and Social Rigidities* (New Haven: Yale University Press, 1984).

30. John Hicks, *Economic Perspectives: Further Essays on Money and Growth* (Oxford: Clarendon Press, 1977).

31. See Mellor, "New Economics of Growth," for data on potential job losses in India due to increasing capital intensity.

32. Kou-shu Liang and T. H. Lee, "Process and Pattern of Economic Development," mimeograph (Taipei, Taiwan: Joint Committee on Rural Reconstruction, 1972).

33. Lele and Mellor, "Technological Change," 426–41.

34. John W. Mellor, Christopher Delgado, and Malcolm J. Blackie, eds., *Accelerating Food Production Growth in Sub-Saharan Africa* (Baltimore: Johns Hopkins University Press, 1987).

4

Models of Agricultural Development

VERNON W. RUTTAN

Prior to this century, almost all increase in food production was obtained by bringing new land into production. There were only a few exceptions to this generalization—in limited areas of East Asia, in the Middle East, and in Western Europe. By the end of this century almost all of the increase in world food production must come from higher yields—from increased output per hectare. In most of the world the transition from a resource-based to a science-based system of agriculture is occurring within a single century. In a few countries this transition began in the nineteenth century. In most of the presently developed countries it did not begin until the first half of this century. Most of the countries of the developing world have been caught up in the transition only since mid-century. The technology associated with this transition, particularly the new seed-fertilizer technology, has been referred to as the "Green Revolution."

During the remaining years of the twentieth century, it is imperative that the poor countries design and implement more effective agricultural development strategies than in the past. A useful first step in this effort is to review the approaches to agricultural development that have been employed in the past and will remain part of our intellectual equipment. The literature on agricultural development can be characterized according to the following models: (1) the frontier, (2) the conservation, (3) the urban-industrial impact, (4) the diffusion, (5) the high-payoff input, and (6) the induced innovation.

FRONTIER MODEL

Throughout most of history, expansion of the area cultivated or grazed has represented the dominant source of increase in agricultural production. The most

VERNON W. RUTTAN is professor of economics and of agricultural and applied economics, University of Minnesota.

Originally titled "How the World Feeds Itself." Published by permission of Transaction Publishers, from *Society* 17, no 6. Copyright © 1980 by Transaction Publishers. Published with omissions and minor editorial revisions and with the permission of the author.

dramatic example in Western history was the opening up of the new continents—North and South America and Australia—to European settlement during the eighteenth and nineteenth centuries. With the advent of cheap transport during the latter half of the nineteenth century, the countries of the new continents became increasingly important sources of food and agricultural raw materials for the metropolitan countries of Western Europe.

Similar processes had occurred earlier, though at a less dramatic pace, in the peasant and village economies of Europe, Asia, and Africa. The first millennium A.D. saw the agricultural colonization of Europe north of the Alps, the Chinese settlement of the lands south of the Yangtze, and the Bantu occupation of Africa south of the tropical forest belts. Intensification of land use in existing villages was followed by pioneer settlement, the establishment of new villages, and the opening up of forest or jungle land to cultivation. In Western Europe there was a series of successive changes from neolithic forest fallow to systems of shifting cultivation of bush and grass land followed first by short fallow systems and later by annual cropping.

Where soil conditions were favorable, as in the great river basins and plains, the new villages gradually intensified their system of cultivation. Where soil resources were poor, as in many of the hill and upland regions, new areas were opened up to shifting cultivation or nomadic grazing. Under conditions of rapid population growth, the limits to the frontier model were often quickly realized. Crop yields were typically low—measured in terms of output per unit of seed rather than per unit of crop area. Output per hectare and per man-hour tended to decline—except in delta areas, such as Egypt and South Asia, and the wet rice areas of East Asia. In many areas the result was increasing immiserization of the peasantry.

There are relatively few remaining areas of the world where development along the lines of the frontier model will represent an efficient source of growth during the last two decades of the twentieth century. The 1960s saw the "closing of the frontier" in most areas of Southeast Asia. In Latin America and Africa the opening up of new lands awaits development of technologies for the control of pests and diseases (such as the tsetse fly in Africa) or for the release and maintenance of productivity of problem soils.

CONSERVATION MODEL

The conservation model of agricultural development evolved from the advances in crop and livestock husbandry associated with the English agricultural revolution and the notions of soil exhaustion suggested by the early German chemists and soil scientists. It was reinforced by the application to land of the concept, developed in the English classical school of economics, of diminishing returns to labor and capital. The conservation model emphasized the evolution of a sequence of increasingly complex land- and labor-intensive cropping systems, the production and use of organic manures, and labor-intensive capital formation in the form of drainage, irrigation, and other physical facilities to more effectively utilize land and water resources.

Until well into the twentieth century the conservation model of agricultural development was the only approach to intensification of agricultural production available to most of the world's farmers. Its application is effectively illustrated by development of the wet-rice culture systems that emerged in East and Southeast Asia and by the labor- and land-intensive systems of integrated crop-livestock husbandry which increasingly characterized European agriculture during the eighteenth and nineteenth centuries.

During the English agricultural revolution more intensive crop-rotation systems replaced the open-three-field system in which arable land was allocated between permanent crop land and permanent pasture. This involved the introduction and more intensive use of new forage and green manure crops and an increase in the availability and use of animal manures. This "new husbandry" permitted the intensification of crop-livestock production through the recycling of plant nutrients, in the form of animal manures, to maintain soil fertility. The inputs used in this conservation system of farming—the plant nutrients, animal power, land improvements, physical capital, and agricultural labor force—were largely produced or supplied by the agricultural sector itself.

Agricultural development, within the framework of the conservation model, clearly was capable in many parts of the world of sustaining rates of growth in agricultural production in the range of 1.0 percent per year over relatively long periods of time. The most serious recent effort to develop agriculture within this framework was made by the People's Republic of China in the late 1950s and early 1960s. It became readily apparent, however, that the feasible growth rates, even with a rigorous recycling effort, were not compatible with modern rates of growth in the demand for agricultural output—which typically fall in the 3–5 percent range in the less developed countries (LDCs). The conservation model remains an important source of productivity growth in most poor countries and an inspiration to agrarian fundamentalists and the organic farming movement in the developed countries.

URBAN-INDUSTRIAL IMPACT MODEL

In the conservation model, locational variations in agricultural development are related primarily to differences in environmental factors. It stands in sharp contrast to models that interpret geographic differences in the level and rate of economic development primarily in terms of the level and rate of urban-industrial development.

Initially, the urban-industrial impact model was formulated in Germany by J. H. von Thunen to explain geographic variations in the intensity of farming systems and the productivity of labor in an industrializing society. In the United States it was extended to explain the more effective performance of the input and product markets linking the agricultural and nonagricultural sectors in regions characterized by rapid urban-industrial development than in regions where the urban economy had not made a transition to the industrial stage. In the 1950s, interest in the urban-industrial impact model reflected concern with the failure of agricultural resource development and price policies, adopted in the 1930s, to remove the persistent regional disparities in agricultural productivity and rural incomes in the United States.

The rationale for this model was developed in terms of more effective input and product markets in areas of rapid urban-industrial development. Industrial development stimulated agricultural development by expanding the demand for farm products, supplying the industrial inputs needed to improve agricultural productivity, and drawing away surplus labor from agriculture. The empirical tests of the urban-industrial impact model have repeatedly confirmed that a strong nonfarm labor market is an essential prerequisite for labor productivity in agriculture and improved incomes for rural people.

The policy implications of the urban-industrial impact model appear to be most relevant for less developed regions of highly industrialized countries or lagging regions of the more rapidly growing LDCs. Agricultural development policies based on this model appear to be particularly inappropriate in those countries where the "pathological" growth of urban centers is a result of population pressures in rural areas running ahead of employment growth in urban areas.

DIFFUSION MODEL

The diffusion of better husbandry practices was a major source of productivity growth even in premodern societies. The diffusion of crops and animals from the new world to the old—potatoes, maize, cassava, rubber—and from the old world to the new—sugar, wheat, and domestic livestock—was an important by-product of the voyages of discovery and trade from the fifteenth to the nineteenth centuries. The diffusion approach rests on the empirical observation of substantial differences in land and labor productivity among farmers and regions. The route to agricultural development, in this view, is through more effective dissemination of technical knowledge and a narrowing of the productivity differences among farmers and among regions.

The diffusion model has provided the major intellectual foundation of much of the research and extension effort in farm management and production economics since the emergence, in the latter years of the nineteenth century, of agricultural economics and rural sociology as separate subdisciplines linking the agricultural and the social sciences. Developments leading to establishment of active programs of farm management research and extension occurred at a time when experiment station research was making only a modest contribution to agricultural productivity growth. A further contribution to the effective diffusion of known technology was provided by rural sociologists' research on the diffusion process. Models were developed emphasizing the relationship between diffusion rates and the personality characteristics and educational accomplishments of farm operators.

Insights into the dynamics of the diffusion process, when coupled with the observation of wide agricultural productivity gaps among developed and less developed countries and a presumption of inefficient resource allocation among "irrational tradition-bound" peasants, produced an extension or diffusion bias in the choice of agricultural development strategy in many LDCs during the 1950s. During the 1960s the limitations of the diffusion model as a foundation for the design of agricultural development policies became increasingly apparent as technical assistance and rural development programs, based explicitly or implicitly on this model, failed to generate either rapid modernization of traditional farms and communities or rapid growth in agricultural output.

HIGH-PAYOFF INPUT MODEL

The inadequacy of policies based on the conservation, urban-industrial impact, and diffusion models led, in the 1960s, to a new perspective—the key to transforming a traditional agricultural sector into a productive source of economic growth was investment designed to make modern, high-payoff inputs available to farmers in poor countries. Peasants in traditional agricultural systems were viewed as rational, efficient resource allocators. This iconoclastic view was developed most vigorously by T. W. Schultz in his controversial book *Transforming Traditional Agriculture*. He insisted that peasants in traditional societies remained poor because, in most poor countries, there were only limited technical and economic opportunities to which they could respond. The new, high-payoff inputs were classified according to three categories: (1) the capacity of public and private sector research institutions to produce new technical knowledge; (2) the capacity of the industrial sector to develop, produce, and market new technical inputs; and (3) the capacity of farmers to acquire new knowledge and use new inputs effectively.

The enthusiasm with which the high-payoff input model has been accepted and translated into economic doctrine has been due in part to the proliferation of studies reporting high rates of return to public investment in agricultural research.[1] It was also due to the success of efforts to develop new, high-productivity grain varieties suitable for the tropics. New high-yielding wheat varieties were developed in Mexico beginning in the 1950s, and new high-yielding rice varieties were developed in the Philippines in the 1960s. These varieties were highly responsive to industrial inputs, such as fertilizer and other chemicals, and to more effective soil and water management. The high returns associated with the adoption of the new varieties and the associated technical inputs and management practices have led to rapid diffusion of the new varieties among farmers in a number of countries in Asia, Africa, and Latin America.

INDUCED INNOVATION MODEL

The high-payoff input model remains incomplete as a theory of agricultural development. Typically, education and research are public goods not traded through the marketplace. The mechanism by which resources are allocated among education, research, and other public and private sector economic activities was not fully incorporated into the model. It does not explain how economic conditions induce the development and adoption of an efficient set of technologies for a particular society. Nor does it attempt to specify the processes by which input and product price relationships induce investment in research in a direction consistent with a nation's particular resource endowments.

These limitations in the high-payoff input model led to efforts by Yujiro Hayami and myself to develop a model of agricultural development in which technical change is treated as endogenous to the development process, rather than as an exogenous factor operating independently of other development processes. The induced innovation perspective was stimulated by historical evidence that different countries had followed alternative paths of technical change in the process of agricultural development.[2]

Technical Innovation

The levels achieved in each productivity grouping by farmers in the most advanced countries can be viewed as arranged along a productivity frontier. This frontier reflects the level of technical progress achieved by the most advanced countries in each resource endowment classification. These productivity levels are not immediately available to farmers in most low-productivity countries. They can only be made available by undertaking investment in the agricultural research capacity needed to develop technologies appropriate to the countries' natural and institutional environments and investment in the physical and institutional infrastructure needed to realize the new production potential opened up by technological advances.

There is clear historical evidence that technology has been developed to facilitate the substitution of relatively abundant (hence cheap) factors for relatively scarce (hence expensive) factors of production. The constraints imposed on agricultural development by an inelastic supply of land have, in economies such as Japan and Taiwan, been offset by the development of high-yielding crop varieties designed to facilitate the substitution of fertilizer for land. The constraints imposed by an inelastic supply of labor, in countries such as the United States, Canada, and Australia, have been offset by technical advances leading to the substitution of animal and mechanical power for manpower. In some cases the new technologies—embodied in new crop varieties, new equipment, or new production practices—may not always be substitutes per se for land or labor. Rather, they are catalysts which facilitate the substitution of relatively abundant factors (such as fertilizer or mineral fuels) for relatively scarce factors.

INSTITUTIONAL INNOVATION

A developing country which fails to evolve a capacity for technical and institutional innovation in agriculture consistent with its resource and cultural endowments suffers two major constraints on its development of productive agriculture. It is unable to take advantage of advances in biological and chemical technologies suited to labor-intensive agricultural systems. And the mechanical technology it does import from more developed countries will be productive only under conditions of large-scale agricultural organization. It will contribute to the emergence of a "bimodal" rather than a "unimodal" organization structure.

During the last two decades a number of developing countries have begun to establish the institutional capacity to generate technical changes adapted to national and regional resource endowments. More recently these emerging national systems have been buttressed by a new system of international crop and animal research institutes. These new institutes have become both important sources of new knowledge and technology and increasingly effective communication links among the developing national research systems.

The lag in shifting from a natural-resource-based to a science-based system of agriculture continues to be a source of national differences in land and labor productivity. Lags in the development and application of knowledge are also important sources of regional productivity differences within countries. In countries such as Mexico and India differential rates of technical change have been an important source of the widening disparities in the rate of growth of total agricultural output, in labor and land productivity, and in incomes and wage rates among regions.

Productivity differences in agriculture are increasingly a function of investments in scientific and industrial capacity and in the education of rural people rather than of natural resource endowments. The effects of education on productivity are particularly important during periods in which a nation's agricultural research system begins to introduce new technology. In an agricultural system characterized by static technology there are few gains to be realized from education in rural areas. Rural people who have lived for generations with essentially the same resources and the same technology have learned from long experience what their efforts can get out of the resources available to them. Children acquire from their parents the skills that are worthwhile. Formal schooling has little economic value in agricultural production.

As soon as new technical opportunities become available, this situation changes. Technical change requires the acquisition of new husbandry skills; acquisition from nontraditional sources of additional resources such as new seeds, new chemicals, and new equipment; and development of new skills in dealing with both natural resources and input and product market institutions linking agriculture with the nonagricultural sector.

The processes by which new knowledge can be applied to alter the rate and direction of technical change in agriculture, are, however, substantially greater than our knowledge of the processes by which resources are brought to bear on the process of institutional innovation and transfer. Yet the need for viable institutions capable of supporting more rapid agricultural growth and rural development is even more compelling today than a decade ago.

NOTES

1. See Robert E. Evenson, "Benefits and Obstacles in Developing Appropriate Agricultural Technology," chap. 24 in *Agricultural Development in the Third World*, ed. Carl K. Eicher and John M. Staatz (Baltimore: Johns Hopkins University Press, 1984).

2. For more details on the induced innovation model see chapter 5.—ED.

5

Induced Innovation Model of Agricultural Development

VERNON W. RUTTAN and YUJIRO HAYAMI

During the 1960s a new consensus emerged to the effect that agricultural growth is critical (if not a precondition) for industrialization and general economic growth. Nevertheless, the process of agricultural growth itself has remained outside the concern of most development economists. Both technical change and institutional evolution have been treated as exogenous to their systems.

In this paper we elaborate the concept of induced technical and institutional innovation which we have employed in our own research on the agricultural development process, and we discuss the implications of the induced innovation perspective for the design of national and regional strategies for agricultural development.

AN INDUCED DEVELOPMENT MODEL

An attempt to develop a model of agricultural development in which technical change is treated as endogenous to the development process, rather than as an exogenous factor that operates independently of other development processes, must start with the recognition that there are multiple paths of technological development.

ALTERNATIVE PATHS OF TECHNOLOGICAL DEVELOPMENT

There is clear evidence that technology can be developed to facilitate the substitution of relatively abundant (hence cheap) factors for relatively scarce (hence expensive) factors in the economy. The constraints imposed on agri-

VERNON W. RUTTAN is professor of economics and of agricultural and applied economics, University of Minnesota. YUJIRO HAYAMI is professor of economics, Aoyama Gakuin University, Tokyo.

Originally titled "Strategies for Agricultural Development." Reprinted from *Food Research Institute Studies in Agricultural Economics, Trade and Development* 9, no. 2 (1972): 129–48, with omissions and minor editorial revisions, by permission of the Food Research Institute, Stanford University, and the authors.

cultural development by an inelastic supply of land have, in economies such as those of Japan and Taiwan, been offset by the development of high-yielding crop varieties designed to facilitate the substitution of fertilizer for land. The constraints imposed by an inelastic supply of labor, in countries such as the United States, Canada, and Australia, have been offset by technical advances leading to the substitution of animal and mechanical power for labor. In both cases the new technology, embodied in new crop varieties, new equipment, or new production practices, may not always be a substitute by itself for land or labor; rather it may serve as a catalyst to facilitate the substitution of the relatively abundant factors (such as fertilizer or mineral fuels) for the relatively scarce factors. It seems reasonable, following Hicks, to call techniques designed to facilitate the substitution of other inputs for labor ''labor-saving'' and those designed to facilitate the substitution of other inputs for land ''land-saving.'' In agriculture, two kinds of technology generally correspond to this taxonomy: mechanical technology to ''labor-saving'' and biological and chemical technology to ''land-saving.''[1] The former is designed to facilitate the substitution of power and machinery for labor. Typically this involves the substitution of land for labor, because higher output per worker through mechanization usually requires a larger land area cultivated per worker. The latter, which we will hereafter identify as biological technology, is designed to facilitate the substitution of labor and/or industrial inputs for land. This may occur through increased recycling of soil fertility by more labor-intensive conservation systems; through use of chemical fertilizers; and through husbandry practices, management systems, and inputs (that is, insecticides) which permit an optimum yield response.

Historically there has been a close association between advances in output per unit of land area and advances in biological technology and between advances in output per worker and advances in mechanical technology. The construction of an induced development model involves an explanation of the mechanism by which a society chooses an optimum path of technological change in agriculture.

INDUCED INNOVATION IN THE PRIVATE SECTOR

There is a substantial body of literature on the ''theory of induced innovation.''[2] Much of this literature focuses on the choice of available technology by the individual firm. There is also a substantial body of literature on how changes in factor prices over time or differences in factor prices among countries influence the nature of invention. This discussion has been conducted entirely within the framework of the theory of the firm. A major controversy has centered around the issue of the existence of a mechanism by which changes or differences in factor prices affect the inventive activity or the innovative behavior of firms.

It had generally been accepted, at least since the publication of *The Theory of Wages* by J. R. Hicks (1932, 124–25), that changes or differences in the relative prices of factors of production could influence the direction of invention or innovation.[3] There have also been arguments raised by W. E. G. Salter (1960, 43–44) and others (Ahmad 1966; Fellner 1961; Kennedy 1964; Samuelson 1965) against Hicks's theory of induced innovation. The arguments run somewhat as follows: firms are motivated to save total cost for a given output; at competitive equilibrium, each factor is being paid its marginal value product; therefore, all factors are equally expensive to firms; hence, there is no incentive for competitive firms to search for techniques to save a particular factor.

The difference between our perspective and Salter's is partly due to a difference in the definition of the production function. Salter defined the production function to embrace all possible designs conceivable by existing scientific knowledge and called the choice among these designs "factor substitution" instead of "technical change" (1960, 14–16). Salter admits, however, that "relative factor prices are in the nature of signposts representing broad influences that determine the way technological knowledge is applied to production" (ibid., 16). If we accept Salter's definition, the allocation of resources to the development of high-yielding and fertilizer-responsive rice varieties adaptable to the ecological conditions of South and Southeast Asia, which are comparable to the improved varieties developed earlier in Japan and Taiwan, cannot be considered as a technical change. Rather, it is viewed as an application of existing technological knowledge (breeding techniques, plant-type concepts, and so on) to production.

Although we do not deny the case for Salter's definition, it is clearly not very useful in attempting to understand the process by which new technical alternatives become available. We regard technical change as any change in production coefficients resulting from purposeful resource-using activity directed to the development of new knowledge embodied in designs, materials, or organizations. In terms of this definition, it is entirely rational for competitive firms to allocate funds to develop a technology that facilitates the substitution of increasingly less expensive factors for more expensive factors. Using the above definition, Syed Ahmad (1960) has shown that the Hicksian theory of market-induced innovation can be defended with a rather reasonable assumption on the possibility of alternative innovations.[4]

We illustrate Ahmad's argument with the aid of figure 1. Suppose that at a point in time a firm is operating at a competitive equilibrium, A or B, depending on the prevailing factor-price ratio, p or m, for an isoquant, u_0, producing a given output; and this firm perceives multiple alternative innovations represented by isoquants, u_1, u_1', . . . , producing the same output in such a way as to be enveloped by U, a concave innovation possibility curve or meta-production function which can be developed by the same amount of research expenditure. In order to minimize total cost for given output and given research expenditure, innovative efforts of this firm will be directed towards developing Y-saving technology (u_1) or X-saving technology (u_1'), depending on the prevailing factor-price ratio, p (parallel to PP) or m (parallel to MM and MM'). If a firm facing a price ratio m develops an X-saving technology (u_1'), it can obtain an additional

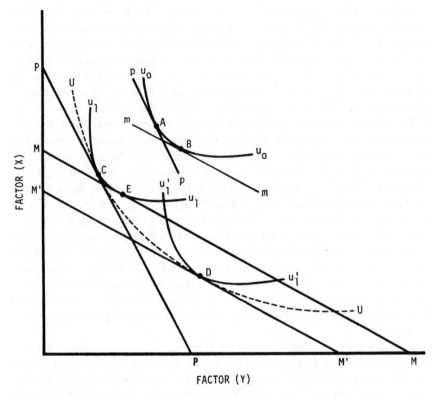

FACTOR (Y)

Fig.1. Factor Prices and Induced Technical Change

gain represented by the distance between M and M' compared with the case that develops a Y-saving technology (u_1). In this framework it is clear that if X becomes more expensive relative to Y over time, in any economy the innovative efforts of entrepreneurs will be directed towards developing a more X-saving and Y-using technology compared with the contrary case. Also, in a country in which X is more expensive relative to Y than in another country, innovative efforts in the country will be more directed towards X-saving and Y-using than in the other country. In this formulation the expectation of relative price change, which is central to William Fellner's theory of induced innovation, is not necessary, although expectations may work as a powerful reinforcing agent in directing technical effort.[5]

The role of changing relative factor prices in inducing a continuous sequence of non-neutral biological and mechanical innovations along the iso-product surface of a meta-production function is further illustrated in figure 2. U represents the land-labor isoquant of the meta-production function, which is the envelope of less elastic isoquants such as u_0 and u_1, corresponding to different types of

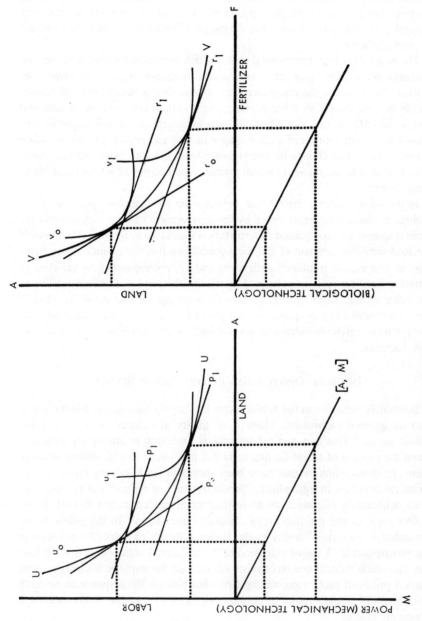

Fig.2. Factor Prices and Induced Mechanical and Biological Innovation

101

machinery or technology. A certain technology represented by u_0 (for example, a reaper) is created when a price ratio, p_0, prevails a certain length of time. When the price ratio changes from p_0 to p_1, another technology, represented by u_1 (for example, a combine), is induced in the long run, which gives the minimum cost of production for p_1.

The new technology represented by u_1, which enables enlargement of the area operated per worker, generally corresponds to higher intensity of power per worker. This implies the complementary relationship between land and power, which may be drawn as a line representing a certain combination of land and power, $[A, M]$. In this simplified presentation, mechanical innovation is conceived as the substitution of a combination of land and power, $[A, M]$, for labor (L) in response to a change in wage relative to an index of labor and machinery prices, although, of course, in actual practice land and power are substitutable to some extent.

In the same context, the relation between the fertilizer-land price ratio and biological innovations represented by the development of crop varieties that are more responsive to application of fertilizers is illustrated in figure 2. V represents the land-fertilizer isoquant of the meta-production function, which is the envelope of less elastic isoquants such as v_0 and v_1, corresponding to varieties of different fertilizer responsiveness. A decline in the price of fertilizer relative to the price of land from r_0 to r_1 creates an incentive for farmers to adopt crop varieties described by isoquants to the right of v_0 and for private seed companies and public research institutions to develop and market such new fertilizer-responsive varieties.

INDUCED INNOVATION IN THE PUBLIC SECTOR

Innovative behavior in the public sector has largely been ignored in the literature on induced innovation. There is no theory of induced innovation in the public sector.[6] This is a particularly critical limitation in attempting to understand the process of scientific and technical innovation in agricultural development. In most countries that have been successful in achieving rapid rates of technical progress in agriculture, "socialization" of agricultural research has been deliberately employed as an instrument of modernization in agriculture.

Our view of the mechanism of "induced innovation" in the public sector agricultural research is similar to the Hicksian theory of induced innovation in the private sector. A major extension of the traditional argument is that we base the innovation inducement mechanism not only on the response to changes in the market prices of profit maximizing firms but also on the response of research scientists and administrators in public institutions to resource endowments and economic change.

We hypothesize that technical change is guided along an efficient path by price signals in the market, provided that the prices efficiently reflect changes in the demand and supply of products and factors and that there exists effective interaction among farmers, public research institutions, and private agricultural supply firms. If the demand for agricultural products increases, due to the growth in population and income, prices of the inputs for which the supply is inelastic will be raised relative to the prices of inputs for which the supply is elastic. Likewise, if the supply of particular inputs shifts to the right faster than that of others, the prices of these inputs will decline relative to the prices of other factors of production.

In consequence, technical innovations that save the factors characterized by an inelastic supply, or by slower shifts in supply, become relatively more profitable for agricultural producers. Farmers are induced by shifts in relative prices to search for technical alternatives that save the increasingly scarce factors of production. They press the public research institutions to develop the new technology and demand that agricultural supply firms supply modern technical inputs that substitute for the more scarce factors. Perceptive scientists and science administrators respond by making available new technical possibilities and new inputs that enable farmers profitably to substitute the increasingly abundant factors for increasingly scarce factors, thereby guiding the demand of farmers for unit cost reduction in a socially optimum direction.

The dialectic interaction among farmers and research scientists and administrators is likely to be most effective when farmers are organized into politically effective local and regional farm "bureaus" or farmers' associations. The response of the public sector research and extension programs to farmers' demand is likely to be greatest when the agricultural research system is highly decentralized, as in the United States. In the United States, for example, each of the state agricultural experiment stations has tended to view its function, at least in part, as to maintain the competitive position of agriculture in its state relative to agriculture in other states. Similarly, national policy makers may regard investment in agricultural research as an investment designed to maintain the country's competitive position in world markets or to improve the economic viability of the agricultural sector producing import substitutes. Given effective farmer organizations and a mission- or client-oriented experiment station system, the competitive model of firm behavior illustrated in figures 1 and 2 can be usefully extended to explain the response of experiment station administrators and research scientists to economic opportunities.

In this public-sector-induced innovation model, the response of research scientists and administrators represents the critical link in the inducement mechanism. The model does not imply that it is necessary for individual scientists or research administrators in public institutions to respond consciously to market prices, or directly to farmers' demands for research results, in the selection of research objectives. They may, in fact, be motivated primarily by a drive for professional achievement and recognition (Niskanen 1968). Or they may, in the Rosenberg terminology, view themselves as responding to an "obvious and compelling need'' to remove the constraints on growth of production or on factor supplies.[7] It is only necessary that there exist an effective incentive mechanism to reward the scientists or administrators, materially or by prestige, for their contributions to the solution of significant problems in the society.[8] Under these conditions, it seems reasonable to hypothesize that the scientists and administrators of public sector research programs do respond to the needs of society in an attempt to direct the results of their activity to public purpose. Furthermore, we hypothesize that secular changes in relative factor and product prices convey much of the information regarding the relative priorities that society places on the goals of research.

The response in the public research sector is not limited to the field of applied science. Scientists trying to solve practical problems often consult with or ask cooperation of those working in more basic fields. If the basic scientists respond to the requests of the applied researchers, they are in effect responding to the needs of society. It is not uncommon that major breakthroughs in basic science are created through the process of solving the problems raised by research workers in the more applied fields.[9] It appears reasonable, therefore, to hypothesize as a result of the interactions among the basic and applied sciences and the process by which public funds are allocated to research that basic research tends to be directed also towards easing the limitations on agricultural production imposed by relatively scarce factors.

We do not argue, however, that technical change in agriculture is wholly of an induced character. There is a supply (exogenous) dimension to the process as well as a demand (endogenous) dimension. Technical change in agriculture reflects, in addition to the effects of resource endowments and growth in demand, the progress of general science and technology. Progress in general science (or scientific innovation) that lowers the ''cost'' of technical and entrepreneurial innovations may have influences on technical change in agriculture unrelated to changes in factor proportions and product demand (Nelson 1959; Schmookler 1966). Similarly, advances in science and technology in the developed countries, in response to their own resource endowments, may result in a bias in the innovation possibility curves facing the developing countries. Even in these cases, the rate of adoption and the impact on productivity of autonomous or exogenous changes in technology will be strongly influenced by the conditions of resource supply and product demand, as these forces are reflected through factor and product markets.

Thus, the classical problem of resource allocation, which was rejected as an adequate basis for agricultural productivity and output growth in the high-payoff input model,[10] in this context is treated as central to the agricultural development process. Under conditions of static technology, improvements in resource allocation represent a weak source of economic growth. The efficient allocation of resources to open up new sources of growth is, however, essential to the agricultural development process.

INSTITUTIONAL INNOVATION

Extension of the theory of "induced innovation" to explain the behavior of public research institutions represents an essential link in the construction of a theory of induced development. In the induced development model, advances in mechanical and biological technology respond to changing relative prices of factors and to changes in the prices of factors relative to products to ease the constraints on growth imposed by inelastic supplies of land or labor. Neither this process nor its impact is confined to the agricultural sector. Changes in relative prices in any sector of the economy act to induce innovative activity, not only by private producers but also by scientists in public institutions, in order to reduce the constraints imposed by those factors of production that are relatively scarce.

We further hypothesize that the institutions that govern the use of technology or the "mode" of production can also be induced to change in order to enable both individuals and society to take fuller advantage of new technical opportunities under favorable market conditions.[11] The Second Enclosure Movement in England represents a classical illustration. The issuance of the Enclosure Bill facilitated the conversion of communal pasture and farmland into single, private farm units, thus encouraging the introduction of an integrated crop-livestock "new husbandry" system. The Enclosure Acts can be viewed as an institutional innovation designed to exploit the new technical opportunities opened up by innovations in crop rotation, utilizing the new fodder crops (turnip and clover), in response to the rising food prices.

A major source of institutional change has been an effort by society to internalize the benefits of innovative activity to provide economic incentives for productivity increase. In some cases, institutional innovations have involved the reorganization of property rights in order to internalize the higher income streams resulting from the innovations. The modernization of land tenure relationships, involving a shift from share tenure to lease tenure and owner-operator systems of cultivation in much of Western agriculture, can be explained, in part, as a shift in property rights designed to internalize the gains of entrepreneurial innovation by individual farmers.[12]

Where internalization of the gains of innovative activity are more difficult to achieve, institutional innovations involving public sector activity become essential. The socialization of much of agricultural research, particularly the research leading to advances in biological technology, represents an example of a public sector institutional innovation designed to realize for society the potential gains from advances in agricultural technology. This institutional innovation originated in Germany and was transplanted and applied on a larger scale in the United States and Japan.

Both Schultz (1968) and Kazushi Ohkawa (1969) have argued that institutional reform is appropriately viewed as a response to the new opportunities for the productive use of resources opened up by advances in technology.[13] Our view, and the view of Ohkawa and Schultz, reduces to the hypothesis that institutional innovations occur because it appears profitable for individuals or groups in society to undertake the costs. It is unlikely that institutional change will prove viable unless the benefits to society exceed the cost. Changes in market prices and technological opportunities introduce disequilibrium in existing institutional arrangements by creating profitable new opportunities for the institutional innovations.

Profitable opportunities, however, do not necessarily lead to immediate institutional innovations. Usually the gains and losses from technical and institutional change are not distributed neutrally. There are, typically, vested interests that stand to lose and that oppose change. There are limits on the extent to which group behavior can be mobilized to achieve common or group interests (Olson 1968). The process of transforming institutions in response to technical and economic opportunities generally involves time lags, social and political stress, and in some cases disruption of social and political order. Economic growth ultimately depends on the flexibility and efficiency of society in transforming itself in response to technical and economic opportunities.

AGRICULTURAL DEVELOPMENT STRATEGY

The induced innovation model outlined above does not possess formal elegance. It is partial in that it is primarily concerned with production and productivity. Yet it has added significantly to our power to interpret the process of agricultural development.

Research that we have reported elsewhere indicates that the enormous changes in factor proportions that have occurred in the process of agricultural growth in the United States and Japan are explainable very largely in terms of changes in factor-price ratios (Hayami and Ruttan 1970, 1971). When we relate the results of the statistical analysis to historical knowledge of advances in agricultural technology, we conclude that the observed changes in input mixes have occurred as the result of a process of dynamic factor substitution along a meta-production function, associated with changes in the production surface, induced primarily by changes in relative factor prices. Preliminary results of the analysis of historical patterns of technical change in German agriculture (by Adolph Weber); in Denmark, Great Britain, and France (by William Wade); and in Argentina (by Alain de Janvry) add additional support to the utility of the induced innovation model in interpreting historical patterns of technological change and agricultural development.

The question remains, however, as to whether the induced development model represents a useful guide to modern agricultural development strategy. In responding to this concern two issues seem particularly relevant.

First, we would like to make it perfectly clear that in our view the induced development model, in which technical change and institutional change are treated as endogenous to the development process, does not imply that agricultural development can be left to an "invisible hand" that directs either technology or the total development process along an "efficient" path determined by "original" resource endowments.

We do argue that the policies that a country adopts with respect to the allocation of resources to technical and institutional innovation, to the capacity to produce technical inputs for agriculture, to the linkages between the agricultural and industrial sectors in factor and product markets, and to the organization of the crop and livestock production sectors must be consistent with national (or regional) resource endowments if they are to lead to an "efficient" growth path. Conversely, failure to achieve such consistency can sharply increase the real costs, or abort the possibility, of achieving sustained economic growth in the agricultural sector.

If the induced development model is valid—if alternative paths of technical change and productivity growth are available to developing countries—the issue of how to organize and manage the development and allocation of scientific and technical resources becomes the single most critical factor in the agricultural development process. It is not sufficient simply to build new agricultural research stations. In many developing countries existing research facilities are not employed at full capacity because they are staffed with research workers with limited scientific and technical training; because of inadequate financial, logistical, and administrative support; because of isolation from the main currents of scientific and technical innovation; and because of failure to develop a research strategy that relates research activity to the potential economic value of the new knowledge it is designed to generate.

The appropriate allocation of effort between the public and private sectors also becomes of major significance in view of the extension of the induced development model to incorporate innovative activity in the public sector. It is clear that during the early stages of development the socialization of much of biological research in agriculture is essential if the potential gains from biological technology are to be realized. The potential gains from public sector investment in other areas of the institutional infrastructure characterized by substantial spillover effects are also large. One of the most important of these areas for public investment is the modernization of the marketing system through the establishment of the information and communication linkages necessary for the efficient functioning of factor and product markets.[14]

In most developing countries the market systems are relatively underdeveloped, both technically and institutionally. A major challenge facing these countries in their planning is the development of a well-articulated marketing system capable of accurately reflecting the effects of changes in supply, demand, and production relationships. An important element in the development of a more efficient marketing system is the removal of the rigidities and distortions resulting from government policy itself—including the maintenance of overvalued currencies, artificially low rates of interest, and unfavorable factor and product price policies for agriculture (Myint 1968).

The criteria specified above for public sector investment or intervention also imply a continuous reallocation of functions among public and private sector institutions. As institutions capable of internalizing a large share of the gains of innovative activity are developed, it may become possible to transfer activities—the production of new crop varieties, for example—to the private sector and to reallocate public resources to other high-payoff areas. Many governments are presently devoting substantial resources to areas of relatively low productivity—in efforts to reform the organization of credit and product markets, for example—while failing to invest the resources necessary to produce accurate and timely market information, establish meaningful market grades and standards, and establish the physical infrastructure necessary to induce technical and logistical efficiency in the performance of marketing functions (Ruttan 1969).

A second issue is whether, under modern conditions, the forces associated with the international transfer of agricultural technology are so dominant as to vitiate the induced development model as a guide to agricultural development strategy. It might be argued, for example, that the dominance of the developed countries in science and technology raises the cost of, or even precludes the possibility of the invention of, location-specific biological and mechanical technologies adapted to the resource endowments of a particular country or region.

This argument has been made primarily with reference to diffusion of mechanical technology from the developed to the developing countries. It is argued that the pattern of organization of agricultural production adopted by the more developed countries—dominated by large-scale mechanized systems of production in both the socialist and nonsocialist economies—precludes an effective role for an agricultural system based on small-scale commercial or semicommercial farm production units (Owen 1969, 1971).[15]

We find this argument unconvincing. Rapid diffusion of imported mechanical technology in areas characterized by small farms and low wages in agriculture tends to be induced by inefficient price, exchange rate, and credit policies which substantially distort the relative costs of mechanical power relative to labor and other material inputs. Nural Islam reports, for example, that as a result of such policies, the real cost of tractors in West Pakistan was substantially below the cost in the United States (1971). The preliminary findings of work by John Sanders in Latin America also stress the role of market distortions in inducing mechanization.

We are also impressed by the history of agricultural mechanization in Japan and more recently in Taiwan. Both countries have been relatively successful in following a strategy of mechanical innovation designed to adapt the size of the tractor and other farm machinery rather than to modify the size of the agricultural production unit to make it compatible with the size of imported machinery.[16]

We do insist that failure to effectively institutionalize public sector agricultural research can result in serious distortion of the pattern of technological change and resource use. The homogeneity of agricultural products and the relatively small size of the farm firm, even in the Western and socialist economies, make it difficult for the individual agricultural producer to either bear the research costs or capture a significant share of the gains from scientific or technological innovation. Mechanical technology, however, has been much more responsive than biological technology to the inducement mechanism as it operates in the private sector. In biological technology, typified by the breeding of new plant varieties or the improvement of cultural practices, it is difficult for the innovating firm to capture more than a small share of the increased income stream resulting from the innovation.

Failure to balance the effectiveness of the private sector in responding to inducements for advances in mechanical technology, and in those areas of biological technology in which advances in knowledge can be embodied in proprietary products, with institutional innovation capable of providing an equally effective response to inducements for advances in biological technology leads to a bias in the productivity growth path that is inconsistent with relative factor endowments. It seems reasonable to hypothesize that failure to invest in public sector experiment station capacity is one of the factors responsible in some developing countries for the unbalanced adoption of mechanical, relative to biological, technology. Failure to develop adequate public sector research institutions has also been partially responsible, in some countries, for the almost exclusive concentration of research expenditures on the plantation crops and for concentration on the production of certain export crops—such as sugar and bananas—in the plantation sector.

The perspective outlined in this paper can be summarized as follows: an essential condition for success in achieving sustained growth in agricultural productivity is the capacity to generate an ecologically adapted and economically viable agricultural technology in each country or development region. Successful achievement of continued productivity growth over time involves a dynamic process of adjustment to original resource endowments and to resource accumulation during the process of historical development. It also involves an adaptive response on the part of cultural, political, and economic institutions in order to realize the growth potential opened up by new technical alternatives. The "induced development model" attempts to make more explicit the process by which technical and institutional changes are induced through the responses of farmers, agribusiness entrepreneurs, scientists, and public administrators to resource endowments and to changes in the supply and demand of factors and products.

NOTES

1. The distinction made here between "mechanical" and "biological" technology has also been employed by Heady (1949). It is similar to the distinction between "laboresque" and "landesque" capital employed by Sen (1959). In a more recent article Kaneda employs the terms "mechanical-engineering" and "biological-chemical" (1969).

2. The term "innovation" employed here embraces the entire range of processes resulting in the emergence of novelty in science, technology, industrial management, and economic organization rather than the narrow Schumpeterian definition. Schumpeter insisted that innovation was economically and sociologically distinct from invention and scientific discovery. He rejected the idea that innovation is dependent on invention or advances in science. This distinction has become increasingly artificial. See, for example, Solo 1951; Ruttan 1959; and Hohenberg 1967. Our view is similar to that of Hohenberg. He defines technical effort as the product of purposive resource-using activity directed to the production of economically useful knowledge: "Technical effort is a necessary part of any firm activity, and is only in part separable from production itself. Traditionally it is part of the entrepreneur's job to provide knowledge to organize the factors of production in an optimum way, to adjust to market changes, and to seek improved methods. Technical effort is thus subsumed under entrepreneurship" (1967, 61).

3. See also the review of thought on this issue in Ahmad 1966.

4. See also discussions by Fellner (1967) and Ahmad (1967a), and by Kennedy (1967) and Ahmad (1967b).

5. The above theory is based on the restrictive assumption that there exists a concave innovation possibility curve (U) that can be perceived by entrepreneurs. This is not as strong a restrictive assumption as it may at first appear. The innovation possibility curve does not need to be of a smooth, well-behaved shape, as drawn in figure 1. The whole argument holds equally well for the case of two distinct alternatives. It seems reasonable to hypothesize that entrepreneurs can perceive alternative innovation possibilities for a given research and development expenditure through consultation with staff scientists and engineers or through the suggestions of inventors.

6. There is a growing literature on public research policy (see Nelson, Peck, and Kalachek 1967). These authors view public sector research activities as having risen from three considerations: (*a*) fields where the public interest is believed to transcend private incentives (as in health and aviation); (*b*) industries where the individual firm is too small to capture benefits from research (agriculture and housing); and (*c*) broad support for basic research and science education (pp. 151–211). For a review of thought with respect to resource allocation in agriculture see Fishel 1971.

7. Rosenberg has suggested a theory of induced technical change based on "obvious and compelling need" to overcome the constraints on growth instead of relative factor scarcity and factor relative prices (1969). The Rosenberg model is consistent with the model suggested here, since his "obvious and compelling need" is reflected in the market through relative factor prices. C. Peter Timmer has pointed out that in a linear programming sense the constraints that give rise to the "obvious and compelling need" for technical innovation in the Rosenberg model represent the "dual" of the factor prices used in our model (1970). For further discussion of the relationships between Rosenberg's approach and that outlined in this section see Hayami and Ruttan 1973.

8. Incentive is a major issue in many developing economies. In spite of limited scientific and technical manpower, many countries have not succeeded in developing a system of economic and professional rewards that permits them to have access to or make effective use of the resources of scientific and technical manpower that are potentially available.

9. The symbiotic relationship between basic and applied research can be illustrated by the relation between work at the International Rice Research Institute in (*a*) genetics and plant physiology and (*b*) plant breeding. The geneticist and the physiologist are involved in research designed to advance understanding of the physiological processes by which plant nutrients are transformed into grain yield and of the genetic mechanisms or processes involved in the transmission from parents to progenies of the physiological characteristics of the rice plant that affect grain yield. The rice breeders utilize this knowledge from genetics and plant physiology in the design of crosses and the selection of plants with the desired growth characteristics, agronomic traits, and nutritional value. The work in plant physiology and genetics is responsive to the need of the plant breeder for advances in knowledge related to the mission of breeding more productive varieties of rice.

10. For a description of the high-payoff input model see chapter 4 in this volume.—ED.

11. At this point we share the Marxian perspective on the relationship between technological

change and institutional development, though we do not accept the Marxian perspective regarding the monolithic sequences of evolution based on clear-cut class conflicts. For two recent attempts to develop broad historical generalizations regarding the relationship between insitutions and economic forces see Hicks 1969; and North and Thomas 1970.

12. For additional examples see Davis and North 1970.

13. See also North and Thomas 1970.

14. Hayami and Peterson (1972) show that the return to investment in improvements in market information is comparable to the returns that have been estimated for high-payoff research areas such as hybrid corn and poultry.

15. Owen argues that differentiation of a rural commercial sector from the rural subsistence sector is the first step towards development of relevant agricultural development policies. The "optimum sized commercial farms will comprise the maximum amount of land that can be farmed at a profit by an appropriate set of labor where the latter uses a relatively advanced level of technology for the particular farming area. . . . the optimum sized subsistence farm plot is one that comprises the minimum amount of land that is necessary to assure to the household concerned the minimum acceptable standard of subsistence living" (1969, 107).

16. This development is reviewed in Hayami and Ruttan 1971.

REFERENCES

Ahmad, Syed. 1966. "On the Theory of Induced Invention." *Economic Journal* 76(302): 344–57.

————. 1967a. "Reply to Professor Fellner." *Economic Journal* 77(307): 664–65.

————. 1967b. "A Rejoinder to Professor Kennedy." *Economic Journal* 77(308): 960–63.

Davis, Lance, and Douglass North. 1970. "Institutional Change and American Economic Growth: A First Step Towards a Theory of Institutional Innovation." *Journal of Economic History* 30(1): 131–49.

Fellner, William. 1961. "Two Propositions in the Theory of Induced Innovations." *Economic Journal* 71(282): 305–8.

————. 1967. "Comment on the Induced Bias." *Economic Journal* 77(307): 662–64.

Fishel, W. L., ed. 1971. *Resource Allocation in Agricultural Development.* Minneapolis.

Hayami, Yujiro, and Willis Peterson. 1972. "Social Returns to Public Information Services: Statistical Reporting of U.S. Farm Commodities." *American Economic Review* 62(1): 119–30.

Hayami, Yujiro, and V. W. Ruttan. 1970. "Factor Prices and Technical Change in Agricultural Development: The United States and Japan, 1880–1960." *Journal of Political Economy* 78(5): 1115–41.

————. 1971. *Agricultural Development: An International Perspective.* Baltimore.

————. 1973. "Professor Rosenberg and the Direction of Technical Change: A Comment." *Economic Development and Cultural Change* 21(2): 352–55.

Heady, E. O. 1949. "Basic Economic and Welfare Aspects of Farm Technological Advance." *Journal of Farm Economics* 31(2): 293–316.

Hicks, J. R. 1932. *The Theory of Wages.* London.

————. 1969. *A Theory of Economic History.* London.

Hohenberg, P. M. 1967. *Chemicals in Western Europe: 1850–1914.* Chicago.

Islam, Nural. 1971. "Agricultural Growth in Pakistan: Problems and Policies." Paper presented at the Conference on Agriculture and Economic Development, Japan Economic Research Center, Tokyo, 6–10 September.

Kaneda, Hiromitsu. 1969. "Economic Implications of the 'Green Revolution' and the Strategy of Agricultural Development in West Pakistan." *Pakistan Development Review* 9(2): 111–43.

Kennedy, Charles. 1964. "Induced Bias in Innovation and the Theory of Distribution." *Economic Journal* 74(295): 541–47.

————. 1967. "On the Theory of Induced Invention—A Reply." *Economic Journal* 77(308): 958–60.

Myint, U. Hla. 1968. "Market Mechanisms and Planning—The Functional Aspect." In *The Structure and Development of Asian Economies*. Tokyo.

Nelson, R. R. 1959. "The Economics of Invention: A Survey of the Literature." *Journal of Business* 33 (April): 101–27.

Nelson, R. R., M. J. Peck, and E. D. Kalachek. 1967. *Technology, Economic Growth and Public Policy*. Washington, D.C.

Niskanen, W. A. 1968. "The Peculiar Economics of Bureaucracy." *American Economic Review* 58(2): 293–305.

North, Douglass C., and R. P. Thomas. 1970. "An Economic Theory of the Growth of the Western World." *Economic History Review*, 2d ser., 23(1): 1–17.

Ohkawa, Kazushi. 1969. "Policy Implications of the Asian Agricultural Survey—Personal Notes." In *Regional Seminar on Agriculture: Paper and Proceedings*. Makati, Philippines.

Olson, Mancur, Jr. 1968. *The Logic of Collective Action: Public Goods and the Theory of Groups*. New York.

Owen, W. F. 1969. "Structural Planning in Densely Populated Countries: An Introduction with Applications to Indonesia." *Malayan Economic Review* 14(1): 97–114.

————. 1971. *Two Rural Sectors: Their Characteristics and Roles in the Development Process*. Indiana University International Developmental Research Center Occasional Paper 1. Bloomington, Ind.

Rosenberg, Nathan. 1969. "The Direction of Technological Change: Inducement Mechanisms and Focusing Devices." *Economic Development and Cultural Change* 18(1, pt. 1): 1–24.

Ruttan, V. W. 1959. "Usher and Schumpeter on Invention, Innovation and Technological Change." *Quarterly Journal of Economics* 73(4): 596–606.

————. 1969. "Agricultural Product and Factor Markets in Southeast Asia." *Economic Development and Cultural Change* 17(4): 501–19.

Salter, W. E. G. 1960. *Productivity and Technical Change*. Cambridge.

Samuelson, P. A. 1965. "A Theory of Induced Innovation along Kennedy, Weisacker [Weizsacker] Lines." *Review of Economics and Statistics* 47(4): 343–56.

Schmookler, Jacob. 1966. *Invention and Economic Growth*. Cambridge, Mass.

Schultz, T. W. 1968. "Institutions and the Rising Economic Value of Man." *American Journal of Agricultural Economics* 50(5): 1113–22.

Sen, A. K. 1959. "The Choice of Agricultural Techniques in Underdeveloped Countries." *Economic Development and Cultural Change* 7(3, pt. 1): 279–85.

Solo, Carolyn Shaw. 1951. "Innovation in the Capitalist Process: A Critique of the Schumpeterian Theory." *Quarterly Journal of Economics* 65(3): 417–28.

Timmer, C. P. 1970. Personal communication, 9 October.

III

Food and Agricultural Policy

Introduction

 During the 1960s and 1970s, most agricultural economists working on policy issues in the Third World framed their analyses in a partial equilibrium context, even though much of the historical literature stressed the interdependence between agricultural growth and overall economic development. The 1980s, however, with its emphasis on structural adjustment, witnessed more frequent efforts to analyze how agricultural policies affected and were affected by the rest of the economy, including international trade. The challenge has been to incorporate adequate microeconomic detail into analyses conceived in a multisectoral or general equilibrium framework.[1]

In the first two chapters in part 3, Mellor and Schuh underscore the need for examining food and agriculture policy in an open economy framework. In chapter 6, Mellor points out the glaring imbalances in world food production, where supply is growing far more rapidly than demand in industrial countries, whereas in many Third World countries, the situation is the reverse. Moreover, the annual collective cost of subsidizing food production in the OECD (Organization for Economic Cooperation and Development) countries was around $125 billion in the late 1980s. The continuing imbalance in world food supplies helps explain the prevalence of food aid in the Third World. Mellor addresses the dual problems of global food imbalances and poverty in the Third World by presenting a two-pronged strategy to promote food security. The first component is to boost food production and the purchasing power of the poor in the Third World in the long run. Increasing productivity and employment are essential parts of any long-term strategy to overcome hunger. Although food subsidy schemes have brought about dramatic *short-run* improvements in nutrition and life span in Sri Lanka, China, and other countries, these programs are difficult to finance over the long run. For example, Sri Lanka's free rice ration scheme cost 15 percent of total government expenditures in 1975. Subsequently the food subsidy program was scaled back through a number of measures, including a shift to food stamps with a fixed nominal value, thereby reducing the fiscal costs to about 3.5 percent of total public expenditures (Pinstrup-Andersen 1988). Nonetheless, simply relying on long-term productivity growth to eradicate hunger would leave many people in the Third World malnourished for years to come (Reutlinger and Selowsky 1976). Therefore, the second component of Mellor's global food strategy involves redistributing food supplies in the short run through food aid from rich countries to poor countries, a topic that Hans Singer also addresses, in chapter 14. This redistribution capitalizes on the availability of food surpluses in the high-income countries to allow low-income countries to launch food distribution programs and employment-oriented growth strategies that would otherwise be precluded by a wage-good constraint (see also Mellor, chapter 3).

The second example of the need to view Third World agriculture in a global context comes from Schuh's analysis of the new macroeconomics of food and agriculture (chapter 7). Schuh points out that "a decade ago, the value of a nation's currency was largely ignored as an issue of domestic food and agricultural policy. Today, it is probably the most important price in the economy." As a consequence, the nature of agricultural policy making has changed dramatically. General macroeconomic and trade policies now often have a greater impact on rural people than do agricultural policies. Furthermore, the move to floating exchange rates and the integration of financial and commodity markets mean that agricultural policies can no longer be made independently of macroeconomic policies or of the policies of major trading partners. As a result of the integration of the world economy, "probably at no time in modern history have such powerful forces been acting to change international comparative advantage." Increasingly, Schuh argues, comparative advantage is becoming based on human capital rather than natural resource endowments, implying high returns to investments in education and research.

Not only have agricultural economists had to broaden their analyses to take into account macroeconomic influences on agricultural policy, they have also become increasingly aware of the political constraints facing policy makers. In 1981, Robert Bates, a political scientist, published his influential *Markets and States in Tropical Africa: The Political Basis of Agricultural Policies*. His central thesis, which is summarized in chapter 8, is that there is a political rationale for seemingly inconsistent agricultural policies in many Third World countries. He argues that politicians often pursue policies detrimental to overall agricultural growth not out of a misunderstanding of economics but because such policies benefit key groups of rural and urban constituents. Therefore, Bates argues, in analyzing agricultural policies, economists need to move away from a model that assumes that policy makers seek to improve the overall welfare of society and instead recognize that "governments are agencies that seek to stay in power." As Timmer points out in chapter 12, adopting such an approach does not obviate the need for economic analysis of food policies, but it places the analysis in a broader, more realistic context.

In chapter 9, the late Raj Krishna examines the interactions between price and technology policies, and he challenges the recommendations of "price fundamentalists," who believe that raising farm prices is the most important way to increase agricultural growth.[2] Krishna argues that, because of low supply elasticities for aggregate agricultural output in most low-income countries, an increase in farmgate prices large enough to stimulate rapid agricultural growth would have adverse macroeconomic effects. Instead of relying solely on price policy, low-income countries should promote technological dynamism in agriculture, within the context of a "congenial price regime" that fosters adoption of new agricultural technology. Krishna goes on to discuss how, in practical terms, a government should go about establishing the support prices necessary to institute this "congenial price regime." Krishna's call for a balanced price and technology policy is timely because many structural adjustment programs in the 1980s zealously promoted pricing policy reform and privatization and failed to give adequate attention to complementary public investments in roads, rural infrastructure, and agricultural research to generate new technology.

The remaining five chapters in part III (chapters 10–14) discuss four interrelated issues: price policy, food security, international trade, and food aid. These four issues coalesce in the area of food policy. Food policy analysis involves determining the mix of production, price, trade, technology, marketing, and other policies needed to achieve the goals a country establishes for its food system. As Timmer points out in chapter 12, most countries set at least four basic objectives for their food systems: (1) efficient growth in the food and agricultural sectors, (2) improved income distribution, (3) satisfactory nutritional status for the entire population, and (4) adequate food security. Achieving these goals involves evaluating the technical, economic, social, and political constraints facing policy makers and developing ways of addressing those constraints. This calls for a detailed understanding of the dynamics of the food system and of its interrelationships with the rest of the economy. It also calls for a political economy approach that explicitly recognizes the limited degrees of freedom facing most policy makers and tries to find ways to increase these degrees of freedom (Timmer, Falcon, and Pearson 1983).

Price policy, especially food price policy and its relationship to technical change in agriculture, is the first of these four components of food policy. As Timmer points out in chapter 12, even in centrally planned economies many day-to-day resource allocation decisions by farmers and consumers are made in response to private incentives, which often take the form of market prices. As Third World economies become increasingly monetized and integrated, a growing number of resource allocation decisions typically are mediated through markets. This has been particularly true during the 1980s, as many countries have undertaken policy reforms aimed at giving the market a larger role in allocating resources. Food price policy is one of the major instruments available to governments for influencing those decisions.

Food prices play a dual role in most economies. First, they serve as incentives to food system participants (farmers, merchants, processors) concerning what to produce, how to produce it, when to produce it and in what quantities, how to process it, where to market it, and so forth. Second, food prices are a major determinant of the real income of much of the population. In their first role, food prices act as signals that guide resource allocation within the agricultural sector and among sectors. Much of the work of neoclassical economists has focused on "getting prices right" so that these signals will guide resource flows efficiently (see, for example, the volume edited by Schultz [1978]). But as Mellor (chapter 10) and Timmer (chapter 12) stress, "getting prices right" is not simple, because food prices also are a major determinant of the real income of a large proportion of the population in low-income countries. When many people spend up to 60 percent of increments to their income on food, changes in food prices substantially affect the level and distribution of real income. Furthermore, because food is the major wage good in most low-income countries, food price policy can strongly influence a country's industrialization efforts (Mellor, chapter 3), and, through effects on the government budget, a host of macroeconomic variables.

The dual role of food prices—incentives to food producers and major determinants of the real income of much of the population—complicates the process of determining an appropriate food price policy. Many governments face a dilemma: high food prices may stimulate long-term growth in agricultural output, but they may also impose severe short-term privation on consumers. Concern for the adverse effects that higher food prices would have on low-income consumers and recognition of the political power of urban consumers explain the reluctance of many governments to increase farm prices, in spite of the urging of international agencies. As Timmer points out "a government that cannot raise food prices because it no longer will be the government will not raise food prices, no matter how critical that is to long-run efficiency." The situation is further complicated by the increasing complexity and interdependence of the world food economy, which makes it very costly for governments to try to insulate domestic food prices from international prices.

Food security is the second major component of food policy analysis. Food security is related to both price policy and technological change in agriculture and is best addressed within a framework that takes account of the linkages among the various sectors of the economy. Food security analysis is a process of determining an appropriate mix of domestic food production, storage, international trade, and other income-generating activities to ensure that "food-deficit countries, or regions or households within these countries, . . . meet target levels of consumption" (Siamwalla and Valdés 1984). A crucial element in food security planning involves trying to ensure adequate effective demand for food among the poor, as well as adequate food supplies. By recognizing that hunger often results from inadequate effective demand rather than simply inadequate total food supplies, food security analysis links hunger with poverty and the lack of productive employment (Reutlinger 1977; Sen 1981; Eicher and Staatz 1986). Food security was given international visibility in 1986 when the World Bank adopted a food security policy statement that was prepared by a team led by Shlomo Reutlinger. The term food security was defined as "access by all people at all times to enough food for an active, healthy life. Its essential elements are the availability of food and the ability to acquire it" (World Bank 1986, 1).

Food security research and policy analysis has generally been concerned with food security at four levels: international, regional, national (or subnational), and household. International food security has focused on the relative efficacy of different mechanisms for ensuring that countries have access to food during periods of low domestic food production or foreign-exchange earnings. The research of Siamwalla and Valdés has made an important contribution by documenting the high cost of trying to ensure food security through a system of international grain reserves. Research by Siamwalla and Valdés (1984) Goreux (1981), and Konandreas, Huddleston, and Ramangkura (1978) was instrumental in convincing the International Monetary Fund (IMF) to expand its compensatory financing facility in 1981 to include a cereal import facility. This facility allows low-income countries to finance above-trend cereal imports through borrowing from the IMF cereal import facility. However, although conceptually good, the cereal import facility has been little used since it was instituted in 1981. Needed modifications in the facility are discussed by Mellor in chapter 6.

Much of the analysis of food security on the international level implicitly assumes that most agricultural production passes through well-functioning markets and that governments hold a significant share of total grain stocks (Lele and Candler 1984). On the other hand, discussions of national food security sometimes focus so narrowly on local production and storage problems that they downplay the potential of interregional and international trade in assuring food security. A major challenge for analysts is to integrate more closely the work on international food security with that on food security at the national and subnational levels.

Research on regional food security has been given high priority in Africa since 1970 because of recurring drought and famines. In 1980, nine nations in Southern Africa set up a regional organization, the Southern African Regional Development Coordination Conference (SADCC), to promote regional development and to reduce dependency, including food dependency, on the Republic of South Africa. But regional food security has been difficult to define and difficult to achieve in practice because regional organizations such as SADCC lack the financial resources to implement schemes such as regional food reserves. Also, to date, regional food security programs in the Sahel and Southern Africa have concentrated on grain storage and trade and have devoted little attention to food access issues (Rukuni and Eicher 1988).

The focus of food security policy analysis during the 1980s shifted from the international and regional levels to the national and household levels. Food security analysis at the national level focuses on how domestic production, marketing, and trade can achieve national food availability and access goals, including adequate nutrition.[3] Such analyses have become increasingly widespread since the mid-1980s, when the goal of food security began replacing that of food self-sufficiency in many Third World countries. This was particularly true in sub-Saharan Africa, where food production grew at half the rate of population between 1970 and 1984.

Analyses of food security were closely linked to efforts at structural adjustment in many countries in the 1980s. In the long term, there is considerable complementarity between structural adjustment, which aims at increasing long-term growth of incomes and employment, and measures to increase food security. Structural adjustments are often needed to get economies on a path of broad-based growth that will help assure long-term access to food. Yet, as the food riots that have accompanied the imposition of structural adjustment programs in many Third World countries testify, the short-term costs of such programs are often high. Therefore, assuring a minimum level of food security to key elements of the population is often a political and economic necessity in order to launch and maintain structural adjustments (Weber et al. 1988, 1044–45). Such actions are also often necessary to prevent nutritionally vulnerable groups from being severely hurt by such programs in the short run (Cornia, Jolly, and Stewart 1987).

Analyzing household food security also increased in popularity during the second half of the 1980s, mainly because of the growing understanding that expanded food production in both high- and low-income countries would not ensure that all families would be able to secure their food needs. For example, it is estimated that about 200 million of India's 800 million people do not have enough land, income, or access to food transfers to secure adequate calories. There has also been increasing recognition of the impact that various policies have on the food security of various groups of the rural poor. For example, during the 1980s, a common donor prescription among African governments was to raise food prices in order to increase farmers' incomes and incentives to produce for the market. Yet recent research has shown that large numbers of smallholders in several African countries are net buyers of staple foods, so that raising their prices would *hurt* many of the rural poor (Weber et al. 1988).[4] A major intellectual contribution to the study of household food security has been the concept of food entitlements, developed by Amartya Sen. Food entitlements describe how people secure a "command over food" via home production, the market, or income transfers. In chapter 11, Sen explains the concept and its use in studying various forms of food insecurity, particularly famines. Sen discusses famine anticipation, forms of relief, the role of food supply and food prices, and long-run strategies for eliminating famines and starvation.

The third component of food policy is defining an appropriate agricultural trade policy. In chapter 13, Myint examines theoretical arguments and empirical evidence in evaluating the debate between import substitution and export-led growth. He finds substantial support for the hypothesis that rapid export expansion leads to faster economic growth. The reasons are not primarily the static efficiency gains predicted by neoclassical theory, however, but the indirect dynamic effects of trade on the economy. These include gains due to better allocation of the flow of investible funds through reductions in product and factor-price distortions, the educative and competitive effects of an open economy on inducing greater X-efficiency (see Leibenstein 1978), and economies of scale and increasing returns from specializing for a wider export market. Myint argues that many countries in Africa and Southeast Asia also have the potential to increase growth through promoting peasant agricultural and handicraft exports, which draw into production previously unused resources.

Capturing the gains outlined by Myint may require active pro-trade intervention by government, not simply removal of existing impediments to freer trade. Greater reliance on and specialization in trade, however, expose a country to the risks as well as the benefits of international markets. Many of these markets are volatile and involve a relatively small number of large-scale commercial and state trading organizations. One way in which primary product exporters have sought to stabilize these markets and gain a measure of countervailing power has been through encouraging the creation of international commodity agreements and export cartels; but, as Schuh points out in chapter 7, such arrangements are increasingly problematic in an era of floating exchange rates, where increases in the nominal prices of goods are quickly offset by exchange-rate adjustments. An alternative, as Schuh suggests, is for developing countries to attempt to manage market risks through forward contracting and the use of international futures and options markets.

The fourth component of food policy is food aid. In chapter 14, Hans Singer tackles the controversial topic of food aid by taking a pragmatic approach, that is, that "food aid is a fact of life." Food aid accounts for about 10 percent of all aid, and the challenge, according to Singer, is to improve its efficiency and its impact. Mellor (1988) supplements Singer's pro–food aid views by arguing that, in an era of structural adjustment lending, food aid can help dampen the immediate impact of adjustment programs on the income and nutritional status of the poor and help lay the foundation for a long-term employment-oriented growth strategy.

NOTES

1. See Mellor, chapter 10 in this volume. In advancing the view that many agricultural policy issues are best addressed within a general equilibrium framework, we do not mean to imply that these issues must necessarily be analyzed using a formal general equilibrium model. Often "an intuitive but sophisticated analysis of the system" is called for, provided that such analysis takes sufficient account of intersectoral linkages (Timmer, chapter 12).

2. See Peterson 1979.

3. For a discussion of nutrition and food security see Von Braun, Kennedy, and Bouis 1988; Berg (1987); Behrman, Deolalikar, and Wolfe 1988; Strauss 1989; Thomas, Strauss, and Henriques, forthcoming; Lipton and Longhurst 1989; and Pinstrup-Andersen, Berg, and Forman 1984.

4. Although researchers and policy makers have recognized for many years that numerous people in rural areas of Asia and Latin America are net buyers of staple foods, until the late 1980s it was widely assumed that smallholders in most African countries were almost all net sellers of food. Research in the major grain producing areas of Mali, Somalia, Senegal, Rwanda, and Zimbabwe indicate, however, that between 15 and 73 percent of all rural families are net buyers of grain in good rainfall years and that only 22 to 48 percent are net sellers (Weber et al. 1988). This suggests that the food price dilemma described by Timmer is much more severe in African countries than was generally thought.

REFERENCES

Bates, Robert J. *Markets and States in Africa*. Berkeley: University of California Press, 1981.

Behrman, Jere, Anil B. Deolalikar, and Barbara L. Wolfe. 1988. "Nutrients: Impacts and Determinants." *World Bank Economic Review* 2 (September): 229–320.

Berg, Alan. 1987. *Malnutrition: What Can be Done?* Baltimore: Johns Hopkins University Press.

Cornia, Giovanni A., Richard Jolly, and Frances Stewart, eds. 1987. *Adjustment with a Human Face*. Oxford: Clarendon Press.

Eicher, Carl K., and John M. Staatz. 1986. "Food Security Policy in Sub-Saharan Africa." In *Agriculture in a Turbulent World Economy*, edited by A. Maunder and U. Renborg, 215–29. Brookfield, Vt.: Gower.

Goreux, Louis M. 1981. "Compensatory Financing for Fluctuations in the Cost of Cereal Imports." In *Food Security for Developing Countries*, edited by Alberto Valdés, 307–33. Boulder, Colo.: Westview Press.

Konandreas, Panos, Barbara Huddleston, and Virabongsa Ramangkura. 1978. *Food Security: An Insurance Approach.* Washington, D.C.: International Food Policy Research Institute.

Leibenstein, Harvey. 1978. *General X-Efficiency Theory and Economic Development.* New York: Oxford University Press.

Lele, Uma, and Wilfred Candler. 1984. "Food Security in Developing Countries: National Issues." In *Agricultural Development in the Third World,* edited by Carl K. Eicher and John M. Staatz, 207–10. Baltimore: Johns Hopkins University Press.

Lipton, Michael, with Richard Longhurst. 1989. *New Seeds and Poor People.* Baltimore: Johns Hopkins University Press.

Mellor, John W. 1988. "Food Policy, Food Aid and Structural Adjustment Programs." *Food Policy* 13, no. 1 (February): 10–17.

Peterson, W. L. 1979. "International Farm Prices and the Social Cost of Cheap Food Policies." *American Journal of Agricultural Economics* 61(1): 12–21.

Pinstrup-Andersen, Per. 1985. "The Impact of Export Crop Production on Human Nutrition." In *Nutrition and Development,* edited by Margaret Biswas and Per Pinstrup-Andersen. New York: Oxford University Press.

Pinstrup-Andersen, Per. 1988. "Food Subsidies: Consumer Welfare and Producer Incentives." In *Agricultural Price Policy in Developing Countries,* edited by John Mellor and Raisuddin Ahmed, 214–52. Baltimore: Johns Hopkins University Press.

Pinstrup-Andersen, Per, Alan Berg, and Martin Forman, eds. 1984. *International Agricultural Research and Human Nutrition.* Washington, D.C.: International Food Policy Research Institute/ACC-SCN.

Reutlinger, Shlomo. 1977. "Malnutrition: A Poverty or Food Problem?" *World Development* 5 (August): 715–24.

Reutlinger, Shlomo, and Marcelo Selowsky. 1976. *Malnutrition and Poverty: Magnitude and Policy Options.* World Bank Staff Occasional Papers, no. 23. Baltimore: Johns Hopkins University Press for the World Bank.

Rukuni, Mandivamba, and Carl K. Eicher. 1988. "The Food Security Equation in Southern Africa." In *Poverty, Policy and Food Security in Southern Africa,* edited by Coralie Bryant, 133–57. Boulder, Colo.: Lynne Rienner.

Schultz, Theodore W., ed. 1978. *Distortions of Agricultural Incentives.* Bloomington: Indiana University Press.

Sen, Amartya. 1981. *Poverty and Famines.* Oxford: Clarendon Press.

Siamwalla, Ammar, and Alberto Valdés. 1984. "Food Security in Developing Countries: Some International Issues." In *Agricultural Development in the Third World,* edited by Carl K. Eicher and John M. Staatz, 189–206. Baltimore: Johns Hopkins University Press.

Strauss, John. 1989. "Households, Communities and Preschool Children's Nutrition Outcomes: Evidence from Rural Côte d'Ivoire." *Economic Development and Cultural Change.* 38(1).

Thomas, Duncan, John Strauss, and Maria-Helena Henriques. Forthcoming. "Child Survival, Height for Age, and Household Characteristics in Brazil." *Journal of Development Economics.*

Timmer, C. Peter, Walter P. Falcon, and Scott R. Pearson. 1983. *Food Policy Analysis.* Baltimore: Johns Hopkins University Press.

Von Braun, Joachim, Eileen Kennedy, and Howarth Bouis. 1988. "Comparative Analyses of The Effects of Increased Commercialization of Subsistence Agriculture on Production, Consumption, and Nutrition." Washington, D.C.: International Food Policy Research Institute, December.

Weber, Michael, John M. Staatz, John S. Holtzman, Eric W. Crawford, and Richard H. Bernsten. 1988. "Informing Food Security Decisions in Africa: Empirical Analysis and Policy Dialogue." *American Journal of Agricultural Economics* 70(5): 1045–54.

World Bank. 1986. *Poverty and Hunger: Issues and Options for Food Security in Developing Countries.* Washington, D.C.: World Bank.

6

Global Food Balances and Food Security

JOHN W. MELLOR

The current world food situation is dramatically different from that of a decade ago. In the mid-1970s the world was beset by acute food shortages; in the mid-1980s it appeared to be awash in food. Only a decade and a half ago it would have seemed naive to analyze food security as purely a distributional problem; the physical inadequacy of global food supplies was too readily apparent. However, in the late 1980s it had become reasonable to focus on food insecurity as the inability of poor countries, poor families, and poor individuals to purchase sufficient quantities of food from existing supplies. Yet, that formulation is also an oversimplification.

Today's global food situation is one of acute structural imbalances. In the developed countries, supply is growing far more rapidly than demand; but in many developing countries the situation is the reverse. Such imbalances are likely to continue, thereby presenting a major opportunity for advancing food security. As always, these imbalances will be punctuated by misleading short periods of weather-induced extreme surplus and scarcity.

The present food security situation is more complicated than scarcity amidst plenty. In most of Asia and Africa, and even much of Latin America, improving food security requires both increasing the purchasing power of the poor and boosting overall food production. This is true because of the importance of food prices in determining the purchasing power of most low-income people, and because of the dominant role of agricultural production as a source of employment for the poor.

These factors suggest the following two-pronged strategy to promote food security. In the long run, efforts must be made to increase the purchasing power of the poor by raising the overall level of food production in the Third World. Increased food supplies and purchasing power must be inextricably linked elements of any long-term food security effort. And in the short run, redistributing food supplies from the developed to the developing world is likely to be the best way to meet the more immediate food security needs of the poor.

JOHN W. MELLOR is director of the International Food Policy Research Institute, Washington, D.C.
Reprinted from *World Development*, Vol. 16, no. 9, pp. 997–1011, 1988. Copyright © 1988 by Pergamon Press, Inc. Published with permission of Pergamon Press and the author.

In the developing world, agricultural production must be stimulated through cost-decreasing technological change. The small farm, food production sector must be at the center of this effort. Food transfers from the structurally food-surplus nations 'ɔ the structurally food-deficit nations must be achieved through mechanisms which boost the purchasing power of the poor, while also increasing the incentives to raise agricultural and food production over the long run. The gross instability of food availability and purchasing power of the poor must also be reduced. This must be done without prejudicing the long-run efforts to increase the supply of food and the necessary purchasing power.

To comprehend the policy needs and potentials, one must understand the underlying nature of current global food imbalances. To achieve the policy objectives of food security will require complex, time-consuming development of national and international institutions. While food security cannot be achieved overnight, it can be achieved soon.

THE STRUCTURAL BASIS OF THE CURRENT GLOBAL FOOD IMBALANCES

The world does seem awash in food. Global cereal stocks in the mid-1980s were almost twice as large as in the mid-1970s. And, in 1985, real world cereal prices were down 30 percent from 1981, compared to an almost twofold increase between 1972 and 1974. Net exports of cereals from developed to developing countries were 80 percent larger in the mid-1980s compared to the mid-1970s.[1]

Review of regional production and consumption trends provides somewhat less sense of the current food surplus than price and stock data. On a global basis, between the early 1960s and 1980s, major food crop production grew at a 2.4 percent annual rate, only half a percent faster than population. That margin has been declining in recent years—largely because of a deceleration of production in the developed countries. In the 1960s, food production grew 1.1 percent faster than population growth, while in the 1970s, production was marginally slower than the rate of population growth. From 1971–73 to 1981–83, food production grew more than twice as fast in the developing countries as in the developed countries. Of course, production has grown much faster than consumption in developed countries and conversely in the developing countries.

Despite the positive margin of production growth over population growth, there is little evidence of a decline in the numbers of malnourished and undernourished people in developing countries. The Food and Agriculture Organization (FAO) of the United Nations estimates adequate caloric standards for people. By those standards it is estimated that somewhere between 340 million and 730 million people have inadequate diets.[2] Sukhatme and others suggest that the human body has capacity to adjust to caloric intakes lower than the FAO standards, leading to a reduced estimate of people with inadequate calorie intake (Sukhatme 1977; Margen 1978). Whatever the estimate, it is clear that levels of food intake below the FAO standards are closely associated with abject poverty.

In countries with very low average incomes and massive poverty, such as India, special programs for ensuring food supplies to the poor may well have reduced the number of people in abject poverty (Mellor and Desai 1985; Dandekar 1988). However, it is notable that in India, which includes some one-third of the malnourished people in the world, there was no measurable trend in the proportion of rural people living below the poverty line. From 1956–67 to 1977–78, the proportion of rural people in India below the poverty line has fluctuated between 40 and 60 percent (Ahluwalia 1985). However, during these years the absolute number of people living in poverty increased.

Thus, we can see that the apparent global abundance of food is the product of very different tendencies in the developed compared to the developing countries, and that the differences in consumption growth are far larger than the differences in production growth. What is the source of these structural differences and how likely are they to continue? The answers to such questions have a profound influence on the choice of policies for ensuring food security to the poor of the world.

In developed countries, the processes of technological change in agriculture have been institutionalized. As a result, the productivity of agricultural resources is continually increasing. Concurrently, because population growth is slight and demand is highly inelastic, consumption of food grows little or not at all. Consequently, in developed countries, the benefits of technological change in agriculture are realized largely through the continuous transfer of resources out of agriculture, rather than from increased consumption of food. Frictions to those adjustments are met by a combination of declining agricultural prices, increased stocks of food, or increased exports. Production growth may be retarded either by accelerating the flow of resources out of agriculture, or by reducing the flow of public resources for stimulating technological change. In general, though, while the outflow of resources from the agriculture of developed countries continues to be rapid, it is not as rapid as the pace of productivity increase.[3]

The problem of surplus agricultural production in developed countries is so intractable because technological change is a dynamic process. The measures necessary to transfer resources out of agriculture require not once-and-for-all policy changes, but continuous adjustments. Reduced public expenditure on research in agriculture is one means to confront the problem, but the resulting reduction in competitiveness threatens farmer interests, especially if such policies are undertaken unilaterally. In any case, with the increasing shift of research to the private sector and continuation of competitive forces, it may be difficult for public action to reduce the flow of new technology. Thus, continued rapid growth in exportable food surplus seems inevitable. That surplus provides the basis for establishing food security programs which can do much to eliminate food insecurity in Third World countries.

The importance of structural demand forces as a dynamic determinant of supply-demand balances is underlined by the record of Eastern Europe. In the 1970s and 1980s, Eastern Europe has been a major source of demand growth for exports from developed countries. From 1961–63 to 1981–83, the rate of food production growth in Eastern Europe was only slightly worse than in Western Europe. However, within Eastern Europe food consumption has grown at a rate 80 percent faster than that for Western Europe. That growth has brought about an explosive rise in the demand for imported cereals, especially cereals for livestock feed. Eventually, however, that rate of growth in demand will level off, and Eastern Europe will cease to be a major cereal importer.

Developing countries are still in the early stages of institutionalizing the processes of technological change in agriculture. Rates of growth in agricultural output are, therefore, relatively slow. Because low-income countries start in a technologically backward situation, they may have short-term surges of very high growth rates, as they catch up with technological advances. During such periods food production growth rates may exceed long-term rates of growth of demand. Although not universally applicable, both Indonesia in the late 1970s and China in the early 1980s experienced such nonsustainable rates of production growth.[4]

In developing countries, demand can grow rapidly—fueled by high population growth rates, income elasticities of demand close to unity even for the basic food staples, and moderately rapid income growth. Since in developing countries, income elasticities of demand are sharply different across income groups, overall growth in demand for food is particularly affected by changes in the incomes of the lower income groups (Mellor 1978; Alderman 1986).

In many developing countries, the ever-increasing demand for food exceeds local production capabilities. In recent years, this has led many Third World countries to import a rising share of their food requirements. Between the early 1960s and the early 1980s, developing countries' share of world cereal imports increased from 36 percent to 46% (USDA 1987). Most striking, the 24 developing countries with the fastest growth rates in basic food staple production from 1961–65 to 1979–83 increased their net imports of food staples by 419 percent.[5] In fact, the developing countries are the major growth market for basic food staples. Given continued growth of employment and incomes, net imports of basic food staples are projected to increase by at least 40 million tons over the next 20 years.[6] High-employment policies, including accelerated growth in the livestock sector with its large direct demand for feed and its employment driven indirect demand for food, could easily expand incremental imports by three times that amount.[7] These latter projections emphasize the impact high-employment policies have in determing food security as well as trade potentials.

But there is an important point in the food import record of those developing countries that have done well in food production growth. It is well known that the comparative advantage of low-income countries lies in their ability to mobilize large, low-productivity labor supplies for increased production. Yet less fully recognized is the fact that labor supply is itself the product of two interacting markets—the labor market per se and the food market (Lele and Mellor 1981). The high marginal propensity of the poor to spend on food requires more food to back up more employment. As Kumar (1988) demonstrates that additional supplies of food are necessary for improved labor productivity and increased demand for labor by small farmers. Her study also indicates that adequate supplies of food, by relieving the labor constraint, indirectly influence the decisions of small farmers to adopt modern technology. Thus, not just food security as a welfare objective, but food supplies as a productive input call attention to the present food imbalances between developed and developing countries.

It follows that, for developing countries, optimal growth will be associated with high rates of growth of employment and greater supplies of food. The capacity of developed country surpluses to ensure those food supplies acts as a very positive force for economic growth, equity, and food security in the Third World. The important fact, here, is not the concessional terms of such food supplies, but their elastic supply. In most cases, abundant supplies of food aid can do much to accelerate employment growth.

AGRICULTURAL GROWTH AND ACCESS TO FOOD

In countries in which a high proportion of employment and income is generated in the rural sector, an agriculture-based growth strategy provides the only possibility of broad-based participation by the poor.[8] Many people in the Third World work in agriculture. Raising the incomes of these people generates a demand for labor-intensive goods and services, which are typically produced in the countryside.[9] For example, smallholder farmers in Bangladesh and Malaysia spend 35 and 40 percent, respectively of their increments to income on locally produced nonagricultural goods and services. Reardon et al. (1988) emphasize the importance of nonagricultural employment in improving food security in the rural areas of Burkina Faso. In addition, small farmers in Nigeria spend as much as 20 percent of their increments to income on locally produced agricultural goods, such as vegetables and livestock, creating additional employment opportunities in the agricultural sector.[10]

Such incremental expenditure by the peasantry provides a structure of demand that facilitates capital widening to a far greater extent than alternative techniques of production. This places a special emphasis on smallholder agricultural production. If there is a high concentration of landholding among wealthy farmers, increased profits will go largely to imports or highly capital-intensive goods, and will not induce the necessary multipliers and linkages from agriculture to promote employment in other sectors. Fortunately, the bulk of Asia and Africa have peasant farmer dominated rural sectors.

This kind of rural-based growth—which provides increased income and employment opportunities to the poor—has two essential components. First, it is technologically based. Agricultural output is stimulated by applying new technology that increases output per unit of input. This is important because agriculture is a sector particularly subject to Ricardian diminishing returns. As attempts are made to stimulate production, the inelastic supply of land causes the productivity of other inputs to decline gradually. It is the rapid growth in real incomes of the farming classes that provides the effective demand for the labor of the poor, partly working to produce the enhanced agricultural output, but far more to produce consumer goods. Note that virtually all programs to increase productivity of the rural poor involve goods for which income elasticities are quite high (Mellor 1978).

Throughout the Third World, the poor spend between 50 and 80 percent of their increments to income on food.[11] Thus, any increase in food prices has a deleterious impact upon their incomes. The vulnerability of the poor in Asia to rising food prices is well known. It is now clear that the poor in Africa are also generally net purchasers of food and hence are also vulnerable to rising food prices. (Lele and Myers 1987; Reardon and Matlon 1989). Since increasing food production by incentives such as higher prices hurts the poor, there is a special need for technological change, which provides incentives to farmers—incentives which are both potentially greater than those provided by higher prices and which have no negative impact on the poor (see Ranade, Jha, and Delgado 1988). Von Braun (1988) analyzes the specific mechanisms through which cost-reducing technological change can be pro-poor, pro-food security.

Second, an agriculture-based development strategy that enhances food security for the rural poor requires massive investment in rural infrastructure. It is increasingly clear that reliable all-weather transport is essential to achieving a high level of intensity of farming, labor input per hectare, wage rates, and rate of growth in nonfarm employment. Ahmed and Hossain (1987) show that in Bangladesh good infrastructure compared to poor infrastructure is associated with 92 percent more fertilizer use per hectare, 4 percent more labor per hectare in farming, 30 percent more nonfarm employment, and a 12 percent higher wage rate (Ahmed and Hossain 1987). Typically, one-third or more of the agricultural area of developing countries is so ill-served with infrastructure as to be left out of these processes (Wanmali, forthcoming).

The size of the requisite investment in rural infrastructure must be quite large if agriculture is to become the centerpiece for any development strategy. Unfortunately, the investment norm in many developing countries is to neglect the countryside, and to concentrate the bulk of resources in a few major urban centers and in highly capital-intensive industries. This inevitably leads to a very small proportion of the labor force working at high productivity and wage rates, with the bulk of the labor force contributing precious little to the development process. Such suboptimal strategies of development are characterized by the import substitution strategies endemic in Latin America, the heavy industry strategy of India and China, and the capital-intensive consumer goods strategy of the Philippines.

Export-led growth typical of South Korea, if fed by massive capital inflows, can bring the mass of people to income levels that provide food security and may eventually pull the rural sector along. But the countries which have done well from the beginning in providing food security are the ones with broad-based agricultural strategies, for example, Taiwan, Thailand, Malaysia, Kenya, and the Ivory Coast (Mellor and Johnston 1984). Such agricultural growth strategies exploit low-income countries' comparative advantage, providing agricultural exports to pay for commercial imports of food as well as capital-intensive intermediate products. The strategy indicated here varies sharply from a pure export-led strategy because, in the present context, demand is initially generated domestically, rather than overseas.

This point can be illustrated by contrasting the recent experiences of Kenya and Tanzania. In the 1980s, Kenya's agricultural sector grew at an average annual rate of nearly 3 percent and was the primary force behind a slightly more rapid growth in GDP. Tanzania, on the other hand, was unable to sustain a rate of growth above 1 percent either for its agricultural sector or in GDP. Growth in the incomes of Kenya's poor was so rapid as to require large imports of food to sustain per capita consumption. Food imports grew at 6.5 percent per year in Kenya, compared to only 3.0 percent in Tanzania from 1970 to 1985. Kenya has been able to provide better food security to its people by promoting more rapid and more equitable growth through an emphasis on its agricultural sector.[12]

If food were more scarce in the world, as in the mid-1970s, an exposition on food security through growth would have given greater emphasis to the need for increased domestic production of food as a wage good. Yet, in a world genuinely awash with food, such wage goods can be imported without substantially raising prices, and it therefore becomes important to emphasize agriculture for its broad-based employment and income-generating potentials. The current global structural imbalances have the potential to reduce the risks of a high employment growth, rural-based agricultural growth strategy.

REDISTRIBUTION OF FOOD

In a world with large food surpluses in wealthy nations, we should not shy from redistribution of food as a short-run ameliorative to food security. Marginal redistribution of income towards low-income people will not in itself achieve food security. A redistributive approach to short-run food security requires distribution of food, not just finances. Such redistribution efforts, however, face a myriad of problems.

To take a simple case within a developing country, say India, if one rupee of purchasing power is taken away from a person in the top 5 percent of the income distribution it will cause a reduction, in constant prices, of 0.03 rupee in foodgrain consumption.[13] That same rupee provided to a person in the bottom 20 percent of the income distribution will provide increased demand for 0.58 rupee of foodgrains. The one-to-one equality of financial transfers is matched by a 19-to-one inequality in material transfers. Thus, a marginal redistribution of income is profoundly inflationary in driving up food prices. In this case, what the left hand of society gives to the poor, the right hand of the market takes away.

Of course, the more prosperous do reduce their consumption by the amount of the lost rupee. Most of this reduced consumption will be for labor-intensive goods and services, including vegetables and livestock. This produces reduced employment opportunities—and income—for the poor. The poor lose if the physical supply of food is not increased, either by lower incomes from reduced employment or from higher prices.

The same principles apply to transfers across nations. Financial transfers to the poor of poor nations will serve only to drive up the domestic price of food, unless these transfers are used to import food. Keep in mind that the short-run supply response of food production to price is slow and the long-run response is related more to complex institutional development.

All of this means that direct transfer of food to the poor represents a feasible and potentially efficient means of achieving food security by redistributing across international boundaries.[14] But it is important that such food transfers actually reach the poor, or else prices will be depressed. Price decreases, of course, benefit the poor, but there is always the danger that such decreases will retard the process of technological change in agriculture (Mellor 1978, 1968).

The very elastic demand for food of the poor in developing countries offers an opportunity for price discrimination that is advantageous to both food producers and poor consumers. By selling at a lower price in the low-income market, increased consumption occurs that reduces supply in the high-income market where demand is inelastic, resulting in a higher average price.[15] It should be noted that given the supply schedule it is advantageous to all producers, not just those in food aid providing developed countries. That is the theoretical basis for food aid from the point of view of exporters and producers.

Let us turn to the relationship of food, purchasing power, and food security to the structural adjustment programs advocated by the World Bank. These adjustment programs are, of course, reactions to unsustainable deficits in government budgets and large trade imbalances. Reducing transfer payments such as food subsidies, and food imports helps deal with both problems. If subsidies to the poor are reduced but the supply of food is maintained, then a significant part of the loss from reducing subsidies will be returned through lower prices.[16] There will, of course, be a net loss to the poor, but not in full proportion to the subsidy reduction. The major damage occurs, if both the purchasing power of the poor and the supply of food is reduced. Then the reduction in subsidy will not be offset by lower market prices. The precise extent of the net loss of the poor depends on the incidence of the subsidy savings. The major damage to the poor occurs if both the purchasing power of the poor and the supply of food is reduced. Then the reduction in subsidy will not be offset by lower market prices.

Food subsidies and accompanying food imports are likely to represent a substantial part of the budget of those developing countries which have poor agricultural growth records. This is because of the importance of cheap food in maintaining political stability in the face of little income growth. Since the subsidies will tend to drive up prices if imports are not increased, there tends to be a commensurate increase in imports.

Because of the close interaction between incomes of the poor and purchase of food, the structural adjustment process may show itself in many guises, but with the same effect in each case. Policies of reduced government expenditure or tighter monetary policy are both likely to reduce the employment and purchasing power of the poor. This will reduce upward pressures on food prices and thus facilitate reduced imports, thereby closing the circle on the food consumption of the poor. Note that government budget imbalances and trade deficits tend to go hand in hand in the context of food security.

Structural adjustment programs are likely to create another food security problem for the poor. The very purpose of those programs is to accelerate growth. Such growth is likely to raise the incomes and purchasing power of laboring class people in the third through the sixth deciles of the income distribution, who have more human capital, in terms of family nutrition, health, and education. As long as the economy is essentially in labor surplus, these people will earn more and will put upward pressure on the price of food. If the bottom two deciles remain unemployed and underemployed, they will have their real incomes reduced by the higher prices.

That seems to be precisely what has happened with structural adjustment in Sri Lanka. The top 75 percent in the income distribution experienced increased incomes and food consumption, despite a drastic reduction in food subsidies; but the bottom 20 percent suffered a lower level of food consumption.[17] Structural adjustment has all the appearances of working, but with a deleterious effect on the very poor, at least in the short run.

Lele (1987) argues that similar problems have plagued the process of structural adjustment in Malawi. She makes the further point that the pace of market liberalization in the structural adjustment process has often outpaced the capacity to build institutions and to remove constraints for increasing the employment of the poor. In such circumstances, special efforts are needed to ensure the food security of the poor.

In many cases, food aid from the developed countries can be effectively used to mitigate the unfavorable effects of structural adjustment on the poor. The key, here, is targeting such food aid to low-income people. Efficient targeting will maximize the extent of market expansion in response to food aid, gratifying producer groups in both developed and developing countries. Thus, the vital questions for food aid in support of structural adjustment are: (1) How can it be targeted to the poor? and (2) How can it also contribute positively to the process of broad-based growth?

The two principal means of targeting food aid to the poor are food-for-work and food subsidies. Food-for-work is usually highly effective at reaching the most poor, because the work is onerous and the pay is low. While food-for-work sometimes misses certain classes of the poor (such as women and the infirm), it is attractive because it helps create the physical infrastructure needed for broad-based growth. In that regard, it is especially attractive in rural areas where, in general, infrastructure is sorely lacking. In much of Africa, for example, the veritable lack of paved roads and complementary institutions presents one of the largest impediments to rural development.

In considering the use of food aid to support the creation of such public works, it is well to remember that developing countries are currently using food as a factor of production (as a wage good to back up increased employment) at a grossly suboptimal level. Thus, earmarking foreign assistance in the form of food aid is biasing expenditures and development allocations in a direction which is initially suboptimal. That may not be the theoretically most efficient way to improve the allocation of resources, but it is effective and correct.

If food-for-work is to make an effective contribution to growth, it must be complemented by other resources—for example, materials for road surfacing and culverts. Ezekiel estimates that in Africa food comprises some 15 to 40 percent of the cost of public works (Ezekiel 1988). Ahmed and Hossain show that without the complement of other resources, food aid is of little productive value. In Bangladesh, rural roads without a hard surface are of little value, but paved roads enjoy a high rate of return (Ahmed and Hossain 1987).

How to find financing to complement food aid in rural public works or other labor-intensive projects is a matter of institutional convenience. One solution is to provide some additional food aid for monetization, that is, for sale in the market. Such sales must not, however, reduce prices below reasonable levels. Those counterpart funds from sales of food aid would then be allocated to food aid projects to cover nonfood costs (Ezekiel and Gandhi 1987). A second solution would be to develop institutional ties between food aid to developing countries and the institutions which provide financial resources. This should be feasible between such multilateral organizations as the World Food Program and the World Bank.

Food subsidies are another means of targeting food towards the poor. They also have a production effect in that they should lead to a somewhat more stable and lower-priced labor force. Food subsidies have the effect of distorting consumption patterns towards food—more food is consumed at a given income level when income comes from food subsidies than when it comes in other forms. (Kumar 1979; Garcia and Pinstrup-Andersen 1987). Such distortions may or may not be desirable from the point of view of the poor, but are considered attractive by most donors.

Broad subsidy schemes, the most extreme of which exist in Egypt, have immense costs and an immense impact on food security. In recent years, Egypt has spent up to 9 percent of its national income and 17 percent of its national budget on food subsidies. These subsidies have accounted for about 16 percent of the total incomes of the poorest quartile of the population.[18] The level of caloric intake of Egypt's poor is high in relation to international norms at that level of income.

Food subsidies may be targeted to the poor by very general measures, such as choosing lower quality foods, or very specifically, by giving the poor food stamps or inviting them to field kitchens. Efforts at narrow targeting are more expensive in poor countries and those with fewer educated people to serve as administrators. It is all too easy for narrow targeting to become less efficient in delivering a given proportion of food to poor people than more generalized subsidies.

A good example of narrow targeting is the pilot scheme in the Philippines, which designated low-income areas and then focused subsidy programs in these areas (Garcia and Pinstrup-Andersen 1987). Yet, in cases like the Philippines, as targeting efforts narrow, they exclude more and more of both the wealthy and the poor. In a sense, efficiency may rise, but deprivation is likely to increase as well.

Bangladesh is a good example of a country using food aid to back both food-for-work and food subsidies. In the mid-1980s, the average value of food aid in Bangladesh equaled 26 percent of annual development expenditure. That provided a substantial quantity of food and the financial means for the government to transfer purchasing power to the poor. It should be emphasized that governments cannot quickly turn income and food redistribution programs on and off. Once programs are introduced even with foreign aid, governments will do their best to maintain them—even at very high costs to long-term development. For example, an econometric analysis of public development expenditures in Bangladesh indicates that during the period 1976 to 1985, every dollar reduction in the supply of food aid was followed by a reduction in public expenditures on development of as much as 18 cents.[19] Similar analysis for Egypt provides even more striking evidence of the extent to which governments will cut other expenditures in order to maintain food subsidies when foreign aid is reduced.

INSTABILITY

Commitment of a Third World government to food security has profound political implications. Such commitment requires a substantial reallocation of resources to rural infrastructure and the technical institutions of agriculture. Growth will no doubt be faster, but with larger, weather-induced fluctuations. Similarly, a more employment-oriented strategy provides political goods to a larger populace, but it is also subject to the vagaries of national weather and international prices.

During the past few decades fluctuations in both food production and international prices have increased markedly. Policies of developed countries are at least partly responsible for these increased price fluctuations (Koester and Valdes 1984). The increased production fluctuations in developing countries may be partially due to volatility in the important input policies associated with the improved food production technology (Anderson and Hazell 1989). Whatever the cause, it is important to devise policies that reduce the burden of such fluctuations of both Third World governments and the poor.

Lele and Candler (1981) draw attention to immense fluctuations in the demand on public food distribution systems in Africa. The predominance of rainfed agriculture and the marginal nature of much of African agriculture results in large fluctuations in food production. These fluctuations affect the ability of poor rural people to co-produce food and obtain employment. Thus, security of food consumption cannot be separated from production stability problems.

In theory, bilateral foreign assistance programs could play a very useful stabilizing role. But bilateral assistance—and especially food aid—is itself inherently unstable (Lele and Agarwal 1987; Huddleston 1984). Thus, a food security orientation can benefit greatly from stabilization efforts by international institutions.

The most important and obvious international device for stabilizing food supplies is the International Monetary Fund's cereal import facility. Although conceptually a good idea, this facility has been little used since it was instituted in 1981.

The lack of use is ostensibly because of the absence of poor weather and other forces driving up food prices. Ezekiel, however, shows that a substantial number of countries have faced fluctuations in their food import costs and should therefore have been eligible to draw on the fund.[20] They could not do so because of various constraints imposed on drawings under the scheme, including those arising from integration with the Compensatory Financing Facility dealing with export fluctuations.

If developing countries are to be encouraged to make commitments to agriculture and food security, they need a facility that treats food as a special commodity, one that is separated from other foreign exchange needs. This calls for significant modification of the present IMF cereal import facility. Such modifications must take into account circumstances in which a country's food aid is suddenly reduced and that country needs to use hard currencies for importing food. A vigorous cereal facility could encourage countries to take up more agriculture-oriented and more food security–oriented development strategies.

Beyond the cereal import facility, there is scope for the international financial institutions, such as the World Bank and the major regional banks, to provide some stablizing effects. These actors should recognize the commitments that developing countries are making to long-term agricultural development and attempt to provide stability in the face of the shifting national emphases of the bilateral donors. This may require structural adjustment lending in the face of poor crop years and high international prices of food. It may also require attention to imports of fertilizer, which are so vital to technological change in agriculture but which probably cannot be stabilized by an IMF-type facility.

Hay and Rukuni (1988) discuss the evolution of domestic policies in Africa to cope with production and price instability, including the use of domestic storage. Although domestic stocks are expensive to maintain, many countries use them in an attempt to stabilize food supply and consumption. Yet, except in situations where transfer costs are extraordinarily high, such as in the landlocked nations of the Sahel and Southern Africa, domestic storage stocks should, in general only be kept at a level to carry consumption in the face of sharp declines in production up to the time at which imports from abroad can be realized. Pinckney and Valdés (1988) make this point explicitly for the case of Kenya and Pakistan. Minimal use of stocks, of course, presumes an efficient international system for ensuring food security—something not yet in place. Of course, given the human and political importance of food security and imperfections in private trade, it is important that government err on the side of somewhat larger stocks rather than on the side of smaller stocks. In addition, where transport costs are high, investment should be made to improve roads and delivery systems, in order to eliminate long-term dependence on domestic storage.[21]

Stocking policy may be influenced not only by efforts to maintain consumption, but also by price-support operations for the agricultural sector. Yet, in cases where new technological breakthroughs combined with good weather bring large increases in production, such stocking efforts may prove extremely expensive. This is the situation India has faced since the mid-1970s. In India, where buffer stocks were targeted at 10 million tons of cereals, total stocks with central and state governments were as much as 22.5 million tons in 1984 and 29.2 million tons in 1985 (Sarma 1988). Such overstocking provides a high degree of food security for consumers, but at a very high cost. Over the period 1975–76 through 1979–80, the Indian public food distribution system incurred additional costs (received subsidies) ranging from 24.40 to 41.20 percent of the wholesale issue price of wheat in order to protect consumers from paying a wholesale market price that was only between 0.66 and 5.70 percent more than that issue price (Ezekiel 1984). Under such circumstances, food prices need to be gradually reduced. That, of course, does not reduce farm incomes, since they have already been raised by the new technological breakthroughs which reduced cost and produced large production increases.

It is important that the benefits of technological change be passed on to consumers. If those benefits pass on quickly through multiplier effects to other sectors of the economy, those higher incomes will themselves serve to maintain prices only marginally lower than their previous level. To the extent that those processes do not work well or involve lags, it will be necessary for agricultural prices to decline to pass on the benefits more directly. Of course, providing the benefits through employment is the preferred action since that raises national income. Stabilization of domestic prices is often necessary to supplement efforts to create employment, particularly in economies where poverty is widespread and targeting food subsidies is ineffective.

SYNTHESIS

The current global food imbalances present an extraordinary opportunity for achieving world food security. To realize that opportunity will require much intelligence, goodwill, and time. It will also require a number of concrete steps on the part of both developed and developing countries.

There is a need for a complex set of interacting national and international institutions in the areas of production, infrastructure building, and financing. With a clear sense of such needs, these structures could be built in time to end hunger and food insecurity by the end of the century. Such pious hopes have been dashed in the past because there has not been an underlying sense of strategy and a recognition of the complex set of institutions that is needed.

NOTES

1. Data in preceding paragraph are from, respectively, Mellor 1986 and USDA 1987.

2. World Bank 1986, pp. 1–3. Estimates vary widely according to definition of malnutrition and statistical techniques. Reutlinger and Selowsky (1976) have estimated that as many as 1.1 billion people suffer from calorie deficient diets. In light of such discrepancies, these estimates seem useful primarily in emphasizing that malnutrition continues to be a huge and pervasive problem in developing countries.

3. See Tweeten 1988 for a discussion of technological and structural changes in U.S. agriculture.

4. Recent studies of food production in those countries include Rosegrant et al. 1987 for Indonesia and Stone 1987 for China.

5. The analysis of countries with rapid food production growth appears originally in Bachman and Paulino 1979. L. A. Paulino, of the International Food Policy Research Institute, has provided these updated estimates from unpublished data derived from unpublished FAO data.

6. Paulino 1986, table 12, p. 42.

7. Paulino 1986, table 15, p. 62 and unpublished data from J.S. Sarma, of the International Food Policy Research Institute.

8. For a detailed discussion of the impact of agricultural growth on the poor, see Mellor 1976.

9. This fact was originally discussed in Mellor and Lele 1973. It was developed further in Mellor 1976; see especially chapter 7.

10. Data on Bangladesh from Ahmed and Hossain 1987, chapter 7. Data on Nigeria and Malaysia from Hazell and Roell 1983, table 6, p. 28.

11. Pinstrup-Andersen 1985, table 1, p. 9.

12. Data on agricultural and GDP growth from World Bank 1987, table 2, p. 204. Import data from Lele 1988, p. 40. For a full comparative analysis of Kenya, Tanzania, and Malawi, see Lele and Myers 1987.

13. Derived from Mellor 1978, tables 1 and 2, pp. 5–7.

14. A number of studies analyze the impact of food aid in developing countries. See, for example, Singer et al. 1987, Caly 1985a, Reutlinger 1983, Sen 1983, and Schultz 1980. Maxwell and Singer (1979) review a number of other studies as well.

15. The concept of food aid as a form of price discrimination is discussed in Mellor 1983 and Srinivasan 1987.

16. For further analysis of the relationship between food security and the purchasing power of the poor, see Sen 1981. In that context, Mellor and Gavian (1987) and Clay (1985b) analyze the importance of food production on the incomes of the poor.

17. Edirisinghe 1987, table 29, p. 48.

18. National income and budget data from Alderman et al. 1982, table 3, p. 16. Data on subsidies as a percent of per capita income from Alderman and von Braun 1984, p. 41. For additional information on the impact of food subsidies in developing countries, see Ahmed 1979, Gavan and Chandrasekera 1979, George 1979, Gray 1982, Scobie 1983, Trairatvorakul 1984, and von Braun and de Haen 1983.

19. Data in this paragraph derived from Ahmed and Hossain 1987 and Ahmed and Bernard 1987.

20. Ezekiel 1985. For analysis of the theoretical developments leading up to the creation of the cereal import facility, see Adams 1983.

21. High transport costs can seriously inhibit efforts to achieve food security through food imports. For an analysis in the context of the Sahelian region of Africa, see McIntire 1981.

REFERENCES

Adams, R. H. 1983. "The Role of Research in Policy Development: The Creation of the IMF Cereal Import Facility," *World Development* 11, no. 7 (July): 549–63.

Ahluwalia, M. S. 1985. "Rural Poverty, Agricultural Production, and Prices: A Reexamination." In *Agricultural Change and Rural Poverty,* edited by J. W. Mellor and G. M. Desai, 59–75. Baltimore: Johns Hopkins University Press.

Ahmed, R. 1979. "Foodgrain Supply, Distribution, and Consumption Policies within a Dual Pricing Mechanism: A Case Study of Bangladesh." Research Report no. 8. Washington, D.C.: International Food Policy Research Institute.

Ahmed, R., and A. Bernard. 1987. "Fluctuations of Rice Prices and an Approach to Rice Price Stabilization in Bangladesh." Washington, D.C.: International Food Policy Research Institute.

Ahmed, R., and M. Hossain. 1987. *Infrastructure and Development of a Rural Economy*. Washington, D.C.: International Food Policy Research Institute.

Alderman, H. 1986. "The Effect of Food Price and Income Changes on the Acquisition of Food by Low-Income Households." Washington, D.C.: International Food Policy Research Institute.

Alderman, H., and J. von Braun. 1984. "The Effects of the Egyptian Food Ration and Subsidy System on Income Distribution and Consumption." Research Report no. 45. Washington, D.C.: International Food Policy Research Institute.

Alderman, H., J. von Braun, and S. A. Sakr. 1982. "Egypt's Food Subsidy and Rationing System: A Description." Research Report no. 34. Washington, D.C.: International Food Policy Research Institute.

Anderson, J. R., and P. B. R. Hazell. 1989. *Variability in Grain Yields: Implications for Research and Policy in Developing Countries*. Baltimore: Johns Hopkins University Press.

Bachman, K. L., and L. A. Paulino. 1979. "Rapid Food Production Growth in Selected Developing Countries: A Comparative Analysis of Underlying Trends, 1961–76." Research Report no 11. Washington, D.C: International Food Policy Research Institute.

Clay, E. 1985a. "Food Aid and Development: Issues and Evidence." World Food Program Occasional Paper, no. 3. Rome: World Food Program.

———. 1985b. "The 1974 and 1984 Floods in Bangladesh: From Famine to Food Crisis Management." *Food Policy* 10, no. 3 (August): 202–6.

Dandekar, V. M. 1988. "Agriculture, Employment and Poverty." In *The Indian Economy: Recent Development and Future Prospects*, edited by R. E. B. Lucas and G. F. Papanek, 93–120. Boulder, Colo.: Westview Press.

Edirisinghe, N. 1987. "The Food Stamp Scheme in Sri Lanka: Cost, Benefits, and Options for Modification." Research Report no. 58. Washington, D.C.: International Food Policy Research Institute.

Ezekiel, H. 1984. "Costs and Benefits of Foodgrain Buffer Stocks and Public Distribution in India." Mimeo. Washington, D.C.: International Food Policy Research Institute.

———. 1985. *The IMF Cereal Import Financing Scheme*. Report of a study prepared for the Food and Agriculture Organization and the International Food Policy Research Institute. Washington, D.C.: IFPRI.

———. 1988. "Food Aid and the Creation of Assets." Paper presented at International Food Policy Research Institute Board Seminar, Mexico City, January.

Ezekiel, H., and V. Gandhi. 1987. "Food Aid and Financial Aid." Washington, D.C.: International Food Policy Research Institute.

Garcia, M., and P. Pinstrup-Andersen. 1987. "The Pilot Food Price Subsidy Scheme in the Philippines: Its Impact on Income, Food Consumption, and Nutritional Status." Research Report no. 61. Washington, D.C.: International Food Policy Research Institute.

Gavan, J. D., and I. S. Chandrasekera, 1979. "The Impact of Public Foodgrain Distribution on Food Consumption and Welfare in Sri Lanka." Research Report no. 13. Washington, D.C.: International Food Policy Research Institute.

George, P.S. 1979. "Public Distribution of Foodgrains in Kerala—Income Distribution Implications and Effectiveness." Research Report no. 7. Washington, D.C.: International Food Policy Research Institute.

Gray, C. W. 1982. "Food Consumption Parameters for Brazil and Their Application to Food Policy." Research Report no. 32. Washington, D.C.: International Food Policy Research Institute.

Hay, R. W., and M. Rukuni. 1988. "SADCC Food Security Strategies: Evolution and Role." *World Development* 16, no. 9 (September): 1113–25.

Hazell, P. B. R., and A. Roell. 1983. "Rural Growth Linkages: Household Expenditure Patterns in Malaysia and Nigeria." Research Report no. 41. Washington, D.C.: International Food Policy Research Institute.

Huddleston, B. 1984. Closing the Cereals Gap with Trade and Food Aid," Research Report no. 43. Washington, D.C.: International Food Policy Research Institute.

Koester, U., and A. Valdes. 1984. "The EC's Potential Role in Food Security fo LDC's: Adjustments in Its STABEX and Stock Policies." *European Review of Agricultural Economics* 11:415–37.

Kumar, S. K. 1979. "Impact of Subsidized Rice on Food Consumption and Nutrition in Kerala." Research Report no. 5. Washington, D.C.: International Food Policy Research Institute.

———. 1988. "Effects of Seasonal Food Shortage on Agricultural Production in Zambia." *World Development* 16, no. 9 (September): 1051–63.

Lele, U. 1987. "Structural Adjustment, Agricultural Development, and the Poor: Some Observations on Malawi." MADIA. Washington, D.C.: World Bank.

———. 1988. "Agriculture Growth, Domestic Policy, and External Assistance to Africa: Lessons of a Quarter Century." Paper presented at the Eighth Agricultural Sector Symposium on Trade, Aid, and Policy Reform for Agriculture, sponsored by Agricultural and Rural Development Department of the World Bank. Washington, D.C.: World Bank.

Lele, U., and M. Agarwal. 1987. "Four Decades of Economic Development in India and the Role of External Assistance." Paper presented at the ICS/World Bank Conference on Aid, Capital Flows and Development, Talloires, France. September.

Lele, U., and W. Candler. 1981. "Food Security: Some East African Considerations." In *Food Security for Developing Countries,* edited by A. Valdés, 101–2. Boulder: Westview Press.

Lele, U., and J. W. Mellor. 1981. "Technological Change, Distributive Bias, and Labor Transfer in Two-Sector Economy." *Oxford Economic Papers* 33, no. 3 (November): 426–41.

Lele, U., and L. R. Myers. 1987. "Growth and Structural Change in East Africa: Domestic Policies, Agricultrual Performance, and World Bank Assistance, 1963–86." MADIA. Washington, D.C.: World Bank.

Margen, S. 1978. Comment on "The Nature of the Nutrition Problem," by Leonardo Mata. In *Nutrition Planning: The State of the Art,* edited by L. Joy, 103–4. London: IPC Science and Technology Press.

Maxwell, S. J., and H. W. Singer. 1979. "Food Aid to Developing Countries: A Survey." *World Development* 7, no. 3 (March): 225–47.

McIntire, J. 1981. "Food Security in the Sahel: Variable Import Levy, Grain Reserves, and Foreign Exchange Assistance," Research Report no. 26. Washington, D.C.: International Food Policy Research Institute.

Mellor, J. W. 1968. "The Functions of Agricultural Prices in Economic Development." *Indian Journal of Agricultural Economics* 13, no. 1 (January/March): 23–38.

———. 1976. *The New Economics of Growth.* Ithaca: Cornell University Press.

———. 1978. "Food Price Policy and Income Distribution in Low-Income Countries." *Economic Development and Cultural Change* 27, no. 1 (October): 1–26.

———. 1983. "The Utilization of Food Aid for Equitable Growth." In *Report of the World Food Programme—Government of the Netherlands Seminar on Food Aid,* 157–65. The Hague: World Food Programme.

———. 1986. "Commentary: The Changing Global Food Scene: Opportunities for Development and Poverty Alleviation." *IFPRI Report* 8, no. 3. Washington, D.C.: International Food Policy Research Institute.

Mellor, J. W., and G. Desai. 1985. "Agricultural Change and Rural Poverty: A Synthesis." In *Agricultural Change and Rural Poverty,* edited by J. W. Mellor and G. Desai, 192–210. Baltimore: Johns Hopkins University Press.

Mellor, J. W., and S. Gavian. 1987. "Famine: Causes, Prevention, and Relief." *Science* 235 (January): 539–45.

Mellor, J. W., and B. F. Johnston. 1984. "The World Food Equation: Interrelations among Development, Employment, and Food Consumption." *Journal of Economic Literature* 22 (June): 531–74.

Mellor, J. W., and U. Lele. 1973. "Growth Linkages of the New Foodgrain Technologies." *Indian Journal of Agricultural Economics* 23 (January-March): 35–55.

Paulino, L. A. 1986. "Food in the Third World: Past Trends and Projections to 2000." Research Report no. 52. Washington, D.C.: International Food Policy Research Institute.

Pinckney, T. C., and A. Valdés. 1988. "Short-Run Supply Management and Food Security." *World Development* 16, no. 9 (September): 1025–34.

Pinstrup-Andersen, P. 1985. "Agricultural Policy and Human Nutrition." Paper presented at Agricultural Policy Workshop, Santiago, Dominican Republic, April.

Ranade, C. G., D. Jha, and C. L. Delgado. 1988. "Technological Change, Production Costs, and Supply Response." In *Agricultural Price Policy for Developing Countries*, edited by J. W. Mellor and R. Ahmed, 308–30. Baltimore: Johns Hopkins University Press.

Reardon, T., and P. Matlon. 1989. "Seasonal Food Insecurity and Vulnerability in Drought-affected Areas of Burkina Faso." In *Seasonal Variability in Third World Agriculture: The Consequences for Food Security*, edited by D. Sahn. Baltimore: Johns Hopkins University Press.

Reutlinger, S. 1983. "Project Food Aid and Equitable Growth: Income Transfer Efficiency First." In *Report of the World Food Programme—Government of the Netherlands Seminar on Food Aid*, 167–78. The Hague: World Food Programme.

Reutlinger, S., and M. Selowsky. 1976. "Malnutrition and Poverty: Magnitude and Policy Options." World Bank Occasional Paper, no. 23. Baltimore: Johns Hopkins University Press.

Rosegrant, M. W., F. Kasryno, L. A. Gonzales, C. Rasahan, and Y. Saefudin. 1987. *Price and Investment Policies in the Indonesian Food Crop Sector*. Final report submitted to the Asian Development Bank (ADB) for the project "Study of Food Demand/Supply Prospects and Related Strategies for Member Developing Countries of ADB, Phase II." Washington, D.C.: International Food Policy Research Institute and Center for Agro Economic Research (Bogor, Indonesia).

Sarma, J. S. 1988. "Determination of Administrative Prices of Foodgrains in India." In *Agricultural Price Policy for Developing Countries*, edited by J. W. Mellor and R. Ahmed. Baltimore: Johns Hopkins University Press.

Schultz, T. W. 1980. "Effects of the International Donor Community on Farm People." *American Journal of Agricultural Economics* 62, no. 5 (December): 837–78.

Scobie, G. M. 1983. "Food Subsidies in Egypt: Their Impact on Foreign Exchange and Trade." Research Report no. 40. Washington, D.C.: International Food Policy Research Institute.

Sen, A. 1981. *Poverty and Famines: An Essay on Entitlement and Deprivation*. Oxford: Clarendon Press.

———. 1983. "Food Entitlement and Food Aid Programmes." In *Report of the World Food Programme—Government of the Netherlands Seminar on Food Aid*, 111–22. The Hague: World Food Programme.

Singer, H., J. Wood, and T. Jennings. 1987. *Food Aid: the Challenge and the Opportunity*. Oxford: Clarendon.

Srinivasan, T. N. 1987. "Food Aid: A Cause or Sympton of Development Failure or an Instrument for Success." Paper presented at the ICS/World Bank Conference on Aid, Capital Flows and Development, Talloires, France, September.

Stone, B. 1987. "Foodcrop Production and Consumption Performance in China and India." Paper presented at the Annual Meetings of the American Association for the Advancement of Science, Washington, D.C., February.

Sukhatme, P. V. 1977. "Nutrition and Poverty." Ninth Lai Bahadur Shastri Memorial Lecture. New Delhi: Indian Agricultural Research Institute.

Trairatvorakul, P. 1984. "The Effects on Income Distribution and Nutrition of Alternative Rice Price Policies in Thailand." Research Report no. 46. Washington, D.C.: International Food Policy Research Institute.

Tweeten, L. G. 1988. "Long-Term Viability of U.S. Agriculture." Report of the Council for Agricultural Science and Technology.

U.S. Department of Agriculture (USDA). 1987. "Production, Supply, and Distribution Tape, 1987." Washington, D.C.: USDA.

von Braun, J., and H. de Haen. 1983. "The Effects of Food Price and Subsidy Policies on Egyptian Agriculture." Research Report no. 42. Washington, D.C.: International Food Policy Research Institute.

Wanmali, S. Forthcoming. "Changes in the Provision and Use of Services in the North Arcot Region." In *Green Revolution Revisited: A Study of the High-Yielding Rice Varieties in Tamil Nadu*, edited by P. Hazell and C. Ramasamy. Baltimore: Johns Hopkins University Press.

World Bank. 1986. *Poverty and Hunger: Issues and Options for Food Security in Developing Countries*. Washington, D.C.: World Bank.

———. 1987. *World Development Report, 1987*. New York: Oxford University Press.

7

The New Macroeconomics of Food and Agricultural Policy

G. EDWARD SCHUH

Food and agricultural development policy today is carried out in a completely different world from that which prevailed even a decade or so ago. In the past, sectoral approaches were appropriate. Today, the food and agricultural sector can be understood only in the context of the larger economy, both national and international.

A decade ago, the emphasis was on food and food self-sufficiency. Today, the emphasis should be on generating income streams and remaining competitive. A decade ago, policy makers were only just beginning to talk about international capital markets. Today, they cannot understand agricultural commodity markets in isolation from international financial markets. A decade ago, the value of a nation's currency was largely ignored as an issue of domestic food and agricultural policy. Today, it is probably the most important price in the economy. A decade ago, a national perspective was appropriate. Today, food and agricultural policies must take account of changes in international comparative advantage. A decade ago, long-term changes in an economy were understood to arise from technological evolution and rising per capita income. Today a powerful new insight sees that rising per capita income has important collateral effects through the rising value of time.

THE EVOLUTION OF AN INTERNATIONAL FOOD AND AGRICULTURAL SYSTEM

One of the remarkable achievements since the end of World War II has been the evolution of an international food and agricultural system built on international trade and supported by a rapidly evolving institutional infrastructure. The key to this evolving system is an international trade structure that enables consumers to

GEORGE EDWARD SCHUH is dean, Hubert Humphrey Institute of Public Affairs, University of Minnesota.

Originally titled "The Changing Context of Food and Agricultural Policy." Published by permission of the Johns Hopkins University Press from *Food Policy,* edited by J. Price Gittinger, Joanne Leslie, and Caroline Hoisington, 1987, pp. 72–88. Published with omissions and with the permission of the author and the Johns Hopkins University Press.

tap supplies of food and agricultural products in almost any part of the world. This global trade structure has become possible because of technical and institutional innovations that have lowered transportation costs and made information available almost instantly around the world.

As with other forms of trade, trade in agricultural products grew rapidly in the 1970s. Virtually all countries now engage in trade of agricultural products of one kind or another, either as exporters or as importers, and thus are bound together in a common system. As a result, domestic and international policies are inseparable in today's world. Developments in the international economy, generally beyond the reach of domestic policies, often change the articulation and effect of domestic policies, making them different from those originally intended.

This system of trade has become an important means of national food security if and when national governments want to take advantage of it. Associated with the international food and agricultural system has been the virtual elimination of major famines except in those cases where national governments do not let the outside world know about food shortages or make them known too late to overcome difficult transportation problems. Even in the recent African famine, the problem was not lack of available food in a global sense or of the means to get food to the distressed areas. People perished because the international community did not know about the problem in time or failed to act quickly enough once it did know.

Parallel to the evolving system of trade, an international infrastructure for the food and agricultural system has been evolving as well. At the end of World War II, this infrastructure consisted primarily of the FAO (Food and Agriculture Organization), with near universal membership, and the General Agreement on Tariffs and Trade among industrialized countries, its agricultural provisions honored primarily in the breach. Various attempts to develop international commodity agreements occurred during the post–World War II period but have not been notably successful. UNCTAD (United Nations Conference on Trade and Development), although it provides a forum for discussion of international commodity problems, has otherwise been of limited effectiveness. In the late 1960s, CGIAR (Consultative Group on International Agricultural Research) was formed to support a network of international centers. Following the World Food Conference in 1974, the WFC (World Food Council) and IFAD (International Fund for Agricultural Development) were established. In the early 1980s, arrangements for financing food imports through the IMF Compensatory Financing Facility came into effect.

The system still has some important deficiencies. The social science research institutions to parallel the international agricultural research centers are lacking and consist primarily of IFPRI (International Food Policy Research Institute) and the modest research capability of the FAO and the World Bank. These institutions are inadequate in the light of the rapid internationalization of the global food and agricultural economy and the changed conditions that development has created for both international trade and domestic policy making in national economies. It may be time to consolidate these institutions according to some well-conceived overall plan and to sort out what is needed and what is not functioning up to standard.

FOOD AND AGRICULTURAL SELF-SUFFICIENCY

The emergence of a well-articulated international food and agricultural system and the potential for increasing productivity change the focus of food and agricultural policy. The motivating force of this policy today should not be food production per se, and above all it should not be food self-sufficiency. Lack of access to food by individual households is almost wholly associated with poverty and will have to be attacked with income- and employment-generating policies, together with income redistribution policies. The emphasis in agricultural development should be to improve the income of the rural population, which in most developing countries is still the main component of poverty, and to improve export performance so as to acquire the resources needed for development.

RISING FOOD PRODUCTION AND LONG-TERM PRICE DECLINES

Brown (1982, 14) echoed a theme commonly heard in discussions of the world food situation: "the period of global food security is over . . . the worldwide effort to expand food production is losing momentum . . . world food supplies are tightening and the slim margin between food production and population growth continues to narrow."

Much of the recent debate exemplified by Brown's comments was engendered in the early 1970s when international commodity prices surged. Yet neither trends in world food production nor those in food prices imply that the world is running out of production potential or that the developing countries are unable to feed themselves, although the per capita food production data suggest a mixed and uneven performance. Indeed, by the end of the 1970s, the very decade which gave rise to so much Malthusian pessimism, food production in the developing countries as a whole had increased an impressive 58 percent over 1961–65, compared to 42 percent in the developed countries as a whole. Africa was the poorest performer. There, food production expanded only 32 percent during this period. Elsewhere, food output expanded by 75 percent in East Asia, by 73 percent in Latin America, and by 68 percent in West Asia.

Even if one takes into account the rapid growth of population, the performance of the developing countries as a whole was still substantial. Total per capita food production in the developing countries was 6 percent more than in 1961–65. The total masks a great deal, however. Per capita food production had declined by some 12 percent in Africa, and the increase for South and West Asia was only 8 percent. Bangladesh actually experienced a significant decline, and per capita production also declined in the Caribbean countries.

Now, a decade after the Malthusian wave of pessimism in the mid-1970s, the situation could not be more different. There is a chronic food problem in Africa, but food production in the rest of the world is relatively abundant. Farmers in the United States are in dire straits as their capacity to produce has outpaced the ability of the market to absorb their output, especially in the face of a strong dollar and the interference of commodity programs with the free play of market forces. India, which in the early 1970s was widely predicted to become an international basket case, has instead become a net exporter of cereals, with substantial potential for output expansion still remaining. China has emerged as an exporter of rice and feedgrains despite rapid short-term increases in per capita income. Brazil has steadily eroded the previously dominant position of the United States in the international soybean market.

The price of food is another measure of scarcity. If the demand for food were outpacing supply, the price of food would increase. Wheat and maize prices during a span of somewhat more than 100 years are plotted in figure 1. The United States has traditionally been a significant exporter of both wheat and maize, so in a very real sense, the U.S. price represents the international opportunity cost of these grains. The story told by this graph is a dramatic one. The real price of wheat has experienced a long-term decline. In constant value terms, its price in the 1980s is approximately half what it was 100 years earlier. This decline occurred despite the enormous increase in world population and significant increases in per capita income for many of the world's inhabitants. The story for maize is somewhat less dramatic in that its decline extends over a relatively shorter period, primarily the period since the end of World War II. The decline, however, is no less significant, since maize is both a foodgrain and an input into the livestock industry for which demand grows fairly rapidly as per capita incomes increase. Demand for maize has, in fact, grown tremendously.

The rising food production of the last two decades and the long-term decline in the price of foodgrains hardly point to a Malthusian crisis. To the contrary, they

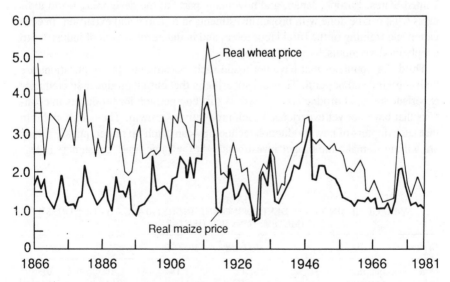

Fig.1. U.S. Wheat and Maize Prices, 1866–1981 (constant 1967 U.S. dollars per bushel). (Source: Martin and Brokken 1982.)

point to a situation of growing abundance, interrupted by short-term problems associated with weather cycles, wars, and international monetary disturbances.

The reason for rising food output and the decline in the real price of food is the use of new agricultural technology. The process started in Europe, Japan, and the United States and in recent years has been extended to the developing countries. The data on yield in table 1 tell a great deal of the story. In the mid-1930s, average yield of cereals was the same in the industrialized countries as in the developing countries. By the mid-1950s, average yield in the industrialized countries had spurted some 19 percent to 1.37 metric tons a hectare, while that in the developing countries stayed at its original level. By the end of the 1960s, yield in the developing countries was finally beginning to increase and had risen 23 percent compared to the mid-1950s, but the yield in industrialized countries had spurted another 56 percent. During the 1980s, grain yield has continued to increase around the world.

The data on food production and productivity have far-reaching implications. First, they demonstrate that production of food and other agricultural products is not based solely on natural or physical resources. Instead, the capacity to produce food and agricultural products is man-made, based on science and technology, new knowledge, and people's skills.

Second, these data support optimism about the ability to feed the world's rapidly growing population. An expanded food supply is based on reproducible human capital, not on the natural endowment of the land. In the United States, food prices in the early part of this century were rising as all available agricultural land was brought under cultivation. Moreover, as noted, grain yield was basically no different from that in countries now referred to as developing. The experience of the United States, Europe, Japan, and now many parts of the developing world indicates what can be done with proper investments in research and extension, in education and training of the rural labor force, and in the development of industries to supply modern inputs.[1]

Third, for countries that have not made such investments, the implications are both sobering and hopeful. They are sobering in that output produced in countries experiencing rapid productivity growth is stiff competition for producers in countries that have not yet experienced such productivity growth. They are hopeful in that late adopters of new production technology can catch up rather quickly if they are willing to make the proper investments. At the same time, consumers in lag-

TABLE 1
AVERAGE GRAIN YIELD, DEVELOPING AND INDUSTRIALIZED COUNTRIES
(METRIC TONS PER HECTARE)

Group	1934–38	1952–56	1967–70	1981–83
Developing countries	1.15	1.15	1.41	2.01
Industrialized countries	1.15	1.37	2.14	2.67

SOURCE: FAO data.

ging countries can benefit from the technological advances elsewhere if those countries play to their own prevailing comparative advantage and earn the wherewithal to have their food produced elsewhere. In any case, consumers worldwide can benefit and have benefited from the technological progress that has occurred to date.

Finally, this analysis points to the poverty or income dimension of the food problem, which has both a production and an income distribution dimension. Building agricultural research capability is no less important than in the past, but the perspective should be one of producting new income streams rather than producing food itself. That will give a very different commodity mix emphasis, with cash, export, and raw material crops emerging to be as important as food crops.

CHANGES IN THE INTERNATIONAL MONETARY SYSTEM

No part of the international system has experienced more change than the international monetary system, nor is there any part of the system for which the changes are more significant. The system is now huge. Recent estimates are that international financial flows are running at a level of approximately $40 trillion a year, while the flow of international trade amounts to approximately $2 trillion a year. Clearly, financial flows dominate the international system and swamp international trade as a factor influencing the value of national currencies in foreign exchange markets.

Parallel to this has been the shift beginning in 1973 from the Bretton Woods system of fixed exchange rates to a system of bloc-floating, with major currencies floated relative to each other, but with a large number of individual currencies pegged to the major floating currencies.

The emergence of a well-integrated international capital market and the shift to a system of block-flexible exchange rates significantly changed the way in which monetary and fiscal policies affect national economies. International capital flows influence the economies of countries with flexible exchange rates by inducing changes in the value of their currencies. These changes in exchange rates in turn shift resources among export- and import-competing sectors and nontraded sectors. For countries in which agricultural commodities are important tradables, agriculture has to bear a large share of the burden of adjustment to changing monetary conditions, with incentives to expand output as conditions in domestic money markets ease and to contract output as domestic monetary conditions tighten. The important change from the old fixed exchange rate system is that it is changes in foreign demand and foreign supply that force adjustments in the agricultural sector, not changes in the domestic cost structure of agriculture.

Another change in the international monetary system was the significant increase in monetary instability that started about 1968, the same time that agriculture in many countries became quite sensitive to changes in monetary conditions. The result has been a significant increase in instability in international commodity markets. Since this instability comes from shifts in foreign demand and supply rather than domestic conditions, it changes the instruments policy makers can use to deal with it. Stability in monetary and fiscal policy is now much more important than grain stocks or reserves as a means to create stable market conditions.

The emergence of a well-integrated international capital market and the shift to flexible exchange rates also established a strong link between financial markets and commodity markets. Somewhat of a link has always existed, since conditions in money markets influenced the cost of carrying stocks. In today's configuration, however, the link is through the exchange rate and its impact on the competitive position of domestic agriculture in international markets. Realignments in exchange rates are reflected immediately in the price of tradable commodities, independently of what is happening on the supply side. This creates very different policy choices and dilemmas than when the price is fluctuating because of changes in supply.

The emergence of a well-integrated international capital market with the shift to flexible exchange rates complicates agricultural policy in a number of additional senses. For instance, minimum price and price support policies become much more difficult to manage. If domestic prices are fixed, realignments in exchange rates that have little to do with the underlying conditions of agricultural supply and demand will influence how competitive tradable agricultural commodities are in foreign markets, with dramatic short-term implications for domestic markets. These disturbances are further complicated when countries that are large in a trade sense are subject to these same conditions. The role of the United States in the international grain and soybean markets is a perfect example. The significant decline in the value of the U.S. dollar in the 1970s caused the price of these commodities to decline in terms of other currencies, thus causing the quantity imported by other countries to increase and U.S. exports to increase as well. This had important dampening effects on the agricultural sectors of other countries, independently of whether they were export competitors or importers. By the same token, the rise in the value of the dollar in the early 1980s led to higher prices of these same commodities in terms of the currencies of other countries. The United States' share of these markets has declined significantly, and the price in other countries has risen. This effect has been exaggerated by the rigidity of the United States' support level, but that only further emphasizes the significance of international interdependence. The agriculture of other countries is affected not only by U.S. monetary and fiscal policies and the changes in the value of the U.S. dollar but also in important ways by the domestic commodity policies the United States implements.

To the extent that national governments isolate their domestic agricultural sectors from international markets, some of these external forces may be attenuated, but the extent to which domestic sectors can be isolated is deceptive. Realignments in exchange rates can bring about implicit changes in domestic relative prices even though domestic and border prices are fixed in relative terms. This can alter the domestic conditions of supply and demand. Consider a country that pegs its currency to the value of the U.S. dollar. If that country is either an exporter or an importer of agricultural commodities, its agriculture will benefit from a decline in the value of the dollar. It will not benefit relative to the United States, of course, but relative to the agriculture of countries whose currencies are rising against the dollar. This includes the agriculture of all those countries that have the value of their currencies pegged to the value of other major currencies. The reverse occurs when the value of the dollar rises, again with important resource allocation effects in these other countries.

Finally, there is the whole issue of international commodity agreements in the context of a flexible exchange rate system. In the new configuration of the international economy, with flexible exchange rates and well-integrated capital markets, such agreements now appear infeasible. Typically, such agreements involve some attempt to support prices in U.S. dollar terms at some agreed-to level, and some means of enforcing that price, by international marketing quotas, imposed production adjustments, or both. Under the fixed exchange rate system, such an agreement was at least feasible in principle. Under a flexible exchange rate system it may not be feasible at all, and with a system of bloc-floating it may be well nigh impossible. Exchange rate realignments induce changes in the domestic prices within member countries. This influences the quantity exported or the quantity imported. More generally, it makes it difficult for some countries to comply with the provisions of the agreement, while creating in other countries very strong pressures to cheat or break out of the cartel.

There are those, of course, who would like to abandon the present flexible exchange rate system because of its perceived instability and go back to the old fixed exchange rate system. That would not be possible, even if it were desirable, unless one were willing to give up all the advantages of a well-integrated capital and financial market and the benefits from trade. The shift to a system of flexible exchange rates in 1973 was nothing more than a tacit recognition that exchange rates could no longer be fixed. Recent attempts to influence the value of the dollar by coordinated and massive central bank interventions have illustrated the difficulties of influencing exchange rates and confirmed the decisions taken in 1973.

This is not to say the system cannot be improved. That will require either that the IMF become an international central bank, that the United States manage its monetary policy as if it were that international central bank, or that there be a great deal of policy coordination among national economies. Part of the present problem arises from the fact that the industrialized countries have never given the IMF resources commensurate with its originally assigned objectives, while the United States has managed its monetary policy primarily as if it were a closed economy when, in fact, since the world is on a dollar standard, the United States is in reality the central banker for the world.

The conditions now unfolding in the international monetary system are cause for serious concern. The rapid growth in barter and countertrade indicates that the international economy is facing a serious liquidity crisis. The emergence of the United States as a debtor country will have major exchange rate and monetary implications. Already it has led to a decline in the value of the dollar. Under circumstances that are quite feasible, the decline could be significant. The result could well be enormous shocks to international commodity markets, to world agriculture, and to the international economy as a whole.

DEVELOPMENTS IN THE SYSTEM OF
INTERNATIONAL TRADE

Developments in the system of international trade are almost as far-reaching as developments in the international monetary system, and almost as poorly perceived and understood. In part this is because of the tendency to consider international economic intercourse as a real trade phenomenon without fully appreciating the significance of the international capital market.

Much of the debate about the current United States trade deficit illustrates the failure to understand the new system. It is popular to predict that the value of the dollar should soon decline because the United States is running a large trade deficit. In point of fact, of course, the United States has a large trade deficit because the dollar is strong, and the dollar is strong because of what is happening in the international capital market. The emergence of the United States as a major debtor country is far more likely to have an effect on the value of the dollar than what happens on the trade account because financial flows are so much larger than trade flows.

The emergence of a well-integrated capital market and the shift to a system of bloc-floating exchange rates has significantly altered the constraints faced by individual nations as they attempt to develop their economies. At the same time, it provides them with new means and opens new development opportunities, but within significant new limitations on international trade policies.

Consider events in the international economy these last three to four years and the dilemmas they present to both developed and devloping countries. To service and repay past debts, the developing countries have to provide a surplus on their trade account. That surplus implies a deficit in the trade accounts of the developed or previously capital-exporting countries, which for the most part the United States has been supplying. For these countries, however, the deficit on the trade account implies that they are capital importers, as illustrated by recent U.S. experience. This, in turn, pulls much-needed capital away from the developing countries.

The opportunities, constraints, and dilemmas are real. Developing countries now have a well-developed capital market they can access for development purposes. Yet if they are to repay that debt and remain good risks for further borrowing, they have to improve their export performance. This forces them to turn outward in the configuration of their economies, to implement policies that use their resources more efficiently, and to develop productive export sectors. It also implies expanded international trade.

Paradoxically, the present crisis in international financial markets may be the harbinger of a brighter future for agriculture in many of the countries most affected by the crisis. Policy makers will be forced to realign their exchange rates to bring their external accounts in line to service and eventually to pay off their debts. They will also have to reduce the import subsidies that have caused food imports to grow so rapidly in some developing countries.[2] Overvalued currency has probably been the single most common policy distortion among developing countries, and the degree of overvaluation is substantial. The implicit export tax from overvaluation of the currency alone in Brazil, for example, ranged from 22 to 27 percent between 1954 and 1966 (Bergsman and Malan 1971; Bergsman 1970). The recent floating of the Mexican peso provides another example of how overvalued currencies often are. Little wonder that the agriculture of these countries has done so poorly. Little wonder also that countries imposing such distortions shift from being net exporters of food to being net importers. After all, the overvalued currency is an implicit import subsidy as well as an implicit export tax.

Trade and exchange rate policies, the main instruments by which governments have intervened to influence food and agricultural prices, have played a major role in shifting the domestic terms of trade against agriculture. The failure to address the effects of trade and exchange rate policy on the domestic terms of trade is ironic in light of the importance the developing countries have attached to the external terms of trade. At the very time many of these countries issued complaints about declining external terms of trade and lack of export opportunities, they have severely overvalued their currency in foreign exchange markets, levied export taxes, and imposed complicated licensing provisions to limit exports. The net effect of these policies has been to divert agricultural output away from viable export markets and to the domestic market. To put it succinctly, limitations on external markets have in important respects been self-imposed.[3]

The developed countries that have been supplying loan capital to developing countries in the past are faced with no less serious policy dilemmas than the debtor countries. If the developed countries want their past credits to be repaid, they must be willing to accept imports from the debtor countries. This places great stress on the traditional sectors of the developed countries, forcing significant restructuring and greater efficiencies in their economies as well as those of the debtors. This is burden sharing at its best, but it is painful for all concerned.

The international economy has been passing through an enormously stressful period. It has accommodated two petroleum crises in the 1970s, suffered from misguided policies in developed and developing countries alike, and learned to live with the system of bloc-floating exchange rates and a burgeoning international capital market. As the international economy recovers from this difficult period, individual countries will have choices to make at the margin between increasing exports or importing capital, and between exporting capital and accepting more imports. In the process, pressures for expanded trade and further integration of the international economy will be great.

One of the major implications of this analysis is the importance of general trade liberalization if international adjustment burdens are to be truly shared. Another is the need for symmetry in conditionality and insistence on policy rationality among the developed countries. Developing countries will not benefit from their domestic policy reforms if the developed countries are unwilling to accept their exports and at the same time supply capital as the demand for it grows.

CHANGES IN INTERNATIONAL COMPARATIVE ADVANTAGE

Probably at no time in modern history have such powerful forces been acting to change international comparative advantage. In the case of world agriculture, there is the growing capacity to produce a modern technology adapted to developing countries, particularly those in the tropics. An important part of this capacity is the CGIAR network of 13 research centers. Of even greater importance is the growing research capacity in many developing countries. India and Brazil are outstanding examples, but many others exist.

Another factor that has great potential to change international comparative advantage in agriculture is the new biotechnology. It is not clear whether this new potential source of technological breakthroughs will benefit developed or developing countries the most. It is likely, however, that this new technology will prove highly transferable, with potentially great effects in the developing countries. For example, a new hormone ready to be adopted in the United States promises to increase a dairy cow's milk production by 40 percent. This hormone ought to be highly transferable.

The rapid diffusion of modern poultry technology is also transforming international agriculture and altering international comparative advantage. Poultry production is a relatively easy way for a country to upgrade the quality of its diet as per capita income increases. An expansion of this sector gives rise to a strong derived demand for feedgrains. As economic development proceeds, therefore, there likely will be a relative shift away from foodgrains as a source of food, with feedgrain use making possible additional value added from local labor and pasture resources.

These examples suggest that a worldwide surge in agricultural technology is under way. That surge can bring enormous benefits, but it can also cause serious adjustment problems. The need to transfer labor out of agriculture will probably be quite great. When agriculture makes up a large part of the economy, managing this adjustment is not easy.

In the industrial sector, the big news is the newly industrialized countries that have already penetrated the developed countries with their exports and forced significant restructuring of their economies. Manufacturing is declining and the service sector is growing. Now, a new round of exporters is coming on the scene, including China, India, Pakistan, and the Philippines. The shocks to trade patterns as important industrial sectors shift from one country to another can be great.

The service sector is probably the least understood sector of the international economy. International trade in services is growing rapidly and can be expected to continue to grow in the future. The service sector probably will be the comparative advantage of the developed countries in the decades ahead.

In today's world, comparative advantage is increasingly influenced by human capital and less and less by the underlying endowment of physical resources. This is a problem for those countries that lag in developing their stock of human capital, but it holds out the promise that in the future countries can, within limits, make their comparative advantage whatever they want it to be. This is not to say that national governments should ignore the principles of comparative advantage when they design their development policy. To the contrary, it is the only viable principle as long as efficiency is important. It is to say that the traditional concept of comparative advantage has to be broadened to include the concept of human capital, and that countries do not have to accept their "original" resource endowment as a basis for their future comparative advantage. Moreover, it implies that investment policy designed to augment and shape a nation's stock of human capital is a more viable way to alter and improve its comparative advantage than protectionist measures, which distort resource use and reduce the ability to compete in the international economy without at the same time building a strong basis for longer-term economic development.

As new agricultural technology becomes increasingly important to agricultural change, individual cultivators must have greater knowledge about opportunities, management choices, and markets, with obvious implications about the education they must receive. Countries will need a whole stock of middle-level workers to provide such services as input and output marketing. Outside agriculture, countries will need an increasingly well-educated work force if they are to take advantage of international trade to energize economic growth. In the case of training the high-level cadres needed for modernization, and in the case of developing the capacity for agricultural research, the resources needed are modest, but the gestation period is long. Most countries need significantly improved human capital services if they are to compete effectively in international markets. These include the capability to analyze trade opportunities, a market information system to give private decision makers an improved basis for decision making, and improved means by which participants in risky markets can transfer that risk to other members of the society through futures markets for commodities and foreign exchange and through marketing instruments, such as warehouse warrants.

CHANGES IN INTERNATIONAL COMPETITIVE ADVANTAGE

Competitive advantage is what is left after policy interventions by governments have had their effect on national economies. Government policies can suppress underlying comparative advantage or they can distort it away from what underlying conditions of supply and demand would imply. The exchange rate can have the same effect. In the absence of large international capital and financial markets, exchange rates were important reflections of underlying comparative advantage. Today, they are more properly a part of competitive advantage, since changes in exchange rates induced by capital and financial flows can distort the extent to which underlying comparative advantage is expressed. Capital flows may reflect differences in savings rates as much as conditions of trade. Until institutional means are developed to create stable international monetary conditions, large shifts in competitive advantage may be expected in response to large swings in the relative values of national currencies.

The international debt crisis that is causing many countries to undertake significant reforms of domestic economic policies is bringing about major shifts in competitive advantage. Subsidies are being phased out, export taxes and other discriminations against exports are being reduced, and exchange rates are being realigned to more realistic levels. These reforms will have major impacts on trade flows in the future.

The manner in which protection is provided to domestic industries has changed significantly over the last 10 to 15 years. Tariff protection has declined as a consequence of multilateral trade negotiations, at least among Western industrialized countries, and nontariff barriers have become more significant. In addition, new forms of protectionism have arisen in the form of voluntary export agreements, semicartel arrangements, and various orderly marketing arrangements. These newer forms of protectionism distinguish themselves by being selective and focusing on one or a small group of countries, by tending to be self-limiting, and by rewarding countries that practice restraint in their exports with economic rents of various kinds. Their negative aspects are that they compensate foreign and domestic producers at the expense of domestic consumers. These selective forms of protectionism are likely to proliferate in the years ahead as the export imperative spreads worldwide. They are an aspect of trade policy that will increasingly have to be taken into account as pressures for exports grow.

Fortunately, the growth of international trade worldwide since the end of World War II has created valuable vested interests against protectionism and in favor of trade liberalization. Protectionist initiatives are tempered by the threat of retaliation as country after country finds it has as much to lose as to gain from the spread of protectionism. This, more than anything else, explains the relative success in staving off protectionism despite enormous realignments in real exchange rates and the emergence of strong new competitors. An important phenomenon that promises to strengthen further these forces against protectionism is the growth in subsector integration across national boundaries. As industries become more international in scope, they generate multicountry forces in favor of freer trade and against protectionism.

It is not well recognized that the new system of bloc-floating exchange rates means there are smaller national gains from protectionist measures of any kind. Both protectionist measures and export subsidies lead to changes in exchange rates. The exchange rate realignments may help spread the burden of adjustment in the domestic economy, but the nation as a whole still has to bear the adjustment. The ability to dump problems abroad, as under the old fixed exchange rate system, is no longer available.

These new dimensions to trade policy are important both in shaping food and agricultural development policy and in shaping economic policy more generally.

CONCLUSION

Food and agricultural development policy in most countries has traditionally been shaped in the narrow confines of sectoral policy, neglecting other sectors of the economy, other aspects of economic policy, and often the international economy. In today's world, that is no longer a sound approach. Policy makers must pay attention to the poverty and income distribution implications of food policy, not just the production implications. The changing international economy, as well as altered concepts of what properly should be paramount in shaping food and agricultural policy, have changed significantly the context policy makers face as they address the complex challenges of improving the welfare of their people in the decades ahead.

NOTES

1. See Bonnen, chapter 15 in this volume.—ED.
2. See de Janvry and Sadoulet, chapter 28 in this volume.—ED.
3. See Myint, chapter 13 in this volume.—ED.

REFERENCES

Bergsman, Joel. 1970. *Brazil: Industrialization and Trade Policies*. London: Oxford University Press.
Bergsman, Joel, and Pedro S. Malan. 1971. "The Structure of Protection in Brazil." In *The Structure of Protection in Developing Countries,* by Bela Balassa and associates. Baltimore: Johns Hopkins University Press.
Brown, Lester R. 1982. "Global Food Prospects: Shadow of Malthus." *Challenge* (January–February).
Martin, Michael V., and Ray F. Brokken. 1982. *Grain Prices in Historical Perspective*. St. Paul: University of Minnesota Department of Agricultural and Applied Economics.

8

The Political Framework for Agricultural Policy Decisions

ROBERT H. BATES

 T. W. Schultz once stated, "Once there are investment opportunities and efficient incentives, farmers will turn sand into gold" (Schultz 1976, 5). Schultz and others are quick to point out that governments in the developing areas often provide distorted economic incentives and that their agricultural policies constitute a major reason for low levels of food production. I shall draw on my earlier work (Bates 1981) to discuss why governments act as they do.

Agricultural policy can be defined as the set of decisions taken by governments that influence the prices farmers confront in the markets which determine their incomes. The level of farm revenues is determined in part by the prices at which sales are made in markets for agricultural commodities. The prices which farmers must pay for farm inputs help to determine their costs and thus, in combination with revenues, the money value of their incomes from farming. And the real value of farm incomes, in turn, is determined by the prices which farmers must pay for consumer items.

THREE APPROACHES TO POLICY ANALYSIS

Research throughout the developing world suggests that governmental policy tends to be antithetical to the interests of most farmers. Governments tend to lower the prices farmers receive for produce. They tend to shelter domestic manufacturers from meaningful levels of economic competition originating both at home and abroad, thereby raising the prices farmers must pay for consumer items. And, while governments often subsidize the price of farm inputs, these subsidies tend to be captured by the larger farmers. The incomes of most farmers are thus adversely affected by the agricultural policies of Third World governments.

Governmental policies thus tend to weaken production incentives for farmers.

ROBERT H. BATES is Henry R. Luce Professor of Political Economy, Duke University.

Originally titled "The Political Framework for Price Policy Decisions." Reprinted from *Food Policy: Frameworks for Analysis and Action*, edited by Charles Mann and Barbara Huddleston, by permission of Indiana University Press and the author.

When governments do emphasize production, moreover, they attempt to secure higher output by building projects rather than by raising prices. And when governments do offer positive incentives for increased production, they tend to do so by lowering costs rather than by increasing gross revenues, that is, by subsidizing the prices of farm inputs rather than by raising the prices of commodities.

Why do Third World governments tend to adopt these kinds of policies? There are several approaches to explaining the behavior of governments, and I will review three of them.

MAXIMIZING SOCIAL WELFARE

The first explanatory approach is the one most often adopted by economists. It treats governments as agencies whose job is to maximize the social welfare; public policy is viewed as a set of choices made by governments to secure society's best interests. In poor societies, this approach holds, the social interest is best served by development, and the behavior of governments is analyzed in terms of its impact on this overriding objective.

There are many problems with this approach. One is its lack of explanatory power. Its basic method is to account for the behavior of governments in terms of social objectives. But a given objective can often be secured through a variety of policy instruments, and noting the underlying objective of a policy program often does not account for the particular choice of instrument. To secure increased food production, for example, governments could pay higher prices to farmers expending the same amount of resources as on food production projects. Under most circumstances, the former would be the more efficient way of securing this social objective, but the latter is more often chosen. Noting the social objectives of government does not account for this systematic bias in governmental policy.

Not only does the approach possess low explanatory power, but when it does make strong predictions, it is often wrong. For example, governments want low-priced food. In the name of this objective, they often strive to impose low food prices. But this choice of policy instrument weakens economic incentives, resulting in lower production and higher food prices. The instrument chosen thus produces an effect precisely opposite to that desired. The objective thus cannot be cited as its cause.

In response to problems such as these, policy analysts often invoke other considerations. They treat the failure of particular governmental policies as "mistakes" and call for "more information" or "better training" for decision makers; or they note that governments often have multiple, often conflicting objectives and so treat the failure to maximize one set of objectives as evidence of efforts to optimize a larger, more complex set. Both responses represent efforts to preserve the welfare-maximizing model of policy formation.

The deeper problem is that unless one is prepared to treat a government as a single, unitary actor—that is to treat it as a single decision maker, be it a planner or a dictator—it is impossible to secure from a government a coherent statement of its objectives that possesses even the most limited set of desirable properties. In this area of policy analysis, the Nobel Prize–winning work of Theodore Schultz (1976) should be coupled with that of Kenneth Arrow (1951). Any approach that treats govenments as agencies for maximizing the best interests of society should be regarded as a normative enterprise rather than as an effort at explanation.

POLICY AS A BARGAINING OUTCOME FOR PRIVATE PRESSURE GROUPS

The pluralist view of policy formation provides an alternative to the assumption of welfare maximization. According to this approach, governments do not pursue transcendent social interests; rather, they respond to private demands. Public policy is regarded as an outcome of political competition among organized groups.

In applying this approach to agricultural policy, we can note forces that shape both the demand and supply of pricing policies. On the demand side, what is striking is the intensity of the pressures for low-priced food. One reason is clear: because urban consumers in the less developed countries are poor, they spend much of their incomes on food. In Africa, for example, urban consumers often spend between 50 and 60 percent of their disposable incomes on food. Changes in the price of food therefore make a major impact on the economic well-being of urban dwellers, and they pay close attention to the issue of food prices.

Another reason is that urban consumers possess the capacity forcefully to register their preferences on the body politic. Urban consumers are geographically concentrated and strategically located. Because of their geographic concentration, they can be organized quickly; and because they control such basic facilities as transport, communications, and public services, they can impose deprivations on others. They are, therefore, an influential force in politics.

The demand for low-priced food is powerful, moreover, because it can form the basis for the formation of coalitions. It is not only the worker who cares about the price of food; it is also the employer. Employers care about food prices because food is a wage good; with higher food prices, wages must rise and, all else being equal, profits fall. Governments care about food prices not only because they are employers in their own right but also because as owners of industries and promoters of industrial development programs they seek to protect industrial profits. Indicative of the significance of these interests is that in Africa, at least, the unit that sets agricultural prices often resides not in the ministry of agriculture but in the ministry of finance or commerce.

When urban unrest begins among food consumers, political discontent often rapidly spreads to upper echelons of the polity; it comes to include those whose incomes come from profits, not wages, and those in charge of major bureaucracies. Political regimes that are unable to supply low-cost food are seen as dangerously incompetent and as failing to protect the interests of key elements of the social order. In alliance with the urban masses, influential elites are likely to shift their political loyalties and to replace those in power. Thus it was that protests over food shortages and rising prices formed a critical prelude to the coup that unseated Busia in Ghana and led to the period of political maneuvers and flux that threatened to overthrow the government of Arap Moi in Kenya.

Many of the factors which account for the potency of the demand for low-priced food suggest why it is not countered by equally strong demands by producers. A prime factor is the cost of organization: while low for urban dwellers, it is high for farmers, who are more numerous and widely scattered. Another is the lack of natural allies, particularly at the upper reaches of the polity. While the ties between governments and rural producers are close in some developing areas, they tend not to be in Africa, and this situation may account for the relatively more adverse set of pricing policies which have been adopted by governments in that continent.

Also important are the factors affecting the supply of public policy. One such factor is the quantity of public resources. A lower bound is placed on low-priced policies by the government's capacity to make up for domestic food shortages; foreign exchange constraints, for example, place limits on food imports. Another factor is the character of the nation's political institutions. Where Third World governments are subject to competitive elections, for example, the evidence suggests they are more sensitive to rural interests, for farmers constitute a political majority in many developing countries. Where there are representative assemblies whose members are accountable to constituencies, then, once again, political pressures will arise for the provision of favorable policies for farmers, for farm districts tend to outnumber urban constituencies in most developing areas. These representative institutions—elections and assemblies—help to offset the anti-farmer bias inherent in pure pressure group politics, as discussed above. At least as important as representative institutions, however, are bureaucracies, particularly those that regulate agricultural markets. Once formed, such bureaucracies secure the resources to reward politicians and thereby come to perpetuate the programs they administer. The agencies in charge of markets accumulate political power, and their vested interests in the government's agricultural programs help to perpetuate these policy commitments even in the face of clear evidence that the policies have failed. Clearly, in understanding agricultural policies, we need to know more about these agencies.

The primary strategy of the pluralist approach, then, is to look at the factors that influence the way in which public demands are processed into public policy. From the pluralist viewpoint, the problem of government is the problem of representation. Viewed in this light, the limitations of the approach become obvious, for in agricultural policy a very small subset of relevant interests receives representation. A third perspective is required—one that explains how governments get away with institutionalizing the interests of political minorities. In nations where commonly over 50 percent of the gross domestic product and over 70 percent of the labor force are in agriculture, how can governments remain in power while maintaining agricultural programs which violate the interests of most farmers?

Using Public Policy to Retain Political Power

The third approach views governments as agencies that seek to stay in power. It underscores the features of agricultural programs that let governments organize political followings and disorganize political opposition, particularly in the rural areas. This approach—which for want of a better term we can label a hegemonic approach to policy analysis—also stresses two general points: that economic inefficiency can be politically useful and that government-controlled markets can be employed as instruments for political power. Economically suboptimal programs, in short, can be politically attractive.

An approach that stresses the role of public policy as a means of retaining political power is useful in explaining several otherwise puzzling aspects of agricultural policy. In seeking increased food production, for example, governments often favor project-based policies over price-based policies. We have already seen that price-based policies can be politically costly—they are resisted by urban interests—but what is also important is that price-based policies offer few political benefits to governments attempting to organize support in the rural areas. For the benefits of higher prices can be reaped by both the supporters and the opponents of governments in power. Projects, however, can be targeted; their benefits can be conferred on those who support the government and withheld from political opponents. Project-based programs thus often provide superior resources to those who seek to organize the rural areas.

Another example illustrates the same point. In seeking increased food production, governments appear far more willing to manipulate incentives by manipulating prices in a way that lowers farm costs than in one that increases farm revenues. We have already discussed one reason for this: the high political costs and low political benefits of offering higher prices for agricultural commodities. Another reason is that subsidy programs create resources for organizing. When governments lower input prices, private sources of supply withdraw from the market, levels of demand increase, and there is excess demand at the government prices. Under such circumstances, markets do not clear, and those in charge of the farm input program achieve the capacity to ration. Those in charge can then employ the program to build an organization. They can target the program's benefits to the politically faithful and withhold them from political opponents. They can also use the program to disorganize. In Ghana, for example, a chief means of breaking the resistance by cocoa farmers to the government's low cocoa prices following self-government was the politicization of farm input programs and the distribution of subsidized farm inputs through the politically loyal faction of farm organizations. Combined with outright coercion, the political manipulation of the supply of farm inputs made it in the private interest of farmers to support a government whose agricultural programs, taken as a whole, violated the interests of agriculture.

Market intervention creates the capacity for political organization in other ways. When governments maintain bureaucracies to lower farm prices, for example, they can use regulated markets to build political machines. Those in charge of the market can selectively grant rights of entry into it, and those who reap the economic rewards from access to the artificially cheapened commodities become their clients and supporters.

SUMMARY

I have moved away from a form of analysis which views policy as the result of efforts to maximize the social welfare. I have moved instead to a set of approaches that looks at public policy as a solution to political problems. The general theme of this chapter, then, is that politicians are rational actors, but they are solving problems that do not take a purely economic form. What appear as economic costs may often offer political benefits: noncompetitive rents or inefficient projects, for example, may be politically attractive in that they offer tools for building loyal organizations.

What economists may evaluate as bad policy, then, is not necessarily the result of poor training, obduracy, or other deficiencies on the part of policy makers. Rather, policy makers may simply be solving a different problem than are economists. As policy analysts, it behooves us to represent explicitly the political problem as perceived by the policy maker and to use our analytic techniques to solve it, both in order to offer better explanations of government behavior and to advocate better policy more effectively.

REFERENCES

Arrow, Kenneth. 1951. *Social Choice and Individual Values*. New York: John Wiley.
Bates, Robert H. 1981. *Markets and States in Tropical Africa: The Political Basis of Agricultural Policies*. Berkeley and Los Angeles; University of California Press.
Schultz, T. W. 1976. *Transforming Traditional Agriculture*. New York: Avon Books.

9

Price and Technology Policies

In the field of price policy, as in the field of growth policy, we have to reckon with the prevalence of fundamentalism. Like agricultural/industrial growth fundamentalism, there is price fundamentalism. The rational escape from the former is provided by the notion of balanced sectoral growth; likewise, a rational answer to price fundamentalism would be a balanced view of the role of price policy and nonprice (technology) policy in promoting growth. The need for balance is clearly suggested by the present state of research on farm supply response.

Although supply response is a heavily researched area, there are surprisingly few studies of the response of aggregate farm output to lagged terms of trade *inter alia*. Such studies are obviously crucial for measuring the marginal leverage of terms of trade as a means of stimulating agricultural growth. In recent survey papers of the World Bank tabulating about one hundred single-crop price elasticities of acreage/supply for developing countries, only two aggregate supply elasticities are recorded: for Argentina and the Punjab (India) (Sobhan 1977, table 1 and p. 13; Scandizzo and Bruce 1980, app. 2, table 1). For Europe and the United States, however, as many as nine of the thirty-six elasticities tabulated by D. G. Johnson (1973, 113) are aggregative. In the OECD region, of course, the (short-run) aggregative elasticities are in the same range (0.25 to 0.45) as single-major-crop elasticities.

The Argentinian (short-run) elasticity came out to be 0.21 to 0.35 in different regressions. The Punjab study yielded a significant positive elasticity (0.22) for the prewar period (1907–46) but a *negative* elasticity (−0.06) for the postwar period. The author explicitly noted that in the postwar period output expanded, while the terms of trade *declined;* and suggested that growth was primarily due to technological change (Herdt 1970).

In order to examine the effect of the terms of trade of agriculture on aggregate farm output, two new equations have been estimated for Japan and India using the available terms-of-trade series.[1]

The late RAJ KRISHNA was professor of economics, Delhi School of Economics.

Excerpts from "Some Aspects of Agricultural Growth, Price Policy and Equity," *Food Research Institute Studies in Agricultural Economics, Trade, and Development* 18, no. 3 (1982). Reprinted with minor editorial revisions by permission of the Food Research Institute, Stanford University, and the author.

Japan (1881–1919)

(J.1) Q_t = constant $-132.80\ P_{t-1}$ + 30.52*** T + 0.17 Q_{t-1}
(*t*) (-0.53) (4.77)   (0.97)
(*e*) $[-0.05]$
$R^2 = 0.90$

India (1952/53–1974/75)

(I.1) Q_t = constant + 0.14* P + 0.49*** W_t + 3.08** Z_t + 0.45** Q_{t-1}
(*t*)   (1.49)   (4.68)   (2.11)   (2.44)
(*e*)   [0.18]   [0.54]   [0.68]
$R^2 = 0.92$

Here: Q = farm output, P = terms of trade, T = time trend, W = weather index, and Z = irrigation ratio. The price coefficient is only marginally significant in the Indian equation, and the price elasticity is about 0.2. In the Japanese case the price elasticity is negative, low (-0.05), and statistically zero. At best these equations (as well as the Punjab and Argentinian results cited above) would suggest a one-period aggregate price elasticity of about 0.2 and a long-run price elasticity of about 0.4.[2]

The terms-of-trade movements do seem to have a positive effect on aggregate output. And a favorable price environment must be considered indispensable for agricultural growth. But for a balanced view of the relative role of price and nonprice factors in promoting growth two implications of supply studies need to be noticed.

First, if we consider, for a moment, price policy as the sole instrument for fostering agricultural development, the order of annual terms-of-trade increases required is certainly more than a poor country can manage on macro grounds. Suppose for instance that the one-period price elasticity is 0.2, the "long run" implied by the usual lag coefficient (0.5) is about five years, and a low-income country needs 3 percent annual growth in farm output. Then the long-run elasticity being 0.4, 16 percent growth over five years would require a once-over 40 percent increase in the real terms of trade of agriculture. This is equivalent to a 7 percent annual increase over the period, which will also, of course, spread out the resulting output growth. This order of terms-of-trade increase is hardly a practical proposition, even assuming that a government can fix terms of trade. (Even if the long-run elasticity is assumed to be 0.6, that is, roughly equal to that for most of the individual cash crops, instead of 0.4, the required 27 percent one-shot increase, or a 5 percent annual increase, in the terms of trade would be infeasible.)

The second important fact relevant here is that in most supply regressions the elasticities of supply with respect to shifter variables (proxies for technological change, like the irrigation ratio) exceed the price elasticities. In the Indian function (I.1) above, the irrigation elasticity (0.68) is more than three times the price elasticity (0.18). In postwar Indian wheat functions the irrigation elasticity (0.75 to 0.80) has been found to be 1.5 times the price elasticity (about 0.5)

(Krishna and Raychaudhri 1979; Krishna and Chhibber 1980). And in an early supply-response study of eleven crops in the Punjab (India) (Krishna 1963, table 1b; 1967) it was observed that the irrigation elasticity exceeded the price elasticity in *every* equation where irrigation was included. The irrigation elasticity was in fact 1.5 to 5.5 *times* the price elasticity in the case of various crops (cotton, millets, and wheat). In the Japanese equation (J.1), the time trend is very strong, while the price coefficient is not even significant.[3] These numbers suggest that a unit percentage change in the important shifter (technology) variable will yield much greater growth than a unit percentage price shift.[4]

There are many episodes in the record of advanced countries in which the (lagged) terms of trade facing agriculture have stagnated, and yet farm productivity has grown 2–3 percent a year for considerable periods (see Johnson 1973 for OECD countries; and Kelley and Williamson 1974 and Hayami, Ruttan, and Southworth 1979 for Japan). Again, the explanation lies in technological dynamism.

The price fundamentalist would, of course, argue that technological change itself is induced by relative price movements. This proposition has a core of proven truth (Hayami and Ruttan 1971).[5] But only some aspects of innovation, in the broadest sense, can be shown to be price-induced. The price milieu determines the relative, privately perceived profitability of different techniques made available by completed applied research and hence influences the rates of their adoption (diffusion). But it cannot by itself explain the evolution of basic scientific knowledge and the level and growth of public investment in research, extension, infrastructure, and human capital in different parts of the world. The growth of basic knowledge has some irreducible nonlinearity, discontinuity, and randomness. And governments have been far less rational than peasants in making investment decisions.

The authors of the "induced innovation" hypothesis have documented the discontinuity of basic breakthroughs, such as the acquisition of the theoretical and empirical knowledge of processes of inheritance, the mastery of crossing techniques, and the development of methods of mass seed production, which added up to the "invention of a method of inventing" varieties and reproducing them (ibid., 147–48).

Public-sector investment in farm research in the United States has been shown to be economically rational since the 1920s (ibid., 151). But it would be hard to prove that the initial setting up of the farm research infrastructure in the late nineteenth century was price-induced. In Japan, too, for three hundred years of the Tokugawa period "constraints of feudalism" left a "substantial backlog of unexploited indigenous technology." And even when a rational research system existed, responses to price changes were very slow (ibid., 156, 162).

As for the currently developing countries, much evidence has been presented to demonstrate (1) the absence of any significant research prior to 1950, except in colonial crops; (2) the utter nonoptimality of the level and allocation of public investment in the production of technology; (3) the continuing neglect of research on noncolonial crops, especially on crops like cassava, coconuts, sweet potatoes, groundnuts, and chickpeas; (4) the necessity and inadequacy of research even to "adapt" imported technologies (varieties, machines, and chemicals); and (5) the failure to promote the genetic improvement of farm animals (ibid., 164–66; and Evenson 1981).[6]

If relative price movements alone were sufficient to generate high-yield technology, this technology should have emerged in the areas of recurrent drought-induced food-price inflations (in South Asia and African societies) in the nineteenth and early twentieth centuries. But it did not develop there; it developed elsewhere and is still to be indigenized and widely adopted in these scarcity-ridden societies.

The upshot seems to be that a congenial price regime is a necessary but not a sufficient condition for agricultural growth. An unbiased listing of growth factors would have to be dualistic, including favorable price movements as well as induced and autonomous technological and institutional innovations. Theoretically, one can conceive of three supply curves (responses): the response to a price increase along an unshifted supply curve (lowest); the response along a supply curve including the effect of price-induced innovations, or shifts (next highest); and the total actual supply growth *associated with* a price increase but including price-induced as well as autonomous shifts. It is tempting for the fundamentalist to attribute the whole or none of the supply shifts to price movements. The true supply response to price would most probably include a part but not the whole of the shift. But so far it has not been possible to identify this part because of the difficulty of identifying induced and autonomous innovations and because of deficiencies of data.

Technological change, by definition, increases the total factor productivity of the aggregate conventional input. Even at unchanged output and input prices, therefore, it must increase the return per unit of cost. To see this, one has only to write the return/cost ratio as the product of terms of trade and total factor productivity. Let the return/cost ratio (r) be written as PQ/pF, where Q and F are total output and total input, and P and p are output and input prices. If the terms of trade are defined as $p^* = P/p$ and total factor productivity is defined as $t^* = Q/F$, then $r = p^*t^*$. In growth rates (denoted by a dot, ˙), $\dot{r} = \dot{p}^* + \dot{t}^*$. Thus profitability r can be raised either by improving the terms of trade (p^*) without innovation ($\dot{t}^* = 0$) or by improving productivity (t^*) at unchanged prices ($\dot{p}^* = 0$), or both.

Successful innovation is thus an alternative, as well as a strong supplement, to an increase in the output-input price ratio, as a means of raising the return/cost ratio and thereby stimulating growth.

In this important sense, a good technology policy is equivalent to a good price policy. A balanced policy should of course include both. But there is a case for giving primacy to a technology policy, for, as we have seen, the (partial) elasticity of output with respect to indices of technical change is generally higher than that with respect to relative price indices and would in all probability remain higher even if the price elasticity were measured to include the effect of price-induced innovations. The measured social return to agricultural research and extension is also known to be very high (48–53 percent) (Hayami and Ruttan 1971).[7] It would perhaps be much higher than the return to price policy alone, if the latter could be measured. National policy makers and international development bankers will therefore do well to devote at least as much attention and effort to the development of *technology, infrastructure,* and *human capital* as to the price environment.

Price policy should not, however, be negative. It is essential that the output-input price ratio for products whose output growth is to be accelerated is not allowed to fall, for the growth-inducing effect of innovation would be reduced. The relevant price ratio is of course net of taxes and subsidies. Abstracting here from tax and subsidy policy, two major issues arise with regard to direct product price policy: (1) the determination of the support-price or the government purchase-price level for any product and (2) the maintenance of appropriate interproduct price relatives in the support/purchase prices.

Despite numerous studies showing the undesirable allocative and distributive effects of price support, it is a safe assumption that support policies will continue in the OECD and developing countries alike, though the mixture of motives for these policies differs between these two sets of countries. In the OECD group it includes income support, stabilization, risk reduction, and/or the discouragement of excess production. In developing countries it covers stabilization, risk reduction, encouragement of production growth, food security, and diversification. (All these concepts carry varying meanings in different countries.)

Taking growth promotion to be the major aim in a poor country, there seems to be no alternative to the adoption of "full average cost" (including the imputed value of family resources at market prices) as the basic principle of support-price fixation for any single crop. This principle has been questioned on many theoretical grounds. First, it has been pointed out that the cost of specialized resources is demand-determined and therefore not independent of the product price. Including this cost in the administered price would involve circularity. Every time the product price rose, the "cost" of these resources would rise, and the administered price would have to be raised. Second, it has been noted that in the presence of uncertainty the cost that determines producer decisions is subjective, opportunity cost. And this cannot be measured objectively for the purpose of price fixation. And third, the variance of cost across farmer groups and regions is very high; therefore the choice of groups and regions whose cost is fully covered by the administered price would be arbitrary (Pasour 1980). But there are counter arguments favoring the full-cost principle. It is of course difficult to estimate the theoretically ideal cost as a basis of support, but for administrative purposes some less than ideal measure has to be chosen. Wherever cost data are generated by regular sample surveys the full-cost principle has proved to be administratively workable (as in India). Second, under certain circumstances the cost principle will entail a lower treasury cost than the parity principle. (It is interesting in this connection that the cost principle has been accepted recently in the

U.S. Food and Agriculture Act of 1977 as an alternative to parity.) Third, the coverage of full average cost provides downward price stability or insurance against the risk of a price decline below cost in the sense most meaningful to the farmers, particularly the small farmers in poor countries. Fourth, the cost-variance problem can be handled for practical purposes by ordering the sample deciles according to their average cost and ensuring that the average cost of a major part of output is covered.[8] And finally, the inclusion of the return to specialized (family-supplied) resources at (lagged) market-determined prices can be viewed as a way of providing a surplus for investment (a necessary incentive for growth in poor countries).

Thus, on balance the cost principle can be used as the least unsatisfactory basis for support. While the support price is a guaranteed minimum, entailing "passive" purchases by the government when the market price goes below it, many governments engage in "active" purchases of grain for running a concessional subsidized grain supply system, or building up public-sector stocks. These purchases need to be made in principle at the going market price even if it is much above the support price. If direct redistribution of income is not feasible and the low-income population of a poor country would suffer unacceptable cuts in food consumption at market-clearing prices, the operation of a concessional (subsidized) food supply system, to serve this population, and the associated dual pricing becomes a second-best necessity, though it has been criticized as a distortion. But the subsidy must be financed from the general revenues and not by forcibly reducing the price realized by (and thus taxing) farmers only.

In many countries supporting the prices of many farm products the interproduct price relatives need to be deliberately rationalized. Otherwise farmers switch resources between products (wheat and rice, cereals and pulses, fine and coarse grains, foodgrains and feedgrains, food crops and cash crops, crops and livestock, and so on) in response to "wrong" signals, generating excess demands and excess supplies in different product markets. This particular problem is often due to the practice of fixing support (purchase) prices for different products one by one, with uncoordinated formulae. The problem can be reduced by fixing a coordinated support-price package for all supported crops. The determination of this package—the consistent price set—can be guided by the solution of a farm-sector equation system for related products with exogenously projected or endogenous final demands. Operational research on such models to derive consistent administered price sets deserves priority.[9]

NOTES

1. For this paper, using series from Hayami, Ruttan, and Southworth 1979; Kelley and Williamson 1974; and Thamarajakshi 1977. Of the three terms-of-trade series available for India, the foodgrains terms of trade yielded relatively more significant coefficients. The simple Nerlovian specification is maintained to get t-estimates comparable with earlier ones.

Figures in the parentheses are t-values of regression coefficients. Figures in square brackets are elasticities at the means of variables. Coefficients significant at the 10 percent, 5 percent, and 1 percent levels are marked by (*), (**), and (***), respectively.

2. The possibility of these elasticities' being underestimates is discussed below. But the recent estimates of the aggregate agricultural supply elasticity ranging from 1.25 to 1.66 (Peterson 1979) would seem to be gross overestimates to the economists of developing countries. It is difficult to believe that sample observations from Japan and Pakistan, the United States and Denmark, Chile and Paraguay, Niger and Upper Volta used in the Peterson study come from the same structural universe. It is also difficult to accept the implication that in the typical developing country, say in Africa or South Asia, all that is required for a 3 percent growth of farm output is a 2.5 percent increase in the real price of output. For price increases of this order have occurred frequently and have continued for many years in these regions, while aggregate output has increased much less or stagnated.

3. In the Asian context at least, the irrigation ratio, or more inclusively, the proportion of area under water control, can be shown to be the best single proxy for the supply shifters. In many studies irrigation growth has been found to have been the critical precondition and most important determinant of the growth of area under high-yielding varieties, fertilizer consumption, and cropping intensity (for India see Jha 1980; and Sanderson and Roy 1979). The World Bank has noted that 50–60 percent of the increase in output over the past twenty years has been due to higher yields on previously or newly irrigated areas (World Bank 1982, chap. 4, p. 13).

In the cases of Meiji Japan and India, the treatment of a major part of irrigation growth as an autonomous or non–price-induced process also seems justified. For in Japan irrigation and water control had been extended to almost all paddy land in the Tokugawa period itself. This is the reason for specifying only time trend and the terms of trade as the main variables in the supply function for the Meiji period. And in India, the development of canal-irrigated area, which now accounts for more than 40 percent of total irrigated area, has been a public-sector activity. Tanks and traditional wells have existed since ancient times. But their renovation, and the recent expansion of pump irrigation, has been largely due to growing public outlays on construction, exploration, and outright grants; and the expansion of subsidized credit. About 20 percent of public irrigation investment goes for "minor irrigation," and medium-term credit from state institutions has been growing at 16 percent a year in the seventies (CMIE 1980). Surely some part of irrigation growth, and the associated technical input growth, is attributable to relative price movements. But it cannot be isolated with the available data. If this effect could be measured, the measured long-run price elasticity would be somewhat greater than 0.4.

4. Ideally, we should compare the elasticities of output with respect to the dollar costs, rather than the direct indexes, of price movements and supply shifters. But studies making such comparisons have yet to be made.

5. See also chapter 5 in this volume.—ED.

6. See Evenson 1981.

7. See Schultz, chapter 22 in this volume.—ED.

8. In practice there are three options: to cover the major part (more than 50 percent) of (*a*) output, (*b*) area, or (*c*) holdings, after ordering sample farms by average cost. (In business-management practice "bulk-line" costing sometimes covers as much as 85 percent of output.) The position taken here is that at least the cost of 50 percent of output (in sample farms ordered by average cost) should be covered. This avoids protecting the higher average cost of relatively inefficient farms. In the term "full average cost," *full* refers to the fact that the imputed value of family resources is included in cost, and *average* is applied to the cost on each farm. It is not necessarily the sample average cost and it is not marginal cost.

9. Attention may be drawn here to the recent work of IIASA on sector modeling (see Parikh and Rabar 1981).

REFERENCES

Center for Monitoring Indian Economy (CMIE). 1980. *Basic Statistics Relating to the Indian Economy*. Vol. 2, *States*. Bombay.

——————. 1981. *Basic Statistics Relating to the Indian Economy*. Bombay.

Ensminger, Douglas, ed. 1977. *Food Enough or Starvation for Millions*. New Delhi: Tata McGraw-Hill.

Evenson, R. E. 1981. "Benefits and Obstacles to Appropriate Agricultural Technology." *Annals of the American Academy of Political and Social Sciences* 458 (November).

Hayami, Y., and V. W. Ruttan, 1971. *Agricultural Development: An International Perspective*. Baltimore: Johns Hopkins Press.

Hayami, Y., V. W. Ruttan, and H. M. Southworth, eds. 1979. *Agricultural Growth in Taiwan, Korea and the Philippines*. Honolulu: University Press of Hawaii.

Herdt, Robert A. 1970. "A Disaggregated Approach to Aggregate Supply." *American Journal of Agricultural Economics* 52(4).

Jha, D. 1980. "Fertilizer Use and Its Determinants: A Review with Special Reference to Semi-Arid Tropical India." Hyderabad, India: International Crops Research Institute for the Semi-Arid Tropics. Mimeo.

Johnson, D. G. 1973. *World Agriculture in Disarray*. London: Macmillan.

Kelley, A. C., and J. G. Williamson. 1974. *Lessons from Japanese Development*. Chicago: University of Chicago Press.

Krishna, Raj. 1963. "Farm Supply Response in India-Pakistan: A Case Study of the Punjab Region." *Economic Journal*, 73(291):477–87.

——————. 1967. "Agricultural Price Policy and Economic Development." In *Agricultural Development and Economic Growty,* edited by H. M. Southworth and Bruce F. Johnston. Ithaca: Cornell University Press.

Krishna, Raj, and Ajay Chhibber. 1981. "Policy Modelling of a Dual Grain Market: The Case of Wheat in India." Stanford: Food Research Institute. Mimeo.

Krishna, Raj, and G. S. Raychaudhri. 1979. "Some Aspects of Wheat Price Policy in India." *Indian Economic Review*, n.s., 14(2):101–25.

Parikh, K., and F. Rabar, eds. 1981. *Food for All in a Sustainable World*. Laxenburg, Austria: International Institute for Applied Systems Analysis.

Pasour, E. C. 1980. "Cost of Production: A Defensible Basis for Agricultural Price Supports." *American Journal of Agricultural Economics* 62(2):244–48.

Peterson, W. L. 1979. "International Farm Prices and the Social Cost of Cheap Food Policies," *American Journal of Agricultural Economics* 61(1):12–21.

Sanderson, F. H., and S. Roy. 1979. *Food Trends and Prospects in India*. Washington, D.C.: Brookings Institution.

Scandizzo, P. L., and Colin Bruce. 1980. *Methodologies for Measuring Agricultural Price Intervention Effects*. World Bank Staff Working Paper, no. 394. Washington, D.C.

Sobhan, Iqbal. 1977. "Agricultural Price Policy & Supply Response: A Review of Evidence and an Interpretation for Policy." Washington, D.C.: World Bank.

Thamarajakshi, R. 1977. "Role of Price Incentives in Stimulating Agricultural Production." In Ensminger 1977.

World Bank. 1982. *World Development Report 1982*. Washington, D.C.

10

Food Price Policy and Income Distribution in Low-Income Countries

JOHN W. MELLOR

Change in relative food prices is, in the short run, one of the most important determinants of change in the relative and absolute real income of low-income people. They spend a high proportion of their income on food and depend directly or indirectly on agriculture for a high proportion of their employment and income. In the longer run, food price policy may affect shifts in the supply function for wage goods and thereby influence the extent to which total wage employment and hence income of the laboring classes can be expanded.

Thus, there are important trade-offs and conflicts among various direct short-run influences and indirect long-run effects of price policy on the real incomes of the poor.[1] Similarly, if the aggregate supply of food is fixed, there are direct income trade-offs for low-income families between change in prices and change in employment as market devices for providing the equilibrium consumption level.

Because the interrelationships among price, supply of wage goods, pattern of production, and income distribution are so complex, only a general equilibrium analysis can unequivocably determine the various effects of specific food price policies on income distribution. In contrast, the substantial literature on agricultural price policy is dominated by analysis of the partial relation between relative agricultural prices and production. Further, economists not only have concentrated their analyses of agricultural prices on production relations rather than on distributional effects but have given least attention to those aspects of production—such as marketable surplus, risk-uncertainty relationships, and shift of resources among enterprises of varying labor intensity—which are most rele-

JOHN W. MELLOR is director of the International Food Policy Research Institute, Washington, D.C.

Reprinted from *Economic Development and Cultural Change* 27, no. 1 (1978): 1–26, by permission of the University of Chicago Press. Copyright © 1978 by the University of Chicago. All rights reserved. Published with omissions and minor editorial revisions by permission of the author.

vant to the absolute and relative incomes of low-income consumers and producers.[2]

The purpose of this paper is to delineate the component parts of a general equilibrium analysis relevant to the relation of price policy to income distribution; to present data as to the relation of price change to a variety of those component parts; and to suggest the nature of the various interactions among those parts. The presentation commences with the more standard, relatively simple, and very limited questions of price influence on income distribution and provides the empirical basis for answers to those questions. It then proceeds to successively more complex questions, indicating the bases for judgments on those matters, but falling increasingly short of a definitive position.

DIRECT EFFECTS OF FOODGRAIN PRICE CHANGE ON DISTRIBUTION OF INCOME AMONG CONSUMERS

Change in foodgrain prices causes a larger percentage change in the real incomes of low-income consumers but a larger absolute change in the real incomes of high-income consumers. The absolute effect on the incomes of high-income consumers may have secondary effects on the poor through changes in consumption of other goods and services and a consequent change in employment in their production.

Thus, in India, the top 5 percent in the income distribution spends over two and a half times as much per capita on foodgrains as the lowest two deciles in the income distribution.[3] However, despite its large absolute expenditure, this upper-income class allocates only 15 percent of its total expenditure to foodgrains, compared with 54 percent for the lower-income class.

Table 1 presents data as to the income effect of an increase in foodgrain price. For high-income nations, this effect is normally considered negligible; but it is a major factor in low-income nations, where the proportion of family income spent on foodgrains is much higher. The analysis uses Indian data because of their availability, because foodgrains are dominant in Indian consumption patterns, and because of the low levels of income.

For the data presented, if foodgrain prices rise by 10 percent, the lowest two deciles in expenditure, which initially spend Rs 4.830 per capita per month on foodgrains, experience a real total expenditure decline of Rs 0.494 per capita per month (table 1). The decline in total real expenditure is, in fact, slightly greater than 10 percent of the initial expenditure on foodgrains because the proportion of total income spent on foodgrains increases in successively lower income classes. In this case, assuming all other prices as well as the proportion of income saved as constant and expressed in constant price terms, the new real expenditure will be Rs 8.44 per capita per month, or a decline of 5.5 percent.

In contrast, the top 5 percent in the expenditure distribution experiences a decline in real total expenditure of Rs 1.01, or somewhat over twice as large an

TABLE 1
DECLINE IN EXPENDITURE CONSEQUENT TO THE INCOME EFFECT OF A 10 PERCENT RISE IN THE PRICE OF FOODGRAINS, BY EXPENDITURE CATEGORIES AND CLASSES, INDIA, 1964/65*
(Rs)

Expenditure Category	Bottom Two Deciles	Decile 3	Deciles 4 and 5	Deciles 6, 7, and 8	Decile 9	Lower Half of Decile 10	Upper Half of Decile 10	Mean for All Classes
Initial total per capita monthly expenditure	8.93	13.14	17.8	24.13	30.71	41.89	85.84	24.43
Decline in monthly per capita expenditure due to the income effect of a 10% rise in food-grain price:								
Foodgrains	0.285	0.260	0.208	0.153	0.115	0.068	0.026	0.147
Milk and milk products	0.034	0.074	0.105	0.125	0.196	0.132	0.113	0.124
Meat, eggs, and fish	0.013	0.021	0.026	0.030	0.031	0.032	0.030	0.030
Other foods	0.004	0.037	0.061	0.085	0.104	0.131	0.210	0.085
Tobacco	0.008	0.010	0.011	0.012	0.012	0.012	0.011	0.012
Vanaspati	0.003	0.008	0.013	0.020	0.022	0.022	0.015	0.019
Other oils	0.020	0.033	0.037	0.034	0.030	0.023	0.010	0.034
Sweeteners	0.022	0.034	0.038	0.038	0.034	0.028	0.006	0.037
Cotton textiles	0.043	0.057	0.062	0.062	0.058	0.055	0.042	0.062
Woolen textiles	†	0.002	0.004	0.006	0.003	0.011	0.021	0.006
Other textiles	†	0.001	0.001	0.002	0.003	0.006	0.033	0.002
Footwear	†	0.006	0.007	0.008	0.009	0.008	0.008	0.008
Durables and semidurables	0.004	0.007	0.012	0.017	0.023	0.032	0.067	0.017
Conveyance	0.004	0.010	0.015	0.025	0.034	0.052	0.062	0.024
Consumer services	0.009	0.015	0.021	0.029	0.035	0.044	0.072	0.028
Education	0.005	0.009	0.015	0.025	0.035	0.054	0.135	0.025
Fuel and light	0.040	0.049	0.051	0.051	0.050	0.052	0.036	0.050
House rent	†	0.005	0.009	0.019	0.029	0.046	0.101	0.018
Absolute decline in total expenditure	0.494	0.638	0.696	0.741	0.772	0.808	1.01	0.728
Decline in total expenditure (%)	5.53	4.86	3.91	3.07	2.51	1.93	1.18	2.98

SOURCE: The data source is the National Council of Applied Economic Research, *All-India Consumer Expenditure Survey*, vol. 2 (New Delhi: NCAER, 1967). These data provide expenditure elasticities of foodgrains and milk and milk products consistent with those from the *National Sample Survey (NSS)* of 1963/64 when fitted to the function used here. R^2 for equations estimated from grouped data for different commodities varied between 0.742 and 0.981. The NCAER data provide more detailed breakdown of expenditure than the *NSS*, but for a sample biased toward higher-income groups. The mathematical functional form used for these calculations was: $\log y = a + b/x + c \log x$, where $y = $ per capita monthly expenditure on a commodity in each expenditure class x and $x = $ per capita monthly total expenditure in each expenditure class. For a more complete discussion of the data see B. M. Desai, *Analysis of Consumption Expenditure Patterns in India*. Occasional Paper 54 (Ithaca: Department of Agricultural Economics, Cornell University–USAID Employment and Income Distribution Project, August 1972).

NOTE: Let the demand function for the ith commodity be

$$Q_i = Q_i(P_1, \ldots, P_i, \ldots, P_m, Y), \tag{1}$$

where $P_i = $ price of the ith commodity; $i = 1, \ldots, N$; and $Y = $ total expenditure. The effect of change in the price of ith commodity on the demand for any commodity, say jth, is given by the Slutsky equation as follows:

$$\frac{\partial Q_i}{\partial P_i} = \left(\frac{\partial Q_i}{\partial P_i}\right) \text{ utility } = \text{constant} - Q_i \left(\frac{\partial Q_i}{\partial Y}\right) \text{ prices } = \text{constant}. \tag{2}$$

This can be written as

$$\frac{\partial P_i Q_i}{\partial P_i} = \left(\frac{\partial P_i Q_i}{\partial P_i}\right) \text{ utility } = \text{constant} - Q_i \left(\frac{\partial P_i Q_i}{\partial Y}\right) \text{ prices } = \text{constant}. \tag{3}$$

In terms of elasticity, equation (3) can be written as:

$$E_{ji} = c_{ji} - b_i \eta_j, \tag{4}$$

where $E_{ji} = $ uncompensated price elasticity of demand for jth commodity with respect to the price of ith commodity, $c_{ji} = $ compensated price elasticity of demand for jth commodity with respect to the price of ith commodity, $b_i = $ budget share of ith commodity, and $\eta_j = $ expenditure elasticity of jth commodity. We further know that

$$\sum_{i=1}^{n} c_{ji} = 0 \text{ and } c_{ji} = c_{ij} \tag{5}$$

for all i and j. Thus, if the ith commodity is foodgrains, then the assumption that all the cross price elasticities are zero would imply that

$$c_{ji} = 0 \tag{6}$$

for all j and i whenever either the jth or ith commodity is foodgrains. Substituting equation (6) into equation (4) we get

$$E_{ji} = -b_i \eta_j \tag{7}$$

for all j. Alternatively, the change in consumer expenditure on the jth commodity as a result of a 10 percent change in foodgrain prices is given by the product of the expenditure on the jth commodity, the expenditure elasticity of the jth commodity, the proportion of expenditure on foodgrains, and the proportionate change in foodgrain prices.

*Assumes no change in the percentage saved.

†Negligible.

absolute decline as that of the lower-income class; but at only 1.2 percent of the initial expenditure, there is less than one-quarter as large a percentage decline as that experienced by the lower-income class. The expenditures of the poor on foodgrains are, of course, far more elastic with respect to the income effects of price than are those of the rich. For the bottom two deciles in the income distribution, the elasticity of response of real expenditure (assuming no substitution effect) to change in foodgrain prices is 0.55, compared with 0.12 for the top 5 percent (table 1).

A number of other relationships important to income distribution are illuminated by this exercise. It is significant that in response to a price increase both the absolute and the percentage declines in real expenditure on foodgrains are greater the lower the income class. Thus, for a 10 percent increase in foodgrain prices, the bottom two deciles reduce their real expenditure on foodgrains by 5.9 percent, compared with a reduction of only 0.2 percent by the upper half of the tenth decile. More important, this top income class reduces its absolute real expenditure on foodgrains by only Rs 0.03, compared with over ten times as large an adjustment by the lower-income class (table 1). These data illustrate that in a market economy the bulk of adjustment to reduced supplies of foodgrains is made by low-income consumers.[4] Given the low initial level of foodgrain consumption in the lower-income deciles, the privation imposed on them by rising grain prices is very great. But any measures that seek to insulate the poor from the necessity to adjust to reduced supplies will force the need for adjustment to those whose demand is much more inelastic—thereby causing proportionately much greater, and perhaps explosive, price increases. It is clear from this analysis that it is essentially impossible to protect the poor from the major income effects of a short crop by market measures.

Further adverse consequences for the poor of a change in relative foodgrain prices may follow from the effects of such a change on the consumption of other commodities. As a result of a rise in foodgrain prices, the absolute decline in expenditure for almost all nonfoodgrain commodities is greater for higher-income classes than for lower-income classes, although of course the percentage decline in expenditure is much greater in each case for the lower-income classes. For example, in response to a 10 percent increase in foodgrain prices, the lowest two deciles in the income distribution reduce consumption of milk and milk products by 33 percent, compared with a reduction of 9 percent by the top 5 percent, though the absolute reduction by the higher-income class is over three times as great as for the lower-income class. Overall, while foodgrain consumption declines only 4 percent, consumption of most other commodities declines between 10 percent and 30 percent.

These relationships suggest, first, that an increase in foodgrain prices may lead to substantially reduced consumption by the poor of agricultural commodities of high nutritive value. It is, of course, conceivable, but neither logical nor likely, that the poor would respond to increased foodgrain prices by some substitution of higher-quality foods which, though more expensive, had not increased in price.

Second, the large absolute reduction in consumption by higher-income groups of goods and services other than foodgrains, and particularly of livestock products and vegetables (the production of which is in Asian countries generally highly labor-intensive), reduces employment. To the extent that such reduction in employment reduces incomes and hence demand by the poor, the increase in price of foodgrains will be dampened. This indirect effect of foodgrain price changes of course complicates empirical analysis: the greater the employment effect, the less will be the price increase. But either way the poor pay—in terms of lower real wages as prices rise or in reduced employment caused by the decline in real income of the upper-income classes.

The foregoing partial analysis is based on the calculation of the income effect of a relative price change. The extent to which observed behavior is consistent with it depends on the extent of the substitution effects and, of course, on the extent to which countervailing or reinforcing employment, income, and stocking effects occur. Substitution effects of relative price changes cannot be determined on an a priori basis and empirically cannot be separated from several other influences. However, useful observations can be made as an extension of the preceding analysis.

First, to the extent that foodgrains are an inferior good for the poor, the income effects will be reinforced. In assuming an inferior-good status, it should be remembered nevertheless that the poor have already reduced consumption of other goods to a very low and perhaps biologically minimal level.

Second, to the extent that higher-income groups have positive substitution effects, the income effects will, of course, be reduced by the substitution effects. However, although in the short run higher-income consumers may substitute livestock products, fruits, and vegetables for grain, the aggregate impact is likely to be small—first, because the same factors of weather and demand are likely to raise prices of those commodities also; and second, because in the longer run those commodities will compete with grain for the same production resources. It seems less likely that strong substitution effects would prevail between grain and nonfood commodities.

Finally, it should be remembered that grain is itself not a homogeneous category, so substitution of lower-priced for higher-priced varieties may allow reduced expenditures without a commensurate reduction in quantity, though with a possible reduction in nutritive value. In the short run, the supply of the inferior types of grain will be inelastic, and the search for a cheaper mix of grains will simply reduce the quality-related price disparities rather than mitigate the effects on consumption.

Substitution effects are probably less important in reducing the effect of production changes on price than are storage effects and employment effects. The market is usually insulated to some extent from declines in the current production of foodgrains by the availability of carryover stocks, unless there is a very large change in production or a succession of bad harvests. There is clear evidence that

TABLE 2

DECLINE IN CONSUMER EXPENDITURE IN DIFFERENT INCOME CLASSES AS A RESULT OF A 10 PERCENT DECLINE IN THE SUPPLY OF FOODGRAINS, BY INCOME CLASS, INDIA, 1964/65

	Bottom Two Deciles	Decile 3	Deciles 4 and 5	Deciles 6, 7, and 8	Decile 9	Lower Half of Decile 10	Upper Half of Decile 10	Mean for All Classes
Per capita monthly consumer expenditure	8.93	13.14	17.80	24.13	30.71	41.89	85.84	24.43
Expenditure on:								
Foodgrains	1.909	1.747	1.396	1.025	0.773	0.455	0.166	0.968
Milk and milk products	0.196	0.497	0.700	0.836	0.884	0.888	0.755	0.828
Meat, eggs, and fish	0.085	0.140	0.176	0.201	0.209	0.213	0.202	0.198
Other foods	0.026	0.248	0.408	0.568	0.698	0.876	1.412	0.567
Tobacco	0.051	0.065	0.075	0.077	0.079	0.079	0.070	0.078
Vanaspati	0.020	0.052	0.086	0.134	0.144	0.145	0.100	0.129
Other oils	0.136	0.220	0.247	0.230	0.200	0.152	0.070	0.226
Sweeteners	0.147	0.227	0.256	0.252	0.227	0.190	0.109	0.228
Cotton textiles	0.286	0.383	0.415	0.418	0.400	0.366	0.279	0.413
Woolen textiles	—	0.011	0.026	0.039	0.056	0.075	0.141	0.038
Other textiles	—	0.004	0.005	0.011	0.112	0.043	0.022	0.011
Footwear	—	0.040	0.050	0.054	0.109	0.058	0.050	0.056
Durables and semidurables	0.026	0.050	0.079	0.113	0.157	0.213	0.451	0.116
Conveyance	0.030	0.065	0.104	0.116	0.230	0.351	0.412	0.161
Consumer services	0.060	0.010	0.142	0.193	0.232	0.295	0.479	0.188
Education	0.031	0.060	0.100	0.165	0.237	0.360	0.922	0.163
Fuel and light	0.266	0.326	0.344	0.343	0.333	0.306	0.245	0.336
House rent	—	0.032	0.059	0.128	0.193	0.310	0.679	0.124
Total decline in real income in each class	3.27	4.17	4.67	4.90	5.27	5.38	6.77	4.89
New real expenditure	5.66	8.97	13.13	19.23	25.44	36.51	79.07	19.95
Decline in real expenditure (%)	36.6	31.7	26.7	20.3	17.2	12.8	7.9	20.0

SOURCE: See table 1.

NOTE: The percentage rise in the prices of foodgrains due to a 10 percent decline in supply is calculated, and then the adjustment made in consumption of all commodities due to the rise in the price of foodgrains is shown in this table. (1) The percentage rise in price of foodgrains $= [(dQ/Q) \times 100]/e$, where dQ/Q is a proportionate decline in the foodgrains supply and e is the price elasticity of demand for foodgrains in the mean class. From table 1, the decline in expenditure on foodgrains corresponding to mean class as a result of a 10 percent rise in the price of foodgrains is 0.147, implying a 1.52 percent decline in foodgrains consumption expenditure. Therefore, the percentage rise in the prices of foodgrains $= 10/0.15 = 67$ percent. (2) This 67 percent rise in the price of foodgrains is reflected in the decline in the consumption expenditure on all commodities. See the footnote to table 1 for the basis of calculation of the decline in expenditure on each commodity.

174

farmers build stocks in good years and deplete them in poor years.[5] Thus, in India, the price response to poor crops was much more substantial in 1966/67 than in 1965/66, a much "worse" year; similarly for 1973/74 compared with 1972/73.

As pointed out above, the secondary effects on employment of an increase in foodgrain prices could be as important in depressing the real incomes of the poor as the direct effects of price on consumption.

With these important caveats in mind, table 2 is of interest in suggesting the distributive impact on consumers of a 10 percent decline in the supply of foodgrains, using the elasticities implicit in the preceding analysis and assuming no compensating decline in employment or secondary effects from the effect of the price change on producers' incomes.

In this analysis, the lowest two deciles in the income distribution of consumers suffer a 36.6 percent decline in real income, compared with a decline of 7.9 percent for the top 5 percent in the income distribution. Similarly, the lowest-income deciles experience a 39.5 percent decline in foodgrain consumption, compared with 1.3 percent for the top income group. The large reduction in consumption of nonfoodgrain commodities shows clearly that there would be large secondary effects on employment, greatly reducing the foodgrain price increases.

The foregoing data show one additional relationship between foodgrain prices and low-income consumers. The poor spend a high proportion of increments to income on foodgrains: the bottom two deciles in the income distribution spend 59 percent of increments to income on foodgrain, compared with only 2 percent for the top half of the tenth decile. Thus, the role of price on the supply function for this crucial wage good must enter importantly into a full analysis of the relation between price and income distribution, particularly given the important role of employment in determining the income of lower-income families.

DIRECT EFFECTS OF FOODGRAIN PRICE CHANGE ON DISTRIBUTION OF INCOME AMONG PRODUCERS

The effects of relative price changes on agricultural producers differ from the effects on consumers in two important respects. First, the income effect, assuming production is constant, is in the same, rather than in the opposite, direction as the price change. Second, the largest effects, both relative and absolute, fall on the producers with the largest marketings (and presumably with the higher incomes).

The effect of a price change that occurs independently of change in the volume of domestic production is easier to analyze than the effect of a price change in response to a production change, perhaps induced by variations in the weather. These two somewhat different cases will be discussed in order, followed by analysis of the effects of price change on production.

The Effect on Producers of Change in Relative Prices with Production Constant

The relationships described below refer to effects of price changes on producers when quantity produced stays constant, as could happen if the price changes were due to a foreign food-aid program. It could also happen as a result of commercial trade, although in that case the relationships are more complex because change in imports and exports of foodgrains would presumably be offset by trade in other commodities, with further price and income effects.

The effect of relative change in agricultural prices on producers' incomes depends on (1) the quantity they produce, (2) the quantity of home consumption and hence of marketings, and (3) the quantity of purchased production inputs. The effect of price changes is much greater in both absolute and percentage terms on larger farms than on smaller farms—the larger farms normally produce more, market a higher proportion of their production, and have a higher proportion of output represented by purchased inputs.

Table 3 illustrates these relationships by relating size classes of farms to level of production, home consumption, and marketings. For the smallest farmers, a price increase actually decreases income, because they are net purchasers of foodgrain, presumably paid for largely by working as laborers. It is only in the fourth and fifth deciles and above that a substantial rise in income occurs. In the upper income deciles, the price effect is more nearly proportionate to income, since the bulk of production is marketed—it is actually less than proportionate because of the fixed share of output assumed to be retained for feed, seed, and waste and because the calculation relates to gross value of output rather than to the value of output net of cash production costs.

The absolute increase in income resulting from a 10 percent price increase is about 60 percent larger for the ninth decile than the average for the sixth, seventh, and eighth deciles and over six times larger in the upper half of the tenth decile than the average for the sixth, seventh, and eighth deciles.

Thus, if a foodgrain price increase is seen as a simple transfer of income from consumers to producers, it largely takes place between high-income consumers, who expend the largest absolute amount on food, and high-income producers, who market the largest absolute quantities. In terms of a percentage change in income, the transfer causes the largest percentage decline in the income of low-income consumers and the largest percentage increase in the income of high-income producers.

The Effect on Producers of Concurrent Change in Production and Price

Changes in the relative price of foodgrains more usually occur as a result of changes in domestic output, due to either short-term weather changes or more permanent technological changes, and thus the effects of price changes on producers are usually offset wholly or in part by production changes.

While a production change in response to the weather or a technological change affects producers' incomes in direct proportion to their levels of production, the countervailing price change is more nearly proportional to marketings. Thus, if price increases by the same percentage as production declines, the incomes of all producers decline at least slightly. If the price increase is half as large in percentage terms as the production decline, producers' incomes, of course, decline more precipitously. In both cases, the percentage decline in income is greater for low-income than for high-income farmers. However, if the price increase is larger than the production decline, then farmers in the upper-income classes will experience an increase in income, while the lowest-income farmers may still experience a decline in income.

These relationships are illustrated in table 3, which depicts the effects of a 10 percent production decline combined with price increases of respectively, 5 percent, 10 percent, or 20 percent, giving the effects of alternative assumptions as to the price elasticity of demand. In general, the price change will be counter to the production change, and since demand is inelastic, the change in price will presumably be more than proportionate to the change in production. Given a 10 percent decline in production, a 10 percent increase in price is consistent with unit elasticity; a 20 percent increase in price is consistent with an elasticity of -0.5; and a 5 percent price increase is consistent with an elasticity of -2.0. The elasticity of -0.5 has often been justified on theoretical and empirical grounds.[6] The price rise of only 5 percent is included to illustrate the comparative effects of a price stabilization program.

It should be noted that price stabilization programs destabilize small producers' real incomes and stabilize consumers' incomes and large producers' incomes. Thus, it is significant that the introduction of a less unstable price (row 8 compared with row 12 of table 3) increases the decline in income in years-of-production decline for the third through the fifth deciles in the income distribution. Reduced price instability stabilizes income for the lowest-income farmers because they are net consumers, and for the highest-income producers because they market a high proportion of what they produce.

THE EFFECT OF RELATIVE CHANGES IN AGRICULTURAL PRICES ON AGRICULTURAL PRODUCTION

A slow rate of increase in food production is increasingly recognized as a major limitation to increase of employment and income of low-income families.[7] Without a commensurate increase in the supply of food, growth in paid employment and the consequent rise in demand for wage goods will cause an increase in food prices, the effects of which may substantially neutralize the benefits from increased employment and indeed force a reversal of high-employment policies. Adequate additional supplies of such wage goods can rarely be mobilized through reallocation of existing domestic supplies or through inter-

TABLE 3
CHANGE IN THE GROSS VALUE OF FOODGRAINS CONSEQUENT TO VARIOUS CHANGES IN PRODUCTION AND PRICE, BY RURAL INCOME CLASS, INDIA, 1964/65

	Bottom Two Deciles	Decile 3	Deciles 4 and 5	Deciles 6, 7, and 8	Decile 9	Lower Half of Decile 10	Upper Half of Decile 10
1. Average gross acres sown per reporting holding	0.29	0.98	3.85	8.05	12.57	20.70	45.50
2. Gross value of foodgrains production*	4.06	13.72	53.91	112.72	176.01	289.85	637.11
3. Foodgrain consumption expenditure	4.83	6.84	8.31	9.58	10.45	11.37	12.80
4. Value of foodgrains marketed	-1.38	4.83	37.51	86.23	139.16	235.00	528.74
5. Effect of 10 percent rise in price of foodgrains, with no change in production, on value of foodgrains marketed	-0.14	0.48	3.75	8.62	13.92	23.50	52.87
6. Row 5 as a percentage of gross value of foodgrains production	-3.4	3.5	7.0	7.7	7.9	8.1	8.3
7. Effect of 10 percent decline in production and 5 percent rise in foodgrains' price on value of foodgrains marketed	-0.44	-0.99	-2.93	-5.75	-8.75	-14.05	-30.42
8. Row 7 as a percentage of gross value of foodgrains production	-10.8	-7.2	-5.4	-5.1	-5.0	-4.8	-4.8
9. Effect of 10 percent decline in production and 10 percent rise in foodgrains' price on value of foodgrains marketed	-0.52	-0.80	-1.29	-1.91	-2.54	-3.53	-6.69

10. Row 9 as a percentage of gross value of foodgrain production	-12.8	-5.8	-2.4	-1.7	-1.4	-1.2	-1.1
11. Effect of 10 percent decline in production and 20 percent rise in foodgrains' price on value of foodgrains marketed	-0.70	-0.44	2.01	5.75	9.88	17.52	40.77
12. Row 11 as a percentage of gross value of foodgrain production	-17.2	-3.2	3.7	5.1	5.6	6.0	6.5

SOURCES: Government of India, Cabinet Secretariat, *The National Sample Survey*, 18th Round, February 1963–January 1964, no. 142, tables with notes on consumer expenditure, 1968; and *The National Sample Survey*, 17th Round, September 1961–July 1962, no. 162, tables with notes on some features of land holdings in rural areas, 1969.

NOTE: In this analysis, expenditure on foodgrains is assumed to remain the same irrespective of changes in production and prices of foodgrains. The difference between production and consumption is due to a 15 percent allowance for feed, seed, and waste. For row 1, the cumulative percentage of rural population in various landholding classes was calculated from *National Sample Survey (NSS)* of landholdings for 1961/62. Similarly from *NSS*, 1963/64, data on consumer expenditure for rural households, the cumulative percentage distribution of rural population in various expenditure classes was calculated. The two cumulative distributions were matched to ascertain the approximate correspondence between level of expenditure and landholding. Then the average area cultivated per reporting holding in each consumer expenditure class was obtained. For row 2, the gross output of rice was obtained on the assumption that all the acreage was planted to rice. Hence, it is considered as gross output of foodgrains. Taking the all-India average yield of rice as 1,078 kg per hectare and the price of rice as Rs 1.925 per kilogram as the price of all foodgrains, the gross value of foodgrain production per annum was obtained. Further, assuming that the average farm family size was five, the gross value of foodgrain production per capita per month was obtained. For row 4, the value of foodgrain marketings per capita per month = the gross value of foodgrain production per capita per month − retentions. Retentions = seed + feed + waste + consumption. Seed, feed, and waste is taken to be 15 percent of gross value of output.

*Per capita per month for this and all subsequent categories.

national trade. Thus, policies on employment, agricultural production, and agricultural prices must be closely linked. Change in relative prices plays at most a very limited role in increasing agricultural production in the context of traditional technology. But if used to complement technological change in agriculture, price policy may speed the growth of production significantly. In this context, too, price policy may encourage the adoption of income-increasing innovation by low-income producers through its influence on profitability as well as on risk and uncertainty.[8]

PRICES AND PRODUCTION IN THE CONTEXT OF STATIC TECHNOLOGY

With technology given, an increase in relative agricultural prices increases the supply of agricultural commodities by movement along the production function. Such an increase in production is, by definition, at an increasing real cost in resources and shifts the distribution of income against low-income consumers. Agriculture in low-income countries is commonly operating near the top of the total product curve, with low marginal returns to added inputs, and is, consequently, often a sector of highly inelastic aggregate supply.[9]

The extent to which the income effect of increased wage employment of the poor will be neutralized by increased food prices depends on (1) the incremental budget share allocated to foodgrains by those in wage employment, (2) the elasticity of supply of foodgrains, and (3) the cross-elasticities of demand for foodgrains. Income increases will be nullified by food price increases as the incremental budget share approaches one, the supply elasticity approaches zero, and the cross-elasticity approaches zero. In a low-income country for which the incremental budget share allocated to foodgrains by the laboring classes may be 0.59, the aggregate supply elasticity for basic foodgrains is as low as +0.1, and the cross-elasticity is low, the income increase to the laboring classes from employment may be largely eliminated by the consequent price increases.

The literature dealing with agricultural supply response is much greater with respect to substitutions among individual commodities than with respect to the more complex, but here more relevant, problem of aggregate supply of foodgrains and of agricultural wage goods more generally. What literature there is suggests quite inelastic aggregate supply, on the order of +0.1 to +0.2.[10]

The supply of basic agricultural wage goods is perhaps likely to be most elastic if a substantial proportion of land and other resources is devoted to annual crops consumed either domestically by high-income people or exported. A transfer of acreage may then be effected with little decline in marginal productivity. In such a case, the use of a price increase policy to encourage food-crop production, and the maintenance of high relative prices as a means of implementing that policy, may be successful.

A few countries have at times followed price policies that have depressed agricultural prices substantially relative to international relationships (for example, Thailand), with consequent low levels of input use by international standards and consequent discouragement of production for the market.[11] Particularly if the production functions are essentially linear, except near the bottom and top of the function, rectification of such policies may have dramatic effects on input use and on production.

In the face of inelastic domestic production, the supply of foodgrains may, of course, be augmented by imports, depending on the elasticities of supply and demand for exports to pay for them and on the elasticity of supply of foodgrains for import. However, the coefficients for these variables too may be quite inelastic, particularly for large countries or large aggregates of small countries. As an alternative policy, the marginal redistribution of income effected by fiscal policy is also unlikely to achieve an adequate transfer of food from high-income to low-income classes, because of the highly disparate marginal propensities to consume at the various income levels.

Thus, one may conclude that in the context of static agricultural technology the gains to the poor from expanded employment are likely to be substantially offset by increased prices of food as increased demand exerts its pressure on an inelastic supply. It is these relationships that turn attention to technological change generally and the role of price policy to technological change in agriculture more specifically.

PRICES AND PRODUCTION IN THE CONTEXT OF TECHNOLOGICAL CHANGE

Efficiency-increasing technological change in agriculture allows an increased supply of wage goods without an increase in price.[12] Thus, incomes of low-income people may increase through employment without an offsetting effect of rising wage-good prices. The benefits of scale-neutral technological change will be distributed among producers more nearly in proportion to output than to marketings and, thus, need be less skewed toward larger producers in their benefits than increased prices. Scale-neutral technological change is, of course, directly a product of development of institutions for research, education, input distribution, and so on, and not of policy for price changes. However, increased prices may play an important indirect role in the adoption of new technology. Insofar as that is the case, there may be a trade-off between short-run losses by the poor from higher agricultural prices and long-run gains from a shift of the agricultural production function, a larger supply of wage goods with favorable employment implications, and eventually lower agricultural prices as equilibrium is reached in agriculture with lower costs of production.

Despite its importance to both growth and income distribution, there is little empirical evidence as to the relation between agricultural prices and the pace of technological change. Of course, increased relative output prices increase further the disequilibrium induced by the lower cost of new technology, thereby accelerating output increase. That influence is thought in agriculture to be particularly strengthened by effects that reduce the incidence of uncertainty. Higher prices reduce the probability of loss from an innovation by increasing expected average profitability. More stable prices may also reduce uncertainty for some farmers.

The relation between price policy and variance in agricultural incomes is highly complex. High variance in net income, at the very least, has an unfavorable effect on income distribution by skewing the pattern of adoption toward already higher-income farmers—reflecting their greater risk-bearing capacity.[13]

However, in agriculture, yield variation due to weather is generally a more important source of variance than price. This is particularly true when a large proportion of output is retained for domestic consumption. And the extent to which price stabilization even increases the stability of producers' incomes is, in practice, dependent on several factors, important among which is the extent to which movements in price are inversely related to movements in production. At the micro level, that depends on the extent to which production changes in a particular area are similar to changes in national aggregates and on the degree of national integration of markets. Thus, Schluter, in a simulation of the effect of changes in price variance, using actual farm data from the Surat District, India, found that in four out of six situations price stabilization actually increased the coefficient of variation of revenue.[14]

Finally, in selecting a price policy to facilitate efficiency-increasing technological change in agriculture, it must be remembered that increased profitability and reduced variance in income may be achieved by appropriate investment in such items as research, education, and irrigation—quite possibly on a more cost-effective basis than through price policy and with lesser short-run deleterious effects on income distribution.

The new high-yielding crop varieties are noted for their generally low elasticity of employment with respect to output. Thus, the primary significance for employment of the new foodgrain technologies lies in their potential to relax the wage goods' constraint and to generate increased farm incomes, which may promote a secondary increase in employment.[15] In this section, three further aspects of the relation between agricultural prices and employment are explored: (*a*) the effect of relative agricultural prices on the labor intensity of the agricultural output mix; (*b*) the effect of relative agricultural input prices on the choice of technique in agricultural production; and (*c*) the effect of relative agricultural prices on the level and structure of nonagricultural employment.

PRICES AND THE AGRICULTURAL OUTPUT MIX

Choice of cropping pattern is one of the most important factors influencing labor requirements in agriculture, and, thus, because of the relative magnitude of the agricultural sector, it is one of the most important determinants of overall employment in a low-income country. B. M. Desai, in a detailed analysis of farm-management data from the Surat District, India, calculates that 90 percent of the differences in income per acre among farms is due to differences in cropping pattern, which affect income largely through differences in labor input, rather than to differences in the intensity of input use in specific crops.[16] Desai and Schluter show from farm management data for the Surat District, India, that human labor use is 60 and 37 days per acre on groundnuts and cotton, respectively.[17] A transfer of one-quarter of the cotton acreage to groundnuts would add over 2.1 million man-days of employment per year in the Surat District. That is about eight times as much employment to be added in that district as by the special "crash scheme for rural employment" intended as a major source of rural employment. In this case, not only do the two crops compete for the same set of nonlabor resources and have substantial differences in labor requirements, but a portion of the domestic supplies of each commodity is also imported. Thus, the relative domestic prices, production, and aggregate employment can be influenced by import policy.

Despite the importance of agricultural output mix on employment and the substantial literature showing significant elasticities of output substitution at the farm level, there has been little policy analysis of this issue. Needed study not only would examine employment and elasticities of substitution among crops but, equally important, would analyze potentials to shift trade policy and domestic demand toward more labor-intensive commodities. Most simply, export and import policy may be used marginally to facilitate a shift in relative domestic prices and production toward more labor-intensive commodities. Temperate-zone nations have done this particularly in the case of sugar—historically a labor-intensive crop. India, in the earlier example, could shift the product mix from cotton toward groundnuts by importing more cotton and less vegetable oil, with a consequent increase in employment. Export subsidies on vegetables could have a similar effect. Such policies are particularly attractive if they compensate for the effects of the labor market and other imperfections, causing suboptimal utilization of labor on small farms.

Domestic demand structure may also be influenced toward more labor-intensive commodities through tax and subsidy schemes. Related and perhaps more important, demands for relatively labor-intensive agricultural commodities tend to be relatively elastic with respect to income, providing a significant opportunity for rising incomes to favor rising employment. Unfortunately, there is a tendency, because of the bulky, perishable nature of many such commodities, for marketing bottlenecks to result in restraint of consumption through price increases that are not transmitted to the farm level. Institutional credit gaps at the farm level for commodities with generally high working-capital requirements may also inhibit the desired expansion of demand. Thus, as for other aspects of agricultural price policy, programs must go beyond the price policies and indicators to substantive aspects of marketing and production. In this context, an employment-oriented price policy should (*a*) recognize the employment implications of alternative price relationships among agricultural commodities, (*b*) see that overt price policies do not discriminate against the relatively labor-intensive commodities, and (c) use movements in market-determined prices as indicators of marketing and production bottlenecks that may be dealt with through other policies.

RELATIVE INPUT PRICES

The dramatic displacement of labor often occasioned by farm mechanization and its frequent association with effective subsidization of farm machinery prices relative to labor has prompted a substantial literature.[18] Given that extensive treatment, attention is here brought to two features that make the statement of effective policy difficult in this area.

First, although inappropriate pricing policy is frequently deplored, there is still controversy as to whether market prices of labor adequately reflect the equivalent of perfect market supply prices.[19] It is thus difficult to know whether or not compensating taxes on machinery may be in order.

Second, and related to the first, considerable controversy exists as to the precise nature of the labor supply, particularly given the complexities of seasonal cycles in both demand and supply of labor.[20] Thus, Donovan shows with a linear programming analysis based on farm-management data for an area in Mysore, India, that the introduction of hand tractors allows a substantial increase in total employment.[21] It does so by shortening land preparation time sufficiently to allow a not otherwise possible second crop. It follows that at such time as mechanization is appropriate for breaking labor bottlenecks it may be as appropriate a recipient of price subsidy and other facilitative measures, particularly for small farmers, as any other element of production and labor-absorbing technological change. The full complexities of policy in this area are underlined by Donovan's analytic position that seasonal labor migration, which of course brings other problems, can meet the labor bottleneck as effectively as mechanization.

Finally, it should be noted that fertilizer and other chemical inputs also substitute for labor, and, hence, subsidization of their prices will reduce employment unless ancillary policies ensure an aggregate increase in output, with a set of direct and indirect employment effects as elaborated in preceding sections.

AGRICULTURAL PRICES AND NONAGRICULTURAL EMPLOYMENT

The basic relationships between agricultural price policy, technological change in agriculture, supply of wage goods, and employment were discussed above. In that argument, relatively low agricultural prices are seen as desirable in the longer run not only to bring about an immediate raising of the real incomes of the poor but also to stimulate longer-term employment growth—as long as technological change effects a continuous upward shift of the supply curve for agricultural commodities.

Relative agricultural prices are often depressed by import and foreign-exchange pricing policies specifically intended to encourage industrial growth. Clearly, such policies may directly encourage industrial employment while in the longer run discouraging production of the basic agricultural wage goods, with a consequent deleterious effect on employment potentials. Whether such policy is desirable hinges on an argument for industry essentially analogous to that for relatively higher agricultural prices intended to encourage accelerated application of efficiency-increasing technological change in agriculture. Policies that boost the domestic production of industrial consumer goods that are relatively efficient and labor-intensive, and eventually effect a reduction in the price of these goods, need have only short-run adverse effects on relative agricultural prices and agricultural production. As they expand, they generate increased demand for agricultural wage goods from increased industrial employment, tending to raise relative agricultural prices.

However, the effects may be quite different when import restrictions are introduced to protect capital-intensive, low-efficiency industrial processes. Protection of this kind generates little increase in employment or in demand for food, and so the depression of relative agricultural prices continues, potentially reducing production in the traditional agricultural sector and weakening incentives for technological change in agriculture.[22] Such an effect may continue indefinitely if those industries remain inefficient relative to foreign sources of supply.

CONCLUSION

The data presented demonstrate dramatically that the income effect on low-income people of food price changes is large and that the bulk of adjustment to reduced food supplies is made by low-income people. Conversely, of course, changes in the income of low-income people are reflected to a large degree as change in the demand for food.

Change in food prices causes a larger percentage change in the real incomes of low-income consumers but a larger absolute change in the real incomes of high-income consumers. Thus, there is potential for substantial secondary effects on employment and incomes of the poor arising from the primary effects on the consumption pattern of the more well-off.

The effects of relative price changes on agricultural producers differ from the effects on consumers in two important respects. First, the income effect, assuming production is constant, is in the same rather than in the opposite direction as the price change. Second, the largest effects, both relative and absolute, fall on the producers with the largest marketings (and presumably with the higher income).

Demand for food may be effectively brought into balance with deficit supply through reduction in employment rather than an increase in price. High-income consumers may prefer policy measures of that type. Similarly, if the increased demand for food accompanying the increased employment of low-income people is not met by an increased food supply, the employment-based increase in real income will be substantially reduced by price increases. Thus, an employment program, or an income-transfer program for the poor, will be inefficient in assisting them unless provision is made for an enlarged supply of basic food commodities. It follows that in designing income and employment programs attention needs to be paid to the material balances and not just the fiscal balances. To state the position clearly, barring a strict rationing system, increased agricultural production may be a necessary precondition for improving the incomes of the poor. It follows, of course, that a program of foreign food aid and, to a lesser extent, commercial imports can be effective in facilitating an employment increase, particularly in the short run.

The importance of an increased supply of food to the effectiveness of employment programs in raising the income of low-income families suggests the appropriate consideration in the analysis of production effects of agricultural price policy. The preponderance of the evidence shows that in the context of traditional technology aggregate food supply will normally be highly inelastic, and hence an upward shift in demand for food will result in magnified upward movements in food prices, with the consequent distribution effects shown above. However, in the context of technological change, higher prices to producers may counterbalance the added risk and uncertainty associated with such change. If experience with new technologies itself reduces risk and uncertainty, higher prices may induce a shift to a new technology, which will not be reversed if prices later decline. Of course, domestic policy may so depress relative agricultural output prices as to virtually eliminate use of certain key inputs, such as fertilizer, for market production, and in that case supply may be highly responsive to even modest changes in prices. Such a situation is often the result of government monopoly pricing. Changes in policy will be most effective if such policy has held production close to the subsistence level. The effect will be further enhanced if there is close interaction of such input use and new technology.

Research and education that dramatically reduce production costs may serve as an alternative to higher prices to induce innovation. Such measures do not have such deleterious effects on low-income consumers as higher prices, can also induce more permanent increases in productivity, and may have a less skewed distribution of net benefits to producers. Thus, price policy may be viewed as a competitor to other measures as well as a complement.

Relative agricultural prices affect employment through the labor intensity of the agricultural output mix, the labor intensity of agricultural technology, and the level and structure of nonagricultural employment. In each case, the importance of interactions of agricultural price policy with other policy measures is important.

Finally, the extent to which a change in terms of trade between agriculture and industry benefits the poor depends very much on the extent of the structural adjustments it encourages. A turn against industry will redress itself if it induces accelerated technological change in agriculture and consequent linkage effects with industry through relaxed wage-goods constraint and increased consumer demand. Conversely, a turn against agriculture will redress itself if it encourages accelerated industrial employment growth, consequent greater demand for agricultural wage goods, and increased efficiency of industrial production. A lack of the conditions for technological change in agriculture and a lack of the conditions for employment growth in industry will cause either of the respective price policies to fail.

NOTES

I am grateful to Shakuntala Desai for her assistance in developing the data and references; to Uma Lele, S. D. Tendulkar, Mohinder Mudahar, C. Ranade, B. M. Desai, and G. Doraswamy for a careful reading and set of comments; and to an anonymous reviewer for most helpful specific as well as general comments.

1. See Timmer, chapter 12 in this volume.—ED.
2. The complexity of the issues and the weight of analysis toward narrow short-run production considerations is reflected in the differences and controversy in the following: M. L. Dantwala, "Incentives and Disincentives in Indian Agriculture," *Indian Journal of Agricultural Economics* 22 (April–June 1967): 1–25; V. M. Dandekar, "Agricultural Price Policy," *Economic and Political Weekly* 3 (16 March 1968): 454–59; John W. Mellor, "The Functions of Agricultural Prices in Economic Development," *Indian Journal of Agricultural Economics* 23 (January–March 1968): 23–37; idem, "Agricultural Price Policy in the Context of Economic Development," *American Journal of Agricultural Economics* 51 (December 1969): 1413–20; Uma J. Lele, "Agricultural Price Policy," *Economic and Political Weekly* 4 (30 August 1969): 1413–19; idem, *Food Grain Marketing in India* (Ithaca: Cornell University Press, 1971); idem, "Considerations Related to Optimum Pricing and Marketing Strategies in Rural Development" (Paper presented at the Sixteenth International Conference of Agricultural Economists, Nairobi, Kenya, 26 July–4 August 1976); Raj Krishna, "Agricultural Price Policy and Economic Development," in *Agricultural Development and Economic Growth*, ed. Herman H. Southworth and Bruce F. Johnston (Ithaca: Cornell University Press, 1968); Theodore W. Schultz, *Transforming Traditional Agriculture*, Studies in Comparative Economics, no. 3 (New Haven: Yale University Press, 1964); E. S. Mason, *Economic Development in India and Pakistan* (Cambridge: Center for International Affairs, Harvard University, 1966). For an effort to look directly at the effects of agricultural price changes on income of various socioeconomic classes see Roberto Echeverria, *The Effect of Agricultural Price Policy on Intersectoral Income Transfers*, Occasional Paper 30 (Ithaca: Department of Agricultural Economics, Cornell University–USAID Employment and Income Distribution Project, June 1970).
3. In India foodgrains represent a major portion of total expenditure and exhibit sharply different marginal propensities to consume across income classes. The same analysis is relevant to countries with higher incomes than India if the subset of food items is defined sufficiently more broadly than foodgrains as to maintain these two characteristics.
4. These calculations in effect assume equating of total expenditure and total income. If the higher-income classes reduce savings, or the lower-income classes increase dissaving, in response to higher foodgrain prices, then the expenditures on various categories of goods will be even less responsive to price. If, as is usually assumed to be the case, the marginal propensity to save is higher for high-income than for low-income classes, then of course the proportion of the total adjustment

that must be made by the lower-income classes is even greater. Similarly, the greater the extent to which foodgrain expenditure of higher-income consumers is for relatively more demand-elastic services associated with the foodgrain, the more this conclusion will be reinforced.

5. For an analysis of this point and estimates of magnitudes see John W. Mellor and Ashok Dar, "Determinants and Development Implications of Foodgrains Prices, India, 1949–50 to 1963–64," *American Journal of Agricultural Economics* 50 (November 1968): 962–74.

6. See, for example, L. M. Goreux, *Demand Analysis for Agricultural Products,* Agricultural Planning Study, no. 3 (Rome: FAO, 1964); and Mellor and Dar, "Determinants and Development Implications."

7. For a full exposition of these relations see John W. Mellor, *The New Economics of Growth: A Strategy for India and the Developing World* (Ithaca: Cornell University Press, 1976). For a more theoretical presentation see Uma J. Lele and John W. Mellor, *Technological Change and Distributive Bias in a Dual Economy,* Occasional Paper 43 (Ithaca: Department of Agricultural Economics, Cornell University–USAID Employment and Income Distribution Project, June 1971). For a briefer, more policy-oriented statement see idem, "Jobs, Poverty and the 'Green Revolution,'" *International Affairs* 48 (January 1972): 20–32.

8. See also Krishna, chapter 9 in this volume.—ED.

9. For a more complete discussion see John W. Mellor, *Economics of Agricultural Development* (Ithaca: Cornell University Press, 1966), chap. 11.

10. For an analysis of aggregate supply elasticities see Robert Herdt, "A Disaggregate Approach to Aggregate Supply," *American Journal of Agricultural Economics* 52 (November 1970): 512–20; Howard Barnum, "A Model of the Market for Foodgrains in India, 1948–64," Technical Report 23 (Berkeley: Project for the Evaluation and Optimization of Economic Growth, Institute of International Studies, University of California, 1970); Krishna, "Agricultural Price Policy"; and Mellor, *Economics of Agricultural Development,* chap. 11.

11. See Jere R. Behrman, *Supply Response in Underdeveloped Agriculture* (Amsterdam: North-Holland Publishing Co., 1968).

12. For a wide range of examples see John W. Mellor and Uma J. Lele, "Growth Linkages of the New Foodgrains Technologies," *Indian Journal of Agricultural Economics* 28, no. 1 (1973): 35–55.

13. Michael G. G. Schluter, *Interaction of Credit and Uncertainty in Determining Resource Allocation and Incomes on Small Farms, Surat District, India,* Occasional Paper 68 (Ithaca: Department of Agricultural Economics, Cornell University–USAID Employment and Income Distribution Project, February 1974).

14. The data were for rice and cotton (for each, fertilized and unfertilized), sorghum, and groundnuts. For 1962–72 the coefficient of variation of revenue (price *x* yield) was reduced slightly with both prices fixed at the mean and prices fixed at 50 percent of the mean for sorghum and groundnuts; the coefficient of variation of revenue was increased by a much larger margin in the other four cases (Schluter, *Interaction of Credit and Uncertainty*).

15. Mellor and Lele, "Growth Linkages."

16. B. M. Desai, *Relationship of Consumption and Production in Changing Agriculture: A Study in Surat District, India,* Occasional Paper 80 (Ithaca: Department of Agricultural Economics, Cornell University–USAID Technological Change in Agriculture Project, February 1975).

17. G. M. Desai and Michael G. G. Schluter, "Generating Employment in Rural Areas," in *Seminar on Rural Development for the Weaker Sections* (Bombay: Indian Society of Agricultural Economics, May 1974), 143–52; and Mellor, *New Economics of Growth,* 86.

18. H. Rao, "Farm Mechanisation in a Labour Abundant Economy," *Economic and Political Weekly* 7 (February 1972): 393–400. [See also chapter 26 in this volume.—ED.]

19. See, for example, the review and analysis in Mellor, *New Economics of Growth,* chap. 4.

20. Ibid.

21. Graeme W. Donovan, *Employment Generation in Agriculture: A Study in Mandya District, S. India,* Occasional Paper 71 (Ithaca: Department of Agricultural Economics, Cornell University–USAID Employment and Income Distribution Project, June 1974).

22. For an analysis of such an effect in the Indian context see Mellor, *New Economics of Growth,* chap. 7.

11

Food, Economics, and Entitlements

AMARTYA SEN

ECONOMICS AND THE ACQUIREMENT PROBLEM

What may be called "instant economics" has always appealed to the quick-witted layman impatient with the slow-moving economist. This is particularly so in the field of hunger and food policy. Of course, the need for speed is genuinely important in matters of food, and the impatience is, thus, easy to understand. But instant economics is also highly deceptive, and especially dangerous in this field. Millions of lives depend on the adequacy of the policy response to the terrible problems of hunger and starvation in the modern world. Past mistakes of policy have been responsible for the death of many millions of people and the suffering of hundreds of millions, and this is not a subject in which short-cuts in economic reasoning can be taken to be fairly costless.

One common feature of a good deal of instant economics related to food and hunger is impatience with investigating the precise mechanisms for acquiring food that people have to use. People establish command over food in many different ways. For example, while a peasant owning his land and the product of his labor simply owns the food produced, a wage laborer paid in cash has to convert that wage into a bundle of goods, including food, through exchange. The peasant does, as it were, an exchange with "nature," putting in labor, etc., and getting back the product, viz., food. The wage laborer does repeated exchanges with others in the society—first, his labor power for a wage and then the wage for a collection of commodities, including food. We cannot begin to understand the precise influences that make it possible or not possible to acquire enough food, without examining the conditions of these exchanges and the forces that govern them. The same

AMARTYA SEN is Lamont University Professor, Harvard University.

This chapter represents a shortened version of the fourth Elmhirst Lecture given at the triennial meeting of the International Association of Agricultural Economists, Malaga, Spain, 26 August 1985. Reprinted from *Lloyd's Bank Review*, no. 160 (1986):1–20. Copyright © The International Association of Agricultural Economists, 1986, and reprinted by permission of Gower Publishing Company Ltd., and Gower Publishing Company. Published with minor omissions by permission of the author.

applies to other methods of acquiring food, for example, through sharecropping and getting a part of the produce, through running a business and making a profit, through selling services and earning an income, and so on. I shall call the problem of establishing command over commodities, in this case food, the "acquirement problem." It is easy to establish that the acquirement problem is really central to questions of hunger and starvation in the modern world.

The acquirement problem is often neglected not only by non-economists, but also by many economists, including some great ones. For example, Malthus in his famous *Essay on the Principle of Population as It Affects the Further Improvement of Society* (1798) leaves the acquirement problem largely unaddressed, though in his less known pamphlet *An Investigation of the Cause of the Present High Price of Provisions* (1800), which deals with more short-run questions, Malthus is in fact deeply concerned precisely with the nitty-gritty of this problem.[1] The result of this neglect in the former work is not without practical consequence, since the popularity of the Malthusian approach to population and food, and of the particular metric of food output per head extensively used in the *Essay on Population,* has tended to give that metric undue prominence in policy discussions across the world.

Malthusian pessimism, based on the expectation of falling food output per head, has not been vindicated by history. Oddly enough, what can be called "Malthusian optimism," that is, *not* being worried about the food problem so long as food output grows as fast as—or faster than—population, has often contributed substantially to delaying policy response to growing hunger (against a background of stationary or rising food output per head). This is a serious enough problem in the case of intensification of regular but non-extreme hunger (without starvation deaths but causing greater proneness to morbidity and mortality), and it can be quite disastrous in the context of a famine that develops without a decline in food output per head, with the misguided focus leading to a hopelessly delayed response of public policy. While Malthus's own writings are by no means unique in focusing attention on the extremely misleading variable of food output per head, "Malthusian optimism," in general, has been indirectly involved in millions of deaths which have resulted from inaction and misdirection of public policy.[2] While fully acknowledging the great contribution that Malthus has made in highlighting the importance of population policy, this negative feature of his work, related to his own bit of instant economics, must also be recognized.

The neglect of the acquirement issue has far-reaching consequences. For many years rational discussion of the food problems of the modern world was distracted by undue concentration on the comparative trends of population growth and the expansion of food output, with shrill warnings of danger coming from very respectable quarters.[3] The fear of population outrunning food output on a global scale has certainly not been realized, and world food output per head has steadily risen.[4] This has, however, gone hand in hand with intensification of hunger in some parts of the world. In many—though not all—of the affected countries, food output per head has in fact fallen, and the anxiety about these countries has often been anchored to the statistics of food output per head, with Malthusian worries translated from the global to the regional or country level. But a causal analysis of the persistence and intensification of hunger and of the development of famines does, in fact, call for something more than attention being paid simply to the statistics of food output per head.

I shall have more to say on the policy questions presently, but before that I would like to discuss a bit further the nature and implications of the acquirement problem. I shall also discuss some arguments that relate to studying food and hunger in terms of what in my book *Poverty and Famines*[5] was called the "entitlement approach."[6] That approach has been extensively discussed, examined, criticized, applied as well as extended, and I have learned a lot from these contributions.[7] But the approach has also been occasionally misinterpreted, and, given the importance of the subject of food policy and hunger, I shall permit myself the self-indulgence of commenting—*inter alia*—on a few of the points that have been made in response to my earlier analysis.

FAMINES AND ENTITLEMENTS

The entitlement approach provides a particular focus for the analysis of famines. It does not specify one particular causation of famine—only the general one that a famine reflects widespread failure of entitlements on the part of substantial sections of the population. Such failure can arise from many different causes.

The entitlement of a person stands for the set of different alternative commodity bundles that the person can acquire through the use of the various legal channels of acquirement open to someone in his position. In a private ownership market economy, the entitlement set of a person is determined by his original bundle of ownership (what is called his "endowment") and the various alternative bundles he can acquire starting respectively from each initial endowment, through the use of trade and production (what is called his "exchange entitlement mapping"). This is not the occasion to go into the formal characterizations of endowments, exchange entitlement mappings, entitlement sets, etc., which were discussed in *Poverty and Famines*.

A person has to starve if his entitlement set does not include any commodity bundle with enough food. A person is reduced to starvation if some change, either in his endowment (e.g., alienation of land, or loss of labor power due to ill health) or in his exchange entitlement mapping (e.g., fall in wages, rise in food prices, loss of employment, drop in the price of the goods he produces and sells), makes it no longer possible for him to acquire any commodity bundle with enough food. I have argued that famines can be usefully analyzed in terms of failures of entitlement relations.

The advantages of the entitlement approach over more traditional analysis in terms of food availability per head were illustrated with case studies of a number of famines, for example, the Bengal famine of 1943, the Ethiopian famines of 1973 and 1974, the Bangladesh famine of 1974, and the Sahel famines in the early seventies.[8] In some of these famines food availability per head had gone down (e.g., in the Sahel famines); in others there was no significant decline—even a little increase (e.g., in the Bengal famine of 1943, the Ethiopian famine of 1973, the Bangladesh famine of 1974). That famines can occur even without any decline in food output or availability per head makes that metric particularly deceptive. Since food availability is indeed the most commonly studied variable, this is a source of some policy confusion. It also makes "Malthusian optimism" a serious route to disastrous inaction. But the point of entitlement analysis is not only to dispute the focus on food availability, but more positively also to provide a general approach for understanding and investigating famines through focusing on variations in endowments and exchange entitlement mappings.

Famine can be caused by various different types of influences, and the common predicament of mass starvation does not imply any one common fundamental cause. Droughts, floods, general inflationary pressure, sharp recessionary loss of employment, and so on, can all in their own way deprive large sections of the population of entitlement to adequate food. A decline in food output or availability can, of course, be one of the major influences on the development of a famine, but even when that is the case (indeed even when food availability decline is the primary proximate antecedent), a serious study of the causal mechanism leading to the famine and the precise form it takes will require us to go into the behavior of the determinants of the entitlements of the different sections of the population.

In *Poverty and Famines,* two broad types of famines were distinguished from each other, viz. boom famines and slump famines. A famine can, of course, occur in a situation of general decline in economic activity (as happened, for example, in the Wollo province of Ethiopia in 1973, due to a severe drought). But it can also occur in overall boom conditions (as happened, for example, in the Bengal famine of 1943, with a massive expansion of economic activity related to war efforts). If economic expansion is particularly favorable to a large section of the population (in the case of the Bengal famine, primarily the urban population, including that of Calcutta), but does not draw into the process another large section (in the Bengal famine, much of the rural laboring classes), then that uneven expansion can actually make the latter group lose out in the battle for commanding food. In the food battle the devil takes the hindmost, and even a boom condition can lead to some groups losing their command over food because of the worsening of their *relative* position vis-à-vis the groups favored by the boom.

THE ENTITLEMENT APPROACH AND ECONOMIC TRADITIONS

It is important to emphasize that the entitlement approach is consistent with many different *detailed theories* of the actual causation of a famine. While the approach identifies certain crucial variables, different theories of the determination of the values of these variables may all be consistent with the general entitlement approach. For example, the entitlement approach does not specify any particular theory of price determination, but relative prices are quite crucial to the entitlements of various occupation groups. The entitlement approach by itself does not provide—nor is it intended to provide—a detailed explanation of any famine, and such an explanation would require supplementation by more specific theories of movements of prices, wages, employment, etc., causing particular shifts in the entitlements of different occupation groups.[9]

What the entitlement approach does is to take up the acquirement problem seriously. Rather than arbitrarily making some implicit assumption about distribution (such as equal division of the available food, or some fixed pattern of inequality in that division), it analyzes acquirement in terms of entitlements, which in a private ownership economy is largely a matter of ownership and exchange (including, of course, production, i.e., exchange with nature). I would claim that this is not in any way a departure from the old traditions of economics. It is, rather, a reassertion of the continuing concern of economics with the mechanism of acquiring commodities. If I had the courage and confidence that Gary Becker shows in his distinguished work in calling his own approach "*the* economic approach,"[10] I would have called the entitlement approach by the same bold name. While the price of timidity is to shy away from assertive naming, I would nevertheless claim that economic traditions stretching back centuries do, in fact, direct our attention to entitlements in analyzing problems of wealth, proverty, deprivation, and hunger.

This is clear enough in Marx's case,[11] but the point is often made that Adam Smith was a great believer in the simple theory of food availability decline in explaining all famines and that he would have thus had little patience for discussion of entitlements and their determinants. Indeed, it is true that in his often-quoted "Digression Concerning the Corn Trade and Corn Laws" in Book IV of the *Wealth of Nations,* Adam Smith did remark that "a dearth never has arisen from any combination among the inland dealers in corn, nor from any other cause but a real scarcity, occasioned sometimes, perhaps, and in some particular places, by the waste of war, but in by far the greatest number of cases, by the fault of the season."[12] However, in understanding the point that Adam Smith is making here, it is important to recognize that he is primarily denying that traders could cause famine through collusion, and he is disputing the view that famines often follow from artificial shortages created by traders, and asserting the importance of what he calls "a real scarcity." I shall have the occasion to take up this aspect of Smith's observation presently when I discuss the issue of anti-famine policy.

We have to look elsewhere in the *Wealth of Nations* to see how acutely concerned Adam Smith was with the acquirement problem in analyzing what he called "want, famine and mortality." I quote Smith from the chapter called "Of the Wages of Labour" from Book I of the *Wealth of Nations:*

> But it would be otherwise in a country where the funds destined for the maintenance of labour were sensibly decaying. Every year the demand for servants and labourers would, in all the different classes of employments, be less than it had been the year before. Many who had been bred in the superior classes, not being able to find employment in their own business, would be glad to seek it in the lowest. The lower class being not only over-

stocked with its own workmen, but with the over-flowings of all the other classes, the competition for employment would be so great in it, as to reduce the wages of labour to the most miserable and scanty subsistence of the labourer. Many would not be able to find employment even upon these hard terms, but would either starve, or be driven to seek a subsistence either by begging, or by the perpetration perhaps of the greatest enormities. Want, famine, and mortality would immediately prevail in that class, and from thence extend themselves to all the superior classes.[13]

Here Adam Smith is focusing on the market-based entitlement of laborers, and its dependence on employment and real wages, and explaining famine from that perspective. This should, of course, come as no surprise. In denying that artificial scarcity engineered by collusive traders can cause famine, Adam Smith was in no way closing the door to the economic analysis of various different real influences on the ability of different groups to command food in the market, in particular the values of wages and employment.

Perhaps it is useful to consider another argument presented by another great classical economist, viz. David Ricardo, attacking the view that a famine cannot occur in a situation of what he calls "superabundance." This was in a speech that Ricardo wrote for delivery in Parliament in 1822, using the third person for himself as if the speech is reported in the *Hansard,* though in the event Ricardo did not actually get to deliver the speech. The reference is to the famine conditions then prevailing in Ireland, and Ricardo examines the point made by another member of Parliament that this could not be the case, since there was superabundance of food in Ireland at that time.

But says the honble. gentn. the people are dying for want of food in Ireland, and the farmers are said to be suffering from superabundance. In these two propositions the honble. gentn. thinks there is a manifest contradiction, but he Mr. R. could not agree with him in thinking so. Where was the contradiction in supposing that in a country where wages were regulated mainly by the price of potatoes the people should be suffering the greatest distress if the potato crop failed and their wages were inadequate to purchase the dearer commodity corn? From whence was the money to come to enable them to purchase the grain however abundant it might (be) if its price far exceeds that of potatoes. He Mr. Ricardo should not think it absurd or contradictory to maintain that in such a country as England where the food of the people was corn, there might be an abundance of that grain and such low prices as not to afford a renumeration to the grower, and yet that the people might be in distress and not able for want of employment to buy it, but in Ireland the case was much stronger and in that country there should be no doubt there might be a glut of corn, and a starving people.[14]

There is indeed nothing surprising in the fact that economists should be concerned with the acquirement problem and dispute the instant economics that overlooks that aspect of the food problem based on confusing supply with command, as the "honourable gentleman" quoted by David Ricardo clearly did. It is a confusion that has recurred again and again in actual discussions of the food problem, and the need to move away from instant economics to serious analysis of the acquirement problem and the entitlement to food is no less today than it was in Ricardo's time.[15]

It is not my purpose to assert that the entitlement approach is flawless as an economic approach to the problem of hunger and starvation. Several "limitations" of the entitlement approach were, in fact, noted in *Poverty and Famines,* including ambiguities in the specification of entitlement, the neglect of nonlegal transfers (e.g., looting) in the disposition of food, the importance of tastes and values in causing hunger despite adequate entitlement, and the relevance of disease and epidemic in famine mortality which extends far beyond the groups whose entitlement failures may have initiated the famine.

To this, one should also add that in order to capture an important part of the acquirement problem, to wit, distribution of food within a family, the entitlement approach would have to be extended. In particular, notions of perceived "legitimacy" of intrafamily distributional patterns have to be brought into the analysis, and its causal determinants analyzed.[16]

Further, if the focus of attention is shifted from famines as such to less acute but possibly persistent hunger, then the role of choice from the entitlement set becomes particularly important, especially in determining future entitlement. For example, a peasant may choose to go somewhat hungry now to make a productive investment for the future, enhancing the entitlement of the following years and reducing the danger of starvation then. For entitlement analysis in a multiperiod setting, the initial formulation of the problem would require serious modification and extension.[17]

These changes and amendments can be systematically made without losing the basic rationale of introducing entitlement analysis to understand the problem of hunger and starvation in the modern world. The crucial motivation is to see the centrality of the acquirement problem and to resist the short-cuts of instant economics, no matter how respectable its source.

POLICY ISSUES

FAMINE ANTICIPATION AND ACTION

Focusing on entitlements and acquirement rather than simply on food output and availability has some rather far-reaching implications for food policy. I have tried to discuss some of these implications elsewhere, but I would like to pick a few issues here for brief comment. In particular, the problems of famine anticipation and relief are among the most serious ones facing the turbulent and traumatic world in which we live, and I shall comment on them briefly from the perspective that I have been outlining.

So far as famine anticipation is concerned, the metric of food output and availability is obviously defective as a basis, for reasons that follow from the preceding discussion. In fact, the anticipation of famines and their detection at an early stage have often in the past been hampered by undue concentration on this index, and specifically by what we have been calling "Malthusian optimism." Early warnings, as they are sometimes called, may not come at all from the output statistics, and it is necessary to monitor other variables as well, which also influence the entitlements of different vulnerable groups. Employment, wages, prices, etc., all have very direct bearing on the entitlements of various groups.

It is also important to recognize that famines can follow from many *different* types of causal processes. For example, while in a boom famine food prices will sharply rise, in a slump famine they may not. If the economic change that leads to mass starvation operates through depressing incomes and purchasing powers of large groups of people, food prices may stay low—or rise only relatively little, during the process of pauperization of these groups. Even when the slump famine is directly related to a crop failure due to, say, a drought, there may possibly be only a relatively modest rise in food prices, if the supply failure is matched by a corresponding decline in purchasing power due to the same drought. Indeed, it is easy to see that in a fully peasant economy in which food is eaten precisely by those who grow it, a crop failure will subtract from demand what it deducts from supply. The impoverished peasants would of course later be thrown into the rest of the economy—begging, looking for jobs, etc.—but they will arrive there without purchasing ability, and thus need not cause any rise in food prices even later. Actual economies are not, of course, that pure, but the impact on prices is very contingent on the relative weights of the different types of system and organization that make up the affected economy.[18]

Neither food output, nor prices, nor any other variable like that can be taken to be an invariable clue to famine anticipation, and once again there is no substitute to doing a serious economic analysis of the entitlements of all the vulnerable groups. All these variables have possible significance, and it is a question of seeing them as contingently important in terms of what they could do to the ability of different groups to acquire food. The search for some invariable indicator on the basis of which even the economically blind could see an oncoming famine sufficiently early is quite hopeless.

One of the major influences on the actual prevention of famine is the speed and force with which early hunger is reported and taken up in political debates. The nature and freedom of the news media, and the power and standing of opposition parties, are of considerable importance in effective prevention of famines.[19] But if the aim is to anticipate a famine even before early reports of hunger, that object cannot be satisfied by some mechanical formula on an "early warning system." The various information on prices, wages, outputs, etc., have to be examined with an economic understanding of the determinants of the entitlements of the different occupation groups and of the rich variety of ways in which the entitlements of one group or another can be undermined.

The different processes involved not only vary a good deal from each other, they may also be far from straightforward. For example, in various famines some occupation groups have been driven to the wall by a fall in the relative price of the food items they sell, for example, meat sold by pastoral nomads in Harerghe in the Ethiopian famine of 1974, fish sold by fishermen in the Bengal famine of 1943. These groups may survive by selling these food items and buying cheaper calories through the purchase of grains and other less expensive food. A decline in the relative price of meat or fish will, of course, make it easier for the richer parts of the community to eat better, but it can spell disaster for the pastoralist and the fisherman. To make sense of them as signals of turmoil, the observed variables have to be examined in terms of their specific roles in the determination of entitlements of vulnerable groups.

RELIEF, FOOD, AND CASH

Turning now from the anticipation to the relief of famines, the traditional form of relief has, of course, been that of providing free food in relief camps and distribution centers. There can be no doubt that relief in this form has saved lives in large scale in various famines around the world. But to understand precisely what free food distribution does, it may be useful to distinguish between two different aspects of the act of providing, which are both involved in the food relief operation. One is to give the destitute the *ability* to command food, and the other is to give him this ability in the actual form of *food itself*. Though they are integrated together in this form of relief, they need not in general be thus combined. For example, cash relief may provide the ability to command food without directly giving the food.

A person's ability to command food has two distinct elements, viz., his "pull" and the supplier's "response." In the price mechanism the two elements are integrally related to each other. But in terms of the logistics of providing the person with food, the two elements may, in some contexts, be usefully distinguishable. If a person has to starve because he has lost his employment and has no means of buying food, then that is a failure originating on the pull side. If, on the other hand, his ability to command food collapses because of absence of supply, or as a result of the cornering of the market by some manipulative traders, then this is a failure arising on the response side.

One way of understanding what Adam Smith was really asserting (an issue that was briefly touched on earlier) is to see his primary claim as being one about the nature of "response failure" in particular, saying nothing at all about "pull failure." His claim was that a response failure will arise only from what he called "a real scarcity," most likely due to natural causes, and not from manipulative actions of traders. He may or may not have been right in this claim, but it is important to note that in this there is no denial of the possibility of "pull failure." Indeed, as is shown by his own analysis of "want, famine and mortality" arising from unemployment and falling wages (I quoted a passage from this earlier), Smith did also outline the possibility of famine originating on the pull side. There is nothing particularly puzzling or internally inconsistent in Smith's various pronouncements on famine, if we distinguish between his treatment of pull and that of response. It is not the case, as is often asserted, that Adam Smith believed that hunger could not arise without a crop failure. Also he was not opposed to public support for the deprived, and in particular he was not opposed to providing relief through the Poor Laws (though he did criticize the harshness of some of the requirements that were imposed on the beneficiaries under these laws).

Smith's point that response failure would not arise from collusive action of traders has a direct bearing on the appropriate form of famine relief. If his point is correct, then relief could just as easily be provided by giving the deprived additional income and leaving it to the traders to respond to the new pull through moving food to the cash recipients. It is arguable that Smith did underestimate the extent to which traders can and do, in fact, manipulate markets, but at the same time the merits of cash relief do need serious examination in the context of assessing policy options.

Cash relief may not, of course, be quick enough in getting food to the starving in a situation of severe famine. Directly moving food to the starving may be the only immediate option in some situations of acute famine. There is also the merit of direct food distribution that it tends to have, it appears, a very immediate impact on nutrition, even in nonfamine, normal situations, and it seems to do better in this respect than relief through income supplementation. These are points in favor of direct relief through food distribution. There is the further point that cash relief is arguably more prone to corruption, and that the visibility of direct food distribution does provide a better check. And the point about the possibility of manipulative actions of traders cannot, also, by any means be simply dismissed. These are serious points in favor of direct food distribution. But cash relief does have many merits as well.

First, the government's inefficiency in transporting food could be a considerable barrier to famine relief, as indeed some recent experiences have shown. In addition to problems of bureaucracy and red tape, there is the further problem that the transport resources (i.e., vehicles, etc.) in the possession of the private sector may sometimes be hard to mobilize, whereas they would be drawn into use if the actual trading and moving is left to the profit-seeking private sector itself. There is here a genuine pragmatic issue of the speed of response, and it cannot be brushed aside by a simple political judgment one way or the other.

Second, as was observed in the Wollo famine in 1973 and the Bangladesh famine of 1984, and most spectacularly in the Irish famines of the 1840s, food often does move *out* of the famine-stricken regions to elsewhere. This tends to happen especially in some cases of slump famine, in which the famine area is short of effective demand. Since such "food countermovement" tends to reflect the balance of pulls of different regions, it may be preventable by distributing cash quickly enough in the famine-affected region.

Third, by providing demand for trade and transport, cash relief may help to regenerate the infrastructure of the famine-stricken economy. This has some merit in contrast with ad hoc use of transitory public intervention, which is not meant to continue, and the lasting benefits from expansion of normal trade and transport may be considerable for the local economy.

Fourth, it is arguable that cash relief is more usable for development investment needed for productive improvement, and this cannot be sensibly organized in relief centers. Even "food for work" programs, which can help in this direction, may sometimes be too unwieldy, given the need for flexibility for such investment activities.

Fifth, living in relief camps is deeply disruptive for normal family life as well as for pursuing normal economic activities. Providing cash relief precisely where the people involved normally reside and work, without having to move them to relief camps, may have very considerable economic and social advantages. Judging from the experience of an innovative "cash for food" project sponsored by UNICEF in Ethiopia, these advantages are indeed quite real.[20]

This is not the occasion to try to form an overall judgment of the "net" advantage of one scheme over another. Such judgments would have to be, in any case, extremely contingent on the exact circumstances of the case. But the general distinction between the "pull" aspect and the "response" aspect of entitlement failures is of immediate relevance to the question of the strategy of famine relief. Adam Smith's long shadow fell over many famines in the British Empire over the last two hundred years, with Smith being cited in favor of inaction and letting things be. If the analysis presented here is accepted, then inaction reflected quite the wrong reading of the implications of Smith's economic analysis. If his analysis is correct—and the honors here are probably rather divided—the real Smithian issue in a situation of famine is not "intervention versus nonintervention," but "cash relief versus direct food relief." The force of the arguments on Smith's side cannot be readily dismissed, and the experience of mismanagement of famine relief in many countries has done nothing to reduce the aptness of Smith's question.

FOOD SUPPLY AND FOOD PRICES

In comparing the merits of cash relief with food distribution, it was not assumed that there would be more import of food with the latter than with the former. That question—of food imports from aboard—is a quite distinct one from the form that relief might take. It is, however, arguable that in a famine situation direct food distribution is more thoroughly dependent on food import from abroad than a cash relief scheme need be. This is to some extent correct, though direct food distribution may also be based on domestically acquired food. But if we compare food distribution combined *with* food imports, on the one hand, and simple cash relief *without* such imports, on the other, then an arbitrary difference is brought into the contrast which does not belong there. In fact, the issue of food import is a separate one, which should be considered on its own.

This relates to an issue that has often been misunderstood in trying to work out the implications of the entitlement approach to hunger and famines, and in particular the implications of recognizing the possibility that famines can occur without any decline in food availability per head. It has sometimes been argued that if a famine is not caused by a decline in food availability, then there cannot be a case for food imports in dealing with the famine.[21] This is, of course, a non sequitur, and a particularly dangerous piece of nonsense. Consider a case in which some people have been reduced to starvation not because of a decline in total supply of food, but because they have fallen behind in the competitive demand for food in a boom famine (as happened, for example, to rural laborers in the Bengal famine of 1943). The fact is that the prices are too high for these victim groups to acquire enough food. Adding to the food supply will typically reduce prices and help these deprived groups to acquire food. The fact that the original rise in prices did not result from a fall in availability but from an increase in total demand does not make any difference to the argument.

Similarly, in a slump famine in which some group of people has suffered a decline in their incomes due to, say, unemployment, it may be possible to help that group by reducing the price of food through more imports. Furthermore, in each case import of food can be used to break a famine through public relief measures. This can be done either directly, in the form of food distribution, or indirectly through giving cash relief to the famine victims combined with releasing more food in the market to balance the additional demand that would be created. There are, of course, other arguments to be considered in judging pros and cons of food imports, including the important problem of incentives for domestic food producers. But to try to reject the case for food imports in a famine situation on the simple ground that the famine has occurred without a decline in food availability (if that is the case) is to make a straightforward mistake in reasoning.

A more interesting question arises if in a famine situation we are, for some reason, simply not in a position to get more food from abroad. Would a system of cash relief then be inflationary, and thus counterproductive? The answer is it would typically be inflationary, but not necessarily counterproductive. Giving the famine victims more purchasing power would add to the total demand for food. But if we want a more equal distribution of food, with some food moving from others to the famine victims, then the only way the market can achieve this (when the total supply is fixed and the money incomes of others cannot be cut) is through this inflationary process. The additional food to be consumed by the famine victims has to come from others, and this may require that prices go up to induce others to consume less, so that the famine victims—with their new cash incomes—can buy more. Thus, while having a system of cash reliefs is not an argument against food imports in a famine situation, that system can have some desirable consequences *even when* food imports are, for some reason, not possible. If our focus is on enhancing the entitlements of famine victims, the creation of some inflationary pressure—within limits—to redistribute food to the famine victims from the rest of the society may well be a sensible policy to pursue.

ENTITLEMENTS AND PUBLIC DISTRIBUTION

So far in this lecture my concentration on policy matters has been largely on what may be called short-run issues, including the anticipation and relief of famines. But it should be clear from the preceding analysis, with its focus on acquirement and entitlements, that long-run policies have to be geared to enhancing, securing, and guaranteeing entitlements, rather than to some simple formula like expanding food output.

I have discussed elsewhere the positive achievements of public food distribution policies in Sri Lanka and China, and also in Kerala in India, along with policies of public health and elementary education.[22] The role of Sri Lanka's extensive "social welfare programmes" in achieving high living standards has been the subject of some controversy recently. It is, of course, impossible to deny that, judged in terms of such indicators of living standard as life expectancy, Sri Lanka's overall achievement is high (its life expectancy of 69 years is higher than that of any other developing country—even with many times the GNP per head of Sri Lanka). But by looking not at the *levels* of living but at their rate of *expansion* over a selected period, to wit 1960–78, it has been argued by Surjit Bhalla and others that Sri Lanka has performed only "in an average manner." Armed with these findings (based on international comparisons of expansion of longevity, etc., over 1960–78), the positive role of Sri Lanka's wide-based welfare programs has been firmly disputed (asking, on the contrary, the general question: when does a commitment to equity become excessive?).[23]

The basis of this disputation, however, is extremely weak. The period 1960–78 is one in which Sri Lanka's social welfare programs themselves did not grow much, and indeed the percentage of GNP expended on such programs *came down sharply*, from 11.8 in 1960–61 to 8.7 by 1977.[24] If the expansion of sowing is moderate, and so is the expansion of reaping, that can scarcely be seen as a sign of the ineffectiveness of sowing!

The really fast expansion of Sri Lanka's social welfare programs came much earlier, going back at least to the forties. Food distribution policies (e.g., free or subsidized rice for all, free school meals) were introduced in the early 1940s, and health intervention was also radically expanded (including taking on the dreaded malaria). Correspondingly, the death rate too fell from 21.6 per thousand in 1945 to 12.6 in 1950, and to 8.6 by 1960 (all this happened *before* the oddly chosen period 1960–78 used in Bhalla's much-publicized "international comparisons" of expansions). There is nothing in the picture of "expansion" that would contradict the fact of Sri Lanka's exceptional performance, if one does look at the right period, that is, one in which its social welfare programs were, in fact, radically expanded, which happened well before 1960.

The diverse policy instruments of public intervention used in Sri Lanka relate closely to "food policy" in the wider sense, affecting nutrition, longevity, etc., going well beyond the production of food. Similar relations can be found in the experience of effective public distribution programs also in other regions, for example, China and Kerala. It is right that the "food problem" should be seen in these wider terms, involving not only the production of food, but also the entitlements to food and to other nutrition-related variables such as health services.

PRODUCTION AND DIVERSIFICATION

The problem of production composition in achieving economic expansion is also, *inter alia,* an important one in long-run food policy. This complex problem is often confounded with that of simply expanding food output as such, treating it as largely a matter of increasing food supply. This is particularly so in the discussions of the so-called African food problem. It is, of course, true that food output per head in sub-Saharan Africa has been falling in recent years, and this is certainly one of the major factors in the intensification of hunger in Africa. But food production is not merely a source of food supply in Africa, but also the main source of means of livelihood for large sections of the African population. It is for this reason that food output decline tends to go hand in hand with a collapse of entitlements of the masses in Africa.

The point can easily be seen by comparing and contrasting the experience of sub-Saharan Africa in terms of food output per head vis-à-vis those of some countries elsewhere. Take Ethiopia and the Sahel countries, which have all suffered so much from famines. Between 1969–71 and 1980–82, food output per head has fallen by five percent in Chad and Burkina Faso, seven percent in Senegal, 12 percent in Niger, 17 percent in Mali, 18 percent in Ethiopia, and 27 percent in Mauritania.[25] These are indeed substantial declines. But in the same period, and according to the same source of statistics, food output per head has fallen by five percent in Venezuela, 15 percent in Egypt, 24 percent in Algeria, 27 percent in Portugal, 29 percent in Hong Kong, 30 percent in Jordan, and 38 percent in Trinidad and Tobago. The contrast between starvation in sub-Saharan Africa and nothing of the sort in these other countries is not, of course, in the least difficult to explain. Unlike the situation in these other countries, in sub-Saharan Africa a decline in food output is associated with a disastrous decline in entitlements, because the incomes of so many there come from growing food, because they are generally poor, and because the decline of food output there has not been outweighed or even balanced by increases in nonfood (e.g., industrial) output. It is essential to distinguish between (1) food production as a source of income and entitlement, and (2) food production as a source of supply of the vital commodity food. If the expansion of food production should receive full priority in Africa, the case for it lies primarily in the role of food production in generating entitlements rather than only supply.

There are, of course, other reasons as well for giving priority to food production, in particular the greater security that the growers of food might then have, since they would not be dependent on market exchange for acquiring food. This argument has been emphasized by many in recent years, and it is indeed an important consideration, the relevance of which is brought out by the role of market shifts in contributing to some of the famines that have been studied. But this type of uncertainty has to be balanced against uncertainties arising from other sources, in particular those related to climatic reasons. In the very long run the uncertainty of depending on unreliable weather conditions in parts of sub-Saharan Africa may well be eliminated by irrigation and afforestation. However, for many years to come this is a serious uncertainty, which must be taken into account along with other factors in the choice of investment policy in sub-Saharan Africa. An argument that is often encountered in public discussion in various forms can be crudely put like this: "Food output in parts of sub-Saharan Africa has suffered a lot because the climate there is so unreliable for food production; therefore let's put all our resources into food production in these countries." This is, of course, a caricature, but even in somewhat more sophisticated forms, this line of argument as a piece of economic reasoning is deeply defective. One does not put all one's eggs in the same highly unreliable basket. The need is surely for diversification of the production pattern in a situation of such uncertainty.

CONCLUDING REMARKS

I have tried to comment on a number of difficult policy problems. The entitlement approach on its own does not resolve any of these issues. But by focusing on the acquirement problem, and on the major variables influencing acquirement, the entitlement approach provides a general perspective that can be fruitfully used to analyze the phenomenon of hunger as well as the requirements of food policy. I have tried to illustrate some of the uses of the entitlement approach and have also discussed what policy insights follow or do not follow from it. The policy issues discussed have included problems of anticipation and relief of famines, forms of relief to be provided (including food distribution versus cash relief), the role of food supply and food prices in famine relief, and long-run strategies for eliminating vulnerability to famines and starvation (with particular reference to Africa).

I have also claimed that the entitlement approach is, with a few exceptions, in line with very old traditions in economics, which have been, in their own way, much preoccupied with the acquirement issue. The challenges of the terrible economic problems of the contemporary world relate closely to those traditional concerns and call for sustained economic analysis of the determination and use of entitlements of diverse occupation groups.

NOTES

1. On the importance of the latter document, which has received much less attention than the former, see my *Poverty and Famines* (Oxford: Clarendon Press, 1981, Appendix B).
2. This issue is discussed in my article "The Food Problem: Theory and Policy," *Third World Quarterly* 4 (1982).
3. The Club of Rome, despite its extremely distinguished leadership, has been responsible for some of the more lurid research reports of doom and decline. However, a later study sponsored by the club undertaken by H. Linnemann, *MOIRA: A Model of International Relations in Agriculture* (Amsterdam: North-Holland, 1981) shows the picture to be both less gloomy and more easily influenced by policy. See also K. Parikh and F. Rabar, eds., *Food for All in a Sustainable World* (Laxenburg, Austria, IIASA, 1981), especially on the role of policy.
4. See, for example, FAO, *The State of Food and Agriculture 1984* (Rome, 1985).
5. See also my "Starvation and Exchange Entitlements: A General Approach and Its Application to the Great Bengal Famine," *Cambridge Journal of Economics* 1 (1977); and "Ingredients of Famine Analysis: Availability and Entitlements," *Quarterly Journal of Economics* 95 (1981).
6. Note that the use of the expression "entitlement" here is descriptive rather than prescriptive. A person's entitlements as given by the legal system, personal circumstances, etc., need not command any

moral endorsement. This applies both to the opulent entitlements of the rich and to the meager entitlements of the poor.

7. Particularly from Kenneth J. Arrow, "Why People Go Hungry," *New York Review of Books* 29 (15 July 1982); Christopher Bliss, "The Facts About Famine," *South* (March 1982); Keith Griffin, "Poverty Trap," *Guardian* (7 October 1981); Teresa Hayter, "Famine for Free," *New Society* (15 October 1981); Vijay Joshi, "Enough to Eat," *London Review of Books* (19 November 1981); Robert M. Solow, "Relative Deprivation?", *Partisan Review* 51 (1984).

8. See *Poverty and Famines*, chapters 6–10.

9. See *Poverty and Famines*, chapters 6–10. See also Peter Svedberg, "Food Insecurity in Developing Countries: Causes, Trends and Policy Options," UNCTAD, 1984; Martin Ravallion, "The Performance of Rice Markets in Bangladesh during the 1974 Famine," *Economic Journal* 92 (1985); Qaisar M. Khan, "A Model of Endowment Constrained Demand for Food in an Agricultural Economy with Empirical Applications to Bangladesh," *World Development* 13 (1985).

10. See Gary S. Becker, *The Economic Approach to Human Behavior* (Chicago: University of Chicago Press, 1976); and Becker, *A Treatise on the Family* (Cambridge: Harvard University Press, 1981).

11. See, for example, the discussion on wages and capital in *Capital*, vol. I (London: Sonnenschein, 1887, parts 6 and 7).

12. Adam Smith, *An Inquiry into the Nature and Causes of the Wealth of Nations*, Book IV, chapter 5, b.5, in the edition edited by R. H. Campbell and A. S. Skinner (Oxford: Clarendon Press, 1976, vol. 1, p. 526).

13. Smith, *Wealth of Nations*, Book I, chapter 8, pp. 90–91.

14. *The Works and Correspondence of David Ricardo*, edited by P. Sraffa, with the collaboration of M. H. Dobb (Cambridge: Cambridge University Press, 1971, vol. 5, pp. 234–35).

15. See Lance Taylor's illuminating critique, "The Misconstrued Crisis: Lester Brown and World Food," *World Development* 3 (1975).

16. The consequences of particular perceptions of "legitimacy" of intrafamily distributions do have something in common with those of legal relationships. Using that perspective "*extended* exchange entitlement" relations, covering both interfamily and intrafamily distributions, have been explored in an integrated structure in my paper, "Women, Technology and Sexual Division," *Trade and Development Review* no. 6, 1985, UNCTAD, Geneva. The interrelations may be of real importance in understanding sex bias, e.g., the effect that outside earnings of women have on the divisions with the family. On this see also Ester Boserup's pioneering study, *Women's Role in Economic Development* (London, Allen and Unwin, 1970); and my *Resources, Values and Development* (Oxford: Blackwell, 1984, essays 15, 16, 19 and 20).

17. See *Poverty and Famines*, p. 50, footnote 11. For some important and original ideas in this direction, see Peter Svedberg, "The Economics of Food Insecurity in Developing Countries" (Stockholm: Institute for International Economic Studies, 1985, mimeographed).

18. In the Ethiopian famine in Wollo in 1973, food price rises seem to have been relatively moderate. Indeed, in Dessie, the capital of Wollo, the mid-famine food prices seem to have been comparable with prices outside the famine-affected province. There was more of a price rise in the rural areas, but again apparently not a catastrophic rise, and prices seemed to come down relatively quickly. On the importance of prices as a monitoring device for famine anticipation, see J. A. Seaman and J. F. J. Holt, "Markets and Famines in the Third World," *Disasters* 4 (1989); and P. Cutler, "Famine Forecasting: Prices and Peasant Behaviour in Northern Ethiopia," *Disasters* 8 (1984): 48–56. See also B. Snowdon, "The Political Economy of the Ethiopian Famine," *National Westminster Bank Quarterly Review* (November 1985).

19. On this see my "Development: Which Way Now?" *Economic Journal* 93 (1983), reprinted in *Resources, Values and Development*, 1984.

20. See B. G. Kumar, "The Ethiopian Famine and Relief Measures: An Analysis and Evaluation," UNICEF, 1985. See also Wendy A. Bjoerck, "An Overview of Local Purchase of Food Commodities (LPFC)," UNICEF, 1984; and R. Padmini, "The Local Purchase of Food Commodities: 'Cash for Food' Project, Ethiopia," UNICEF, 1985.

21. For a forceful presentation of this odd belief, see Peter Bowbrick's paper (with a truly flattering title), "How Professor Sen's Theory Can Cause Famines," presented at the Agricultural Economics Society Conference, 1985, at the Annual Conference of the Development Studies Association. For a revised version of Bowbrick's paper see P. Bowbrick, "The Causes of Famine: A Refutation of Professor Sen's Theory," *Food Policy* 11 (1986) and my reply, "The Causes of Famine: A Reply," *Food Policy* 11 (1986).

22. See my "Public Action and the Quality of Life in Developing Countries," *Oxford Bulletin of Economics and Statistics* 43 (1981); and "Development: Which Way Now?" *Economic Journal* 93 (1983).

23. See Surjit Bhalla, "Is Sri Lanka an Exception? A Comparative Study of Living Standards," World Bank, 1985, to be published in T. N. Srinivasan and P. Bardhan, eds., *Rural Poverty in South Asia* (Columbia University Press, vol. 2). Bhalla's findings have been used for drawing negative policy conclusions regarding social welfare programs, by several economists (e.g., Hla Myint, "Growth Policies and Income Distribution," discussion paper, World Bank, March 1985; and Jagdish Bhagwati, "Growth and Poverty," text of the Center for Advanced Study of International Development Lecture, Michigan State University, spring 1985).

24. These figures are given by Bhalla himself in a different context. He does not give the figure for 1978, but in his table the percentage had further dropped to 7.7 by 1980. Other sources confirm these overall declining trends during the 1960s and 1970s taken together.

25. *World Development Review 1984* (Oxford: Oxford University Press, 1984, table 6).

12

Developing a Food Strategy

C. PETER TIMMER

POLICY PERSPECTIVE

What does it mean for a country to "develop a food strategy"? How does a country do it? What should be its objectives, where does it turn for help, what lessons can it learn from others, and what must it learn from the painful but effective techniques of trial and error?

These questions have no set answers. Each must be addressed in the context of individual country and temporal settings. Each must also be addressed analytically, and that is the purpose of this paper. The analytical perspective permits us to distinguish the set of answers—the actual building blocks of a country's food policy—from the process of identifying the right questions to ask as the first step in the design and ultimate assembly of those building blocks.

This paper is about the design process. Although the way the analytical design process is defined places some boundaries on the dimensions of the resulting food strategy, it is still possible, indeed necessary, to distinguish between what an "optimal" food policy looks like for all worlds and the analytical process that frames the right set of questions. These questions emerge from the need for a national food strategy to satisfy four basic objectives: (1) efficient growth in the food and agricultural sectors; (2) improved income distribution, primarily through efficient employment creation; (3) satisfactory nutritional status for the entire population through provision of a minimum-subsistence floor for basic needs; and (4) adequate food security to ensure against bad harvests, natural disasters, or uncertain world food supplies.

Three assumptions define the philosophical starting point for this chapter. They are as much intuitive perspective as based on verifiable reality, and their efficacy no doubt varies from country to country and from time to time. It is best,

C. PETER TIMMER is Thomas D. Cabot Professor of Development Studies, At-Large, Harvard University.

Reprinted, with minor editorial revisions, from *Proceedings of the Conference on Food Security in a Hungry World*, International Food Policy Conference, San Francisco, 4–6 March 1981, cosponsored by the University of California, Davis, and Castle and Cooke, Inc. Published by permission of the conference organizers and the author.

however, to lay these assumptions out ahead of time rather than to discover them lurking at the core of the results.

First, the four basic objectives listed above are taken as representative of the broad set of goals most policy makers in poor and rich countries alike have for their food and agricultural sectors. Growth, jobs, a decent minimum standard of living, and security against famine or extreme food shortages capture most of what might ideally be delivered by a successful food strategy. If not all objectives are simultaneously satisfied from a given set of policies (and typically they are not), it will be necessary to understand which objectives are most important. While development plans may say all four objectives are equally important, actual budget, price, and trade policies for the food and agricultural sector usually indicate otherwise. Hence the first important starting point is a political economy perspective organized around understanding national objectives for the food and agricultural sector.

The second starting point is a concern for moving from here to there, that is, for the process of incremental change that moves a country slowly but increasingly surely toward the simultaneous achievement of all four food strategy objectives. Such a marginalist perspective is surely inappropriate in some, perhaps even many, national environments. Without radical restructuring of assets and basic production relations, little progress can be made toward any of the four objectives in such countries. This paper, however, is not about revolution but rather the search for feasible improvements in the individual components of a food strategy in those environments where the four objectives are taken seriously by some sector of the government.

What is feasible depends on what constraints the political and economic system is under. Such constraints are highly heterogeneous. They range from the political base of the national regime and the potential, for instance, to find a million workers and students in the streets when food prices rise, to the diminishing returns in additional rice production from incremental fertilizer applications when fertilizer use is already high, to the inability of national, provincial, or local bureaucracies to identify and reach the truly poor (and only the truly poor) with real resources. None of these three constraints on government policies seeking to reach the four objectives is the sort that economists normally identify as factors limiting government action. The more normal constraints—availability of foreign exchange, of domestic savings, of budgetary resources, even of talented analytical capacity—are real and important. But so too are the other, more nebulous political, economic, or technical constraints. A genuine concern for policy movement, for change in the right direction, requires that the full range of constraints be identified and incorporated into the analysis.

The third major starting point for this paper is a strong belief that understanding markets is critical to the development of an efficient and equitable food strategy. This market orientation grows out of the belief, buttressed by a now impressive range of empirical experience, that in a global economic environment undergoing rapid, almost radical change in the prices, and hence the relative scarcities, of important factors of production and commodities, the efficiency and rapidity of market decision making will generate substantially better economic progress than will strong central planning or heavy reliance on public enterprises operated according to central directives. No food system anywhere in the world is centrally planned, although some (those of the Soviet Union, China, or Cuba, for example) are more heavily influenced by planners' allocations than others. Throughout the world, however, in the fields and in the households, largely private decisions are being made in response to private incentives. How hard to work, which inputs to use, and which foods to consume are decisions that are made mostly through habit and a private calculus. Since a food strategy is designed to change many of these decisions, it is necessary that the analysis leading to the design of that food policy reveal a full understanding of the context in which the decisions are made.

Few would quarrel with this market orientation on efficiency grounds. It is the equity of the outcome, or the resulting nutritional status of the population, that is of concern. The fundamental argument of this paper is that the role of analysis and design of a food policy is to find a feasible way to use market efficiency to help provide nutritional equity. Such analysis is faced with a basic food policy dilemma: in many poor countries, especially in the heavily populated South and Southeast Asian countries, the set of incentives necessary to induce rapid and efficient growth of food production will, in the short run, simultaneously increase the hunger of the urban and rural landless poor, who are already on the nutritional margin of survival.

A food policy that deals with this basic dilemma by keeping food prices low and thus dampening agricultural incentives can partially succeed in the short run as long as food resources are available to implement the policy. The long-run consequence of such a food price policy, however, is a shortage of those essential food resources. The alternative, a food price policy designed specifically for its positive long-run productivity effects, has as a short-run consequence the significant reduction in food intake among the poor whose incomes are not linked fairly directly to food prices. This is, unfortunately, a very sizeable number of people.

Analysis that copes directly with this food price policy dilemma is at the core of the design of any successful food strategy. Recognizing this is to recognize a fundamental revolution in development thinking: macro price policy is the cutting edge of economic development; projects and programs are the cutting edge of reducing nutritional inequities. The critical bridge requires two supports: (1) understanding the nutritional consequences of that efficient macro price policy and (2) designing and implementing targeted food programs that reach the poor within reasonable budget limits.

This perspective on food policy design suggests four components to the analytical process: (1) to determine the feasible set of policies, (2) to extend the degrees of freedom for policy choice, (3) to determine what investments are needed to break the binding constraints on policy choice, and (4) to devise policies to deal with the short-run consequences of efficient long-run food sector development.

The first step is to determine the feasible set, or at least the nature of potential policies and programs that are actively discussed and debated even if considered infeasible or unlikely in the near term. Part of this process involves understanding the perceived constraints on infeasible policies and programs. Do policy makers see these constraints in budget terms, in political risks, or in unresponsive rice plants, farmers, or consumers?

The next step in this policy analysis is a search for ways to extend the degrees of freedom for policy choice. Policy makers do not live in an efficient world where all alternatives are clearly defined with costs and benefits attached, merely awaiting the nod of a person with power to decide. Many policy choices are constrained by myopic visions and faulty analysis of too aggregated a picture of the world. The first instinct of a good food policy analyst is to disaggregate, to take the data apart by producers and consumers, by income class, by commodity, by region, by urban and rural status. The poor—the ultimate focus of a successful food strategy—are different from the middle- and upper-income groups. They consume different foods, live in different places, have different kinds of jobs, and different-sized families. A full analytical understanding of these differences frequently suggests whole new policy approaches to dealing with food problems.

Assembling the basic ingredients of an effective food strategy is frequently prevented by real constraints on what committed policy makers can do. Discovering this is critical for food policy analysis. It is important to know when good policy analysis can suggest additional degrees of freedom and when the effective constraints really are binding. In the latter case the third step in the analytical process is to determine what investments are needed to break the binding constraints on policy choice. It may require investments in building the capacity to generate greater budgetary resources; investments in agricultural research to build the foundation for a locally adapted, high-yielding agriculture; investments in communications and building public trust and understanding with respect to basic policy dilemmas; or investments in analytical capacity. All of these investments no doubt have high payoffs most of the time. Good food policy analysis will identify which investments are *critical* to the design and implementation of a successful food strategy.

The fourth element of creative food policy analysis is facing squarely the short-run welfare consequences of efficient long-run food sector development strategies. Two easy approaches are possible, and both are usually wrong. The first assumes that efficient long-run policies also solve short-run welfare and nutritional problems. In this view all that is lacking is "political will." The second approach recognizes that efficient development strategies do carry severe short-run welfare costs, but the answer is to be seen in neutral fiscal transfers from the wealthy to the poor via the budget. Political will is the missing ingredient in this view of the world as well.

Both approaches beg the important question, How can good policy analysis identify the needed bridging programs that enable policy makers to make difficult choices? A government that cannot raise food prices because it will no longer be the government will not raise food prices, no matter how critical that is to long-run efficiency. A government that cannot collect income taxes cannot make neutral fiscal transfers, no matter what political will it has. Ration shops, subsidized inferior foods consumed primarily by the poor, or even direct food distribution may be feasible programs that would cushion the food consumption consequences of efficient food production strategies. It would be a wonderful world where food consumption decisions could be separated from food production decisions, but it is not the world we live in. Food prices link the two, and food policy analysis begins with this understanding.

ANALYTICAL APPROACH

An implicit hypothesis behind the search for successful food policies is that neither nutrition policies nor agricultural policies can solve the basic hunger problem. In short, "one-sided" analytical approaches, whether from the production side or from the basic needs side, fail to provide for the central role of the food system, particularly food markets and prices. Production approaches focus on the role of new technology, or, more recently, the efficiency and productivity of small farmers, but these approaches fail to integrate the demand side apart from rural farm income. Both on Java and in the United States more than half of rural income is earned from nonfarm sources,[1] and much urban poverty and hunger has no food production link at all. Similarly, despite the impressive accomplishments of nutrition planners in identifying and measuring the extent and consequences of hunger and malnutrition, their "nutritional requirements" approach to allocating resources usually runs into a contrary market economy. Nutrition simply does not have many policy levers to pull.

The alternative is to approach the hunger problem explicitly through the food sector, recognizing the linkages through that sector from the agricultural sector and to the food consumption endpoint. The advantage of such a food policy approach, apart from its central focus on food markets, is the ease with which macroeconomic influences, especially via the budget and macro price policy, and international influences can be linked to the hunger problem.

At this stage the problem sounds sufficiently complicated to require complicated models to understand it. Such models exist, and they test the ingenuity of even the brightest graduate students in their design and interpretation. Agricultural sector models nearly captured the entire agricultural development profession before the rapid changes in the 1970s revealed such models to be essentially static in nature. Not enough is known about even the agricultural growth process in the context of radically evolving macroeconomic and international environments to have much faith in the capacity of such models to capture the subtle linkages between the micro and macro sectors that now are important driving mechanisms in the modernization of agriculture.

Macro-consistency models with separate foodgrain sectors and even disaggregated income classes face many of the same problems. There is no question that changes in food policies in most Third World countries and many industrialized countries have important macroeconomic repercussions that few agricultural economists are trained to understand. Recognizing and roughly quantifying these macroeconomic effects are important, but two provisos limit the usefulness of the formal and complicated macroeconomic models for this purpose. First, the complexity of real-world patterns of food, services, and industrial goods production, of price formation, of income generation, and of food consumption patterns by income class of various important food commodities is such that all macro models are greatly simplified and frequently require important counterfactual assumptions in order to be "calculable." Second, most such macro models are built on Keynesian assumptions about surplus industrial capacity, closed economies or economies with foreign-exchange "constraints," and cost-plus price formation. Many, but not all, of the major countries with serious food problems more nearly resemble classical economies in the Lewis sense, where labor alone, rather than labor and industrial capacity, is in surplus supply. Such economies have important macroeconomic linkages to their food sectors, but such linkages are not always mediated by Keynesian mechanisms.

What is the alternative to such formal, complicated models if the goal remains to understand the food system and its horizontal linkages to agriculture and nutrition and its vertical linkages to the international economy and to macro price policy? Given the complexity of these linkages and of the individual components themselves, such an understanding can be generated only by an intuitive but sophisticated analysis of the system. Informal modeling of interrelationships and linkages among components of the food sector, combined with an analytical sensitivity both to the important issues and to what seems to be driving the system, is probably the best that can be achieved in the foreseeable future.

Many economists are concerned that there is more art than science to this, and certainly no two creative food policy analysts are likely to emerge with exactly the same sense of how the system works and what the policy options might be. There is, however, a reality driving the complexity. The more skilled the analysts, the more their respective visions of what is possible will correspond.

Three separate sensibilities are required of such analysts. The first is a welfare sensitivity from a macroeconomic policy perspective. This is manifested as a concern for income distribution and the food consumption consequences of budgetary, fiscal, and macro price policy changes. The concern comes from the top down.

The second sensitivity requires a macro understanding from a nutritional or food consumption perspective. The design of nutritional intervention intended to make an impact on the magnitude of basic hunger must be sensitive to budget priorities and the nature of national policy objectives and constraints. An understanding of the macroeconomic and productivity impact of food price changes must condition nutrition policy at the same time that concern for replicability and the aggregate impact of feeding interventions must condition the design of nutrition programs. This concern comes from the bottom up.

A last sensitivity is perhaps most critical of all. Food policy analysis is the search for second-best solutions in an imperfect and poorly understood world. First-best solutions are best, and the designer of food strategies will fight for them whenever they appear even reasonably attainable. But there must be a sensitivity to what is possible. A food policy analyst need not abandon ideals or principle, for these motivate the search for degrees of freedom, but the search must be in the real world and not in a model.

UNDERSTANDING THE FOOD SYSTEM

CONSUMPTION

For the food policy analyst, food consumption is the variable of proximate concern. Nutritional status is strongly influenced by water and sanitation conditions, health status, food preparation techniques, and a host of other variables that intervene between the quantities of food entering the household and how well-nourished the household members are. In most circumstances, however, it is the quantity of food consumed by the household members that determines whether hunger is a significant factor in their lives. Consequently, food policy analysis focuses major analytical attention on food consumption patterns, even to the extent of starting the analysis with this component of the food system.

Two separate analyses—one in aggregate, the other disaggregated—must be conducted and ultimately reconciled. First, it is necessary to generate an understanding of the major market demand parameters for basic foodstuffs. When average per capita GNP rises, how much is market demand for rice likely to increase? market demand for wheat? for cassava? for corn? for meat? How much meat is grain-fed, and what impact will increased meat demand have on demand for grain? How sensitive is market demand to absolute and relative food prices? If all foodgrain prices rise relative to nonfood prices, how much does demand drop? When rice prices rise, does wheat consumption rise while rice consumption falls?

Answering these questions is important because the resulting income, own-price, and cross-price elasticities provide necessary linkages from macro price policy and macroeconomic performance to food consumption and, through the food marketing sector, to incentives for agricultural production. Obtaining these aggregate market demand parameters with any real confidence is seldom easy. Time series data are frequently short and of dubious accuracy when domestic foodgrain production makes up a significant part of total consumption. Mechanical regression analysis seldom gives plausible parameters. A combination of intuitive judgment, talking to traders, evidence from household surveys, simple graphical and statistical analysis of available data, and familiarity with similar parameters in other countries is frequently the best that can be achieved. Economic theory suggests some basic consistency relationships; reality suggests that parameters can change from year to year for many reasons, including changing expectations. Aggregate demand parameters are important; they are seldom precise.

The second step in food consumption analysis is to disaggregate the first step. The motivation for this step, however, is quite different from the need to know aggregate market demand parameters to understand the macro linkages in the food sector. The disaggregated consumption understanding is needed in order to trace the effects of various price and income policies on the food intake of the poor. Indeed, it is quite possible to focus this stage of the food consumption analysis specifically on the poor. Additional insights can be gained by similar analysis of the food consumption patterns of the middle class and wealthy, especially with respect to the impact that demand for grain-fed livestock will have. If time and analytical resources are a binding constraint, however, understanding what the poor eat and why should receive first priority.

The starting point is to discover what the poor actually eat. Everyone knows that they eat less than the rich, but in virtually all societies the composition of foods the poor eat is also significantly different from the middle-income and wealthy diet. The point can usually be demonstrated and suitably quantified by preparing separate food balance sheets for three or four income classes in a society and comparing them with the aggregate food balance sheet that is published by most governments. The information needed to do this is normally available from household expenditure surveys (if not published, then in the file drawers of the statistical bureau). Any country that publishes a cost of living index has such data, although the base year may not be recent. Failing this, careful interviews with a dozen representative consumers in each income category will substitute and will not fail to provide fascinating perspectives on the variations in food habits across income classes.

Good food policy analysts should always go this far in understanding disaggregated food consumption patterns. It is critical to get the commodities and the amounts right. Whether it is then possible to disaggregate the demand parameters by income class will depend on data availability, computer facilities, and analytical capacity. With the right combination of these factors, as in Indonesia and Thailand, very powerful analysis of the determinants of food intake by income class can be conducted. Such analysis is conducted commodity by commodity, income class by income class, using extremely large household expenditure surveys conducted by statistical bureaus for other purposes. Only the analytical costs are attributable to food policy analysis.

The results of the few such analyses that have been conducted are both satisfying and exciting. Intuitive prior judgments that the poor are significantly more responsive to economic signals—both income and price signals—are strongly borne out in the analysis. The analysis has also demonstrated significant variations in food consumption levels and in parameters of change by geographic region, by age and sex, and especially by season of the year. It may not help a malnourished child to have enough food on average for the year if it is going to die during a three-month ''hungry season.''

PRODUCTION

Food production is also a legitimate starting point for food policy analysis. The fundamental fact is that food cannot be consumed unless it has been produced. Society cannot borrow from next year's production for this year's consumption needs (although in desperate times societies have eaten the seed for next year's production). Somehow food must be produced, and understanding that process is an important component of food policy analysis.

What should society ask of its food production sector? The question is harder to answer than it seems. Most people's immediate instinct is that the domestic food producing sector should provide the society's food consumption "needs." But then the thoughtful hedges begin. The United States should not grow all of its sugar and bananas, Japan should not grow all of its wheat, Europe need not grow all of its soybeans. In fact, the same four basic objectives for an overall food strategy can also be held out, with different weights, to the food producing sector as well.

Generation of farm income through efficient agricultural production provides the real productivity base from which all other objectives can be discussed. Without efficient income generation the entire rural sector will act as a drag on both macroeconomic performance and the ability of policy makers to deal with hunger and malnutrition. Knowing which crops, which new crop technologies, which size farms, which rural infrastructure investments, and which production techniques will generate that efficient agricultural productivity is partly the responsibility of policy analysis, public investment, and macro price policy and partly the responsibility of millions of farmers who typically make rational decisions within the constraints of their own household and resource environment.

Food production policy has three major tasks: (1) ensuring the availability of efficient agricultural technology for the various agro-climatic zones of the country; (2) providing a set of macro price policies—prices for capital, labor, foreign exchange, and food—which at the least do not actively discriminate against the rural sector and which ideally would provide more positive incentives for food production; and (3) developing a rural marketing system for inputs and outputs with equal access for all classes of farmers at a minimum and preferential access for small farmers as an ideal.

Each of these public policy roles with respect to efficient food production has an implicit or explicit income distribution consequence. The ideal policies build a concern for income distribution specifically into the policy and program design, for the evidence suggests that rural income distribution can worsen in the context of efficient growth in agricultural production without such specific attention.

Food production analysis must ask many of the same questions a food consumption analysis asks, but it is probably better to begin with the disaggregated perspective. For each of the major agro-climatic zones in a country, what yields are farmers actually obtaining? What is the seasonal pattern of land use relative to temperatures, rainfall, or water availability? Are crops grown in mono-culture stands or are they extensively intercropped? What are the substitute crop possibilities for any given season? Nothing may compete with paddy rice in the rainy season, but soybeans, peanuts, maize, and cassava may all be possibilities for the same plot immediately after the rice harvest. Little area response to changed rice prices is likely in such an environment, while extreme sensitivity to relative soybean to peanut prices may exist.

What prices are farmers receiving at the farm gate for their output, and how do such prices compare with international prices suitably discounted to local levels? The answer to this question is quite revealing about the extent of incentive or disincentive to domestic farmers for their respective crops. If farms are receiving high prices for their crops but are producing very low yields, both by world standards, then a visit to the local agricultural experiment station is in order. It is possible that the farmers simply do not know how to use available crop technology very efficiently, and then a vigorous agricultural extension program is called for. Historically, however, such circumstances have been explained by an absence of a high-yielding crop technology that worked reliably on a farmer's field with available inputs.

How these three empirical relationships—farmers' yields, farm-gate incentives, and available technology—compare with each other provides strong clues as to where government agricultural policy should focus its attention. Most developing countries have provided their farmers with very poor incentives and, until recently, with little modern biological technology. For most countries this record of neglect and discrimination must be reversed if the domestic food production sector is to play a dynamic role in the overall modernization process, if income distribution between urban and rural areas is to be more equal, and if domestic food security is to be improved without increasing resort to unstable world markets.

Three more micro aspects of agricultural production are also important to policy makers. First is the composition of commodity output. Many countries would like their farmers to produce domestically needed quantities of basic food grains at very low prices before turning to more profitable cash and export crops. China has had some, but not unlimited, success in implementing such a policy through centrally determined grain acreage allocations. Countries with less control over their population, and even China at the margin (and more recently in general), have found their farmers quite recalcitrant about growing relatively unprofitable crops. If the balance of commodities produced is undesirable from a social point of view, either the technology or the incentives, and frequently both, will have to be changed.

The second micro issue is choice of technique in agricultural production.[2] How farmers combine factors of production to produce agricultural output is critical for three reasons: (1) depending on the extent of labor hiring, techniques chosen alter the income distribution within rural areas; (2) some techniques use considerably more foreign exchange than others, with resulting macroeconomic consequences; and (3) some techniques are more natural resource–intensive than others, especially in their use of liquid fuels or care with which fragile soils are cultivated. Many choices about technique are strongly influenced by macro price policy, and the choice of technique issue in agricultural production has strong linkages to macro and international economic policies.

The third micro production issue for policy makers is the responsiveness and flexibility of the agricultural system. Traditional agriculture evolved in a variable year-to-year internal environment but a static external world. There is some evidence that the weather may be becoming even more variable, but the external world is clearly no longer static. An agricultural system that is efficient in production and responsive to new signals about what is desired as output will be an essential foundation for a successful food strategy for the 1980s.

MARKETING

The need for responsiveness and flexibility in food production is transmitted from food consumers via the marketing system. If the signals do not get through efficiently, both sides of the food system are frustrated. Since foods as consumed are nearly always different in time, place, or form from foods as produced, nearly all foods must be marketed in the technical sense. Not all foods must enter the marketing system, however, since the three marketing functions are often provided by the farm household itself as it transports grain from the field, stores it, and mills it before consumption. The process of economic modernization raises the opportunity cost of such household activities, and the marketing system tends to supply an ever larger share of these services relative to household production. For food policy analysts the important questions about the marketing system involve its static efficiency with respect to time, space, and form transformations and the dynamic capacity and flexibility to handle varying and especially larger quantities.

Market efficiency refers to whether the marketing system equates costs of storage, transportation, and processing with temporal, spatial, and product form price differences. High marketing margins do not necessarily denote inefficient markets if costs are commensurately high. High costs typically reflect inadequate physical and institutional infrastructure in the marketing system (poor roads accessible to trucks only in the dry season, lack of central market places where price formation is competitive and resulting prices are publicly announced and broadcast to farmers, shortage of fertilizer go-downs close to the point of fertilizer use, inadequate milling facilities), and public policy should normally focus on high-payoff investments that will improve the physical capacity of the marketing system to handle both the inputs and output. Greater capacity usually means lower short-run marginal costs when supplies increase sharply; hence the flexibility of the system to respond to variations is also improved.

Food policy analysts must be alert to two common biases in developing country food marketing systems. First, most traditional peasant households have always sold at least a small portion of their basic grain output in order to buy a few cash goods necessities—salt, cloth, cooking ware. The traditional marketing system evolved to handle limited quantities of grain flowing out of the countryside to commercial centers, and small quantities of consumer goods flowing back to the countryside. Such a marketing system is frequently incapable of providing large quantities of agricultural inputs to the countryside or of returning a sizeable increase in the net marketed output.

The second market bias has built up in regions with heavy reliance on a single export commodity, for example, cocoa, peanuts, sugar. The marketing system then tends to be efficient at moving the export commodity out to ports and possibly at moving foodstuffs and other consumer goods back to the growing region. Even fairly strong demand for food from other parts of the country, especially the commercial and governmental centers, may not be transmitted back to potential growers. The argument is not that cocoa farmers should grow rice or peanut farmers, millet, but that the marketing system may be more efficient at transmitting both commodities and price signals for some goods than for others and in one direction rather than both directions.

The marketing system must not only transmit price signals efficiently but also serve as the arena for price formation for many agricultural commodities. Most countries have national food price policies for their basic staple grain (and frequently for many more commodities), and such policies are normally implemented by special trade arrangements at the international border with respect to imports and exports of the commodity. Even with such a macro food price policy, however, the marketing system must still transmit the desired price signals up to consumers and down to farmers. For other commodities that frequently are very important for farm income—fruits, vegetables, livestock, pulses—the marketing system must provide the price formation arena itself. The institutions by which governments encourage or discourage this activity heavily influence the net returns to farmers and the retail prices to consumers.

The income distribution consequences of inefficient price formation or transmittal of policy-determined price signals are almost uniformly bad. High marketing costs do not imply high incomes for the "middleman," but they do tend to imply high returns to those who can take the real risks of a costly marketing venture. Secondly, even in efficient and low-cost marketing systems many middlemen who are transporting and storing grain will tend to make windfall profits when food prices rise suddenly and unexpectedly. Although no one notices their losses when food prices fall unexpectedly, speculative profits on holding food grain during the food shortage seem antisocial, if not criminal, and many societies have treated the middleman as both. Honest profits are to be made in food marketing, and the role of public policy should be to see that such profits, and only such profits, are a normal component of the cost of providing food to consumers.

MACROECONOMIC ENVIRONMENT

Domestic Macro Policy

If policy is the cutting edge of development, then domestic macro policy conditions the development environment in which a food strategy is designed and implemented. Unfortunately, this macro environment is usually hostile to several of the objectives of a food policy, especially the critical one of efficient (and even equitable) growth in agricultural production. Macro policy has three essential components from the perspective of the food system: (1) fiscal, budgetary, and monetary policy; (2) macro prices for labor, capital, and land (food prices); and (3) the foreign-exchange rate.

Fiscal policy encompasses the overall tendency toward expansion or contraction of the economy; budgetary policy entails the actual sectoral allocations of the fiscal total; and monetary policy tends to be the instrument that accommodates fiscal policy when tax revenues fall short of budgetary expenditures. Monetary policy can be operated independently of fiscal policy, but in most cases the money supply tends to expand to fill fiscal deficits. The inevitable result is chronic and frequently rapid inflation. Inflation is a characteristic of the usual macro policy context in which food policies are framed.

The second essential component of macro policy is the real level of an economy's macro prices—the prices for the basic factors of production: labor, capital, land. Most countries influence land prices through the urban-rural terms of trade (although land also serves as a hedge against inflation), and these terms of trade are heavily influenced by prices for basic food staples. Thus the macro prices are wages, interest rates, and food prices as a proxy for the broader rural-urban terms of trade.

All three macro prices also tend to be biased against efficient agricultural production, at least to the extent that governments are able to implement their policy intentions. Since prices are meant to signal relative scarcity to decision makers in the economy, policy-dictated macro prices that are sharply at variance with actual scarcity values will tend not to be widely applicable as actual decision variables. Low interest rates can be maintained for a few preferential customers through a rationing system and an accommodating monetary policy, but such rates will depress savings and force informal credit rates, especially rural rates, to higher levels than otherwise.[3] High minimum wages can be enforced in large industries but reduce the demand for labor and force wages lower in the much larger informal labor market, also heavily rural. Low food prices, if enforced only by statute, will tend to generate a black market where nonpreferred customers, especially the poor, must pay much higher prices for their foods while forced market deliveries from food surplus areas depress agricultural incentives.[4] The typical macro price policy set, although perfectly understandable as a political reaction to the very difficult pressures of economic modernization, tends to place a very heavy burden on an effective food strategy.

Low food prices can also be maintained, usually more effectively, by appropriate food import or export policy controlled by the government. Restricting food exports or subsidizing imports will reduce domestic food prices. Restricting food exports usually provides a government budget surplus, as in Thailand, so it is a doubly popular policy with urban-based government officials. Since subsidizing imports requires a budget allocation, the costs of such a low food price policy are more apparent.

The third component of macro policy, however, typically hides some of these costs behind an overvalued exchange rate. The foreign-exchange rate—also a macro price because it is set and defended by the central bank—measures the price of a unit of foreign exchange, say a dollar, in terms of the number of units of domestic currency, say the Indonesian rupiah, required to purchase it. Thus the Indonesian exchange rate between August 1971 and November 1978 was Rp 415 per U.S. dollar and is now Rp 625 per U.S. dollar. From 1974 to 1978 the rupiah became increasingly overvalued as domestic inflation ran much faster than international inflation. Food prices were kept low domestically, not by large budget subsidies on imports, but by large imports valued at an overvalued exchange rate. The burden on rural producers and the benefits to urban consumers came through the overvalued exchange rate (permitted in this instance by petroleum revenues) that made imported commodities appear cheaper to the domestic economy than they should have. With the sharp devaluation in 1978 this bias was eliminated, and the costs of maintaining low food prices were transferred directly to the budget. The visibility of such costs changes the nature of food policy discussions from trying to show a bias to examining the costs and benefits of the bias. A devaluation also tends to increase sharply the terms of trade for rural commodities that are not specifically subsidized by domestic macro price and trade policy. Rural areas almost always benefit from devaluations of domestic currencies to reflect more accurately long-run scarcity.

Broad-based macroeconomic reforms encompassing all three components of macro policy—fiscal, budgetary, and monetary policy; macro prices for labor, capital, and food; and the foreign-exchange rate—are not likely to be carried out at the behest of food strategists. But first, they should be carried out anyway if the country is concerned about growth and equity, and second, food strategists should be on the right side rather than the wrong side of the macro policy debate.

Where is the side of the angels? The first point is to understand that macro policy reform will have significant short-run food consumption consequences and large political costs. Programs to deal with both should be in place before a major reform is implemented rather than assembled in a scramble after problems begin to appear. In effect, understanding the need for such programs and assisting in their design is the basic role of good food policy analysis.

With this step taken, the components of effective macro policy are fairly straightforward, even classical: (1) a reasonably balanced budget with restrained monetary growth leading to stable prices by the standards of international trading partners and (2) macro prices set to reflect long-run opportunity costs of the factors of production—determined by their marginal productivity in producing tradeables at an equilibrium exchange rate. Such opportunity costs should not be read from international prices with a narrow, short-run, or mechanical vision. The first leaves out environmental costs, the second is unduly influenced by temporary fluctuations in highly leveraged international markets, especially for sugar and foodgrains, and the third implies that some formula can translate border prices into appropriate domestic price policy. With these provisions, however, such a macro policy reform will end up reflecting the reality of the domestic economy rather than the shadows of planners' wishes.

INTERNATIONAL ELEMENTS IN A DOMESTIC FOOD STRATEGY

Few countries have tried and even fewer have succeeded in isolating themselves from the international economy. Global interdependence brings great benefits, but it also magnifies the costs of contrary domestic policies. Long-term autarky is almost never a good policy, but a short-term hiatus from relatively free trade may be essential for some countries in the early stages of nation building. In general, however, international trade is beneficial to a young and unbalanced economy. It is fair to ask who benefits from the gains to such trade, and this is a task of food policy analysis. The burden of proof, however, falls on those who wish to show harm, and not vice versa.

This perspective suggests that the international economy serve as the standard by which domestic resource allocations are made, at least before income distribution consequences are factored into the policy decision. Tradeable goods, especially most output from the rural sector, can be imported or exported at the margin, and that marginal cost relative to domestic costs of production indicates the efficiency in income generation of a domestic project. Such an efficiency comparison need not dictate the ''go–no go'' decision if income distribution arguments are compelling, but the calculation should always be done.

If international opportunity costs are going to be held up as a standard of comparison to domestic production (and consumption) costs, then some understanding of the long-run functioning of major international commodity markets should be in the bag of tools carried by good food policy analysts. Such commodity markets are often said to be highly leveraged, unstable, and controlled by multinational corporations for the benefit of the industrialized world. There is enough truth in the appearance of some of these markets for the charges to have some validity, especially with respect to leverage and instability. Domestic food strategy planning would be made much easier if world food markets could be stabilized with some assurance of adequate food reserves for years of bad harvests—but planning *domestically* for such stabilization *internationally* would be foolish in today's world. Domestic planners should invest in understanding how the world grain markets actually perform, while encouraging their diplomats to search for ways to improve that performance.

World commodity markets are in fact tightly interconnected by technical and economic relationships, primarily through the livestock feeding industry and, in the not-too-distant future, possibly also through the sweetener and the alcohol fuel industries. Thus cassava, corn, wheat, and soybeans are linked through these mechanisms. Wheat and rice are linked in the world market by China through a calorie arbitrage implemented by shifting domestic food demand patterns with its urban grain rationing system. Understanding interdependence is the essence of understanding international commodity markets.

What international instruments of assistance are available to domestic food strategy planners? None is important enough that it should influence the basic strategic design for the food sector, but food aid can be useful as a short-run consumption support to a bridge linking existing food price policy with greater long-run price incentives to the domestic agricultural sector. The World Bank and other assistance agencies can provide useful funding and design assistance for critical urban and rural infrastructure, and their support of the International Agricultural Research Institutes is absolutely critical for developing the long-run technological base for rapid improvement in domestic agricultural productivity. Finally, analytical assistance is available for the design of effective food strategies. This design process is extraordinarily complex and requires personnel trained to think creatively about such complexity. No country has a monopoly on such personnel or on the training institutions that produce them. Here the gains to international trade are impressive indeed.

SUMMARY: ELEMENTS OF A FOOD STRATEGY

Three important summary points come out of the above discussion. First is the critical importance of recognizing the explicit need for a reconciliation between food consumption/nutrition objectives and the policy set necessary for efficient growth in agricultural production and farm incomes. Reconciliation is not the same as compromise, at least in the sense of giving each side half. Doing so might turn out to be the worst of all possible worlds, serving neither efficiency nor equity. Rather, reconciliation involves creative disaggregation of food consumption problems in the search for targeted interventions that do not require impossible budget subsidies or bureaucratic resources.

Second, food policy analysis involves a frame of mind for finding order in complexity. It is sophisticated, intuitive, even artistic. At its best such analysis uses a set of filters accumulated with experience and training to sort out (1) what is driving the food system at any given time and (2) how policy levers might be used to affect its direction and speed.

Third, food policy analysts will have three important starting points: food consumption patterns, food production potential, and how the macro policy environment conditions both. These three sectors are obviously not independent. They are connected by the domestic food marketing sector and conditioned by the international economic environment. Food prices turn out to be the critical short-run link joining all the pieces of the system, while the distribution of increases in income provides a second important, long-run link. Successfully integrating the short-run and long-run perspectives on behavior and performance of the food system is the goal of a food strategy.

NOTES

1. See Chuta and Liedholm, chapter 19 in this volume.—ED.
2. See Timmer, chapter 18 in this volume.—ED.
3. See Adams and Vogel, chapter 21 in this volume.—ED.
4. See Mellor, chapter 10 in this volume.—ED.

13

Exports and Economic Development of Less Developed Countries

HLA MYINT

INTRODUCTION

The question of how far exports, particularly primary exports, are capable of providing the underdeveloped countries with a satisfactory basis of economic development has been extensively discussed during the last two decades and may still be regarded as something of an open question. Prima facie, the broad facts relating to the export and development experiences of these countries during the period seem to support those who advocated policies of freer trade and export expansion rather than those who advocated policies of protection and import substitution. Thus, despite the ''export pessimism'' of the latter, which persisted well into the 1960s, the period 1950–70 has turned out to be a period of very rapid expansion in world trade, and those underdeveloped countries that responded to the buoyant world market conditions have been able to expand their exports rapidly, typically above 5 percent per annum. This export expansion included not only the primary exports produced by the large mining and plantation enterprises but also those produced by the small peasant farmers. In addition, a smaller group of countries have expanded their exports of manufactured and semiprocessed products. Furthermore, the countries that expanded their exports have also tended to enjoy rapid economic development, and significant correlations have been found between the growth of export and the growth of national income among the underdeveloped countries by cross-section studies; by time-series studies; or by a

HLA MYINT is professor of economics, London School of Economics.

Reprinted from *Economic Growth and Resources,* Volume 4: *National and International Policies,* edited by Irma Adelman. Copyright © 1979 by the International Economic Association. Reprinted by permission of the International Economic Association, St. Martin's Press, Inc., New York, and Macmillan Press Ltd., London. Published with minor editorial revisions by permission of the author.

combination of both methods (Emery 1967; Maizels 1968; Kravis 1970a, 1970b; and Chenery 1971). Conversely it has been found that the countries that concentrated on import substitution tend to have lower rates of growth than those that expanded their exports (Balassa 1971).

In this paper, we shall be concerned both with the causal analysis and with the policy implications of the relationship between the exports and the economic development of the underdeveloped countries. In section I, we shall consider this relationship, not as a simple one-way causation running from exports to economic development, but as a mutual interrelationship involving other important elements of the economic system. In section II, we shall argue that it is necessary to take into account not only the "direct gains" from trade in terms of the allocative efficiency of resources but also the "indirect effects" of trade on the productive efficiency of resources in a broader sense in order to have a better understanding of why the export-oriented underdeveloped countries tend to enjoy a more rapid rate of economic growth than those that have pursued import-substitution policies. In section III, we shall argue that the expansion of peasant exports from the "traditional sector" of the underdeveloped countries tends to promote economic development, directly by a fuller and more effective utilization of their underutilized resources in the "subsistence sector" and indirectly by extending and improving their domestic economic organization, which is incompletely developed. In section IV, we conclude that the outcome of our analysis is to support the prima facie view that freer trade and export expansion policies tend to promote the economic development of the underdeveloped countries.

I. POSSIBLE CAUSAL RELATIONSHIPS

A positive statistical association between the expansion of exports and the growth of national incomes among the underdeveloped countries does not tell us much about causal relationships. It may mean (a) that export expansion is the cause of economic development; or (b) that economic development is the cause of export expansion; or (c) that both are caused by some third factor. Further, the causal link running in each direction can be interpreted in a variety of ways. Without attempting to be exhaustive, we may review some of these potential elements in the mutual interrelationships between export and economic development.

(a) The hypothesis that the expansion of exports is the cause of economic development may be interpreted in three ways: (a.1) The first is the conventional free trade argument that the expansion of exports according to comparative costs will increase the direct gains from trade and thus help to promote economic development. (a.2) Next, we have the widely held belief that exports contribute to economic development mainly by providing the underdeveloped countries with the foreign exchange necessary for the purchase of capital goods and inputs from abroad. (*a*.3) Third, we may think of the "indirect effects" of freer trade and export expansion on domestic productive efficiency, such as the "educative effect" of an open economy, facilitating the spread of new wants and activities and new technology and new economic organization; or the gains in the productivity and the economies of scale from specialization for the export market.

It is fair to say that (*a*.1), viz., the direct gains from trade through a more efficient allocation of resources, provided the theoretical basis on which freer trade policies were advocated for the underdeveloped countries during the last two decades. Yet the causal link running from the direct gains from trade to economic development appears to be rather weak. During the decades 1950–70, the growth rates of the underdeveloped countries with rapid export expansion have been typically between 5.5 percent and 7 percent, while those with slow or stagnant exports have been about 3–4 percent; and the difference in the growth rates between the two types of countries became more pronounced during the decade 1960–70 (cf. Chenery 1971; Balassa 1971; and Meier 1970). On the other hand, it seems to be widely held that the static gains from the removal of the distortions created by protection tend to come out as a rather "small" percentage of the aggregate national product (Harberger 1959; and Corden 1975). Even if the whole of this gain is reinvested, this would seem to be too small and short-lived to explain the difference in growth rates between the successful and the unsuccessful countries. Later, we shall see that the picture may be modified by extending the concept of the "direct" gains and losses to include those arising from the allocation of the investible funds. But even so, we shall find it necessary to go beyond the "direct gains" to the "indirect effects" of the type listed under (*a*.3).

Leaving (*a*.2) and (*a*.3) for later consideration, let us now go on to the second hypothesis (*b*), viz., that economic development is the cause of export expansion. This may be interpreted in two ways: (*b*.1) Economic development may lead to an expansion of exports via increasing the supply of exportable goods. This is most easily seen when we assume exports as a constant proportion of a growing national output, but this proposition will hold so long as the share of exports does not decrease sufficiently to counteract the effects of the growth in total output. (*b*.2) Economic development may act via the increase in demand and the widening of the domestic market, having beneficial effects both upon the domestic industries and upon the export industries. Both these propositions are unexceptionable and may be included in the process of interaction between exports and economic development. The crucial question here is not whether a given increase in national output and income will tend to increase exports, but what is to be regarded as the main cause of this increase in output and income.

This leads up to the third hypothesis (*c*), viz., that both the expansion of exports and economic development are caused by a third factor. Here we approach the central battleground of the debates on trade and aid policies during the postwar decades, for it turns out that the choice of the "third factor" is nothing short of the choice of a theory of economic development that shapes our views about the relationship between exports and economic development. There are two main theories here.

(c.1) The first is deeply rooted in the thinking of the 1950s, when the supply of resources available for capital investment was regarded as the central problem of economic development. In this view, the level of investment (financed out of domestic savings and aid) is regarded as the "third factor" which will increase the total national product according to some assumed capital-output ratio and thus increase the supply of the exportable commodities. Combined with the "export pessimism" and the jaundiced attitude towards international trade which prevailed well into the 1960s, this has led to the familiar "inward-looking" policies.

(i) It was held that an underdeveloped country seeking a rapid rate of economic growth should step up the rate of capital investment oriented towards its internal investment opportunities independently of its external economic opportunities, which were assumed to be unfavorable.

(ii) Earlier on, these internal investment opportunities were supposed to be generated by a "balanced growth" between the domestic manufacturing and the domestic agricultural sectors. But given the prevailing faith in the power of modern manufacturing industry based on capital-intensive advanced technology to promote economic development, both domestic agriculture and primary exports came to be increasingly neglected in favor of the import-substituting manufacturing industry.

(iii) The expansion of the modern manufacturing industries, however, required imports of capital goods and other inputs and materials. Thus, the importance of foreign exchange as the means of acquiring the imported capital goods came to be emphasized. However, since it was assumed that the world market demand for primary exports would be extremely inelastic, it did not lead to export expansion policies (suggested by *a*.2 above), but to the restrictions on the imports of consumer goods to save foreign exchange for the imports of capital goods and to the renewed pleas for greater international aid to fill the "foreign exchange gap."

(c.2) The alternative view regards both the expansion of export and economic development as being caused not so much by the level of domestic investment per se as by the appropriate domestic economic policies that enable a country to allocate its resources more efficiently, taking into account both its internal and external economic opportunities. This is the position adopted by most economists who advocated policies of freer trade during the last two decades. They emphasized that an underdeveloped country would not be able to reap fully the direct gains from international trade unless it also pursued appropriate domestic policies, viz.: (1) appropriate pricing policies in both factor and product markets that remove discriminatory treatment of different lines of economic activities, both within the domestic economy and between the domestic and the foreign trade sectors; (2) appropriate macroeconomic policies that prevent overvaluation of the foreign exchange rate and avoid the need for ad hoc import restrictions and quantitative controls resulting in an unplanned protection arising from a chronic foreign exchange shortage; and (3) appropriate investment policies that reflect the country's comparative costs by valuing both the inputs and the outputs of investment projects at world market prices (cf. Johnson 1967; Little, Scitovsky, and Scott 1970; and Little and Mirrlees 1974).

It is fair to say that there are considerable empirical and theoretical grounds for supporting (*c*.2) against (*c*.1).

First, most economists would agree nowadays that the earlier approach to economic development in terms of increasing the *supply* of resources available for capital investment has turned out to be seriously inadequate and that in a fundamental sense economic development involves the raising of the productive efficiency in the use of resources. Despite the low ratios of domestic savings to their GDPs in the early 1950s, the overall rate of growth of the underdeveloped countries during the 1950–60 decade was about 4.5 percent per annum—much higher than was generally expected. This growth rate in GDP was maintained between 4.5 percent and 5 percent during the 1960–70 decade. During this time, the ratio of their domestic savings also increased to some 15 percent of the GDPs. A comparison of the savings ratio and the growth rates serves to bring out the modest contribution of capital to economic development. Thus if we follow Cairncross (1962) and assume the average rate of return on capital investment in the underdeveloped countries to be 10 percent, then the 15 percent saving ratio would have contributed no more than 1.5 percent of the total growth rate between 4.5 percent and 5 percent. If the level of domestic investment cannot explain the average growth rate of the underdeveloped countries as a whole, it is also not able to explain the difference in the growth rates between the successful and the unsuccessful countries. There does not seem to be any striking difference in the level of domestic investment between the successful countries that pursued export expansion policies and the less successful countries that pursued import-substitution policies (Bruton 1967).

Second, in the perspective of the 1950–70 decades, during which world trade expanded at an unprecedented rate, it is now difficult to maintain the extreme type of export pessimism that dominated discussions on trade and development well into the 1960s. Of course, it is anyone's guess whether world trade will resume its previous rate of expansion after the current recession. But even so, a more reasonable hypothesis would be that "under normal conditions" most underdeveloped countries could expand their exports, provided they pursued appropriate domestic economic policies. Kravis (1970a, 1970b) has taken considerable pains to dispel the fatalistic view that the underdeveloped countries' exports depend solely on the world market factors over which they have no control. He has shown that successful export performance among the underdeveloped countries during the postwar decades is determined mainly by domestic supply factors and "competitiveness." Thus the successful countries expanded their primary exports mainly by increasing their shares of the world market for their traditional exports and, to some extent, by diversifying into new exports. De Vries (1967) has also shown that some underdeveloped countries have succeeded in expanding their "minor" exports substantially by controlling their domestic rate of inflation with given exchange rates.

Third, the limitations of the concept of the "foreign exchange gap," popularized by UNCTAD economists during the 1960s, have been extensively discussed (for example, in Findlay 1973), and here we need touch upon only one aspect of the subject. We have seen above that the once-for-all gains obtainable from the removal of the static distortions are likely to be a small percentage of the GDP and that therefore the reinvestment of these once-for-all gains would have a very small effect on economic development. But this is not to deny that losses can be great and economic development can be seriously retarded when the *annual* flow of investible funds, including the supply of foreign exchange, is directed into unproductive channels by the import-substitution policies. This suggests an important qualification of the role of foreign exchange in economic development.

In the standard case in which a country acquires imports as final consumption goods, the "direct" gains from trade can be readily identified with the cheaper imports leading to a greater consumers' welfare. In the case of an underdeveloped country wishing to acquire the imports, not for final consumption but as capital goods and inputs for further production, the concept of "direct" gains from trade has to be defined more carefully. Following Hicks (1959), we may picture the country as being faced with a problem of choice in two stages. In the first stage, the country has the choice of converting its given savings into capital goods either by producing them at home or by converting the savings into exports which can be exchanged for the imported capital goods from abroad. Having acquired the capital goods in one way or another, the country has the further choice of either using them to produce the final consumer goods at home or using them to produce exports which can be exchanged for the imported consumer goods from abroad. Comparative advantage enters into both stages of choice, and the country will not maximize its final consumer gains unless the correct choices have been made at both stages.

We can now see why we need to qualify the popular argument that foreign exchange plays a crucial role in economic development by enabling an underdeveloped country to purchase the much-needed capital goods and technical inputs that it could not produce at home except at a prohibitive cost. This is true enough as far as it goes, but the gain from the opportunity to import the capital goods is only a potential gain; it can be turned into an actual welfare gain only if the imported capital goods are *economically* suitable, that is to say, only if the technology they represent fits in with the factor proportions of the country and the final products they produce are in accordance with the country's comparative costs. If the "wrong" type of capital goods is imported because of the protection of the domestic manufacturing industry and if, moreover, the importation of the wrong type of capital goods is actively encouraged by the provision of cheap capital funds and foreign exchange by government policies, it is not difficult to see that the potential gain from the availability of foreign exchange may be reduced or even turned into an actual loss (cf. Johnson 1967; and Myint 1969). Bruton's study (1967) of import substitution of five Latin American countries vividly illustrates this point. According to him, during the war period 1940–45, when these countries could not obtain their supplies of capital equipment and materials from abroad, the productivity of domestic resources rose through a process of improvisation and adaptation of the existing capital equipment to fit the local market size and the product to fit the local market demand, resulting in a fuller utilization of the productive capacity. In contrast, in the post-1955 period, when import-substitution policies were actively pursued with overvalued exchange rates and subsidies on the import of capital goods and technically necessary inputs, there was virtually no increase in the "pure" productivity of resources. On the contrary, with a growing inappropriateness of input mix of production due to the overvaluation of currency and distortions in the factor markets, and with a growing inappropriateness of the composition of output due to protection and to a decline in competition, "an industrial structure has tended to emerge that is so alien to factor endowments that full utilization of existing capacity came to depend more, not less, on a constant flow of imports" (Bruton 1967, 1112–13).

In this section we have been considering the mutual interrelationship between exports and economic development in terms of its constituent elements: (a) the effects of export expansion on economic development; (b) the effects of economic development on export expansion, through both an increase in total supply and an increase in total demand; and (c) the effects on both export expansion and economic development of a "third factor," notably the appropriate domestic economic policies. We have found that the causal link running from the direct gains from trade to economic development (a.1) is rather weak but that the static theory of comparative costs can be effectively extended to explain the *negative* proposition as to why the countries that pursued import-substitution policies tended to enjoy a lower growth rate through a misdirection of the investible resources. This has also suggested an important qualification to the proposition (a.2), viz., exports can contribute to economic development through the foreign exchange earnings only if these are correctly reinvested, according to comparative costs. We now turn to (a.3), the "indirect effects" of exports on economic development through their effects on the productive efficiency of the domestic economic system.

II. INDIRECT EFFECTS OF TRADE ON PRODUCTIVE EFFICIENCY

If we adhere strictly to the assumption of the static comparative costs theory and the "perfect competition" model on which it is based, then there would be little scope for the indirect effects of trade to operate on the domestic economic system. In such a model, the country's maximum production possibility frontier is supposed to be determined in an unambiguous manner by the autonomously given resources and technology. The country is assumed to be already on the production possibility curve before trade takes place, and it responds to the opportunity to trade by reversible movements along this curve. Since the country's production possibility curve cannot be shifted except by autonomous changes in the supply of resources and technology, all that trade can do is to change the allocation of resources. The possibility that the country's productive efficiency in a broader sense might be affected, either favorably or unfavorably, by the process of adapting its capacity to the requirements of international trade is ruled out by assumption.

(1) The possible increase in productive efficiency through the "educative effect" of an open economy in facilitating the spread of new skills and technology is ruled out if we adhere strictly to the assumption of "perfect knowledge," which implies a zero cost of search for information and transmission of knowledge. Thus "given" the technology in the outside world, the producers within a country supposedly would be able to adopt this technology in an instantaneous and costless manner.

(2) The possible increase in productive efficiency through the response of the domestic entrepreneurs to the pressure of foreign competition is similarly ruled out. Each producer is already supposed to be operating on his production function representing the minimum combinations of inputs required to produce a given output. With the given technology, these production functions are assumed to be determinate and can be changed only through an autonomous technological change.

(3) The possible increase in productive efficiency through the process of specialization for a wider export market in a genuine sense, involving the adaptation in the quality of resources and investment in durable productive capacity and human capital to meet a specific international demand, is ruled out by the static assumptions. Movements along the production possibility curve are reversible, and resources of each type are assumed to be homogeneous and divisible. There are no differential rents arising out of the differences in the quality of the resources and their suitability to international demand; all that adjustments to trade can bring about are the changes in the relative scarcities of different types of resources or their scarcity rents. The assumption of perfect divisibility of resources rules out the economies of scale. If there are no gains in productivity from specialization for the export market, there are also no risks or commitments in specialization. The economic system is assumed to be able to allocate resources either to expand or to contract exports in a smooth and flexible manner.

(4) Finally, it is assumed that with a given physical endowment of resources and given technology, the production possibility curve of a country cannot move upwards through a fuller utilization of these given resources. Resources are assumed to be fully employed, given the assumptions of their perfect mobility and the flexibility of their prices. This is reinforced by the assumption of "perfect knowledge," according to which the producers are supposed to know about the availabilities of the resources within the country in the same way as they are supposed to know about the available technology in the outside world. Further,

the "perfect competition" model has an implicit assumption that is of considerable importance to our later analysis, viz., that the domestic economic organization of a trading country, including its market system and network of transport and communication, is sufficiently well developed to bring the physically available resources into full utilization. This excludes the possibility that the process of international trade might introduce improvements of the organizational framework of the domestic economic system resulting in a fuller utilization of its existing resources.

Let us now consider how far we can combine these indirect effects of trade on the broader productive efficiency of the domestic economic system with the direct static gains from trade.

(1) The "educative effect" of an open economy arises not only from free commodity trade but also from the auxiliary functions of trade in facilitating the spread of new wants and activities and new methods of production and economic organization through a greater degree of international mobility of resources and human contacts. The conditions favorable for the "educative effect" are thus not identical with the static optimum conditions of free trade. A moderate degree of tariff or indirect controls on trade (as distinct from detailed quantitative controls) need not reduce the "educative effect," provided other aspects of international economic contacts are relatively free. Similarly, some of the concepts of static welfare analysis, such as "the tariff equivalent" of quantitative controls, may be inappropriate for the analysis of the "educative effect." But on the whole there does not seem to be any inherent logical difficulty in combining it with the static gains from trade.

(2) It is not clear how far the possible increase in productive efficiency or X-efficiency arising from the response of domestic entrepreneurs to the "pressure of foreign competition" can be grafted on to the static framework of analysis. A protectionist can argue that while the sheltering from foreign competition may lead to entrepreneurial inefficiency, exposure to the pressure of competition, particularly from the producers in the advanced countries, may present the domestic producers of the underdeveloped countries with an excessive challenge which outclasses them, and that they are likely to succumb rather than respond to such a challenge. In spite of this indeterminacy, there can be no disagreement about the proposition that under the typical conditions in which import-substitution policies are pursued by means of a network of controls, the domestic entrepreneurs of the underdeveloped countries would find it more profitable to direct their energies to the task of procuring the government licenses or exploiting the loopholes in the regulations rather than to the task of raising productivity. Thus a removal of such controls and a redirection of entrepreneurial incentives would tend to raise productive efficiency in addition to the purely static gains from the correction of the distortions.

(3) We shall definitely have broken out of the static framework of the comparative costs theory when we try to broaden the argument for export expansion by incorporating the gains from "specialization" for a wider export market involving the adaptation of the quality of resources and the building up of special

skills and productive capacity to meet the specific requirements of the export market. These gains represent a nonreversible outward shift of the production possibility curve of a country in the direction of export production. In order to obtain them, a country would usually have to commit its resources to export production on a large enough scale to overcome the indivisibilities in the production process or in the auxiliary facilities such as transport and communications. This is likely to take the country beyond the static optimum point indicated by the given comparative advantage before the process of specialization takes place and is therefore likely to impose some initial sacrifice of static gains from trade and also the risks of specialization. On the other hand, there is a general presumption, dating back to Adam Smith, that a country is likely to increase its productive efficiency by taking advantage of the opportunity to exploit the economies of scale and specialization in certain selected lines of export production for a wider world market instead of matching its resource allocation to the pattern of domestic demand inside the narrow home market.

There is some empirical evidence to suggest that indirect effects of this nature are more relevant for the understanding of the higher growth rates of the export-oriented underdeveloped countries than the conventional approach in terms of the removal of the static distortions. Bhagwati and Krueger (1973) have found that some of the export-oriented countries, such as South Korea, appear "to have intervened virtually as much and as 'chaotically' on the side of promoting new exports as others have on the side of import substitution" and that their success cannot be attributed to "the presence of a neo-classically efficient allocating mechanism *in toto* in the system." Similarly, one may deduce that the need for the "free trade zones" in other export-oriented countries such as Taiwan and Mexico implies that the rest of the economy, outside these zones, is not so free. Bhagwati and Krueger suggest that the success of the export-oriented countries may be attributed to the factors emphasized by the older writers on international trade, viz., the built-in budgetary constraints preventing excessive export subsidization; the relatively greater use of indirect rather than direct interventions in export promotion; the pressure of international competition on the producers of the subsidized exports; and the economies of scale.

The protectionist case against primary exports is based entirely on the alleged unfavorable indirect effects of such exports on the long-run productive efficiency of the domestic system contrasted with the external economies and "linkages" from the manufacturing industry. Since the whole argument is based on the presumption that it is normally worthwhile for an underdeveloped country to sacrifice some of the direct gains from trade to secure these longer-run indirect benefits, the issues of the debate are not properly joined so long as the free trade argument is limited to the direct gains from trade. We have to go on to consider the adverse indirect effects attributed to the expansion of primary export production.

The belief that primary exports tend to create the colonial-type "export enclaves" and tend to "fossilize" the economic structure of the underdeveloped countries still exerts a powerful influence and requires a critical examination.

Basically, the argument envisages the primary exports as being produced by the larger mining and plantation enterprises operated by direct private foreign investment. The objections usually advanced against such exports may be summarized as follows: (1) There may be "unfair" distribution of the gains from trade because the foreign investors have been able to obtain cheap concessions to exploit the country's natural resources, paying less than the "economic rent" for the use of these resources. (2) An "export bias" may be created because too large a portion of government revenues from the exports and the external supply of capital has been devoted to the type of social overhead capital, such as transport and communications and research, which benefits the larger enterprises in the export sector rather than the small peasants in the domestic sector. (3) This tends to "fossilize" the production structure, trapping resources in special lines of primary export production in the face of a long-run decline for the world market demand for primary products. (4) Primary export production tends to result in "enclaves" with few "linkages" with the rest of the economy, in contrast to the manufacturing industry's capacity to create such linkages and external economies.

(1) Leaving aside the complications introduced by the exhaustible natural resources, the possibility of "unfair" distribution of the gains from trade is an argument for the government of an underdeveloped country to charge the full economic rent on its natural resources rather than an argument against allowing either the foreign or the domestic investors to use these resources for the production of primary exports (see Myint 1972 for a fuller discussion of the issues). It does, however, serve to bring out a weakness in the standard Heckscher-Ohlin type of trade theory, based on the assumption of homogeneous resources and concerned with the effects of trade on the relative scarcities or the scarcity rents of the different types of homogeneous resources. Typically the "economic rents" on the natural resources required for primary exports largely consist of "differential rents" arising from the qualitative differences in a country's natural resources, including their location. This means that the direct gains from trade from primary exports are likely to be much larger than the conventional gains in terms of allocative efficiency based on the assumption of homogeneous resources. If withdrawn from export production, the earnings of special types of natural resources, such as land bearing mineral deposits or suitable for particular types of tropical product, would drop sharply in their alternative uses in domestic production. Thus so long as the governments of the underdeveloped countries are able to extract the full economic rent from the investors (and they have increasingly proven their ability to do so), this argument strengthens the case for primary export production.

(2) There are two different versions of the "export bias" argument. The first is directed against the flow of external capital into the underdeveloped countries for the construction of social overhead capital to facilitate the primary exports from the mines and plantations. But since this type of capital investment is "induced" by the specific purpose of expanding these exports and would not have been available to the country for other purposes, the country does not suffer

from foregone opportunities of investment elsewhere. It is true, for example, that a railway line running straight from the seaport to the mines, without the "feeder" lines to develop the surrounding countryside, may give little stimulus to domestic economic development. But it would not have come into existence without the mines, and it does not hinder domestic development in any way. It may be easier subsequently to build the feeder lines because of the existence of the trunk routes than if they had not existed. Further, the mines should provide the government with the revenues for domestic economic development. This brings us to the second version of the "export bias" arguments, viz., that in the past the colonial governments have devoted too much of the country's revenue for the benefit of the larger mining and plantation enterprises in the export sector rather than for the benefit of the small peasants in domestic agriculture. Whatever the truth of this allegation, it would now be entirely within the control of the independent governments of the underdeveloped countries to correct this bias against the "domestic sector." Unfortunately, however, in many underdeveloped countries the "domestic sector" has come to be identified with the modern manufacturing industry in the urban centers rather than with the small peasant producers in traditional agriculture. Thus the small peasant producers in the traditional sector may have suffered doubly—under the old "dualism" because of the colonial governments' encouragement of the larger-scale mining and plantation enterprises and under the new "dualism" because of the independent governments' encouragement of the modern manufacturing industry.

(3) The argument that the underdeveloped countries would tend to "fossilize" their domestic economic structure by specialization in primary exports has two aspects. The first stems from pessimistic views of the long-term patterns of world market demand for primary exports. These have proved unfounded in the light of the experiences of the postwar decades and the present concern with raw-materials shortage and exhaustible resources. In particular, Porter (1970) has shown that while the demand for primary products may be typically very price-inelastic or very income-inelastic, they are not both price- and income-inelastic and that the advanced countries of North America and Western Europe have managed to become dominant producers of the income-elastic primary products at least partly through an ability to cut costs. The second strand of the "fossilization" argument stems from the view that it is more difficult to shift resources out of primary production than out of manufacturing industry. Here, as we have seen, any genuine process of specialization in an export production, involving specific investment in durable productive capacity and infrastructure, is bound to give rise to heavy costs of readjustment in output, not taken into account in the conventional trade model with reversible movements along the production possibility curve. The question is whether it is significantly more difficult to shift out of specialization in primary production than from specialization in manufacturing industry. Although this is widely assumed to be true, it is difficult to find cogent theoretical or historical reasons for it. Historically, it is not difficult to find instances of successful switches from one line of primary exports to another.

Thus Malaysia switched from coffee production to her highly successful rubber industry and is in the process of switching at least some of her land to palm oil. Brazil is in the process of shifting from coffee to soya beans. Conversely, the British textile industry has for long been a well-known example of "fossilization" in manufacturing industry following an early leadership in the export market (cf. Allen and Donnithorne 1957; and Kindleberger 1961. See also, however, Chenery 1976, where it is argued that few governments would have sufficient foresight to switch out of primary exports in time, as though this "foresight" in an operational sense could be obtained from broad cross-section average relationships between the level of per capita incomes and the share of manufacturing industry in GNP).

(4) Finally, we come to the widely held opinion that primary exports are inherently less capable than manufacturing industry of creating "linkages" with the rest of the economy. On the face of it, there are as many technical possibilities for primary export production to create "forward linkages"—say, by increasing the supply of locally produced raw materials for processing industries—as for manufacturing industry to create "backward linkages" by setting up demand for locally produced inputs. How far these technical possibilities in either case can be economically realizable depends on the relative costs and prices of inputs and outputs; in other words, on the comparative costs principle that operates on the pattern of vertical international specialization between different intermediate stages of production in the same way that it operates on the pattern of horizontal international specialization between different final products. Advantages in location and the saving of transport costs may help with the creation of linkages. Here, as we shall see, the expansion of primary exports by peasant producers located in the traditional sector of the underdeveloped countries may be more favorable for the generation of some kinds of linkages than manufacturing industry located in the urban centers.

III. PEASANT EXPORTS AND ECONOMIC DEVELOPMENT

So far we have been concerned with the exports from the "modern sector" of the underdeveloped countries. We may now turn to the peasant exports from the "traditional sector" and their effect on economic development. At this point, it is necessary to reexamine the two related assumptions of the conventional trade theory, viz., that the domestic economic organization of the trading country, including its market system and its internal network of transport and communications, is fully developed before trade takes place; and that its resources are fully employed, given that they are internally mobile and that their prices are flexible. These two assumptions effectively rule out the possibility that the process of "opening up" an underdeveloped country to international trade will extend and improve its domestic economic framework and thereby enable it to utilize its "given" resources more fully and effectively.

There is, however, considerable historical evidence that in the early stages of development, peasant exports from the underdeveloped countries typically expanded, not by a contraction of domestic outputs, as implied by the full employment assumption of the comparative costs theory, but by bringing in the hitherto underutilized resources of the "subsistence sector," as suggested by the "vent-for-surplus" theory (Myint 1958). On the demand side, there were the foreign merchants and entrepreneurs, who actively searched for the sources of the exportable peasant products from the underdeveloped countries and subsequently built up the channels of trade consisting of the chains of transport and communications and retail-wholesale links that connected the traditional sectors of these countries to the world market. On the supply side, there were the peasant producers, who responded vigorously to the stimulus of new or cheaper imported consumer goods by clearing more land and by devoting the labor they did not require for subsistence production to export production. This historical process started in the late nineteenth century, but its potentialities were by no means exhausted in the postwar decades, particularly for the peasant export economies of Africa and Southeast Asia (Lewis 1969; and Myint 1972). Thus the rapid rate of economic growth of some of the export-oriented countries, such as the Ivory Coast and Thailand during the decade 1960–70, may be largely accounted for in terms of the vent-for-surplus theory. The direct gains from trade obtainable by bringing in the underutilized resources from the subsistence sector into export production offer a more convincing explanation of their growth than the conventional gains in terms of an increase in the static allocative efficiency of the "given" and fully employed resources.

The protectionist reaction to this type of export expansion policy would be to say that since the extension of peasant production takes place on the basis of unchanged agricultural techniques, it would sooner or later be stopped by the limits of the cultivable hinterland and that in order to forestall this and obtain a self-sustained basis for economic growth, the proceeds from peasant exports should be used to finance domestic industrialization. There has been no shortage of underdeveloped countries that have followed this protectionist domestic industrialization policy, in spite of the fact that their resource endowments and stage of development would seem to indicate that they could still greatly benefit from the expansion of peasant exports. Thus Ghana and Burma have used the device of state agricultural marketing boards with considerable ruthlessness to extract the revenue from their peasant exports of cocoa and rice for the purposes of domestic industrialization. Their poor performance both in export and economic growth contrasts sharply with that of their respective neighbors, the Ivory Coast and Thailand.

The idea that unlike manufacturing industry, peasant export production is incapable of generating "linkages" and should therefore be treated merely as the milch cow for the domestic industrialization programs is very widespread. It arises from a failure to appreciate the strategic position that peasant exports occupy in the incompletely developed domestic economic organization of the underdeveloped countries.

First, there is the familiar "dualism" in their economic organization, characterized by the coexistence of a "modern sector," consisting of the larger scale economic units engaged in mining, plantation, or manufacturing industry, and a "traditional sector," consisting of small economic units engaged in peasant agriculture and handicraft industries. The larger economic units in the modern sector are well provided with the auxiliary facilities such as transport, communications, power, and so on, and have access to a modern banking system and organized capital market. Even with a neutral government policy, the small economic units would have been handicapped by the incomplete development of the domestic economic organization, by the higher transport and transactions costs in retail trade, by the higher risks and costs of organizing a credit supply for small borrowers, and by the higher administrative costs of providing transport and communications and other public services to the widely dispersed small economic units in the rural areas. These natural handicaps are greatly aggravated when the government pursues a deliberate policy of encouraging domestic industrialization by discriminating in favor of the larger economic units engaged in the import-substituting manufacturing industry.

Second, although all types of peasant agriculture are handicapped compared with the economic activities in the modern sector, peasant export production is relatively favored under free market conditions compared with subsistence production and with cash production of food crops for the local or the domestic market. Thus peasant export crops are better served with marketing, transport, and credit facilities than are cash crops for the local market. Few other types of peasant products would enjoy a nationwide marketing network normally associated with the export products. Now the vent-for-surplus theory is concerned with the process whereby the surplus land and labor not required for "subsistence production" are attracted into export production in the early stages of the development of the traditional sector. At a later stage of development, it becomes necessary to consider also the relationship between the staple export crops and the development of cash crops for the domestic market and of the new subsidiary export crops. It is in this context that the full employment assumption of the conventional trade theory has to be modified.

An underdeveloped country that has apparently exhausted the more obvious possibilities of extending cultivation into the unused hinterland may nevertheless possess considerable "pockets" of underutilized resources which can be brought into fuller use by improvements in transport and communications and by widening of the local markets that extend the marketing facilities to cover some of the "gaps" in the existing network. In this setting of an incompletely developed domestic economic organization there would be possibilities for *complementary* relationships between the expansion of peasant exports and the development of cash production for the domestic market and the new peasant exports. The full employment assumption stresses the *competitive* relationship in allocating the "given" resources between one use and another. But if there were considerable "slacks" arising from the gaps in the organizational framework, the complementary relationships might be more important than the competitive relationships. Thus it has been observed that in some of the West African countries, the trade credit advanced by the export-import firms to the middlemen for the purchase of cocoa is frequently turned over two or three times to finance the local food crops before it is used for its original purpose of purchasing the export crop (Jones 1972, 251). Similarly, the "slacks" in other trading and transport facilities in the staple export crop can be used in the marketing of local food crops and subsidiary exports. Thus the effect of introducing state agriculture marketing boards into the export economies of West Africa and Southeast Asia has been not only to retard the growth of peasant exports by fixing buying prices well below the world market prices but also to repress the growth of the credit and marketing institutions in the traditional sector by replacing the private middlemen with state purchasing agencies at the local level.

Third, it is true that in the past, peasant exports have expanded on the basis of more or less unchanged methods of production, relying mainly on the possibility of extending cultivation into unused land. But this is not to say that peasant exports are inherently incapable of technical improvement. They may also indirectly contribute to the productive efficiency of the resources in the traditional sector in a number of ways. (i) First, there are the gains in productive efficiency from the division of labor and specialization through the widening of the local markets. In the initial stages, peasant producers entered into export production on a spare-time basis while continuing to produce all their subsistence requirements. At a later stage, some of them would specialize or devote all their resources to export production, so setting up a cash demand for locally produced foodstuffs. The consequent development of specialized food producers for the local markets tends to stimulate the growth of a marketable food surplus for the country as a whole, so enabling a labor-abundant underdeveloped country to take up its potential comparative advantage in labor-intensive exports of manufactured and semiprocessed products. (ii) The growth of cash crops both for the export and the domestic markets should in turn facilitate the adoption of the improved cash-intensive methods of production based on purchased inputs, such as high-yielding seeds, fertilizer, and more efficient farm equipment. So far, these improved agricultural methods introduced by the "Green Revolution" have been mainly taken up by the food-deficit countries for the purpose of attaining "national self-sufficiency" in food, based on a considerable amount of agricultural protection. Freer trade and export expansion policies have an important role of counteracting this tendency towards import substitution in agriculture and in bringing out the potential export possibilities of peasant agriculture after the introduction of these new methods. (iii) Finally, the development of both the product and the factor market within the traditional sector, which is perhaps the most important indirect effect of the expansion of peasant exports, should serve to improve the information network linking up the technology available in the outside world with the local availability of resources within the traditional sector. Since agricultural technology is "location-specific," this should facilitate the adaptation of new technology to local requirements.

To sum up: the expansion of peasant exports would tend to promote the economic development of the underdeveloped countries, both directly, through the "vent-for-surplus" mechanism, and indirectly, through the extension and improvement of their domestic economic organization, particularly in relation to the traditional sector of their economy. These indirect effects will continue to be important as long as these countries are characterized by a pronounced "dualism" between the modern and the traditional sectors and so long as a considerable proportion of resources in the traditional sector still remains in subsistence production.

IV. EXPORT POLICY AND ECONOMIC DEVELOPMENT

The result of our analysis is to support the prima facie impression that the economic development of the underdeveloped countries is likely to be promoted by freer trade and export-expansion policies rather than by protection and import-substitution policies. This result has been arrived at both in terms of the "direct gains" from trade within the conventional framework of the comparative costs theory and in terms of the broader "indirect effects," which take us beyond the confines of the conventional theory.

(1) The conventional approach yields the negative proposition that the countries that pursue import-substitution policies tend to suffer from a lower rate of growth. Thus, although the reinvestment of the once-for-all gains obtainable from the removal of static distortions may only have a small effect in increasing the growth rate, the misallocation of the *annual* flow of investible funds into inappropriate channels dictated by the import-substitution policies is likely to lead to serious losses and a significant retardation of economic growth.

(2) In order to put forward the positive proposition that freer trade and export expansion policies are likely to lead to a higher growth rate, it is necessary to bring in the "indirect effects" of trade. These include the "educative effect" of the open economy, the pressure of foreign competition in stimulating productive efficiency, and the economies of scale and increasing returns from specializing for a wider export market. The last type of gain involves a commitment of resources on a large enough scale to overcome indivisibilities and may require a pro-export policy instead of a strict neutrality between exports and domestic production implied by the static comparative costs theory. It also involves changes in the production structure that can be reversed only at considerable cost. But, on the other hand, genuine specialization in any line of economic activity, whether in manufacturing or primary products, would entail the commitment of resources and the risk of wrong or excessive investment. Specialization for the export market at least exposes the country to the discipline of international competition. These "indirect effects" are not theoretically demonstrable in the same way as the "direct" static gains from trade and are not susceptible of accurate measurement. But they are based on widely acceptable general presumptions that are, at least in principle, capable of empirical verification.

Our analysis of the relationship between the expansion of peasant exports and economic development gives an additional support to our general conclusion. The expansion of peasant exports tends to promote economic development, both directly, through the "vent-for-surplus" mechanism, and indirectly, by improving the domestic economic organization of an underdeveloped country.

REFERENCES

Allen, G. C., and A. Donnithorne. 1957. *Western Enterprise in Indonesia and Malaya*. London: Allen & Unwin.

Balassa, B. 1971. "Trade Policies in Developing Countries." *American Economic Review* 61(2): 178–87.

Bhagwati, J., and A. Krueger. 1973. "Exchange Control, Liberalization and Economic Development." *American Economic Review* 63(2): 419–27.

Bruton, H. J. 1967. "Productivity Growth in Latin America." *American Economic Review* 57(5): 1099–1116.

Cairncross, A. K. 1962. *Factors in Economic Development*. Chap. 4. London: Allen & Unwin.

Chenery, H. B. 1971. "Growth and Structural Change." *Finance and Development Quarterly* 8(3).

———. 1976. *Transitional Growth and World Industrialization*. Nobel Symposium on the International Allocation of Economic Activity, Stockholm.

Corden, W. M. 1975. "The Costs and Consequences of Protection. A Survey of Empirical Work." In *International Trade and Finance: Frontiers for Research*, edited by Peter B. Kenen. Cambridge: Cambridge University Press.

De Vries, B. A. 1967. *The Export Experience of Developing Countries*, World Bank Staff Occasional Papers, no. 3. Washington, D.C.

Emery, R. F. 1967. "The Relation of Exports to Economic Growth." *Kyklos* 20, fasc. 2.

Findlay, R. 1973. *International Trade and Development Theory*. Chap. 10. New York: Columbia University Press.

Harberger, A. C. 1959. "Using the Resources at Hand More Effectively." *American Economic Review, Proceedings* 49(2): 134–46.

Hicks, J. R. 1959. *Essays in World Economics*. Chap. 8. Oxford: Clarendon Press.

Johnson, H. G. 1967. "The Possibility of Income Losses from Increased Efficiency or Factor Accumulation in the Presence of Tariffs." *Economic Journal* 77(305): 151–54.

Jones, W. O. 1972. *Marketing Staple Food Crops in Tropical Africa*. Chap. 9. Ithaca: Cornell University Press.

Kindleberger, C. P. 1961. "Foreign Trade and Economic Growth: Lessons from Britain and France, 1850–1913." *Economic History Review* 14(2).

Kravis, I. B. 1970a. "Trade as a Handmaiden of Growth: Similarities between the Nineteenth and Twentieth Centuries." *Economic Journal* 80(320): 850–72.

———. 1970b. "External Demand and Internal Supply Factors in LDC Export Performance." *Banca Nazionale del Lavoro Quarterly Review* 93(June): 157–79.

Lewis, W. A. 1969. *Aspects of Tropical Trade*. Stockholm: Almqvist and Wicksell.

Little, I., T. Scitovsky, and M. Scott. 1970. *Industry and Trade in Some Developing Countries: A Comparative Study*. London: Oxford University Press for the Organisation for Economic Cooperation and Development.

Little, I., and J. Mirrlees. 1974. *Project Appraisal and Planning for Developing Countries*. London: Heinemann.

Maizels, A. 1968. *Exports and Economic Growth of Developing Countries*. Cambridge: Cambridge University Press.

Meier, G. M. 1970. *Leading Issues in Economic Development*. 2d ed. New York: Oxford University Press.

Myint, H. 1958. "The 'Classical' Theory of International Trade and the Underdeveloped Countries." *Economic Journal* 68(270): 317–37.

———. 1969. "International Trade and The Developing Countries." In *International Economic Relations*, edited by P. A. Samuelson. London: Macmillan.

———. 1972. *South East Asia's Economy: Development Policies in the 1970s*. Harmondsworth: Penguin Books.

Porter, R. 1970. "Some Implications of Post-war Primary Product Trends." *Journal of Political Economy* 78(3):586–97.

14

Food Aid

HANS W. SINGER

This article is not a balanced presentation of the pros and cons of food aid. Rather it is a "criticism of the critics" who, in the author's view, have gone much too far and have often been inconsistent in their hostility to food aid. For this reason it is only fair at the very outset to make two broad concessions to the critics. One, their criticism has been extremely valuable and useful in forcing the advocates and practitioners of food aid to rethink and improve their approaches and procedures. And second, it is clear that food aid, like financial aid and in fact any other economic resource, whether domestic or foreign exchange, can be badly or well used—and also badly or well given. It is not claimed that food aid is a shining exception to this rule.

For a corner of aid which accounts for a mere 10 percent of total aid, food aid has attracted an extraordinary amount of controversy and criticism (but also of hope and support). Why? I believe the main reason why food aid has attracted such a disproportionate volume of criticism is a mistaken identification of food aid with the policy framework in which it is given and received.

Let me explain: food aid is given by donors from the surplus food mountains that are accumulating among the major industrial countries as a result of enormous subsidy payments, open and concealed, and other protective measures for the benefit of their own farmers. The Common Agricultural Policy (CAP) of the European Community is perhaps the best-known example. These policies have been rightly criticized as harmful to developing countries, harmful to the industrial countries, and harmful to North-South relations in the world economy. Historically, food aid is inextricably linked with the existence of these surpluses. If we leave aside the Marshall Plan—a big chunk of which consisted of food aid—the whole food aid business began in 1954 in the United States with Public Law 480, when food aid was still honestly called "surplus disposal," or "food for starving children," but the cloven hoof of surplus food is still there. It is an open question whether food aid in its new incarnation as "food for development" would survive the abandonment of

HANS SINGER is a Professorial Fellow at the Institute for Development Studies, University of Sussex. Originally titled "A Pioneer's Response to Food Aid Critics." Reprinted from *CERES, the FAO Review*, no. 123 (vol. 21, no. 3), May–June 1988, pp. 44–47, by permission of the publisher, the Food and Agriculture Organization of the United Nations, and the author.

the crazy agricultural policies of the North and the disappearance of surpluses. But it is an entirely academic question since the food mountains seem to be merrily increasing all the time; the only thing that would put an end to them, at least in the EEC, would seem to be the bankruptcy and collapse of the EEC, which nobody would want.

MISTAKEN IDENTITY

Often the critics of food aid are really criticizing the policies which lead to the food surpluses, which in turn have led and are still leading to food aid—so their criticism is a case of mistaken identity. Some of the critics, aware of this danger of mistargeting, have argued that the opportunity of reducing the surplus mountains through food aid gives an incentive to the donors to continue their harmful agricultural policies. But this seems a far-fetched link, considering the small, almost minute, size of food aid in relation to the enormous surplus mountains; surely, if food aid were a significant reason for the present agricultural policies, it would be much larger than it is. Moreover, as will be subsequently argued, much, probably most food aid in fact takes the place of commercial imports by the recipient countries; to the extent it obviously does not reduce the surplus mountains. We must assume that the line of causation runs from surpluses to food aid, not the other way. This does not mean that the existence of surplus stocks is not a reason for donors' willingness to give food aid—but such self-interested motives are not inconsistent with developmental and humanitarian effects, nor are they in any way peculiar to food aid as distinguished from financial aid.

On the recipient side, food aid is often given to countries which fail to produce as much domestic food for their own consumption as they could or should. Here the critics' case is often directed at such neglect of their own food production by recipient countries rather than at food aid as such. But again, as in the case of donors' motives, the reply of the critics would be that food aid is a causal factor in encouraging recipient governments to neglect their own food production. It must be admitted that this causal link between food aid and bad policies is more plausible and more serious than in the case of the donors. I think it is also more serious than the more frequently alleged link between food aid and disincentives to local producers through lower prices which result from the augmentation of supply through food aid. We shall consider this latter case in more detail later, but the more serious criticism of food aid leading to bad policies of "urban bias," involving a neglect of local food production by recipient governments, deserves a closer look.

Would developing countries, in the absence of food aid, have shown less urban bias and done more to increase their own food production? This is one of those counterfactual questions to which no compelling answer can be given. But it is clear that the forces making for such urban bias as existed are much deeper and go much beyond the existence of food aid. They include the increasing trend toward urbanization which gives greater numbers and greater political power to urban groups: the fact that urban pressures and urban interests are closer to the seat of power and have much more political leverage (you get urban food riots while the rural poor starve quietly in inaccessible rural areas or remote refugee camps and need foreign journalists and television cameras to make their plight known); and the desire for industrialization, which is rightly identified as an essential part of economic development (although wrongly identified with large-scale and urban industries only). If, in the light of these pressures, governments are determined to show urban bias, it could even be argued that without food aid they would squeeze their local farmers even harder to extract surpluses for the urban population. As it is, with part of the food constraint relaxed by supplies of food aid, developing countries can better afford to relax the monopoly grip of parastatal marketing organizations and permit farmers to sell their surplus food at free-market prices.

One may add that criticism of developing countries for neglecting their own food production and for urban bias does not come well from countries which themselves show such distortions and extreme forms of "rural bias" in their own agricultural policies: structural adjustment must be a two-way business. In the overall picture, the "disincentive" due to low international food prices (in turn due to the overhanging surpluses resulting from the CAP and similar policies) encouraging imports is certainly more important than any disincentive due to food aid. Nor does such criticism come well from neoliberal critics who preach the virtues of "outward orientation" for developing countries: replacing food imports by domestic production is an act of import substitution, and the use of land for export crops rather than food for domestic consumption is the result of "outward orientation" and the pressure to earn foreign exchange to repay debts.

Food aid provides for those governments keen to promote their own food production plenty of opportunity to do so. In the first place, much of food aid is supplied in bulk and in fact takes the place of commercial imports (in spite of "Usual Market Requirements" rules). This foreign exchange can be used to import fertilizers, insecticides, agricultural tools and machinery, irrigation equipment, and other inputs into domestic food production; and also essential consumption goods, such as clothing, shoes, blankets, and soap, which farmers need as an inducement to sell surplus food—or better still the capital goods needed to produce such essential consumption goods domestically. In the second place, the government can use the revenue obtained from the sale of food aid or the counterpart funds arising from food aid, for the promotion of domestic agriculture, for example, rural public works or transport and irrigation projects.

India was by far the largest recipient of food aid in the 1960s under PL480 and it can be argued that this flood of food aid provided the Indian government with the funds to finance the infrastructure and investment needed for the Green Revolution in the Punjab. In the third place, the relaxation of the food constraint provided by food aid enables the recipient government to be more expansionist in its general policies. This, in a degree dependent on the pattern of expansion, is bound to increase the demand for local food and hence raise prices. Again taking India as an example, some commentators have maintained that the expansion of demand for local food in India, due to the expansion made possible by food aid, easily compensated for any tendency of the additional food supply to depress prices.

LINKING FOOD AID WITH PRODUCTION

Moreover, where a government cannot be trusted to use the relaxation of the food constraint in a manner favorable to domestic food production, food aid offers plenty of opportunities to the donors to insist on a shift in policy. Food aid can be given directly for agricultural purposes; it can be given as part of a structural adjustment program; it can be linked with an agreed food strategy; or the use of counterpart funds can be made subject to agreement and this leverage can be used to direct them into the rural sector. All these are not theoretical possibilities but describe a spreading practice of linking food aid with the promotion of domestic food production. Multilateral food aid through the World Food Programme and UNICEF, which is essentially on a project basis, has always favored the rural sector and can hardly be accused of urban bias. The monetization of food aid will offer new opportunities to combine the administrative and logistic advantages of using food aid for distribution in the urban areas with the objective of giving food aid in the context of maximum encouragement of national food production.

In any case, the idea that the governments of developing countries eagerly seize on food aid as an opportunity to neglect domestic food production is hardly plausible politically. Developing countries, particularly those whose independence is relatively recent, are very keen to establish and safeguard their national sovereignty. Dependency on food imports and specifically on food aid is clearly incompatible with this political priority objective. Who *likes* to be dependent on food aid?

In addition to the issue of a possible policy disincentive for the recipient government, there is another, closely related criticism of food aid as a source of fiscal disincentives. The point here is that food aid supplied in bulk for local sale—normally representing about two-thirds of total food aid—provides the government with "easy revenue." This, so the criticism goes, may tempt the government into relaxing its efforts to mobilize domestic savings through taxation. For some recipients of food aid (Bangladesh would be a good recent example) it is true that receipts from food aid may form a considerable part of government revenue, and it is important that this should not lead to slack fiscal policy and consequent "fiscal dependence." However, once more the critics are in danger of being inconsistent. To the extent that they are now preaching liberalization, greater reliance on the market, and limitation of the public sector as a recipe for development, one should have thought that they would welcome this effect of food aid, namely, that it reduces the burden of taxation and enlarges the resources at the disposal of the private sector. The critics cannot have it both ways. Moreover, insofar as a relaxation of the tax grip reduces the tax burden on the rural sector and on farmers, it can only help with the agreed objective of promoting local food production.

THREE MORE CRITICISMS

There are three other major criticisms of food aid which will have to be dealt with more briefly. These relate to harmful effects on local food producers through lower prices, the inferiority of food aid to financial aid, and the distortion of consumption patterns and the creation of "taste dependence."

The first of these criticisms, that food aid tends to depress local food prices and thus provides disincentives for local food producers, has dominated the earlier discussions largely because it relates to the image of free-market prices determined by the interplay of supply and demand on which all economists have been nurtured by the economics textbooks. Answers to this criticism are many. First, food prices in developing countries are normally not determined by the interplay of supply and demand in a "free market"; they are normally determined by regulation, often combined with a monopolistic or strong position of marketing boards or similar parastatal bodies. Second, as already pointed out, much, perhaps most of food aid replaces commercial imports and hence does not add to total supply. Third, we have already pointed out that food aid, by making possible an expansion of the economy, should lead to an increase in demand for food which should offset the increase in supply, even in a free-market analysis. Fourth, the additional revenue obtained by the government from food aid should enable it to use such additional resources to support local agriculture, by subsidizing inputs such as fertilizers, or by creating rural infrastructure providing better links with urban markets, or most directly by offering higher prices to local food producers. The latter action would in fact establish a dual price structure of cheap, subsidized food in the urban areas and higher prices for local food producers, with the difference covered from the revenue or counterpart funds arising from food aid. Fifth, it should always be possible for the donors of food aid to link it with a policy dialogue and food strategy which provides proper—which often means enhanced—incentives to local food producers. Sixth, insofar as food aid consists of "triangular transactions," buying food from other developing countries, such as maize from Zimbabwe or rice from Thailand, it would have a positive effect on food production and incentives to local food producers in such food-exporting developing countries. Triangular transactions are an increasingly significant feature of food aid and deserve to be more fully developed. Seventh, among the complex and numerous incentives and disincentives for local food production, price is only one of many factors and not nearly as important as the economic textbooks and the neoliberal doctrine of "getting prices right" as a universal remedy for underdevelopment would suggest. If food aid helps to finance agricultural research, or agricultural extension services, or through public works and feeding programs helps to make farmers' families better fed and healthier, or through school meals gives incentives to farmers to send their children to school, that would normally be an important factor in raising productivity in food production on a sustainable basis. But the critics are right in drawing attention to the need for encouragement of local food production, including proper output prices for local producers.

The second criticism was that food aid is an inferior substitute for financial aid. Here again there are some brief answers: First, food aid is at least partially additional to, rather than a substitute for, financial aid. There are political and commercial as well as humanitarian and legal reasons (such as international commitments under the Food Aid Convention) which make donors inclined to give food aid where they would refuse to give an equivalent amount of financial aid. Second, to the extent that food aid replaces commercial imports, it sets free foreign exchange and is therefore equivalent to or even better than financial aid—better because the foreign exchange released is not subject to conditionality. Third, financial aid is also often tied both by commodity and source of supply. Fourth, food aid can be monetized, thus sharing the flexibility of financial aid. Fifth, food aid is superior to financial aid in that a higher proportion of it goes to the poorer developing countries; and in spite of great difficulties of reaching the poorest of the poor, it is likely that food aid benefits the poor in the recipient countries more than does financial aid. But once again, the critics have served to remind us that food aid ought to be additional and specific and not at the expense of financial aid.

Finally, the distortion of consumption patterns: Here the chief answer to the critics must be that this shift in consumption patterns, say toward wheat and dairy products, is mainly a result of urbanization. The data do not suggest any clear correlation between the amount of food aid and shifts in consumption patterns.

Some of the critics would reply that food aid going to the urban areas for cheap distribution increases the rate of urbanization, but this also is difficult to trace. Much more fundamental forces seem to be at work. Moreover, this criticism would not apply to triangular transactions when the products supplied under food aid represent a traditional standard food of the recipient country. Once again, however, the critics are right in reminding us that the choice of products given in food aid must be carefully considered; for example, the share of dairy food aid in the EEC food aid program is almost certainly excessive and should be reduced.

To sum up, the voice of the critics in this debate has been too loud and strident and the voice of the defenders has been too muted. The defenders should listen carefully to the critics—but the critics should listen equally carefully to the defenders. Food aid is a fact of life and more likely to expand than to contract, so the natural approach should be to develop and improve it. A healthy debate is an essential part of this process.

REFERENCES

Cassen, Robert, and associates. 1986. *Does Aid Work?* Oxford: Clarendon Press.

Clay, E. J., and Hans W. Singer. 1985. "Food Aid and Development: Issues and Evidence." World Food Programme Occasional Paper, no. 3. Rome.

Riddell, Roger C. 1987. *Foreign Aid Reconsidered.* London: James Curry, in association with the Overseas Development Institute.

Shaw, John, and Hans W. Singer, eds. 1988. "Food Policy, Food Aid and Economic Adjustment." Special issue of *Food Policy* 13.1.

Singer, Hans W., John Wood, and Tony Jennings. 1987. *Food Aid: The Challenge and the Opportunity.* Oxford: Clarendon Press.

World Food Programme and Government of the Netherlands. 1984. Report of Food Aid Seminar, The Hague, 3–5 October 1983. WFP and Government of the Netherlands.

IV

Transforming Agriculture and the
Rural Economy

Introduction

The 1980s can be described as the decade of policy reform, the rise and decline of farming systems research, and increased emphasis on markets, institutions, and sustainability. The thirteen chapters in part IV draw heavily on empirical research on the relationships between technical change, markets, institutions, and policy reform. The emphasis on markets, market failure, institutions, and agricultural development arises out of a long overdue recognition that agricultural development involves more than transferring resources (technology, food aid, capital grants) to the Third World. Today, it is recognized that some of the basic differences between industrial and Third World countries are differences in economic organization, how factors of production interact, and how institutions mediate these interactions. "Among the most important of these institutions are markets" (Stiglitz 1989, 197).

Several chapters show that innovations in rural areas have important intersectoral as well as intrasectoral effects. As a result, agricultural innovations cannot be analyzed solely in terms of their impact on agriculture. For example, technical change in rice processing may affect the demand for labor in rural areas and the price of rice and hence wage rates in the cities. The primary emphasis of the articles in part IV, however, is on understanding how to accelerate agricultural growth and transform the rural economy, including improvement of farm production, marketing, processing, rural labor markets, and rural small-scale industry.

Growth in agricultural output occurs in three ways: through changes in the use of existing factors of production, through the development and use of new factors of production (technological change), and through changes in institutions, which alter the incentives and rights to use existing factors of production and develop new ones.[1] All three sources of agricultural growth are discussed in part IV. Chapters 16–21 examine how the market and other institutional structures influence the use of land, labor, and capital (including human capital) in farming and in rural nonfarm enterprises. Chapters 22–24 focus on technological change in agriculture while chapter 25 examines the distribution of costs and benefits from technological change in agriculture.

Bonnen introduces part IV by analyzing the need to coordinate and carefully sequence investments in human capital, technology, and institutional reforms when designing an agricultural development strategy. Drawing heavily on the experience of the United States, he points out that the payoffs to investments in any single activity, such as basic research, extension, or farming systems research, will be low unless there is a high degree of coordination with investments in complementary activities. Yet, given the scarcity of public resources in most Third World countries, not all investments can be made simultaneously. Hence, the question of the sequence in which investments are made becomes critical. Bonnen emphasizes the long-term institution building and human-capital improvement required for a highly productive agricultural sector. But he points out that institution building must go beyond research and training institutions to include organizations to deal with topics such as soil and water conservation, credit, rural infrastructure, and market regulation. Some institutions will be public, some private, with the mix depending on a nation's history, institutions, and political philosophy. Bonnen concludes by observing that the lesson to be learned from the past is that a search for complementarities between public and private roles and a pragmatic focus on problem solving is more important than an exclusive ideological commitment to any particular "ism," such as capitalism or socialism.

In chapter 16, Nobel laureate T. W. Schultz reiterates Alfred Marshall's dictum that "knowledge is the most powerful engine of production; it enables us to subdue nature and satisfy our wants." Considered the father of human capital theory, Schultz has a straightforward message: "while land per se is not the critical factor in being poor, the human agent is: investment in improving population *quality* can significantly enhance the economic prospects and welfare of poor people."

Schultz points out the critical importance of "investing in people" as part of a development strategy. Traditionally, the bulk of such investment in many Third World countries has been in improving the income-earning skills of men. As development economists began paying increasing attention to income distribution issues, in the 1970s, they also became more aware of the enormous contributions of women to the rural economy, the differential impact of development projects and programs on men and women, and hence the need to invest in improving women's income-earning skills and access to resources. The UN declared 1976–85 the "Decade for Women," and development agencies launched numerous projects aimed at improving the welfare of rural women. In chapter 17, Buvinić and Mehra demonstrate the substantial economic contributions of women to the rural economy, analyze the failure of many traditional development efforts to reach women, and examine the record of women-in-development projects launched during the Decade for Women. The authors show that many projects aimed at increasing women's incomes often became sidetracked into providing welfare services and training in "traditional female skills (sewing, cooking, and crafts, among others)." Although these projects demonstrated that donors were doing something about rural women, they ultimately had little impact on improving the welfare of women.

Learning from these failures, new approaches launched during the late 1980s stressed micro-enterprise and other income-generating projects for women (Deere and Leon 1987). Buvinić and Mehra examine the issues in designing such projects and conclude that, above all, women in the Third World "need to increase their productivity and income in agriculture and related rural enterprises in order to improve their own and their families' welfare." Thus, the strategic issues for helping women in the 1990s include improving the productivity of smallholder farming (as long as women as well as men benefit), income generation through micro-enterprise projects, human capital formation, and removing the racial, class, and institutional barriers to helping women become participants and beneficiaries in Third World development.

In chapter 18 Timmer uses the example of rice milling in Java to illustrate the type of economic analysis that is useful in selecting techniques appropriate for agricultural processing in low-wage economies.[2] Timmer undertook this analysis because the government of Indonesia was considering importing several large, capital-intensive milling facilities in order to "modernize" the Javanese rice processing industry. Timmer shows that if Indonesia had imported technology appropriate to high-wage countries like the United States (large rice processing mills), it would have resulted in much higher milling costs and increased unemployment, as expensive imported capital displaced inexpensive domestic labor. Using neoclassical analysis, Timmer demonstrates the superiority, from an efficiency standpoint, of the small-scale rice mills adopted spontaneously in Java during the late 1960s. These mills outperformed both large, capital-intensive facilities and hand pounding of rice.

In their comment on Timmer's paper, Collier et al. point out that, although the small mills may have been economically efficient given the existing property rights, the costs and benefits of shifting from hand-pounding to small mechanized mills were borne very unevenly. The major cost was in the form of increased unemployment among low-income women who previously had hand-pounded the crop, while the benefits were in the form of lower consumer rice prices and increased incomes for rice millers.

The Timmer–Collier et al. interchange raises the issue of whether mechanisms are needed to compensate those hurt by technical change. The exchange also demonstrates the large array of detailed engineering, economic, and social data needed to understand the production and income-distribution consequences of technical change.[3]

Development theory and practice during the 1950s and 1960s devoted little attention to rural nonfarm activities such as processing, carpentry, tailoring, and trading. In chapter 19, Chuta and Liedholm review empirical studies from the 1970s and 1980s and reaffirm that rural nonfarm enterprises are major sources of output, employment, income, and intermediate demand for agricultural products in many Third World countries. Rural small-scale industry is particularly important in providing agricultural equipment adapted to local conditions and slack-season rural employment for farm laborers. Nevertheless, because of the interdependencies between agriculture and rural nonfarm enterprises, the profitability of nonfarm enterprises is crucially linked to the growth of farm income. Despite the importance of rural small-scale industries in terms of their efficiency and rural income and employment generation, there are few widely applicable policy measures to assist small-scale firms other than "leveling the playing field" between small- and large-scale firms by removing discriminatory tariffs, taxes, and licensing requirements for small-scale firms (DeSota 1989). Chuta and Liedholm stress the need to link rural small-scale industries, credit, and marketing initiatives. Promising examples of such integration include the Grameen banks in Asia and micro-enterprise projects for women. But more research is urgently needed on the dynamics of rural industries (Liedholm and Parker, 1989) and on developing cost-effective and targeted interventions to reach particular groups.

During the 1950s and 1960s most economists investigating land tenure issues concluded that tenure reforms were often necessary in order to give small farmers incentives to invest in land improvements and to adopt new technologies that required more purchased inputs.[4] Although the 1960s and early 1970s witnessed a number of land reforms in Latin America and Asia, by the late 1970s land reform in most parts of the world was relegated to historians (Powelson and Stock 1987). In chapter 20, Binswanger and Elgin address two questions—land reform and farm size. Land reform, although still important in political rhetoric, is seldom implemented today in the Third World. After reviewing the experience of reforms during the past four decades, the authors conclude that land reform is unlikely to be a major tool for improving the welfare of the poor because of political resistance by large farmers and estate (plantation) owners. Hence, other measures have to be developed to improve the access of the rural poor to land, including land registration (Barrows and Roth 1989), land settlement, tenancy reform (Otsuka and Hayami 1988), and helping the poor increase rural nonfarm incomes.[5]

Turning to the economics of farm size, Binswanger and Elgin draw on the definitive study by Berry and Cline (1979) showing that, in many countries, productivity is higher on small farms than large farms because family members have a higher incentive to work on their own farms because they receive a share of profits, there are no hiring and search costs for family labor, and each family member takes a share of risk. But in some countries, large estates and plantations coexist with small farms. The usual justification for plantations is that these large firms can more efficiently perform the tight coordination between harvesting, processing, and international marketing. For example, to ensure high quality, bananas must be put in a refrigerated ship within 24 hours of harvest. There is, however, substantial evidence that smallholders are competitive with large farms if class and racial barriers are removed and creative institutions are developed to achieve the vertical and horizontal integration necessary to supply inputs to smallholders, purchase their products, and find "windows of opportunity" for these products in international markets. Such arrangements often take the form of contract farming, linking smallholders to larger firms, which may be privately or cooperatively owned (Minot 1986). For example, smallholder cotton is competitive with plantation cotton in French-speaking countries in Africa through a French-directed multicountry, integrated research, extension and marketing system (Lele, van de Walle, and Gbetibouo 1989). But it takes political support, vision and institutional innovations to help smallholders compete with large agribusiness firms.

Development theorists during the 1950s viewed the lack of physical capital as a crucial constraint on both agricultural and industrial growth. Concern about capital shortages in agriculture grew during the 1960s as the Green Revolution technology, with its heavy reliance on purchased inputs, was introduced into many countries. This concern led to greatly expanded efforts to channel subsidized credit to Third World farmers. In fact, Adams and Graham (1984) estimate that donors poured over $5 billion into rural credit projects in the 1960s and 1970s. A major debate of the 1960s and 1970s centered on whether specialized lending agencies should subsidize interest rates to small farmers in order to offset the administrative costs and risks of lending to small farmers, and on the alleged monopoly profits in private capital markets and the price distortions in other parts of the economy, such as low farm-gate prices due to heavy agricultural taxation. Many researchers argued that subsidized interest rates were an extremely inefficient means of counteracting price distortions, that they tended to undermine incentives for rural savings mobilization and that they worsened income distribution. The work of scholars like Adams and Graham (1984), Adams and Vogel (chapter 21 in this volume), and Von Pischke, Adams, and Donald (1983) has led some donors and Third World governments to deemphasize subsidized agricultural credit and to charge positive real rates of interest.[6] In chapter 21, Adams and Vogel review the arguments for and against specialized small-farmer lending institutions and subsidized interest rates. The authors point out that there are often politically powerful groups that benefit enormously from subsidized credit programs and therefore favor their continuation. Like so many other aspects of agricultural policy, farm credit needs to be analyzed within a broad political economy framework (Von Pischke et al. 1983).

Technical change in agriculture is covered in chapters 22–27. In chapter 22, T. W. Schultz argues that investment in agricultural research should be analyzed like any other economic activity because it uses scarce resources to produce valuable outputs. Schultz maintains that many Third World countries have underinvested in agricultural research because they have erroneously assumed that agricultural technology could be imported from high-income nations and the international agricultural research centers with little or no local adaptive research. Reviews by Evenson (1984) and Judd, Boyce, and Evenson (1986) of studies on the rate of return on investment in agricultural research emphasize that these rates are generally high in industrial countries, as well as in Asia and Latin America. But the rates of return cited have to be interpreted with caution, because such studies typically focus only on successful research programs and, as Bonnen points out in chapter 16, they often understate the strategic role of complementary services, such as extension. Moreover, it takes about a decade, on the average, to generate and/or import, test, and adapt technology to local environments. For example, although the rate of return on investment in research on hybrid maize in the United States was 35–40 percent (Griliches 1958), plant geneticists created hybrid corn in the 1930s only after twenty-three years of research. The average lag time between agricultural research spending and the full realization of its benefits is ten years (Evenson, 1984, p. 357). Therefore, although there may be significant payoffs to agricultural research, it must be viewed in a long-term perspective; research is not a "quick fix" to the food problems of the Third World.

Because agricultural production is a biological process, local environmental conditions can often hinder the transferability of agricultural technology, particularly of the biogenetic type. This implies that there may be a high payoff to decentralizing a national agricultural research system by developing local research stations in each of a country's major agroecological zones. Bonnen (chapter 15) stresses the contribution that decentralization made to the productivity of the U.S. agricultural research system. But, as Schultz points out in chapter 22, decentralization can be carried too far, to the point where regional research stations lack a critical mass of professional staff, thereby reducing research productivity.

Bonnen also stresses that research, extension, other forms of human capital formation, and improvements in input and output markets should be viewed as complementary investments. Returns to investment in basic and applied research would be very low unless means existed to diffuse research results to farmers, facilitate their purchase of needed inputs, and allow them to market the resulting output profitably.[7]

Farming systems research (FSR) is a multidisciplinary approach to problem solving that was developed in the late 1970s in response to the realization that many national agricultural research systems were not producing technologies appropriate to small farmers. In other words, the induced innovation mechanism described by Hayami and Ruttan in chapter 5 was not generating technologies appropriate to small farmers' circumstances. FSR strives to develop technologies consistent with farmers' goals and with the constraints imposed by the entire farming system rather than simply increasing production of a few major commodities.

In chapter 23, "FSR Revisited," four CIMMYT researchers examine the contributions and shortcomings of farming systems research from the mid-1970s to 1989. They point out that FSR has played an important role in making on-station researchers more aware of farmers' constraints but that its direct contribution to developing new technologies has been limited. There has also been a tendency of FSR advocates to see it as a substitute for, rather than a complement to, on-station, commodity-oriented research.[8] The challenge in the 1990s is to incorporate the positive features of FSR into the entire research system and to draw upon the experience with FSR in coming to grips with natural resource and sustainable agriculture projects in the 1990s.

Sustainability of agricultural systems has received increased attention since the mid-1980s, with the rise of the environmental movement in Europe and the publication of the Bruntland Commission Report, *Our Common Future,* in 1987 (World Commission on Environment and Development 1987).[9] As Ruttan points out in chapter 24, there are close similarities between the conservation model of agricultural growth discussed in chapter 4 and the current sustainability models. Both approaches focus on the need to recycle "natural" nutrients and to design production systems that protect fragile environments. Deforestation and environmental degradation in many parts of the Third World resulting from agricultural expansion and intensification lend credence to calls for sustainable agricultural systems. The challenge, as Ruttan points out, is to devise approaches that help preserve environmental quality and long-term agricultural productivity while at the same time generating the rates of growth of output needed to sustain rapidly growing populations. In arguing that "sustainability is not enough," Ruttan cautions that some advocates of sustainability are pressing for the adoption of agricultural practices whose productivity and feasibility are as yet unproven. Pushing for widespread adoption of untested technologies in the name of sustainability could hurt the poor if these technologies reduced the rate of growth of food production in the Third World, thereby leading to higher food prices. Ruttan suggests that the concept of sustainability needs to be more clearly defined and that substantial additional research is required to develop sustainable technologies.

The benefits and costs of technological change in agriculture are seldom shared equally among the members of society. Many observers have expressed the fear that new, high-yielding grain varieties would benefit mainly large farmers living in well-irrigated regions, while smallholders and tenants, particularly in upland areas, would be made relatively, and perhaps absolutely, worse off. In chapter 25, Scobie and Posada examine the distribution of costs and benefits from rice research in Colombia, while in chapter 26, Hayami reviews evidence on the income-distribution consequences of the Green Revolution in Asia.

Scobie and Posada isolate, by income stratum and by area of residence (rural or urban), the incidence of the costs and benefits of the Colombian research program on new varieties of rice for irrigated land. The rapid and widespread adoption of the new varieties led to a substantial increase in production and a concomitant fall in the price of rice. The authors show that 70 percent of the net benefits of the research program accrued (in the form of lower rice prices) to the over one million low-income Colombian consumers who receive only 15 percent of national income.[10] As a result of the fall in the price of rice, the incomes of small upland rice farmers who could not adopt the varieties were substantially reduced from what they would have been without the research program, as were the incomes of some owners of large irrigated farms. The authors stress, however, that the research resulted in a small number of losers relative to winners: over one million low-income consumers benefited from lower rice prices, while fewer than twelve thousand small upland rice farmers had their incomes reduced by the research program. "Hence, under any plausible set of welfare weights, the . . . losses would be more than offset by the gain . . . implying an overall gain (albeit uncompensated) in some measure of social welfare." The analysis by Scobie and Posada demonstrates the importance of looking beyond farmers when analyzing the welfare effects of technological change in agriculture.

The Green Revolution has been a controversial topic in the literature since its introduction in India in 1965. Today the modern varieties of cereals, developed through improved plant breeding, add at least 50 million tons to Third World grain output per year (Lipton and Longhurst 1989). But Ruttan and Thirtle observe that "the Green Revolution is still largely confined to irrigated rice and wheat in Asia" (Ruttan and Thirtle 1989).[11] Moreover, Lipton and Longhurst contend, in *New Seeds and Poor People* (1989), that the modern varieties have been of little help in reducing malnutrition and rural poverty. Their analysis, however, focuses almost entirely on the modern varieties' lack of impact in ecologically disfavored areas. As Scobie and Posada point out in chapter 25, an evaluation of the consequences of the modern varieties for the poor should also take account of how increased production resulting from these varieties has lowered food prices and hence increased the real income of those who depend on the market for food.

Although many early evaluations of the income-distribution consequences of the Green Revolution in Asia were impressionistic (e.g., Frankel 1971; Griffin 1974), they did serve as warnings that the high-yielding varieties were not a cure-all for rural poverty. In chapter 26, Hayami reviews more recent evidence on how the modern grain varieties have affected farm output, employment, and income distribution within villages in Asia. Hayami argues that the new seed/fertilizer technology is both scale-neutral and factor-neutral. Therefore, in most instances small farmers have adopted the new varieties as quickly as large farmers, and the new technology by itself has not led to labor-displacing farm mechanization. Where such mechanization has occurred, it has resulted from factor-price distortions (particulary subsidized interest rates and overvalued domestic currencies) unrelated to the new technology. Hayami does not deny that the income distribution in rural Asia has become more unequal in recent years, but he disputes the conclusion of authors such as Pearse (1980), who attribute the growing inequality to the effects of high-yielding varieties. Rather, Hayami says, the empirical evidence strongly supports the position that growing population pressure on the land is the core problem and that the worsening income distribution has resulted from too little, not too much, technical change in agriculture (Hayami 1988).

The final essay in part IV focuses on the food-population race in Asia in the 1990s. In chapter 27 Byerlee voices concern that the struggles of the 1960s may reappear in the 1990s because there have been no major breakthroughs in raising the yield potential of cereals in Asia since the 1960s, and none are likely to occur in the 1990s. With population projected to grow at 1.5 percent in East Asia and 2.0 percent in South Asia from 1987 to 2000 (World Bank 1989, 215) and incomes projected to grow at one to two percent, the increase in food demand in Asia will be 2.5 to 3.5 percent per year. Byerlee identifies a number of measures to boost food production in Asia, such as giving priority to expanding food production in favorable areas, as India did when Green Revolution technologies were introduced in the mid-1960s. But there can be no blanket recommendation on this issue, because the direct and indirect effects of investing in favorable and less favorable areas, including the consequences for income distribution, will vary widely by country.

NOTES

1. Although reallocation of existing factors of production in technologically stagnant agriculture may result in small increases in production, reallocation may be a much more important source of growth in technologically dynamic agriculture characterized by frequent disequilibria (Schultz 1964). Increasing farm specialization, often cited as a major source of agricultural growth, frequently involves all three of the mechanisms mentioned above.

2. For similar analyses of the choice of technique in farming see Sen 1960; and Binswanger 1978.

3. Byerlee et al. (1983) extended Timmer's approach to analyze the output, employment, and foreign-trade consequences of alternative rice processing techniques in Sierra Leone. The articles by Timmer, Collier et al., and Byerlee et al. illustrate how the debate on the choice of technique can be furthered by empirical research.

4. Raup (1967) presents an excellent summary of these views. Most authors argued that land ownership per se was not necessary for small farmers to be technologically dynamic: many improvements could be achieved through reform of rental agreements.

5. Lewis (1954) and Nelson (1973) analyze the reasons why land settlement schemes have so frequently failed in the Third World.

6. In theory, real market interest rates have four components: a pure interest rate, an administrative premium, a risk premium, and monopoly profit.

7. The literature on agricultural extension in the Third World is vast, but there has been little consensus about which approaches to extension are most appropriate in different institutional environments. For recent studies see Roling 1988; Howell 1988; Roberts 1989; and Krueger, Michalopoulos, and Ruttan 1989.

8. FSR has also frequently failed to live up to its avowed aim of involving farmers in a multidisciplinary approach to solving their production problems. In a review of 158 abstracts of FSR studies, Herdt (1987) found that 70 percent were carried out by a researcher from a single discipline and that, of the 30 percent carried out by multidisciplinary teams, only 9 percent involved farmers in the on-farm trials.

9. Classic references on sustainability include Boserup 1965, 1981; Pingali, Bigot, and Binswanger 1987; and Ruthenberg 1980.

10. This finding is consistent with Mellor's analysis in chapter 10 of the income-distribution consequences of changes in food prices.

11. The impact of the Green Revolution has been exceedingly small in Africa. As of 1983, modern wheat and rice varieties totaled 800,000 hectares in Africa, or about one-fourth the annual cropped area of Zimbabwe, one of 45 countries in sub-Saharan Africa (Eicher 1989).

REFERENCES

Adams, Dale W and Douglas H. Graham. 1984. "A Critique of Traditional Agricultural Credit Projects and Policies." In *Agricultural Development in the Third World,* edited by Carl K. Eicher and John M. Staatz, 313–28. Baltimore: Johns Hopkins University Press.

Barrows, Richard, and Michael Roth. 1989. "Land Tenure and Investment in African Agriculture: Theory and Evidence." Madison: University of Wisconsin, Land Tenure Center. Mimeo.

Berry, R. A., and William R. Cline. 1979. *Agrarian Structure and Productivity in Developing Countries.* Baltimore: Johns Hopkins University Press.

Binswanger, Hans P. 1978. *The Economics of Tractors in South Asia: An Analytic Review.* New York and Hyderabad: Agricultural Development Council and International Crops Research Institute for the Semi-Arid Tropics.

Binswanger, Hans P., and Vernon W. Ruttan. 1978. *Induced Innovation: Technology, Institutions, and Development.* Baltimore: Johns Hopkins University Press.

Boserup, Ester. 1965. *The Conditions of Agricultural Growth: The Economics of Agrarian Change and Population Pressure.* Baltimore: Johns Hopkins University Press.

———. 1981. *Population and Technological Change: A Study of Long-Term Trends.* Chicago: University of Chicago Press.

Byerlee, Derek, Carl K. Eicher, Carl Liedholm, and Dunstan S. C. Spencer. 1983. "Employment-Output Conflicts, Factor Price Distortions and Choice of Technique: Empirical Results from Sierra Leone." *Economic Development and Cultural Change* 31(2): 315–36.

Deere, Carmen Diana, and Magdalena Leon. 1987. *Rural Women and State Policy: Feminist Perspectives on Latin American Agricultural Development.* Boulder, Colo.: Westview.

DeSota, Hernando. 1989. *The Other Path.* New York: Harper and Row.

Eicher, Carl K. 1989. *Sustainable Institutions for African Agricultural Development.* ISNAR Working Paper, no. 19. The Hague: International Service for National Agricultural Research (ISNAR).

Evenson, Robert. 1984. "Benefits and Obstacles in Developing Appropriate Agricultural Technology." In *Agricultural Development in the Third World,* edited by Carl K. Eicher and John M. Staatz, 348–61. Baltimore: Johns Hopkins University Press.

Frankel, Francine R. 1971. *India's Green Revolution: Economic Gains and Political Costs.* Princeton: Princeton University Press.

Griffin, Keith. 1974. *The Political Economy of Agrarian Change: An Essay on the Green Revolution.* Cambridge: Harvard University Press.

Griliches, Zvi. 1958. "Research Costs and Social Returns: Hybrid Corn and Related Innovations." *Journal of Political Economy* 66:419–31. Reprinted in *Agriculture in Economic Development,* edited by Carl K. Eicher and Lawrence Witt, 369–86. New York: McGraw-Hill, 1964.

Hayami, Yujiro. 1988. "Asian Development: A View from the Paddy Fields." *Asian Development Review* 6(1): 50–63.

Herdt, Robert. 1987. "Whither Farming Systems?" In *How Systems Work: Proceedings of the Farming Systems Research Symposium, 1987,* 3–7. University of Arkansas and Winrock International Institute for Agricultural Development.

Howell, John, ed. 1988. *Training and Visit Extension in Practice.* London: Overseas Development Council.

Judd, Ann M., James K. Boyce, and Robert E. Evenson. 1986. "Investing in Agricultural Supply: The Determinants of Agricultural Research and Extension Investment." *Economic Development and Cultural Change* 35, no. 1 (October): 77–113.

Krueger, Anne O., Constantine Michalopoulos, and Vernon W. Ruttan. 1989. *Aid and Development.* Baltimore: Johns Hopkins University Press.

Lele, Uma, Nicolas van de Walle, Mathurin Gbetibouo. 1989. *Cotton in Africa: An Analysis of Differences in Performance.* MADIA Study. Washington, D.C.: World Bank.

Lewis, W. Arthur. 1954. "Thoughts on Land Settlement." *Journal of Agricultural Economics* 11 (June): 3–11. Reprinted in *Agriculture in Economic Development,* edited by Carl K. Eicher and Lawrence W. Witt, 299–310. New York: McGraw-Hill, 1964.

Liedholm, Carl, and Joan Parker. 1989. "Small Scale Manufacturing Growth in Africa: Initial Evidence." MSU International Development Working Paper, no. 33. East Lansing: Michigan State University, Department of Agricultural Economics.

Lipton, Michael, with Richard Longhurst. 1989. *New Seeds and Poor People.* Baltimore: Johns Hopkins University Press.

Minot, Nicholas W. 1986. "Contract Farming and Its Affects on Small Farmers in Developing Countries." MSU International Development Working Paper, no. 31. East Lansing: Michigan State University, Department of Agricultural Economics.

Nelson, Michael. 1973. *The Development of Tropical Lands: Policy Issues in Latin America.* Baltimore: Johns Hopkins University Press.

Otsuka, Keijiro, and Yujiro Hayami. 1988. "Theories of Share Tenancy: A Critical Survey." *Economic Development and Cultural Change* 37(1): 31–68.

Pearse, Andrew. 1980. *Seeds of Plenty, Seeds of Want: Social and Economic Implications of the Green Revolution.* New York: Oxford University Press.

Pingali, Prabhu, Y. Bigot, and H. P. Binswanger. 1987. *Agricultural Mechanization and the Evolution of Farming Systems in Sub-Saharan Africa.* Baltimore: Johns Hopkins University Press.

Powelson, John P., and Richard Stock. 1987. *The Peasant Betrayed: Agriculture and Land Reform in the Third World.* Boston: Oelgeschlager, Gunn and Hain, in association with the Lincoln Institute of Land Policy.

Raup, Philip M. 1967. "Land Reform and Agricultural Development." In *Agricultural Development and Economic Growth,* edited by Herman M. Southworth and Bruce F. Johnston, 267–314. Ithaca: Cornell University Press.

Roberts, Nigel, ed. 1989. *Agricultural Extension in Africa.* Washington, D.C.: World Bank.

Roling, N. G. 1988. *Extension Science: Information Systems in Agricultural Development*. Cambridge: Cambridge University Press.

Ruthenberg, Hans. 1980. *Farming Systems in the Tropics*, 3rd ed. Oxford: Clarendon Press.

Ruttan, Vernon W., and Colin Thirtle. 1989. "Induced Technical and Institutional Change in African Agriculture." *Journal of International Development* 1(1): 1–45.

Schultz, Theodore W. 1964. *Transforming Traditional Agriculture*. New Haven: Yale University Press.

Sen, Amartya. 1960. *Choice of Techniques: An Aspect of the Theory of Planned Economic Development*. Oxford: Basil Blackwell.

Stiglitz, Joseph. 1989. "Markets, Market Failures and Development." *American Economic Review* 79(2): 197–203.

Von Pischke, John D., Dale W. Adams, and Gordon Donald. 1983. *Rural Financial Markets in Developing Countries: Their Use and Abuse*. Baltimore: Johns Hopkins University Press.

World Bank. 1989. *World Development Report, 1989*. Washington, D.C.

World Commission on Environment and Development. 1987. *Our Common Future*. Oxford: Oxford University Press.

15

Agricultural Development: Transforming Human Capital, Technology, and Institutions

JAMES T. BONNEN

INTRODUCTION

Increased agricultural productivity is commonly explained solely in terms of technological change. Technology, in turn, is often seen as the exclusive product of research and development. Both notions are erroneous. Implicit in the attitudes of many scientists is the even more erroneous belief that "basic research" is the true and ultimate source not only of all technology but of all increased productivity. This frequently produces the view that everything else is of some lower order of scientific interest and importance to society, and thus to be relegated to second-rate minds, that is, to bureaucrats, politicians, applied researchers, and other inferior orders.

Conscious technological innovation predates science by centuries, and even today we often produce new technologies without recourse to science, especially basic science. In any case, the origins of specific changes in productivity are more complex and multiple than is commonly appreciated. Many criticisms of agricultural research arise out of confusion over the sources of agricultural productivity, as well as from a profound ignorance of the characteristics imposed on the search for agricultural productivity by its biological nature.

This chapter argues that increases in productivity arise not from technological change alone but from institutional innovation, improvements in human capital, as well as changes in the availability of biological and physical capital. Any careful reading of the history of the development of agriculture and its institutions and people will demonstrate this. Moreover, the data on returns to agricultural research have independently begun to substantiate this view (Evenson, Waggoner, and Rut-

JAMES T. BONNEN is professor of agricultural economics, Michigan State University.

Reprinted from *U.S.-Mexico Relations: Agriculture and Rural Development*, edited by Bruce F. Johnston, Cassio Luiselli, Celso Cartas Contreras, and Roger D. Norton, 1987, pp. 267–300. Copyright © 1987 by the Board of Trustees of the Leland Stanford Junior University. Published with revisions and deletions by permission of Stanford University Press and the author.

tan 1979; Ruttan 1982, 237–61). The chapter also illustrates these points by describing the evolution of the system of developmental institutions in U.S. agriculture, and it examines the significance of the organizational characteristics of this system for other nations.

RELATIONSHIPS BETWEEN SCIENCE, TECHNOLOGY, HUMAN CAPITAL, AND INSTITUTIONS

Change in productivity, as measured by economists, is the unexplained residual in output after accounting for conventional inputs (land, labor, capital, etc.). This residual is attributable both to new technology and to the new human capital and institutional innovations that are almost invariably preconditions for or adaptive complements to any technological innovation. Because technology, human capital, and institutional innovations tend to be complementary inputs in production, it is impossible to separate their relative influences with much accuracy. In some recent studies of the returns to agricultural research, variables for human capital and technological change have been introduced into regression models to explain changes in agricultural productivity and to measure the internal rates of return to these investments. To my knowledge, no one has yet found a way even crudely to conceptualize and represent separately in such models the aggregate effect of institutional innovations.[1]

Institutional innovation seems to depend on prior human capital accumulation, just as technological innovation does (Schultz 1968; Shaffer 1969). Both are embodied human capital. Like technological changes, institutional innovations represent a change not just in the opportunity sets of individuals or groups but in the aggregate or social opportunity set. Thus, institutional changes are transformations of social production functions in much the same sense that technological changes are transformations of the production functions of conventional economic theory. The problem is how to conceptualize and measure production functions in society's marketplace for social and political transactions.

I will not dwell long on human capital. Anyone who does not now appreciate what the quality of the human agent means to productivity growth and development has missed one of the most important dimensions of the economic literature over the last 20 years. In the United States, the land-grant colleges' historical contribution in educating farmers, providing broad access to higher education, forcing high schools into existence nationwide, and helping to create science as a profession by introducing it into college curricula cannot be overemphasized. Before there can be science, scientists must be trained. Indeed, the leadership that created the land-grant system and the U.S. Department of Agriculture (USDA) came not from farmers, but primarily from an educated middle class of professionals—lawyers, clergy, doctors, and journalists—who shared a faith in the idea of progress and saw access to education as the road to individual opportunity, as well as the primary assurance of a vital democratic social order. Educated professionals created and then staffed the USDA, the land-grant colleges, and other public universities. These institutional innovations eventually made a significant difference in the economic productivity of the United States. In short, the slow accumulation of human capital in an educated middle class preceded and led to an institutional innovation, the land-grant-USDA system, which in turn led to a greater accumulation in human capital through the growing access to higher education and through agricultural research and extension. New science-based agricultural technologies have flowed from and were preceded by many decades of investment in human capital and related institutional innovation. This has been an iterative and interactive development process without a clearly conceived blueprint.

The concept of human capital in its modern form is the intellectual contribution of Nobel laureate Theodore W. Schultz. Improvements in human capital increase the ability of the human agent to identify, define, and deal with problems, or as Schultz puts it, "the ability to deal with disequilibria" (Schultz 1975). In the development of agriculture, this ability to deal with disequilibria shows up dramatically in the early contribution of improved farm management to agricultural productivity. As new agricultural technologies are introduced, factor combinations inevitably are left in less-than-optimal proportions. Many scientists and traditional farmers commonly attribute to the new technology the productivity that farmers in the aggregate could never have realized if they had not taught themselves and been taught how to make rational economic decisions. The traditional practices of farmers are invariably made inefficient in some degree by technical change. Continuous technical change makes traditional practices obsolete, and to achieve efficiency requires a conscious system of management decision based on economic as well as biological and physical science knowledge—that is, farm management.

Thus, new technologies not only arise out of prior investments in human capital and institutions but have a potential for increasing productivity that generally cannot be realized until the new technologies are combined with some appropriate, complementary improvement in agricultural institutions and in the human agents managing agriculture. Whereas new institutions generally depend on prior human capital accumulation, improved human capital frequently depends on prior institutional innovation. The creation of farm management research and extension in the United States as a function of the college of agriculture was a prerequisite to improving the farmers' ability to capitalize on the stream of new physical and biological technologies that began to flow from science in this century.[2] Thus, the factors of technology, individual human capability, institutions, and biophysical capital, interact in a continuing process of innovative disturbance in one factor, followed by the managed adaptation of the other factors to find a new, more efficient equilibrium of resource use.

Under such conditions, it is a major intellectual misunderstanding to attribute the entire increment of any increase in productivity to one factor, as is commonly done in agriculture in discussing the role of technology in transforming productivity. An even greater misunderstanding allows the media and some scientists to talk about basic science as if it were the only factor necessary to create new technologies. As important as basic science is, this is a naive understanding of the development process. Basic science must be interactively linked with various types of applied research and that linked in turn with technology development and ultimately with technology- and knowledge-transfer mechanisms. If these other activities or linkages are missing, some basic science knowledge will remain undeveloped or be developed so slowly that significant part of its value will be lost, and the social return to that investment in basic science reduced or lost. As a consequence, some of the potential growth in productivity is lost to society (Knutsen and Tweeten 1979).

To extract the full potential in productivity, the creation of knowledge and its development must be coordinated and interlinked in some systemic manner all the way to its use. This cannot be achieved accidentally or solely by market forces. To achieve the highest potential levels of productivity requires a sustained national policy with clear goals to guide the development of the necessary public and private institutions and to assure the investments in human capital and institutions that are prerequisite to, as well as complements in, creating new technologies.

In their organization and evolution, the developmental institutions of U.S. agriculture directly reflect this understanding of the relationship between scientific knowledge, effective technology development and use, investments in human capital, and institutional development. It is the creative process of innovative disruption and selective adaptation that the system of developmental institutions in U.S. agriculture historically managed so well. To understand the lessons for the potential of science and the sources of productivity in agriculture, we must understand the system of developmental institutions.

THE U.S. SYSTEM OF DEVELOPMENTAL INSTITUTIONS

Man, not science, transformed U.S. agriculture. Men and women, acting through the institutions they had created, developed scientific knowledge, changed human values and aspirations, modified old institutions and built new ones as they saw the need, and step by step transformed the productivity and welfare of U.S. farmers. A set of diverse institutions supporting public policy slowly evolved around a common goal of agricultural development. By the 1930s it constituted a coherent, science-based system that subsequently transformed U.S. agriculture.

Five sets of institutions compose the core of this developmental system. These are (1) a web of diverse farmer organizations, (2) the land-grant colleges of agriculture, (3) the U.S. Department of Agriculture, (4) the private-sector markets and firms that provide purchased inputs to farmers and market farm products as well, and (5) the political bodies, federal and state, responsible for agricultural policy. These last two sets of institutions, one private and the other public, help coordinate the other three and provide closure to the social system. If separate institutions are to constitute a system with a common purpose, their behavior must be coordinated. Private markets provide the information necessary to coordinate the marketing decisions of farmers and agribusiness firms as well as the purchasing decisions of public institutions. However, it is national, state, and local governments that set many of the rules for markets. Governments, of course, provide the financial support and the policy direction to coordinate the public institutions of agriculture. Since the nineteenth century, as the fundamentally different institutions of agriculture coalesced into a single system for agricultural development, these two quite different coordination processes have behaved as one interactive, tension-ridden communications and coordination system. Over time these public and private institutions and policies have become more and more interactive, until now their embrace is so intimate and longstanding that the line between public and private is often difficult to draw. In short, the public and private institutions of U.S. agriculture are part of and respond to signals out of both of these coordination processes.

The Birth of New Institutions, 1850–1880

The institutions that evolved into a developmental system in U.S. agriculture were created during the middle decades of the nineteenth century and grew quite separately until the 1880s. The first farm organization to have an impact on national economic and farm policy matters was the Patrons of Husbandry, commonly called the Grange. Founded in 1867, the Grange grew rapidly during the 1870s as the forces of agrarian discontent fed on depressed economic conditions. The first land-grant college, Michigan State University, was established in 1855. The Morrill Act, creating a national system of land-grant colleges, was enacted by Congress in 1862. Most of the colleges were in place by 1880, except in the West. The U.S. Department of Agriculture was founded the same year the land-grant system was established; but in the early years it followed its own evolutionary course, focusing almost exclusively on developing a research program while the colleges were struggling to develop a curriculum. These early decades were a period of great conflict, in which agrarian leaders fought over the need for and the nature of the institutions that had been created. Battles raged inside and around each institution over its appropriate activities, organizational form, and social purpose. Survival was a daily battle, especially in the colleges. Great struggles over what an appropriate agricultural curriculum should be took place through the 1870s and 1880s between practical men, who saw agriculture as a vocation, and a small but growing body of scientists and professionals, who believed in the potential of science for transforming agriculture. This stuggle lasted well into the twentieth century (Bonnen 1962). The curriculum and organization that finally evolved was a compromise between science and a vocational commitment to farming and its improvement.

Growing Links between Institutions, 1880–World War I

Attempts to apply science to agriculture forced a search for appropriate organizational forms. The first U.S. agricultural experiment station (an innovation borrowed from Germany) was established as an independent institution in Connecticut in 1875. Further efforts by agricultural leaders with an understanding of the potential for science in agriculture led to congressional passage of the Hatch Act of 1887, providing federal funds for the establishment of stations in all the states and for an office in the USDA to coordinate the flow of scientific knowledge between the two systems (True 1929). Legislation of this kind requires consensus, coordinated effort, and political activity. The consensus and the movement that led to the Hatch Act grew out of annual informal meetings between representatives of the colleges and the USDA during the early 1880s. In 1887, the colleges formalized their collaboration by establishing the Association of American Agricultural Colleges and Experiment Stations, subsequently renamed the American Association of Land-Grant Colleges. Legislation raising the Department of Agriculture to cabinet status (1889) was this coalition's next legislative achievement. The Adams Act (1906) strengthened the support for experiment stations, especially in basic science, and clarified the USDA and land-grant college roles in agricultural research.

From 1897 to 1913, scientific agricultural research came to full maturity within the USDA. A systematic structure of applied and problem-oriented bureaus was created. The organizational structures of the USDA and the land-grant colleges were now strikingly similar, and they were staffed by a similar cadre of scientists. By the beginning of World War I, the USDA was the world's finest agricultural research organization. Although it had been assigned regulatory activities as early as 1884, its primary functions were agricultural research and education (Baker et al. 1963).

In 1914 Congress passed the Smith-Lever Act, which established a national extension system organized on roughly the same pattern as the research system, with the USDA and the colleges linked in a loose structure for coordination. The American Association of Land-Grant Colleges was the early political arm of this coalition of federal and state research and educational organizations. The USDA worked toward the same goals in the formal budget processes of the executive and legislative branches. The Congress and its agricultural committees grew accustomed to dealing with the USDA, the land-grant colleges, and the farm organizations as clientele of federally funded agricultural research and education programs. In sum, the period from the 1880's through World War I was one of growing interdependence and institutional linkage between these research and education institutions.

A fundamental change in the system had begun to take place in the early 1900s, when the colleges experimented with full-time representatives at the county level to extend to farmers the growing body of new scientific knowledge. The Smith-Lever Act of 1914 transformed this idea into a national system of county extension agents, financed from federal, state, and local (county) government sources but responsible to a director of agricultural extension in the state colleges of agriculture. An agency was created within the USDA to assist in coordination of the system. The existence of this linkage to the local level created for the land-grant colleges and for the USDA a grass-roots organization that communicated new agricultural technologies and knowledge directly to farmers in a systematic and continuing way, while sending back to the colleges and the USDA information about farming problems that needed research and policy attention.

THE SYSTEM MATURES, 1920–1950

The early county extension agents were frustrated in their efforts to get farmers interested in learning how to improve farm practices. After a brief national debate, extension began organizing farm bureaus in the local chambers of commerce for this purpose. They recruited the more progressive, often better-educated farmers and gave them special attention. Once organized, these farmers wanted to influence national policy. This quickly led to the organization of state farm bureaus and, in 1920, to the American Farm Bureau Federation (AFBF), which pursued the economic and business interests of members at state and national levels. The AFBF opened an office in Washington, D.C., and quickly became the dominant farm organization in the United States.

Although the land-grant college extension agents created the county farm bureaus as their political action arm, the AFBF soon controlled the local and state farm bureaus as well as the county extension offices. When the Farm Bureau spoke, the colleges, the USDA, and the U.S. Congress all listened intently. County agents did not travel to Washington to represent extension; the AFBF's state president took care of that chore. The AFBF generally supported the interests of the land-grant colleges and the USDA, as well as those of the more successful farmers. This awkward marriage ultimately led to a separation of the public extension and private farm organization structures.

The rise of politically effective modern farm organizations, especially the AFBF, strengthened political support for the colleges but complicated life for their presidents and deans of agriculture. Conflicts arose between educational objectives and farmers' political goals and eventually led to a physical, financial, and organizational separation of the county farm bureaus from the land-grant college county extension offices. A strong political coalition remains to this day in many states in which the American Farm Bureau is the only or the dominant general farm organization. And the history of close ties with the politically strong Farm Bureau have made relations between the colleges and other general farm organizations difficult at best.

The experience gained from nineteenth-century failures in farm organization became the basis for their success in the twentieth century. Unlike the nineteenth-century farm organization, the contemporary farm organization is an interest group that is careful not to compete with political parties. Its business activities are managed quite separately from its lobbying and other political activities. Business services at advantageous prices are made available only to members, which stabilizes membership and ensures a continuing organizational base for political and policy activities (Olson 1971; Salisbury 1970).

Since the 1930s the National Farmer's Union, the American Farm Bureau Federation, and, on occasion, the National Grange have had a substantial impact on national agricultural policy decisions. Other, more recently formed general farm organizations are the National Farmers Organization and the American Agriculture Movement.

Modern farm organizations have considerable economic and political strength at the national, state, and county levels. By the late 1920s, farmers had become one of the best-organized economic groups in the United States. The extremely low farm prices that prevailed during the 1920s led to what was known as the "farm bloc" in the U.S. Congress, a coalition of senators and congressmen from farm states who were backed by and responsive to the farm organizations. Although the farm bloc was a loose coalition, it represented an absolute majority of both the House and the Senate.

CHARACTERISTICS OF THE SYSTEM OF DEVELOPMENTAL INSTITUTIONS

The system of developmental institutions that evolved in U.S. agriculture up through the 1940s had several key characteristics that contributed to the great increase in the productivity and adaptive capability of U.S. agriculture. First and perhaps *most* significantly, it was a *system* of institutions linked one to another in various ways. It is interesting how much this aspect is discussed and how little it is understood. Its significance, however, has not escaped the notice of astute observers.

Perhaps agriculture's strongest claim to consideration as a scientific undertaking has come with the rise of cybernetics, or systems theory—the theory of how the diverse elements of systems interact through time to produce change. Even in oral traditions, agriculture has always been perceived as a system; hundreds of generations of farmers have understood the interaction of stock, soil, water supply, climate, supply and demand. Today these elements are understood better than ever; they can be quantified; they can even be controlled. More than ever, the science of agriculture stands at the center of a broader system integrating human society and its physical environment. The further study of this system demands the coordination of all the sciences from physics to sociology (Mayer and Mayer 1974).

ARTICULATED LINKAGE OF INSTITUTIONAL COMPONENTS

The performance of a successful institutional system comes to more than the sum of its parts. To say that a set of institutions is a system is to say that its individual components are interlinked or articulated, that the separate institutions are connected, that they communicate and cooperate in action to achieve some common goal. This does not mean that U.S. agricultural institutions have pursued or now pursue totally compatible or common goals. They are not mechanical but human social systems, after all. In the United States there has in fact been a continuing tension and contest between the USDA, the land-grant colleges, and farm organizations over their appropriate roles and activities. In research, the USDA and the state colleges, as well as the various experiment stations, have competed for federal funds ever since the states first began to expand their experiment stations. Farmer organizations periodically tell colleges of agriculture what they should be teaching and researching and on occasion even try to tell them what they should not be teaching and researching. In turn, the colleges attempt to instruct farmers and their organizations on the appropriate policies and roles for farmer action. Much of this tension is constructive. Indeed, it is through such continuing tension and the associated communication between institutions that the commonality of goals is repeatedly rediscovered, adapted to change, and revalidated.

A constructive tension holds the system in place and allows it to adapt to changes in the economic and political environment. But periodically the tension becomes excessive and destructive, threatening the very fabric of the system. So far the system has proved quite durable, although it is rarely without some serious problems, usually the result of prior policy or decision failures or a failure to recognize problems early enough.

The system of institutions exists by virtue of various types of articulated linkage that join differing functions and levels of the system. The U.S. college of agriculture is an institution that internally manages three very different functions: research, teaching, and extension. Here the linkage is internal to a single organization and is administered by one officer, the dean, although there are great variations across the states in degree of decentralization and delegation of authority. This direct linkage produces far more complementarity, coordination, and thus productivity than can be extracted from systems where each of these functions— teaching, research, and extension—is embedded in a separate institution that is a creature of national government and controlled by a different ministerial bureaucracy. Farmers tend to distrust and ignore information delivered by a bureaucracy that is also responsible for national agricultural policies. Extension has enough difficulty maintaining credibility with farmers when it restricts itself to an educational role.

The problems and conditions of production agriculture are location specific, embedded in local ecosystems. Research agendas that are set unilaterally in national capitals by organizations without interactive linkage to state and local levels rarely reflect regional or local research priorities and problems. To have a locally governed institution for teaching, extension, and research working from a common knowledge base appears to have a high payoff in agricultural productivity. These functions are usually well integrated in the U.S. system, since researchers and on-campus extension specialists do almost all the teaching and the extension specialist often does much of the applied research and is usually housed with researchers in the same academic department. Again, there has been quite a bit of variation historically, but the system is converging at present on a model in which all three functions are integrated and administered at the departmental level in colleges of agriculture.[3]

There are fifty states in the U.S. and about sixty land-grant colleges. Coordinating a group of this diversity has never been easy, but it has repeatedly achieved major goals. When the Hatch Act of 1887 established a national system of state experiment stations and when the Smith-Lever Act of 1914 established a national system of state extension services, two small offices, now the Cooperative State Research Service and the Federal Extension Service, were created within the USDA to facilitate communication and to manage the transfer of congressional appropriations to the states. The National Association of State Universities and Land-Grant Colleges meets annually and is a forum for debate and policy formation between the various states and regions, as well as between the states and the USDA's research and extension managers. The USDA's top political leaders once participated effectively in this forum, but no longer do so.

The agricultural colleges and the USDA, thus are held together in a loosely coordinated structure. At the national level this system integrates and coordinates basic science for agriculture, applied research, technology development, extension, and the formal education of scientists and other agricultural professionals. Finally, and just as importantly, it must be recognized that this system is also coordinated and linked through markets and the political process at both the state and the national level. Indeed, these last two sources supply, validate, and sustain some of the most important values that drive this system of developmental institutions.

Historically, a strong, if uneven, political commitment has been made at the state level to education and research in agriculture. At the national level, a strong continuing commitment has been made to education (1862), research (1887), and extension (1914), and to the institution building involved in creating these means to achieve improved agricultural productivity and welfare. In addition, very important and highly complementary national public investments have been made in developing institutions and programs for farm credit, soil conservation, reclamation and water development, rural electrification, rural free delivery of mail, rural roads and highways, market regulation, and market stabilization. This investment in infrastructure facilitated the industrialization of agriculture, the growth of agricultural markets, and the increase in agricultural productivity. The returns to agricultural research would have been lower without these physical, human, and institutional investments—and vice versa.

In short, basic research, although necessary, is not sufficient to achieve high levels of agricultural productivity. The same is true of all other elements: applied research and technology development, extension of knowledge and technologies to the private sector including farmers, education for farmers and scientists, credit, electricity, and so forth. The most important issue is the systematic integration of decisions about institutional development and the combination, timing, and coordination of the various factors. Failure to link together in the same goal-driven system public and private decisions about investments in basic science, applied research, technology development, extension, and education will reduce the level of productivity that can be extracted from a given social investment in agriculture or in any other industrial sector.

DECENTRALIZATION OF DECISION MAKING

Another obvious characteristic of the U.S. agricultural support system is decentralization. Although it is a national system, authority is not concentrated solely at the national level. This is an important strength of the system, not because decentralization is inherently superior organizationally to centralization, but because decentralization is responsive to the nature of the problems the system addresses. First, to manage agricultural research or almost anything else over an area as large as the United States requires some decentralization of decision making for the sake of both efficiency and effectiveness. However, decentralization is particularly suitable for research that must deal with countless combinations of climatic conditions, soils, topography, flora, and fauna. The creation of basic scientific knowledge is only the first step toward greater national agricultural productivity. Basic scientific research creates potential that cannot be fully realized until it is successfully adapted to many specific ecosystems. This requires extensive adaptive research and technology development—that is, applied research. In addition, to get new technologies and knowledge adopted by farmers often requires further adaptive work in the sense of devising extension strategies to deal with historical differences in farming practice as well as ethnic and other cultural differences. The private sector faces the same problem in technology development and transfer.

While articulation of the system of developmental institutions is necessary, to keep many diverse functions coordinated, decentralization is necessary for the successful adaptation of science and technology to the highly varied local ecospheres that characterize agricultural production. There are, in addition, all sorts of political, cultural, and social variations that make it necessary to accommodate the institutional structure to local polities and resources to ensure a politically inclusive, legitimized, and coordinated system. To do otherwise in the United States would leave fifty subnational polities free to develop potentially conflicting, duplicate, and, in the aggregate, inefficient agricultural policies.

Many of the states, finding that a single experiment station was inadequate to deal with the multiple ecosystems within their borders, established multiple field stations or substations to work on different soil types, specific crops or animal products, and other problems peculiar to a local area. There were well over 350 such substations in the United States in 1981 (USDA 1981). Thus, the U.S. system is far more decentralized than the existence of fifty to sixty "state experiment stations" would imply.

Consensual Decision Making

A less obvious characteristic of the U.S. system is that decisions that affect all or large parts of the system must be developed by consensus, if they are to be accepted as legitimate and implemented effectively. Unilateral power plays to achieve something that substantially affects the whole system generally create excessive conflict and end in failure. Attempts at unilateral or external command do not work in systems of separate institutions held together by a few common goals and the tensions of interdependence. Given the steady relative decline of federal support for agricultural research in the U.S., further attempts to command the system from the federal level are likely to cause the states to consider opting out of the system rather than cooperating.

Balanced Pursuit of Basic and Applied Research

Another characteristic of U.S. agriculture institutions is the combination and management of societal problem solving and the pursuit of science for its own sake in a single system. The pragmatism and political expediency necessary to sustain effective societal problem solving involve organization, values and expectations that are inconsistent with the organization, values and expectations associated with the scientific pursuit of knowledge for its own sake. When managed in the same system, they exist in a perpetual tension. Nevertheless, the productivity achieved in agriculture has arisen from the sustained linkage of these functions and the management of the resulting tensions to maintain a workable balance.

The four characteristics discussed above—a well-articulated linkage of institutional components, a decentralization of decision making, consensual decision making, and a balanced pursuit of basic and applied science, technology development, and transfer—are not unique to the U.S. system; they are fundamental to the success of science-based developmental systems throughout the world.

But there are two serendipitous elements in the evolution of the U.S. system that should be noted. The first is that the legislation that established the nationwide system of land-grant colleges in 1862 came well before that which established the nationwide system of experiment stations in 1887. Had the timing been reversed, the research function might have been assigned to institutions independent of the colleges, as has been done in most countries. The same is true of extension. With the land-grant colleges in command of the state's agricultural science resources and "political turf," it was logical for the Congress to establish the extension service in 1914 as part of the existing agricultural system; but it might have been otherwise.[4]

Equally important is the fact that the Morrill Act did not establish colleges just to teach agriculture. It set forth the broad goal of improving the welfare of the working classes and ensuring their social equity and political freedom in the face of the growing concentration of economic and political power in an industrializing nation. This egalitarian vision, combined with the pragmatism of the strong vocational commitment to the welfare of the farm family, constrained and balanced the inherent intellectual narcissism that can turn a university into a gaggle of isolated disciplines and an engine of social elitism. The "land-grant idea" has been a great force for both democracy and national development in U.S. history. These values have given cohesion and purpose to the developmental institutions of U.S. agriculture.

The other major serendipitous element in the development of the U.S. system is the relatively small size of most of the states. This created a very decentralized system from the beginning, ensuring systematic research on many different ecosystems and an adaptive capability that the agricultural research programs of many industrialized nations do not have even today.

RECENT EROSION OF THE U.S. SYSTEM

The clarity and singleness of purpose of the U.S. system of developmental institutions began to erode in the late 1930s. Until the 1930s, legislation affecting farmers was usually broad social legislation that affected all farmers as a group (e.g., homesteading laws, the Morrill Act, the Hatch Act, the Smith-Lever Act, and the farmer cooperative and early farm credit legislation). During the Great Depression, Congress introduced price support programs for individual commodities, to stablize farm markets and maintain farm incomes. Such legislation, in bringing direct economic benefits not to all but to specific groups of farmers, immediately created an incentive for those groups to organize in pursuit of their special interests. These relationships quickly evolved into what has come to be called a "triangle of power" or subgovernment composed of the federal administrator of a particular commodity program, the congressional committees that control it, and the national group or groups representing its beneficiaries (Bonnen 1980).

By 1945, the relationship between the USDA and the Congress was dominated by the new farm programs and the specialized farmer organizations that developed around them. Life grew more complicated for the general farm organizations and the land-grant colleges, and their political influence was diluted. Even the general farm organizations shifted their strongest support to the areas where direct farm benefits were concentrated. Thus, representation of farmer interests was narrowed—to commodity programs, credit, conservation, electrification, and regulation. With the organization of these concentrated economic interests, the research and education coalition among the USDA, the colleges, and the AFBF grew progressively weaker after 1933 and began to unravel rapidly after World War II (Lowi 1965).

In 1915, agricultural research accounted for one-quarter of the USDA's budget (OTA 1981). Today, a far larger research enterprise accounts for only about 2 percent of the USDA's budget. The regulatory role of the USDA grew rapidly from the 1890s onward, as scientific research identified needs that resulted in regulations ranging from standards for fertilizer and seeds to food safety and animal health. Beginning in the 1930s, the USDA was transformed from a research and educational organization into a conventional government agency managing programs that provided direct economic benefits to (or imposed costs on) a specific set of farmer and agribusiness interests. USDA research is a matter of minor political concern at the congressional level today. In fact, in recent decades the congressional interest in agricultural research has focused on creation and expansion of federal research laboratories in specific states. Despite the quality of some of these facilities, this trend has progressively isolated, distorted, and fragmented the USDA's national research capability, especially since little or no new operating money has been appropriated to sustain these new laboratories, some of which stand unused.

From the 1880s through World War II, the USDA provided most of the scientific and administrative leadership that established national priorities for the agricultural sciences, performed most of the basic science research, and made major investments in the long-term intellectual and social capital of agriculture. Since the 1940s, colleges of agriculture have slowly inherited the intellectual mantle of research leadership.

Starting in the 1940s, the scientific knowledge produced by the colleges and the USDA was combined with the earlier mechanical revolution (Rasmussen 1977), greater price stability, and access to credit to industrialize U.S. agriculture. This led to far more intense specialization and growing economic interdependence, within agriculture and between agriculture and the rest of the economy. Specialization fragments economic interest, creating rising levels of conflict among farmers and introducing other political actors with legitimate interests into the agricultural policy scene. The first new actor to organize a continuous policy presence was agribusiness, when land was withdrawn from production in the mid-1950s to reduce farm surpluses, with the consequence that business profits declined. A succession of others followed rather quickly in the 1960s, when labor, consumer, and welfare organizations arose to champion food stamp and other supplemental food and food safety programs. Finally, through the 1970s, shortages in world commodity markets and weakening U.S. dollar greatly expanded U.S. exports of farm commodities, thus adding to the policy arena those organizations with substantial economic interests in international trade in agricultural products, including parts of the federal bureaucracy such as the White House Special Trade Representative and the Treasury and State departments. Thus, the monopoly control of political power in agriculture that various producer groups exercised through commodity organizations and the "triangles of power" in the 1940s and 1950s was progressively fragmented by an increasing number of participants with conflicting interests (Heinz 1962). As a result, although the farm commodity groups that were formed in the 1930s are still strong, they have lost ground as a political coalition and are in frequent disarray. In public policy for agriculture, the United States today faces not only greater market instability but a decision-making process that is itself less stable.

One of the clear lessons from successful agricultural development the world over is necessity of a centralized national investment in agricultural research complemented by and coordinated with a decentralized capacity in adapting agricultural research to the highly varied local ecospheres within which agriculture is practiced. Together this is what the land-grant colleges and the USDA originally accomplished. Their performance was magnificent. The focus of the USDA today, however, is on the immediate economic benefits created by special programs that are controlled or fought over by a growing swarm of special interest groups. Although the administrative linkages between the USDA and the land-grant colleges and their legislated roles remain intact, the attention of USDA political leadership is no longer on research and education. The USDA neglects its own research functions, which today constitute a declining force within the agricultural science research community. Congress appears neither to understand nor care much about agricultural research today. National research has faltered, and research budgets have all but ceased to grow in real terms since 1967. The federal commitment to agricultural research has faded and now lies in the balance. Without an effective national agricultural research policy and without an influential national research focus, coordination of the agricultural research system has been deteriorating slowly for decades. This is primarily a failure of political institutions and political leadership, but the institutions of agricultural science also seem to lack a coherent vision of a politically viable future.

CONCLUSIONS

Clearly a nation that cannot sustain long-term institution building and human capital improvement will never have a highly productive, industrialized agriculture. Just as clearly, long-term institution building and human capital accumulation must involve more than the research and educational institutions. Physical capital and conventional input development are necessary for soil and water conservation, reclamation, and development; for long-term, intermediate, and short-term credit; for rural roads, mail service, and eventually electronic communications; and for the development of modern market institutions, common market standards, regulation, and, if necessary, market stabilization. These investments improve the capacity and productivity of agriculture and thereby the productivity of agricultural research as well.

Some institutional development will be public, some private. The mix will differ depending on a nation's history, institutions, and political philosophy. One lesson to be learned from past failures is to avoid extreme, exclusive ideological commitment either to free market capitalism or to socialism, with their demands that institution building take place entirely in the private sector or entirely in the public sector. The search for complementarities between public and private roles and a pragmatic focus on problem solving appear to form a more effective and more efficient approach. The U.S. experience also involved a partnership between public universities and state and national research institutions. If the universities do not do some of the basic research in agriculture, where does the next generation of well-trained scientists come from? Some applied research, the benefits of which spill over to the entire nation, must be done at the national level, if it is to get done at all. These are some of the lessons from the U.S. experience. Despite all its free enterprise values and rhetoric, the United States has imposed significant government regulation on and has socialized important activities of its agricultural sector. Despite a major investment in a national, centralized R&D institution (the USDA), the United States also developed a decentralized, location-specific R&D capacity to contend with the diverse ecosystems inherent in nature.

The evolution of the developmental system of institutions in U.S. agriculture was a pragmatic process of piecing together solutions to problems identified at state, local, and national levels. It used existing institutions and created new ones, public and private, to achieve results that reflected interests and needs at all levels of organization. It was a decision-making process in which all the major institutions shared the common nineteenth- and early twentieth-century goal of increasing human welfare through greater agricultural productivity. They made major national decisions by mobilizing a consensus, not by command. This takes a strong commitment by individuals and institutions to a reasonably common set of specific social values. It also requires strong and sustained leadership. One cannot, after setting off on an institution-building path, reverse directions or reorganize every few years to let some politician "put his stamp on things" or to test some new theory of public accountability. Unilateral changing of the rules in the middle of the game of long-term institutional development breeds suspicion and conflict instead of cooperation and leads to a breakdown in the linkage between separately governed institutions. If this occurs, some of the benefits of decentralization are eventually lost as cooperation across institutions and levels of government decays, and the system's ability to extract the full potential of increased productivity from any social investment declines.

There are large differences between the situation faced by the United States and those of other nations in developing a modern agricultural sector. The United States is a large continental land mass. It is exceptionally well endowed with natural resources and is blessed with a good climate for agriculture. Until about World War I, labor was short but land very plentiful. U.S. political institutions were democratic in a Western European, mostly Anglo-Saxon, tradition while its economic institutions were free-market oriented and capitalistic.

Agricultural development across the world has many common requirements, even though the opportunity sets nations face can be quite different. A small nation with few ecosystems and climatic variations to deal with has much less need for decentralization of its agricultural institutions. If it is very small, it may face problems of resource base too small to sustain all of the scientific specializations needed for a fully effective agricultural research effort. Thus, many small Third World countries need to develop an efficient capacity to borrow, screen, and adapt technologies from neighboring countries, regions, and the international research system.

Nations less well endowed than the U.S. face many more constraints. A poor country cannot invest in everything at once. So the question of the most effective sequencing of complementary investments becomes critical to successful development.

By the middle of the nineteenth century the United States was highly literate and by the twentieth century was a well-educated society, so collecting market information to allow agricultural markets to function more efficiently was possible very early in U.S. development. The U.S. legal system, building on British common law traditions, protected property rights in transactions, reducing many of the risks and costs of commerce.

The fundamental lesson is clear. It takes more than research to increase productivity. It takes more than basic research. It takes an articulated-systems approach that coordinates a broad research investment with the creation of biological and physical capital, new human capital, new technologies, and an adaptive response to their use. It takes sustained national policy and institution building focused on clear common goals over long periods of time.

NOTES

1. Some models do, however, provide limited insights into the impact of certain institutional characteristics of a research system, such as its degree of decentralization and/or articulation, on returns to
investments in agricultural research. See, for example, Evenson, Waggoner, and Ruttan 1979.

2. The same reasoning applies to all major educational investments made in U.S. agriculture in both
the public and the private sector.

3. In only six of the fifty states, Maine and five southern states, is extension organized separately
from research at the academic department level. Extension followed a different evolutionary path in the
South than in the rest of the United States.

4. Seaman Knapp, the "father" of modern extension, was adamantly opposed to putting county
agents under the control of the deans of agriculture, whose objectives he saw as parochial and generally
limited to their own states. Knapp wanted to make the extension system part of the U.S. Department of
Agriculture, an organizational model similar to that followed in most countries today. He died before
Congress passed the Smith-Lever Act of 1941, establishing a national extension system controlled at the
state level by individual colleges of agriculture.

REFERENCES

Baker, Gladys L., Wayne Rasmussen, Vivian Wiser, and Jane M. Porter. 1963. *Century of Service: The First 100 Years of the U.S. Department of Agriculture.* Washington, D.C.: U.S. Department of Agriculture.

Bonnen, James T. 1962. "Some Observations on the Organizational Nature of a Great Technological Payoff." *Journal of Farm Economics* 44, no. 5: 1279–94.

———. 1980. "Observations on the Changing Nature of National Agricultural Policy Decision Processes, 1946–76." In *Farmers, Bureaucrats and Middlemen: Perspectives on American Agriculture,* edited by Trudy H. Peterson, 309–27. Washington, D.C.: Howard University Press.

Evenson, Robert E., Paul E. Waggoner, and Vernon W. Ruttan. 1979. "Economic Benefits from Research: An Example from Agriculture." *Science* 205, no. 14: 1101–7.

Heinz, John P. 1962. "The Political Impasse in Farm Support Legislation." *Yale Law Journal* 71:945–70.

Knutson, Marlys, and Luther G. Tweeten. 1979. "Toward an Optimum Rate of Growth in Agricultural Production Research and Extension." *American Journal of Agricultural Economics* 61, no. 1:70–76.

Lowi, Theodore J. 1965. "How Farmers Get What They Want." In *Legislative Politics U.S.A.,* edited by Theodore J. Lowi 132–39. Boston: Little Brown.

Mayer, Andre, and Jean Mayer. 1974. "Agriculture and the Island Empire." *Daedalus* 103, no. 3:83–95.

Office of Technology Assessment (OTA). 1981. "An Assessment of the United States Food and Agricultural Research System." Washington, D.C.: Office of Technology Assessment, pp. 201–6.

Olson, Mancur. 1971. *The Logic of Collective Action.* Cambridge: Harvard University Press.

Rasmussen, Wayne D. 1977. "Technology and American Agriculture: An Historical View." In *Technology Assessment: Proceedings of an ERS Workshop, April 20–22, 1976,* pp. 20–25. Washington, D.C.: USDA Economic Research Service, AGERS-31.

Ruttan, Vernon W. 1982. *Agricultural Research Policy.* Minneapolis: University of Minnesota Press.

Salisbury, Robert H. 1970. "An Exchange Theory of Interest Groups." In *Interest Group Politics in America,* edited by Robert H. Salisbury, 32–67. New York: Harper and Row.

Schultz, Theodore W. 1968. "Institutions and the Rising Economic Value of Man." *American Journal of Agricultural Economics* 50, no. 5: 1113–22.

———. 1975. "The Value of the Ability to Deal with Disequilibria." *Journal of Economic Literature* 13, no 3: 827–46.

Shaffer, James D. 1969. "On Institutional Obsolescence and Innovation—Background for Professional Dialogue on Policy." *American Journal of Agricultural Economics* 51, no. 2: 245–67.

True, Alfred Charles. 1929. *A History of Agricultural Education in the United States, 1785–1925.* USDA Miscellaneous Publication, no. 36. Washington, D.C.: U.S. Department of Agriculture.

U.S. Department of Agriculture (USDA). 1981. *1980–81 Directory of Professional Workers in State Agricultural Experiment Stations and Other Cooperating State Institutions.* Agricultural Handbook 305. Washington, D.C.: USDA.

16

Investing in People

THEODORE W. SCHULTZ

THE ECONOMICS OF BEING POOR

Most people in the world are poor. If we knew the economics of being poor, we would know much of the economics that really matters. Most of the world's poor people earn their living from agriculture. If we knew the economics of agriculture, we would know much of the economics of being poor.

Economists find it difficult to comprehend the preferences and scarcity constraints that determine the choices poor people make. We all know that most of the world's people are poor, that they earn a pittance for their labor, that half and more of their meager income is spent on food, that they reside predominantly in low-income countries, and that most of them earn their livelihood in agriculture. What many economists fail to understand is that poor people are no less concerned about improving their lot and that of their children than rich people are.

What we have learned in recent decades about the economics of agriculture will appear to most reasonably well informed people to be paradoxical. Agriculture in many low-income countries has the potential economic capacity to produce enough food for the still-growing population and also improve the income and welfare of poor people significantly. The decisive factors of production in improving the welfare of poor people are not space, energy, and cropland; the decisive factors are *the improvement in population quality and advances in knowledge.*

In recent decades the work of academic economists has greatly enlarged our understanding of the economics of human capital, especially the economics of research, the responses of farmers to new and profitable production techniques, the connection between production and welfare, and the economics of the family. Development economics has, however, suffered from several intellectual mistakes. The major error has been the presumption that standard economic theory is inadequate for understanding low-income countries and that a separate economic theory is needed. Models developed for this purpose were widely acclaimed, until it be-

THEODORE W. SCHULTZ is professor emeritus, Department of Economics, University of Chicago, and a Nobel laureate.

This chapter is based on his Nobel lecture, given 8 December 1979, Stockholm, Sweden, copyright © the Nobel Foundation, 1979. Reprinted from *Investing in People: The Economics of Population Quality,* 1981; with minor omissions, by permission of the University of California Press and the author.

came evident that they were at best intellectual curiosities. Some economists reacted by turning to cultural and social explanations for the alleged poor economic performance of low-income countries, although cultural and behavioral scholars are understandably uneasy about this use of their studies. Increasing numbers of economists have now come to realize that standard economic theory is as applicable to the scarcity problems that confront low-income countries as to the corresponding problems of high-income countries.

A second mistake is the neglect of economic history. Classical economics was developed when most people in Western Europe were barely scratching out subsistence from the poor soils they tilled and were condemned to a short life span. As a result, early economists dealt with conditions similar to those prevailing in low-income countries today. In Ricardo's day, about half of the family income of laborers in England went for food. So it is today in many low-income countries. Marshall tells us that "English labourers' weekly wages were often less than the price of a half bushel of good wheat" (Marshall 1920) when Ricardo published his *Principles of Political Economy and Taxation* (1817). The weekly wage of a ploughman in India is currently somewhat less than the price of two bushels of wheat (Schultz 1980). Knowledge of the experience and achievements of poor people over the ages can contribute much to an understanding of the problems and possibilities of low-income countries today. Such understanding is far more important than the most detailed and exact knowledge about the surface of the earth, or of ecology, or of tomorrow's technology.

Historical perception of population is also lacking. We extrapolate global statistics and are horrified by our interpretation of them—mainly that poor people breed like lemmings headed toward their own destruction. Yet when people were poor in our own social and economic history, that is not what happened. Expectations of destructive population growth in today's poor countries are also false.

LAND IS OVERRATED

A widely held view—the natural earth view—is that the land area suitable for growing food is virtually fixed and the supply of energy for tilling the land is being depleted. According to this view, it is impossible to continue producing enough food for the growing world population. An alternative view—the social-economic view—is that man has the ability and intelligence to lessen his dependence on cropland, traditional agriculture, and depleting sources of energy and to reduce the real costs of producing food for the growing world population. By means of research, we discover substitutes for cropland which Ricardo could not have anticipated, and, as incomes rise, parents reveal a preference for fewer children, substituting quality for quantity of children, which Malthus could not have foreseen. Ironically, economics, long labeled the dismal science, shows that the bleak natural earth view with respect to food is not compatible with history, which demonstrates that we can augment resources by advances in knowledge. I agree with Margaret Mead: "The future of mankind is open-ended." Mankind's future is not foreordained by space, energy, and cropland. It will be determined by the intelligent evolution of humanity.

Differences in the productivity of soils do not explain why people are poor in long-settled parts of the world. People in India have been poor for ages, both on the Deccan Plateau, where the productivity of the rainfed soils is low, and on the highly productive soils of South India. In Africa, people on the unproductive soils of the southern fringes of the Sahara, on the somewhat more productive soils on the steep slopes of the Rift landform, and on the highly productive alluvial lands along and at the mouth of the Nile all have one thing in common: they are very poor. Similarly, the much-publicized differences in land-population ratio throughout the low-income countries do not produce comparable differences in poverty. What matter most in the case of farmland are the incentives and associated opportunities farm people have to augment the effective supply of land by investments that include the contributions of agricultural research and the improvement of human skills. An integral part of the modernization of the economies of high- and low-income countries is *the decline in the economic importance of farmland and a rise in that of human capital—skills and knowledge.*

Despite economic history, economists' ideas about land are still, as a rule, those of Ricardo. But Ricardo's concept of land, "the original and indestructible powers of the soil," is no longer adequate, if ever it was. The share of national income that accrues as land rent and the associated social and political importance of landlords have declined markedly over time in high-income countries, and they are also declining in low-income countries.

Why is the Ricardian law of rent (which treats it as a result rather than a cause of prices) losing its economic sting? There are two primary reasons: first, the modernization of agriculture has over time transformed raw land into a vastly more productive resource than it was in its natural state; second, agricultural research has provided substitutes for cropland. With some local exceptions, the original soils of Europe were poor in quality. They are today highly productive. The original soils of Finland were less productive than the nearby western parts of the Soviet Union, yet today the croplands of Finland are superior. Japanese croplands were originally much inferior to those in Northern India; they are greatly superior today. In both high- and low-income countries these changes are partly the consequence of agricultural research, including the research embodied in purchased fertilizers, pesticides, insecticides, equipment, and other inputs. There are new substitutes for cropland, or land augmentation. The substitution process is well illustrated by corn: the corn acreage harvested in the United States in 1979, 33 million acres less than in 1932, produced 7.76 billion bushels, three times the amount produced in 1932.

THE QUALITY OF HUMAN AGENTS IS UNDERRATED

While land per se is not the critical factor in being poor, the human agent is: investment in improving population quality can significantly enhance the economic prospects and welfare of poor people. Child care, home and work experience, the acquisition of information and skills through schooling, and other investments in health and schooling can improve population quality. Such investments in low-income countries have been successful in improving economic prospects wherever they have not been dissipated by political instability. Poor people in low-income countries are not prisoners of an ironclad poverty equilibrium that economics is unable to break. No overwhelming forces nullify all economic improvements and cause poor people to abandon the economic struggle. It is now well documented that in agriculture poor people do respond to better opportunities.

The expectations of human agents in agriculture—farm laborers and farm entrepreneurs who both work and allocate resources—are shaped by new opportunities and by the incentives to which they respond. These incentives, explicit in the prices farmers receive for their products and in the prices they pay for producer and consumer goods and services, are greatly distorted in many low-income countries. The effect of these government-induced distortions is to reduce the economic contribution that agriculture is capable of making.

Governments tend to introduce distortions that discriminate against agriculture because internal politics generally favor urban at the expense of rural people, despite the much greater size of the rural population (Schultz 1978). The political influence of urban consumers and industry enables them to exact cheap food at the expense of the vast number of rural poor. This discrimination is rationalized on the grounds that agriculture is inherently backward and that its economic contribution is of little importance despite the "Green Revolution." The lowly cultivator is presumed to be indifferent to economic incentives and strongly committed to traditional ways of cultivation. Rapid industrialization is viewed as the key to economic progress. Policy gives top priority to industry and keeps foodgrains cheap. It is regrettable but true that this doctine is still supported by some donor agencies and rationalized by some economists in high-income countries.

Farmers the world over, in dealing with costs, returns, and risks, are calculating economic agents. Within their small, individual, allocative domain they are entrepreneurs tuning so subtly to economic conditions that many experts fail to recognize how efficient they are (Schultz 1964). Although farmers differ in their ability to perceive, interpret, and take appropriate action in responding to new information for reasons of schooling, health, and experience, they provide the essential human resource of entrepreneurship (Welch 1970; Evenson and Kislev 1975). On most farms women are also entrepreneurs in allocating their time and using farm products and purchased goods in household production (Schultz 1974). Allocative ability is supplied by millions of men and women on small-scale producing units, for agriculture is in general a highly decentralized sector of the economy. Where governments have taken over this entrepreneurial function in farming, they have been unsuccessful in providing an effective allocative substitute capable of modernizing agriculture. The allocative roles of farmers and farm women are important and their economic opportunities matter.

Entrepreneurship is also essential in research, always a venturesome business, which entails organization and allocation of scarce resources. The very essence of research is that it is a dynamic venture into the unknown or partially known. Funds, organizations, and competent scientists are necessary, but not in themselves sufficient. Research entrepreneurship is required, be it by scientists or by others engaged in the research sector of the economy. Someone must decide how to distribute the limited resources available, given the existing state of knowledge.

THE INEVITABILITY OF DISEQUILIBRIA

The transformation of agriculture into an increasingly productive state, a process commonly referred to as modernization, entails adjustments in farming as better opportunities become available. The value of the ability to deal with disequilibria is high in a dynamic economy (Schultz 1975). *Such disequilibria are inevitable.* They cannot be eliminated by law, by public policy, and surely not by rhetoric. Governments cannot efficiently perform the function of farm entrepreneurs.

Future historians will no doubt be puzzled by the extent to which economic incentives have been impaired during recent decades. The dominant intellectual view is antagonistic to agricultural incentives, and prevailing economic policies depreciate the function of producer incentives. D. Gale Johnson (1978) has shown that the large economic potential of agriculture in many low-income countries is not being realized. Technical possibilities have become increasingly favorable, but the economic incentives that are required for farmers in these countries to realize this potential are in disarray, either because the relevant information is lacking or because the prices and costs farmers face have been distorted. For want of profitable incentives, farmers have not made the necessary investments, including the purchase of superior inputs. Intervention by government is currently the major cause of the lack of optimum economic incentives.

ACHIEVEMENTS IN POPULATION QUALITY

I now turn to measurable gains in the quality of both farm and nonfarm people. Quality in this context consists of various forms of human capital. I have argued elsewhere that while a strong case can be made for using a rigorous definition of human capital, it will be subject to the same ambiguities that continue to plague capital theory in general, and the concept of capital in economic growth models in particular (Schultz 1972). Capital is two-faced, and what these two faces tell us about economic growth, which is a dynamic process, are, as a rule, inconsistent stories. It must be so because the cost story is a tale of sunk investments; for example, once a farmer invests in horse-drawn machinery, such machinery has little value for use with tractors. The other story pertains to the discounted value of the stream of services such capital renders, which changes with the shifting sands of growth. But worse still is the assumption, underlying capital theory and the aggregation of capital in growth models, that capital is homogeneous. Each form of capital has specific properties: a building, a tractor, a specific type of fertilizer, a tube well, and many other forms not only in agriculture but also in all other production activities. As Hicks has taught us, this capital homogeneity assumption is the disaster of capital theory (Hicks 1965). It is demonstrably inappropriate in analyzing the dynamics of economic growth afloat on capital inequalities because of the differences in the rates of return, whether capital aggregation is in terms of factor costs or in terms of the discounted value of the lifetime services of its many parts. Nor would a catalogue of all existing growth models prove that these inequalities are equals.

But why try to square the circle? If we were unable to observe these inequalities, we would have to invent them, because *they are the mainspring of economic growth*. They are the mainspring because they are the compelling economic signals of growth. One of the essential parts of economic growth is thus concealed by such capital aggregation.

The value of additional human capital depends on the additional well-being that human beings derive from it. Human capital contributes to labor productivity and to entrepreneurial ability valuable in farm and nonfarm production, in household production, in the time and other resources that students allocate to their education, and in migration to better job opportunities and better locations in which to live. Such ability also contributes importantly to satisfactions that are an integral part of current and future consumption.

My approach to population quality is to treat quality as a scarce resource, which implies that it has an economic value and that its acquisition entails a cost. The key to analyzing the human behavior that determines the type and amount of quality acquired over time is the relation between the returns from additional quality and the cost of acquiring it. When the returns exceed cost, population quality will be enhanced. This means that an increase in the supply of any quality component is a response to a demand for it. In this supply-demand approach to investment in population quality, all quality components are treated as durable, scarce resources useful over some period of time.

My hypothesis is that the returns on various quality components are increasing over time in many low-income countries; the returns that entrepreneurs derive from their allocative ability rise; so do the returns on child care, schooling, and improvements in health. Furthermore, the rates of return are enhanced by reductions in the cost of acquiring most of these quality components. Over time, the increased demand for quality in children, and on the part of adults in enhancing their own quality, favors having and rearing fewer children (Becker and Tomes 1976). The movement toward quality thus contributes to the solution of the population problem.

INVESTMENT IN HEALTH

Human-capital theory treats everyone's state of health as a stock, that is, as health capital, and its contribution as health services. Part of the quality of the initial stock is inherited and part is acquired. The stock depreciates over time and at an increasing rate in later life. Gross investment in human capital entails acquisition and maintenance costs, including child care, nutrition, clothing, housing, medical services, and care of oneself. The service that health capital renders consists of "healthy time" or "sickness-free time" which contributes to work, consumption, and leisure activities (Williams 1977; Grossman 1972).

The improvements in health revealed by the longer life span of people in many low-income countries have undoubtedly been the most important advance in population quality. Since about 1950, life expectancy at birth has increased 40 percent or more in many of these countries. The decline in mortality among infants and very young children is only part of this achievement. The mortality of older children, youths, and adults is also down.

Ram and Schultz deal with the economics of these demographic developments in India (Ram and Schultz 1979). The results correspond to those in other low-income countries. From 1951 to 1971, life expectancy at birth of males increased by 43 percent in India, and that of females by 41 percent. For both males and females, life spans over the life cycle after age ten, twenty, and on to age sixty, were also decidedly longer in 1971 than in 1951.

The favorable economic implications of these increases in life span are pervasive. While the satisfactions that people derive from longer life are hard to measure, Usher (1978) has devised an ingenious extension of economic theory to determine the utility that people derive from increases in life expectancy. His empirical analysis indicates that the additional utility increases substantially the value of personal income (Usher 1978).

Longer lifespans provide additional incentives to acquire more education, as investments in future earnings. Parents invest more in their children. More on-the-job training becomes worthwhile. The additional health capital and the other forms of human capital tend to increase the productivity of workers. Longer life results in more years of participation in the labor force, and brings about a reduction in "sick time." Better health and vitality in turn lead to more productivity per man-hour at work.

The Ram-Schultz study provides evidence of the gains in the productivity of agricultural labor in India realized as a consequence of improvements in health. Most telling is the productivity effect of the "cycle" that has characterized the malaria program.

INVESTMENT IN EDUCATION

Education accounts for much of the improvement in population quality. But in reckoning the cost of schooling, the value of the work that young children do for their parents must be included. Even for very young children during their first years of school, most parents sacrifice the value of the work that children traditionally perform (Rosenzweig and Evenson 1977). Another distinctive attribute of schooling is what might be called the vintage effect, as more education per child is achieved. Starting from widespread illiteracy, older people continue through life with little or no schooling, whereas the children on entering adulthood are the beneficiaries of schooling. The population of India grew about 50 percent between 1950–51 and 1970–71. School enrollment of children aged six to fourteen rose over 200 percent, and the rate of increase in secondary schools and universities was much higher. Since schooling is primarily an investment, it is a serious error to treat all educational outlays as current consumption. This error arises from the assumption that schooling is solely a consumer good. It is misleading to treat public expenditures on schooling as "welfare" expenditures, and a use of resources that has the effect of reducing "savings." The same error occurs in the case of expenditures on health, both on public and private account.

Expenditures on schooling, including higher education, are a substantial fraction of national income in many low-income countries. These expenditures are large relative to the conventional national accounting measures (concepts) of savings and investment. In India, the proportional cost of schooling in relation to national income, savings, and investment is not only large, but has tended to increase substantially over time.

THE HIGHLY SKILLED

In assessing population quality, it is important not to overlook the increases in the stock of physicians, other medical personnel, engineers, administrators, accountants, and various classes of research scientists and technicians.

The research capacity of a considerable number of low-income countries is impressive. There are specialized research institutes, research units within governmental departments, industrial sector research, and ongoing university research. Scientists and technicians are university trained, some of them in universities abroad. Research areas include, among others, medicine, public health (control of communicable diseases and the delivery of health services), nutrition, industry, agriculture, and even some atomic-energy research. I shall touch briefly on agricultural research, because I know it best and because it is well documented.

The founding and financing of the international agricultural research centers, originally initiated by the Rockefeller Foundation in cooperation with the government of Mexico, is an institutional innovation of a high order. But these centers, good as they are, are not a substitute for national agricultural research enterprises, as demonstrated by the increases in the number of agricultural scientists in twenty-two selected low-income countries between 1959 and 1974. All told, the number of man-years devoted to agricultural research in these countries increased more than three times during this period. By 1974, there were over 13,000 such scientists, ranging from 110 in the Ivory Coast to over 2,000 in India (Boyce and Evenson 1975). Indian agricultural research expenditures between 1950 and 1968 also more than tripled in real terms. An analysis by states within India shows that the rate of return has been approximately 40 percent, which is high indeed compared to the returns from most other investments to increase agricultural production (Evenson and Kislev 1975).

While there remains much that we do not know about the economics of being poor, our knowledge of the economic dynamics of low-income countries has advanced substantially in recent decades. We have learned that poor people are no less concerned about improving their lot and that of their children than those of us who have incomparably greater advantages. Nor are they any less competent in obtaining the maximum benefit from their limited resources. Population quality and knowledge matter. A good number of low-income countries have a positive record in improving population quality and in acquiring useful knowledge. These achievements imply favorable economic prospects, provided they are not dissipated by politics and governmental policies that discriminate against agriculture. As Alfred Marshall wrote, "knowledge is the most powerful engine of production; it enables us to subdue Nature and satisfy our wants."

Even so, most people throughout the world continue to earn a pittance from their labor. Half, or even more, of their meager income is spent on food. Their life is harsh. Farmers in low-income countries do all they can to augment their production. What happens to these farmers is of no concern to the sun, or to the earth, or the behavior of the monsoons and the winds that sweep the face of the earth; farmers' crops are in constant danger of being devoured by insects and pests: Nature is host to thousands of species that are hostile to the endeavors of farmers. Nature, however, can be subdued by knowledge and human abilities.

NOTE

I am indebted to Gary S. Becker, Milton Friedman, A. C. Harberger, D. Gale Johnson, and T. Paul Schultz for their helpful suggestions, as well as to my wife, Esther Schultz, for her insistence that what I thought was stated clearly was not clear enough.

REFERENCES

Becker, Gary S., and Nigel Tomes. 1976. "Child Endowments and the Quality of Children." *Journal of Political Economy* 84, part 2 (August): S143–S162.

Boyce, James K., and Robert E. Evenson. 1975. *National and International Agricultural Research and Extension Programs.* New York: Agricultural Development Council.

Evenson, Robert E., and Y. Kislev. 1975. *Agricultural Research and Productivity.* New Haven: Yale University Press.

Grossman, M. 1972. *The Demand for Health.* National Bureau of Economic Research, Occasional Paper, no. 119. New York: Columbia University Press.

Hicks, John. 1965. *Capital and Growth.* Oxford: Oxford University Press.

Johnson, D. Gale. 1978. "International Prices and Trade in Reducing the Distortions of Incentives. In Schultz, *Economics of the Family,* 195–215.

Marshall, Alfred. 1920. *Principles of Economics,* 8th ed. New York: Macmillan.

Ram, Rati, and Theodore W. Schultz. 1979. "Life Span, Health, Savings and Productivity." *Economic Development and Cultural Change* 27 (April): 399–421.

Rosenzweig, Mark R., and Robert E. Evenson. 1977. "Fertility, Schooling and the Economic Contribution of Children in Rural India." *Econometrica* 45 (July): 1065–79.

Schultz, Theodore W. 1964. *Transforming Traditional Agriculture*. New Haven: Yale University Press. Reprinted New York: Arno Press, 1976; Chicago: University of Chicago Press, 1983.

———. 1972. "Human Capital: Policy Issues and Research Opportunities." In *Human Resources*. New York: National Bureau of Economic Research.

———, ed. 1974. *Economics of the Family: Marriage, Children and Human Capital*. Chicago: University of Chicago Press.

———. 1975. "The Value of the Ability to Deal with Disequilibria." *Journal of Economic Literature* 13 (September): 827–46.

———. 1978. "On Economics and Politics of Agriculture." In *Distortions of Agricultural Incentives*, edited by T. W. Schultz, 3–23. Bloomington, Ind.: Indiana University Press.

———. 1980. "On the Economics of the Increases in the Value of Human Time over Time." In *Economic Growth and Resources*. Vol. 2, *Trends and Factors*, edited by R. C. O. Matthews. London: Macmillan.

Usher, Dan. 1978. "An Imputation to the Measure of Economic Growth for Changes in Life Expectancy." In *The Measurement of Economic and Social Performance*, edited by Milton Moss, 193–236. New York: National Bureau of Economic Research.

Welch, Finis. 1970. "Education in Production," *Journal of Political Economy* 78 (January-February): 35–59.

Williams, Alan. 1977. "Health Service Planning." In *Studies in Modern Economic Analysis*, edited by M. J. Artis and A. R. Nobay, 301–5. Edinburgh: Blackwell.

17

Women and Agricultural Development

MAYRA BUVINIĆ AND REKHA MEHRA

INTRODUCTION

Before 1970, analyses of women's roles in Third World agriculture were found mostly in ethnographic studies of traditional societies. Ester Boserup, an economist, deserves full credit for placing this subject squarely within economic development. In 1970 she presented the first comprehensive, empirically based analysis of women's participation in agriculture and linked the evolution of farming systems to population pressures, technological change in agriculture, and the participation of women in the labor force.

Boserup (1970) distinguished three types of agricultural systems: female, male, and mixed. Female farming systems in some countries in Africa and Latin America and in certain areas of India are characterized by slash and burn agriculture, communal land ownership, and the use of the hoe. Except for land clearing, most of the work is done by women, who support themselves and their children. These women tend to be economically independent and mobile. If they generate an agricultural surplus, they engage in trade to supplement their subsistence earnings with cash income.

Male farming systems, found in Asia, are based on land ownership, settled production patterns, and the use of draft animals and the plow. Field labor is done almost entirely by men and is supplemented by hired labor; if women contribute to farming at all, it is during harvest time or at other peak periods. Women are often secluded and are dependent on men for economic support.

Mixed farming, which follows and shares many of the characteristics of male farming systems, emerges with rapidly growing populations. Increasing land pressure requires year-round intensive cultivation and multiple cropping, which are facilitated with irrigation. Labor demand is high and, despite social norms to the contrary, women are drawn into such tasks as weeding, transplanting, and harvesting.

MAYRA BUVINIĆ is director and REKHA MEHRA is an agricultural economist at the International Center for Research on Women, Washington, D.C.

Boserup attributes the disappearance of female farming systems to population pressure and the introduction of cash crops during the colonial period. Population pressure caused a shift to permanent agriculture. The plow replaced the hoe, plowing became men's work, arguably because it required physical strength and/or physical mobility, and men took over many of the farming activities. For example, in colonial Africa, European administrators and technical advisers introduced cash crops and modern agricultural technologies to men. Men, therefore, took credit for developing a highly productive export-oriented farming sector while women were left behind in the traditional low-yielding subsistence sector. As a consequence, women lost control over farming as well as the economic autonomy derived from farming.

Without question, Boserup's work provided much of the substance for the increased attention to women's issues by the United Nations, development agencies, and nongovernmental organizations (NGOs) starting in 1975, when an International Women's Year conference was held in Mexico City. Until this conference, international donors, national governments, and NGOs had channeled development resources to women only in their roles as mothers and homemakers. Women's roles as economic producers—farmers as well as wage laborers—had been ignored.

The 1975 Mexico City conference used Boserup's analysis to promote action that focused on women as producers and redressed sex-based inequities in development programs. But the weakness of these early efforts stressing women's economic participation was the inability of researchers and advocates to marshall convincing empirical evidence of the multiple economic roles of women and the negative impact that development had often had on women. In part as a result of lack of knowledge, the bulk of development assistance in the decade following the Mexico conference did not revise its assumptions about women. A variety of women-only projects were implemented over the 1976–85 period, with limited funding from donors. Although these projects demonstrated that donors were "doing something about rural women," ultimately they brought little improvement to the welfare of women. We shall now summarize findings on women's roles in farming systems, describe the impact of agricultural technologies on women in agriculture, and present an agenda for improving their situation in the 1990s.

THE RESEARCH EVIDENCE ON WOMEN'S ROLES IN FARMING SYSTEMS

Two decades of research have largely supported Boserup's (1970) insights in terms of variations in women's participation in different farming systems. But by analyzing in more detail the less visible work activities (such as domestic production and seasonal wage labor), the research has also shown that women's contributions to agriculture are greater than those postulated by Boserup. It is well accepted nowadays that women make substantial contributions to food production and agricultural wage labor, even when they are secluded or in male-dominated farming systems. Unfortunately, reliable statistics on the actual size and composition by sex of the agricultural work force are still lacking. More importantly, research has yielded useful information on the nature and determinants of women's work in agriculture and has revealed complex interactions between women's market and home production roles, household consumption, and family nutrition.

Although subject to considerable socioeconomic and agroecological variations, there is a traditional division of farm work by sex. Women are particularly active in growing food for subsistence, in weeding, post-harvest storage and processing, small-scale marketing of agricultural produce, and the care of livestock. Men grow cash crops for sale in local, national, and international markets. In many parts of Africa, for instance, where women's participation in farm work is traditional and well recognized, and female farming systems in a sense still survive, there are "female crops" (i.e., cassava and other roots and tubers) and "male crops" (maize and cotton). But the division of farm tasks by sex is more rigid in cultural convention than in reality. It breaks down easily in response to changes in demand for farm wage labor and household labor. Rural poverty and the shortage of farm labor expand women's participation into "male" ascribed farm tasks; for example, they plant tobacco in commercial farms in Honduras, pick coffee in Colombia, and harvest subsistence crops in nearly landless households in the Peruvian sierra.

Variations in women's participation in agricultural work depend on supply and demand factors linked to economic growth and agricultural modernization. Countries with high rates of urbanization and female-dominated rural-to-urban migration, like Latin American nations in the last two decades, experience shortages in the supply of female farm labor. Conversely, countries with low rates of urbanization (like many in sub-Saharan Africa) have an abundant supply of female farm workers. The demand for female farm work varies with land tenure patterns, the commodity being produced, and the degree of integration of agriculture into the market economy. Women's participation in agriculture is greater, as is their contribution to farm income, in small farms oriented to local rather than export markets (Dixon 1983). The demand for female farm labor has also increased with male labor migration and with agricultural policies that foster the development of agribusiness, in which women comprise the bulk of the work force. The time women spend in farm activities supplementing male labor as well as farming their own plots has increased notably among small farmers who grow groundnuts and cotton for export in Senegal, snowpeas for an agribusiness firm in Guatemala, and flowers for export in Ecuador. Export fruit companies in Chile and Costa Rica rely almost exclusively on female labor for harvesting, processing, and packing fruits.

Despite women's extensive and varied participation in agriculture, they continue to have less access than do men to modern agricultural inputs. As a result, their farm work is labor-intensive and yields meager economic returns. This work pattern of high female participation with low productivity and low earnings has been documented across regions and is especially evident among women who head farm households with absent spouses.

THE NATURE AND CONTRIBUTIONS OF RURAL WOMEN'S HOME AND SUBSISTENCE WORK

The unpaid home and farm activities of women are very time consuming; nevertheless, these activities make vital contributions to the economy of poor rural households in Third World countries. The poorer the country, the more hours women work and the greater are their contributions to the economy and family welfare. Rural women in developing economies work longer hours than both their urban female counterparts and rural men.

In parts of East Africa women work up to 16 hours a day doing housework, caring for children, preparing food, and growing between 60 and 80 percent of the food for the family (Fagley 1976). Rural Javanese women work 11 hours a day, compared to 8 ½ hours for men (Nag, White, and Peet 1978). Home production includes some activities that can be called housework proper, such as cooking, child care, and sweeping, and a host of other tasks that in industrial economies would fall under agricultural or agroindustrial production or services. They include collecting water and firewood, storing and processing grains for home consumption, managing household wastes, and building floors and walls, among others. Because this is unpaid work, these activities have remained outside of official statistics that measure economic and agricultural output.

Recently, however, economists have begun to measure the economic contribution of women to family income. To quantify this contribution, economic activities, such as housework, that can be delegated to a paid outsider have been measured, by the number of hours women spend doing them (from time-use studies), the economic value of this time (what wage a person would earn if hired to do the work), the volume of production (e.g., the amount of firewood collected), or the value of what a woman produces (the price of the cassava that women process). Numerous studies have obtained valuable information on the allocation of work and leisure time in poor households by sex and age. Table 1 summarizes the results of twelve rural time allocation studies and shows that women's daily work, including production, marketing, and household activities, ranges from a low of 5.79 hours per day to a high of 12.49 hours per day. The corresponding figures for men range between 5.17 and 10.8 daily work hours. Men do significantly more market work than women but substantially less home work.

Women's time allocation patterns are less fixed than those of men. Men's use of time does not vary much during their adult working lives. In contrast, time allocation by women and children is flexible, changing with the number and ages of children in the household and the annual cycle of agriculture and schooling (if children go to school at all). As the demand for childrearing time and for cash income increases over the household's life cycle, the burden of meeting this demand falls primarily on the wife and, as they grow older, on the children.

In the rural Philippines, fathers' time spent in domestic chores is 1 to 2 hours daily, whether there is one child or seven. Filipino women spend about 2 ½ hours per day in market production (wage employment, farming, fishing, and income-

TABLE 1
HOURS PER DAY SPENT ON PRODUCTIVE ACTIVITY IN RURAL AREAS IN THE THIRD WORLD (BY GENDER)

Country and Year of Study	Reference	Gender	Home Production[a]	Agriculture Market and Nonmarket Work[b]	Other Market Work[c]	Unspecified Wage Work	Total Hours Worked
Latin America							
Peru (1975)	Johnson 1975	women	4.07	1.72	0.00	—	5.79
		men	.53	4.43	.21	—	5.17
South and Southeast Asia							
Bangladesh (1976) (Char Gopalpur District)	Cain 1980	women	7.65	.55	.05	.45	8.70
		men	.90	4.25	1.20	2.40	8.75
Bangladesh (1976) (Char Gopalpur District)	Cain, Khanam, & Nahar 1979	women	5.40	1.71	.35	.84	8.30
		men	1.27	2.80	1.01	3.24	8.32
Indonesia (1972–73) (Java)	Nag, White, & Peet 1978	women	5.61	1.50	4.54	—	11.65
		men	.69	4.29	2.64	—	7.62
Indonesia (1972) (Java, Jogjakarta)	White 1975	women	4.13	2.17	5.67	—	11.97
		men	.75	4.24	3.36	—	8.35
Nepal (1972–73)	Nag, White, & Peet 1978	women	4.86	7.23	.40	—	12.49
		men	2.17	6.13	1.88	—	10.18
Nepal (n.d.)	Acharya & Bennett 1981	women	6.13	3.76	.91	—	10.80
		men	1.53	4.33	1.66	—	7.52
Philippines (1977) (Laguna)	Folbre 1983	women	7.37	—	2.41	—	9.78
		men	.49	—	7.06	—	7.55
Philippines (1977) (Laguna)	King & Evenson 1983	women	5.20	1.85	1.89	—	8.94
		men	1.08	3.59	3.99	—	8.66
Africa							
Tanzania (1976) (Bukoba District)	Kamuzora 1980	women	3.47	4.24	.01	—	7.72
		men	1.13	4.20	.82	—	6.15
Cote d'Ivoire (1979)	FAO 1983	women	6.89	1.64	.13	—	8.66
		men	.75	3.14	.04	—	3.93
Burkina Faso (1979)	McSweeney 1979	women	3.28	7.43	.82	—	11.53
		men	.12	3.48	2.60	—	6.20

NOTE: Reciprocal labor exchange has not been included in this chart.

[a]Home production includes activities such as food preparation, child care, hygiene, firewood collection, house construction, attending the sick, and food collection.

[b]Agriculture market and nonmarket work includes activities such as hunting and gathering, garden labor, animal care, crop production, rice cultivation, and processing crops for storage or sales.

[c]Other market work includes activities such as trading, handicraft production, and food preparation for market sale.

earning work at home) and 7 to 8 hours in home production. Older children often substitute for father's time in home chores and care of siblings. When there are seven or more children, men actually reduce their child care time (to about 10 minutes a day) and increase their leisure time (King and Evenson 1983). In rural Peru as well, it is mothers and children who substitute for each other in cooking, hauling water, and animal care (Deere 1983).

Women's subsistence activities in some rural areas of Botswana, Cameroon, and Nepal amount to 54 to 70 percent of total household income; domestic activities contribute another 30 percent. In rural Malaysia, subsistence and domestic activities, contribute 56 percent of household monetary income (Goldschmidt-Clermont 1983). The estimated mean value of home production for a farm wife in a polygamous household in Burkina Faso is 61 percent of the income generated through crop production. This value increases with the number of young children at home and the use of animal traction technology in the farm. It decreases in households that have many wives or older female children, who substitute in the wife's work at home (Singh and Morey 1987).

Studies have repeatedly shown that the earnings of adult women are proportionately more important in poor than in better-off families. In Indonesia, women and girls of poor landless families devote almost as much time to wage labor as men and boys (Hart 1980). In the sierra region of Peru, women from landless peasant households provide 35 percent of the total number of family labor days devoted to agricultural production, while women from the middle-class and rich peasantry provide only 21 percent. Furthermore, the poor peasant household is affected prejudicially by the differential returns to male and female labor, for it is primarily the women of the near landless and smallholder households who work as wage laborers or artisans to generate income (Deere 1983).

HOUSEHOLDS AND HOUSEHOLD STRUCTURES

Women's work throughout the world is more strongly affected by family arrangements than men's work. Household structure (i.e., man-headed, woman-headed, or jointly-headed) and household dynamics, or the distribution of labor and resources within the household by sex and age, intervene and affect women's economic behavior. The life stage of the household, including the numbers and ages of children, is also a powerful determinant of women's economic participation, as is, in many cases, women's marital status and the access to resources correlated with their status. In turn, women's work, and their access to earnings, have powerful and direct effects on family welfare.

Household Models

The reality of families and households in the Third World is very different from the constructs surrounding families and households in development theory and research. The latter have used an ideal family model with a *pater familias* as the head of household. Along with this notion of a male head has been the convenient assumption in microeconomic theory that he is the single decision maker in the household and that other household members share his interests and follow his decisions. Neither assumption is true, as recent research has revealed. Female-headed households have been traditional in some African societies and have emerged recently in many others as a result of economic pressures and labor migration. Jointly-headed households are also increasingly common; they are the result of modernization and women's integration into the modern work force as well as of poverty and the need for multiple sources of household income.

Throughout the world, household members have differing interests that cannot be subsumed by the interests of the head. Inequalities within the household in the distribution of work and resources by sex and age are pervasive, as are negotiations among family members over household assets. Overall, men and boys have the upper hand over women and girls in the distribution of household resources, particularly when these are scarce (Sen 1985). In addition, there are both cultural and economic variations in spending patterns and responsibilities by sex. In some societies there are distinctive and separate male and female economies, while, in others, resources are pooled. In many parts of West Africa, men and women have independent sources of income and independent spending responsibilities. In parts of South Asia, on the other hand, households behave more like the ideal model of one purse and one decision maker, although these households often exhibit significant intrahousehold inequalities in the distribution of resources (Dwyer and Bruce 1988).

Variations in household headship and household dynamics affect who gains and who loses during the introduction of technological change in agriculture. Unfortunately, most farming systems researchers and extension workers consider the household as a homogeneous unit of production and consumption and ignore differing household arrangements and interests (Poats et al. 1988). For example, extension schemes often do not assist women who head farm households.

Woman-headed Households: Empirical Evidence from Africa

"Left-behind" women, de facto heads of farm households (whether they are farm owners or not), are increasingly common in rural areas with high rates of male migration. Unfortunately, census and household survey data have not yielded reliable assessments of the incidence and prevalence of these households. But, in Africa in particular, household surveys illustrate the interplay between household structures, women's work in agriculture, and family welfare.

Estimates of woman-headed households in Kenya vary from 22 to 40 percent in rural areas (Clark 1984). Staudt (1978) found that 40 percent of the farms in two areas of Western Kenya were female-managed farms where the male was absent. Women both worked on the farm and functioned as the de facto household heads. In comparing female-managed with jointly-managed farms (that is, farms with a man present and sharing farm management decisions), Staudt found that jointly-managed farms were 4 times more likely to have a household member trained by an extensionist and 14 times more likely to have detailed loan information. Over time, the extension services' preference for targeting male over female farmers negatively affected the productivity of females and increased the income gap between the sexes.

In Botswana, the largest proportion of woman-headed households is in the rural areas; they are also poorer than male-headed households. Kossoudji and Mueller (1983) found that 36 percent of the households in a rural income distribution survey were female-headed with no man present, because males had migrated to work in the South African mines. The female-headed households were smaller and had a higher child dependency burden; lacking a second adult (male) worker, they faced acute shortages of labor; and their income was less than half that of male-headed households, even when transfer payments were included in total income. Male-headed households owned three times more cattle than female-headed households. Having fewer oxen for plowing, female-headed households had less than half the value of equipment and cultivated less land than male-headed households. The lower income of female-headed households in this study was not due to educational differences between the sexes, women's higher preference for leisure (in fact, women worked 20 percent more than men and had 20 percent less leisure time), or greater inefficiency at work. Women were poorer because they had similar economic burdens but less access to the productive assets (land, cattle, labor) needed to increase agricultural production and income.

The Botswana study also found that girls and boys in woman-headed households received more education than in male-headed households (Kossoudji and Mueller 1983). Using the same data set, Chernichovsky and Smith (1979) had earlier found that this effect persisted after allowance was made for differences in income, number of school age children, and location. Similarly, Kumar (1985) found a significantly higher level of child nutrition in Zambia at any given income level in woman-headed households than in jointly-headed and polygamous households. In southwestern Kenya, Kennedy and Cogill (1987) report that children from female-headed households did significantly better on long-term measures of nutritional status (height-for-age and weight-for-age). Greer and Thorbecke (1986) found in rural Kenya that, after controlling for land size and household composition, female-headed households still allocated a greater proportion of income toward high-calorie foods.

The unexpected positive findings from resource-poor woman-headed households stress the importance of understanding intrahousehold dynamics and variations by sex in the use of labor and resources. The results are best explained by hypothesizing that there are gender differences in expenditure preferences and that women's greater preference to invest in children can be realized more effectively or easily in a household situation where women make more decisions (or are the sole decision makers) and face fewer intrahousehold conflicts (between men and women) over the use of household resources. The next section illustrates the role of household variables in mediating the effects of technological change in agriculture.

THE IMPACT OF NEW TECHNOLOGY ON WOMEN FARMERS

Following Boserup's lead, a number of researchers have hypothesized that technological change would increase women's workload, displace women wage earners, reduce women's income, and, indirectly, lower family nutritional status. More recent research has shifted to analyzing how the inclusion of gender in technological change can help bring about improved output, economic growth, and household welfare. Many of the empirical studies are on rice and smallholder production systems in Asia and Africa. Methodologically, the studies are more descriptive than analytical and rely primarily on qualitative analysis and descriptive statistics. Only 6 of 21 studies reviewed for this chapter used statistical methods to test hypotheses. The major findings are summarized below.

LABOR USE AND EMPLOYMENT

The empirical evidence on the effects of technological change on labor use and employment is mixed, and it depends on, among other things, the crop and the technology, the household's access to land, women's socioeconomic standing, and intrahousehold dynamics. In examining the effects of high-yielding rice varieties (HYVs), it is important to distinguish between seed-fertilizer technology packages and mechanical field, harvest, and post-harvest operations that often accompany the new technology. Agarwal (1984) and Ghosh and Mukhopadhyay (1988) found that the adoption of HYVs in India increased total labor use and raised the demand for women's labor relatively more than for that of men. But Agarwal also found that the increased income from HYVs enabled women in larger landholding households to withdraw from field work. Where mechanical operations were adopted along with the HYVs, women's work intensity decreased, as did wage employment opportunities, both in rice (Acharya and Patkar 1985) and non-rice production (Rassam and Tully 1988).

Two studies in South and East Asia examined the effects of mechanical milling on the demand for labor in rice processing. Both Begum (1985) and Scott and Carr (1985) found that mechanization of post-harvest operations in Bangladesh reduced women's labor input in large- and small-landed households, increasing leisure time in the first case and reducing the work burden in the second. However, mechanization also displaced landless female labor from wage employment. The few mill jobs were not sufficient to meet the work demands of displaced women workers and, in any case, the mills either exclusively hired or gave preference to men. Unlike men, women displaced as workers or farmers were not offered training for alternative employment.

In the Gambia in West Africa, women worked on male-owned or communal plots rather than on their own plots when time constraints were introduced by new rice technologies and the allocation of irrigated land to men (Dey 1981, 1985). This substitution effect appeared in situations where women traditionally engaged in rainfed rice production on their own plots and where the development project consciously made an effort to encourage women to retain their own production (von Braun and Webb 1989). Similar increased farm labor and substitution effects have been found with the introduction of other crops, such as high-value vegetables and commercialized dairy production.

Only a few studies have addressed changes in women's roles associated with technological innovations and farm output. Dey (1981) concluded that the production increase due to irrigation in the Gambia was not as significant as it might have been if women's expertise in dryland rice production had been tapped.

Von Braun (1989) found that women's farm work increased 78 percent in a non-traditional vegetable production project in Guatemala. Women had to substitute farm work for off-farm income-generating work, losing control over economic resources, since men controlled the income from the highly profitable farm work.

WAGES AND INCOMES

Increases in the demand for women's labor as a result of HYVs are not always associated with improved wages and incomes, although there is the possibility that observed reductions in woman's wages could have been greater without the introduction of HYVs. A more relevant measure is how women's real wages changed relative to changes in men's wages. The small amount of available evidence on this issue is mixed. Acharya and Patkar (1985) found that the new technology had a positive income effect for females and slightly reduced the gap between men's and women's wages in each of five states in India represented in their sample. On the other hand, in Cameroon, with the introduction of irrigated rice as a cash crop, women became wage workers on their husband's rice farms; and, while they earned their opportunity wage, this amounted to less than one-fourth of the net increase in household income generated by their labor (Jones 1986). Von Braun and Webb (1989) found that the adoption of irrigated rice by men in the Gambia resulted in less rice marketing and a switch by women into cash crop production. Because women did not have access to labor-saving tools and had less time than men to devote to agriculture, due to competing demands from household work, their labor productivity was consistently lower than men's by an average of roughly 70 percent.

Numerous studies have shown that mechanization has displaced women and reduced their income and employment. Scott and Carr (1985) estimated that the displacement of landless labor due to rice mechanization in Bangladesh reduced the incomes of the poorest 5 percent of women by 55 percent annually. This represented a loss of 15 percent of family income. In Indonesia, mechanical rice processing eliminated about 1.25 million woman days of labor in Java alone—the equivalent of $50 million in annual earnings.[1] Von Braun's (1989) study of the production in Guatemala of nontraditional vegetable crops for export showed a loss of economic independence among women as they substituted farm for off-farm income-generating work.

Nutrition and Welfare

There is growing evidence on the nutritional impact of agricultural innovations mediated by changes in women's work roles. Some researchers have postulated, but without empirical evidence, that family nutritional levels have been threatened by women's diversion to cash crop production (Dey 1985). However, von Braun and Webb (1989) have provided evidence that the expansion of rice production under irrigation in the Gambia resulted in higher caloric consumption for both men and women. Although women's incomes fell and women's role in rice production declined, rice became a communal crop and more rice was retained for domestic consumption than for market sale.

Von Braun, Kennedy, and Bouis (1988) summarize the result of five studies, including their research in the Gambia, on the effects of commercialization of smallholder agriculture on consumption and nutrition. While there are variations across settings, they conclude that women's direct control over income from the new cash crops was much less than men's and was often disproportional to their labor input. However, household food expenditures, as well as other expenditures with high welfare content, increased in absolute terms as incomes controlled by men rose; and this increase had a positive, although not large, effect on child nutritional status.

The increases in women's wage rates accompanying technological change in agriculture could have a negative effect on nutritional levels, because the cost of women's time spent on home production (and child rearing) increases. In particular, the concern has been that increased market work might cause women to curtail breastfeeding, as well as other health care activities that are critical to preventing child malnutrition. However, a recent review of the empirical evidence on the relationship of women's market work to infant feeding practices and child nutrition reveals that there is no clear association between women's work status and breastfeeding patterns or child nutritional status. In most studies the prevalence of breastfeeding was not related to women's work status. A few studies found that child nutrition had been negatively affected, but a number of others found a positive association, particularly among children of higher-income working mothers (Leslie 1988).

In summary, the literature shows that technological change in agriculture has specific and highly heterogeneous effects on women's labor, control of income, and child nutrition. These effects are often different from those on men's labor and are uniquely linked to household consumption patterns and child nutritional status. The effect of agriculture technology on women, as on men, can be to either displace or increase women's farm labor, decrease or increase women's wage rates, and can lead to substitution effects between women's off- and on-farm work or between women's and other household members' labor in home production.

A review of the evidence indicates the need for empirical work that disaggregates the effects of technology adoption by sex, measures effects on labor use, wages, and degree of control over income, and integrates the intervening variables of intrahousehold dynamics and social stratification into analyses of the social and economic impacts of technological change.

PROJECTS FOR RURAL WOMEN

The emphasis on income generation, training, and credit projects for poor rural women was a response to the project orientation that dominated development work in 1970s. Projects were then the main units for implementation, analysis, and evaluation (Lewis 1988). The project orientation was compatible with the limited financial resources allocated to studying women's issues, the restricted access of women development workers to policy makers in Third World countries, and the need to build up a concrete record by the end of the "Women's Decade" in 1985. In the late 1970s, a large percentage of development funds on behalf of women went to NGOs, because these organizations were generally more receptive than government agencies were to addressing the problems of poor women. NGOs were also easier to work with than cumbersome governmental bureaucracies. But this choice restricted the impact that women's projects had on policy and institutional reforms, which are more easily accomplished by government action than by NGO intervention.

The bulk of the development projects for rural women over the 1976–85 period provided training in traditional female skills (e.g., sewing, cooking, and crafts), credit programs for microenterprises, and income-generation schemes to bring rural women into the market economy. Notably absent were interventions that could develop and provide agricultural technologies, credit, and extension to women farmers, redistribute land to women, or increase the demand for women's paid labor in rural areas. Interventions in these areas could have dramatically strengthened women's roles in agriculture. By failing to support these reforms, donors, NGOs, and governments limited the impact their earmarked funds could have on poor rural women.

These women might also have benefited from the general funds assigned to agriculture and rural development. Especially during the 1970s, international donors made large investments in smallholder agriculture and integrated rural development projects. But these projects were designed to raise the welfare of farm and landless families, rather than of individuals, and did not generally succeed in improving women's economic opportunities. Ironically, the existence of funds earmarked for women, and the special women-in-development activities that they encouraged, made it easier not to deal with women's concerns in mainstream development projects. The result was that women were effectively denied access to the resources and expertise that mainstream activities commanded.

MICROENTERPRISE PROJECTS

Microenterprise projects became very popular in the 1980s, in part because they reinforced a private-sector orientation that was much in vogue in development assistance and in part because they targeted a sector that increases in importance in the face of economic crises and modern-sector unemployment.

Microenterprise projects deliver short-term flexible loans with few collateral requirements to entrepreneurs who operate very small scale businesses in rural and urban informal markets. A distinctive feature of these projects, which in part accounts for their relative success, is that they are directed to women and men who are already integrated into market production and need only to strengthen their productivity and earnings rather than join the market economy. For instance, microenterprise projects provide working capital to basket weavers, rice huskers, beer brewers, tortilla producers, and others who pursue home-based enterprises of the sort that rural women commonly operate. Success is measured by high repayment rates, ability to reach a relatively large number of beneficiaries, and significant short-term increases in net business earnings. The more successful or better-performing projects are run by specialized agencies that focus on a particular task and provide the single missing ingredient rather than integrated services. In these projects individual clients carry out familiar or easily mastered tasks, they are not required to engage in collective production, and they undertake an economic activity for which there is a shortfall in supply and an established demand (Tendler 1989). Densely populated areas help guarantee local demand, so these projects have proliferated in rural Asia and in Latin American cities, areas with high population densities. Sparsely populated rural communities in sub-Saharan Africa and Latin America have had limited success with these types of schemes. In summary, microenterprise projects have proven to be a successful vehicle for helping poor women.

INCOME-GENERATION PROJECTS AND THEIR MISBEHAVIOR

Why do production- and income-generating projects frequently misbehave and end up pursuing welfare goals? We shall address this question by first examining two project histories. In 1979 a private voluntary agency set up an income-generation project for rural women in the western province in Kenya. A group of 50 women was organized into a cooperative to produce potholders from banana fiber rings for sale in Nairobi. Two years later, the women were losing 0.50 Kenyan shillings for every potholder they produced and sold, even before including the implicit cost of their labor (the unit cost of the fiber was 3 shillings and the retail price of the potholders was 2.50 shillings). Moreover, capital that had been donated to finance and replicate the project through a revolving fund had been depleted. The project, nonetheless, continued operating with donated funds and survived its financial misfortunes, because social or community development goals were perceived as appropriate or beneficial for poor women even if the productive component failed.

In Bolivia, a large integrated rural development scheme financed by an international donor agency and implemented by the government was launched in the highlands to increase alpaca and llama wool production and modernize the herd management and shearing practices of Bolivian peasants. But information collected during the appraisal of the project revealed that herding and shearing were women's work and, as a result, the design of the project was revised to include a production-oriented women's component. Project implementation was assigned to a government social welfare agency rather than the Ministry of Agriculture. The social welfare agency redirected the production-oriented component towards something that they were familiar with: developing women's skills in nutrition, cooking, and embroidery. Highland peasant women, whose principal duties were to herd and shear animals, manage household finances, and supervise the day-to-day activities of the household, were instead organized into groups and given training in a number of unfamiliar and (for them) complicated tasks such as nutrition and cooking, embroidery, sewing, knitting and crochet, and paper and papier mache flower making. Women were given what was essentially welfare rather than production-oriented training because it was wrongly assumed that this training would enhance tasks they had traditionally performed.

The experience of these two projects illustrates the typical unfolding of income-generation projects for poor women in the Third World. During implementation, many projects "misbehave" and many of the production goals are gradually replaced by welfare activities, which deliver information or free handouts (food, clothes, or money) to poor women in their roles as wives and mothers (Buvinić 1986). The welfare slant in the execution of women's projects is explained by three specific project characteristics that interfere with the execution of production objectives and cause projects to misbehave. First, there are common misperceptions about women's lives and what is good or appropriate for poor rural women. Projects often concentrate on stereotypical Western female tasks, such as sewing and embroidery, because they are perceived to be simple and familiar to poor rural women. But in the Third World these activities are largely unfamiliar to poor rural women, who have difficulty performing them effectively. Badly executed activities lead to loss of motivation among project participants and economic failure. Second, most welfare-oriented projects are designed to help groups of women identify their felt needs in a participatory fashion and arrive at group decisions, while economic programs require centralized decision making for successful implementation. The participatory style of women's projects is conducive to the implementation of social rather than economic objectives. The preference for this working style, therefore, helps explain the survival of projects that are financial failures.

The third characteristic of production projects that misbehave is that they are often staffed by female volunteers with limited technical qualifications. Women are usually called to staff these projects because of the largely untested belief that women work best with other women. The lack of technical expertise of women advisers in areas such as agricultural extension, accounting, and marketing is a major hindrance to the success of projects directed toward increasing women's income.

The design choices of the typical woman's project are easily explained by some of the organizations that have been most frequently invited to implement them: nongovernmental volunteer organizations that focus on women's issues, along with the social welfare, children's, and women's sections of governmental agencies. Most of the women's NGOs have substantial expertise in welfare projects, since they were widely utilized by international relief agencies to distribute services and free goods in the 1950–70 period. These organizations, which had acquired large numbers of women volunteers to distribute relief, were asked during the 1970s to revise their charters and implement productive programs for poor women. They did so, but because they knew how to implement welfare rather than productive programs, they transformed productive designs into welfare projects. From an organizational perspective, this was the rational choice for institutions with a welfare history, successful performance in welfare activities, and no technical expertise in productive projects.

These NGOs and the welfare, children's, and women's sections of government agencies are both willing to work with poor women and do so more cheaply than does anyone else. The women who volunteer cost nothing and the female government staff are, on average, paid lower salaries than male staff. In an environment where financial resources for development programs are tight, the lower cost of these NGOs and agencies helps explain why they are often chosen to implement women's projects, even if the agencies lack the technical qualifications to do so. The misperception that women can work only with women, combined with the lower costs of women's organizations[2] and the lower status of working on woman's issues, often leads to project misbehavior.

Unfortunately, the misbehavior of income-generating projects has led to unjust criticism of women's organizations, skepticism about the effectiveness of directing resources to poor women, and, worst of all, misuse of poor women's valuable and scarce time. Obviously, in some instances the social benefits of projects may outweigh the financial costs to poor women, but the multiplication of this type of project during the Women's Decade did little to improve the economic situation of poor rural women (Flora 1987).

Fortunately, many donor and implementing agencies have become aware of these project pitfalls and, along with replicating their more successful microenterprise projects, are revising their approaches to working with poor rural women. These revisions include a renewed focus on needed institutional and policy reforms and greater attention to technical issues.

AN AGENDA FOR THE 1990s

Above all, rural women in the Third World need to increase their productivity and income in agriculture and related rural enterprises, to improve their own and their families' welfare. Because of the critical differences in the type of work men and women perform, and in the ways in which they utilize their income, interventions aimed at the family are not effective in alleviating rural women's poverty nor, in most cases, the welfare of children, for whom, almost universally, women are responsible. One of the most effective ways to attack rural poverty and increase rural women's incomes is to increase the productivity of smallholders, provided that such efforts benefit female as well as male farmers. Agricultural projects, therefore, must be oriented toward smallholders and should use a targeted approach that takes into account women's roles as farmers and resource managers. This approach should focus on the individual farmer (men and women) within farm households rather than the household as a whole.

The initial step in a chain of events to increase the productivity of female farmers is research that goes beyond the farming system and examines the entire food system of the dominant staple foods in the area. This approach helps identify the constraints on both men and women in production, marketing, processing, and trade (Jiggins 1986).[3] Research is also needed on the nutritional effects of alternative production technologies (Pinstrup-Andersen, Berg, and Forman 1984). This research needs to be followed by policies that provide women farmers incentives to adopt agricultural innovations and by institutional changes that increase women's access to agricultural services. International donors can influence the nature of investments in agricultural research at international and national levels, the adoption of appropriate national agricultural policies, and the implementation of reforms in agricultural institutions so that women can have access to agricultural technologies, training, credit, and extension. Governments should be encouraged to implement land tenure reforms that will benefit *all* small farmers, men and women.

Structural adjustment and other policy reform programs worldwide have produced a number of unforeseen problems because the role of women in various economic activities has not been taken into account. To be effective, such reforms must be structured to assist women, not only men, respond to price and other incentives. Agriculture, for instance, is typically targeted by short- and medium-term structural adjustment programs to increase production of exports or import substitutes, to improve a country's balance of payments. For example, structural adjustment programs typically include measures to increase price incentives for export crops. But increasing the relative profitability of export crops may force women to work more hours, recruit the help of their children, or accept a decrease in their real incomes. Each of these options may have a negative impact on the family, on national food security, and on the long-term success of structural adjustment policies. Stepping up export-oriented production at the expense of locally grown food may cause a dysfunctional dependence on food imports.

There is a case, therefore, for balancing policy reform with effective sectoral strategies for raising the productivity of women's work in agriculture and microenterprises. Agricultural extension efforts should help women improve food production while allowing them to shift more of their labor to export production. Similarly, changes in legal, financial, and educational systems must be undertaken in order to enhance women's social and economic contributions to rural development in the long term. There is a need to examine carefully the implications of land tenure laws and regulations for women. Financial policies that encourage biases against, or reduce the profitability of, the types of borrowing that poor women seek must be revamped to increase the productivity of women's work. And educational policies and funding must be changed to reflect the very high social and economic returns to women's primary education and literacy.

NOTES

This paper was supported by a Ford Foundation grant to the International Center for Research on Women (ICRW). Parts of the paper draw from the following ICRW publications: Buvinić 1986; Buvinić and Lycette 1988; and Leslie, Lycette, and Buvinić 1988.

1. See chapter 18, by Timmer, and the reply by Collier et al.—ED.

2. However, although the total budgetary cost of female based NGOs may be lower than other organizations, the unit cost of output (e.g., per dollar increase in the income of the poor women being assisted by the project) may be high, because of the low productivity of the projects assisted by the NGO agencies. Low productivity may result from the lack of technical, managerial, and financial expertise of the NGO staff.

3. In Southern Africa, SADCC (Southern African Development Coordination Conference) and ICRISAT (International Crops Research Institute for the Semi-Arid Tropics) recently launched a research program on the sorghum food system, including research on household and village processing of sorghum with the assistance of the International Development Research Centre and the Canadian International Development Agency.

REFERENCES

Acharya, Meena, and Lynn Bennett. 1981. *The Rural Women of Nepal: An Aggregate Analysis and Summary of Eight Village Studies.* Kathmandu, Nepal: Centre for Economic Development Administration.

Acharya, Sarthi, and Praveen Patkar. 1985. "Technological Infusion and Employment Conditions of Women in Rice Cultivation Areas." In *Women in Rice Farming,* 287–305. International Rice Research Institute, Proceedings of a conference on women in rice farming systems, Manila, Philippines, September 1983. Brookfield, Vt.: Gower.

Agarwal, Bina. 1984. "Rural Women and High-Yielding Variety Rice Technology." *Economic and Political Weekly* 19, no. 13 (March 1984): A39–A52.

Begum, Saleha. 1985. "Women and Technology: Rice Processing in Bangladesh." In *Women in Rice Farming,* 221–41. (See Acharya and Patkar 1985.)

Boserup, Ester. 1970. *Woman's Role in Economic Development.* New York: St. Martin's Press.

Buvinić, Mayra. 1986. "Projects for Women in the Third World: Explaining Their Misbehavior." *World Development* 14(5): 653–64.

Buvinić, Mayra, and Margaret A. Lycette. 1988. "Women, Poverty and Development in the Third World." In *Strengthening the Poor: What Have We Learned?,* edited by John P. Lewis, 149–62. New Brunswick, N.J.: Transaction Books.

Buvinić, Mayra, Margaret A. Lycette, and William Paul McGreevey, eds. 1983. *Women and Poverty in the Third World.* Baltimore: Johns Hopkins University Press.

Cain, Mead. 1980. "The Economic Activities of Children in a Village of Bangladesh." In *Rural Household Studies in Asia,* edited by Hans Binswanger et al. Singapore: Singapore University Press.

Cain, Mead, S. R. Khanam, and S. Nahar. 1979. "Class, Patriarchy, and the Structure of Women's Work in Rural Bangladesh." Center for Policy Studies Working Paper, no. 43. New York: Population Council.

Chernichovsky, Dov, and Christine Smith. 1979. "Primary School Enrollment and Attendance in Rural Botswana." Washington, D.C.: World Bank. Photocopy.

Clark, Mari H. 1984. "Women-headed Households and Poverty: Insights from Kenya." *Signs* 10 (Winter 1984): 338–54. (Special issue on women and poverty.)

Deere, Carmen Diana. 1983. "The Allocation of Familial Labor and the Formation of Peasant Household Income in the Peruvian Sierra." In *Women and Poverty in the Third World,* edited by Mayra Buvinić, Margaret A. Lycette, and William Paul McGreevey, 104–29. Baltimore: Johns Hopkins University Press.

Deere, Carmen Diana, and Leon Magdalena, eds. 1987. *Rural Women and State Policy: Feminist Perspectives on Latin American Agricultural Development.* Boulder, Colo.: Westview.

Dey, Jennie. 1981. "Gambian Women: Unequal Partners in Rice Development Projects." *Journal of Development Studies* 17, no. 3 (April 1981): 109–22.

———. 1985. "Women in African Rice Farming Systems." In *Women in Rice Farming,* 419–44. (See Acharya and Patkar 1985.)

Dixon, Ruth. 1983. "Land, Labor, and the Sex Composition of the Agricultural Labor Force: An International Comparison." *Development and Change* 14 (July 1983): 347–72.

Dwyer, Daisy, and Judith Bruce. 1988. *A Home Divided: Women and Income in the Third World.* Stanford: Stanford University Press.

Fagley, R. M. 1976. "Easing the Burden of Women: A Sixteen-Hour Workday." *Assignment Children* 36 (1976): 9–28.

Flora, Cornelia Butler. 1987. "Income Generation Projects for Rural Women." In *Rural Women and State Policy: Feminist Perspectives on Latin American Agricultural Development,* edited by Carmen Diana Deere and Magdalena Leon, 212–38. Boulder, Colo.: Westview Press.

Folbre, Nancy. 1983. "Household Production in the Philippines: A Neo-Classical Approach." Michigan State University Working Paper, no. 26. East Lansing: Michigan State University.

Food and Agriculture Organization (FAO). 1983. "Time Allocation Survey: A Tool for Anthropologists, Economists, and Nutritionists." Food Policy and Nutrition Division. Rome: FAO.

Ghosh, Bahnisikha, and Sudhink Mukhopadhyay. 1988. "Gender Differentials in the Impact of Technological Change in Rice-Based Farming Systems in India." In *Gender Issues in Farming Systems Research and Extension,* 253–68. (See Poats et al. 1988.)

Goldschmidt-Clermont, Luisella. 1983. *Economic Evaluations of Unpaid Household Work: Africa, Asia, Latin America and Oceania.* Women, Work and Development Series, no. 14. Geneva: International Labour Organization.

Greer, Joel, and Erik Thorbecke. 1986. "Food Poverty Profile Applied to Kenyan Smallholders." *Economic Development and Cultural Change* 35, no. 1 (October 1986): 115–42.

Hart, Gillian. 1980. "Patterns of Household Labor Allocation in a Javanese Village." In *Rural Household Studies in Asia.* Hans Binswanger et al., eds. Singapore: Singapore University Press.

Jiggins, Janice. 1986. *Gender Related Impacts and the Work of the International Agricultural Research Centers.* CGIAR Study Paper, no. 17. Washington, D.C.: World Bank.

Johnson, Allen. 1975. "Time Allocation in a Machiguenga Community." *Ethnology* 14(3): 301–10.

Jones, Christine. 1986. "Intra-Household Bargaining in Response to the Introduction of New Crops: A Case Study from North Cameroon." In *Understanding Africa's Rural Households and Farming Systems,* edited by Joyce Lewinger Moock. Boulder, Colo.: Westview Press.

Kamuzora, C. Lwechungura. 1980. "Constraints to Labour Time Availability in African Smallholder Agriculture: The Case of Bukoba District, Tanzania." *Development and Change* 11:123–35.

Kennedy, Eileen T., and Bruce Cogill. 1987. *Income and Nutritional Effects of the Commercialization of Agriculture in Southwestern Kenya.* Research Report, no. 63. Washington, D.C.: International Food Policy Research Institute.

King, Elizabeth, and Robert E. Evenson. 1983. "Time Allocation and Home Production in Philippine Rural Households." In *Women and Poverty in the Third World* (Buvinić, Lycette, and McGreevey 1983), 35–61.

Kossoudji, Sherrie, and Eva Mueller. 1983. "The Economic and Demographic Status of Female-headed Households in Rural Botswana." *Economic Development and Cultural Change* 31, no. 4 (July 1983): 831–59.

Kumar, Shubh K. 1985. "Women's Agricultural Work in a Subsistence-Oriented Economy: Its Role in Production, Food Consumption, and Nutrition." Paper presented at the Thirteenth International Congress of Nutrition, Brighton, England, August 1985. Washington, D.C.: International Food Policy Research Institute.

Leslie, Joanne. 1988. "Women's Work and Child Nutrition in the Third World." *World Development* 16, no. 11: 1341–62.

Leslie, Joanne, Margaret Lycette, and Mayra Buvinić. 1988. "Weathering Economic Crises: The Crucial Role of Women in Health." In *Health, Nutrition and Economic Crises: Approaches to Policy in the Third World,* edited by David E. Bell and Meichall R. Reich. Dover, Mass.: Auburn House.

Lewis, John P. 1988. "Strengthening the Poor: Some Lessons for the International Community." In *Strengthening the Poor: What Have We Learned?,* edited by Valeriana Kallab and Richard E. Feinberg, 3–26. Washington, D.C.: Overseas Development Council.

McSweeney, B. G. 1979. "Collection and Analysis of Data on Rural Women's Time Use." *Studies in Family Planning* 10:379–83.

Nag, M., B. N. F. White, and R. C. Peet. 1978. "An Anthropological Approach to the Study of the Economic Value of the Children in Java and Nepal." *Current Anthropology* 19:293–306.

Pinstrup-Andersen, Per, Alan Berg, and Martin Forman, eds. 1984. *International Agricultural Research and Human Nutrition.* Washington, D.C.: International Food Policy Research Institute.

Poats, Susan V., Marianne Schmink, and Anita Spring, eds. 1988. *Gender Issues in Farming Systems Research and Extension.* Boulder, Colo.: Westview Press.

Rassam, André, and Dennis Tully. 1988. "Gender Related Aspects of Agricultural Labor in Northwestern Syria." In *Gender Issues in Farming Systems Research and Extension* (Poats et al. 1988), 287–313.

Scott, Gloria L., and Marilyn Carr. 1985. "The Impact of Technology Choice on Rural Women in Bangladesh." World Bank Staff Working Papers, no. 731. Washington, D.C.: World Bank.

Sen, Amartya K. 1985. "Women, Technology and Sexual Divisions." UNCTAD/TT/79. New York: United Nations.

Singh, Ram D., and Mathew J. Morey. 1987. "The Value of Work-at-Home and Contributions of Wives' Household Service in Polygymous Families: Evidence from an African LDC." *Economic Development and Cultural Change* 35, no. 4: 743–65.

Staudt, Kathleen. 1978. "Administrative Resources, Political Patrons, and Redressing Sex Inequalities: A Case from Western Kenya." *Journal of Developing Areas* (July 1978).

Tendler, Judith. 1989. "What Ever Happened to Poverty Alleviation?" *World Development* 17, no. 7, 1033–44.

von Braun, Joachim. 1989. "Effects of New Export Crops in Smallholder Agriculture on Division of Labor and Child Nutritional Status in Guatemala." In *Women's Work and Child Welfare in the Third World,* edited by Joanne Leslie and Michael Paolisso. AAAS Selected Symposium 10. Boulder, Colo.: Westview Press.

von Braun, Joachim, Eileen Kennedy, and Howarth Bouis. 1988. "Comparative Analyses of the Effects of Increased Commercialization of Subsistence Agriculture on Production, Consumption, and Nutrition." Final report prepared for the U.S. Agency for International Development. Washington, D.C.: International Food Policy Research Institute.

von Braun, Joachim, and Patrick J. R. Webb. 1989. "The Impact of New Crop Technology on the Agricultural Division of Labor in a West African Setting." *Economic Development and Cultural Change* 37, no. 3 (April 1989): 513–39.

White, Benjamin. 1975. "The Economic Importance of Children in a Javanese Village." In *Population and Social Organization,* edited by M. Nag, 127–40. The Hague: Mouton.

18

Choice of Technique in Rice Milling on Java

C. PETER TIMMER

INTRODUCTION

A technological revolution has swept across Java virtually unnoticed. As recently as 1971 informed estimates assumed that as much as 80 percent of Java's rice crop was hand-pounded, both for subsistence consumption and for local marketings. The figure now (1973) is certainly less than 50 percent and may well be as little as 10 percent—there are no direct statistics from which to judge. The number of small mechanical rice processing facilities has increased dramatically. The economic and social impacts are only beginning to be felt, and any assessments of these changes in the countryside and villages are necessarily for the future.

This article will try to answer three questions about the recent changes in rice processing: (1) What has happened, in rough quantitative terms? (2) What explains the shift from hand-pounding to small rice mills and why not to larger mills? and (3) What has happened to rural employment with the decline of hand-pounding? The secondary data are taken from an anonymous report from the Asian Development Bank (ADB),[1] a Rice Marketing Study (cited in this paper as RMS) prepared by a U.S. consulting firm,[2] and two publications by the author.[3]

TECHNOLOGY CHOICES

Three rice processing techniques are in use in Indonesia: hand-pounding, small rice mills, and large rice mills. The overall patterns of what has happened technologically to rice milling in the past few years are very clear: hand-pounding has declined drastically. But the large-scale mills have not been the beneficiaries of the decline in hand-pounding. Rather, a whole new rice-milling industry has sprung up, composed of an assortment of machinery but with one overriding

C. PETER TIMMER is Thomas D. Cabot Professor of Development Studies, At-Large, Harvard University.

This paper and the following comment and reply are reprinted from *Bulletin of Indonesian Economic Studies* 9, no. 2 (1973), with omissions and minor editorial revisions, by permission of the publisher—the Research School of Pacific Studies of the Australian National University—and the authors.

characteristic: all of the facilities are small in scale and labor-intensive. A quote from ADB, *Rice Processing Report,* makes the point explicitly:

> Why pay more than 40,000 Dollars for a large rice mill when the same output can be attained by a small mill with an investment of 7,400 Dollars? Naturally the cheap unit requires far more labour, but that does not count much in a country where a mill labourer is paid Rp 100–150 (U.S. Dollars 0.24 to 0.36) per working day. The differences in rendement (extraction) rate (less than 1 percent) and broken percentage (around 3 percent) are also insignificant compared to the high debt service for the large-scale mill.

The type of machinery used to mill rice—from wooden pounding pole and pestle to large-scale multistage mills with bulk storage and drying—is, then, a function of labor and capital costs. The results of a formal economic analysis of the question of choice of technique in rice milling strongly confirm the "common sense" of the quote above.[4] Both the methodology and the results of the analysis are presented below.

The analytical technique is purposefully textbookish: the aim is not to confuse the choice of technique issue with fancy methodology but to be as simple-minded as the problem will allow. Consequently, an isoquant has been constructed that represents several different techniques, in terms of relative capital/labor ratios, of producing a unit amount of value added in rice processing. After going step by step through the data, the assumptions and the manipulations, we end up with a standardized isoquant in the two dimensions of investment cost and labor cost.

Five different processing techniques form the basis of the analysis: hand-pounding (HP); small rice mills (SRM); large rice mills (LRM); small bulk facilities (SBF); and large bulk facilities (LBF). The first three techniques are at present in operation in Indonesia—hand-pounding is millennia old. The small rice mills can be thought of as ranging from the now obsolete double Engelberg-type huller/polisher combinations to the smaller self-contained Japanese rice milling units and rubber roll huskers connected to Engelberg-type or pneumatic polishers. All these together are taken as the class "small rice mills." They do not have mechanical drying equipment but rely solely on sun drying. Consequently, the small rice mills (SRM) are assumed to suffer high physical (and monetary) losses during processing, not so much in the milling per se but from a lack of control in drying.

Fewer "large rice mills" are seen in Indonesia, although all the older multi-stage milling equipment fits this category if mechanical drying facilities are also available. The major feature of this category is the combined use of mechanical and sun drying with modern milling equipment, either Japanese-type or conventional multi-stage.

The fourth and fifth techniques—bulk facilities—represent proposed improvements to the Indonesian rice processing sector. "Bulk facilities" is a shorthand way of describing a rice mill/storage system. The rice mill produces high-quality milled rice which is stored in vertical silos of varying capacity. No example of either the small bulk facility or the large bulk facility exists at present in Indonesia, although even the larger facility is not large by international grain-handling standards. The small bulk facilities have a milling and drying capacity of three tons per hour and forty-five hundred tons of vertical steel storage. The large bulk facilities can process nine tons of rough rice per hour and contain fifteen thousand tons of bulk storage in vertical steel silos for rough rice and conventional multi-stage gradual-reduction milling machinery. A continuous-flow dryer attached has a capacity of twenty tons per hour.

CONSTRUCTING UNIT ISOQUANTS

The data and calculations necessary to construct a unit isoquant in value added by rice processing are presented in table 1. The isoquant is drawn in the two dimensions of total investment cost and number of unskilled workers needed to run each facility. A "budget" or "iso-cost" line can then be drawn tangent to the isoquant in order to determine the optimum capital/labor ratio for rice processing. Since the capital axis is in total investment cost and not in annualized capital charges, it is necessary to convert annual laborers' wages into a lifetime "wage fund." This is done by discounting a laborer's annual earnings for his lifetime (fifty years) by an appropriate discount rate (12 percent, 18 percent, or 24 percent) to calculate the present value of the cost of a laborer.

Three basic steps are necessary to construct the isoquant, and all three are carried out in table 1. The "Data Per Unit" section simply reports capacity, investment cost, and number of manual laborers required per operating shift for each facility. These data are then standardized in terms of one thousand tons of rough rice input per year. The data for the small rice mill do not change, since its initial capacity was one thousand tons per year, but each of the larger facilities is scaled down to a comparable one-thousand-ton capacity. Obviously, it is not possible to install one-twentieth of a large bulk facility, but this technique merely keeps the numbers manageable without losing any of the scale economies of the larger facilities. Conceptually it is equally possible to use the large bulk facility capacity of 21,600 tons as the standard and multiply the number of smaller units to be on a comparable basis. Nothing is lost by keeping the numbers smaller and more manageable.

PHYSICAL AND MONETARY CONVERSIONS

The next step is to convert the one thousand tons of rough rice input per facility into a value of output. There are two parts to the process: a physical conversion and a monetary conversion. Table 1 shows the conversion rates for both processes. The first is merely the rendement or extraction rate. How much milled rice does each facility produce per ton of rough rice? No fixed rates are really applicable, since this extraction rate depends so critically on quality of

TABLE 1
DERIVATION OF A UNIT ISOQUANT IN VALUE ADDED FROM RICE PROCESSING

	Hand-Pounding HP (s)[a]	Small Rice Mill SRM (s)[a]	Large Rice Mill LRM (s/m)[a]	Small Bulk Facility SBF (m)[a]	Large Bulk Facility LBF (m)[a]
			Data per Unit		
Milling capacity (tons per year)[b]	—	1,000[c]	2,500[d]	7,200	21,600
Investment cost (U.S. dollars)[e]	0	$8,049[c]	$90,511[d]	$453,283	$2,605,926
Operative laborers (number per shift)	—	12[c]	16[d]	27	39
		Data per 1,000 Tons of Rough Rice Input per Year			
Investment cost (U.S. dollars)	0	$8,049	$36,204	$62,956	$120,645
Operative laborers (number)	22.00[f]	12.00	6.40	3.75	1.81
Milled rice output (tons)	570	590	630	650	670
Market price (Rp/kg)	40.0	45.0	48.0	49.5	50.0
Value of output (million Rp)	22.8	26.6	30.2	32.2	33.5
Value added[g] (million Rp)	4.8	8.6	12.2	14.2	15.5
		Data per Rp 10 Million in Value Added per Year			
Investment cost (U.S. dollars)	0	$9,359	$29,675	$44,335	$77,835
Operative laborers (number)	45.83	13.95	5.25	2.64	1.17

[a]The s in parentheses indicates that the facility uses sun drying; m indicates mechanical drying.
[b]Milling capacity is measured in tons of rough rice input per year, assuming the facility can operate 2,400 hours per year.
[c]The technical and cost data for the small rice mill relate specifically to a locally manufactured flash-type husker with an input capacity of three-quarters of a ton per hour linked to an Engelberg-type polisher with an input capacity of half a ton per hour. A thresher shed and sun-drying pad are provided, but no additional storage capacity. This facility is taken as "representative" of the entire range of small rice milling facilities.
[d]The technical and cost data for the large rice mill relate specifically to a Japanese self-contained milling unit integrated with 756 tons of rough rice storage capacity: 300 tons in bagged storage and 456 tons in upright bulk steel bins. A mechanical dryer with three-quarters ton per hour capacity is provided along with a sun-drying pad. The milling capacity is 1.0 to 1.1 tons per hour of rough rice.
[e]Costs of building and machinery (including a diesel-powered thresher) are included, but not land.
[f]This assumes that one worker hand-pounds about 150 kg of gabah (unhusked rice) per day, with a yield of approximately 95 kg of rice.
[g]Value added is calculated assuming a gabah cost of Rp 18 per kg, which is above the Rp 16 per kg floor price for "village dry" gabah at the mill. The cost (and value added) of reducing the moisture to "mill dry" is included as a mill activity.

input, moisture, variety, by-product rates, and so on, but the average figures shown in table 1 capture the general trend: the larger and more capital-intensive facilities have significantly higher extraction rates. Thus the hand-pounding rate is taken as 57 percent, the small mill rate as 59 percent, the large mill rate as 63 percent, and the small and large bulk facility rates as 65 percent and 67 percent, respectively. As was noted earlier, these differences are not to be taken as strictly due to different milling techniques, but capture the overall impact of the significantly different drying and storage facilities connected with each type of mill.

Apart from the sheer differences in physical output per ton of input, each facility is presumed to produce an output with varying consumer value. Thus one kg of hand-pounded rice sells for only Rp 40, while the output of the large bulk facility is valued at Rp 50 per kg; facilities between these two extremes sell at appropriate values in between, as shown in table 1. Although the different values include some allowance for better by-product retention in the larger facilities, these prices still somewhat overstate the actual market differences that consumers are willing to pay for rice quality per se, as opposed to varietal price differentials, which are substantial. Should these consumer preferences ever be developed, however (or if they were ever imposed by Bulog),[5] the smaller facilities and especially hand-pounding would be at a severe disadvantage.

The overall impact of the physical and monetary conversions is that one thousand tons of rough rice input is transformed into Rp 22.8 million in output by hand-pounding, Rp 26.6 million by small rice mills, Rp 30.2 million by large rice mills, Rp 32.2 million by small bulk facilities, and Rp 33.5 million by the large bulk facilities. That is, the large bulk facilities are able to produce 47 percent more value of output from a given input than hand-pounding and 26 percent more output than the small rice mills. The differences in value added, when Rp 18 million is subtracted from value of output as the cost of the rough rice input, are even more dramatic. The large bulk facility produces more than 200 percent more value added than hand-pounding and almost double the value added from small rice mills. At this stage of the analysis the larger facilities seem to hold a very substantial competitive edge.

The last step required in the construction of a unit isoquant is to calculate the investment cost and numbers of laborers needed to produce a given amount of value added—Rp 10 million in table 1. Since the small rice mill produced only Rp 8.6 million in value added from one thousand tons of rough rice input, it is necessary to increase the investment-cost and number-of-laborers data under that heading by 10/8.6, or 1.16. Thus to produce Rp 10 million in value added, the small rice mill needs $8,049 × 1.16 = $9,359 in investment cost and 12 × 1.16 = 13.95 operative laborers. The calculations for the other facilities are similar, and the results are shown in the last two lines of table 1.

These numbers are the "x, y coordinates" of the desired isoquant, which is drawn in figure 1. Because only five different processing techniques are considered in table 1, the isoquant in figure 1 does not look exactly like the smooth, twice-differentiable isoquants shown in neoclassical production economics textbooks. But the family resemblance is very close. In the linear-segmented world shown in figure 1 smooth tangencies of iso-cost lines to the isoquant must give way to corner tangencies. Thus it is that all three iso-cost lines shown are (corner) tangent at small rice mills. This means that small rice mills are the least-cost facilities for producing value added in rice processing, at least at the wage levels shown in figure 1.

The wage level used to calculate the iso-cost lines was $200 per year, a level used by the *RMS Report* to evaluate their recommendations. The present value of a $200 wage payment each year for fifty years was calculated using three different time rates of discount: 12 percent, 18 percent, and 24 percent. Although it is

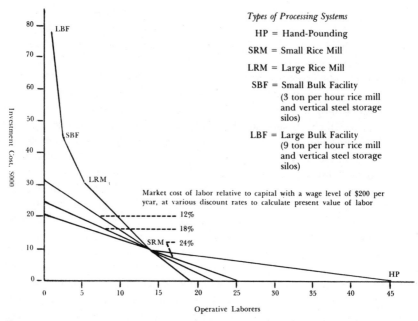

Fig.1. Isoquant Relating Investment Cost and Laborers Needed to Produce Rp 100 Million in Value Added Assuming Rough Rice Costs Rp per kg

always difficult to determine the appropriate social discount rate under any circumstances, investment calculations in rice milling on Java should use something close to the social opportunity cost of capital. Most observers would place this closer to the 24 percent end of the spectrum, with 12 percent clearly reflecting a substantial subsidy. Thus at the opportunity cost of capital—24 percent—a wage of $200 per year has a present value of $833. This means that the slope of the ''24 percent'' iso-cost line in figure 1 is the same as a line that connects $833 on the Investment Cost axis with one Laborer on the horizontal axis.

Table 2 presents the present values of a range of wage levels discounted at the three different discount rates. The three iso-cost lines drawn in figure 1 (all of them with corner tangencies at SRM) represent the highest assumed wage under consideration. Two other wage levels, not shown in figure 1, are also worth consideration. The $80 wage is close to an actual market wage for unskilled labor for large parts of Java. The $40 wage represents a shadow wage to take account of the high degree of surplus labor on Java, although this may actually be close to a market wage in certain heavily populated rural areas.

The striking effect of discounting to obtain the present value of wages stands out in table 2. The $200 wage for fifty years is a total wage bill of $10,000, but its present value is only $1,661 when discounted at 12 percent per year, the subsidized rate of interest for medium-/long-term investment credits in Indonesia. Using a market interest rate of 24 percent reduces the present value wage

TABLE 2
PRESENT VALUE OF ALTERNATIVE WAGE RATES
($)

| Assumed Wage Levels per Year | Discounted Present Value of Wages[a] | | |
	12% Discount Rate	18% Discount Rate	24% Discount Rate
$200 (RMS)	$1,661	$1,111	$833
$80 (Market)	664	444	333
$40 (Shadow price)	332	222	167

[a]The present worth factor for fifty years is as follows:

Discount Rate (%)	Present Worth Factor
12	8.304
18	5.554
24	4.167

to $833. Market wages ($80) discounted at market interest rates have a present value of $333, while a shadow wage rate equal to half the market wage has a present value of less than $200. Whether one is calculating annual capital charges on a fixed investment or determining the present value of a worker's lifetime earnings, the effect of discounting, the only known way of evaluating future economic events at the present time, is dramatic indeed.

What would the optimal rice processing technique be at the lower market and shadow wage rates? And what happens if the selling price of rice is held constant (by competition or imports) while the price of rough rice paid by the milling facilities increases? Both these questions are answered in table 3, where the maximum present value wage at which each rice processing technique remains optimal for various rough rice prices is shown. Thus for a rough rice price of Rp 18 per kg (the value used to construct the isoquant in table 1 and figure 1), hand-pounding is the optimal technique until the present value wage exceeds $294; small rice mills are optimal from a present value wage of $295 to $2,335, beyond which large rice mills, small bulk facilities, and ultimately large bulk facilities become optimal.

Similarly, the maximum present value wage a facility can afford and still remain optimal declines as the rough rice price increases. At a price of Rp 18 per kg for rough rice the small rice mill can pay up to $2,335, but at Rp 20 per kg it can pay only $1,956. At a price of Rp 26 per kg the mill would have to be subsidized to remain optimal; that is, it would have to receive $260 per worker (for his lifetime services). At Rp 28 per kg the small rice mill actually produces a negative value added—its output sells for less than the cost of its rough rice input. No subsidy can make the firm optimal, although obviously a large enough subsidy would permit the small rice mill to survive (but never to produce a positive value added).

TABLE 3
MAXIMUM PRESENT VALUES OF WAGE RATES THAT YIELD CORNER TANGENCIES
TO THE ISOQUANT

Corner Solution at	Maximum Present Value Wage at Which the Indicated Facility is Optimal for Various Rough Rice Prices Rp/kg					
	18	20	22	24	26	28
Hand-pounding (HP)	294	202	70	a	a	a
Small rice mills (SRM)	2,335	1,956	1,457	766	−260	a
Large rice mills (LRM)	5,617	5,034	4,265	3,197	1,699	−728
Small bulk facilities (SBF)	22,789	21,829	20,468	18,879	16,296	12,316
Large bulk facilities (LBF)[b]	greater than the value shown for SBF					

[a]Negative value added.

[b]Just for comparison, it is worth noting that the discounted present value of $6,000 per year at 8 percent is $73,400. Thus the relative capital intensity of even the large bulk facilities (LBF) is low by U.S. standards.

The interesting comparisons are between the various present value wages of table 2 and the maximum wages that yield optimum solutions in table 3. At either $200 per year or the market wage of $80 per year, for all three discount rates, the small rice mills remain the optimal rice processing facility at normal rough rice prices. When the price reaches Rp 24 per kg, the large rice mills are optimal at the highest wage for all three discount rates. The small bulk facilities only enter the picture when the rough rice price reaches Rp 28 per kg, so high that the small rice mills yield negative value added. This situation could only come about by full "modernization" of Indonesia's entire rice processing system or a rigidly enforced price policy that used imports to control retail price and large-scale facilities (or large subsidies to smaller mills) in connection with a vigorous floor price. The general point ought to be clear, however: in a squeeze between rough rice and milled rice prices only the technically more efficient facilities can survive.

It is not hard to see, then, the reasons why few large rice mills (or bulk facilities) have been installed in recent years in Indonesia. Where market forces—low wages, high interest rates, and cheap rice prices—have been allowed to work, the overwhelming superiority of small rice mills as a generic class has been apparent to investors, and these facilities have indeed mushroomed throughout Java. Some large mills have been built, but they have been either government- or army-sponsored (where market forces are little felt in the decision making) or close to cities, where wage rates are higher than in rural areas, rough rice prices relatively higher, and when investment capital at 12 percent was available. Under these circumstances investment in the larger rice mills is understandable, though it may not be socially desirable.

At the other end of the spectrum, the economies of hand-pounding are fascinating. If market wages of about $80 per year (say Rp 100 to Rp 150 per day) must be paid, hand-pounding is not optimal unless the discount rate is greater than 24 percent or unless the *gabah* price falls below Rp 16 per kg (at the same time that the retail price is Rp 40 for the end product). So it is not hard to see why hand-pounding has virtually disappeared from Java as a cash-hire activity. And yet it is still frequently profitable for the farmer or his family to hand-pound their rice for home consumption if the perceived opportunity cost of the labor spent is not great. For example, hand-pounding is economically optimal (despite the very large losses that are assumed) if the wage rate is $40 per year and is discounted at 18 percent or higher, at least for rough rice prices less than Rp 20 per kg, as they are likely to be in many rural areas. And in fact, of course, some rural families still do hand-pound their rice.

The evidence from the countryside, which showed literally thousands of small rice mills installed on Java in the past three years, is thus strongly corroborated by the economic analysis. Only at the extremes of economic conditions existing in Indonesia could hand-pounding or large rice mills be explained. The small rice mills were shown to be socially and privately optimal over a wide range of circumstances in between. There are exceptions to be sure: exporting rice would require facilities not optimal in this analysis, and Bulog may have some special needs that are not fully met by all small rice mills. But in total this is a good example of where "getting prices right" has helped the development effort at minimal cost and effort to the scarce planning manpower in the government. Not all development problems are so easy, of course, but some are made harder by inappropriate pricing policies. Indonesia's rice processing sector still faces some difficult problems, especially with regard to drying and storage. But milling has been largely removed as a constraint.

EMPLOYMENT IN RICE MILLING

The employment potential of the entire rice economy—production, harvesting, processing, transporting, storing, selling—is enormous. Rice marketing, defined broadly, is only part of this potential, and rice processing but part of this part. Still, the total employment figures must be large indeed. No reliable survey data are available to serve as a reference here, but table 4 provides a rough point of departure for discussion.

The intent of table 4 is to work backward from the input/output micro data used to generate the isoquant to an overall estimate of the number of workers needed to process the entire 1971 rice crop, assuming only a single technique were used. This is obviously an artificial number. But somewhere within the range of the 399,000 full-time workers needed to hand-pound the crop to only 33,000 workers needed if large bulk facilities were used lies the actual full-time employment potential. (If work sharing is pervasive, the numbers actually earning a livelihood in rice processing could be much larger.) It is interesting that each technique employs roughly double the number of workers of the next most

TABLE 4
EMPLOYMENT AND INVESTMENT IN RICE PROCESSING IN 1971 USING
ALTERNATIVE MILLING TECHNIQUES

| | Inputs | | | |
| | Per 1,000 Tons of Rough Rice | | For 1971 Harvest[a] | |
Milling Technique	Investment Cost ($)	Operatives (Number)	Investment Cost ($m)	Operatives (Thousands)
Hand-pounding (HP)	$ 0	22.00	0	399[b]
Small rice mills (SRM)	8,049	12.00	146	217
Large rice mills (LRM)	36,204	6.40	656	116
Small bulk facilities (SBF)	62,956	3.75	1,141	68
Large bulk facilities (LBF)	120,645	1.81	2,186	33

SOURCE: Calculated from table 1.

[a]For each technique, the figure shows the investment and employment required to process the 1971 rice crop of 18.123 million tons of rough rice, assuming that particular technique is the only one utilized. Obviously this shows alternative hypothetical magnitudes only, and none of the figures should be interpreted as representing actual employment levels in rice milling.

[b]This is the full-time equivalent required for hand-pounding. More than 399,000 laborers would be needed if hand-pounding were done only part-time.

capital-intensive technique. This is simply a repeated and forceful demonstration that this particular part of the economic system does not exhibit fixed technical relationships between capital and labor. Indeed, the "wrong" choice of technique, whether by government decision directly or by private investors reacting to inappropriate price signals, can easily cost many thousands, in fact, hundreds of thousands, of jobs. The choice between small and large rice mills depended very much on the government's interest rate policy, its rice price policy, and unskilled wage levels. Given that a dramatic transformation to mechanized rice processing had been occurring at private initiative in Indonesia in the past few years, the country was fortunate indeed to have those critical policies more or less in order.

As recently as 1971 it was assumed that as much as 80 percent of Java's rice crop was hand-pounded. Although hand-pounding has certainly not been eliminated over the past few years, the evidence does suggest that it no longer accounts for more than perhaps 20 percent of the crop, at least in Java. Upwards of 100,000 jobs have probably been lost (at least jobs in the sense of an opportunity cost income—the "return" to milling is no longer captured by the family but by the miller). This loss of jobs should be kept in perspective, however. The farmer having his rice milled is frequently one of the laborers in the small rice mill, thus capturing part of the milling cost for his family. In addition, little cash income has been forgone, and the small rice mills are frequently so much more technically efficient that the farmer appears to go home with more rice than if he had hand-pounded it. (But since the farmer ate the bran if the rice were hand-pounded, whereas the miller keeps it for himself, this is probably not usually the case.) Lastly, hand-pounding is drudgery, and the people obviously welcome its demise.

SUMMARY

Two main points have been presented in this paper. The first is that economic analysis shows labor-intensive (but mechanical) rice processing facilities to dominate both hand-pounding and more capital-intensive techniques. And this is a result amply confirmed by recent evidence on actual investments in rice processing facilities in the countryside. A second, more general point is that the employment effects of the choice of technique decision are not trivial and are critically dependent on parameters directly subject to government control. "Getting prices right" is not the end of economic development. But "getting prices wrong" frequently is.

NOTES

1. Anonymous, "Report from the Agricultural Credit Specialist" (1972); "Rice Processing in Java" (Manila: Asian Development Bank, August 1972), cited hereafter as ADB, *Rice Processing Report*.

2. Weitz-Hettelsater Engineers, "Rice Storage, Handling, and Marketing Study: Economics and Engineering Aspects" (Kansas City, Mo., 1972). The final draft was submitted to the Republic of Indonesia in December 1972. This report is referred to in this article as Rice Marketing Study (RMS).

3. C. Peter Timmer, "Employment Aspects of Investment in Rice Marketing in Indonesia," *Food Research Institute Studies in Agricultural Economics, Trade, and Development* 11, no. 1 (1972); and idem, "Choice of Technique in Indonesia" (Cambridge: Harvard Center for International Affairs, Occasional Papers, 1973).

4. Ibid.

5. Bulog is the Indonesian state food logistics agency.—ED.

A Comment

WILLIAM L. COLLIER, JUSUF COLTER, SINARHADI,
AND ROBERT D'A. SHAW

Over the past few years, nothing short of a revolution has occurred in the process of rice cultivation in Java. Probably one of the most rapid and widespread changes of all has been the displacement of traditional hand-pounding techniques by rice hullers. Perhaps the most interesting and widely debated aspect of these changes is the distribution of the benefits arising from them. Dr. Timmer implied that villagers in general welcome the demise of hand-pounding, since those engaged in the activity gained little income from it. Recent information suggests that this proposition is not tenable. It appears that Dr. Timmer's estimate of the number of jobs lost is far too low. More important in terms of rural poverty, he has failed to give sufficient weight to the large number of women who, prior to the introduction of hullers, gained a sufficient share of their income from hand-pounding. Moreover, it seems that Dr. Timmer overestimated the amount of employment created by rice hullers.

These differences are very important when they are considered in the aggregate. While Dr. Timmer thinks that "upwards of 100,000 jobs" may have been destroyed, our estimate using the same assumptions is much higher. Of even greater consequence is our estimate that earnings of laborers engaged in hand-pounding of rice on Java may have been reduced by as much as $50 million annually. Most of those losing work and sources of income from hand-pounding are likely to be members of the poorest families in the rural areas, those with little or no access to land. Thus the spread of rice hullers has, in our opinion, probably worsened the distribution of income in a substantial way.

These opinions are based on surveys carried out in twelve villages in Java by the Agro-Economic Survey in August and September 1973. Approximately four hundred farmers, laborers, village leaders, and owners of rice hullers were interviewed in these surveys of rural change in rice production. The interviews included information about hand-pounding and mechanical hulling. The material is supplemented by some additional information from eight other villages in the Agro-Economic Survey sample that were surveyed earlier in 1973. ·

WILLIAM L. COLLIER, JUSUF COLTER, and SINARHADI are agricultural economists in Bogor, Indonesia. ROBERT D'A. SHAW is director of special programs, Aga Khan Foundation.

Even though we believe that more of the total rice crop on Java is still being hand-pounded than is indicated in Dr. Timmer's model, this factor is more than compensated for by his overestimation of the amount of rice that can be hand-pounded per day. The actual amounts hand-pounded per day and per hour by workers in our sample villages vary from 12.5 kg to 50.0 kg of *padi* per day. Much of the variation is accounted for by the number of hours worked by each woman. Usually this is five to six hours per day, but in those villages where women undertake contracts for hand-pounding it stretches up to an amazing thirteen hours per day. Thus the average weight of *padi* pounded per hour per person was 5.0 kg, with the range varying from 3.1 to 7.8 kg. This average translates into 3.9 kg of *gabah* per hour and 2.4 kg of *beras* (milled rice) per hour.

Dr. Timmer, however, used an estimate of 150 kg of *gabah* per day. If we assume that he was using a working day of eight hours, this converts to 18.7 kg of *gabah*, or nearly 12 kg of *beras* per hour. Since this is about five times the figure found in our survey, it seems clear that his estimate has little empirical basis.

However, Dr. Timmer's models have additional problems. In the first place, while the title of his article and his coefficients apply to Java alone, Timmer's employment estimates are made on the basis of the total Indonesian rice crop. Information about the rice processing situation outside Java is, in fact, conspicuously inadequate. At the same time, it is probably fair to assume that the greater availability of employment in the other islands makes this technological change less important in terms of human welfare. We will therefore limit our estimates on the impact of mechanical hulling to Java, where nearly two-thirds of the population of Indonesia live and approximately one-half of the country's rice is produced.

Moreover, within Java, Dr. Timmer's estimates for the employment and income effects of hullers would seem to be misleading in the following important ways:

(1) His estimate of the percentage still hand-pounded is probably too low—20 percent against our estimate of 40 percent.
(2) While the above mitigates the unemployment resulting from the use of hullers, this is more than offset by our findings that he used estimates of the hand-pounding capacity of women that seem to be five times too high.
(3) The importance of wage labor in hand-pounding was almost entirely neglected by Dr. Timmer. In our estimate, this may have involved half the total crop on Java.
(4) Lastly, Dr. Timmer may have exaggerated the employment created by hullers by a factor of two.

Let us now take a schematic look at these changes to give an indication of the orders of magnitude of their importance on Java. For this purpose, we shall use a figure of 12 million tons of milled (*gabah*) rice for the total Indonesian rice crop.[1] Typically, half of the total is produced in Java—a total of 6 million tons in our example. If we further assume that 50 percent of this would have been hand-pounded by wage laborers in the absence of hullers, this amounts to 3 million tons that would have created wage employment. Let us now postulate conservatively that one woman can hand-pound enough *gabah* in an hour to obtain 3 kg of *beras* (cf. our estimate of 2.4 kg). To hand-pound 3 million tons would take 1 billion woman-hours, or 125 million woman-days. At a wage of Rp 180 per day, this amounts to earnings of Rp 22.5 billion in a year, or just under $55 million.

To estimate the earnings of employees in SRM hulling this amount, if we assume that one SRM can hull 1,000 tons of *gabah* per year (or approximately 620 tons of *beras*), then to obtain 3 million tons of *beras* requires nearly 5,000 SRM. At an average wage bill of $80 per month, the annual earnings of laborers in these SRM would be just under $5 million.

Thus the total loss in laborers' earnings attributable to the introduction of hullers seems to be of the order of $50 million annually in Java, where the cash incomes of the rural poor are exceedingly low and where the possibilities of alternative employment opportunities are often slight. This represents a substantial diminution of income for large numbers of households of landless laborers and small farmers. Three million tons of rice could provide wages for one million women every day for four months each year.

The beneficiaries of the new technology are those farmers who would otherwise have hired laborers to pound their rice, the huller operators and the buyers of rice, to whom prices of milled rice may be around Rp 5 per kg lower than those that would have prevailed if hand-pounding had remained in force.[2] The losers, on the other hand, are those wives of small farmers and landless laborers who gain additional income from hand-pounding. These are the people who can least afford such a drop in income, as the number of alternative work opportunities is so limited.

The major conclusion we draw from this rough approximation of the impact of the introduction of hullers is that this redistribution of income in favor of relatively large farmers and SRM operators requires, as an urgent matter of public policy, massive programs to create additional income opportunities for the rural disadvantaged. In contrast to our estimate of 125 million woman-days of wage labor lost in Java, the *kabupaten* public works program in 1972–73 provided 43.6 million man-days of employment throughout Indonesia. This program is an excellent start but clearly inadequate to meet the needs.

NOTES

1. The actual total for 1971–72 was estimated at 12.8 million tons.
2. Whether such potential savings have in fact been passed on to rice buyers is impossible to determine because of the very rapid rise in rice prices over the last two years for other reasons.

A Reply

Everyone stands in debt to Messrs. Collier, Colter, Sinarhadi, and Shaw (henceforth acronymized in good Indonesian fashion as CCSS) for providing a substantial body of empirical material dealing with the impact of changing technology in rice milling. I am especially pleased to have some firm evidence on the technical coefficients for hand-pounding. This was a topic of so little concern to the Weitz-Hettelsater Rice Marketing Study[1] that hand-pounding was completely ignored in its report. The coefficient of forty workers per one thousand tons of *gabah* per year used in its final report was picked up from a draft of my first paper on this topic. Since I relied on that document for the great bulk of my technical and cost data, I am not surprised to find that the crude estimates were fairly far off the mark.

Granting this, however, it is important not to lose sight of the meaning and impact of the new numbers provided. The first issue is how they affect the economic analysis of the choice of technique; the second issue is their impact on a social analysis of the economic results. For space reasons, my article does not deal at all with the relationship between an economic analysis and a social analysis, but my earlier article on "Employment Aspects of Investment in Rice Marketing in Indonesia"[2] provided a framework for comparing these two viewpoints (and others). An economic analysis can be done with either market prices or shadow prices. The shadow price analysis results in the largest national income possible when all prices are taken at their social rather than their private values (and this should include distributional and employment considerations). A social analysis carries the concern for unemployment and an unfavorable distribution of income into the political sphere, with the possible (but not inevitable) result that measures taken to relieve unemployment in specific situations would actually have an adverse impact on social equity for the entire economy and society. Only the economic perspective (with both market and shadow prices) is presented in this article, with the exception of the short section on employment impact. It is on this section that CCSS focus their comments, but the data have significant implications for the economic analysis as well.

Picking even the most optimistic figures about hand-pounding productivity and hours worked from the CCSS data, it is evident that the coefficient I used in the choice of technique analysis was off by a minimum of a factor of two and perhaps on average by a factor of four or five. That is, hand-pounding is at most only one-half as productive as I assumed and probably less. The bias I built into the analysis was in favor of hand-pounding entering the tableau of optimal economic activities under a realistic set of circumstances, and, of course, that was one of the striking results of the analysis. Even with the high productivity of hand-pounding that I assumed, it did not become optimal under any set of market price conditions on Java, but it still seemed to make economic sense for farm families (and harvesters) to hand-pound for their own consumption if their opportunity labor costs were below the market wage rate.

The new data provided by CCSS dash this economic rationality completely. Hand-pounding makes sense only when the opportunity wage is virtually zero and not even then if there is any significant squeeze between *padi* prices and milled rice prices. Hand-pounding quickly succumbs to negative value added in such a price squeeze (perhaps caused by a too narrow range between the floor and ceiling prices, which is defended by large-scale imports) because of its technical inefficiency. It is important that we understand this result. From an economic viewpoint, hand-pounding is shown by the CCSS data to be a completely inappropriate technique under present market conditions on Java and would make sense only if labor were shadow priced at a near zero wage (and the government paid the difference between this level and the market wage) and the shadow value of rice were well below present market prices (and the government could afford this subsidy as well).

Having just argued that the only significant effect of the CCSS data is to make hand-pounding nearly impossible to justify on economic grounds, I do agree with the major thrust of the social concern demonstrated by the authors. The distribution impact of the SRM has been higher incomes for large farmers and for operators of the SRM, but at the expense of the poor village women who have lost a source of case income and are now pressing into the harvest labor forces, with serious economic and social consequences. I fully accept the conclusions of CCSS with respect to lost cash income potential of village women. Their numbers without doubt more correctly assess the impact here than my own, based as they were on very rough estimates. But even as early as 1971 hand-pounding as a cash-hire activity was a rapidly vanishing phenomenon. My whole perspective on this particular issue was colored by this *fait accompli*. In historical terms the loss of cash wages by the poor women villagers is important, but it had little immediate bearing on the policy issue directly before the government, namely, Would Indonesia be best served by investment in large bulk facilities for drying, milling, and storing rice? We should all be very thankful to CCSS for redirecting our attention to the neglected social issue now that the immediate policy issue has been resolved. Their pleas for a vastly expanded rural works program will be met with enthusiasm by all whose consciences are moved by the plight of the rural (and urban) poor in Indonesia.

This brings us to the other side of the distributional impact of the new milling technology. Rice prices to consumers are perhaps "Rp 5 per kg lower than those that would have prevailed if hand-pounding had remained in force" (CCSS). As CCSS point out, it is hard to tell, with rice prices in such turmoil over the past few years, whether these cost reductions have actually been passed on to the consumer, but let us work with this magnitude and examine its implications. Do lower consumer prices for rice for a given farm price hurt income distribution or help it? I would argue that a Rp 5 per kg reduction in consumer rice price while farm prices are held constant has an enormous welfare impact on the lower half or two-thirds of the income distribution. The magnitudes are just as impressive as the $50 million quoted by CCSS as wage losses to the rural poor. A Rp 5 per kg cost saving to the new technology applied to a 13-million-ton rice crop gives a resulting saving to consumers of $165 million. Even if only half of this benefits the lower half of the population—a very conservative assumption—its gain exceeds $80 million.

We must also put in the balance the greater outturn of rice from a given volume of *gabah* achieved by the machine technology. The new data on extraction rates provided by CCSS raise the savings to truly important proportions. The difference between 57 percent extraction for hand-pounding and 66 percent for the SRM on average is 9 percent. For a *gabah* crop of 18 million tons a milling industry composed entirely of SRM would yield *over one and a half million tons more milled rice* than if the crop were hand-pounded. At a very conservative price of $200 per ton this is an added value to society of more than $300 million. Again, the exact distributional nature of this gain is not clear, but it is hard to see how the unemployed women are made worse off by this aspect of the technological change.

Losing the efficiency gains by banning small rice mills (thus forcing a return to hand-pounding) would be an enormously costly way of helping the displaced women whose primary source of wages during the harvest has been removed. We must set the $50 million loss to these women against a gain to society of more than $450 million, and some of that gain accrues to these very same women, although not a sufficient amount to offset their losses. But surely with the comprehensive and statistically documented picture presented by CCSS to create awareness of the problem, a mechanism can be found that would redistribute 10–15 percent of the social gain to the private losers.[3]

Lastly, I should like to enter a confession. I started this entire area of research with the intention of demonstrating in simple, clear-cut terms that both economic planners and engineering consultants would understand that the large-scale rice mills and bulk silo terminals were inappropriate in the Indonesian countryside. The battle to be fought in the planning agency was not hand-pounding versus small rice mills but large bulk facilities versus small rice mills. I was nearly laughed out of court for defending the small rice mills, but the analysis spoke for itself and still does. In terms of prevailing market prices and any imaginable modification of them (including reasonable shadow prices), facilities in the generic class "small rice mills" are the most appropriate for Indonesia.

NOTES

1. Weitz-Hettelsater Engineers, "Rice Storage, Handling, and Marketing Study: Economics and Engineering Aspects" (Kansas City, Mo., 1972).

2. Timmer, "Employment Aspects of Investment in Rice Marketing in Indonesia," *Food Research Institute Studies in Agricultural Economics, Trade, and Development* 11, no. 1 (1972).

3. Another distributional issue that neither CCSS nor I have treated is nutrition. The primary source of the B-vitamin complex for the poorer half of the population is the bran left on hand-pounded rice. A complete shift to the white rice made possible by well-operated small rice mills could easily result in serious vitamin deficiencies that could be offset only by a fairly expensive vitamin fortification program. I have no way of knowing how these costs would compare with the gains already cited nor with the wage losses cited by CCSS.

19

Rural Small-Scale Industry: Empirical Evidence and Policy Issues

ENYINNA CHUTA and CARL LIEDHOLM

The role of rural small-scale industries in providing productive employment and earning opportunities has recently emerged as an important research concern in development economics and has become a hotly debated topic among policy makers and international donor agencies.[1] This heightened interest has paralleled the increased international concern for equity and employment objectives and the growing realization that the large-scale urban industrialization strategies of the 1960s generally failed to solve the problems of underemployment and poverty. Moreover, empirical research has begun to demonstrate that small rural manufacturing enterprises have been substantially underreported in official publications and that these smaller firms might be more effective vehicles for meeting a country's growth and equity objectives than their larger-scale urban counterparts.

In spite of the importance of this topic, there have been few analytical or empirical studies of small rural industries. The World Bank (1978a), for example, concluded that "there is little concrete evidence" on many of the important characteristics of these activities. As a result, policy makers and planners charged with the formulation of policies and programs to assist rural small-scale industry in the Third World are often forced to make decisions that are "unencumbered by evidence."

The purpose of this paper is to fill the gap in the literature on rural industries in the Third World. We shall begin with a descriptive profile of rural industries and then examine the role of rural small-scale industries in development. In the final section we shall discuss major policy and program issues.

ENYINNA CHUTA is dean, School of Management Sciences, University of Maiduguri, Yola, Nigeria. CARL LIEDHOLM is professor of economics and agricultural economics, Michigan State University.

DESCRIPTIVE PROFILE

Rural industries, which include manufacturing, processing, and repair activities, form one component of a larger set of rural nonfarm activities. Commerce, services, construction, and transport are also important activities within the rural nonfarm sector. Although these activities fall outside the purview of this paper, the overall importance of the rural nonfarm sector needs to be examined briefly at the outset, in order to place the discussion of rural industry in a proper perspective.

OVERALL MAGNITUDE

Just how significant are rural industries and other nonfarm activities in developing countries? The evidence available from national censuses and various regional and rural surveys indicates that nonfarm activities provide an important source of *primary* rural employment in developing countries. In the vast majority of the eighteen developing countries where relatively recent data on the subject are available, one-fifth or more of the rural labor force is *primarily* engaged in nonfarm activities (table 1). Although the rural nonfarm percentage ranged from 14 percent to 49 percent, in over three-quarters of the countries the percentage fell between 19 percent and 28 percent.

TABLE 1
PERCENTAGE OF THE RURAL LABOR FORCE WITH PRIMARY EMPLOYMENT IN
RURAL NONFARM ACTIVITIES

Country	Year	Coverage	Percentage of Rural Labor Force Primarily Employed in Nonfarm Sector (%)
Guatemala	1964	All rural	14%
Thailand	1970	All rural	18
Sierra Leone	1976	Male–rural	19
South Korea	1970	All rural	19
Pakistan	1970	Punjab only	19
Nigeria	1966	Male—3 districts, Western State	19
India	1966	All rural	20
Uganda	1967	Four rural villages	20
Afghanistan	1971	Male—Paktia Region	22
Mexico	1970	All—Sinaloa State	23
Colombia	1970	All rural	23
Indonesia	1971	All rural	24
Venezuela	1969	All rural	27
Kenya	1970	All rural	28
Philippines	1971	All rural	28
W. Malaysia	1970	All rural	32
Iran	1972	All rural	33
Taiwan	1966	All rural	49

SOURCE: Chuta and Liedholm 1979.

The figures provide a minimal estimate of the magnitude of primary employment in nonfarm activities in rural areas. First, they generally reflect the employment characteristics of the rural villages with populations below five thousand; if the larger rural towns were included, the rural nonfarm percentage would likely be larger.[2] Second, there are certain measurement errors that cause systematic undercounting of nonfarm activities. In some African countries rural respondents will report farming to be their main occupation even if they engage in this activity only part-time. In addition, women's participation in nonfarm activities is often substantial, but frequently it is not measured or included in labor-force figures. In Honduras, for example, one study revealed that over 60 percent of the rural industrial entrepreneurs were women, a fact not reflected in the country's official statistics (Stallmann and Pease 1979).

These primary employment statistics also understate the magnitude of rural nonfarm activities, because they fail to reflect those farmers who engage in nonfarm activities on a part-time or seasonal basis. Data on secondary employment are not generally available for most countries. The limited evidence indicates that 10–20 percent of the rural male labor force undertakes nonfarm work as a secondary occupation. In western Nigeria, for example, 20 percent of the rural males engaged in nonfarm work on a part-time basis, while in Sierra Leone, Afghanistan, and Korea the figures were 11 percent, 16 percent, and 20 percent, respectively (Chuta and Liedholm 1979).

There are significant monthly variations in the amounts of rural farm and nonfarm employment over the agricultural cycle. Farm and nonfarm employment move in opposite directions. There is no period when nonfarm employment disappears; thus, nonfarm employment does compete somewhat with farm employment during periods of the peak agricultural demand for labor. Data from Nigeria reveal that the peak in nonfarm labor use is nine times the use in the slack periods (Norman 1973). The fluidity of labor between a number of activities on a seasonal basis is thus a striking feature of rural households.

In summary, rural industries and other rural nonfarm activities appear to provide a source of primary or secondary employment for 30–50 percent of the rural labor force in developing nations.[3] Consequently, in terms of employment, nonfarm activities are quantitatively an important component of the rural economy that should not be overlooked in the design of rural development policies or programs.

In view of the magnitude of rural nonfarm employment, it is not surprising that rural industries and other nonfarm activities also provide an important source of income for rural households. Although data on rural incomes are generally lacking for most countries, evidence from those countries where information is available indicates that nonfarm earnings account for over one-fifth of total rural household income. Indeed, in Sierra Leone, where a detailed rural household survey was recently undertaken, nonfarm income was found to provide 36 percent of rural household income, while in Taiwan the comparable figure was 43 percent (Chuta and Liedholm 1979).

COMPOSITION

What are the most important types of activities within the rural nonfarm sector? In most developing countries, rural industries, rural commerce, and rural services tend to dominate. For the nine countries for which the required data are available, rural industry accounts for 22–46 percent of total nonfarm employment, rural commerce ranges from 11 percent to 35 percent, while rural services range from 10 percent to 50 percent.[4] Other nonfarm activities, such as construction, transport, and utilities, generally account for less than 25 percent of rural nonfarm employment (see Chuta and Liedholm 1979 for more details).

The relative importance of rural industrial activity as a component of the rural economy may appear surprising. Even more surprising, perhaps, is how important rural industries appear when compared with urban industries in many developing countries. Indeed, there is evidence that employment in small rural industrial enterprises typically exceeds that in large urban industrial firms (Liedholm and Mead 1987). In Sierra Leone 86 percent of the total industrial-sector employment and 95 percent of the industrial establishments were located in rural areas (Chuta and Liedholm 1985). The percentage of rural industrial employment in other countries ranged from 70 percent in Bangladesh (Bangladesh Institute of Development Studies 1979) to 67 percent in Jamaica (Davies et al. 1979) and 63 percent in Malaysia (World Bank 1978b). These figures may actually understate the true magnitude of rural industrial activity, because country censuses often fail to pick up the very small rural enterprises. A rural industry survey in Honduras (Stallmann and Pease 1979) found that rural industrial employment had been underestimated in Honduras by almost one-half. A similar survey in Bangladesh indicated that in one rural district the number of rural industrial firms was twenty times greater than indicated by the official statistics (Ahmed, Chuta, and Rahman 1978).

Within rural industries there is a surprising diversity of activities. The most important activity in the majority of countries appears to be clothing production, followed by woodworking, metalworking, and food processing. Clothing production, for example, accounted for 53 percent of the rural manufacturing employment in Sierra Leone, 41 percent in Korea, 24 percent in Taiwan, 32 percent in western Nigeria, and 52 percent in rural Bangladesh (Chuta and Liedholm 1979).

SIZE

What is the average size of these rural industries? The available empirical evidence is limited, but it does indicate that the vast majority of rural industrial activities are undertaken by very small "micro" firms, which have fewer than ten workers.[5] In Sierra Leone the average rural industrial firm employed 1.6 workers, and 99 percent of the firms employed fewer than 5 individuals (Chuta and Liedholm 1985). In rural Jamaica (Davies et al. 1979) the average rural industrial enterprise engaged 1.8 workers. The results of a similar survey undertaken in rural Honduras (Stallmann and Pease 1979) revealed that 59 percent of the industrial firms were one-person endeavors and that 95 percent employed fewer than 5 workers. These findings indicate that most rural enterprises are very small and thus may be potentially an important target group for policy makers concerned with the rural poor.

Growth Potential

Finally, in a dynamic sense, do rural industries decrease as rural incomes rise and opportunities for trade increase? On this issue there has been a divergence of views. The issue was sparked by the 1969 paper "A Model of an Agrarian Economy with Nonagricultural Activities," by Stephen Hymer and Stephen Resnick. The authors develop a model of the rural economy in which rural industrial and other nonfarm activities, denoted as Z goods, are hypothesized to decline as rural incomes rise and opportunities for trade increase. Resnick, in a subsequent article (1970), provided empirical evidence for the contention by tracing the decline of rural industry in Burma, the Philippines, and Thailand from 1870 to 1938. Comprehensive times series data were not available, however, and Resnick was forced to rely on fragments of evidence from various sources. Consequently, the results of the study, while interesting, cannot be considered conclusive.

The empirical evidence available for more recent periods indicates that in the aggregate, rural industrial and other nonfarm employment and output have been increasing, rather than decreasing, with development (see Liedholm and Kilby 1989 for details). Although much of the available evidence is anecdotal or episodic, some time series data are available for countries such as the Philippines (Anderson and Khambata 1981), Sierra Leone (Chuta and Liedholm 1982), and India (Little, Mazumdar, and Page 1987). These data indicate that employment growth in industrial establishments tends to be directly related to the size of the locality (Liedholm and Parker 1989). Thus, there is a gradual shift in the locus of activity over time from smaller villages to larger regional towns. There are also important variations in growth by firm size. Data from India (1961–71) and Sierra Leone (1974–80) indicate that a direct relationship exists between growth rates and firm size (Liedholm and Mead 1987). In both countries, the growth in the number of rural industrial firms is highest in the 10–49 employee size category, for example, and lowest in the one-person firm category. Indeed, in Sierra Leone, the number of one-person rural industrial firms actually declined during the time period covered by the study. Moreover, in terms of firm expansion, recent evidence suggests that relatively few rural "micro" enterprises, particularly in Africa, graduate through the size structure; most remain "micro" firms (Liedholm and Parker 1989).

There are also variations in the growth performance by type of rural industry. The available evidence indicates that tailoring, dressmaking, furniture making, baking, and rice milling have all continued to grow in importance even after large-scale domestic factory production in these subsectors has begun. Shoe production, leather production, and pottery making appear to have generally declined in importance.[6] A mixed record appears for blacksmithing and for spinning and weaving.[7] The kinds of activities undertaken by some of the important artisan groups have also been evolving. In some countries, for example, rural blacksmiths, who previously were primarily engaged in the production or servicing of hand tools, now also produce or service animal-drawn or mechanized farm equipment and irrigation equipment (Liedholm and Kilby 1989; Child and Kaneda 1975). Moreover, several newer types of artisan activities, such as bicycle, auto, and electrical repair, have grown particularly rapidly in recent years. These newer activities reflect the increasing service orientation of many artisan activities as incomes and urban factory production increase. In addition, certain types of craft-oriented artisan activities designed for the international market, such as gara (tie-dyed) cloth in Sierra Leone (Chuta and Liedholm 1985) and woodcarving in Haiti (Haggblade, Defay, and Pitman 1979), have also been growing rapidly in certain countries. Finally, a few "modern" factory activities, some of which have emerged from small enterprises such as metal-working factories in India (Berna 1960) and cement block production and essential oils (luxury perfume) production in rural Haiti (Haggblade, Defay, and Pitman 1979), have also begun to increase in importance.[8]

Recognizing these differential growth patterns is important in the design of programs and policies for rural industry. Government policies, particularly with respect to large, modern industries and agriculture, influence growth patterns of individual activities within each country.[9] Although some new rural industrial activities will emerge, the sheer magnitude of existing informal artisan activities in most countries indicates that any major transformation will take many years to complete. Stewart (1972) has estimated that it will take several decades before the "formal" sector will begin to absorb even the additions to the labor force in most developing countries. Consequently, attention must continue to be directed towards enhancing the types of activities represented in the existing structure of rural enterprises, even if, in the longer run, many of them will eventually decline in importance or disappear.[10]

DETERMINANTS OF THE ROLE OF RURAL INDUSTRY

What are the main determinants of both future and existing patterns of rural industrial employment and income? These can be usefully understood by focusing on the set of factors influencing the demand for and supply of these activities.

DEMAND PROSPECTS

Several important issues relate to the nature of the demand for the goods and services produced by rural industries. One crucial issue, on which there has been a divergence of opinion, is whether the demand for these activities increases as rural incomes increase. Hymer and Resnick (1969) have argued that rural industrial activities produce inferior goods, that is, that the demand for them would be expected to decline as rural incomes rise. Mellor (1976), Chuta and Liedholm (1979), and various International Labour Office missions (1972, 1974), on the other hand, have contended that there is a strong, positive relationship between income and the demand for these activities. Recent research, based on analyses of household expenditure surveys in Asia and Africa, however, provides support for the latter position (King and Byerlee 1978; Liedholm and Kilby 1989; Haggblade and Hazell 1989).

Another demand-related issue is whether there are strong backward and forward linkages between rural industrial activities and other sectors of the economy, particularly agriculture. Hirschman (1958) has contended that linkages between agriculture and other sectors are quite weak,[11] while others, such as Mellor (1976) and Johnston and Kilby (1975), have argued that the linkages between rural industries and agriculture, in particular, are or could be potentially very strong. The available empirical evidence indicates that these linkages are quite important. Their magnitude is related to the size distribution of farms and the type of agricultural strategy adopted. The capacity among small producers for "idiosyncratic design adaptation" to meet the equipment and tool needs of small farmers is particularly noteworthy (Liedholm and Kilby 1989). Rural industries are influenced by the pattern of agricultural growth and can themselves influence the course and rate of agricultural development. Finally, there is some empirical and analytical evidence that the international market is an important component of demand for certain types of rural industrial products (see Chuta and Liedholm 1979).

SUPPLY FACTORS

With respect to supply, the key issue is whether rural small-scale industrial firms in developing countries are efficient users of economic resources, particularly when compared with their larger-scale, urban counterparts. Both partial and comprehensive measures of economic efficiency have been used in attempting to answer this question.

The labor-capital (labor intensity) and the output-capital (capital productivity) ratios are the economic efficiency measures most frequently used in empirical studies. These partial efficiency measures are based on the assumption that labor is abundant and capital is the only scarce resource. Virtually all the aggregate and most industry studies reveal that small-scale industries generate more employment per unit of scarce capital than do their larger-scale counterparts. The available evidence on relative capital productivities is somewhat limited and more mixed (Little, Mazumdar, and Page 1987; Liedholm and Mead 1987).

Only a few studies have used one of the analytically more correct comprehensive economic efficiency measures, in which all scarce resources are included in the analysis and are evaluated at "shadow" or social prices that reflect their scarcity values in the economy. The findings of such studies are mixed. Moreover, rural industries are rarely examined explicitly in these analyses.

To assist in filling this void, Liedholm and Kilby (1989) used a social benefit-cost analysis to compare the relative efficiency of small rural manfacturing enterprises with their larger-scale urban counterparts in Sierra Leone, Honduras, and Jamaica. The ratio of the enterprise's value added to the cost of its capital and labor, both valued at their shadow or "social" prices, was used to measure economic efficiency. The primary data were generated from detailed small-scale industry surveys, in which hundreds of rural firms in each country were interviewed twice weekly over a twelve-month period to obtain daily information on revenues and costs.[12] The information on the large-scale enterprises was obtained from the worksheets used to construct the industrial censuses. Among the industry groups examined were baking, wearing apparel, shoes, furniture, and metal products.

The key finding from this three-country analysis was that the small rural manufacturing enterprises were found to use fewer resources per unit of output than their larger-scale counterparts in a majority of the industry groups considered. In over two-thirds of the industrial groups examined, the social benefit-cost ratios of the small rural firms not only exceeded one, but also were greater than the comparable ratios for the large-scale firms in those particular industries and countries. These findings, while not conclusive, do indicate that in several lines of activity small rural industries are economically viable.

The efficiency of individual rural firms, however, varies by their production characteristics, particularly their size, input composition, and location. A review of various rural industry surveys (Liedholm and Mead 1987) reveals some important patterns. The rural firms most likely to be economically efficient tend to possess a number of characteristics, many of which can be discerned on the basis of ocular evidence. Such firms generally use hired workers, operate in workshops away from the home, operate in localities with more than 2,000 inhabitants, and are involved in selected product lines with better economic prospects, such as tiles, furniture, baking, and repair activities. A particularly striking finding is that the one-person rural firms are frequently on the margin of economic viability. Judiciously and cautiously applied, such indicators can provide the analyst with useful insights into those types of rural industries most likely to be economically viable.

MAJOR POLICY AND PROJECT ISSUES

Given the favorable characteristics of rural industries with respect to employment, income generation, and income distribution issues, many governments are showing increasing interest in incorporating these activities into their development strategies. Governments can assist these enterprises by general policy measures that affect the environment in which rural industries operate and by providing direct project assistance.

GENERAL POLICY MEASURES

A wide panoply of policies—ranging from those affecting capital and labor markets to agriculture, trade, and income distribution—affect the efficiency, employment, and size distribution of enterprises in the rural economy. The overall policy environment in most countries, however, is not neutral with respect to firm size and location and is typically biased against small rural industries (Haggblade, Liedholm and Mead 1986). Consequently, great care must be exercised in policy selections, as many government actions seemingly unrelated to rural industrial activities can inadvertently have adverse effects on them.

Factor-Price Distortions

Policies that result in input price distortions, for example, have significant, though often unintended, negative effects on rural industries. Two of the major sources of input price distortions, interest and tariff rates, will be discussed here.

With respect to interest rates, two distinct capital markets—the "formal" and the "informal"—exist in most developing countries.[13] Banks and similar institutions constitute the formal market, while moneylenders, raw material suppliers, and purchasers constitute the bulk of the informal market. Interest rates vary widely between the two. Official interest rates, where government-imposed ceilings frequently exist, generally run from 10 percent to 20 percent, while the non-official rates are frequently 100 percent or more (see Chuta and Liedholm 1979). Particularly under inflationary conditions, the formal real rates become very low, sometimes negative. Thus, not surprisingly, banks have tended to lend only to the established, large-scale firms, which may appear to the banks to involve lower risks and lending costs. Most of the recipients are urban-based, and their operations have tended to become more capital-intensive than they would have been had they been forced to borrow at the opportunity cost of capital. The removal of interest rate ceilings can constitute a step towards ensuring that interest rates for borrowers of all sizes more closely approximate the opportunity cost of capital.

The import duty structure can also be an important source of differential treatment for urban large-scale industries compared with rural small-scale industries. For most developing countries, import duties are lowest for heavy capital goods and become progressively higher through intermediate and consumer durable goods categories. Yet, many items classified as intermediate or consumer goods in tariff schedules are capital goods for rural small-scale firms. In Sierra Leone the sewing machine, an important capital item for tailoring firms, was classified as a luxury consumer good and taxed accordingly (Chuta and Liedholm 1985).

Further escalating the distortion in capital cost is the frequent practice of granting concessions or even total waivers of import duties on capital goods or raw materials for specified periods as an inducement for industrial development. In some cases, small firms may technically qualify for similar consessions but may be unaware of this opportunity or, even when they are aware, may find the process so complicated and time-consuming that it is not economic for them to exercise the option. In many other cases small firms do not even qualify.

Other Policy Measures

Government policies with respect to infrastructure, industry, and agriculture also have important indirect effects on the expansion of rural industrial employment and income opportunities. Because of the strong linkages between agricultural and rural industrial activities, agricultural policies and programs, in particular, have a strong influence on rural small-scale enterprises. The analyses in the earlier section of this paper revealed that the primary demand for most rural industrial goods and services stems from the agricultural sector and that this demand is transmitted through both income and production linkages. Since the available evidence indicates that the rural households' income elasticity of demand for rural industrial goods is positive and that agriculture generates the largest share of rural incomes, policies designed to increase agricultural output and/or income have an important indirect effect on the demand for these activities. Consequently, government actions ranging from improvements in the terms of trade between agriculture and the larger-scale urban sector to specific investment programs and policies designed to increase, directly or indirectly, agricultural production and income can generate an increased demand for a wide array of rural industrial goods and services.

The nature and composition of these agricultural policies and programs should also be considered, however, since they can have important, differential effects on the demand for products from rural industries. There is some evidence that higher-income rural residents have a somewhat lower income elasticity of demand for rural industrial products than do lower-income individuals, the majority of whom are small-scale farmers (see King and Byerlee 1978; Haggblade and Hazell 1989). Moreover, the agricultural inputs, such as tractors and fertilizers, used by large-scale, high income farmers are less likely to be produced in rural localities than are the inputs used by the small-scale farmers (see Johnston and Kilby 1975).[14] Consequently, policies and programs designed to benefit a larger number of small-scale, low-income farmers are likely to generate a larger demand for rural industrial activities and services than those designed to benefit a few larger-scale farmers. These differential effects on rural industrial activities must be recognized when designing agricultural policies or rural development strategies.

DIRECT PROJECT ASSISTANCE

Projects rather than policy reforms have been the primary vehicle used to date by governments and international donor agencies for fostering rural enterprise growth. Small rural enterprises are difficult targets to reach through direct project assistance, however. The firms are numerous, widely dispersed and not easy to assist in a cost-effective manner. Indeed, virtually all rural enterprise surveys reveal that only a tiny fraction of the entrepreneurs have heard of the programs intended for them and even fewer have been aided by them. These same studies indicate that the constraints facing such firms and thus the types of direct assistance needed vary from industry to industry and from country to country. The major types of direct project assistance used to promote rural industries include a broad spectrum of interventions: credit, technical, management, and marketing assistance and the provision of common facilities, usually industrial estates.

Financial Assistance

Credit assistance is one of the most frequently used mechanisms to aid rural small-scale industries. An important issue in the design of such assistance is determining the extent of effective demand for this credit by rural industries. Some evidence appears to indicate that this demand is quite sizable. Rural entrepreneurs, for example, when asked directly to identify their greatest assistance needs and greatest perceived bottleneck, will usually list credit and capital first (see Kilby, Liedholm, and Meyer 1984). There is also evidence that for many types of rural industrial enterprises the rates of return on existing capital are substantial. These high rates of return indicate that the *potential* demand for credit could be quite large.

Yet, other evidence indicates that the rural industrial enterprises' demand for credit may be less extensive than indicated above. Detailed analyses undertaken in Sierra Leone (Chuta and Liedholm 1985) and Kenya (Harper 1978) revealed that although entrepreneurs perceived the lack of credit to be the crucial bottleneck, other problems, such as inadequate management or raw material procurement difficulties, proved to be the crucial basic constraints facing many small enterprises. Unless these other difficulties are recognized and dealt with, the simple provision of credit could, at a minimum, be wasteful and could actually harm rural industrial enterprises by inducing overcapitalization.

Another demand issue relates to the composition of the credit demand from rural industrial enterprises. In particular, is the credit demand primarily for fixed or working capital? The composition of credit demand does appear to vary somewhat depending on the size and type of rural industrial enterprise. For the smallest enterprises, which account for the bulk of the sector, the primary credit demand appears to be for working capital (see Kilby, Liedholm, and Meyer 1984 for more details on working capital). It is important to ascertain how much of the apparent working capital demand is simply a manifestation of some other problem, such as a raw material shortage, inadequate management, or a lack of demand for final products.

An important supply issue centers on determining the appropriate channel for providing financial services to rural industries. In most developing countries, formal credit institutions such as commercial banks, specialized small enterprise banks, specialized divisions of development banks, credit unions, and cooperative and worker banks have typically been used to channel funds to these enterprises. Although such devices as rediscounting facilities, guarantees, and ear-marked funds are frequently introduced to entice these "formal" institutions into expanding their lending to rural industrial enterprises, it is not yet clear that these inducements have been successful in significantly expanding the amount of formal credit available to these enterprises, particularly the smaller ones.[15] Indeed, the vast majority of these rural industries have never even applied for funds from formal credit institutions.[16] Most of their capital is obtained from family or internal sources.

Several innovative credit schemes, however, appear to have been quite successful in providing financial resources to even the smallest rural enterprises. Among them are the Grameen Bank in Bangladesh (Hossain 1988) and the BKK project in Indonesia (Goldmark and Rosengard 1983). There are several characteristics common to such schemes. First, loans are provided primarily for working capital rather than for fixed capital. Second, loans are screened in locally based institutions on the basis of the borrower's character. Third, loans are initially made for small amounts and for short periods to encourage and facilitate high repayment rates. Since these lending practices are closely akin to those of the informal credit institutions, it would appear that the nearer banks and other formal institutions can come to the operating procedures of informal lenders, the more likely it is that they will be successful in making loans to small producers (Liedholm and Mead 1987). Yet, no single delivery system has emerged as a solution for providing credit to the wide array of rural industries. Indeed, rural industries may derive greater long-term economic and social benefits from the development of sound rural financial markets than from specialized, rural industry lending schemes.[17]

Nonfinancial Assistance

Nonfinancial direct assistance to small enterprises involves the delivery of such things as technical, managerial, marketing, and infrastructure inputs. It is frequently argued that the rural firm's demand for such service is generally quite small and that a large volume of resources ends up being concentrated on a relatively limited clientele.

A review of the limited number of nonfinancial assistance projects indicates that most were not particularly successful in terms of benefit-cost analysis (see Liedholm and Mead 1987). Nevertheless, some were successful, and these possessed several common characteristics. First, the projects addressed situations where a single "missing ingredient" needed to be supplied to the firm rather than an integrated set of multiple ingredients (see Kilby 1979). An implication of this finding is that projects assisting existing firms are more likely to be successful than those attempting to establish new firms. Second, the successful projects were industry and task specific. Third, before these projects or schemes were launched, prior surveys were undertaken to uncover the demand for the activity and the number and type of "missing ingredients." Finally, successful projects tended to be built on proven existing institutions, even informal ones.

SUMMARY

International donor agencies and the governments of many developing nations have recently begun to devote increased attention to a previously neglected component of the rural economy, rural industries. The accumulating empirical evidence indicates that these activities not only generate a significant amount of rural employment and output but also provide an important source of income for rural households. Moreover, there is mounting evidence that several kinds of rural industries may be more economically efficient than their larger-scale urban counterparts. With judicious governmental policies and carefully formulated direct assistance measures, the contribution of rural industries in providing employment and income to rural households can be significantly enhanced.

NOTES

1. India and China, two countries with relatively long experience in rural industrialization, began to introduce policies and programs to foster village and cottage industries in the 1950s. In India, cottage or household-type industries, which generally employed traditional technologies, frequently stressed the goal of absorbing surplus labor; these enterprises were frequently protected and subsidized and were not always closely linked with local demands or the agricultural sector. In China, communally

organized industries using improved techniques were designed to meet local demands and were generally closely linked to the agricultural sector (see Gupta 1980).

2. See, for example, the evidence cited in World Bank 1978a. The dividing line between "rural" and "urban" is arbitrary, particularly in census data collected in most countries. The boundary lines are often framed in terms of urbanization characteristics rather than minimum size or occupational structure; consequently, settlements of a few thousand are often classified as "urban." The United Nations includes localities with fewer than twenty thousand inhabitants in its definition of "rural areas." This broader definition, which includes small- and medium-sized towns, is used in this paper. Haggblade and Hazell (1989), in a recent review of population census data for 43 countries, report that rural nonfarm enterprises account for 14 percent of primary employment in rural Africa, 26 percent in rural Asia, and 28 percent in Latin America; these figures are based on official census definitions of rural, which typically include only rural locations with 5000 inhabitants or less. When rural towns are included (none exceeding 250,000), the rural nonfarm percentages rise to 19 percent, 36 percent, and 47 percent, respectively.

3. There is evidence that the figure may be as high as 50 percent in some countries. Luning (1967), in a survey of villages in northern Nigeria, reports that 48 percent of the employed males engaged either full- or part-time in rural nonfarm activities, while Norman (1973) reports that in the same area 47 percent of male labor *time* was devoted to these activities.

4. Agricultural processing and marketing activities are reflected in these figures; fishing and livestock activities are not. See Chuta and Liedholm 1979 for more details.

5. "Small-scale" is not a precisely defined concept. At least fifty different definitions are used in seventy-five countries (see, for example, Staley and Morse 1965). As a working definition for this paper, "small-scale" includes those establishments employing fewer than fifty persons, while "micro" enterprise includes those with less than ten workers.

6. Additional evidence on the decline of these particular activities is found for India (Prasad 1963), Ethiopia (Karsten 1972), and Burma (Resnick 1970).

7. Spinning and weaving have declined in the Philippines and Sierra Leone but have increased, since Independence, in India.

8. For an excellent listing of the types of "modern" small enterprises, both urban and rural, likely to increase in importance see Staley and Morse (1965, 97ff.) Locational, process, and market influences are stressed.

9. In India handloom production declined from 1901 to 1947 under colonial rule (Prasad 1963, table 14) but increased after Independence with government encouragement.

10. Investments in most "informal" rural enterprises, for example, would be fully amortized within ten to twenty years.

11. Two reasons why Hirschman perceived few linkages were: (1) he implicitly was using a two-sector model in which *all* rural activities are labeled "agriculture"; and (2) he was writing in the context of a technologically stagnant agriculture.

12. For data on the profits and productivity of small-scale industries in other countries see Liedholm and Mead 1987.

13. See Adams and Vogel, chapter 21, in this volume, eds.

14. Small-scale farmers are also more likely to use primarily smaller rural-based agricultural processing establishments, while large-scale farmers might be expected to make more use of larger-scale urban-based processing plants.

15. For a review of alternative institutional arrangements see Kilby, Liedholm and Meyer 1984.

16. In Haiti, 94 percent had never applied (Haggblade, Defay, and Pitman 1979), while in Sierra Leone the figure was 96 percent (Chuta and Liedholm 1985).

17. See chapter 21 in this volume.

REFERENCES

Ahmed, S., E. Chuta, and M. Rahman. 1978. "Rural Industries in Bangladesh: Research and Policy Implications." *Journal of Management* (University of Dacca) April: 25–37.

Anderson, Dennis, and Farida Khambata. 1981. "The Financing of Small and Medium Enterprises in the Philippines: A Case Study." World Bank Working Paper, no. 468. Washington, D.C. Mimeo.

Bangladesh Institute of Development Studies. 1979. "Rural Industries Study Project—Phase I Report." Dacca. Mimeo.

Berna, J. J. 1960. *Industrial Entrepreneurship in Madras State, India.* Bombay: Asia Publishing House.

Child, Frank D., and Hiromitsu Kaneda. 1975. "Links to the Green Revolution: A Study of Smallscale, Agriculturally Related Industry in the Pakistan Punjab." *Economic Development and Cultural Change* 23:249–75.

Chuta, Enyinna, and Carl Liedholm. 1979. *Rural Non-Farm Employment: A Review of the State of the Art.* Michigan State University Rural Development Paper, no. 4. East Lansing: Michigan State University, Department of Agricultural Economics.

———. 1982. "Employment Growth and Change in Sierra Leone Small Scale Industry, 1974–1980." *International Labour Review* 121(1):101–12.

———. 1985. *Employment and Growth in Small-Scale Industry: Empirical Evidence and Policy Assessment from Sierra Leone.* New York: St. Martin's Press.

Davies, Omar, Yacob Fisseha, Annette Francis, and C. Kirton. 1979. "A Preliminary Analysis of the Small-Scale, Non-Farm Sector in Jamaica." Kingston, Jamaica: Small-Scale Enterprise Survey Unit, Institute of Social and Economic Research, University of the West Indies. Mimeo.

Goldmark, Susan, and J. Rosengard. 1983. "Credit to Indonesian Entrepreneurs: An Assessment of the BKK Program." Washington, D.C.: Development Alternatives.

Gupta, Devendra. 1980. "Government Policies and Programmes of Rural Industrialization with Special Reference to the Punjab Region of Northern India." World Employment Research Paper WEP 2-37/WP5. Geneva: International Labour Organization. Mimeo.

Haggblade, S., Jacques Defay, and Bob Pitman. 1979. "Small Manufacturing and Repair Enterprises in Haiti: Survey Results." Rural Development Series Working Paper, no. 4, East Lansing: Michigan State University, Department of Agricultural Economics. Mimeo.

Haggblade, Stephen, and P. Hazell. 1989. "Agricultural Technology and Farm-Nonfarm Growth Linkages." *Agricultural Economics* 3, 4:345–64.

Haggblade, Stephen, Carl Liedholm, and Don Mead. 1986. "The Effect of Policy and Policy Reform on Non-Agricultural Enterprises and Employment in Developing Countries: A Review of Past Experiences." EEPA Discussion Paper, no. 1. Cambridge: Harvard Institute for International Development.

Harper, Malcolm. 1978. *Consultancy for Small Business.* London: Intermediate Technology Publications.

Hirschman, A. O. 1958. *The Strategy of Economic Development.* New Haven: Yale University Press.

Hossain, Makabub. 1988. "Credit for Alleviation of Rural Poverty: The Grameen Bank in Bangladesh." Research Report, no 5. Washington, D.C.: International Food Policy Research Institute.

Hymer, Stephen, and Stephen Resnick. 1969. "A Model of an Agrarian Economy with Nonagricultural Activities." *American Economic Review* 50:493–506.

International Labour Office. 1972. *Employment, Incomes and Equality: A Strategy for Discovering Productive Employment in Kenya.* Geneva: ILO.

———. 1974. *Sharing in Development: A Programme of Employment, Equity and Growth for the Philippines.* Geneva: ILO.

Johnston, Bruce F., and Peter Kilby. 1975. *Agriculture and Structural Transformation: Economic Strategies in Late-Developing Countries.* London: Oxford University Press.

Karsten, Detlev. 1972. *The Economics of Handicrafts in Traditional Societies.* Munich: Weltforum Verlag.

Kilby, Peter, 1979. "Evaluating Technical Assistance." *World Development* 7, no. 3.

Kilby, Peter, Carl Liedholm, and Richard Meyer. 1984. "Working Capital and Nonfarm Rural Enterprises." In *Undermining Rural Development with Cheap Credit,* edited by D. Adams and J. Von Pischke. Boulder, Colo.: Westview Press.

King, Robert P., and Derek Byerlee. 1978. "Factor Intensities and Locational Linkages of Rural Consumption Patterns in Sierra Leone." *American Journal of Agricultural Economics* 60:197–206.

Liedholm, Carl, and Peter Kilby. 1989. "Nonfarm Activities in the Rural Economy." In *The Balance between Industry and Agriculture in Economic Development,* vol. 2, edited by J. Williamson and V. Panchamukhi. New York: St. Martin's Press.

Liedholm, Carl, and Don Mead. 1987. "Small Scale Industries in Developing Countries: Empirical Evidence and Policy Implications." MSU International Development Papers, no. 9. East Lansing: Michigan State University.

Liedholm, Carl, and Joan Parker. 1989. "Small Scale Manufacturing Growth in Africa: Initial Evidence." MSU International Development Paper, no. 33. East Lansing: Michigan State University.

Little, Ian, Dipak Mazumdar, and John Page. 1987. *Small Manufacturing Enterprises: A Comparative Study of India and Other Countries.* New York: Oxford University Press.

Luning, H. A. 1967. *Economic Aspects of Low Labor Income Farming.* Agricultural Research Report, no. 699. Wageningen, Netherlands: Centre for Agricultural Publications and Documentations.

Mellor, John W. 1976. *The New Economics of Growth.* Ithaca: Cornell University Press.

Norman, David W. 1973. *Methodology and Problems of Farm Management Investigations: Experiences from Northern Nigeria.* African Rural Employment Paper, no. 8. East Lansing: Michigan State University, Department of Agricultural Economics.

Prasad, Kedamath. 1963. *Technological Choice under Developmental Planning (A Case Study of the Small Industries of India).* Bombay: Popular Prakashan.

Resnick, Stephen. 1970. "The Decline of Rural Industry under Export Expansion: A Comparison among Burma, Philippines and Thailand, 1870–1938." *Journal of Economic History* 30:51–73.

Staley, Eugene, and Richard Morse. 1965. *Modern Small Scale Industry for Developing Countries.* New York: McGraw-Hill.

Stallmann, Judith, and James Pease. 1979. "Characteristics of Manufacturing Enterprises by Locality Size in Four Regions of Honduras: Implications for Rural Development." East Lansing: Michigan State University, Department of Agricultural Economics. Mimeo.

Stewart, Frances. 1972. "Choice of Technique in Developing Countries." *Journal of Development Studies* 9:99–121.

World Bank. 1978a. *Rural Enterprise and Nonfarm Employment.* Washington, D.C.: World Bank.

———. 1978b. *Employment and Development in Small Enterprises.* Washington, D.C.: World Bank.

20

Reflections on Land Reform and Farm Size

HANS P. BINSWANGER AND MIRANDA ELGIN

INTRODUCTION

Land reform gives poor people ownership rights or permanent cultivation rights to specific parcels of land. It makes sense when it increases their income, consumption, or wealth. And it fails if their consumption does not increase—or is reduced.

The Zamindari Abolition Act for Eastern India and the postwar land reforms in Iran, Japan, and China are outstanding examples of successful land reforms. China's creation of family farms from collectives—under the household responsibility system—in 1978 and the Philippines' tenancy reform in 1972 are other examples of successful land reforms. Neither provided ownership rights to the farmers or tenants, but they did provide permanent cultivation rights; and by fixing ceilings on rents, they gave farmers a portion of the land rent. Under both of these reforms, agricultural productivity started to grow faster. Between 1978 and 1984 output in Chinese agriculture increased by 61 percent. Otsuka's study (1988) of the impact of the 1962 Philippines Land Reform Code and its implementation in 1973 concludes that the reform has successfully broken up large ownership holdings. The result has been greater social equity and higher agricultural productivity, as tenants adopt the modern seed technology.

Another success is Kenya's Land Settlement program in the 1960s. Soon after independence, with funding from the British, the government bought large estates from white farmers, subdivided the land into small farms, and redistributed them to the African farmers. Incomes and productivity shot up almost immediately.

By contrast, Algeria's nationalization of French estates in 1964 created large cooperative farms that gave few direct incentives to workers. The state retained ownership of the land and appointed managers to run the farms. It paid cooperative members what amounted to a wage, giving them neither ownership nor cultivation

HANS P. BINSWANGER is an agricultural economist with the World Bank, Washington, D.C. MIRANDA ELGIN is a consultant to the World Bank.

Originally titled "What Are the Prospects for Land Reform," this paper was presented at the Twentieth International Conference of Agricultural Economists, Buenos Aires, 24–31 August 1988. It is reprinted by permission of the International Association of Agricultural Economists and the authors.

rights. Consequently, the real rate of growth in agriculture fell from 1 percent a year in the 1960s to 0.2 percent in the period 1969/71 to 1978/80 (Cleaver 1982).

Today, in recognition of this failure, the Algerian government is reforming the state farm sector. Under its 1987 land reforms, the government dismantled the state farms—which had about 60 percent of the country's agricultural potential—and replaced them with about 25,000 newly formed collectives. These new collectives give permanent and inheritable cultivation rights to groups and individual households. But the sudden switch in policy has yet to convince farmers of the permanency of their new land rights. And the lack of government guarantees in the law may mean that investments and the maintenance of land improvements will remain suboptimal.

WHY DOES LAND REFORM MAKE ECONOMIC SENSE?

If efficient small farms replace inefficient large farms, there is a benefit. But if smaller farms are not as efficient, there is a loss. Berry and Cline (1979) have shown that, in many countries, productivity is higher on small farms than larger farms (table 1). However, many question whether these findings really mean that transfers of land from large to small farms increase output. Some critics have tried to show that the observed differences in efficiency disappear when differences in land quality are accounted for, arguing that larger farms often are on poorer quality land. Bhalla (1983) used the Indian Fertilizer Demand Survey to try to eliminate the land quality differences statistically. He found that when soil quality variables are introduced, the inverse relationship declines for almost all the states. This de-

TABLE 1
PRODUCTIVITY DIFFERENCES BY FARM SIZE FOR SELECTED COUNTRIES

Farm Size[a] *(Hectares)*	*Northeast Brazil[b]*	*Punjab, Pakistan[c]*	*Muda, Malaysia[d]*
Small farm	563 (10.0–49.9)	274 (5.1–10.1)	148 (0.7–1.0)
Largest farm	100 (500+)	100 (20+)	100 (5.7–11.3)

SOURCE: Berry and Cline 1979.

[a] 100 = largest farm size compared with second smallest farm size. Second smallest farm size used in calculations to avoid abnormal productivity results often recorded for the smallest plots.

[b] Table 4-1, Berry and Cline 1979. Northeastern Brazil, 1973: Production per Unit of Available Land Resource, by Farm Size Group (p. 46). Index taken using average gross receipts/area for size group 2 (small) and 6 (large), averaged for all zones excluding zone F, where sugarcane and cocoa plantations skew productivity average for large farms.

[c] Table 4-29. Relative Land Productivity by Farm Size: Agricultural Census and FABS Survey-based Estimates Compared, 1968–69 (p. 84). Index taken using value added per cultivated acre for second smallest size group and largest.

[d] Table 4-48. Factor Productivity of Muda River Farms by Size, Double Croppers, 1972–73 (p. 117). Index taken from value added in agriculture/relong (0.283 ha = 1 relong).

cline is observed for both the magnitude and the significance of the coefficient for land. Kutcher and Scandizzo's (1981) similar work in Northeast Brazil shows that productivity differences between large and small farms do decline, but that they do not disappear. Even after adjusting for the proportion of farmland used for crops and for land value, they still came up with declines in productivity with respect to farm size, with an average elasticity of -0.69 (excluding the humid Southeast, where sugarcane and cocoa plantations skew productivity in most large farms).

WHY SMALL FARMS ARE MORE EFFICIENT THAN LARGE FARMS

Binswanger and Rosenzweig's theoretical study (1986) shows that the main reason for the lower productivity of large farms is that they use more hired labor than do smaller family farms, and family workers are cheaper and more efficient than hired workers. First, family members receive a share of profits and therefore have more incentive than hired wage workers to work for given supervision. Second, there are no hiring and search costs for family labor. And third, unlike hired labor, each family member takes a share of the risk.

The diseconomies of scale associated with hired labor can be partly circumvented by rental markets for land. Over the course of history, most large land owners have realized that family labor is cheaper than hired labor. So, rather than manage hired labor, they rent their land to tenants, taking advantage of the lower cost of family labor. Even if the optimum farm operation is small, the size of land holdings can be large since it is fairly simple to subdivide and rent out smaller holdings.

The subdivision of plantations into small tenant farms in the southern United States after the Civil War illustrates this point. When cheap slave labor became unavailable, the Southern farmers soon found that output and incomes rose if they subdivided and rented out their holdings. Similarly, the Zamindars in Eastern India, and the landlords in China, Japan, Taiwan, and Iran all developed closely supervised, subdivided holdings that they rented out. The systems allowed the landowners to circumvent the higher labor cost of large farming operations and to take advantage of cheap family labor.

Tenancy has its own incentive problems, because sharecroppers do not receive their marginal product. But here, too, landlords have ways to structure their contracts with tenants to circumvent or minimize these problems. The landlords might share in the cost of fertilizers and seeds, tightly supervise the operations of farms, and provide the tenant with credit.

Although these ways of restructuring contracts can reduce the incentive problems, they cannot overcome them. Shaban (1987) shows that in six South Indian villages, inputs and outputs per acre are higher on the owned plots of a mixed sharecropper than on fully sharecropped plots. The difference ranges between 19 and 55 percent for inputs and is 33 percent for output. These differences may be upper bounds, because mixed sharecroppers have the opportunity to divert inputs from the sharecropped plots to their own plots. Otsuka and Hayami's (1988) review shows that the difference between plots of pure sharecroppers and pure owner-operators are smaller. The upshot of the long debate is that tenants are less efficient than owners, but not as much as expected.

Where large landlords have used whole farm tenants on a large scale and constituted a hated class of absentee owners, land reform has succeeded. Land reforms in Iran, Japan, and Taiwan, and under the Zamindari Abolition Act in India were a simple transfer of the land to the former tenant. The reforms owe their success to the fact that the farmers knew the land, had draft animals, family labor, implements, and farm management skills. Today, there are almost no such large-scale opportunities left.

Collective farms suffer from the same labor disincentives as hired labor. These effects are often aggravated by an ideological reluctance to use piece rates and other output-based payment systems. In addition, households in collectives have to take savings and investment decisions jointly—an extremely difficult task if there are wide differences in preferences for consumption over time.

The size of these disincentives can be enormous. A large proportion of Soviet agricultural output is produced not by the state and collective farms but by plots allocated to individuals. Comparing productivity on collectively and privately farmed plots is complicated because the product mix differs and land quality may not be the same. Moreover, inputs may be diverted from collectively managed plots to private plots. Nevertheless the productivity differences are so large as to be noteworthy. Private household plots in the USSR, held by 23 million families (Shamelev 1982), account for only 3 percent of the total sown area, but they produce more than 25 percent of gross agricultural output. These private plots produce more than 30 percent of the country's total meat and milk and around 60 percent of the fruit and vegetables (Johnson and Brooks 1983). In China, agricultural output rose by 61 percent between 1978 and 1984, following the introduction of the household responsibility system. Data on post-1978 Chinese agricultural performance suggest that just over three-quarters of the measured productivity increase is due to change in individual incentives and the remainder to price increases to farmers.

Decollectivization could, as it did in China, substantially increase productivity in, for example, the Ethiopian State farms, the Soviet Union, some Eastern European systems, and Vietnam. The problems of resettlement or of financing a reform do not arise in centrally planned states, since the governments own the land, the farmers are present, and it is a simple matter to redistribute the land to members of the collectives.

MECHANIZATION AND PRODUCTIVITY

Karl Marx and his followers believed that, as in manufacturing, the economies of scale associated with agricultural mechanization were so large as to make the family farm obsolete. Without question, lumpy inputs such as draft animals or tractors give rise to initial economies of scale of farm holdings—that is, the average costs decrease as the size of the holdings increase. And technical change implies that larger tractors and machines operate at lower unit costs, so optimum operational farm sizes will increase.

So, does mechanization make very small *ownership* holdings obsolete? No. Small owners can rent out their land rather than sell it—and still keep the advantage of owning the land to raise credit (Binswanger and Rosenzweig 1984, 1986). Again, tenancy makes the ownership distribution partly independent of the operational distribution. So, the initial economy of scale associated with machines does not imply that reverse land reform is needed in areas with many small ownership holdings.

Moreover, rental markets for machines can circumvent the economies of scale inherent in machines—but only partly. In the late nineteenth century, mechanical threshers in European agriculture were too large for individual farms. Since threshing can be done at any time of the year, the machines would rotate between farms during the winter months, threshing the individual farm's output. Similarly, today's expanded use of threshers in developing countries reflects a well-developed, efficient rental market for threshers. Tractors are widely rented out to small farms for ploughing in Asia, Africa, and Latin America, but the markets are not as problem-free as for threshers (World Bank 1984). Rental markets are often infeasible for time-bound operations, such as seeding in dry climates, or harvesting where climatic risks are high. Farmers compete for first service and prefer to own their own machines.

Rental markets for machines figure prominently in recent decollectivization efforts. In China, the responsibility system has generated very small farms. Some households specialize in renting machines to these small farms. The system assumes that rental markets for equipment can completely overcome the economies of scale inherent in large equipment. That may be over-optimistic, and some farms seem to be growing in size. Conversely, in Algeria, the 1987 land reforms reduced farm sizes from 1,000 to 80 hectares per farm. The government hoped that these 80 hectare farms would be large enough to use a complete set of machinery. However, Krafft, Rogers, and Rooney (1988) suggest that without rental markets, the small farms cannot use the machines to full capacity. They predict that the increased pressure for a rental market will lead to some households or collectives switching out of farming and specializing in machine rentals.

As Hanumantha Rao (1977) showed, the negative relationship between farm size and productivity initially disappeared with the introduction of tractors in northwest India. But once the size of operational holdings rose, small farms re-emerged with higher productivity rates than large farms. Economies of scale for machines increase the minimum efficient farm size, but by less than expected, because of rental markets.

MODERN TECHNOLOGY, MANAGEMENT, AND FARM SIZE

Management, like a machine, is an indivisible and lumpy input. So the need for management initially gives rise to economies of scale: the better the manager, the larger the optimal farm size. The argument goes like this: modern fertilizer, pesticides, credit, and marketing require modern managerial skills. Therefore optimal farm sizes will tend to increase with technical change.

But too much can be made of this. Some management skills can be rented. If technology becomes too complex, farmers can hire private extension officers by the hour or the day to advise them. The training and visit (T and V) agricultural extension system has been a successful way of reaching and advising small farmers on new technology (Feder and Slade 1984). Another solution to the management problem is contract farming, where large firms provide technical advice, finance, and marketing services to small farmers.

Once again, however, rental markets for management and alternative contractual arrangements can circumvent the lumpiness of management skills only partly: actual farming decisions and the supervision of labor cannot be bought in a market. Managers have to do these tasks themselves. Nor is there any substitution for the important plot-specific experience of the farmer or manager. So the minimal *operational* size for farms may rise over time with the introduction of machines and other technology.

CAN PLANTATIONS BE REDISTRIBUTED?

We have just discussed why small farms are more efficient than large farms. Then why are there plantations—large operational farms—using permanent or semipermanent hired workers rather than family labor? The explanation is that for certain crops, economies of scale in processing and marketing are transmitted to the farm via the necessity of tight coordination between harvesting and processing.

Consider the coordination between harvesting and processing. For products that are easily stored in raw form, such as wheat and rice, a large mill can simply buy the grain at harvest time in the open market and store it for milling throughout the year. This shows that economies of scale in processing alone are not a sufficient condition for plantations—explaining why plantations or contract farming for wheat and other foodgrains have never survived.

In contrast with wheat, the harvesting and processing of sugarcane must be well coordinated. If cut cane is left unprocessed for more than 12 hours, the sugar is lost to fermentation. So the manager must carefully stagger the planting and harvesting to keep the sugar factory operating throughout a large part of the year. Some of the cane must be planted at sub-optimal times of the year, when farmers would be unwilling to do so without compensation. To get around this problem, sugar factories run their own plantations, using a single manager who decides on the tradeoffs between the costs of growing cane and the costs of processing it.

The coordination problems of growing and processing bananas for export are an extreme example. Mature bananas must be put into a cold boat within 24 hours of their harvest to arrest further ripening. This represents an immense challenge for the plantation and the shipping company. The coordination is possible if the planter operates a large enough number of plantations in a given area to ensure that a boat will get filled and if he can be sure that a boat will arrive when the bananas mature. So, some of the world's largest owner-operations are banana companies whose holdings include dozens of plantations operated by hired managers. Local banana markets, by contrast, can be served by trucks or rail. These markets are usually served by small owner-operators.

Contract farming can, depending on the crop, substitute for the plantation. For sugarcane, contracting with small farmers is widespread throughout India, Thailand, for example. For bananas, however, the quality controls are so rigorous that contract farming is less feasible. Hayami, Adriano, and Quisumbing (1987) have proposed redistributing the Philippine banana plantations to smallholders, who would then produce under contract. The proposal is to create farms of perhaps 20 to 30 hectares, but this farm size would preclude distribution of land to the poor. Holdings of 5 to 6 hectares are too small to meet the demands of tightly scheduled contracts. In Central America, when legislation prevented the multinationals from owning large plantations, the major banana companies increased their supplies from contract farms. But these farms typically have hundreds of hectares, and their contracts are so tight that they are virtually managed by the multinationals. For this reason, the proposal to split the banana plantations into small operational holdings would be unlikely to lead to an internationally competitive banana industry.

REMAINING OPPORTUNITIES FOR LAND REFORM

Most of the large ownership holdings operated by tenants have disappeared or been reformed—those in India, Iran, and China, to name a few. Left are the agricultural systems that are difficult to reform for political and economic reasons. Where large farms—30–40 hectares—are interspersed with medium and smaller farms, as in parts of South Asia, large farms are owner-operated and are difficult to reform. The same is true of collective farms in the Soviet Union, Eastern Europe, Vietnam, and Ethiopia. As we just described, plantations cannot easily be distributed without efficiency losses.

The only remaining opportunities for reform are the large-scale farms in Brazil, Nicaragua, Guatemala, and other Latin American countries, and in Zimbabwe and South Africa. During colonial times, landowners in these countries ousted the native populations from much of the most fertile areas and forced them into generally infertile mountain or dryland areas. As late as 1964 in Zimbabwe, less than six thousand white farmers consolidated their occupation of nearly half the land—and it was the best land—leaving 800,000 African farms on the other half, which was poor quality land. Despite attempts since 1979 to reform and resettle the African farmers, the situation remains largely unchanged. The sizes of the large estates in these countries exceed what could be justified by the economies of scale of machines or management skills. Farm size productivity differences between these estates and smallholdings are often huge, providing strong economic justification for land reform.

However, land reform in these countries would require resettlement which is a complex process. First, the resettled people have to acquire capital and farming skills appropriate to the new area. This is an important difference between resettlement and simply giving the land to preexisting tenants. Second, the settlers may not be compatible ethnically. Third, new settlements of this kind require costly infrastructure and support services.

Some of these problems can be avoided. Large Latin American farms used to be operated with tenants, hired labor, or as Haciendas. Under the hacienda system, wage-earning laborers are given small plots of land for their own cultivation. In the last 30 years, however, tenants and workers have been driven off these holdings (de Janvry and Sadoulet 1986). Ironically, they have been driven off by well-meaning but perverse reforms—tenancy and labor law reforms. In Brazil, for example, the 1964 Estatuta da Terra imposed ceilings on fixed rents, limits on the share of output that an owner could obtain from the tenant, and provisions giving security to long-term tenants, leading to a practical loss of ownership. In addition, labor laws made it illegal for workers to receive payments in kind. Under such circumstances, any rational owner would try to evict tenants and long-term workers. Alternatively, owners might try to sell their land, but subsidies for mechanization and for credit have provided impressive "gifts" to large farmers. The government's policy mix has encouraged large farmers to mechanize or convert to ranching and to shed laborers and tenants, systematically destroying the poor's opportunities for employment or self-employment.

HOW TO PAY FOR LAND TRANSFERS

SPECIAL PROBLEMS OF POOR FARMERS

Despite the difficulties of reforming these remaining systems of large farms, the economic benefits would probably be large. The question then remains, If small farms are so much more efficient, why do small, poor farmers not buy land from large farmers? The main reason is that even under ideal circumstances, they cannot buy that land without curtailing their consumption, because they have no equity.

Given a perfect market situation, the value of land reflects the present value of agricultural profits, capitalized at the opportunity cost of capital. If the poor have to use credit to buy land at its present value, the only income stream they have available for consumption is the imputed value of family labor. They must use the remaining profits to pay for the loan. If the poor can get the same wage in the labor market, they are not any better off as landowners than they would be as workers. This example is, moreover, an ideal situation, in which the interest rate paid by the poor is equal to the interest rate that the most creditworthy borrowers can get. The poor generally have to pay higher interest rates and therefore have to reduce consumption below what they could have earned in the labor market.

If, in a less than ideal situation, the value of the land exceeds the capitalized agricultural profits, the poor must cut consumption below the imputed value of family labor to pay for the land. Anything that drives the land price above the capitalized value of the agricultural income stream thus makes it impossible for the poor to buy land without reducing consumption.

In most real world situations, several other income streams are capitalized into the land price. First, with populations growing and the demand for land increasing, some of the expected future real appreciation of the land price is capitalized into the current land price. The only way a poor person could have access to that income stream is by selling off a small parcel of land every year to pay for his interest cost. This is clearly infeasible for smallholders.

Second, where land ownership becomes attractive as a hedge against inflation, an inflation premium is built into the real land price, as is clearly shown by Brandao and Rezende (1988) for Brazil.

Third, tax breaks are often capitalized in the land price. Most countries exempt agricultural income from income tax; and even where there is no general exemption, depreciation allowances are so generous that nobody with agricultural income pays any income tax on it. But, since the poor have a zero tax rate anyway, they receive no such benefit from the income tax break.

Fourth, owners of large holdings have a cost advantage in securing credit, even in the absence of credit subsidies, and these credit cost advantages are capitalized into land values as well (Binswanger and Rosenzweig 1986). Official credit systems often allocate the bulk of credit to large farmers, further increasing this credit cost advantage. Brandao and Rezende (1988) demonstrate econometrically how these credit subsidies are capitalized into land prices.

In sum, real future appreciation, inflation premium, income tax exemptions, and credit cost advantages of large ownership holdings raise the land price far beyond the capitalized value of agricultural profits. Agricultural economists know this problem well. When they try to compute the overall rate of return of capital invested in agriculture, they usually find that the opportunity cost of capital exceeds the rate of return in agriculture. In Switzerland the ratio is 5:1. And according to every farm management study in India, agriculture is unprofitable when measured at the opportunity cost of capital. Given this situation, the productivity advantage of the small farmers would have to be immense to enable the assetless poor to finance land purchases out of agricultural profits. So, a land market generally cannot substitute for a land reform.

Making a Land Reform Stick

If governments introduce a land reform into a distorted environment that favors large farms, one would expect the recipients—small farmers—to sell out to the large farmers, defeating the purposes of land reform. Because such distortions as income tax exemptions or credit distortions favor the rich, a precondition for a land reform is the prior elimination of all distortions favoring large farms. For example, to institute a land reform under the current policy regime in Brazil would be foolhardy. Tough policy choices eliminating explicit and implicit subsidies to large farmers must be made in order for a land reform to stick.

Progressive Land Taxes and the Land Market

With a progressive land tax, the price of land in large ownership holdings would drop. Could governments impose a large enough land tax to reduce land prices to a level that the poor could afford? The World Bank has considered this idea in Zimbabwe, and a land tax has been proposed as the main component of a Philippine land reform. Brazil actually has a progressive land tax in place.

In principle, governments can impose a large enough land tax to offset any non-agricultural premium on land prices in large farms. But this is unlikely to benefit the truly poor, because they still need some equity capital to buy the land. Even under the best of circumstances, a progressive land tax redistributes land from the rich to the middle class. And circumstances are seldom the best, because governments have used land taxes to try to raise agricultural productivity, cutting the tax rate for large farms that use land intensively or are very productive. In Brazil, farmers can cut their land tax rate in half by converting idle land or land under forestry into pasture; with modest crop production, they can cut their land tax almost to zero. So, all the Brazilian system does is provide an additional incentive to ranching or extensive crop production.[1] It does not increase the number of land sales from large farmers to small farmers.

HAVING BENEFICIARIES PAY FOR A LAND REFORM

If governments cannot use the voluntary land market to reform the size of land holding, can the beneficiaries of compulsory reform be made to pay? Here again the typical proposal is for the Philippines and Brazil. The state buys the land and compensates the owners at market prices with land reform bonds, instead of cash. It services the interest and principal payments, which it then recovers from the beneficiaries. Sometimes, private agencies, like the Guatemala Rural Development Foundation, execute such programs of land redistribution. The private agency buys large estates, subdivides them, and sells the plots to settlers. Of course, if the land price contains any premium reflecting nonagricultural income streams, the beneficiaries of these schemes will not be able to pay.

If such schemes are implemented in the face of these problems, there are three likely outcomes. First, the beneficiaries default and the program stops. Many ambitious land reform plans simply peter out; this has been a common outcome in Latin American countries (de Janvry and Sadoulet, 1989). Second, bonds may have built-in features that erode their real value over time. So, although landowners receive their nominal value, time erodes the real market value and the government makes no compensation for this loss. Most landowners naturally oppose such thinly disguised expropriation. Third, governments may fail to repay loans from foreign lenders, making the programs effectively funded by a grant.

Since the beneficiaries of a land reform cannot pay for their land, the land purchases must be financed by foreign grants, internal tax revenues, or inflationary monetary expansion, or by a combination of the three. The grants provide the equity that the poor lack. Credit to beneficiaries can play a supplementary but only minor role.

Because the poor cannot pay for land reform, we believe that the outlook for land reform is very bleak. Landowners will oppose any form of open or disguised expropriation, foreign grants will not materialize, and governments will not allocate domestic resources for the purpose.

INCREASING THE OPPORTUNITIES FOR THE POOR
IN AGRICULTURE

Many governments have tried to improve the tenancy terms of poor sharecroppers by legislation, but these attempts have largely had perverse results. First, owners have many ways of getting around the legislation—say, by reducing the size of plots allocated to tenants or by reducing credit, fertilizer, or other inputs they might provide the tenant. Second, if owners cannot circumvent the laws, they expel tenants and revert to self-cultivation. As discussed earlier, the impact of many of these tenancy reforms has reduced the welfare of tenants.

If land reform cannot be financed and tenancy reform leads to perverse results, other policies and programs must be pursued to assist the landless poor and small farmers. Such approaches, far from being new, are the standard fare of small farmer development programs, and they have enjoyed much success. They continue to be valid, and they should be pursued:

First, governments should reform the policies that favor large farmers and that lead to large land premiums over the capitalized value of agricultural profits. Also, they should eliminate income tax exemptions for agriculture and subsidized credit for large farmers.

Second, governments should eliminate explicit and implicit subsidies to machines. As an example, the 1986 U.S. Tax Reform Act lengthened the recovery rates on such depreciable assets as agricultural machinery from five to seven years and repealed the investment tax credit for farmers.

Third, governments should undo perverse tenancy reforms and perverse labor laws, allowing people to rent out their land again or make more intensive use of labor. Hayami's proposal for the newly planned reforms in the Philippines calls explicitly for the abolition of all constraints on tenancy. In Latin America, the abolition of such constraints would greatly benefit self-employment in agriculture.

Fourth, governments should redistribute the land they already own, but with some reasonable ceilings on the size of holdings. In the Brazilian Amazon, squatters can obtain up to 3,000 hectares of land if they clear trees from half of it. This accelerates deforestation and drastically reduces the land available to smallholders. A more sensible policy would be a land ceiling of 50 to 100 hectares. A good example of a successful redistribution scheme, using a smaller land allocation, is the U.S. Homestead Act, which opened the Midwest to settlers in the nineteenth century.

Fifth, efforts should be made to give smallholders adequate titles. Even if their claims to the land are secure, they cannot compete for official credit without titles. Gershon Feder's 1988 study of land titling in Thailand shows how large the disadvantages can be for small farmers lacking deeds of ownership. As mentioned earlier, the recent land reforms in Algeria have not given firm guarantees of land tenure to the new farmers, so the farmers there will continue to have difficulty in raising loans from banks.

Sixth, special efforts should be devoted to programs that assist small farmers.

Very popular in the 1970s, these projects are still an integral part of the World Bank's poverty alleviation strategy. Such schemes as area development programs, the T and V extension programs, and the large dairy projects along the lines of the Anand Dairy Cooperative have done much to help small farmers. Despite these successes, discussion in recent years has often focused on failed small farm projects. These occurred where general economic policies were stacked against the farm sector or where the project design was excessively complex for the implementation capacity of the agricultural services. In sub-Saharan Africa, many projects have also focused on zones with very little agroclimatic potential and where no new high pay-off technology exists. So the failures do not put in question the small farmer development programs, but rather provide lessons of how better to design them.

CONCLUSION

Land reform is unlikely to be a major tool for improving the welfare of the poor in developing countries. Even where it would make a lot of economic sense, it will not happen, because the beneficiaries cannot pay for the land reform, implying the need for confiscating appropriations or imposing large tax costs, neither of which is politically palatable. Consequently, other measures have to be devised to improve poor people's access to land or to increase their income from agriculture. But these measures can help small farmers only if governments abandon policies that favor large farms and that put premiums on land prices. A much stronger commitment from governments and agencies is thus needed to tackle these policy issues and thereby reduce incentives to accumulate large ownership holdings, increase agricultural production, and assure greater equity and self-employment in agriculture.

NOTES

1. This is one measure which de Janvry and Sadoulet (1989) describe as part of the state's strategy to force large farmers to modernize as an alternative to land reform. Other elements of the strategy are the credit subsidies discussed earlier in this paper. Also see de Janvry and Sadoulet, chapter 28 in this volume. —ED.

REFERENCES

Berry, R. A., and W. R. Cline. 1979. *Agrarian Structure and Productivity in Developing Countries.* Baltimore: Johns Hopkins University Press.

Bhalla, G. S. 1983. *The Green Revolution and the Small Peasant: A Study of Income Distribution among Punjab Cultivators.* New Delhi: Concept Publishers.

Binswanger, H. P., and M. R. Rosenzweig, eds. 1984. *Contractual Arrangements, Employment, and Wages in Rural Labor Markets in Asia.* New Haven: Yale University Press.

———. 1986. "Behavioural and Material Determinants of Production Relations in Agriculture." *Journal of Development Studies* 22, no. 3 (April).

Brandao, A., and G. Rezende. 1988. "The Behavior of Land Prices and Land Rents in Brazil." Paper presented at the Twentieth International Conference of Agricultural Economists, Buenos Aires, August 24–31.

Cleaver, Kevin M. 1982. *Agricultural Development Experience of Algeria, Morocco, and Tunisia: A Comparison of Strategies for Growth.* Washington, D.C.: World Bank.

de Janvry, Alain, and Elisabeth Sadoulet. 1989. "A Study in Resistance to Institutional Change: The Lost Game of Latin American Land Reform." *World Development* 17, no. 9 (September): 1397–1408.

Feder, G. 1988. "The Implications of Land Registration and Titling in Thailand." Paper presented at the Twentieth International Conference of Agricultural Economists, Buenos Aires, August 24–31.

Feder, G., and R. Slade. 1984. *Aspects of the Training and Visit System of Agricultural Extension in India: A Comparative Analysis.* Staff Working Paper 656. Washington, D.C.: World Bank.

Hayami, Y., L. S. Adriano, and A. R. Quisumbing. 1987. *Agribusiness and Agrarian Reform: A View from the Banana and Pineapple Plantations.* Los Baños, University of the Philippines, November.

Johnson, D. G., and K. M. Brooks. 1983. *Prospects for Soviet Agriculture in the 1980s.* Bloomington: Indiana University Press.

Krafft, N., R. Rogers, and C. Rooney. 1988. "Algeria After Land Reform: Implementing the Break-up of the State Farms." Washington, D.C.: World Bank.

Kutcher, G. P., and P. L. Scandizzo. 1981. *The Agricultural Economy of Northeast Brazil.* Washington, D.C.: World Bank.

Otsuka, Keijiro. 1988. *The Determinants and Consequences of Land Reform Implementation in the Philippines.* Los Baños: International Rice Research Institute.

Otsuka, Keijiro, and Yujiro Hayami. 1988. "Theories of Share Tenancy: A Critical Survey." *Economic Development and Cultural Change* 37, no. 1 (October): 31–68.

Rao, Hanumantha. 1977. *Technological Change and Distribution of Gains in Indian Agriculture.* New Delhi: Macmillan.

Shaban, R. A. 1987. "Testing between Competing Models of Sharecropping." *Journal of Political Economy* 95 (5): 893–920.

Shamelev, G. 1982. "Social Production and Personal Household Plots." *Problems of Economics* 25 (June): 39–54.

World Bank. 1984. *Agricultural Mechanization—A Comparative Historical Perspective.* Washington, D.C.: World Bank.

21

Rural Financial Markets in Low-Income Countries

DALE W ADAMS AND ROBERT C. VOGEL

INTRODUCTION

During the past two decades many low-income countries (LICs) have rapidly expanded the volume of their agricultural loans as well as the number of rural offices of financial intermediaries. Governments have often used credit programs to promote agricultural output and have also attempted to help the rural poor through cheap credit. As with most development efforts, these programs have included both successes and failures. Some credit efforts, for example, have encountered serious loan recovery problems, and many LICs have found it easier to expand the volume of short-term credit than to increase long-term rural loans. Loan recovery problems, combined with relatively large transaction costs, have sometimes caused lenders to collapse.

Over the past few years a large number of studies, evaluations, and publications have challenged traditional views on rural finance. Since most of these new views are summarized in Donald (1976), Von Pischke et al. (1983), and Adams et al. (1984), we cite extensively from these sources as we outline the major points of controversy between the new and traditional views. Our presentation is divided into eight parts. The next section provides a brief discussion of the contribution that rural financial markets (RFMs) make to development. Following sections cover the main controversies, lessons, and conclusions that emerge from the recent experience with RFMs in low-income countries.

FINANCE AND RURAL DEVELOPMENT

Most financial markets conform to the contours of the societies they serve. In those societies where economic management is centralized, lending decisions tend to be rigid, concentrated, and programmed, while in societies where production decisions are dispersed, financial markets must be flexible. In most cases financial

DALE W ADAMS is professor of agricultural economics, Ohio State University. ROBERT C. VOGEL is a consultant in agricultural economics, Great Falls, Virginia.

Reprinted from *World Development* 14, no. 4, 477–87, 1986 by permission of Pergamon Press and the authors. Copyright © 1986 Pergamon Press.

markets play a more dynamic role in market-oriented countries than in centrally-planned economies.

Typically, intermediaries in rural financial markets are diverse across countries but there is more uniformity in agricultural credit policy objectives, rural financial policies, and in problems encountered. It is common for RFMs to suffer more severe problems than are found in other segments of a country's financial system, because of the difficulty of serving clients who are widely dispersed, borrowers who make large numbers of small transactions, and clients who operate in an industry that experiences unanticipated changes in prices, incomes, and yields. Also, because adversities in rural areas often affect a large number of households at the same time, it is difficult for lenders to diversify portfolios to cushion economic shocks.

Evaluations of RFM projects are often misleading because the fungibility of financial instruments is poorly understood. Fungibility, or interchangeability, means that one unit of money, be it owned or borrowed, is just like any other unit of money (Von Pischke et al. 1983). An example may clarify how fungibility accompanies borrowing. Assume that, without borrowing, a farm household has two units of money and plans to spend one unit on consumption and the other on agricultural production during a given time period. Further assume that, a short time later, an agricultural bank lends the household additional money, which increases the household's money holdings to three units, and that the lender specifies that the loan be used for agricultural production.

The household can make three choices as a result of the loan: (1) It can double its expenditure on agricultural production by using all of the borrowed money to buy agricultural inputs. This would result in 100 percent additionality, because all of the marginal liquidity provided by the loan would be spent for agricultural inputs—fulfilling the loan objectives. (2) Alternatively, the household may decide to apply the borrowed money to buying agricultural inputs, but use all of its own money, two units, to double household consumption. This choice would result in 100 percent financial substitution and fulfill the letter of the loan agreement, but not the spirit. The loan would cause increased consumption, not increased use of agricultural inputs, an outcome lenders find virtually impossible to control. Some financial substitution is involved in virtually every loan. (3) It is also possible that the household may decide to divert all of the borrowed funds, as well as owned-funds, to consumption, effectively tripling consumption. The additional liquidity provided by the loan may allow the household to buy some costly consumer item that it was unable to buy with just its own funds. While this diversion of funds may be illegal, it is difficult to control when large numbers of borrowers are involved and they are geographically dispersed. Low and uncertain returns to farm investments nurture loan diversion. Moreover, granting loans in kind does not obviate fungibility because borrowers can usually sell unwanted inputs provided by the lender in secondary markets and realize cash to buy any good or service that is available in the market.

Because of fungibility and the numerousness of borrowers and lenders that par-

ticipate in decentralized RFMs, it is virtually impossible for policy makers to allocate loans effectively in accord with a credit allocation plan (Adams et al. 1984).
For example, policy makers may program cheap loans for a crop such as rice and
try to force financial intermediaries to extend loans for that purpose. The intent
may be to compensate rice farmers for low rice prices through cheap credit, but the
low rice prices cause the expected returns from investments in rice growing also to
be low. Under these circumstances borrowers will divert the additional liquidity
provided by rice loans to activities that provide higher returns (Adams et al. 1984).
Because of fungibility and the large number of participants in RFMs, the ability of
credit planners to target loans to specific activities is illusory.

INSTITUTIONAL FORM

During the past thirty years many institutions have been formed to provide rural
financial services in LICs (Von Pischke et al. 1983). The organizational form has
depended on the dominant economic philosophy of the country, the nature of the
formal financial system, and the interests of international donors at the time. As a
result, a large variety of rural financial intermediaries is found across LICs, and
these can be grouped into four categories: cooperatives, various types of government-owned agricultural banks, rural private banks, and credit activities included
in multipurpose development agencies. Most countries have experimented with
more than one institutional form and often sustain several types of rural lending
agencies.

Initially, many newly created credit agencies were modeled after those in high-
income countries. Examples of this are the farmers' associations in Taiwan and
South Korea that were patterned after farmers' associations in Japan; rural private
banks in Vietnam and the Philippines based on similar banks in the United States;
and credit unions in Africa and Latin America similar to credit unions in North
America (Von Pischke et al. 1983). A number of countries, especially in Latin
America, have also formed supervised credit programs for small farmers, similar
to the Farmers Home Administration's activities in the United States. Relatively
few of these programs, however, persisted for long. In some cases the technical
assistance provided was of little use to the borrower, and in most cases the cost of
providing supervision was prohibitively expensive for the intermediary (e.g.,
Colombia, Jamaica, Dominican Republic, El Salvador). Even in the best-run programs, administrative costs are a quarter or more of the value of the loans made,
well in excess of the intermediary's interest income. In some cases loan supervision
turned out to be an expensive form of loan collection.

Recently, there has been greater emphasis on developing financial intermediaries
unique to LICs or on strengthening existing intermediaries. Also, there is now less
emphasis on substituting formal for informal credit. Recent research from various
countries has shown that monopoly profits in informal lending are less than had
been widely assumed and that informal lenders provide some financial services
more efficiently than formal credit programs do (Von Pischke et al. 1983). Several

countries, including Malaysia, have even experimented with marketing intermediaries as retail outlets for loans from government credit agencies. An expansion of the formal credit system often causes growth in informal finance, results in more competition, and reduces any monopoly profits found in informal lending.

LESSONS

Most institutional forms for providing financial services in rural areas have had serious shortcomings or have failed in some LICs, while in other countries virtually every institutional form has been at least moderately successful (Schaefer-Kehnert and Von Pischke 1984). While certain institutions, such as cooperatives, work better in some societies than in others, it appears that any financial intermediary will flounder if the sector it serves is heavily taxed or if financial intermediaries themselves are taxed through interest rate ceilings or targeted credit programs. Institutions that mobilize savings as well as lend are more likely to be viable than intermediaries that only lend. Policies, not organizational form, appear to be the main determinant of institutional success or failure.

ECONOMIC RETURNS IN AGRICULTURE

The well-being of financial markets partly depends on the economic vitality of the clients they serve. If farmers receive low prices for their products because of distorted exchange rates, food price controls, imports of cheap food, or inefficient markets, their ability to use financial markets will be diminished; they will be less willing to borrow, less able to repay loans, and will have less capacity to save. Low and unstable yields and lack of public investment in agriculture reinforce adverse effects of low farm prices. It is much easier to develop RFMs that are self-sustaining when returns to agricultural investments are high and relatively stable and rural incomes are increasing.

It is common for governments to attempt to compensate farmers for adverse effects of other economic policies by providing loans at low interest rates. The government may realize that farmers are "taxed" through low product prices resulting from food price controls and that this tax decreases farm production. The government may also believe that it is impossible to remove this tax and, as a result, decide to use a second-best policy of giving farmers an offsetting "subsidy" through cheap credit. Policy makers hope that the cheap credit will encourage borrowers to increase production and that the low-interest-rate subsidy will make up for farmers' income losses.

The second-best argument has serious shortcomings when used to justify cheap credit as an equitable and efficient way to compensate farmers for the adverse effects of other policies. When it is in their interest to do so, lenders—like borrowers—exercise fungibility and substitute targeted funds for owned funds in their loan portfolios, thus defeating the plans of policy makers who program loans. Low interest rates induce both borrower and lender to concentrate loans in the hands of the well-to-do (Adams et al. 1984). Lenders have powerful incentives to minimize their cost of lending by concentrating cheap credit in loans to a select few: for example, those who have borrowed previously, those with excellent loan collateral, and those who take large loans. At the same time, borrowers with clout have strong incentives to capture as much of the cheap credit as possible. These reinforcing incentives result in a small number of farmers getting most of the inexpensive credit.

Because only those who receive cheap loans are subsidized by low interest rates, while all who produce the low-priced product are taxed, there is an inefficient match between the incidence of the tax and subsidy. Those with no loans, or those receiving only small amounts, get little or no compensation (Von Pischke et al. 1983). Those who do not receive loans cannot be expected to increase the output of products with depressed prices resulting from government policy. Even those producers who receive cheap loans are not induced to make investments that are privately unprofitable. In most cases, changes in the interest rate on a loan do not alter the relative profitability of an investment alternative whose returns may be depressed because of government action or inaction.

Also, because cheap loans tend to be concentrated in relatively few hands, second-best policies result in less equitable income distribution. Since the size of the interest rate subsidy is proportional to the amount of the loan, large borrowers receive large subsidies while borrowers of small amounts receive small subsidies (Adams et al. 1984). Since the majority of farmers do not get any cheap loans, they realize no subsidy. Because credit access and loan size are highly correlated with income levels and assets, the well-to-do benefit most from cheap credit. As a result, the second-best argument comes up short on both equity and efficiency grounds.

LESSONS

It is unrealistic to expect RFMs to work well if the sector they serve is not economically healthy. Moreover, cheap credit, even if abundant, cannot compensate for low incomes or low returns to investment agriculture. Cheap credit does not make an unprofitable investment profitable and is largely captured by the well-to-do, thereby worsening income distribution.

POLICIES AND REGULATIONS

It has been common for governments to attempt to influence lender behavior through regulations. Many such regulations are aimed at tilting the behavior or performance of the financial system toward a preferred group or activity: for example, small farmers, medium- and long-term loans, or land reform participants. Techniques used to target loans can be grouped into five categories: loan portfolio requirements, rediscount facilities, crop or loan insurance, regulations on bank branching, and nationalization of banks.

LOAN PORTFOLIO REQUIREMENTS

Governments commonly try to influence lenders through loan portfolio requirements. This may include setting floors or ceilings on certain types of lending and placing limitations on loan size. For example, in the Philippines, Thailand, India, and Colombia, banks have been required to make at least a certain percentage of their total loans for agricultural purposes. In the Dominican Republic the government has set maximum sizes on loans made by the government-owned agricultural bank. The main problem with a portfolio restriction is that it is relatively easy for the lender to conform to the restriction yet evade its intent. For example, a lender may make multiple medium-sized loans to one individual to evade a loan-size ceiling, or a lender can redefine the purpose of a loan—a loan for purchasing a truck becomes an agricultural transportation loan.

REDISCOUNT FACILITIES

Another popular policy tool has been rediscount facilities. These are windows at the central bank allowing final lenders to discount targeted loans with the central bank and receive funds at concessionary interest rates. Most of the LICs that have large and relatively well-developed financial markets make extensive use of these rediscount facilities. Governments and donor agencies have been particularly aggressive in promoting these facilities as ways of moving their funds into RFMs (Von Pischke et al. 1983). Typically, final lenders are allowed an attractive spread between the concessionary rate paid to the central bank and the rate charged final borrowers. Wide spreads are thought to be an effective way of inducing the lender to stress targeted loans.

There are two weaknesses in rediscount facilities. First, the concessionary interest rates on rediscount lines are usually lower than the rates that intermediaries would otherwise pay to mobilize voluntary private savings. This provides powerful incentives for intermediaries to ignore private deposits, which, in the long run, may result in fewer funds for agricultural lending. Second, concessionary discount facilities have a weak effect on lenders' loan decisions. As mentioned earlier, intermediaries, as well as final borrowers, exercise fungibility when it is in their interest to do so. If governments, for example, impose a low ceiling on the price that farmers receive for their crop, final lenders may be very hesitant to expand lending for the crop in question because expected farm returns for that activity will be low. Lenders typically react to this by transferring their regular clients who satisfy the target criteria to the rediscount line, thereby expanding the volume of funds available for non-target lending.

LOAN AND CROP GUARANTEES

Several LICs (e.g., Mexico and Costa Rica) have made extensive use of guarantees or insurance to lessen lenders' risks from loan default. Loan guarantees from a governmental agency may insure that the bank will be reimbursed for a certain percentage of loan defaults, or the guarantee may be crop insurance that is payable to the intermediary (e.g., the Philippines, Sri Lanka, and India), as the insurer agrees to pay the lender a certain percentage of the loan after crop damages have been verified. The main objective of these guarantees is to induce lenders to extend more loans to a target group by transferring part of the loan recovery risk to other agencies.

There are several problems with loan and crop guarantee programs. First, they are often expensive, as governments may be forced to provide large subsidies to pay for costs of insured defaults not covered by premium payments (as happened in Sri Lanka and Costa Rica). Second, the government is also often required to subsidize administrative costs, particularly in crop insurance programs in the tropics. Third, because crop damage in these areas often affects numerous producers at the same time, a large staff is required to make timely assessments of crop damage. Finally, insurance may weaken the resolve of lenders to collect overdue loans.

RURAL BANK BRANCHES

A few LICs have been very aggressive in promoting new rural banks or rural branches of existing banks. In India and Bangladesh commercial banks are forced to open a certain number of rural branches before they can receive permission to open additional, more profitable urban branches. In Vietnam, the Philippines, and Ghana, donor or government funds have been used to induce the formation of private rural banks, with the funds given or lent to the new bank on concessionary terms. In some cases these funds provide part of the equity needed by the new owners.

Banks may respond to government pressure by building token branch offices in rural areas that are open only a few hours a week or that offer only a limited range of services. In extreme cases, new rural branches may simply mobilize rural savings for use in urban areas because banks may not have incentives to offer a broader range of services (India and Bangladesh).

BANK NATIONALIZATION

A number of LICs have nationalized some or all of their commercial banks. This may occur as a colony becomes an independent nation or as part of an attempt to give governments greater control over financial intermediaries. Costa Rica, for example, nationalized most of its banks over forty years ago, while Mexico has done so within the past several years. India, Pakistan, Sudan, and Bangladesh also have banking systems that are largely nationalized.

Nationalized banks in the subcontinent have been particularly effective in increasing the number of bank branches. It is less clear, however, if nationalized banks are more effective than other financial intermediaries in increasing the financial services available to the rural poor, increasing the amounts of medium- and long-term loans for farmers, providing attractive deposit services, lowering transaction costs associated with financial intermediation, and creating rural financial institutions that are innovative and self-sustaining. Recent research in Costa Rica, for example, has shown that the government-owned financial system is having difficulty extending loans to a larger number of the rural poor. Costa Rica's performance appears no better than that of other LJCs that do not have nationalized banks.

LESSONS

The results of various policy measures aimed at altering lender behavior in favor of a target group or commodity have been mixed. In a few cases the results have been quite different from those intended, and in other cases they have been accompanied by undesirable side effects. In many cases the net result of these policies has been to orient the financial intermediaries away from mobilizing private savings in rural areas and toward obtaining loanable funds from governments and donors.

TRANSACTION COSTS

The resources used for transactions by RFM participants are important measures of performance. Like well-oiled and efficient machines, financial markets that perform with little friction create few transaction costs for participants. Transaction costs for the lender include the expenses of mobilizing funds for on-lending, costs of collecting information about potential borrowers, and costs of extending, maintaining, and collecting loans. A significant portion of these costs may result from loan targeting requirements placed on the lender by policy makers. It is often overlooked that borrowers and savers also incur transaction costs. For small and new borrowers and savers, these costs can be large relative to the size of their transactions. Loan transaction costs, including the time taken to negotiate loans, can be several times the interest paid on loans.

Recent research has shown that the costs of financial intermediation are not shared by borrowers and lenders in fixed proportions (Adams et al. 1984). Under some circumstances lenders may find it in their interest to absorb, for preferred clients, some of the loan transaction costs normally incurred by borrowers. At the same time, a lender may force nonpreferred clients to incur transaction costs normally absorbed by the intermediary, as a way of discouraging them from asking for a loan. An analogous situation can occur for depositors.

Interest rate ceilings limit the ability of intermediaries to ration borrowers, so that increased collateral requirements and reallocation of transaction costs to borrowers are often used as substitute rationing mechanisms. When intermediaries are eager to obtain borrower or saver business, they may reduce transaction costs for preferred clients by sending mobile banks to villages (e.g., the Philippines, Sri Lanka, and Pakistan). They may also allow preferred borrowers to negotiate new loans by phone or by visiting a bank's office only once. Meanwhile, nonpreferred clients may be forced to visit the intermediary many times to negotiate, obtain, and repay the loan (e.g., Sudan, Belize, Brazil), to wait in long lines during each visit, to fill out numerous forms to obtain the loan (e.g., Haiti, Tunisia, Portugal), and also to give gifts to the loan officer for rapid and favorable attention.

Formal lenders in many LICs have experimented with loans to small informal groups of borrowers as a way of reducing loan transaction costs and increasing loan recovery rates (Adams et al. 1984; Von Pischke et al. 1983). Typically, one loan is made to a group of five to twenty farmers, and the loan is negotiated and repaid by a representative of the group (e.g., Ghana, the Philippines, the Dominican Republic, the Ivory Coast, Thailand, and Turkey). Ideally, this procedure would reduce the intermediary's lending costs and reduce the overall costs of obtaining formal loans.

Recent research on group lending shows results that are less positive than originally hoped. While group lending generally reduces loan transaction costs for borrowers, it has had a less positive impact on lenders' transaction costs and on loan recovery. Group loans appear to work best where groups have noncredit reasons for collective actions.

LESSONS

The amount of transaction costs and the way in which they are shared tell a great deal about how RFMs perform. These costs also reveal how intermediaries react to regulations. If financial markets are improving, the total costs of financial intermediation per unit of money handled should decline over time for intermediaries, borrowers, and savers. In most countries, those who work in financial markets are creative, but when markets are heavily regulated, a large part of this creativity is directed to innovations that dilute the effect of regulations on the financial intermediary. Such innovations often increase, rather than decrease, the total cost of financial intermediation.

When loans are targeted, the government or donor agency usually requires intermediaries to adopt new procedures to reach those targeted and also to provide periodic reports on the extent to which program objectives are met. Often, the effect of this targeting is to increase sharply the lender's cost. Extensive loan targeting increases the amount of friction in financial markets and also reduces their operating efficiency.

LOAN REPAYMENT PERFORMANCE

Loan delinquency and default have plagued agricultural credit programs in LICs, especially agricultural development banks (Donald 1976). It is not uncommon to find a quarter or more of loans outstanding with payments overdue, and this is often a substantial underestimation of the problem, because of loan refinancing. Accounting practices used in many LICs also disguise the extent of loan recovery problems.

The traditional view of loan delinquency is that borrowers become delinquent for one of two basic reasons: they are unable to repay or they are unwilling to repay. The inability to repay may result from inadequate incomes, which, in turn, are explained by unexpected events such as bad weather, pests, sudden price declines, or by structural deficiencies such as inadequate markets, weak infrastructure, or poor technology. The main reasons given for the unwillingness to repay are that loans are viewed as grants or political patronage or simply that borrowers plan from the beginning not to repay.

Most empirical research on loan delinquency in LICs involves asking delinquent borrowers why they have failed to repay loans. Not surprisingly, most delinquent borrowers report they were unable to repay, not that they were unwilling to repay. This often leads to the conclusion that little can be done about loan delinquency, short of basic structural reforms in agriculture. Agricultural development banks, especially those that lend to small farmers, are thereby given an excuse for tolerating high rates of loan delinquency.

In recent work on loan delinquency in LICs, it has been shown that delinquency rates are not always high on agricultural loans, even when the lenders are state-owned banks with development objectives (Vogel 1981). In fact, in Costa Rica, delinquency rates were found to be lower on agricultural than on nonagricultural loans and lowest on loans to small farmers. This performance is explained, in part, by the efficient techniques that banks have developed to gather information about potential rural borrowers and also by incentives for bank employees to achieve low delinquency rates and for borrowers to repay promptly in order to maintain access to cheap credit. Other authors have pointed out that patronage and politics are often paramount in the operation of state-owned development banks, so that bank employees may have few incentives to reduce loan delinquency (Von Pischke et al. 1983; Adams et al. 1984).

Increasing awareness of the importance of incentives for both lenders and borrowers in determining loan delinquency can be termed the new view of delinquency, in contrast to the traditional view, in which borrowers are seen as either unable or unwilling to repay. The point of departure for the new view is the costs and benefits to a borrower of repaying or not repaying a loan. A model along such lines has been developed recently in which a utility maximizing borrower is seen as choosing to play either of two lotteries—to repay or to become delinquent (Christen and Vogel 1984). The main advantage to the borrower of playing the repayment lottery is the probability of receiving a larger loan in the future, on which a positive rate of return can be expected. Against this must be weighed the explicit financial charges on the possible new loan, the transactions costs involved in repaying and then negotiating and receiving a new loan, and the timeliness of the new loan. When a borrower chooses to play the delinquency lottery, two main outcomes are possible. The lender may do nothing, in which case the borrower keeps the current loan but is denied future loans from that lender. Or the lender may take strong action so that borrowers lose collateral pledged for loans, in addition to which they may be denied future loans from other lenders. The possible loss from failing to receive new loans may be larger than any other sanction that a lender imposes on a delinquent borrower.

This model has been applied to a sample of some 6,000 loans made by 30 credit unions in Honduras. Results of the sample support the usefulness of this new approach in explaining loan delinquency. The most important factors in determining whether a loan was likely to be delinquent were those related to the borrower's assessment of the probability of obtaining a new larger loan in the future on a timely basis. In contrast, variables traditionally associated with the willingness or ability to repay, such as the stated use of the loan, were not helpful in explaining delinquency.

LESSONS

Some borrowers may fail to repay because they are unable to do so, and other defaulters may never intend to repay under any circumstances. However, the new view of loan delinquency suggests that it is more fruitful to analyze the incentives that borrowers have to repay on time or to become delinquent. Borrowers will find it attractive to repay on time and maintain a good credit rating if they view the lender as able to provide new larger loans in the future on a timely basis with modest borrower transactions costs. The new view is clearly skeptical about the extent to which loan delinquency is beyond the control of the lender and is, hence, skeptical about recommendations to generously refinance over-due loans.

APPROPRIATE INTEREST RATE POLICIES

The traditional view of appropriate interest rates for agricultural loans is that they should be kept low to promote agricultural development and to assist the rural poor. However, it became clear by the early 1970s that agricultural credit projects based on low interest rates were encountering serious difficulties in most LICs (Donald 1976). Some observers began to argue that these widespread difficulties were not due to problems that were unique in each country but rather to the low interest rate policies themselves (Adams et al. 1984; Von Pischke et al. 1983). Cheap loans did not appear to increase agricultural output or encourage the adoption of new technologies and often failed to reach the rural poor. Moreover, low interest rates frequently undermined the financial viability of lenders and discouraged the mobilization of voluntary savings by financial institutions.

To analyze low interest rate policies, it is essential to define what is meant by low and to distinguish among different measures of interest rates. With the prevalence of inflation in LICs over the past decade, it has become necessary to distinguish between nominal and real rates of interest, real rates being those adjusted for the rate of inflation.[1] This adjustment is required because most formal loans are made and repaid in nominal terms (i.e., in money), so when inflation is significant the nominal rate of interest may seem high while the real rate is actually low or even negative. When the real rates are negative (i.e., when the rate of inflation exceeds the nominal rate of interest), borrowers repay lenders less in terms of goods and services than they initially borrowed.

It is also useful to distinguish between the stated rate of interest on a loan and the effective rate; the effective rate takes into account all charges on a loan, including not only fees and commissions but also whether interest is collected in advance and whether compensating balances are required. When governments attempt to set interest rates on loans significantly below equilibrium, lenders often respond by imposing additional charges and conditions that raise effective rates above stated rates. Borrowers will largely be willing to accept these additional charges and conditions as long as effective interest rates remain below what would be paid in competitive markets. Moreover, government regulators will find it difficult to keep up with lenders' innovations that raise effective interest rates above stated rates. These innovations might also be associated with the transfer of loan transaction costs to borrowers.

There are three policies that governments can use to influence interest rates on deposits and formal loans in rural areas: (1) provide concessionary rediscount facilities that effectively cap the rate that intermediaries will pay on rural deposits, (2) directly set ceilings on rates intermediaries may pay on deposits, and (3) establish ceilings on rates that intermediaries may charge on formal loans. As mentioned earlier, concessionary rediscount facilities alone dampen the interest of intermediaries to mobilize voluntary savings in rural areas, and may also stimulate intermediaries to increase the transactions costs of individuals who have savings accounts. Without other restrictions, ceilings on rates paid on savings accounts also limit the ability of intermediaries to attract savings deposits through interest incentives and may induce them to offer noninterest rewards for savings as a way of avoiding the effects of the interest rate ceiling on deposits. Ceilings on the interest rates that intermediaries may charge on their loans are the most damaging of the three policies. As mentioned earlier, interest rate ceilings on agricultural loans force lenders to ration rural loans more severely, encourage the lender to transfer funds to loans that have less restrictive interest rate ceilings, stimulate lenders to transfer part of their normal loan transaction costs to nonpreferred borrowers, and force lenders to set even lower rates on deposits. Thus, these loan rate ceilings distort both the lending and the mobilizing efforts of the intermediary and can result in significant net outflows of funds from rural areas.

LESSONS

The new view of interest rate policies rejects the traditional approach of low-interest loans. These traditional policies have generally failed to achieve their primary objectives of promoting agricultural production and assisting the rural poor and have, instead, often undermined the financial viability of the lenders involved. The traditional approach has usually overlooked the distinction between real and nominal interest rates and has generally failed to recognize the importance of effective, as opposed to stated, interest rates, in addition to the relationship between interest rates and transaction costs. The main recommendation of the new view is that interest rates must be high enough that depositors can be adequately compensated and lenders can cover their costs.

SAVINGS MOBILIZATION BY AGRICULTURAL LENDERS

Savings mobilization is the forgotten half of rural finance. The role of financial intermediaries is not only to lend but also to provide deposit facilities for savers.

Nevertheless, almost all rural finance projects in LICs have stressed low-interest loans for agriculture and have neglected savings mobilization. The bias toward lending is also reflected in the literature on rural finance (Donald 1976). The studies that do deal with savings generally ignore savings mobilization by financial intermediaries and focus instead on the determinants of the portion of income that is saved rather than consumed.

The neglect of savings mobilization can perhaps be explained by the often-heard arguments that savings cannot or should not be mobilized in rural areas. It is said that most of the rural population has no margin for saving and does not respond to higher interest rates. It is also argued that if financial institutions were encouraged to mobilize savings aggressively, savings would simply be diverted from one institution to another or from rural to urban areas, as higher interest payments to depositors drive institutions toward bankruptcy or force them to lend outside of rural areas, where higher returns are available. A more basic explanation for the neglect of savings mobilization may be that it is inconsistent with low-interest-rate lending.

Three main arguments support a policy emphasizing rural savings mobilization. The first notes that more equitable income distribution is an important objective of rural finance projects, and traditional projects based on low-interest-rate lending have tended to bias the distribution of income away from the rural poor for reasons discussed earlier. Policies to improve savings opportunities can, however, efficiently help the rural poor. An essential function of financial intermediaries is the pooling of funds, that is, bringing together small amounts from many savers so that loans for relatively large projects involving economies of scale can be made. Hence, by their nature, formal financial intermediaries should serve many more savers than borrowers. On the average, depositors will have lower incomes than borrowers. Policies that focus on improving services for savers are therefore a better way to help the rural poor than is cheap credit.

If most of the rural population had no savings, the rural poor would have become extinct long ago with the onset of the first emergency (Von Pischke et al. 1983). The rural poor, more than any others, must have a liquid reserve to meet emergencies. Even the moneylender will not lend to someone with no accumulated or potential surplus; and friends and relatives, as well as rotating savings and credit associations, usually require the ability to reciprocate. Bouman (1983) has emphasized the widespread importance of savings in informal financial arrangements in LICs, and other authors have reported numerous instances of significant savings capacity among the rural poor (Von Pischke et al. 1983).

The most important service that financial institutions can provide for rural savers is the opportunity to hold liquid deposits which pay interest rates that are at least positive in real terms. Without this, the rural poor are forced to hold a variety of inflation hedges, many of which earn low or negative rates of return, and to pay an inflation tax on cash that is held to meet current obligations. The non-poor, by contrast, can often avoid these alternatives because they have access to a wider range of investment possibilities.

The myth that most of the rural population does not respond to interest rate incentives is often based on tepid responses to pseudo interest rate reforms in which rates are raised somewhat, but continue to be negative in real terms. In other cases, interest rates on deposits are raised significantly but financial institutions are expected to continue to lend at low rates of interest or to meet very high reserve requirements on deposits. These institutions respond quite logically by discouraging deposits through the imposition of high transaction costs on depositors in the form of inconvenient locations and hours, slow service, excessive paperwork, and high minimum balance requirements. Recent research has shown substantial responsiveness by savers to appropriate policies such as higher real rates of interest (Von Pischke et al. 1983).

Improved resource allocation is the second major argument for increased emphasis on savings mobilization. Deposit mobilization by financial intermediaries draws resources away from low-return investments, especially inflation hedges, as the opportunity is provided to make deposits that earn positive real rates of interest. Funds mobilized can be on-lent by financial intermediaries for those activities that promise the highest rates of return. Some arguments frequently heard against savings mobilization can actually help to clarify the ways in which savings mobilization can improve resources allocation. It is often said, for example, that aggressive savings mobilization by one institution will only divert deposits from other institutions with no gain to society. However, this neglects the gain to savers, who would not have moved their deposits without being better off, and the fact that financial institutions earning the highest risk-adjusted returns on the funds entrusted to them will be able to compete most effectively for savings.

Critics of the new views also argue that no additional savings will be generated, because the rural population will not save more because of higher interest rates. Such arguments confuse the flow of savings from income with the allocation of a stock of savings among competing assets, while also raising the question of whether savings allocated to inflation hedges, such as inventories of commodities, should be counted as saving or consumption. Regardless of whether more is saved out of income, which is an open question both theoretically and empirically, effective savings mobilization can help deploy the stock of assets of the rural population in more productive ways.

The beneficial effect of savings mobilization on the viability of financial institutions is the third major argument for greater emphasis on savings mobilization. Financial institutions that neglect savings mobilization are incomplete institutions (Adams et al. 1984). They not only fail to provide adequate services for rural savers, but they also make themselves less viable, as can be seen most clearly from high rates of loan delinquency. When financial institutions deal with clients only as borrowers they forgo useful information about the savings behavior of these clients that could allow them to improve estimates of creditworthiness. Furthermore, borrowers are more likely to repay promptly and lenders to take greater responsibility for loan recovery when they know that funds come from neighbors, rather than from government or donors.

Financial institutions that mobilize savings effectively are likely to have a continual flow of funds available for lending, while those that neglect savings mobilization are inevitably subject to the feast-or-famine cycle of government and donor funding. Financial institutions are likely to have little interest in savings mobilization or loan recovery when cheap funds are available through government loans, central bank rediscounts, or loans from international donors. It is generally overlooked that the volume of funds that can be obtained through effective programs of savings mobilization and loan recovery is potentially far greater than the most optimistic estimates of the amount of subsidized loans and grants available from governments and donors. There is mounting evidence that substantial amounts of savings can be mobilized in the rural areas of LICs and that certain techniques, such as positive real rates of interest for depositors, are particularly effective in mobilizing these savings (Von Pischke et al. 1983).

LESSONS

Research indicates that savers place considerable importance on access to future loans when selecting a financial institution and that innovative institutions can be quite successful in mobilizing savings (Von Pischke et al. 1983). However, financial intermediaries have often been used by governments or donors for purposes like low-interest lending that are inconsistent with aggressive savings mobilization, and in these cases savings mobilization has been neglected and the institutions have often performed poorly (Von Pischke et al. 1983). Savings mobilization that can assist the rural poor, improve resource allocation, and make financial institutions more viable, has been forgotten because of powerful incentives against savings mobilization. When savings mobilization is discouraged the total amount of funds available for lending in rural areas will generally be lessened.

LOOKING AHEAD

Continued population growth, shortfalls in agricultural production, and widespread rural poverty will force policy makers to continue to promote agricultural development in low-income countries. If the past is any guide to the future, agricultural credit will continue to be a major part of these efforts. Moreover, the problems and controversies that exist in rural financial markets in LICs are likely to persist. The tendencies of governments to use policies that turn the terms-of-trade against agriculture while repressing RFMs through low interest rate policies will not provide healthy environments for the growth of RFMs in the future. The subtle and complex nature of RFMs makes it possible for hard-pressed policy makers to assume success in agricultural credit projects, though careful analysis shows substantial shortcomings. Few policy makers in LICs take the time and effort to undertake careful assessment of the performance of their RFMs. This lack of analysis allows policy makers to sustain wishful thinking rather than to face reality.

An alternative view is that the political system finds the current performance of RFMs *satisfactory* (Ladman and Tinnermeier 1981). That is, political forces in the country may be more than satisfied with the results of distortions introduced by negative real rates of interest in RFMs, because they result in the allocation of political patronage, in the form of implied income transfers, to those influential people in the economy who end up receiving most of the cheap credit (Robert 1979). Distortions in interest rates, as well as other price distortions, caused by fixed exchange rates, import and export regulations, and licenses allow the political system to allocate "administrative profits." If interest rates were raised to equilibrium levels, the political system would have no cheap credit to grant to its favored patrons and strong supporters.[2]

The main lesson to be learned from this review of recent research and evaluation is that RFMs could play a more efficient and equitable role in development if appropriate policies were adopted. These policies include much more emphasis on mobilization of voluntary private savings in rural areas, interest rate policies that sustain positive real rates of interest most of the time, and more stress on improving the overall quality of financial services provided by these markets.

NOTES

1. The real rate of interest is defined as $[(1 + i)/(1 + p) - 1$, where i is the nominal rate of interest and p is some index of the annual change in prices.

2. This paragraph is taken from Adams and Graham 1981, p. 362.

REFERENCES

Adams, Dale W, and Douglas H. Graham. 1981. "A Critique of Traditional Agricultural Credit Projects and Policies." *Journal of Development Economics* 8, no. 3 (June): 347–66.

Adams, Dale W, Douglas H. Graham, and John D. Von Pischke, eds. 1984. *Undermining Rural Development with Cheap Credit.* Boulder, Colo.: Westview Press.

Bouman, F. J. A. 1983. "Indigenous Savings and Credit Societies in the Developing World." In Von Pischke, Adams, and Donald 1983, 262–68.

Christen, Robert P., and Robert C. Vogel. 1984. "The Importance of Domestic Resource Mobilization in Averting Financial Crises: The Case of Credit Unions in Honduras." Ohio State University. Unpublished paper.

Donald, Gordon. 1976. *Credit for Small Farmers in Developing Countries.* Boulder, Colo.: Westview Press.

Ladman, Jerry R., and Ronald L. Tinnermeir. 1981. "The Political Economy of Agricultural Credit: The Case of Bolivia." *American Journal of Agricultural Economics* 63 (February): 66–72.

Robert, Bruce L., Jr. 1979. "Agricultural Credit Cooperatives in Madras, 1893–1937: Rural Development and Agrarian Politics in Pre-Independent India." *Indian Economic and Social History Review* 16: 163–84.

Schaefer-Kehnert, Walter, and John D. Von Pischke. 1984. "Agricultural Credit Policy in Developing Countries." World Bank Reprint Series, no. 280, Washington, D.C.

Vogel, Robert C. 1981. "Rural Financial Market Performance: Implications of Low Delinquency Rates." *American Journal of Agricultural Economics* 61, no. 1 (February): 58–67.

Vogel, Robert C., and Paul Burkett. 1985. "Deposit Opportunities for Small Savers." Financial Development Unit, Industry Department, World Bank, Washington, D.C. Unpublished paper.

Von Pischke, John D., Dale W Adams, and Gordon Donald, eds. 1983. *Rural Financial Markets in Developing Countries: Their Use and Abuse.* Baltimore: Johns Hopkins University Press.

22

The Economics of Agricultural Research

THEODORE W. SCHULTZ

The future food supply depends in large measure on the achievements of agricultural research. Whether or not we will succeed in doing the necessary research is of no concern to the sun, or to the earth and the winds that sweep her face. Our popular doomsday activists know it will be impossible for agricultural research to save us from disaster. For them the history of the struggle of mankind to produce enough food is irrelevant. What is odd, however, is that most scientists have virtually no historical perspective. Why know history?[1] Although the common man cherishes his roots, scientists do not waste their time on history. Nor do most economists as they become more "scientific." This is an age of ever more minute specialization. Avoid history, discover a little new knowledge, and you have the makings of another crisis. Without history, current events produce much pessimism. He who is an optimist is either isolated or committed to the belief that there is a thread of historical continuity in the human condition and that it is not altogether bad.

The case for history and utility of the sciences in agriculture has been stated imaginatively as follows: "Few scientists think of agriculture as the chief, or the model science. Many, indeed, do not consider it a science at all. Yet it was the first science—the mother of all sciences; it remains the science which makes human life possible; and it may well be that, before the century is over, the success or failure of Science as a whole will be judged by the success or failure of agriculture."[2]

I shall treat research as an economic activity because it requires scarce resources and it produces something of value. It is a specialized activity that calls for special skills and facilities that are employed to discover and develop new and

THEODORE W. SCHULTZ is professor emeritus, Department of Economics, University of Chicago, and co-winner of the 1979 Nobel prize for economics.

Originally titled "The Economics of Research and Agricultural Productivity," this paper was presented at the Seminar on Socio-Economic Aspects of Agricultural Research in Developing Countries, 7–11 May 1979, Santiago, Chile, and was subsequently published as an IADS Occasional Paper, 1979. Reprinted with minor editorial revisions by permission of the International Agricultural Development Service and the author.

371

presumably useful information. The resources that are allocated to various re-search enterprises are readily observed and measured. But the value of the new information that these enterprises produce is always hard to determine. Orga-nized agricultural research has become an important part of the process of mod-ernizing agriculture throughout the world. It has been increasing at a rapid rate, and annual expenditures on research are in the billions of dollars.

The economics of agricultural research has long been high on the Ph.D. research agenda of our graduate students at the University of Chicago. I am much indebted for their contributions and for what others have done.[3] Needless to say, there are unsettled economic questions that await analysis. Much as I am tempted to elaborate on these questions, I have decided to leave this task to others. What I plan to do is of five parts. I begin with some estimates of the growth and magnitude of agricultural research throughout the world and in Latin America and with some observations on the increases in agricultural productivity from this research. I then consider what I deem to be a very important question, namely, Who should pay for agricultural research? I then proceed to the organizational quandary. I close with two very brief parts: one deals with the harm that is done to agricultural research by the distortions in agricultural prices, and the other comments on the function of research entrepreneurship.

EXPENDITURES ON RESEARCH AND AGRICULTURAL PRODUCTIVITY

Annual expenditures on agricultural research throughout the world have in-creased over fivefold since 1951. I view the rapid growth of this sector as a response to its success. When one adds up the annual costs of the national agricultural research systems and of the agricultural research that industrial firms are doing and also that of related university research, as Evenson and Kislev have done,[4] and which has been extended by Boyce and Evenson,[5] the estimates covering the period from 1951 to 1974, in constant 1971 U.S. dollars, show the total world expenditure for this purpose increased from $769 million to $3,841 million. I have extrapolated these estimates under very conservative assump-tions. My estimate for 1979 is $4,130 million in terms of 1971 constant dollars. In 1979 prices it would total over $7,000 million for the current year. By the same reckoning, using the Boyce-Evenson estimates, the expenditures on agri-cultural research throughout Latin America rose from $30 million in 1951 to $183 million in 1979 in constant 1971 dollars. Adjusted for the decline in the dollar, this 1979 figure comes to over $300 million.[6] It should be noted, howev-er, that in terms of the percentage of total research expenditure relative to the value of the agricultural products of a region, Latin America devotes fewer resources to this research than any of the other five major regions of the world.[7] Has this relationship improved in Latin America since Boyce and Evenson made their estimates? Why should this region have lagged as recently as 1974?

Returning to the total world agricultural research expenditures, this research sector is obviously no longer an infant. Many parts of it have all the earmarks of maturity. Are there signs of senility in any of these parts? In the language of economists, are there specific classes of agricultural research where diminishing returns indicate that it is no longer worthwhile? It will not do for us to be silent on this issue. To answer this question requires both the knowledge of scientists pertaining to scientific possibilities and that of economists with respect to the value of the required resources compared with the potential value of such research contributions.

Allocative decisions, however, must be made on the basis of limited information. But in fact we know a good deal. I consider actual allocative behavior as useful information. The observed rapid growth tells me that those who have made and are making the allocative decisions do so because they deem it to be worthwhile. There are also a fairly large number of competent economic studies that show that the rates of return on investment in various specific classes of agricultural research have been much higher than the normal rates of return.[8] It is true that those research endeavors that have not been successful have not been identified in these studies. Nevertheless, the classes of agricultural research that have been analyzed are of major economic importance in agricultural production, especially so in the case of food, feed, and fiber crops.

Recent economic history provides additional useful information on the value of the contributions of agricultural research. I rate this historical information highly for the purpose at hand. The following achievements are pertinent:

1. No doubt agriculture throughout the world will find it increasingly costly to increase the area of cropland. Agricultural research, along with complementary inputs, has been very successful in developing substitutes for cropland (some call this land augmentation). Actual increases in yield per hectare have held and may well continue to hold the key to increases in crop production. For example, during my first year at Iowa State College, 1931, the U.S. yield of maize was 1,500 kg/ha, a normal crop. In 1978 this yield came to 6,300 kg/ha. Although the maize area harvested in 1978 was 16 million hectares less than in 1931, total production was over 175 million metric tons, compared with 65 million tons in 1931. No wonder the estimated rates of return on maize research in the United States are exceedingly high. The achievement with sorghum is even more dramatic. Taking 1929 as a normal year, the yield of sorghum grain rose from 870 kg/ha to 2,800 kg/ha in 1978, despite the fact that the area devoted to this crop increased from 1.8 to 6.7 million hectares. Total production in 1978 was 19 million tons, which is over 15 times as much as that in 1929.

2. It is no longer true that a large per capita supply of beef can be produced only in countries with a sparse population and with a lot of good grazing land. As maize and sorghum have become cheaper than grass in the United States, producers of beef have turned increasingly to feed grains. Here

again, one sees the large economic effects of maize and sorghum research, along with complementary inputs on the reduction of the real costs of production and on increases in supply. The per capita consumption of beef in the United States doubled between 1940 and 1975 (retail weight, civilian population: 19.7 kg in 1940 and 40.3 kg in 1975). The rise in real per capita income tells most of the story of this extraordinary increase in the demand for beef. The decline in the real price of feed grains as a consequence of much higher yields and lower costs in turn tells most of the story that explains the threefold increase in domestic beef slaughter and the approximately constant real producer beef price trend, with fluctuations, to be sure, about that trend.[9]

3. The returns to poultry research are well known.[10] Add to them the effects of research on the supply of poultry feed and the result is a major improvement in the production of poultry products and a large gain for consumers. In the United States per capita consumption in terms of retail weight increased almost threefold between 1940 and 1975 (from 7.9 kg to 22.5 kg).

4. The last item on my partial list of research achievements pertains to wheat. The real costs of producing wheat have declined very much. As yet, the costs of producing rice have not come down as they have for wheat. Back in 1911–15, the world prices of these two primary food grains per ton tended to be equal. During 1947–62 wheat sold at about 60 percent of the price of rice. Between 1965 and 1970 the wheat price had declined to half of that of rice. My most recent date is August 1978, when wheat was quoted at 35 percent relative to rice, namely wheat at $129 and rice at $366 per ton.[11] When will the real costs of producing rice come tumbling down?

WHO SHOULD PAY FOR AGRICULTURAL RESEARCH?

In my view, Who should pay for agricultural research? is a critical question. There is, I regret to say, a good deal of confusion on this issue. The international agricultural research centers have prospered. They are a successful innovation.[12] The donors who have provided the funds have been generous. In view of their success, why not have these centers expand further and do most of the necessary agricultural research? The answer is that these centers, good as they are, will not suffice. They are not a substitute for national agricultural research enterprises. Nor are they capable of doing more than a small part of the required basic research in this area.

Since basic research is very expensive and what may be discovered is subject to much uncertainty, why not let the rich countries do it and pay for it? Presumably they can afford to do it. The implication of this view is that low-income countries can be "free riders" when it comes to basic research related to agriculture. It is, however, a shortsighted view because even to be a free rider requires a high level of scientific competence. To take advantage of such advances in the pertinent sciences, achieved elsewhere throughout the world, calls for a corps of highly skilled scientists. The unique requirements of agriculture by countries is still another important consideration in this context.

The conclusion that I come to at this point is that it would be a serious mistake for Chile or any other major country in Latin America to assume that the international agricultural research centers, along with the ongoing agricultural research in high-income countries, are substitutes for first-rate national agricultural research enterprises.

Who, then, within a country should pay for agricultural research? Economists, of course, will raise their hands wanting to be heard. They will, however, modify the question and proceed to comment on who pays the bill. Accordingly there are two quite different questions.

Consider the activities of experiment stations and those of universities related to agriculture. They do not normally sell their products; they make their findings available to the public. Nor do they provide the funds that cover the costs of doing the research in which they engage. Who benefits and who bears the costs of agricultural research requires some elaboration.

I shall begin with the agricultural research that is being done by private industrial firms, because in terms of economics it is the least difficult to present. Industrial firms, understandably, restrict their agricultural research to projects from which they expect to derive a profit. A good example has been the research of private firms pertaining to the medication of poultry feed and to the optimum mix of poultry feed ingredients at the lowest cost as the relative prices of the various feed ingredients change. Some types of research on insecticides, pesticides, animal antibiotics, drugs, location-specific seeds (such as hybrid maize) and various types of engineering research oriented to the requirements of agriculture are profitable for firms to undertake. In an advanced industrial economy there are many such research opportunities. About 25 percent of all expenditures on agricultural research in North America and Oceania is accounted for by the industrial sector.[13] In Latin America, industrial firms account for about 5 percent of all agricultural research; note, however, that given the state of industrial development, it would not make sense for governments to attempt to mandate that their industrial firms increase their share of expenditures for this purpose. In an open market economy these firms will increase their expenditures on agricultural research when it becomes evident that it is profitable for them to do so.[14]

The same economic logic is sometimes used to argue that farmers should pay for the research from which they profit because private farms are in principle like private industrial firms in undertaking activities that are profitable. It is true that landlords with large land holdings have engaged at various periods in something akin to agricultural research. Landlords in England in the past took much pride in developing various breeds of livestock. What they did, however, required very little scientific knowledge. I recall my impressions while in Uruguay in 1941: the large livestock farms were at best relying on the advice from individuals with a bachelor's degree in livestock with a modicum of knowledge about genetics, whereas at the small agricultural experiment stations in South Uruguay the plant breeding projects were designed and carried out by highly competent geneticists with full knowledge of R. A. Fisher's experimental design.

Individual farms the world over are obviously too small to undertake scientific research on their own. Nor are commodity organizations of farmers capable of doing it. The scale of the research enterprise and the continuity required to recruit and hold competent scientists entails a capability that is beyond that of the individual farmer or that of various farm organizations.

It is necessary at this point to consider who actually benefits from agricultural research. Under the assumption that the contributions of this research reduce the real costs of producing agricultural products, the reduction in cost results in either a producer surplus or a consumer surplus, or some combination of the two. Under market competition over time the benefits derived from this research accrue predominantly to consumers. It enhances their real income and welfare. Some farmers benefit during the early stages, when, for example, a new high-yielding variety is being adopted. Those farmers who are among the first to adopt and who are successful at it benefit, often substantially so. Once, however, all farmers have adopted such a variety, the reduction in costs under competition results in a lower supply price to the benefit of consumers. When such a high-yielding variety is for a time location-specific, as in the case of Mexican wheat in the Punjab of India and Pakistan, farmers, landowners, and farm laborers have profited. In general, if the commodity that is produced is solely for domestic consumption, domestic consumers are the primary beneficiaries; if the commodity is solely for export, consumers abroad benefit, and farmers in other countries who produce the same commodity and sell in the world market will experience a decline in their comparative advantage.[15] Although the consumer surpluses derived from the contributions of agricultural research are real and over time they are large, it is not feasible for consumers here or elsewhere to organize and finance modern agricultural research enterprises. The complexity of university-related basic research raises additional issues on who can and will finance this type of research.

In summing up, the implications of my arguments on paying for agricultural research are as follows:

• International agricultural research centers are not substitutes for national research enterprises.
• Nor do the large agricultural research institutions in high-income countries serve the unique requirements of Latin American countries.
• Industrial firms within any country will undertake only strictly applied research from which they can derive a profit. In countries where the industrial sector is small and not highly developed, their expenditures on agriculturally related research are, for good reasons, a very small part of the total agricultural research that is required.

• It is beyond the capacity of the individual farmer to do the required research on his own; nor are farmers collectively up to organizing and financing national agricultural research.

• Although over time most of the benefits from agricultural research accrue to consumers, it is not feasible for them to organize and finance national agricultural research enterprises.

• The only meaningful approach to modern agricultural research is to conceptualize most of its contributions as *public goods*. As such they must be paid for on public account, which does not exclude private gifts to be used to produce public goods.

THE ORGANIZATION QUANDARY

Organized agricultural research has a long history. Despite the constraints and difficulties that have been encountered and the mistakes that have been made, viewed historically, organized agricultural research has been a remarkable success. I featured some of its achievements at the outset. We may learn from past mistakes, and we should ponder the puzzles. I have a little list.

1. Why did many of the states in the United States establish all too many tiny agricultural substations? Many of them were inefficient. They could not recruit competent scientists. The staff that could be had was in general isolated intellectually, having all too little interaction with the principal experiment station of the state and with scientists at the land-grant college.[16] Whatever the reasons, the same mistake is occurring in many low-income countries.

2. Agricultural laboratories established to do research on agricultural product processing, where the scientists are off by themselves far removed from university scientists, are a mistake. The puzzle is, why did the U.S. government establish various expensive regional laboratories of this type? It behooves other countries not to repeat this costly mistake.

3. There are many examples throughout the world of important crops that are receiving all too little attention when it comes to agricultural research.[17] Who is to blame? For example, in the United States there is, in my view, a gross underinvestment in soybean research, compared with funds devoted to wheat, cotton, and maize research, relative to the value of these various crops. The value of the annual soybean crop is as large as the value of the wheat and cotton crops combined.[18] It is hard for me to believe that geneticists who are also plant breeders have no theories from which to derive research hypotheses to improve the genetic capacity of the soybean. Why this underinvestment in soybean research?

4. All too much of the foreign aid for agricultural development has undervalued agricultural research. When it has supported such research, it has been, in general, short-term aid, notwithstanding the fact that the gestation period in research is a matter of years and it should for that reason be

approached as a long-term investment. The commitment to obtain quick results has been the bane of most foreign aid, not only with respect to research but also in other program areas. It continues to be the better part of wisdom for low-income countries not to rely on foreign aid in financing their agricultural research enterprises.

5. It is difficult to understand why any of the major private foundations should assume that the necessary research results for agricultural modernization are at hand and, on that assumption, proceed to support various communications activities. The dissemination of existing knowledge, better communication, featuring new approaches in extension activities, has been and continues to be the announced policy of the Kellogg Foundation. The prestigious Ford Foundation made the same mistake during its early agricultural programs in India. It is to the credit of the Rockefeller Foundation that it has had the wisdom to see that research must come first, and it has consistently held to that policy.

6. It is still a puzzle for me why so few worthwhile agricultural research results were available throughout Latin America at the time when President Truman's Point Four Program was launched. It was my responsibility during the early 1950s, with ample foundation funds and with five competent colleagues, to make an assessment of the achievements of the Point Four programs. Our studies and publications were labeled TALA, Technical Assistance Latin America. We roamed over all parts of Latin America. We found that in the area of agriculture, Point Four had accomplished very little. Agricultural extension work was prematurely emphasized.[19] In general the extension work supported by Point Four was empty for lack of available agricultural research results. Where some funds were allocated to agricultural research, they were used far less effectively than the funds of the Rockefeller Foundation, jointly with those of the Mexican government in Mexico, in what is now CIMMYT.

7. The last point on my little list reaches far back in time. It serves the purpose of deflating our self-acclaimed importance in augmenting the production of food. It is a disconcerting puzzle. Whereas Neolithic women invented agriculture and developed many of the food crop species that we have today, our highly skilled plant breeders have produced only one new food species, triticale. Norman Borlaug,[20] the agricultural Nobel Laureate, puts it this way, "The first and greatest green revolution occurred when women decided that something had to be done about their dwindling food supply." Neolithic men in hunting for meat were failing to bring home enough to eat. Try to explain and ponder the implications of the achievements then and now.

Important as it is to avoid making the mistakes that other countries have made in organizing and administering agricultural research, there are various other considerations. Robert E. Evenson's recent essay on the organization of research[21] is an important contribution to the allocation of research funds by commodities. By his criteria,[22] the allocation of funds for cotton or rubber research is twice as large as that for wheat or sugar cane, and that allocated for rice, maize, millet, and sorghum or livestock and its products is only half as large as that for wheat or sugar cane. Pulses, groundnuts, oilseeds, and roots and tubers are among the really neglected crops. Evenson also deals competently with the allocation of research resources by environmental regions and with the issues pertaining to single-commodity, multiple-commodity, and discipline-oriented research.

My own experience and observations lead me to stress the following organizing decisions:

1. Once the commodities have been selected, the state of the market for the services of the scientists who are required to do the research becomes an important consideration.
2. It is all too easy to become enamored of the phrase "interdisciplinary research." What matters is the actual value that is to be realized from the complementarity between the scientists who have different professional skills. So-called interdisciplinary research is as a rule weak on theory and soft in the quality of research that gets done.
3. The effects of various incentives on research workers' productivity is of major importance. The built-in incentives that characterize organized agricultural research in most low-income countries are bad. All too often agricultural scientists are worse off in this respect than high-class clerks in the bureaucracy of the government.
4. Too little attention is given to the effects of alternative accountability requirements on research efficiency. Unnecessary paper work abounds. Those who provide the funds call the accounting rules; they are rarely aware of the sharply diminishing returns to the burdensome accounting that they call for. On this score, in my view, the international agricultural research centers are no exception.
5. The trade-off, or call it the compromise, between the loss from fragmentation and the gain from location-specific research within a country is a choice that has to be made. The mistakes that various high-income countries have made on this issue in their organizational decisions are instructive on what not to do.
6. Each of the major Latin American countries must have its own corps of competent agricultural scientists. The long-term payoff on this investment is very high. The ever-present strong desire of those who make the organizational decisions for quick results is a serious obstacle in recruiting and maintaining a corps of competent scientists. Where the main agricultural experiment station is an integral part of a university, it is possible to give due attention to basic research oriented to agriculture, provided that the decisions of the government in allocating funds do not thwart the basic research.
7. In economics there is the concept of the optimum scale of an enterprise.

Although it is difficult to apply this concept in determining the optimum scale of an agricultural experiment station, it is nevertheless relevant. There is a strong tendency in agricultural research to violate all scale considerations by ever more centralization of its administration.

THE HARM DONE TO RESEARCH BY PRICE DISTORTIONS

The scarcity of agricultural resources—land relative to labor and both of these relative to the stock of reproducible forms of physical capital—is a major consideration in determining the forms of useful knowledge that are appropriate for an economy. The historical responses of agricultural research in various countries to resource scarcity considerations are presented by Hayami and Ruttan in their well-known book on agricultural development.[23]

The scarcity of the factors of production is not self-evident. It requires proof, and proof calls for measurement. The price of the services of each of the factors of production in an open competitive market is a unit of measurement of scarcity. When the market is rigged, be it by governmental intervention or by means of private monopoly pricing, the resulting prices are distorted. The price signals that are a consequence of such distortions do not reveal the true scarcity of the factors of production, and for that reason they are beset with misinformation. The allocation of funds for agricultural research and the use to which these funds are put are not immune to the adverse effects of such price misinformation.

The overpricing of sugar beets in Western Europe and the United States, and the associated expenditures on sugar-beet research, is a case in point. The expenditures on rice research in Japan have not been immune to the enormous overpricing of rice in that country.[24] In India on rice it is the other way around. There is no end to examples. The harm that is being done throughout the world to agricultural research as a consequence of the distortions in prices and in agricultural incentives is very substantial.[25]

THE FUNCTION OF RESEARCH ENTREPRENEURSHIP

The dynamic attributes of research are pervasive both in the domain of economic growth and in the conduct of actual research. Advances in useful knowledge are compelling dynamic forces. Such new knowledge is the mainspring of economic growth. Were it not for advances in knowledge, the economy would arrive at a stationary state and all economic activities would become essentially routine in nature. Over time, new knowledge has augmented the productive capacity of land, and it has led to the development of new forms of physical capital and of new human skills. The fundamental dynamic agent of long-term economic growth is the research sector of the economy.

The concept of meaningful research conducted to enhance the stock of knowledge that is useful in production and consumption is inconsistent with static, unchanging, routine work on the part of scientists. The very essence of research is in the fact that it is a dynamic venture into the unknown or into what is only partially known. Research, in this context, is inescapably subject to risk and uncertainty. Whereas funds, organization, and competent scientists are necessary, they are not sufficient. An important factor in producing knowledge is the human ability that I shall define as *research entrepreneurship*. It is an ability that is scarce; it is hard to identify this talent; it is rewarded haphazardly in the not-for-profit research sector; and it is increasingly misused and impaired by the over-organization of our research enterprises. What is happening in agricultural research is on this score no exception.

Who are these research entrepreneurs? In business enterprises that are profit-oriented, the chief executive officers perform the entrepreneurial function. The skilled factory worker is not an entrepreneur in doing his job. In research it is otherwise. Whereas administrators who are in charge of a research organization may be entrepreneurs, much of the actual entrepreneurship is a function of the assessment by scientists of the scientific frontiers of knowledge. Their professional competence is required to determine the research hypotheses that may be worthwhile pursuing.

Briefly and much simplified, my argument is that in the quest for appropriations and research grants, all too little attention is given to that scarce talent which is the source of research entrepreneurship.[26] The convenient assumption is that a highly organized research institution firmly controlled by an administrator will perform this important function. But in fact a large organization that is tightly controlled is the death of creative research, regardless of whether it be the National Science Foundation, a government agency, a large private foundation, or a large research-oriented university. No research director in Washington or Santiago can know the array of research options that the state of scientific knowledge and its frontier afford. Nor can the managers of foundation funds know what needs to be known to perform this function. Having served as a member of a research advisory committee to a highly competent experiment station director for some years and having observed the vast array of research talent supported by funds that we as a committee had a hand in allocating, I am convinced that most working scientists are research entrepreneurs. But it is exceedingly difficult to devise institutions to utilize this special talent efficiently. Organization is necessary. It too requires entrepreneurs. Agricultural research has benefitted from its experiment stations, specialized university laboratories, and from the recently developed international agricultural research centers. But there is the ever-present danger of over-organization, of directing research from the top, of requiring working scientists to devote ever more time to preparing reports to "justify" the work they are doing and to treat research as if it were some routine activity.

NOTES

1. Here I draw briefly on my "What Are We Doing to Research Entrepreneurship?" in *Transforming Knowledge into Food in a Worldwide Context*, ed. William F. Hueg, Jr., and Craig A. Gannon (Minneapolis: Miller Publishing Co., 1978), 96–105.

2. André Mayer and Jean Mayer, "Agriculture: The Island's Empire," in *Science and Its Public: The Changing Relationship, Daedalus* 103, no. 3 (1974): 83–95. See also the excellent essay by Edward Shils, "Faith, Utility and the Legitimacy of Science," in the same issue of *Daedalus.*

3. My debt to scientists concerned about agricultural research is large. I learned much from R. E. Buchanan, who was director of the Agricultural Experiment Station during my years at Iowa State College. Albert H. Moseman has also contributed a good deal to my understanding of agricultural research in low-income countries, beginning with the symposium that he organized for the American Association for the Advancement of Science, "Agricultural Sciences for the Developing Nations," 1964, and his comprehensive analysis, *Building Agricultural Systems in Developing Nations* (New York: Agricultural Development Council, 1970)

4. Robert E. Evenson and Yoav Kislev, "Investment in Agricultural Research and Extension: An International Survey," *Economic Development and Cultural Change* 23, no. 3 (1975): 507–21.

5. James K. Boyce and Robert E. Evenson. *National and International Agricultural Research and Extension Programs* (New York: Agricultural Development Council, 1975).

6. This estimate for expenditures in Latin America does not account fully for the recent expansion of the agricultural research activities in Brazil, and to this extent it is too low for Latin America.

7. See table 1.5, for the year 1974, in Boyce and Evenson, *National and International Agricultural Research.*

8. See Evenson and Kislev, 1975.

9. T. W. Schultz, "The Politics and Economics of Beef" (Paper presented at the Conference on Livestock Production in the Tropics, 8–12 March 1976, Acapulco, Mexico, published by the Banco de Mexico in their *Proceedings,* 1976).

10. See Willis Peterson, "Returns to Poultry Research in the United States" (Ph.D. diss., University of Chicago, 1966).

11. Why there has not been more substitution of wheat for rice, inasmuch as the nutritive value of rice and wheat is virtually the same, presents a puzzle (see my "Reckoning the Economic Achievements and Prospects of Low Income Countries" [James C. Snyder Memorial Lecture, Purdue University, 22 February 1979]).

12. It should be noted that the Rockefeller Foundation, in cooperation with the government of Mexico, was the first to launch this type of venture. Not to be overlooked is the importance of research entrepreneurship in this connection. I shall have more to say on research entrepreneurship later on in this paper.

13. This estimate and the one that follows for Latin America are for 1974, based on table 1.1 in Boyce and Evenson, *National and International Agricultural Research.*

14. Experience in the United States indicates that there is a tendency for some agricultural experiment stations to hold on to research work that has been successful and has reached the point where private firms would continue it, as occurred in the case of the southern experiment stations' holding on to the development and production of hybrid maize for seed.

15. The economics of the preceding arguments is greatly simplified. Much depends on the elasticity of the demands and on the shifts in the supply curves as a consequence of the production effects of the contributions derived from agricultural research.

16. These interactions among agricultural scientists contribute to their research productivity, but they do not solve the institutional requirements for useful working interactions between farmers and scientists. The more centralized the agricultural research establishment of a country becomes, the fewer the actual working contacts that scientists have with on-farm production problems. Robert E. Evenson, in his comments on this paper, made the point that one of the overlooked contributions of substations is that they provide agricultural scientists with some of these much needed working contacts with actual farm conditions (see also Robert E. Evenson, Paul E. Waggoner, and Vernon W. Ruttan, "Economic Benefits from Research: An Example from Agriculture," *Science,* 14 September 1979, 1101–7).

17. See Evenson and Kislev, 1975.

18. The size of the area devoted to soybeans in the United States in 1979 exceeded that devoted to maize. The anticipated soybean crop at current future harvest prices implies a value of $14,000 million.

19. See chapter 1 in this volume.—ED.

20. Norman E. Borlaug, "The Green Revolution: Can We Make It Meet Expectations?" *Proceedings of the American Phytopathological Society* 3 (1976).

21. Robert E. Evenson, "The Organization of Research to Improve Crops and Animals in Low Income Countries," in *Distortions of Agricultural Incentives,* ed. Theodore W. Schultz (Bloomington: Indiana University Press, 1978).

22. See table 3, p. 230, in Evenson, "The Organization of Research."

23. Yujiro Hayami and Vernon W. Ruttan, *Agricultural Development: An International Perspective* (Baltimore: Johns Hopkins Press, 1971). See also Hans P. Binswanger et al., *Induced Innovation: Technology, Institutions and Development* (Baltimore: Johns Hopkins University Press, 1978). [See also chapter 5, by Ruttan and Hayami.—ED.]

24. Keijiro Otsuka, "Public Research and Rice Production—Rice Sector in Japan, 1953–76" (Ph.D. diss., University of Chicago, 1979).

25. For an extended treatment of the adverse effects of the distortions in agricultural incentives, including their effects on the adoption of research results and on providing the wrong price signals to guide agricultural research, see Schultz, *Distortions of Agricultural Incentives.*

26. This closing paragraph is a slightly revised part of my "What Are We Doing to Research Entrepreneurship?" cited in n. 1 above.

23

Farming Systems Research Revisited

ROBERT TRIPP, PONNIAH ANANDAJAYASEKERAM,

DEREK BYERLEE, AND LARRY HARRINGTON

INTRODUCTION

In the mid-1970s, while the results of the "Green Revolution" were still being assessed and debated, a new approach to agricultural technology development began to take shape. It was concerned with the fact that many resource-poor farmers, especially in less favorable environments, had not yet benefited from new agricultural technology. Proponents of this approach argued that a more careful understanding of the conditions and constraints under which farmers in these more difficult environments operated would lead to technology better suited to their needs. Various institutions were involved in developing this approach, including international agricultural research centers (IARCs), universities, donor agencies, and national agricultural research systems (NARSs). This range of interests led, not surprisingly, to a wide array of research methods, philosophies, and projects. Much of this work found itself described under the rubric of farming systems research (FSR). FSR quickly progressed from a rough amalgam of ideas regarding technology development to become a dominant concept in the 1980s in both the literature of agricultural development and the organization of agricultural research and extension systems (CGIAR/TAC 1978; Simmonds 1985).

By the early 1970s it had become clear that a broader approach was needed to follow the successes of the seed-fertilizer strategy of the Green Revolution in Asia. In the favorable environments where this strategy had its greatest impacts, the introduction of new early-maturing rice and wheat varieties opened the way for further increases in cropping intensity and the need for research to evaluate new cropping patterns. At the same time, attention shifted to the less-favored environments (especially rainfed areas) where the seed-fertilizer technology had had little im-

ROBERT TRIPP is anthropologist at CIMMYT, Mexico; PONNIAH ANANDAJAYASEKERAM is regional economist, CIMMYT, Kenya; DEREK BYERLEE is an economist at CIMMYT, Mexico; and LARRY HARRINGTON is regional economist, CIMMYT, Thailand. CIMMYT is the International Maize and Wheat Improvement Center, Mexico, D.F.

pact. Consequently, the rationale and complexity of managing a variety of crops and livestock on a small holding became the focus, and the range of economic and social parameters affecting the farm household gave credence to analyzing such farms as *systems* and to seeing technology development as being system-specific. Meanwhile, following the successes in wheat and rice breeding, many national programs were reorganized along commodity lines in order to focus research resources on key commodities. However, in many cases there was little communication across commodity research programs, even though commodities were often produced by the same farmers as part of complex systems.

Thus there emerged considerable justification for FSR as an approach to adaptive agricultural research that is sensitive to the biological, economic, and social factors that influence the management of farming systems. The practices, problems, and interests of the farm household are incorporated into a research program in order to design technology compatible with the farming system. Such technologies are then tested and assessed on farmers' fields, under their conditions and using their criteria (Byerlee, Harrington, and Winkelman 1982; Byerlee 1987).

Over the past decade, FSR has enlisted the energies and skills of thousands of biological and social scientists in scores of countries and has attracted considerable funding. FSR has made important contributions to the way agricultural research is conceived and organized. However, FSR has also produced an uneven record of accomplishment, and some FSR work has been extravagant, impractical, and divisive. This chapter reviews the origins of FSR, assesses its accomplishments and failures, and provides guidelines for FSR in the 1990s.

ROOTS OF FSR

Although FSR responded to practical concerns about the effectiveness of agricultural and rural development strategies of the early 1970s, it is in fact the logical outgrowth of earlier initiatives (Brush and Turner 1987). For example, some geographers (e.g., Grigg 1974) and economists (e.g., Ruthenberg 1971) had found the systems concept a useful way to describe variations in world agriculture. Schultz (1964) had earlier offered his dictum that Third World farmers were "poor but efficient," and this stimulated a number of detailed micro-level studies to examine the complexity and rationale of traditional farming practices (Collinson 1972; Norman 1977; Harwood 1979).

FSR also has clear antecedents in the history of technology development. In developed countries, much of the pre–World War II problem-solving work in farm management had a systems and farm-household perspective (Johnson 1982). Simmonds (1985, 14) compares some of the British colonial research in Africa and Asia to FSR, and early work in India (Heinemann and Biggs 1985) and Taiwan (Lionberger and Chang 1970) presents many similarities to FSR. Some agricultural research in Francophone Africa also developed a systems perspective, as in Les Unites Experimentales in Senegal (Fresco 1984), which came to be included as part of FSR (Gilbert et al. 1980, 113).

Nevertheless, it took a series of specific projects and experiences to establish FSR as a research strategy. Two efforts in Latin America, the Caqueza Project, an integrated rural development effort sponsored by the International Development Research Centre (IDRC) in Colombia (Zandstra et al. 1979), and Plan Puebla, sponsored by the Rockefeller Foundation in Mexico (Jimenez 1970), both demonstrated the importance of assessing technologies under farmers' conditions. Rockefeller support was also instrumental in the establishment of a national agricultural research institute in Guatemala (Hildebrand 1976) which featured the incorporation of a social science component and a strong farming systems orientation. Meanwhile, in Africa, earlier work on describing and analyzing local farming systems began to be used as a basis for designing technological interventions that were taken to farmers' fields for evaluation under representative conditions (Norman et al. 1979).

Beginning about 1975, the International Agricultural Research Centers initiated FSR studies. The International Rice Research Institute (IRRI) developed a set of methods and an extensive network of collaborators in Asia in cropping systems research (Zandstra et al. 1981). The International Maize and Wheat Improvement Center (CIMMYT), based on early experience in eastern Africa (Collinson 1982) and Latin America (Moscardi et al. 1983), developed methods for commodity-based on-farm research with a farming systems perspective (Byerlee et al. 1982). Some of the IARCs established separate farming systems programs with a goal of developing *new* farming systems for difficult environments. Examples of this approach include the work of the International Crops Research Institute for the Semi-Arid Tropics (ICRISAT) on vertisol management and watershed development in India and that of the International Institute of Tropical Agriculture (IITA) to develop technology in the humid and subhumid tropics of Africa. With this base, FSR also caught the notice of donor agencies.[1]

A BRIEF OVERVIEW OF FSR

THE FARMING SYSTEMS PERSPECTIVE

A great deal of effort has been spent on deciding exactly what constitutes research on a farming system. The CGIAR/TAC (Consultative Group on International Agricultural Research, Technical Advisory Committee) review team described a farming system as "a complicated interwoven mesh of soils, plants, animals, implements, workers, other inputs and environmental influences with the strands held and manipulated by a person called the farmer, who, given his [sic] preferences and aspirations, attempts to produce output from the inputs and technology available to him [sic]" (CGIAR/TAC 1978, 8). This definition highlights the complexities of farming systems and the role of the farmer in shaping the perspectives and methods used by FSR researchers. System complexities are the product of several characteristics of small-farm agriculture. Long growing seasons allow for multiple cropping and intercropping. Uncertain markets and climates make risk an important factor in farmers' decisions. Farm households consume a significant proportion of their production, thus making household food security a key objective in farm management. Labor and other household resources often exhibit considerable heterogeneity and lead to complex management strategies. The combination of these factors often leads to complex and varied farming systems.

FSR has led to a wide variety of research strategies and projects, and several attempts have been made to place them in some sort of order. Simmonds (1985) divides the FSR universe into three general categories. The first is the academic study of entire farming systems, or what he calls "FSR *sensu stricto*." The second is research devoted to the development of entirely new systems to replace current practices, or "new farming systems development." The third is research that uses an understanding of the farming system to identify opportunities for introducing stepwise change to farming practices, or "on-farm research with a farming systems perspective." The latter definition is the major activity described as FSR in national research systems and is the focus of the remainder of this chapter. For reasons of simplicity and historical continuity it will be referred to simply as FSR; in practice it may cover a range of research activities from adaptive research on component technology, such as variety or fertilizer levels for a specific crop or livestock enterprise, to research aimed at overcoming major systemwide constraints, through introduction of more radical changes to the system, such as a new crop or a new early-maturing variety or new tillage technique to facilitate increased cropping intensity.

FSR RESEARCH PROCEDURES

Despite the variety of approaches to FSR, most work is distinguished by a set of research procedures that emphasizes the following sequence of activities:

Diagnosis. This includes various methods for describing the area where research is to be carried out, understanding current farming practices, and eliciting farmers' problems and interests.

Planning. Diagnostic information is used to set research priorities, propose improved technologies, and design an experimental program.

Testing. On-farm experiments test promising technologies on farmers' fields, under their conditions.

Assessment. Experimental results are assessed using formal agronomic, statistical, and economic criteria, as well as being reviewed to assure that the conclusions are compatible with farmers' concerns and the characteristics of the farming system.

Recommendation and extension. Various methods are used for diffusing the results of the research to farmers and monitoring its impact.

CHARACTERISTICS OF FSR

Beyond these methodological similarities, FSR is usually described in terms of certain characteristics that distinguish it from other approaches to agricultural research. A brief examination of these characteristics is helpful, not only for reviewing the contributions of FSR, but also for understanding some of the problems that have arisen in its implementation. Because many of these characteristics conflict with other aspects of research organization or have at times been applied in extreme form, they have been the source of numerous misunderstandings.

System-oriented. Virtually all FSR is said to be "system-specific," but the definition of the system boundaries has been problematic (Merrill-Sands 1986). A farming systems perspective does not necessarily imply a broad research agenda. Research may concentrate on key enterprises or cropping patterns in the farming systems where success in introducing technological innovations will have a major impact on system productivity. However, research on these key enterprises takes account of interactions with other elements of the system (table 1). These include direct interactions between production activities, generated by intercropping or crop rotation practices; interactions due to competition and complimentarity in resource use between different production activities; interactions due to trade-offs among the multiple objectives of the farm household; and interactions between crop and livestock production.

Some FSR projects have been too ambitious in the conception of their responsibilities and have investigated all farm enterprises in the system simultaneously. The impression that FSR necessarily involves studies of multiple cropping, crop-

TABLE 1
CLASSIFICATION OF FARMING SYSTEM INTERACTIONS

Type of Interaction	*Examples*
Direct interaction between crops	
Interactions in space	Interactions due to intercropping
Interactions over time	Conflicts in planting crop in relation to harvest of previous crop
	Carry-over of soil structure and crop residues from preceding crop
	Carry-over fertility from previous crops
	Carry-over and build-up of weed seeds and other pest populations from previous crops
Interactions between crops and livestock	Use of crops and crop residues for fodder
	Use of farmyard manure as crop nutrient source
	Use of animals for draft power
Resource competition and complementarity	Conflicts in labor use and cash needs between enterprises, including nonfarm enterprises
	Competition for irrigation water between enterprises
Meeting multiple objectives of farm households	Choice of multiple crops, livestock, and production practices to manage risk
	Planting and storage of food crops to balance seasonal food needs and off-farm work to provide seasonal cash needs

SOURCE: Byerlee and Tripp 1988.

livestock systems, or broader rural development issues has, at times, contributed to a breach between FSR activities and commodity or disciplinary research. This is illustrated in a recent World Bank review that urges "commodity research when appropriate and farming systems or problem-oriented research when needed" (1985, 52). This division has made commodity programs suspicious of data developed through FSR and has meant that FSR has sometimes failed to pursue research themes of value to commodity research (Kydd 1989).

Interdisciplinary. The problem-solving emphasis in FSR requires the participation of various disciplines in the research effort, including social scientists who had previously not participated in the process of technology generation. Achieving such interdisciplinary collaboration has proven difficult, however, and many FSR efforts are dominated by either social or biological scientists. FSR is often looked upon as being "a social scientists' invention" (Chambers and Jiggins 1986, 11). In some national programs there is a confusion between FSR and social science research. On the other hand, a recent study has shown that although social scientists may be instrumental in establishing FSR activities, their participation in on-going programs is often minimal (Merrill-Sands et al. 1989).

Location-specific. FSR usually claims to be location-specific, in that it carries out research activities on particular kinds of farming systems in specific geographical or agro-ecological zones. Such strategies have obvious potential for improving the focus of research and the coordination between research and extension. But too little attention has been paid to efficiency considerations in the size and number of study areas or research sites. It is not uncommon to see exhaustive work carried out in relatively small areas, where the possibilities for extrapolation to a wider area are unclear. This imposes very high costs (in terms of staff, vehicles, and budgets) per farmer and per hectare, and reduces the efficiency of research. This inward-looking tendency also means that FSR projects have often failed to link their work to the broader policy context.

For resource-poor farmers. FSR has its origins in concerns for more equitable strategies for technology development. Since the system focus is particularly appropriate to resource-poor farmers with diversified enterprise patterns, resources, and objectives, this has led to some confusion between research methods and targets. Some opposition to FSR, for instance, has been based on the perception that it is a methodology suitable for developing technologies for resource-poor farmers only. In practice, the principles and methods of FSR are applicable to a wide range of farming populations. Decisions regarding the utility of FSR must distinguish between the choice of clients for agricultural research and appropriate methods.

On-farm. Most FSR activities are carried out on farmers' fields, but on-farm activity per se is not necessarily a sign of well-focused research. Unless on-farm experiments are properly conceived and analyzed they may provide little useful information. In addition, it is often forgotten that research on experiment stations such as crop breeding work, laboratory support, and long-term experiments are usually critical to the success of FSR. Rather than contributing to an optimal mix of on-farm and on-station work, FSR has sometimes been responsible for the formation of two separate research camps, contemptuous of the lack of rigor or relevance, respectively, in each other's work.

Adaptive. FSR is often seen as a way of adapting technologies that are "on the shelf" to specific farming conditions, but in many instances improved technology is not available. Nevertheless, some FSR efforts have assumed that good will and systems analysis are sufficient to bring productive innovations to less favorable environments, and this has led to an overinvestment in on-farm experimentation. When improved technology is not available for adaptation, FSR researchers can help orient an applied research program to develop appropriate technology (much of which will be done on the experiment station). But in most cases this potential for feedback from FSR programs to experiment stations has not been realized (Merrill-Sands et al. 1989).

THE CONTRIBUTIONS OF FSR

After more than a decade of prominence, FSR is losing some of its luster. Hence, it is appropriate to describe areas in which FSR has made contributions and areas where it has not fulfilled the expectations of research managers and donors.

The principal contributions of FSR to strengthening agricultural research have been in the areas of research orientation, methods, and organization, and only secondarily in technology development. FSR has been responsible for permanent and significant changes in the way research is conceived and carried out. The introduction of FSR, under various guises, has altered the way researchers look at their clients, the farmers. The force of the FSR movement has led both its supporters and its detractors to concentrate more on the conditions and problems of resource-poor farmers. FSR can take some credit for the fact that an increasing number of researchers can provide good descriptions of local farming practices, explain their rationale, and offer examples of how technology must be tailored to farmers' needs. For example, there is now much more awareness of the rationale and benefits of intercropping than a decade ago, when almost all research was conducted on sole-crops, even though intercropping is the dominant practice over much of the Third World. Likewise, researchers now evaluate the maturity of a variety not only in terms of the potential length of the growing season, but also in terms of cropping patterns, staggered planting practices, and the food supply calendar of farm households. Researchers also give much more attention to the value of crop residues as a fodder and the role of draft animal nutrition in crop production. This greater awareness by biological researchers of the circumstances and needs of small farmers represents an important accomplishment of FSR.

FSR has stimulated an immense amount of work on research methods, and although this has been accompanied by an inevitable profusion of jargon and a certain number of false starts, the net result has been positive. FSR provides a cost-effective alternative to the formal survey methods used by economists, which are often applied in a mechanical fashion to diverse farming situations. One of FSR's most significant contributions has been the idea of initiating research with an informal survey (Collinson 1981) or "sondeo" (Hildebrand 1981), which places an interdisciplinary group of researchers in the field for several days, talking to farmers, observing their fields, and gradually building up a set of hypotheses about local practices and problems. A review of FSR projects would reveal a range of survey techniques, from exclusive reliance on informal surveys to extensive multiple-visit questionnaires. But there is a definite trend towards more efficient problem-oriented survey techniques and more imaginative methods for involving farmers in identifying research priorities (Ashby et al. 1987) and monitoring experimental work (Norman et al. 1988).

Although researchers have been planting experiments and demonstrations in farmers' fields for decades, FSR has been responsible for developing and promoting a more rigorous approach to the planning, design, and analysis of on-farm experiments. Guidelines are available to help researchers identify high-priority factors for on-farm experiments (Tripp and Woolley 1989) and for the design and management of cropping pattern testing (Zandstra et al. 1981). Considerable experience has been gained regarding appropriate experimental designs and analytical techniques for assessing technologies under farmers' conditions (e.g., Woolley 1987; Mutsaers et al. 1986). Also, more interest has been shown in the possibilities of farmer management of experiments (Barker and Lightfoot 1988) and the role of farmers in setting experimental parameters (Sumberg and Okali 1988). In addition, methods are well established for the economic analysis of on-farm experiments (CIMMYT 1988).

FSR has contributed to changes in the organization of agricultural research. It has helped give a definite role to economists and other social scientists in the process of technology generation and has greatly stimulated the field of microeconomic research. Until the 1980s, most farm-level research in developing countries concentrated on standard farm management methods borrowed from developed countries, especially the construction of farm enterprise budgets or production functions based on aggregated categories of inputs such as land, labor, purchased inputs, and capital. Who the clients were for this work was never clear, in part because it lacked a problem-solving orientation (Collinson 1981). FSR has stimulated economists to consider more integrated and pragmatic approaches to *understanding* the complexity of farming systems, approaches that recognize physical and biological parameters and risk and food supply management. FSR has changed the role of the economist from one of simply providing an ex post evaluation of technologies to that of helping set the research agenda. Economists and other social scientists now have a recognized ex ante role in the definition of research problems and the organization of field research (Byerlee and Tripp 1988; IRRI 1982; Rhoades 1984).

Finally, FSR has led to the development of useful technologies, which in some cases have been widely adopted by farmers. Location-specific on-farm research, carried out by national program and IARC staff, has brought new technology to farmers for improved tillage in Panama (Martinez and Sain 1983), pest control and plant stand management in Indonesia (Dahlan et al. 1987), improved maize varieties and planting practices in Ghana (Tripp et al. 1987), and new bean varieties and methods of disease control in Colombia (Woolley et al. 1988). Donor-sponsored FSR with national programs has also produced technologies that have been taken up by farmers (see Ruano and Fumagalli (1988) for evidence from Guatemala). The work of the Asian Rice Farming Systems Network has been instrumental in fostering the intensification of rice-based cropping patterns in several Asian countries, through the introduction of early rice varieties, new tillage and planting technologies, and new crops, especially in the Philippines (Morris 1984), Indonesia (Siwi et al. 1986), and Nepal (Mathema 1986). Virtually all of these examples involve commodity-based FSR that has focused on a few high-priority problems within a farming system.

However, even taking account of the time required for technology development and the effort necessary to establish a new orientation to research, the current assessment must be that FSR has not yet repaid its intellectual and financial investment with increases in productivity for resource-poor farmers. The limited number of success stories to date gives cause for serious concern about the efficiency with which past FSR activities have been conducted, and even about the future of FSR itself.

FSR IN THE 1990s

Although FSR is no longer the fashionable theme that it once was, it is not about to fade into obscurity. It will continue to have its promoters and its critics, to engender debate and controversy, and to challenge researchers to address clients' needs. It is important that its contributions be recognized and utilized and that its excesses be acknowledged and incorporated into lessons for the future.

There are a number of opportunities for FSR to play a more productive role in agricultural research, but there is considerable division of opinion regarding the most desirable strategy to follow. We shall review several of the most prominent ideas currently being discussed. These include suggestions for further elaboration of FSR methods and more farmer participation in research. Other suggestions are concerned with the institutional environment in which FSR is carried out and urge more attention to extension programs and policy formulation. In addition, there is growing interest in the issue of sustainable agriculture, and this is seen as complementing FSR. Finally, although each of these ideas has some merit, the strengthening of organizations and management capacities for national research and extension systems is seen as the most important prerequisite for the utilization of FSR methods.

Elaboration of FSR methods. FSR provides an opportunity to examine a wide variety of issues and to develop new research methods, but there is the temptation to explain slow progress in the development of technology by the failure to investigate particular themes in greater depth. Many FSR programs have become mechanical exercises for establishing extensive programs of on-farm experimentation. In some cases in sub-Saharan Africa, scores of experiments have been run to refine fertilizer dosages, even though the main issue is the unavailability of fertilizer or inappropriate price policies. In other areas, such as South or Southeast Asia, where fertilizer use is well established, the information generated by fertilizer experiments has not been usefully synthesized by researchers or utilized by extension services.

Similar problems exist for FSR diagnostic studies. For example, FSR activities have provided insights into household dynamics and the differential impact of agricultural technology on rural women (Moock 1986; Poats et al. 1988). The issue having been successfully brought to the fore, the question now is whether further study and methodological innovation will benefit rural women (McKee 1986) or whether the focus should be on better targeting of the services and knowledge that already exist. The costs of refinements in FSR methodologies must be balanced against the likely benefits. There is the danger that in-depth FSR studies may run far ahead of the capacity to respond with technology or may ignore both the policy and extension environments in which the research is being carried out.

Farmer participation. An alternative to researchers studying the complexities of farming systems in more depth is providing opportunities for farmers to direct and carry out research, which has led to recent interest in farmer participatory research as a substitute for, or complement to, FSR (Farrington and Martin 1988). This interest stems partially from an assessment that, although FSR promised to "give voice" to small farmers (Norman 1980), much FSR has been carried out in a superficial manner that pays only lip service to farmers' interests. Beyond this, there is the feeling that fitting complex technologies to heterogeneous environments requires that more decision making be in the hands of farmers. There are a number of examples of increased farmer participation in research proving useful (Tripp 1989), but there are definite limits in efficiency and technical feasibility for farmers doing their own research. No matter what the future holds for FSR, incentive systems must be devised to direct researchers towards farmers' problems, and these must be balanced by opportunities for farmers to apply political pressure on research and extension services to address their concerns.

Extension. It is easy to blame extension for the slow rate of adoption of new technologies, but the situation is more complicated than that. Although one of the justifications for FSR has been that it would forge better links between research and extension, there are relatively few examples of effective collaboration. Training and Visit (T&V), a major effort at organizing extension promoted by the World Bank in many countries (Benor and Harrison 1977), has been developed parallel to FSR, with few obvious connections. The T&V extension method assumes that technology is available for farmers and that the critical factor is the organization of clear extension messages and methods for delivering them. But FSR has not yet developed a backlog of technology for delivery, and extension has not yet accepted that effective transfer of technology often begins with a better understanding of clients' needs. Hence, there remains much room for improvement on both sides. In the 1990s, much more emphasis must be placed on the development of stronger research-extension linkages and more direct participation of extension staff in the technology generation process.

Policy. FSR has at times been encouraged to include wider policy issues within its purview (Davidson 1987). It is true that many FSR projects have taken a conservative stance by assuming that the policy environment is fixed, and hence a lot of effort has been devoted to "tinkering" with the existing system (e.g., comparing intercropping combinations or dates of weeding) when the real payoffs may come only by introducing new technology based on increased use of purchased inputs. Data from on-farm research can be highly relevant to policy issues, especially the issue of input supply (Yates et al. 1988); but FSR should not see itself as providing the nucleus for agricultural development policy formation. FSR can provide information to help resolve policy-related issues impeding technological change, but FSR should not be presented as a substitute for conventional policy research on issues such as marketing, input distribution, or pricing (Herdt 1987). Instead, methods and channels of communication need to be developed so that policy formation can better utilize the unique information on the technical and socioeconomic circumstances of farmers that is now being generated by FSR programs.

Sustainable agriculture. To the extent that FSR in the 1970s and 1980s encapsulated a number of concerns and captured the interest of donor and scientific communities, its successor for the 1990s is likely to be the theme of sustainability (Davis and Schirmer 1987). It is true that FSR has emphasized the development of technologies acceptable to farmers using short-term criteria rather than analyzing the longer-run issues of sustaining productivity and maintaining the natural resource base. But it is not likely that the concerns raised by sustainable agriculture can be addressed properly while ignoring the experience of FSR. In particular, the sustainable agriculture movement must avoid the trap of believing that problem identification can substitute for technology development.[2] A considerable amount of applied research will have to be combined with widespread, location-specific, adaptive research before much progress can be made towards developing sustainable agricultural systems.

Research organization. The greatest challenge for FSR in the 1990s, and the only hope for taking full advantage of its potential contributions, is for it to find its place in the context of the entire agricultural research organization. Donors and IARCs have not often thought sufficiently about the organization or integrity of NARS in promoting FSR, and FSR often finds itself imposed from the outside, rather than being adapted to particular institutional environments (Heinemann and Biggs 1985). Many projects aimed at strengthening agricultural research in Africa, for example, have been piecemeal, with inadequate long-term commitment, and without a strategy for institutional development (Eicher 1989). Often, FSR projects have relied on the youngest and least experienced researchers for their implementation. The effectiveness of FSR is highly dependent on the way in which it is institutionalized within NARS. Interdisciplinary work demands clear definitions of responsibilities and the establishment of channels for communication. A client focus requires changes in the way that research priorities are set. On-farm work requires changes in personnel deployment and incentives. When these factors are not addressed by research managers, any attempt to maintain FSR in a national program context quickly runs into problems, as a comprehensive study of the institutionalization of FSR has shown (Merrill-Sands et al. 1989).

FSR has tended to be seen as a separate entity, complementary to or competitive with other research activities. In addition, the variants of FSR have been presented as rigid sets of steps, complete with their own procedures and vocabulary, and research organizations have been forced to choose among them. The urgency of looking for a common ground in FSR has been recognized (IARCs 1987), and there is strong evidence that it exists (Harrington et al. 1989).

Although FSR programs typically focus on relatively small areas, the payoffs to FSR can be greatly increased if information generated on technological needs of farmers can be effectively fed back to influence the design of technology and technology development on the research station (Byerlee et al. 1986; Merrill-Sands and McAllister 1988). In the future, more emphasis should be placed on ensuring the relevance of all research, whether on-station or on-farm, to farmers' circumstances. More opportunities need to be created for researchers *at all levels* to interact with representative farmers and observe their fields. Furthermore, the emphasis of FSR on stratifying farmers for the purpose of technology design and dissemination should be applied throughout the research system. In the 1990s, research organizations need to learn how to target their scarce resources efficiently towards the more important problems and farm populations. The perspective and methods of FSR, if properly integrated into research and extension institutions, can play an important role in that task.

SUMMARY

The FSR movement has been responsible for focusing attention on resource-poor farmers as clients for agricultural research. It has placed agricultural research scientists in much closer contact with farmers and has provided a wide variety of innovative research methods to help understand farmers' priorities and to test and assess technologies under farmers' conditions and criteria. But FSR has often been implemented in NARS with little thought to clear definitions of staff responsibilities, interdisciplinary communication, or the setting of research priorities within the larger institution. The consequence has been a much slower rate of technology generation than expected, and often a perceived split between farming systems researchers on the one hand and commodity and disciplinary researchers on the other. The principal challenge for the 1990s is to use the perspective and methods of FSR to improve the efficiency of entire research and extension organizations and to help them participate more effectively in the formulation of agricultural development policy.

NOTES

1. USAID played a leading role in the promotion of FSR by sponsoring a comprehensive review of FSR methods (Shaner et al. 1982), funding FSR projects in a number of countries, establishing the Farming Systems Support Project at the University of Florida, and sponsoring an annual farming systems symposium at Kansas State University. In the 1980s, the World Bank substantially increased its lending for adaptive on-farm research (World Bank, 1985), and a number of European donors developed FSR projects in eastern and southern Africa. Similarly, IDRC provided strong support for the Asian Rice Farming Systems Network.

2. See Ruttan, chapter 24 in this volume.

REFERENCES

Ashby, J. A., C. A. Quiros, and Y. M. Rivera. 1987. *Farmer Participation in On-Farm Varietal Trials.* Overseas Development Institute Network Discussion Paper 22. London.

Barker, R., and C. Lightfoot. 1988. "On-Farm Trials: A Survey of Methods." *Agricultural Administration and Extension* 30:15–23.

Benor, D., and J. Q. Harrison. 1977. *Agricultural Extension: The Training and Visit System.* Washington, D.C.: World Bank.

Brush, S. B., and B. L. Turner II. 1987. "The Nature of Farming Systems and Views of Their Change." In *Comparative Farming Systems,* edited by B. L. Turner and S. B. Brush. New York: Guilford Press.

Byerlee, D. 1987. *Maintaining the Momentum in Post Green Revolution Agriculture: A Micro-Level Perspective from Asia.* MSU International Development Paper, no. 10. East Lansing: Michigan State University, Department of Agricultural Economics.

Byerlee, D., M. Collinson, et al. 1980. *Planning Technologies Appropriate to Farmers: Concepts and Procedures.* Mexico, D.F.: CIMMYT.

Byerlee, D., L. Harrington, and D. Winkelmann. 1982. "Farming Systems Research: Issues in Research Strategy and Technology Design." *American Journal of Agricultural Economics* 64:897–904.

Byerlee, D., P. Hobbs, B. Khan, A. Majid, M. R. Akhtar, and N. Hashmi. 1986. *Increasing Wheat Productivity in the Context of Pakistan's Irrigated Cropping Systems: A View from the Farmer's Field.* PARC/CIMMYT Paper 86–7. Islamabad, Pakistan: PARC.

Byerlee, D., and R. Tripp. 1988. "Strengthening Linkages in Agricultural Research through a Farming Systems Perspective: The Role of Social Scientists." *Experimental Agriculture* 24:137–51.

CGIAR, Technical Advisory Committee (TAC). 1978. *Farming Systems Research at the International Agricultural Research Centers.* Rome: TAC Secretariat.

Chambers, R., and J. Jiggins. 1986. *Agricultural Research for Resource Poor Farmers: A Parsimonious Paradigm.* Discussion Paper 220, Institute of Development Studies. Sussex, England.

CIMMYT. 1988. *From Agronomic Data to Farmer Recommendations.* Mexico, D.F.: CIMMYT.

Collinson, M. 1972. *Farm Management in Peasant Agriculture.* New York: Praeger.

Collinson, M. 1981. "A Low Cost Approach to Understanding Small Farmers." *Agricultural Administration* 8:433–50.

Collinson, M. 1982. *Farming Systems Research in Eastern Africa: The Experience of CIMMYT and some National Agricultural Research Services, 1976–81.* MSU International Development Paper, no. 3. East Lansing: Michigan State University, Department of Agricultural Economics.

Dahlan, M., Heriyanto, Sunarsedyono, S. Wahyuni, C. E. Van Santen, J. Ph. Van Staveren, and L. W. Harrington. 1987. *Maize On-Farm Research in the District of Malang.* Malang, Indonesia: Malang Research Institute for Food Crops.

Davidson, A. P. 1987. "Does Farming Systems Research Have a Future?" *Agricultural Administration and Extension* 24:69–77.

Davis, T. J., and I. A. Schirmer, eds. 1987. *Sustainability Issues in Agricultural Development. Proceedings of the Seventh Agriculture Sector Symposium.* Washington, D.C.: World Bank.

Eicher, C. K. 1989. *Sustainable Institutions for African Agricultural Development.* ISNAR Working Paper, no. 19. The Hague: ISNAR.

Farrington, J., and A. Martin. 1988. *Farmer Participation in Agricultural Research: A Review of Concepts and Practices.* Overseas Development Institute Agricultural Administration Unit Occasional Paper, no. 9. London.

Fresco, L. O. 1984. "Comparing Anglophone and Francophone Approaches to Farming Systems Research and Extension." Paper presented at the 4th Annual Conference on Farming Systems Research, Kansas State University, Manhattan, Kansas.

Gilbert, E. H., D. W. Norman, and F. E. Winch. 1980. *Farming Systems Research: A Critical Appraisal.* MSU Rural Development Paper, no. 6. East Lansing: Michigan State University, Department of Agricultural Economics.

Grigg, D. B. 1974. *The Agricultural Systems of the World.* Cambridge: Cambridge University Press.

Harrington, L. W., M. D. Read, D. Garrity, J. Woolley, and R. Tripp. 1989. "Approaches to On-Farm Client-Oriented Research: Similarities, Differences, and Future Directions." Paper presented at the International Workshop on Developments in Procedures for FSR/OFR, Bogor, Indonesia.

Harwood, R. 1979. *Small Farm Development.* Boulder, Colo.: Westview.

Heinemann, E., and S. D. Biggs. 1985. "Farming Systems Research: An Evolutionary Approach to Implementation." *Journal of Agricultural Economics* 36:59–65.

Herdt, R. 1987. "Whither Farming Systems." In *How Systems Work. Proceedings of Farming Systems Research Symposium 1987.* University of Arkansas and Winrock International Institute for Agricultural Development.

Hildebrand, P. 1976. *Generating Technology for Traditional Farmers: A Multidisciplinary Methodology.* Guatemala City: ICTA.

Hildebrand, P. 1981. "Combining Disciplines in Rapid Appraisal: The Sondeo Approach." *Agricultural Administration* 8:423–32.

IARCs. 1987. *Proceedings of the Workshop on Farming Systems Research.* Patancheru, India: ICRISAT.

IRRI. 1982. *The Role of Anthropologists and Other Social Scientists in Interdisciplinary Teams Developing Improved Food Production Technology.* Los Baños, Philippines: IRRI.

Jimenez, L. 1970. "The Puebla Project: A Regional Program for Rapidly Increasing Corn Yields among 50,000 Small Holders." In *Strategies for Increasing Agricultural Production on Small Holdings,* edited by D. Myren. Mexico, D.F.: CIMMYT.

Johnson, G. L. 1982. "Small Farms in a Changing World." In Proceedings of Kansas State University 1981 Farming Systems Research Symposium, edited by W. Sheppard. Manhattan, Kansas: Kansas State University.

Kydd, J. 1989. "Maize Research in Malawi: Lessons from Failure." *Journal of International Development* 1:112–44.

Lionberger, H. F., and H. C. Chang. 1970. *Farm Information for Modernizing Agriculture: The Taiwan System.* New York: Praeger.

Martinez, J. C., and G. Sain. 1983. *The Economic Returns to Institutional Innovations in National Agricultural Research: On-Farm Research in IDIAP Panama.* CIMMYT Economics Program Working Paper 04/83. Mexico, D.F.: CIMMYT.

Mathema, S. B. 1986. "Adoption and Effects of Technologies Generated by the Cropping Systems Program in Nepal." Unpublished Ph.D. diss., University of the Philippines, Los Baños.

McKee, K. 1986. "Household Analysis as an Aid to Farming Systems Research: Methodological Issues." In J. Moock, ed.

Merrill-Sands, D. 1986. "Farming Systems Research: Clarification of Terms and Concepts." *Experimental Agriculture* 22:87–104.

Merrill-Sands, D., P. Ewell, S. Biggs, and J. McAllister. 1989. "Issues in Institutionalizing On-Farm Client-Oriented Research: A Review of Experiences from Nine National Agricultural Research Systems." *Quarterly Journal of International Agriculture.* Forthcoming.

Merrill-Sands, D., and J. McAllister. 1988. *Strengthening the Integration of On-Farm Client-Oriented Research and Experiment Station Research in National Agricultural Research Systems (NARS): Management Lessons from Nine Country Case Studies.* OFCOR Comparative Paper, no. 1. The Hague: ISNAR.

Moock, J., ed. 1986. *Understanding Africa's Rural Households and Farming Systems.* Boulder: Westview Press.

Morris, R. A. 1984. "A Decade of On-Farm Research in Lowland Rice-Based Farming Systems: Some Lessons." Paper presented at the 4th Annual Conference on Farming Systems Research, Manhattan, Kansas.

Moscardi, E., V. H. Cardoso, P. Espinosa, R. Soliz, and E. Zambrano. 1983. *Creating an On-Farm Research Program in Ecuador.* CIMMYT Economics Program Working Paper 01/83. Mexico, D.F.: CIMMYT.

Mutsaers, H. J. W., N. M. Fisher, W. O. Vogel, and M. C. Palada. 1986. *A Field Guide for On-Farm Research.* Ibadan, Nigeria: IITA.

Norman, D. 1977. "Economic Rationality of Traditional Hausa Dryland Farmers in the North of Nigeria." In *Tradition and Dynamics in Small-Farm Agriculture,* edited by R. D. Stevens. Ames, Iowa: Iowa State University Press.

Norman, D. 1980. *The Farming Systems Approach: Relevancy for Small Farmers.* MSU Rural Development Paper, no. 5, East Lansing: Michigan State University, Department of Agricultural Economics.

Norman, D., D. Baker, C. Heinrich, and F. Worman. 1988. "Technology Development and Farmer Groups: Experiences from Botswana." *Experimental Agriculture* 24:321–31.

Norman, D. W., D. H. Pryor, and C. J. N. Gibbs. 1979. *Technical Change and the Small Farmer in Hausaland, Northern Nigeria.* African Rural Economy Paper, no. 21. East Lansing: Michigan State University.

Poats, S. U., M. Schmink, and A. Spring, eds. 1988. *Gender Issues in Farming Systems Research and Extension.* Boulder: Westview Press.

Rhoades, R. 1984. *Breaking New Ground: Agricultural Anthropology.* Lima, Peru: International Potato Center.

Ruano, S., and A. Fumagalli. 1988. *Guatemala: Organización y Manejo de la Investigación en Finca en el Instituto de Ciencia y Tecnología Agrícolas (ICTA).* OFCOR Case Study, no. 2. The Hague: ISNAR.

Ruthenberg, H. 1971. *Farming Systems in the Tropics.* Oxford: Clarendon Press.

Schultz, T. W. 1964. *Transforming Traditional Agriculture.* New Haven: Yale University Press.

Shaner, W. W., P. F. Philipp, and W. R. Schmehl. 1982. *Farming Systems Research in Development: Guidelines for Developing Countries.* Boulder: Westview Press.

Simmonds, N. W. 1985. *Farming Systems Research. A Review.* World Bank Technical Paper, no. 43. Washington, D.C.: World Bank.

Siwi, B. H., et al. 1986. *The Impact of Cropping Systems Research in Indonesia.* Bogor, Indonesia: Central Research Institute for Food Crops.

Sumberg, J., and C. Okali. 1988. "Farmers, On-Farm Research, and the Development of New Technology." *Experimental Agriculture* 24:333–42.

Tripp, R. 1989. *Farmer Participation in Agricultural Research: New Directions or Old Problems?* IDS Discussion Paper 256. Sussex, England.

Tripp, R., K. Marfo, A. A. Dankyi, and M. Read. 1987. *Changing Maize Production Practices of Small-Scale Farmers in the Brong-Ahafo Region, Ghana.* Kumasi, Ghana: Ghana Grains Development Project.

Tripp, R., and J. Woolley. 1989. *The Planning Stage of On-Farm Research: Identifying Factors for Experimentation.* Mexico, D.F.: CIMMYT and CIAT.

Woolley, J. 1987. *The Design of Experiments in On-Farm Research.* Cali, Colombia: CIAT.

Woolley, J., J. A. Beltran, R. A. Vallejo, and M. Prager. 1988. *Identifying Appropriate Technologies for Farmers: The Case of the Bean and Maize Systems in Ipiales, Colombia, 1982–1986.* CIAT Working Document, no. 31. Cali, Colombia: CIAT.

World Bank. 1985. *Agricultural Research and Extension: An Evaluation of the World Bank's Experience.* Washington, D.C.: World Bank.

Yates, M., J. C. Martinez, and G. Sain. 1988. *Fertilizer in Les Cayes, Haiti: Addressing Market Imperfections with Farm-Based Policy Analysis.* CIMMYT Economics Working Paper 88/01. Mexico, D.F.: CIMMYT.

Zandstra, H., E. Price, J. Litsinger, and R. Morris. 1981. *Methodology for On-Farm Cropping Systems Research.* Los Baños, Philippines: International Rice Research Institute.

Zandstra, H., K. Swanberg, C. Zulberti, and B. Nestel. 1979. *Caqueza: Living Rural Development.* Ottawa: International Development Research Centre.

24

Sustainability Is Not Enough

VERNON W. RUTTAN

Any definition of sustainability suitable as a guide to agricultural practice must recognize the need for enhancement of productivity to meet the increased demands created by growing populations and rising incomes. The sustainable agricultural movement must define its goals sufficiently broadly to meet the challenge of enhancing both productivity and sustainability in both the developed and the developing world. I will illustrate the problems of achieving these goals with some historical examples.

AMBIGUITY ABOUT TECHNOLOGY

The productivity of modern agriculture is a result of a remarkable fusion of science, technology, and practice. This fusion did not come easily. The advances in tillage equipment and crop and animal husbandry which occurred during the Middle Ages and until well into the nineteenth century evolved almost entirely from husbandry practice and mechanical insight. The power that the fusion of theoretical and empirical inquiry has given to the advancement of knowledge and technology since the middle of the nineteenth century has made possible advances in material well-being that would not have been imagined in an earlier age.

These advances have also been interpreted as contributing to the subversion of traditional rural values and institutions and to the degradation of natural environments. They led, in the 1960s and 1970s, to the emergence of a new skepticism about the benefits of advances in science and technology. A view emerged that the political power created by the fusion of science and technology was dangerous to the modern world and could lead to the failure of the human race.

This ambiguity about the impact of science and technology on institutions and environments has led to a series of efforts to increase the sensitivity of scientists and science administrators and to reform the decision processes for the allocation of research resources. These efforts have typically attempted to find rhetorical

VERNON W. RUTTAN is Regents Professor, Department of Agricultural and Applied Economics and Department of Economics, and adjunct professor, Hubert H. Humphrey Institute of Public Affairs, University of Minnesota, St. Paul.

Reprinted from *American Journal of Alternative Agriculture* 3, nos. 2 and 3, Spring/Summer, 1988: 128–30, by permission of the Institute for Alternative Agriculture, Inc. and the author.

400

capsules that would serve as a banner under which efforts to achieve reforms might march. Among the more prominent have been "appropriate technology," "integrated pest management," "low-input technology," and, more recently, "sustainability."

REFORMING AGRICULTURAL RESEARCH

It is not untypical for such rhetorical capsules to achieve the status of an ideology or a social movement even before acquiring a methodology, a technology, or even a definition. If the reform movement is successful in directing scientific and technical effort in a productive direction, it becomes incorporated into normal scientific or technological practice. If it leads to a dead-end, it slips into the underworld of science, often to be resurrected when the conditions which generated the concern again emerge toward the top of the social agenda.

Research on new uses for agricultural products is an example. It was promoted in the 1930s under the rubric of chemurgy and in the 1950s under the rubric of utilization research as a solution to the problem of agricultural surpluses. It lost both scientific and political credibility because it promised more than it could deliver. It emerged again, in the late 1970s and early 1980s, in the guise of enhancing value added.

The "sustainability" movement, like other efforts to reform agricultural research, has experienced some difficulty in arriving at a definition that can command consistency among the diverse and sometimes incompatible reform movements that are marching under its banner. Readers who recall the more populist conservation literature of the 1950s, such as *Topsoil and Civilization* (1955) by Tom Dale and Vernon Carter, and *Malabar Farm* (1947) by Louis Bromfield, will recognize the poetry that has emerged in some of the new sustainability literature. Fortunately, we can draw on several historical examples of sustainable agricultural systems.

SUSTAINABLE AGRICULTURAL SYSTEMS

One example of sustainable agriculture was the system of integrated crop-animal husbandry that emerged in Western Europe in the late Middle Ages to replace the medieval two- and three-field systems (Boserup 1965). The "new husbandry" system emerged with the introduction and intensive use of new forage and green manure crops. These in turn permitted an increase in the availability and use of animal manures. This permitted the emergence of intensive crop-livestock systems of production through the recycling of plant nutrients in the form of animal manures to maintain and improve soil fertility.

A second example can be drawn from the agricultural history of East Asian wet rice cultivation (Hayami and Ruttan 1985). Traditional wet rice cultivation resembled farming in an aquarium. The rice grew tall and rank; it had a low grain-to-straw ratio, and grain was recycled into the flooded fields in the form of human and animal manures. Mineral nutrients and organic matter were carried into and deposited in the fields with the irrigation water. Rice yields rose continuously, though slowly, even under a monoculture system.

A third example is the forest and bush fallow (or shifting cultivation) systems that were practiced in most areas of the world in premodern times and still are today in many areas of tropical Africa (Pingali, Bigot, and Binswanger 1987). At a low level of population density, these systems were sustained over long periods of time. As population density increased, short fallow systems emerged. Where the shift to short fallow systems occurred slowly, as in Western Europe and East Asia, systems of farming that permitted sustained growth in agricultural production emerged. Where the transition to short fallow has been forced by rapid population growth, the consequence has often been soil degradation and declining productivity.

SUSTAINING AND ENHANCING PRODUCTIVITY

This brings me to the title of this paper. The three systems I have described, along with other similar systems based on indigenous technology, have provided inspiration for the emerging field of agroecology. But none of the traditional systems, while sustainable under conditions of slow growth in demand for food, has the capacity to respond to modern rates of growth in food demand generated by some combination of rapid increase in population and in growth of income. Some traditional systems were able to sustain rates of growth in the 0.5–1.0 percent per year range, but modern rates of growth in demand are in the range of 1.0–2.0 percent per year in the developed countries. Rates of growth of demand in the less developed and newly industrializing countries are often in the range of 3.5–5.0 percent per year.

In searching the literature on sustainability, I do not find sufficient recognition of the challenge that modern rates of growth in food demand impose on agriculture. If the concept of sustainability is to serve as a guide to practice, it must include the use of technology and practices that both sustain and enhance productivity.

In the United States, the capacity to sustain the necessary increases in agricultural production will depend largely on our capacity for institutional innovation. If we lose our capacity to sustain growth in agricultural production, it will be a result of political and economic failure. Failure to reform agricultural commodity programs in a manner that will contribute to both sustaining and enhancing productivity will mean a loss of one of the few industries in the United States that has managed to retain world-class status—that is capable of competing in world markets (von Witzke and Ruttan 1988).[1]

It is quite clear, however, that the scientific and technical knowledge is not yet available that will enable farmers in most tropical countries to meet the current demand their societies are placing upon them or to sustain the increases that are being achieved. Further, the research capacity has not yet been established to provide that knowledge and technology. In these countries, achievement of sustainable agricultural surpluses is dependent on advances in scientific knowledge and on technical and institutional innovation.

IMPLICATIONS FOR RESEARCH

I am deeply concerned about a weakening commitment to creating in both developed and developing countries the research capacity necessary to achieve productive and sustainable agricultural systems. I am also concerned that the sustainability movement is pressing for adoption of agricultural practices under the banner of sustainability before either the science has been done or the technology is available.

It has been surprisingly difficult to find careful definitions of the term *sustainability*. This is at least in part because sustainability, if it is to provide a useful rhetoric for reform, must be able to accommodate the several traditions that must march under its banner. These include the organic agriculture tradition, the land stewardship movement, the agroecological perspective, and others. In my judgment, any attempt to specify the technology and practices that meet the criteria of sustaining and enhancing productivity would be premature. *At present it is useful to define sustainability in a manner that will be useful as a guide to research rather than as an immediate guide to practice.* Thus, it seems useful to adhere to a definition that includes (1) the development of technology and practices to maintain and/ or enhance the quality of land and water resources, and (2) the improvement in plants and animals and the advances in production practices to facilitate substitution of biological technology for chemical technology.

Furthermore, it is desirable to learn what is achievable in the above objectives, primarily from a biological perspective. Maximum yield experiments represent a useful analogy: the objective of a maximum yield experiment or trial is not to provide a guide to farm practice; it is to find out how a plant population performs under high-level input stress. The research agenda on sustainable agriculture needs to define what is biologically feasible without being excessively limited by present economic constraints.

NOTE

1. See Bonnen, chapter 15 in this volume.—ED.

REFERENCES

Boserup, E. 1965. *Conditions of Agricultural Growth*. Chicago: Aldine Publishing Company.
Bromfield, L. 1947. *Malabar Farm*. Harper, New York.
Dale, T., and V. G. Carter. 1955. *Topsoil and Civilization*. Normal: Oklahoma University Press.
Hayami, Y., and V. W. Ruttan. 1985. *Agricultural Development: An International Perspective*. Baltimore: Johns Hopkins University Press.

Pingali, P., Y. Bigot, and H. P. Binswanger. 1987. *Agricultural Mechanization and the Evolution of Farming Systems in Sub-Saharan Africa.* Baltimore: Johns Hopkins University Press.
von Witzke, Harold, and V. W. Ruttan. 1988. "International Agricultural Policy Coordination." *Atlantic Community Quarterly* 26 (Fall/Winter): 321–29.

25

The Impact of Technical Change on Income Distribution: The Case of Rice in Colombia

GRANT M. SCOBIE AND RAFAEL POSADA T.

The contribution of technical change to agricultural productivity in developing countries has been widely recognized and increasingly documented (Arndt, Dalrymple, and Ruttan 1977). The generation of that technical change through agricultural research is now viewed as an economic activity to which scarce resources can be devoted and measurable output defined (Schultz 1970).[1]

In the appraisal of potential or past research strategies, two central economic issues arise: efficiency and equity. While earlier studies were concerned primarily with the efficiency goal, increasing attention has been given to the distribution of social benefits stemming from programs of agricultural research. Akino and Hayami (1975) and Ramalho de Castro and Schuh (1977) examine the distribution of the gross social benefits between consumers and producers, while others have considered the impact on the functional distribution of income (for example, Ayer and Schuh [1972]; Schmitz and Seckler [1970]; Wallace and Hoover [1966]).

In this chapter we analyze the impact of technological change in the Colombian rice industry, giving particular attention to the consequences for the household income distribution. "It appears that relatively little theoretical and empirical work has been done on the welfare or income distributional effects of technical change. This is unfortunate, for a considerable amount of research funds is spent each year by both private and public institutions to develop new technologies for agriculture" (Bieri, de Janvry, and Schmitz 1972, 801). After sketching the background of the research program, we present some estimates of

GRANT M. SCOBIE is a consultant in agricultural economics, Hamilton, New Zealand. RAFAEL POSADA T. is economist, Centro Internacional de Agricultura Tropical (CIAT), Cali, Colombia.

Reprinted from *American Journal of Agricultural Economics* 60, no. 1 (1978): 85–92, with omissions and minor editorial revisions, by permission of the American Agricultural Economics Association and the authors.

the social benefits: the rate of return (efficiency) and the impact on household income distribution (equity). Both costs and benefits of the research program are used in deriving the distributional consequences.

BACKGROUND

In 1957 a national rice research program was formed within the Ministry of Agriculture with the cooperation of the Rockefeller Foundation (Rosero 1974). At that time, the tall U.S. variety, Bluebonnet-50, was extensively grown; but in 1957 it was attacked by a virus disease, causing extensive losses. Imports of rice rose substantially, and the real domestic retail price was higher in 1957 than in any year since 1950 (and in fact up to 1974). These events stimulated the formation and funding of a national rice research program whose primary objective was the selection of varieties resistant to the virus. It was hoped that by this mechanism domestic output could be increased, partly eliminating the need for rice imports and lowering domestic prices. This strongly consumer-oriented policy contrasts with the vacillation of public policy between a consumer and a producer focus which had been characteristic of Colombian rice policy since the thirties (Leurquin 1967).

This research effort did produce new varieties, but their impact was limited (Hertford et al. 1977). In 1967 the newly formed rice program of the Centro Internacional de Agricultura Tropical (CIAT) joined in a collaborative effort with the Colombian program, and dwarf lines from the International Rice Research Institute in the Philippines were introduced. This was followed by the local development and release of four disease-resistant dwarf rices. The rate of adoption of these modern varieties has been spectacular. In 1966, 90 percent of the irrigated sector was sown to the traditional variety (Bluebonnet-50); by 1974 virtually all the irrigated rice production came from dwarf varieties.

The research program, especially since 1967, has been oriented to the irrigated sector. The modern varieties have been best suited to areas with good water control and high levels of other inputs. Thus, while widely adopted throughout the irrigated sector, they had little impact in the upland or rainfed sector. Given the possibility of rapid increases in national output through the introduction of new varieties suited to irrigated culture, this was undoubtedly a rational choice. The rate of technological progress that could have been achieved with the same research resources surely would have been less had attention been directed to the upland sector. A further explanation of the particular ecological orientation adopted lay in the close collaboration between FEDEARROZ, the National Rice Growers' Federation (founded and supported principally by the large rice growers), and the research program.

As a consequence of the emphasis on the irrigated sector, together with the rapid adoption of the modern varieties, yields and production in that sector rose dramatically. In contrast, the relatively disadvantaged upland sector, which experienced little or no technical change, declined in importance from 50 percent of the national output in 1966 to 10 percent in 1974.

THE MODEL

The approach taken closely follows the formulation of Ayer and Schuh (1972).[2] A more detailed statement of the model and the estimation of the parameters is given in Scobie and Posada 1977. The model estimates the total gross social benefits and their division between Colombian rice producers and consumers, but extends existing formulations (following Bell 1972) by distinguishing between upland and irrigated producers. This distinction was made as a consequence of the differential impact of the research program on the two sectors. It is suggested that the proposed formulation would have general applicability in analyzing the differential impact of a new technology whose relevance is restricted for whatever reason to a subset of the producing firms.

RESULTS

Gross Benefits

The changes in consumer and producer surpluses resulting from the introduction of modern varieties were estimated for each year from 1964 to 1974 and are summarized in table 1. Consumer benefits are positive because in the absence of modern varieties, the volume of rice entering the domestic market would have been much lower, with a concomitant higher internal price. However, for the same reason, both upland and irrigated producers have forgone rents to factors of production whose mobility is limited in the short run. Changes in producer surplus follow as a consequence of some inelasticity in the supply of rice, imparted by rising short-run marginal cost curves. Such changes would be transitory if, in the long run, the supply elasticities of all factors to rice production approached infinity. Despite the overall reduction in short-run producer sur-

TABLE 1
GROSS BENEFITS OF NEW RICE VARIETIES IN COLOMBIA TO
CONSUMERS AND PRODUCERS, IN $(COL.) MILLION

Gross Benefits Accruing to:	1964–69	1970–74
Consumers	1,404	17,542
Producers		
Irrigated	−368	−6,468
Upland	−517	−3,878
Total	519	7,196

NOTE: Each entry is the sum of the annual deflated values (1964 = 100).

pluses, some gains undoubtedly accrued to "early adopters" in the irrigated sector.

Had Colombia not mounted a successful research program, upward pressure on domestic prices may well have been contained by allowing rice imports. Even in the absence of such approval, illegal imports from neighboring Venezuela and Ecuador may have had a price-depressing effect. Higher imports of rice would have reduced the amount of foreign exchange available for other imports and put upward pressure on the exchange rate. However, estimating the distributional consequences of this scenario would lead us far beyond the more modest scope of this investigation.

NET BENEFITS

The distribution of gross benefits between producer and consumer groups is a relatively blunt tool for analyzing the distributional impact of technological change. We attempt two extensions: first we will consider the incidence of the research costs, and so derive net benefits to producers and consumers; subsequently we will examine the distribution of the gross benefits and research costs by income level within groups.

The costs of the research program were borne by three entities: (*a*) the national rice program of the Instituto Colombiano Agropecuario (ICA); (*b*) the contribution of the growers through FEDEARROZ under Law 101 of 1963, which created the *Cuota de Fomento Arrocera*. This law requires the collection of $(Col.) 0.01/kg from all growers and authorizes FEDEARROZ to administer the funds for support of research, regional testing, publishing technical bulletins, presenting training courses to field agronomists, and financing the Technical Division of FEDEARROZ; and (*c*) international cooperation, originally through the Rockefeller Foundation and subsequently through the rice program of the Centro Internacional de Agricultura Tropical (CIAT).

No attempt is made to include any costs incurred by the International Rice Research Institute (IRRI) in the development of IR-8 and IR-22, which occupied up to almost 60 percent of the area sown in Colombia. Hence, for these varieties we will overstate the net global benefits by allowing their contribution to production without discounting their full costs. However, if the measurement of net benefits is viewed from Colombia's standpoint, then it is valid to include only those costs incurred by Colombia in testing, multiplying, and releasing the IRRI materials.

The distribution of gross social benefits, research costs, and net benefits for producers and consumers is shown in table 2. The gross social benefits were totaled for the period 1964–74 and expressed in $(Col.)million 1970, compounding forward the years 1964–69 and discounting 1971–74, both using an estimate of 10 percent for the social opportunity cost of capital in Colombia (Harberger 1972, 155).

In a similar manner the costs of the research from the three sources were

TABLE 2

SIZE AND DISTRIBUTION OF BENEFITS AND COSTS OF MODERN RICE VARIETIES IN
COLOMBIA, 1957–74, IN $(COL.) MILLION

Item	Producers			Consumers	Total Colombia	International Cooperation[a]
	Upland	*Irrigated*	*Total*			
Gross benefits	−3,542	−5,293	−8,835	14,939	6,104	—
Costs of research						
FEDEARROZ	8	30	38	—	38	—
ICA[b]	1	2	2	22	25	—
Total	9	32	40	22	63	19
Net benefits	−3,551	−5,325	−8,875	14,917	6,042	—

NOTE: All data expressed in 1970 pesos; minor discrepancies are due to rounding.

[a]From Ardila 1973, and personal communication from the Centro Internacional de Agricultura Tropical (CIAT).

[b]From Ardila 1973, and personal communication from the Instituto Colombiano Agropecuario (ICA).

summed and are shown in table 2. The costs of the ICA program were assumed to come from general tax revenue and were divided between consumers and producers on the basis of urban and rural proportions of total tax revenues in 1970 (Jallade 1970). The producer contribution was further broken down between upland and irrigated producers on the basis of the production coming from each sector in 1970. The contributions from FEDEARROZ were distributed between the upland and irrigated sectors assuming a 45 percent collection rate (FEDEARROZ 1975), except that no contributions were assumed for upland producers with less than ten hectares. Expressed in 1970 pesos, $(Col.)82 million were devoted to rice research between 1957 and 1974.

In order to assess the sensitivity of the net benefits to varying assumptions about the supply-demand elasticities, the results in table 3 were calculated. The demand elasticity was varied from −0.3 (a typical lower bound found in a review

TABLE 3

NET BENEFITS IN 1974, IN $(COL.) MILLION, AND INTERNAL RATES OF RETURN
FOR DIFFERING ELASTICITIES OF SUPPLY AND DEMAND

Elasticity of Supply (ϵ)	Elasticity of Demand (η)		
	−0.300	*−0.449*	*−0.754*
0.235	9,052	3,981	2,174
	89%	94%	89%
1.500	8,627	3,556	1,749
	96%	87%	79%

NOTE: In each cell, the upper figure is the net benefits to Colombia of the rice research program in 1974, and the lower figure is the internal rate of return based on the period 1957–74, with the last year's costs and returns assumed to continue until 1986. The combination of $\eta = -0.449$ and $\epsilon = 0.235$ was used in calculating the results presented in tables 1 and 2.

of numerous studies in developing countries) to -0.449 (based on Pinstrup-Andersen, de Londoño, and Hoover 1976, 137) to -0.754 (Cruz de Schlesinger and Ruiz 1967). The supply elasticity of 0.235 is from Gutiérrez and Hertford 1974, with an arbitrarily chosen upper value of 1.5.

The internal rate of return on the investment is consistently high and relatively insensitive to varying elasticities. These high returns are not uncommon in agricultural research. Ayer and Schuh (1972, 581) report an internal rate of return of 89 percent for cotton in São Paulo, Brazil; Akino and Hayami (1975, 8) report values up to 75 percent for rice in Japan; Peterson (1967, 669) reports 20–30 percent for poultry in the United States; Barletta (1971) reports 75 percent for wheat in Mexico; Griliches (1958) reports 35 percent for corn in the United States; Ardila (1973) reports 58–82 percent for rice in Colombia up until 1971; and Montes (1973) reports 76–96 percent for soybeans in Colombia. One should resist the conclusion that all agricultural research would show such payoffs—the literature is not replete with evaluations of failures.

While the net benefits in 1974 vary little with the supply elasticity, they fall markedly with higher absolute demand elasticities (table 3). However, our concern here is more with the relative distribution of the net benefits within groups than with establishing their absolute magnitude.

DISTRIBUTION OF NET BENEFITS BY INCOME LEVEL

To evaluate the distributional impacts of the technological change, the gross benefits, the costs of the research program, and the consequent net benefits were distributed across income groups for consumers and upland and irrigated producers. In each case the annual average impact for 1970 was estimated by summing the gross benefits and costs (expressed in 1970 pesos) and dividing by the appropriate number of years.

Gross benefits to consumers were assumed to be directly proportional to the quantity of rice consumed, while their contributions to the research costs were distributed in proportion to tax receipts from each income stratum. The resulting net benefits to consumers by income level are shown in table 4.

Rice is now virtually the most important foodstuff in Colombia; between 1969 and 1974 total domestic consumption doubled (U.S. Department of Agriculture 1976, 11), and rice is the major source of calories and the second major source of protein (after beef) in the Colombian diet (Departamento Nacional de Planeación 1974). As rice is disproportionately consumed by the lower-income groups, who make limited tax contributions, the net benefits of the research program were strongly biased toward them in both absolute and relative terms. While the lower 50 percent of Colombian households received about 15 percent of household income, they captured nearly 70 percent of the net benefits of the research program.

In the case of producers, the annual average change in producer surplus was

TABLE 4
DISTRIBUTION OF NET BENEFITS, HOUSEHOLDS, AND HOUSEHOLD INCOME

1970 Income Level ($[Col.]000)	Annual Average Net Benefits ($[Col.])	Net Benefits as a Percentage of Income[a]	Cumulative Percentage of:		
			Net Benefits	Households[b]	Household[b] Income
0–6	385	12.8%	18%	19%	2%
6–12	642	7.1	50	39	8
12–18	530	3.5	67	52	15
18–24	333	1.6	77	64	23
24–30	348	1.3	83	71	29
30–36	353	1.2	88	76	35
36–48	342	0.8	93	82	43
48–60	200	0.4	95	86	51
60–72	128	0.2	96	89	57
72+	138	0.2	100	100	100

[a]Relative to the midpoint of the interval.
[b]From Jallade, 1974, 22.

distributed across farm sizes in proportion to estimates of the production based on census data. The research costs were also distributed by farm size, assuming that tax payments were proportional to production (in the case of the ICA costs), and by the method already discussed for the research levy. The sum of the forgone income and the research costs were then expressed as a percentage of the estimated 1970 average net income by farm size for the entire rural sector (table 5). This last step is clearly less than satisfactory.

Ideally, income distribution data are required for upland and irrigated rice producers by size of farm. As no such data are known to exist, resort was made to a distribution of rural income by farm size for 1960 (Berry 1974, 610), inflated to 1970 values. We have no basis for knowing whether rice producers would have higher or lower incomes than the rural average for each farm size group. However, again, our principal interest is in the relative rather than absolute distribution of benefits by income level.

The group most severely affected was the small (that is, low-income) upland producers. For these producers, the annual average income forgone through lower rice prices (and no compensating technological change) represented a high proportion of their assumed 1970 income. To the extent that their incomes were below the rural sector average, this impact would have been even more pronounced. On the other hand, the forgone income to the irrigated producers varied more erratically depending on the size group, with the heaviest relative burden falling on the 200–500- and 500–1,000-hectare groups. However, the absolute impact may well be overstated if irrigated producers had incomes above the national average for rural income earners.

In summary, the net benefits of the technological change accrued to con-

TABLE 5
ANNUAL AVERAGE DISTRIBUTIONAL IMPACT OF RICE RESEARCH PROGRAM ON
UPLAND AND IRRIGATED PRODUCERS

		Change in Producer Surplus Plus Research Costs as a Percentage of 1970 Income	
Farm Size (hectares)	Average Income[a] ($[Col.])	Upland Sector	Irrigated Sector
0–1	1,500[b]	−58%	−56%
1–2	3,647	−53	−39
2–3	5,330	−60	−25
3–4	6,508	−71	−38
4–5	7,406	−75	−53
5–6	10,295	−60	−43
10–20	15,652	−48	−47
20–30	18,934	−41	−48
30–40	23,394	−35	−47
40–50	28,620	−30	−45
50–100	35,904	−29	−48
100–200	66,759	−26	−53
200–500	155,398	−18	−79
500–1,000	287,513	−21	−69
1,000–2,000	532,389	−19	−49
2,000+	1,480,199	−11	−36

[a]From Berry 1974, 610, adjusted to 1970.
[b]Assumed value.

sumers, with the lowest-income households capturing a disproportionate share. As Hayami and Herdt (1977) note, "The decline in the price of a food staple due to technical progress in its production has the effect of equalizing income among urban consumers." The forgone income to producers appeared to fall most heavily on the small upland producers. Even if the average annual consumer benefits are included as benefits to upland producers, the small upland producers still appear as the most severely affected, a not surprising result, given the orientation of the research program toward the irrigated sector. However, some notion of the relative magnitudes of the different groups should be borne in mind. In 1970 (prior to the major impact of the modern varieties) there were only an estimated twelve thousand upland producers with less than five hectares. Hence, under any plausible set of welfare weights, their losses would be more than offset by the gain to more than one million low-income consuming households, implying an overall gain (albeit uncompensated) in some measure of social welfare.

Caution should be exercised in generalizing from this conclusion. The urban and nonlandowning rural poor of Colombia are very much more numerous than the small farmers. In less urbanized countries with a large semisubsistence rural population, the lowest-income households may benefit from technological advances specifically designed for the small-farm sector (Valdés, Scobie, and Dillon 1979).

CONCLUDING COMMENTS

Concern is periodically voiced for the distributional implications of technological change in developing agriculture. One is often led to feel that the introduction of new technology has been only a qualified success because of its apparent failure to solve a broad spectrum of social ills. But frequently it is the well-being of only the rural poor (both the small farmer and the landless worker) that is the focus of attention. The presence of large concentrations of urban poor who are potential beneficiaries of expanded production of basic foodstuffs is sometimes neglected when castigating the "green revolution."

Throughout much of Latin America, the rural poor tend to be concentrated (for historical reasons) in the less favored ecological zones. The development of technology suited to such areas is presumably a more difficult process, which, *ceteris paribus*, would divert research resources from the discovery of technologies that can result in rapid increases in total output from the more favored commercial agricultural sector.

The results presented for the case of Colombian rice exemplify this trade-off. By focusing on the distribution between consumers and producers and, more important, by isolating both the costs and benefits by income strata, we have endeavored to quantify some of the dimensions of this trade-off. Concentrating the research on the upland producers would presumably have entailed forgone benefits to the numerous urban poor (without guaranteeing that small upland producers would have benefitted in the long run).

In this chapter we have attempted some preliminary extensions of the commonly used approaches to analyzing the distributional impact of technological change: (*a*) a model that allows for differential impact of technological change on two classes of producers is introduced; (*b*) the incidence of research costs is considered in the distribution of the social benefits to different groups; and (*c*) the distributional impact (at the national level) on consumer and producers households by income strata is analyzed. These extensions have come only at a price. We have ignored the consequences for the employment of resources released from the rice sector due to the differential impact of the new technology; and the lack of data to analyze the distributional consequences for household income led us to a formidable number of assumptions, we hope not excessively cavalier.

NOTES

The research on which this article is based was conducted while the authors were economists in the rice program of the Centro Internacional de Agricultura Tropical (CIAT), Cali, Colombia. The support and interest of John L. Nickel, director-general of CIAT, and Peter R. Jennings, of the Rockefeller Foundation, are gratefully acknowledged. G. Edward Schuh, Paul R. Johnson, Alberto Valdés, Per Pinstrup-Andersen, Reed Hertford, and two reviewers for the *American Journal of Agricultural Economics* all offered insightful comments.

1. See also Schultz, chapter 22 in this volume.—ED.
2. Hertford and Schmitz (1977) provide a review of the procedures involved in estimating changes

in consumer and producer surplus. A valuable survey with discussion of some of the contentious issues is given by Currie, Murphy, and Schmitz (1971), while some apparent inconsistencies between alternative formulations are noted by Scobie (1976).

REFERENCES

Akino, M., and Y. Hayami. 1975. "Efficiency and Equity in Public Research: Rice Breeding in Japan's Economic Development." *American Journal of Agricultural Economics* 57:1–10.

Ardila V., J. 1973. "Rentabilidad social de las inversiones en investigación de arroz en Colombia." Master's thesis, ICA-Universidad Nacional, Bogotá.

Arndt, T. M., D. G. Dalrymple, and V. W. Ruttan, eds. 1977. *Resource Allocation in National and International Agricultural Research*. Minneapolis: University of Minnesota Press.

Ayer, H. W., and G. E. Schuh. 1972. "Social Rates of Return and Other Aspects of Agricultural Research: The Case of Cotton Research in São Paulo, Brazil." *American Journal of Agricultural Economics* 54:557–69.

Barletta, A. N. 1971. "Costs and Social Benefits of Agricultural Research in Mexico." Ph.D. diss., University of Chicago.

Bell, C. 1972. "The Acquisition of Agricultural Technology: Its Determinants and Effects." *Journal of Development Studies* 9:123–59.

Berry, R. A. 1974. "Distribución de fincas por tamaño, distribución del ingreso y eficiencia de la producción agrícola en Colombia." In *Lecturas sobre desarrollo económico colombiano*, edited by H. Gomez O. and W. Weisner D. Bogotá: Fundación para la Educación Superior y el Desarrollo.

Bieri, J., A. de Janvry, and A. Schmitz. 1972. "Agricultural Technology and the Distribution of Welfare Gains." *American Journal of Agricultural Economics* 54:801–8.

Cruz de Schlesinger, L., and L. J. Ruiz. 1967. *Mercadeo de arroz en Colombia*. Bogotá: Centro de Estudios sobre Desarrollo Económico.

Currie, J. M., J. A. Murphy, and A. Schmitz. 1971. "The Concept of Economic Surplus and Its Use in Economic Analysis." *Economic Journal* 81:741–800.

Departamento Nacional de Planeación. 1974. *Plan nacional de alimentación y nutrición*. Doc. DNP-UDS-DPN-011. Bogotá.

FEDEARROZ (Federación Nacional de Arroceros). 1973. *Informe de Gerencia*. Bogotá.

———. 1975. *Informe de Gerencia*. Bogotá.

Griliches, Z. 1958. "Research Costs and Social Returns: Hybrid Corn and Related Innovations." *Journal of Political Economy* 66:419–31.

Gutiérrez A., N., and R. Hertford. 1974. *Una evaluación de la intervención del gobierno en el mercadeo de arroz en Colombia*. Technical pamphlet no. 4. Cali, Colombia: Centro Internacional de Agricultura Tropical.

Harberger, A. C. 1972. *Project Evaluation*. London: Macmillan and Co.

Hayami, Y., and R. W. Herdt. 1977. "Market Price Effects of Technological Change on Income Distribution in Semisubsistence Agriculture." *American Journal of Agricultural Economics* 59:245–56.

Hertford, R., and A. Schmitz. 1977. "Measuring Economic Returns to Agricultural Research in Colombia." In Arndt, Dalrymple, and Ruttan 1977.

Hertford, R., J. Ardila V., A. Rocha, and C. Trujillo. 1977. "Productivity of Agricultural Research in Colombia." In Arndt, Dalrymple, and Ruttan 1977.

Jallade, J. P. 1974. *Public Expenditures on Education and Income Distribution in Colombia*. World Bank Staff Occasional Paper 18. Washington, D.C.

Leurquin, P. P. 1967. "Rice in Colombia: A Case Study in Agricultural Development." *Food Research Institute Studies in Agricultural Economics, Trade and Development* 7:217–303.

Montes, G. 1973. "Evaluación de un programa de investigación agrícola: el caso de la soya." Master's thesis, Universidad de Los Andes, Bogotá.

Peterson, W. L. 1967. "Return to Poultry Research in the United States." *Journal of Farm Economics* 49:656–69.

Pinstrup-Andersen, P., N. R. de Londoño, and E. Hoover. 1976. "The Impact of Increasing Food Supply on Human Nutrition: Implications for Commodity Priorities in Agricultural Research and Policy." *American Journal of Agricultural Economics* 58:131–42.

Ramalho de Castro, J. P., and G. E. Schuh. 1977. "An Empirical Test of an Economic Model for Establishing Research Priorities: A Brazil Case Study." In Arndt, Dalrymple, and Ruttan 1977.

Rosero M., M. J. 1974. *El Cultivo del arroz.* ICA-FEDEARROZ, Assistance Manual, no. 9. Palmira, Colombia: FEDEARROZ.

Schmitz, A., and D. Seckler. 1970. "Mechanized Agriculture and Social Welfare: The Case of the Tomato Harvester." *American Journal of Agricultural Economics* 52:569–77.

Schultz, T. W. 1970. *Investment in Human Capital: Role of Education and Research.* New York: Free Press.

Scobie, G. M. 1976. "Who Benefits from Agricultural Research?" *Review of Marketing and Agricultural Economics* 44:197–202.

Scobie, G. M., and R. Posada T. 1977. "The Impact of High-Yielding Rice Varieties in Latin America with Special Emphasis on Colombia." Centro de Documentación Económica para la Agricultura Latinoamericana (CEDEAL), Series JE-01. Cali, Colombia: Centro Internacional de Agricultura Tropical.

U.S. Department of Agriculture. 1976. *Foreign Agricultural Circular* FR-1. Washington, D.C.

Valdés, A., G. M. Scobie, and J. L. Dillon, eds. 1979. *Economic Analysis and the Design of Small-Farmer Technology.* Ames: Iowa State University Press.

Wallace, T. D., and D. M. Hoover. 1966. "Income Effects of Innovation: The Case of Labor in Agriculture." *Journal of Farm Economics* 48:325–36.

26

Assessment of the Green Revolution

YUJIRO HAYAMI

In a recent article, Richard Grabowski has applied the Hayami-Ruttan model of induced innovation to the analysis of dualistic rural economies.[1] He argues that in the economies characterized by bimodal distribution of assets and income, the induced innovation mechanism dictates technological change in a socially inefficient and inequitable direction.

According to Grabowski, in the situations of dualistic agrarian structure, large landholders, because of their monopsonistic position, face factor price relations different from those faced by smallholders and the landless. Landed elites usually have better access to institutional credit and subsidized modern inputs, with the result that the cost of nonlabor inputs for them are lower than social opportunity costs. The demand of the powerful elites based on such biased price signals will induce public agencies to generate technological changes that have labor-saving effects and are more profitable for large-scale operations. Thus the inequitable distribution of assets and income in dualistic rural communities will be aggravated further.

I share Grabowski's perspective that in situations where the rural sector consists of more than one group with sharply conflicting interests, the induced innovation mechanism may fail to generate socially desirable innovations or may produce innovations that are socially undesirable for both efficiency and equity reasons—a perspective entirely consistent with Hayami and Ruttan's.[2] Indeed, we often observe cases in which factor market distortions and concentration of land assets induced inefficient and inequitable technological changes, such as labor-displacing mechanization in the labor-abundant economies where the social opportunity cost of labor was low relative to that of capital.

YUJIRO HAYAMI is professor of economics, Aoyama Gakuin University, Tokyo.

Originally titled "Induced Innovation, Green Revolution, and Income Distribution: Comment," this paper was a comment on the article by Richard Grabowski cited in n. 1, below. Reprinted from *Economic Development and Cultural Change* 30, no. 1 (1981): 169–76, by permission of the University of Chicago Press. Copyright © 1981 by The University of Chicago. All rights reserved. Published with minor editorial revisions by permission of the author.

My major disagreement is with Grabowski's view on the "Green Revolution"— the development and diffusion of modern semidwarf varieties of rice and wheat in tropical countries with heavier application of fertilizers and chemicals. He considers that the Green Revolution represents a typical case in that the induced innovation mechanism worked in dualistic situations to generate technological changes biased toward the benefit of landed elites at the expense of smallholders and landless laborers.

THE GREEN REVOLUTION AND INCOME DISTRIBUTION

In this perspective Grabowski shares the criticism of the Green Revolution popular among radical political economists and sociologists.[3] Their arguments run as follows: Green Revolution technology tends to be monopolized by large commercial farmers, who have better access to new information and better financial capacity. Modern varieties (MV) can profitably use higher applications of modern inputs such as fertilizers and chemicals. Adoption of MV is said to be difficult for small subsistence farmers, who have little financial capacity to purchase these inputs. A large profit resulting from the exclusive adoption of MV technology by large farmers stimulates them to enlarge their operational holdings by consolidating the farms of small nonadopters through purchase or tenant eviction. As a result, polarization of rural communities into large commercial farmers and landless proletariat is promoted. Furthermore, the large commercial farms have an intrinsic tendency to introduce large machinery for ease of labor management, which reduces employment opportunities and wage rates for the landless population, resulting in more inequitable income distribution.

Indeed, such arguments are not groundless. It is not difficult to find cases in which significant trends toward polarization and more inequitable income distribution have developed side by side with the diffusion of MV. The point of major controversy is the causal relationship between new technology and polarization phenomena. Does the adoption of new technology in fact tend to be monopolized by largeholders because of constraints in information and credit to smallholders? Does the technology make large-scale operations relatively more efficient and profitable? Is there a technical complementarity between MV and labor-displacing machinery? The issue is an empirical question and should be resolved as such.

EMPIRICAL EVIDENCE

In fact, there is little empirical evidence that the use of MV has been monopolized by large farmers. Of thirty-six villages selected throughout Asia for the international cooperative study on the process of adoption of new rice technology, in only one village was there a significant lag of small farmers behind large farmers in the adoption of MV.[4] This exceptional village was the one studied by

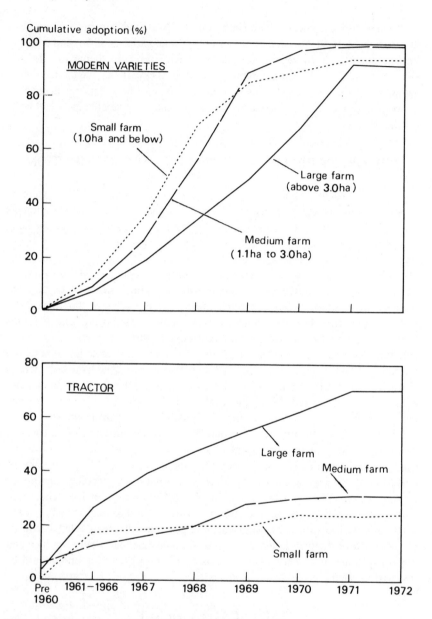

Fig.1. Cumulative Percentage of Farms in Three Size Classes Adopting Modern Varieties (*top*) and Tractors (*bottom*) in Thirty Selected Villages in Asia (IRRI, *Interpretive Analysis of Selected Papers from Changes in Rice Farming in Selected Areas of Asia* [Los Baños, Philippines, 1978], 91)

Parathasarathy and Prasad, which Grabowski refers to as evidence for the differential adoption of MV technology among large and small farms.[5] On the average, small farmers were even faster in the MV adoption than were large farmers (fig. 1, top). The pattern of MV diffusion paths among different farm-size classes contrasts sharply with the diffusion pattern of tractors, in which large farmers achieved distinctly faster and higher rates of adoption (fig. 1, bottom).

The contrasting diffusion patterns suggest that the MV and tractor technologies differ. The latter is characterized by indivisibility or lumpiness in the use of capital and therefore requires a large farm size for efficient operation, whereas the former is divisible into any small units at equal efficiency. In other words, the MV technology is neutral with respect to scale. The scale neutrality of MV technology was supported by the econometric test on wheat production in the Indian Punjab by Sidhu.[6]

The data collected from selected villages in Asia show that there was no significant difference in the average paddy yield per hectare between large and small farmers adopting MV, except for Indonesia (table 1), and that there was no difference in the percentage of farmers reporting increases in profit from rice production and level of living after the introduction of MV (table 2). These data are consistent with the hypothesis of scale neutrality of MV. Similar results were reported in a large body of micro studies for various parts of Asia.[7] After a careful review of those micro studies, Ruttan concluded that "neither farm size nor tenure has been a serious constraint to the adoption of new high yielding grain varieties" and "neither farm size nor tenure has been an important source of differential growth in productivity."[8]

Another major issue revolves around the direction of factor-saving bias in new technology. If MV has a labor-saving bias, the income position of landless laborers and tenants will deteriorate even if the technology is neutral with respect to the scale of farm operation. The econometric test by Sidhu for Punjab wheat

TABLE 1
AVERAGE PADDY YIELDS ON LARGE VERSUS SMALL FARMS ADOPTING MODERN
VARIETIES IN 32 ASIAN VILLAGES, 1971/72 WET SEASON

	Villages (N)	Paddy Yield (tons per hectare)		
		Small Farmer (S)	Large Farmer (L)	Difference (L–S)
India	12	3.8	4.6	0.8
Pakistan	2	3.3	3.4	0.1
Indonesia	5	3.7	5.3	1.6
Malaysia	2	2.4	2.2	−0.1
Philippines	9	2.7	2.5	−0.2
Thailand	2	3.4	3.4	0
All villages	32	3.3	3.8	0.5

SOURCE: IRRI, *Interpretive Analysis*, 96.

TABLE 2
AVERAGE PERCENTAGE OF FARMERS REPORTING INCREASES IN PROFIT FROM
RICE AND LEVEL OF LIVING AFTER THE INTRODUCTION OF MODERN VARIETIES IN
SELECTED ASIAN VILLAGES, 1971/72

| | | Farmers Reporting Increases (%) | | | |
| | | Profit from Rice | | Level of Living | |
	Villages (N)	Small Farmer	Large Farmer	Small Farmer	Large Farmer
India	8	72%	80%	59%	73%
Indonesia	5	80	79	65	67
Malaysia	2	67	53	60	45
Philippines	12	62	64	55	62
Thailand	3	41	55	41	48
All villages	30	66	69	57	63

SOURCE: IRRI, *Interpretive Analysis*, 108.

production shows that the MV wheat represented a neutral technological change not only with respect to scale but also with respect to the factor use.[9] A similar study by Ranade and Herdt on rice in the Philippines suggests that the MV technology is biased in the direction of land saving, though the evidence is not conclusive.[10]

Although more econometric investigations are required to confirm the direction of factor-saving bias in the MV technology, available evidence shows that the MV technology resulted in a significant increase in labor demand. Data assembled for various parts of Asia by Barker and Cordova show that labor inputs per hectare for rice production were higher for MV than for traditional varieties (TV) in the order of 10–50 percent.[11] Similar results were drawn from a review of other studies.[12] Typically, labor application for land preparation was reduced by use of tractors, but the reduction was more than compensated for by increases in labor use for weeding, other crop-tending requirements, and harvesting. Grabowski cites Bardhan's study for North India as evidence for the insignificant effect of the green revolution on the increase in rural labor demand.[13] However, Lal shows clearly that Bardhan's study refers to an early period of MV diffusion and that as MV diffused more widely, the net effect of the resultant increase in labor demand was a significant rise in real wages in the Punjab and Haryana at a time when real wages were constant or declining in parts of India where the diffusion of MV technology was limited.[14]

A popular argument is that even if the MV technology may itself be neutral or labor using, it stimulates the introduction of labor-displacing machinery through either technical complementarity or increased income for large farmers to enable the purchase of machinery. However, such a conjecture is not supported by empirical observations. As shown in figure 1, increases in the adoption of tractors by large farmers began earlier than the introduction of MV, and there was no sign that the tractor adoption was accelerated by the dramatic diffusion of MV from the late 1960s to the early 1970s. Much of the growth in the use of tractors in South and Southeast Asia can be attributed to distortions in the price of capital by such means as overvalued exchange rates and concessional credits from national governments and international lending agencies.[15]

CONDITIONS OF GREATER INEQUALITY

The empirical evidence fails to identify the MV technology (in combination with irrigation and fertilizer) as a factor promoting more unequal income distribution. In general, both small and large farmers adopted MV at more or less equal rates and achieved efficiency gains of the same order. It is likely that the MV technology was neutral or biased in the land-saving and labor-using direction and resulted in increases in labor demand, despite the concurrent progress of mechanization.

Contrary to the popular belief, we see a real danger of growing inequality in rural communities not because of the MV technology but because of insufficient progress in the technology under the strong population pressure on land. Rural economies in developing countries have been experiencing a rapid deterioration in the man/land ratio, with the average number of workers per hectare of arable land doubling within a fifty-year period.

If technological progress of the land-saving type is not sufficiently rapid, the increase in labor demand will fail to keep up with the increase in labor supply arising from rapid population growth. The wage rate is bound to decline and the return to land to rise, and the income position of laborers and tenants will deteriorate relative to that of landowners. The process approximates the world predicted by classical economists such as Ricardo.[16] As the growth of population presses hard on limited land resources under stagnant technology, cultivation frontiers are expanded to more marginal land and greater amounts of labor are applied per unit of cultivated land. The cost of food production increases, and food prices rise. In the long run, laborers' income will be lowered to a subsistence minimum barely sufficient to maintain stationary population, and all the surplus will be captured by landlords in the form of increased land rent.

The increased rate of return to land provides a strong incentive to accumulate more land, especially under the condition of an underdeveloped capital market, because alternative investment opportunities, such as stocks and securities, are not easily available. The concentration of landholdings induced by the higher rate of land rental makes the income distribution more skewed, which promotes further concentration of land—a vicious circle producing polarization. This trend is accelerated further by the development of labor-displacing mechanical technology which was induced by market distortions through a process correctly perceived by Grabowski.

It is not easy to stop this process simply by instituting land-reform laws and regulations or trying to protect smallholders by such means as subsidizing credit and input prices, as Grabowski suggests. In many cases such government interventions have the effect of promoting polarization, especially under the power structure of dualistic rural communities. It is a common observation that rich farmers, through their pull with government agencies, manage to receive a disproportionate share of subsidized input and credit.[17] Land-reform regulations, such as rent control or the prospective plan of land confiscation and redistribution, often have resulted in the large-scale eviction of tenants in order to establish landlords' direct cultivation by use of agricultural laborers.[18]

If the real economic force underlying polarization and greater misery of the poor is the decline in the return to labor relative to the return to land, agrarian reform programs—such as land reform and institutional credit programs—will have little chance of success to achieve more equitable distributions of income and assets unless they are supported by the efforts to counteract the decreasing return to additional labor applied per unit of land area. One critical effort, among others, should aim at the development of labor-using and land-saving technology or at least neutral technology in order to raise the marginal productivity of labor on limited land resources.

In this perspective, the Green Revolution can be considered an induced innovation in response to growing population pressure on land, without which both the wage rate and the income level of the rural working population would have degenerated further. As Grabowski rightly points out, in dualistic situations the induced innovation mechanism can dictate technological change toward a socially inefficient and inequitable direction, as evidenced by labor-displacing mechanization in many parts of labor-abundant economies. However, the Green Revolution does not seem to represent such a case. Empirical evidence is more consistent with the hypothesis that the growing inequality in the rural sector of developing countries has been a result not of Green Revolution technology but of insufficient progress of the Green Revolution technology in overcoming growing population pressure on land.

NOTES

1. Richard Grabowski, "The Implications of an Induced Innovation Model," *Economic Development and Cultural Change* 27 (July 1979): 723–34. [For details on the induced innovation model see chapter 5 in this volume.—ED.]

2. "Usually the gains and losses from technical and institutional change are not distributed neutrally. There are, typically, vested interests which stand to lose and which oppose change. There are limits on the extent to which group behavior can be mobilized to achieve common or group interests. The process of transforming institutions in response to technical and economic opportunities generally involves time lags, social and political stress, and, in some cases, disruption of social and political order" (Yujiro Hayami and Vernon W. Ruttan, *Agricultural Development: An International Perspective* [Baltimore: Johns Hopkins Press, 1971], 61).

3. The radical criticism is typically expressed in Harry M. Cleaver, "The Contradictions of the Green Revolution," *American Economic Review* 72 (May 1972): 177–88; Ali M. S. Fatami, "The

Green Revolution: An Appraisal,'' *Monthly Review* 2 (June 1972): 112–20; Francine R. Frankel, *India's Green Revolution: Economic Gains and Political Costs* (Princeton: Princeton University Press, 1971); and Keith Griffin, *The Political Economy of Agrarian Change: An Essay on the Green Revolution* (Cambridge: Harvard University Press, 1974).

4. International Rice Research Institute (IRRI), *Changes in Rice Farming in Selected Areas of Asia* (Los Baños, Philippines, 1978).

5. G. Parathasarathy and D. S. Prasad, ''Response to, and Impact of, HYV Rice according to Land Size and Tenure in a Delta Village, Andhra Pradesh, India,'' *Developing Economies* 12 (June 1974): 182–98; see also G. Parathasarathy, ''West Godavari, Andhra Pradesh,'' in IRRI, *Changes in Rice Farming*, 43–70.

6. Surjit S. Sidhu, ''Economics of Technological Change in Wheat Production in the Indian Punjab,'' *American Journal of Agricultural Economics* 56 (May 1974): 217–26.

7. For India, Bandhudas Sen, *The Green Revolution in India: A Perspective* (New Delhi: Wiley Eastern, 1974); for Indonesia, Irlan Soejono, ''Growth and Distributional Changes in Paddy Farm Income in Central Java,'' *Prisma*, May 1976, 26–32; for Pakistan, K. M. Azam, ''The Future of the Green Revolution in West Pakistan: A Choice of Strategy,'' *International Journal of Agrarian Affairs* 5 (March 1973): 404–29; for the Philippines, Mahar Mangahas, Virginia A. Miralaro, and Romana P. de los Reyes, *Tenants, Lessees, Owners: Welfare Implications of Tenure Change* (Quezon City, Philippines: Ateneo de Manila University Press, 1974).

8. Vernon W. Ruttan, ''The Green Revolution: Seven Generalizations,'' *International Development Review* 19 (August 1977): 16–23.

9. Sidhu, ''Economics of Technological Change.''

10. Chandra G. Ranade and Robert W. Herdt, ''Shares of Farm Earnings From Rice Production,'' in IRRI, *Economic Consequences of the New Rice Technology* (Los Baños, Philippines, 1978), 87–104.

11. Randolph Barker and Violeta Cordova, ''Labor Utilization in Rice Production,'' in ibid., 113–36, esp. 117.

12. Ifmkhar Ahmed, ''Employment Effects of the Green Revolution,'' *Bangladesh Development Studies* 4 (January 1976): 115–28; William G. Bartsch, *Employment Effects of Alternative Technologies and Techniques in Asian Crop Production: A Survey of Evidence* (Geneva: International Labour Office, 1973); and Edward J. Clay, ''Institutional Change and Agricultural Wages in Bangladesh,'' *Bangladesh Development Studies* 4 (October 1976): 423–40.

13. Pranab Bardhan, ''Green Revolution and Agricultural Laborers,'' *Economic and Political Weekly* 5 (July 1970): 1239–46.

14. Deepak Lal, ''Agricultural Growth, Real Wages, and the Rural Poor in India,'' ibid. 11 (June 1976): A47–A61.

15. Randolph Barker et al., ''Employment and Technological Change in Philippine Agriculture,'' *International Labour Review* 106 (August–September 1972): 111–39; and Bart Duff, ''Mechanization and Use of Modern Rice Varieties,'' in IRRI, *Economic Consequences*, 145–64.

16. David Ricardo, *On the Principle of Political Economy and Taxation*, ed. Piero Sraffa, 3d ed. (Cambridge: Cambridge University Press, 1951).

17. See Adams and Vogel, chapter 21 in this volume.—ED.

18. Kalyan Dutt, ''Changes in Land Relations in West Bengal,'' *Economic and Political Weekly* 12 (December 1977): A106–A110; P. C. Joshi, ''Land Reform in India and Pakistan,'' ibid. 5 (December 1970): A145–A152; Dharm Narain and P. C. Joshi, ''Magnitude of Agricultural Tenancy,'' ibid. 4 (September 1960): A139–A142; Doreen Warriner, *Land Reform in Principle and Practice* (Oxford: Clarendon Press, 1969).

27

Technological Challenges in Asian Agriculture in the 1990s

DEREK BYERLEE

This chapter outlines the technological challenges for Asian agriculture in the 1990s. I first briefly recapitulate the major sources of growth in Asian agriculture in recent decades—that is, the spread of modern rice and wheat varieties accompanied by increased use of fertilizer and improved irrigation. I argue that the contribution of these factors to increased food production in the future will be much smaller compared to the past two decades and that, to sustain growth into the 1990s and beyond, we need to seek new sources of growth. The prognosis is that, without a renewed effort in food grain production, the 1990s will be a period of increasing foodgrain deficits in some of the major countries of Asia, which have been self-sufficient for much of the period since 1970. The critical ingredients of a strategy to reverse these trends are discussed with emphasis on the technical-scientific and the institutional issues in technology development and transfer.

TECHNOLOGICAL CHANGE IN CEREALS SINCE THE 1950s

Over the past three decades, there has been a major switch from area increases to yield increases as the major source of growth in world cereal production. This phenomenon is true for the developing world as a whole and is especially marked in Asia. As recently as the 1950s, expanding area was the major source of increased cereal production in much of Asia. For many countries, area increases now make a negligible contribution to raising cereal production; and in some cases, notably China, the area sown to cereals has actually declined in the past decade, with increasing competition for land from cash crops and urbanization.

DEREK BYERLEE is director of the economics program, CIMMYT, Mexico, D.F.

Background paper prepared for the USAID workshop Strategic Planning for Asia and the Near East, Rabat, Morocco, 19–24 February 1989. Reprinted with omissions by permission of the author.

TECHNOLOGICAL CHANGE IN FAVORABLE AREAS

Three important changes in production technology have contributed to rapid yield increases in favorable (mostly irrigated) environments, but each is now showing definite signs of slowing.

Modern varieties. The story of the rapid spread of modern varieties of wheat and rice in Asia is well known (Dalrymple 1985). Less spectacular but significant gains have also been made in maize, sorghum, and millet over much of Asia. However, in the favorable environments where modern varieties have had their greatest impact, almost all the area is now sown to modern wheat and rice varieties and there is little scope to exploit the switch from traditional to modern varieties as a future source of growth. Moreover, since the mid-1960s there have been no additional *major* breakthroughs in raising the yield potential of cereals, and none are likely to occur in the 1990s, at least at the farm level. Yield potential in new wheat varieties has risen at a steady rate of 0.7–1 percent per year since the release of the first semidwarf materials in the 1960s (CIMMYT 1989). In rice, no increase in yield potential has been achieved since the 1960s, although important gains have been made in earliness and disease and insect resistance (Pingali 1988).

Irrigation water. Increased supplies of irrigation water made a major contribution to raising yields in the 1960s and 1970s in much of Asia. For example, over the past twenty years the percentage of wheat area under irrigation rose from 50 percent to 72 percent in India and from 66 percent to 83 percent in Pakistan. However, in recent years, expansion in irrigated area has slowed drastically as the easier and less expensive irrigation sites have been developed (Levine et al. 1988).

Fertilizer. Fertilizer use per hectare of cultivated land has expanded rapidly in the past two decades at over 10 percent per year to reach 78 kg/ha in Asia. In both wheat and rice production, fertilizer levels have reached modest to high levels of over 100 kg/ha of nutrients in irrigated areas of Asia, and there are diminishing returns to increased fertilizer doses *at current levels of fertilizer efficiency.* At the margin, grain-nutrient ratios in wheat (the amount of grain produced for each kilogram of fertilizer nutrient applied) appear to have fallen to less than 7:1 in India and less than 5:1 in Pakistan, compared to ratios of over 10 in the early years of the "Green Revolution."

Together, modern varieties, improved supplies of irrigation water, and increased fertilizer doses accounted for over 75 percent of the total yield increases in rice and wheat in Asia in the 1970s and 1980s (Herdt and Capule 1983; CIMMYT 1989). But, there is clear evidence that the contributions of each of these factors to yield increases in favorable environments have reached a stage of rapidly diminishing returns. There is already evidence that rates of cereal yield increase have slowed in some countries that were the early beneficiaries of the Green Revolution (e.g., Pakistan, India, and Turkey in the case of wheat).

The gap between farmers' yields and those on experiment stations has also tended to narrow in the original Green Revolution areas. In the area surrounding the International Rice Research Institute (IRRI) in the Philippines, the highest yields obtained by farmers now surpass yields recorded on the IRRI experiment station (Pingali 1988). A similar trend for wheat has been observed in the Indian Punjab, where farmers' yields in Ludhiana District now average over 4 t/ha. Furthermore, much of the remaining yield gap in these areas is not economically recoverable (Herdt 1988). Hence, in the most advanced areas, farmers have successfully adopted most of the newer technologies, and there is little technology waiting "on the shelf" to be transferred to farmers.

Nevertheless, there are still large areas in favorable environments, such as Pakistan's irrigated Punjab, where yields remain low (2 t/ha) relative to potential yields, even though all farmers have adopted the improved wheat varieties and use modest to high levels of fertilizer. There is substantial potential to increase yields in these areas through a number of relatively small and incremental management changes that are specific to each area, such as better plant stand establishment, minimum and zero tillage, improved weed control, balanced fertilizer doses, and improved timing of irrigation water application. These factors could profitably increase wheat yields at the farm level by up to 50 percent in Pakistan's Punjab (Byerlee et al. 1986).

Finally, there are worrying indications that yields or productivity are falling in some of the best production areas. Flinn and De Datta (1984) have documented a decline in yields obtained on IRRI's experiment stations. In Pakistan's Punjab, farm yields of improved wheat varieties have remained unchanged since 1970 despite a steady increase in inputs supplied (especially fertilizer, which has risen from 40 kg/ha nutrients in 1970 to 114 kg/ha in 1986), indicating a possible decline in productivity. The reasons for this decline are not yet well understood but may relate to soil micronutrient problems, soil structure, soil health, poor stand establishment, low-quality irrigation water from tubewells, and worsening weed problems. Clearly, sustaining cereal yields and productivity in these favorable areas is a critical challenge in the 1990s.

TECHNOLOGICAL CHANGE IN LESS FAVORABLE AREAS

The use of modern varieties and fertilizer has also expanded steadily into less favorable areas, especially in the past decade. For example, 50 percent of the sorghum and millet area in India is estimated to be sown to modern varieties, much of it in marginal areas. Semidwarf wheat varieties have spread to most of the rainfed areas receiving over 500 mm of rainfall annually, and they are diffusing slowly into the dry areas receiving less than a 500-mm annual rainfall (CIMMYT 1989). However, the yield impact of semidwarf varieties in marginal areas is much smaller, in part because of lower yield potential and in part because use of purchased inputs is less profitable and more risky. CIMMYT estimates that in irrigated areas of South Asia semidwarf wheat varieties grown with modest levels of fertilizer provided a 40–50 percent jump in yields over traditional varieties. In dry rainfed areas, the equivalent gain in yields of the semidwarfs is estimated to be less than 10 percent. Similarly, Barker and Duff (1986) estimated expected yield gains from rice research in favorable rainfed areas to be twice those in less favorable rainfed areas.

THE CHALLENGE OF FOODGRAIN SUPPLY IN THE 1990s

Almost all recent projections indicate a growing gap between supply and demand for food products in the 1990s in Asia, given current trends. The FAO (Food and Agricultural Organization of the United Nations) projects an increase in demand for all food of 3.1 percent per annum for the region and 2.5 percent for cereals. Food and feed demand will be increasingly driven by rapidly rising incomes in the region, projected to average 3 percent per year. Demand will increase fastest for income-elastic products such as livestock products and their derived demands for feed grains (FAO 1987). The FAO projections indicate a widening gap between supply and demand for cereals in the region and more in-depth projections for rice and wheat support this conclusion (Barker and Herdt 1985; CIMMYT 1989).

These projections do not suggest that famine will return to Asia. Rather they indicate that, if the food-feed demands of the growing populations and economies of Asia are to be satisfied in the 1990s, either substantial efforts will have to be made in agricultural research, extension, and irrigation, or food- and feedgrain imports will increase sharply.

TECHNICAL CHALLENGES IN THE 1990s

PLANT BREEDING AND BIOTECHNOLOGY

Plant breeding has made a major contribution to increased food production over the past two decades. There are still substantial opportunities to achieve improved technology for specific problem environments and needs, such as wheat varieties for late planting in intensive cropping systems and rice varieties for nonirrigated environments. But, the rates of yield gains in these stressed environments will generally be much slower (CIMMYT 1989; Barker and Duff 1986). A large share of plant breeding research is now devoted to enhancing yield stability, especially the maintenance of disease and pest resistance in the face of evolving pest biotypes. Research managers and policy makers must recognize that substantial research resources will be required simply to maintain current yield levels in favorable environments.

Despite the excitement about the potential contributions of biotechnology to agriculture, the impact of this technology at the farm level will be small in Asia in the 1990s. Some commercial applications may be available, especially in rice (Anderson and Herdt 1988); however, they will consist largely of the incorporation of new sources of disease or pest resistance, based on a single or a few gene traits, to improve yield stability, rather than on changes that increase yield potential. Nonetheless, it will be important for countries in Asia to establish a capacity for bio-technological research on major crops to provide the technology for the even more challenging period beyond 2000.

CROP AND RESOURCE MANAGEMENT

Crop and resource management in the 1990s will need to play a much larger role in increasing productivity by exploiting the yield potential of available technology and in sustaining productivity gains while preserving the resource base. In addition, the trend toward reduced input subsidies and increasingly open economies will require greater production efficiency. In favorable environments, the emphasis will be on increasing the efficiency of water and fertilizer use, on minimum tillage and integrated pest control, and on sustaining cropping intensification over the long term.

Crop management will also increase in complexity because cropping intensity will be greater and because more emphasis will be given to input efficiency and sustainability (Pingali 1988; Byerlee 1987). Gains will be more incremental and less profitable than the gains from the Green Revolution technologies of the recent past. Hence, crop management will be more knowledge-intensive (a good example is integrated pest control) and will require more institutional support from extension, input suppliers, and irrigation systems (see below). Also, in marginal areas the key to increasing productivity will often be through crop management (in the form of improved tillage techniques, weed control, and rotations to conserve and efficiently exploit moisture) rather than through improved varieties.

Research on crop and resource management will need to be strengthened at the two extremes of adaptive and strategic research. Adaptive research is needed to tailor available technology to local conditions in relatively small and homogeneous areas. Few countries have developed the capacity to effectively undertake this type of location-specific and problem-oriented research. Second, strategic crop management research is needed for some major cropping systems to address widespread problems, such as the apparent decline in productivity in some systems, and to develop the knowledge and technology base for arresting this decline.

INTENSIFICATION AND DIVERSIFICATION

Three trends characterize many cropping systems in Asia—intensification, diversification, and specialization. Increases in cropped area now come largely from greater cropping intensity rather than expansion of the cultivated area. Diversification is driven by increased demand from a higher-income population for oilseeds, vegetables and fruits, and feedgrains. In some cases, these crops may displace basic foodgrains, but, given the necessity of maintaining foodgrain production, much of the area needed for "diversification crops" will come from fitting these crops into existing cropping systems to increase overall cropping intensity (Tetlay, Byerlee, and Ahmad 1989). Finally, with improved infrastructure and markets, there is a trend toward regional specialization that leads to the dominance of one or two major cropping patterns within a region and diversification across regions.

These trends in intensification, diversification, and specialization further increase management complexity and the importance of the sustainability issues discussed above. They also mean that varietal breeding of diversification crops, such as oilseeds and feed grains, will have to emphasize characteristics (especially earliness) that will allow those crops to fit into existing cropping systems.

SOME INSTITUTIONAL ISSUES FOR THE 1990s

Many institutional issues will have a bearing on whether the technical challenges of the 1990s are met successfully. Three issues are examined here: 1) national agricultural research programs, 2) private sector research and technology transfer, and 3) international agricultural research centers.

NATIONAL AGRICULTURAL RESEARCH SYSTEMS (NARSs)

The success of the Green Revolution stimulated a rapid increase in agricultural research expenditures. In the 1970s in Asia, research expenditures rose by 10 percent per year in real terms. In the 1980s, this growth rate has slowed considerably, and in a number of important countries such as the Philippines and Indonesia research expenditures appear to have fallen in recent years. Most large countries in Asia now have well-established research programs for plant breeding in basic food crops, but even the stronger programs in the region experience cycles of maturity and decline (Ruttan 1986). National agricultural research systems (NARSs) are often unable to respond to changes in the environment, such as increasing cropping intensity or the outbreak of new diseases and pests. Research on crop and resource management is often still weak and fragmented among disciplinary groups. Above all, many NARSs lack a functional mechanism for diagnosing high-priority problems and setting the research agenda accordingly. Social science research capacity, which can help in diagnosing problems and evaluating technology, is still in its infancy in most NARSs. Continued investment in NARSs, both to sustain established programs and to broaden and improve the relevance of the research agenda, will be necessary in the 1990s.

Research management will need to develop appropriate incentive systems for promoting problem-solving research. Most NARSs still lack an effective mechanism by which the clients of the research system, the farmers, can effectively influence the selection of research priorities. Producer and commodity organizations, perhaps with a role in financing research, may be one way to more effectively link research and farmers (Ruttan 1986). Another recurring management issue is the low share of operating funds in the total research budget of many NARSs, which immobilizes researchers and restricts access to farmers and their fields. Investment in human resource development will also be a continuing need of many NARSs in Asia.

Agricultural research systems in the 1990s will require greater support from extension, input supply, irrigation management, and rural education to transfer and efficiently use available technology. Farmers' information and skills are much more important for the managerially complex, science-based agriculture now characteristic of much of Asia (Jain 1985). The Training and Visit extension system promoted by the World Bank has reformed many of the extension systems of the region, but in many cases the emphasis is still on a "recipe" approach to crop production, rather than the development of the broad understanding that farmers need to adapt and use the new technology efficiently. The level of rural education continues to be low in many areas of South Asia and West Asia and appears to be a growing constraint on improving productivity (Byerlee, 1987). The role of extension and education is likely to be particularly important in helping farmers to successfully utilize the results of crop and resource managment research with its greater complexity, emphasis on input efficiency, and relatively small incremental changes.

PRIVATE SECTOR RESEARCH AND TECHNOLOGY TRANSFER

The private sector is playing an increasing role in plant breeding research in certain crops, especially in coarse grains and oilseeds, for which hybrid-seed industries are potentially profitable. Private sector research is also important for chemical and mechanical technologies, although most of such research still involves testing and adapting of technologies developed for the industrialized countries.

Private sector research usually places emphasis on areas with the largest market potential. This emphasis implies that research will initially focus on more favorable areas and on commercial farmers and may widen the differences between small farmers in marginal areas and their counterparts in favorable areas. Also, research on chemical technologies in the private sector will not necessarily promote input efficiency and sustainability by, for example, using such approaches as integrated pest management. Hence, public sector research systems will need to develop a strong complementary role to private sector research to ensure that social welfare objectives, such as equity and environmental issues, are adequately addressed.

Although the role of the private sector in research is limited to some crops, there is clearly an increasing role for the private sector in technology transfer. In many cases, input supplies, especially seed production and distribution, are still handled by the public sector and lack vigorous market promotion. The private sector can also play a larger role in supplying the information needs of farmers, especially in providing information on using purchased inputs more effectively (Byerlee 1987).

INTERNATIONAL AGRICULTURAL RESEARCH
CENTERS (IARCs)

The role of international agricultural research centers (IARCs), such as CIMMYT (International Center for Maize and Wheat Improvement) and IRRI (International Rice Research Institute), has evolved considerably over the past decade. The IARCs play a vital role in germplasm and information exchange among NARSs, including strong NARSs in Asia, in India and China for instance. That role must be maintained into the 1990s. The IARCs are moving a larger share of resources from routine plant breeding research to strategic research, especially research related to stress tolerance and durable resistance to pests and diseases, and exploring new ways to increase yield potential. The international centers will also play a lead role in strategic research on crop and resource management that addresses major problems common to several countries.

An important part of the strategic research agenda of the IARCs for the 1990s will be investment in the new techniques of the so-called biotechnology. Given that much of this research will be conducted by the private sector for agriculture in industrialized countries, IARCs will at first have a potentially important role in adapting and applying the new techniques to problems of Third World agriculture, with the purpose of increasing the efficiency of conventional plant breeding programs. As discussed above, much of this work will emphasize pest and disease resistance, to enhance yield stability rather than to increase yield potential.

A major strength of IARCs in taking on these roles has been their relative isolation from political considerations and their sustained and assured budgetary support. It will be important to preserve these critical roles into the 1990s.

MARGINAL ENVIRONMENTS AND THE POOR

Development thought is notably "faddish," moving from an emphasis on community development in the 1950s to the "high-payoff input" model of technological change in the 1960s and 1970s to farming systems research, privatization, free markets, and policy reform in the 1980s. In the process of promoting growth-oriented approaches to development in the 1980s, we may have forgotten that the ultimate purpose of development is to reduce poverty, both relatively and absolutely. A critical instrument for achieving both growth and equity is the reduction in foodgrain prices through technological change. The 1990s should be a period of rededicating development efforts to alleviating poverty.

An important debate in the war on poverty in the 1990s will be the relative emphasis to be placed on favorable versus less favorable or marginal environments. Mellor (1988) estimates that about 500 million people live below the poverty line and that the absolute number of rural poor in Asia is evenly divided between favorable and less favorable environments. These statistics, plus the evidence presented earlier on expected lower payoffs to research investments in less favorable areas, suggest that caution is needed in abruptly shifting research attention from favorable to less favorable areas. Also there is evidence that technological progress in favorable areas will often benefit less favorable areas through "technological spillovers," labor migration, and lower food prices to the poor, including small farmers in less favorable areas, who are usually net food purchasers. Clearly, more research is needed to understand these complex relationships, but for the moment technological change in basic foodgrains in high-potential areas seems to be one of the most effective means to improve the incomes of the poor.

These conclusions also suggest that, although concern with sustainability of natural resources is often associated with marginal and fragile environments, the emphasis in the 1990s should be on sustainability in favorable areas, where increasing crop intensification and specialization appear to have important implications for sustaining productivity.

CONCLUSION

The rapid technological advances of the past two decades, especially in wheat and rice, should be seen as an extraordinary period of growth in world food production, especially in Asia. In the future we can expect much slower growth from the main sources of yield increases in recent years—spread of modern varieties, increased fertilizer use, and improved supplies of irrigation water. In the 1990s, ways must be found through improved crop and resource management to exploit this yield potential at the farm level, to promote input efficiency, and to sustain the resource base. Added to this challenge will be the need to increase the production of income-elastic food products, especially feedgrains, in the rapidly growing economies of the region, and the special challenge of increasing productivity and maintaining the resource base in less favorable areas. Rapid technological progress in foodgrain production *is* possible in the 1990s, but it will require a new research strategy, focusing on small incremental changes, and it will be more difficult to organize and manage.

REFERENCES

Anderson, J. R., and R. W. Herdt. 1988. "The Impact of New Technology on Foodgrain Productivity to the Next Century." Paper presented at the Twentieth International Conference of Agricultural Economists, Buenos Aires, Argentina, August 24–31.

Barker, R., and B. Duff. 1986. "Constraints to Higher Rice Yields in Seven Rice Growing Environments in South and Southeast Asia." Paper presented at the annual meeting of the Rockefeller Program on the Genetic Engineering of Rice. Philippines: International Rice Research Institute.

Barker, R., and R. W. Herdt, with B. Rose. 1985. *The Rice Economy of Asia*. Washington, D.C.: Resources for the Future.

Byerlee, D. 1987. *Maintaining the Momentum in Post–Green Revolution Agriculture: A Micro-Level Perspective from Asia*. MSU International Development Paper, no. 10. East Lansing: Michigan State University, Department of Agricultural Economics.

Byerlee, D., P. Hobbs, B. R. Khan, A. Majid, R. Akhtar, and N. Hashmi. 1986. *Increasing Wheat Productivity in the Context of Pakistan's Irrigated Cropping Systems: A View from the Farmer's Field*. PARC Research Report 86/6, Islamabad, Pakistan: Agricultural Research Council.

CIMMYT. 1989. *1987–88 World Wheat Facts and Trends: The Wheat Revolution Revisited: Recent Trends and Future Challenges*. Mexico, D.F.: CIMMYT.

Dalrymple, D. G. 1985. "The Development and Adoption of High Yielding Varieties of Wheat and Rice in Developing Countries" *American Journal of Agricultural Economics* 67(5):1067–73.

Flinn, J. C., and S. K. De Datta. 1984. "Trends in Irrigated-Rice Yields under Intensive Cropping at Philippine Research Stations." *Field Crops Research* 9(1):1–15.

Food and Agriculture Organization. 1987. *Agriculture: Toward 2000*. Rome.

Herdt, R. W. 1988. "Increasing Crop Yields in Developing Countries: Sense and Nonsense." Paper presented at the annual meeting of the American Agricultural Economics Association, July 30–August 3, Tennessee.

Herdt, R. W., and C. Capule. 1983. *Adoption, Spread, and Production Impact of Modern Rice Varieties in Asia.* Los Baños, Philippines: International Rice Research Institute.

Jain, H. K. 1985. "India's Changing Agriculture: Its Management, Genetic Vulnerability and Diversification." *Proceedings of the Indian Academy of Science (Plant Science)* 94:465–74.

Levine, G., et al. "Irrigation in Asia and the Near East in the 1990s: Problems and Prospects." Paper prepared for HIID/USAID Symposium on Agriculture in the 1990s, Washington, D.C.

Mellor, J. 1988. "Agriculture Development Opportunities for the 1990s and the Role of Research." Paper presented at International Centers Week of the Consultative Group on International Agricultural Research, Washington, D.C.

Pingali, P. L. 1988. "Intensification and Diversification of Asian Rice Farming Systems." Paper presented at the International Rice Research Conference, Los Baños, Philippines.

Ruttan, V. 1986. "Toward a Global Agricultural Research System: A Personal View." *Research Policy* 15:307–27.

Tetlay, K. D., D. Byerlee, and Z. Ahmad. 1989. "The Role of Tractors, Tubewells, and Plant Breeding in Increasing Cropping Intensity in Pakistan's Punjab." *Agricultural Economics.*

V

Case Studies of Economic Policy Reforms

Introduction

The dual themes that this book has been exploring are the sources of agricultural growth and development and understanding the evolving role of agriculture in national economic development. The use of case studies of economic policy reforms helps integrate these themes as well as illustrate the complex interactions between technology, institutions, and policy. Throughout the 1980s a large number of countries introduced significant policy reforms to speed agricultural growth and increase the contribution of the agricultural sector to national development. For example, structural adjustment programs were under way in 32 of the 45 countries in sub-Saharan Africa in 1989. The case studies in part V illustrate these significant policy reforms.

De Janvry and Sadoulet (chapter 28) analyze agricultural development in Latin America over the past thirty years, emphasizing the economic expansion of the 1960s and 1970s, the economic crisis of the 1980s, and the emergence of agriculture as the leading sector in many Latin American countries in the 1980s. For example, while during the 1970s the average rate of growth of agriculture in Latin America was only about half that of gross domestic product (GDP), it grew at nearly double the rate of GDP between 1980 and 1986, a period of generally slow overall economic growth.

Latin America's stabilization (structural adjustment) policies were launched five to seven years before similar programs in Africa and many parts of Asia. Thus, the Latin American experience may be a harbinger of developments in these other countries. The dramatic agricultural growth in Latin America during the 1980s provides evidence that a lagging agricultural sector can be spurred on by an appreciation of the real exchange rate, as might be induced by devaluation of the domestic currency. For this to occur, however, there must exist sufficient effective demand either domestically or internationally for the country's agricultural products, as well as the capacity of the agricultural sector, to produce the desired supply response. Hence, relying on changes in the real exchange rate to spur rapid agricultural growth may require prior or parallel complementary investments in rural infrastructure, agricultural technology generation and diffusion, and market development.

The second part of de Janvry and Sadoulet's chapter focuses on additional, complementary policies needed to utilize such growth to alleviate rural poverty. Their presentation illustrates Timmer's point in chapter 12 about the need to disaggregate data when conducting food policy analysis. The authors show that rural poverty in Latin America is highly differentiated socially, requiring different strategies to

437

reach different groups of the poor. For example, for those living in Ecuador on farms of less than one hectare, farm output accounts for only 28 percent of total income. For these families, increasing the productivity of their nonagricultural activities may be the most direct way of reducing their poverty. In contrast, for those rural poor who are net sellers of food, increasing agricultural prices through devaluation may benefit them the most. The authors review how a combination of policy actions discussed earlier in this book, from land reform to reinforcing intersectoral linkages, can be melded into an antipoverty strategy that is financed by agricultural growth.

Some of the most fundamental policy reforms in the late 1980s took place in the centrally planned economies, whose approach to economic development had served as a model for many Third World nations during the 1960s and 1970s. In chapter 29, Brooks examines Soviet agrarian reform in historical perspective, from the early days of collectivization in 1929 to Gorbachev's announcement of the new farm policy in 1989. She analyzes the causes and the effects of the high costs of collectivized agriculture by concentrating on two periods in Soviet agrarian history: 1930 to 1953 under Stalin, when the institutions of collective agriculture were put into place, and 1965 to the present, when Brezhnev's modernization campaign dominated agricultural policy. During Stalin's era, she argues, the aim of agricultural policy was to use the collective farm to transfer resources—cheap food and labor—to the industrial sectors. Having achieved such a transfer, albeit at high cost, the Soviet economy was poised for rapid economic growth after Stalin's death in 1953. But the structure of decision making in collective agriculture, the lack of farmer incentives, and the failure to invest adequately in the off-farm elements of the food and fiber system, such as input and output distribution, shackled agricultural growth. Hence, after 1953, when Soviet agriculture should have assumed a new role as an efficient user of industrial inputs to produce cheap wage goods and raw materials for the rest of the economy, agricultural productivity remained low. Increasingly, the failure of agriculture to grow adequately served as a drag on the rest of the economy. For example, by the late 1980s, farming and the agroindustrial complex (including input manufacture and processing) absorbed about 25 percent of the state budget. Furthermore, slow productivity growth in agriculture resulted in Soviet consumers spending a large proportion of their disposable income on food in comparison with consumers in other middle- and high-income countries.[1]

The policies launched by Gorbachev in 1989 aimed at reforming this system. Brooks analyzes the difficulties of such policy reform in a system where 60 years of collective agriculture have created numerous vested interests as well as strong pressures for change. The debate over the new agricultural program announced in March 1989 essentially boils down to one over how much Soviet society will be willing to pay to retain some or all of the institutions of collectivized agriculture, and who should pay: consumers through higher prices, producers through low earnings, or taxpayers through massive subsidies. The Soviet experience illustrates both the difficulties of agricultural reform and the consequences of failing to reform.

The world's other huge centrally planned economy, China's, also launched fundamental economic reforms in the late 1970s. Agriculture was in the vanguard of those reforms. Since one in five people in the world is Chinese, China's agricultural development experience is of great interest to social scientists, agriculturalists, and policy makers throughout the world.

Economic policy in China has undergone numerous cyclical changes since 1949, its emphasis fluctuating between material incentives and ideological incentives (Tang 1984; Skinner and Winkler 1969; Eckstein 1975). It is, therefore, risky to predict how Chinese policy will evolve in the future.[2] Nonetheless, the three central debates in agricultural policy that are discussed in chapter 30 have recurred throughout the history of the People's Republic: the choice of the appropriate unit of production and accounting in agriculture, the design of the land tenure system, and the determination of how agriculture should be linked to the rest of the economy through the input and output distribution system. In chapter 30, Lin, Yao, and Wen analyze how policies in these areas have evolved since the reforms of 1978. In so doing, they illustrate the motivation for and obstacles facing the reforms.

The forty years of Chinese agrarian reform from 1949 to 1989 can be divided into three periods: the 1949–58 postindependence reform period, culminating in the introduction of communal farming in 1958; the communal farm era, which lasted twenty years, 1958–78; and the period of rural reforms and liberalization since 1978. The 1978–89 period was dominated by the replacement of the communal system with one of individualized farms, known as the household responsibility system, movement to a more market-oriented economy, rapid agricultural growth from 1978 to 1985, and stagnant grain production from 1985 through 1989.

Lin, Yao, and Wen concentrate on three critical issues during the 1978–89 period: evolution of the household responsibility system, experimentation with alternative land tenure systems to achieve both food production and equity goals, and grain marketing reforms, including the movement towards a more market-driven agriculture. Their analysis illustrates many of the points raised earlier in this book: the use of the land tenure and marketing systems to extract the agricultural surplus for use in other sectors, the constraints imposed on agricultural pricing reforms when the government feels compelled to maintain a high level of consumer subsidies, the need to structure the land tenure and marketing systems in a way that creates incentives both to produce in the short run and invest over the long run, and the impact of agriculture on other sectors through intersectoral linkages. For example, the authors point out that while the commune system was effective in mobilizing large amounts of labor for infrastructure development, it limited farmers' individual incentives to produce. The shift to the household responsibility system increased farmers' incentives and sharply reduced the problem of monitoring agricultural labor. But because mechanisms were not created to replace those of the commune system for mobilizing local resources for infrastructure development, the question of the long-term productivity of agriculture under the household responsibility system becomes problematic. Similarly, the analysis of the shift to a more market-oriented agriculture illustrates the problems of achieving such a shift when many of the legal prerequisites of a market economy, such as secure property rights and a commercial code, are missing. More generally, the Chinese experience illustrates a problem common to all major policy reforms, that of institutions evolving at different speeds, thereby generating conflicts and contradictions in the economy. Dealing with such conflicts and contradictions is at the heart of policy analysis and formulation.

The most vexing global agricultural problem in the 1990s will be in the 45 countries of sub-Saharan Africa, a subcontinent of 500 million people dominated by poverty, rapid population growth, fragile institutions, and a low level of technological inputs. In chapters 31 and 32, Eicher and Lele examine Africa's agrarian stagnation in historical perspective. In 1960, when 17 African nations won their independence, the continent was a major exporter of traditional export crops such as cocoa, oil palm, and groundnuts and was a modest net exporter of food. Blessed with favorable weather, Africa's first decade of independence in the 1960s was highly successful in production of both food and export crops. But the 1968–74 Sahelian drought in West Africa helped turn Africa into a net food importer. From 1970 to 1984, Africa's food production grew at half the population growth rate. Moreover, since 1970 Africa has lost world market shares in meat, bananas, groundnuts, sugar, coffee, cocoa, spices, palm oil, natural rubber, and cotton (UNCTAD, 1989). But there are considerable differences among individual countries. For example, while Ghana and Nigeria lost their shares of the world cocoa market, Côte d'Ivoire increased its share of world cocoa exports from 11.0 to 30.1 percent over the 1970–87 period.

In chapter 31, Eicher examines three interlinked problems: breaking the famine cycle, increasing food production, and combating malnutrition and hunger. Eicher stresses the diversity and complexity of African agriculture, and the need to examine Africa's three food battles in a broad historical, political economy context. He contends that most countries in Africa are at an early stage of development (Stage I in the Timmer scheme) where "getting agriculture moving" requires massive and long-term investments in human capital, rural infrastructure, and agricultural research, that is, the "Prime Movers of Agricultural Development."

Lele (chapter 32) draws on the results of a five-year comparative study of agricultural development in six countries in Africa carried out under a project called Managing Agricultural Development in Africa (MADIA). Lele documents the agricultural growth process in six countries in eastern and in western Africa. She recommends a smallholder agricultural strategy and urges both African governments and donors to adopt a balanced approach, emphasizing both food and export crop production. Lele stresses the need for improved policy analysis at the country level and the need for African governments to concentrate on designing and implementing a consistent long-run agricultural growth strategy, country by country. Such a strategy needs to be based, she argues, on a firm understanding of the mechanisms of agricultural growth and the role of agricultural growth in overall economic development, as discussed by Timmer in chapter 2 and Mellor in chapter 3. Finally, because Africa is the most aid-dependent continent in the world, Lele advances a number of urgent measures to improve donor coordination, a prerequisite to improving the effectiveness of aid.

NOTES

1. In 1989, families with per capita earnings twice the official poverty level spent an average one-third of the disposable income on food.

2. Especially in light of the crackdown on the democracy movement and "bourgeois economics" following the pro-democracy demonstrations in China in June 1989.

REFERENCES

Eckstein, Alexander. 1975. *China's Economic Development*. Ann Arbor: University of Michigan Press.

Lele, Uma. 1989. "Sources of Growth in East African Agriculture." *The World Bank Economic Review* 3, no. 1 (January): 119–44.

Skinner, G. William, and Edwin A. Winckler. 1969. "Compliance and Succession in Rural Communist China: A Cyclical Theory." In *A Sociological Reader on Complex Organizations*, 2nd ed., edited by Amitai Etzioni, 410–38. New York: Holt, Reinhart, and Winston.

Tang, Anthony M. 1984. "A Critical Appraisal of the Chinese Model of Development." In *Agricultural Development in the Third World*, edited by Carl K. Eicher and John M. Staatz, 403–19. Baltimore: Johns Hopkins University Press.

UNCTAD. 1989. *UNCTAD Commodity Yearbook, 1988*. New York: United Nations.

28

Investment Strategies to Combat Rural Poverty in Latin America

ALAIN DE JANVRY AND ELISABETH SADOULET

An attempt to reduce rural poverty in Latin America must be based on two building blocks. The first is the current macroeconomic context, where balance-of-payments deficits and inflationary crises have required the implementation of drastic stabilization policies and structural adjustment programs. The second is the analysis of the long-run determinants of rural poverty and the short-run impact of structural adjustments on the rural poor.

The first two parts of this chapter provide quantitative information on these two building blocks. In the third part, we outline a strategy for agricultural and rural development that is consistent with the current macroeconomic context and with the determinants of rural poverty. The agricultural strategy is based on the role that agriculture can play in generating foreign exchange, in reducing inflationary pressures, and in creating effective demand for other economic sectors. Since rural poverty is highly differentiated socially, a rural-development strategy must correspondingly be tailored to the different types of rural poor and to their specific sources of income. In the final part, we show how selective components of rural development programs must aim at (1) enhancing productivity growth in small farms, (2) assisting households on marginal farms to engage in a portfolio of productive activities, (3) giving the landless and marginal farmers greater access to productive assets, (4) generating more employment opportunities in agriculture and rationalizing rural labor markets, and (5) creating off-farm employment in rural areas. These programs provide the basis for identifying investment opportunities to combat rural poverty.

ALAIN DE JANVRY is professor and ELISABETH SADOULET is assistant adjunct professor and assistant research economist, Department of Agricultural and Resource Economics, University of California, Berkeley.

Reprinted from *World Development* 17, no. 8 (1989): 1203–21, by permission of Pergamon Press. Copyright © 1989 Pergamon Press, Inc. Published with omissions by permission of the authors.

THE PERFORMANCE OF AGRICULTURE DURING THE ECONOMIC CRISIS OF THE 1980s

The economic crisis of the 1980s brought thirty years of sustained economic expansion in Latin America to an end (FAO 1988). While agriculture was also negatively affected by the crisis, its growth rate, which was only about half that of gross domestic product (GDP) in the 1970s, became nearly double that of GDP between 1980 and 1986. Thus, agriculture became the relatively most dynamic sector of the economy in the period of structural adjustment. This was due to a combination of stabilization policies leading to appreciation of the real exchange rate, which favored the production of tradable goods (which is the nature of most agricultural goods in Latin America); liberalization policies resulting in low export taxes on agriculture and reduced protectionism on industrial inputs; the coming to maturation of numerous investment projects realized during the period of debt accumulation and plentiful public budgets; and a low-income elasticity of demand for agriculture in general compared to industry and services.[1]

Within agriculture, the production of crops was least affected by the crisis. Food crops performed relatively well in countries such as Brazil, Chile, Ecuador, and Peru, indicating important gains in import substitution stimulated by real exchange rate adjustments. Livestock products, with a higher income elasticity of demand, were, by contrast, seriously hurt by the crisis. While their production was growing faster than that of total agriculture during the prior decade of strong economic expansion, income gains, and shifts in consumption patterns toward higher quality foods, it fell below that of total agriculture during the economic crisis of the 1980s.

With production incentives for tradables and reduced domestic absorption due to falling real incomes, the balance of agricultural trade improved significantly and agriculture became a major source of foreign exchange savings and earnings. Consequently, the volume of agricultural exports increased at an annual growth rate of 3.1 percent between 1980 and 1986, while that of agricultural imports fell at a rate of 2.7 percent. Self-sufficiency ratios, which had declined continuously between 1960 and 1980, increased between 1980 and 1985 as a result of increased exports, import substitution, and falling domestic demand. For cereals, self-sufficiency increased from 93 percent in 1980 to 95 percent in 1985. Because of the sharp deterioration in many international agricultural prices, however, the rapidly rising volume of exports was not sufficient to compensate for falling prices, and the value of agricultural exports actually declined at an annual rate of 3.2 percent between 1980 and 1986.

Compared with other economic sectors, this relatively better performance of agriculture suggests the possibility of capitalizing on a dynamic agriculture as an important element of a strategy of economic recovery for the Latin American countries. This strategy, however, remains subject to several difficulties which have restricted the performance of agriculture and which will need specific attention in the future.

1. Real exchange rates fell sharply during the 1970s due to the rapid accumulation of debt and commodity export booms in many countries (e.g., oil in Mexico, Ecuador, and Venezuela). After 1980, nominal exchange rates were massively devalued to adjust to the crisis of the external sector, and the real exchange rate appreciated in virtually every country. As one would expect, this benefited the production of tradables—and, hence, agriculture—over that of nontradables. International prices of many agricultural commodities, however, fell sharply after 1980. Thus, between 1980 and 1986 the world market prices of wheat, corn, rice, sugar, and cotton fell, in nominal terms, by as much as 55, 49, 53, 74, and 44 percent, respectively. In contrast, other commodities, such as coffee and bananas, increased by 5 and 30 percent. This raises the question as to whether the terms of trade for Latin American agricultural exports have increased or not as a result of the net effect of raising exchange rates and falling prices for many commodities.

   While the price index of agricultural exports indeed fell by 14 percent for Latin America as a whole between 1980 and 1986, it increased for a majority of countries. The overall decline is due to dominance in the aggregate of the large exporters in the Southern Cone (Argentina, Chile, Paraguay, and Uruguay), where cereals are the main product. For most of the other countries, however, tropical products dominate exports, and their prices (particularly those of coffee and bananas) have increased during that period. The general appreciation of the real exchange rate in Argentina has more than compensated for falling international prices and has led to an increase in the terms of trade in agricultural exports. In most other countries, real exchange rate appreciation has further enhanced the terms-of-trade effect of rising international prices, creating the *possibility* of highly favorable terms of trade for agricultural exports.

   This does not mean, however, that the terms of trade for the whole of agriculture have improved. Falling international prices have indeed resulted in mixed terms-of-trade signals for agriculture. Between 1976 and 1984, terms of trade significantly improved in half of the countries for which data are available but fell sharply in a quarter of the countries.

   We conclude that low international prices and continued policy biases, in limiting the passing through of real exchange-rate effects, have reduced the potentially beneficial impacts on agriculture of stabilization and liberalization. In addition, the high rates of inflation induced by exchange-rate devaluations have created considerable uncertainty in the interpretation of price signals, suggesting the need for successful stabilization of both the foreign account and inflationary pressures before economic liberalization can result in maximal investment incentives in agriculture (Corbo and de Melo 1987).

2. New investments in agriculture have fallen sharply since 1980, as a consequence of public budget austerity, public credit constraints, rising interest rates, and higher prices of imported capital goods. For example, tractor and fertilizer imports fell by 40 and 15 percent, respectively, between 1980 and

1985. Government expenditures in agriculture, as a share of total government expenditure, also fell, from an average of 6.7 percent in 1980 to 4.5 percent in 1984, indicating the loss of priority given to agricultural investment in a period of enhanced competition for shrinking government outlays (Twomey 1987). This is particularly serious since a high elasticity of supply response and productivity growth in agriculture both depend upon a continuous flow of new investments. In addition, for structural adjustment to be successful in reallocating resources toward the production of tradable goods and factors toward the use of nontradables requires a high elasticity of substitution between nontradables and tradables on both the product and factor sides as well as new investments. Unless explicit priority is given to agricultural investment in the national allocation of public investable funds, it is unlikely that the current performance of agriculture can be sustained over time. Alleviation of the debt burden and access to new international loans are also essential to increasing the availability of funds for agriculture. For countries that are net importers of food, low international prices create the possibility of taxing imports to generate investable funds that can be used to promote import substitution in agriculture as well as investment in other sectors with international comparative advantages.

3. A successful policy of real exchange rate adjustment and trade liberalization will be effective only if the elasticity of export demand for Latin American agriculture is high. This requires active development of new markets, promotion of nontraditional exports, and expansion of intraregional trade.

4. Continued international aid to Latin American agriculture needs to be ensured, because this type of aid has an important role to play in the promotion of agricultural research and technological change in the agriculture of less developed countries. This type of aid should be continued even though it may be in conflict with United States and European Economic Community agricultural export interests in the short run, because the rapid growth of Latin American economies is in the medium- and long-run interest of agricultural exporters in developed countries. Harmony between aid and trade requires the promotion of productivity growth in sectors of the economy beyond agriculture and promotion of feed-based livestock production to satisfy changes in consumption patterns induced by income effects which greatly accelerate the demand for cereals (de Janvry and Sadoulet 1988).

THE STRUCTURE AND DYNAMICS OF RURAL POVERTY

Important progress has been made in the provision of basic needs amenities to the rural areas during the decades of rapid economic growth in the 1960s and 1970s. During this period, there was a significant decline in infant mortality and improvements in life expectancy and adult literacy. But the absolute number of rural poor has failed to decline. Income inequality has also either worsened or stayed at the same high level as in the 1960s. In addition, rural poverty remains much higher than urban poverty: while 26 percent of urban households were below the poverty line in the 1970s, the figure for rural areas reached 62 percent (Altimir 1982). Food and Agriculture Organization estimates for the late 1970s and early 1980s show that the percentage of rural population in absolute poverty remained staggeringly high. The percentage in absolute poverty was 65 in Ecuador, 67 in Colombia, 68 in Peru, 73 in Brazil, 78 in Haiti, and 85 in Bolivia (Scott 1987). Even before the crisis of the 1980s, rural poverty evidently had long-run structural determinants that made its eradication immutable to economic growth.

By far the leading causes of rural poverty are the lack of access to sufficient land and the low productivity of land for a majority of the rural population. Over the past forty years, there has been a continuous increase in the number of subfamily farms in almost every Latin American country. Available data for 17 countries reveal that the number of small farms increased at an annual compound growth rate of 2.2 percent between 1950 and 1980. The average size of these farms declined from 2.4 hectares in 1950 to 2.1 hectares in 1980, and there was increasing concentration of land on large farms. The bulk of Latin American poverty is located on small farms. Available data reveal the deepening dualism of the agrarian structure and the incapacity of the economy to generate sufficient employment opportunities to absorb the surplus rural labor force. This is indicated by the fact that the incidence of rural poverty is observed to increase with the share of the labor force in agriculture (de Janvry, Sadoulet, and Wilcox 1986). In the period of rapid economic growth, the main factor that helped to alleviate rural poverty was labor absorption in other sectors of the economy. Commercial agriculture, by contrast, has been unable to create additional employment opportunities (in spite of significant economic growth), because of mechanization, land concentration, and substitution of crops by extensive livestock operations. The result is that employment in commercial agriculture increased by only 16 percent between 1960 and 1980, as compared with 41 percent in the peasant sector.

The availability of off-farm sources of income is also crucial in determining the level of household income in subfamily farms. It is likely that as much as two-thirds of the farm households across Latin America derive more than half of their income from off-farm sources—principally in wages from employment in agriculture and in a wide variety of other activities, many of which are linked to agriculture through forward, backward, and final-consumption linkages. A strategy aimed at reducing rural poverty must, therefore, address the issues of access to land (land reform and settlement schemes), labor productivity on family and subfamily farms (rural development programs), and rural employment generation and the level of wages in agriculture and in rural nonagricultural activities.

Several important structural transformations of the rural labor market that occurred during the 1960s and 1970s have generally not favored peasant households. Permanent workers have increasingly been displaced by temporary workers, worsening the problems of seasonal unemployment. Increasingly fewer agricultural workers are recruited from subfamily farms and more come from households surrounding rural towns and cities. At the same time, the share of rural economically active population in nonagricultural activities has also increased very rapidly, reaching 23 percent in Brazil, 16 percent in Ecuador, 41 percent in Costa Rica, and 42 percent in Mexico. This increasing market integration has induced a convergence between agricultural and other wages, with real agricultural wages rising faster than nonagricultural wages. It has, however, reduced employment opportunities for marginal farmers, who are competing with workers in towns, which have lower recruitment costs (Klein 1984).

A social poverty map is useful in the analysis of rural poverty and the identification of programs to combat it. Such a map categorizes the rural poor by access to land and by sources of income within a region. Table 1 does this for the Sierra region of Ecuador and reveals that rural poverty there is highly differentiated and that multiple approaches are needed to combat it. The map also shows that a large

TABLE 1
SOCIAL POVERTY MAP FOR THE SIERRA REGION OF ECUADOR

	Land-less	0.1-1	1-2	2-5	5-20	20+
			Farm Size (Hectares)			
			Percent			
Households	14.6	28.1	14.7	16.9	15.9	9.8
Assets						
Farms	0	34.1	20.0	23.0	16.1	6.8
Land	0	1.7	3.1	8.0	17.6	69.6
Livestock	a	7.3	7.2	15.0	22.1	48.4
Family labor allocation						
Male, on farm	0	21.7	28.0	35.4	42.9	46.7
Female, on farm	0	46.8	48.5	44.9	44.3	44.1
Male, off farm	50.0	28.1	21.5	18.3	11.0	8.6
Sources of income						
Farm income	0	28.4	49.8	66.7	76.9	74.6
Agriculture	0	19.0	43.7	62.0	70.8	70.4
Handicrafts and trade	0	9.4	6.1	4.7	6.1	4.2
Wage income	85.9	53.8	45.1	26.6	11.4	4.6
Agriculture	32.6	20.2	22.9	14.6	5.2	1.3
Nonagriculture	53.3	33.6	22.2	12.1	6.2	3.3
Other nonfarm income	14.1	17.8	5.1	6.7	11.7	20.8
			1985 U.S. Dollars			
Net income						
Per household	548	663	499	652	1,178	6,639
Per capita	103	125	96	123	186	1,236

SOURCE: IFAD, "Special Programming Mission to Ecuador," preliminary draft (Rome: International Fund for Agricultural Development, 1987).

ᵃData not available.

majority of the rural poor cannot be assisted by increasing the productivity of land use. For example, on the 34 percent of farms of less than 1 hectare, agriculture only generates 19 percent of total household income. Moreover, rural landless households and marginal farmers (farms less than 1 hectare) represent 43 percent of the total rural population. Therefore, programs must be directed toward the income-generating capacity of the particular portfolios of activities that characterize the different categories of rural households, and these programs must look beyond the farm toward employment creation in rural-based nonfarm activities linked to agriculture.

Table 2 extends the poverty map of the Sierra region of Ecuador to account for social differentiation in access to government benefits. It shows that the benefits of education and health are received principally by the landless who live in rural towns. By contrast, the benefits of agricultural development programs such as irrigation and reforestation are disproportionately captured by the largest farmers. It is only the expenditures on land reform and rural development programs that assist family farms (1 to 20 hectares). But these programs represent only 3.1 percent of total government expenditures on rural benefits.

The economic crisis of the 1980s has also had highly differentiated effects on the welfare of rural households, according to their assets and their sources of income. Rising food prices due to real exchange rate appreciation, falling employment opportunities, particularly in the nontradable sectors (construction and services), and sharply falling real wages in all sectors of the economy have had devastating effects, not only on the urban poor but also on rural households who are net buyers of food and highly dependent on the availability of off-farm employment.

Agricultural wages, which had registered steady real gains between 1965 and 1980 in a majority of the Latin American countries, fell sharply and systematically

TABLE 2
SOCIAL POVERTY MAP FOR THE SIERRA REGION OF ECUADOR:
PER CAPITA IMPUTED GOVERNMENT BENEFITS
(U.S. DOLLARS PER YEAR)

Government Programs	Rural Landless	Farm Sizes			
		0–1	1–5	5–20	20+
		Hectares			
Education	91.5	17.2	25.0	16.8	26.4
Health	34.4	0.8	1.5	2.3	8.3
Irrigation	0	0.4	2.0	3.7	35.3
Reforestation and others	28.5	4.9	9.5	8.2	159.2
Land reform	0	0.4	2.0	2.4	1.3
Rural development	0	0.8	3.9	4.5	0
Total	154.4	24.5	43.9	37.9	230.5

SOURCE: Kouwenaar (1986).

across all countries except Colombia between 1980 and 1984. For Latin America as a whole, real wages declined during the crisis at the average annual rate of 6 percent in agriculture and 8.4 percent in nonagriculture. In the latter, the largest fall was in the nontradable sector (construction and services), which had offered important off-farm sources of income for the landless and marginal farmers during the years of economic boom.

Small net sellers of food, by contrast, have often been able to benefit from adjustment in the terms of trade, provided the price gains have not been captured by merchants through rising marketing margins. Since the production technology of small farmers is less intensive in capital and in imported inputs than that of larger farmers, the former are potentially the ones who can benefit most from adjustment. As table 1 shows, however, they constitute only a small fraction of the rural poor.

Welfare losses due to falling real incomes for the landless and marginal farmers have been compounded by falling expenditures on public goods and services for the rural areas as stabilization policies severely restricted fiscal outlays. Between 1981 and 1984, public expenditures on health fell in real terms by 5 percent in Costa Rica, 14 percent in Peru, 16 percent in Chile, 10 percent in Brazil, 22 percent in Venezuela, and 30 percent in Uruguay (Scott 1987).   .

While data are still largely unavailable, we can safely conclude that the rural landless and small farmers who are net buyers of food have been particularly hurt. Because they already were the poorest group in Latin American society, they are the group most in need of an effective investment strategy to reduce rural poverty.

AN AGRICULTURE-LED GROWTH STRATEGY

Starting from an analysis of the economic expansion of the 1960s and 1970s and of the adjustments to the crisis of the 1980s, a growth strategy that is centered on the role of agriculture can be spelled out. In this role, agriculture is not looked on as a source of economic surplus to be transferred to the urban-industrial sector, as it was during the periods of import-substitution industrialization and of Dutch disease created by the oil boom and/or the rapid accumulation of an external debt. On the contrary, we start from a situation where agriculture is able to retain and freely dispose of a large part of the surplus it produces, a situation consistent with the effects of recent structural adjustments on agriculture. The contributions of agriculture to economic growth are, consequently, markedly different in this strategy from those which the classical and neoclassical growth models of the 1960s and 1970s attributed to it (see Adelman 1984). A growth strategy led by agriculture can make the following contributions to development:

1. The agricultural sector can generate foreign exchange through agricultural exports or by saving foreign exchange through import substitution. The availability of foreign exchange facilitates the import of raw materials, capital equipment, and intermediate goods for the industrial sector.
2. Agricultural development can reduce the price of nontradable agricultural

products and of tradables whose prices previously were maintained above international levels through government intervention. Reducing the price of food, the main wage good, allows employers to simultaneously increase real wages and reduce nominal wages. This increases the welfare of workers and stimulates employment and growth in industry by lowering labor costs (Lele and Mellor 1981). The key instrument with which to induce this price effect is the diffusion of land-saving technological innovations.

3. The agricultural sector can generate employment and retain an economically active population in agriculture and the rural sector, as opposed to labor being freed for industrial employment (neoclassical model) or a labor suplus being generated in order to keep the real industrial wage low (classical model) (Jorgenson 1969). The main effect of employment creation in agriculture is to raise incomes and effective demand for agriculture itself as well as for the nontradable sectors of the economy.

4. The growth of agricultural income can broaden the domestic market for industry through the activation of linkage effects with agriculture. While the forward and backward linkages of agricultural production are important, the most significant are the final-demand linkages that have their origin in the expenditure of agricultural incomes (Hirschman 1958). By retaining a larger share of the surplus that it generates, agriculture can serve as a dynamic market for rural small industries with high labor intensity and low import content.

In summary, a strategy of economic development centered on agriculture can open up a productive role to peasants and capitalize on the growth and employment multipliers induced by the growth of agricultural incomes.

The logic of an agriculture-led growth strategy and the manner in which it can serve to identify investment strategies for combating rural poverty are summarized in figure 1. On the agricultural supply side, there are two entry points. First, a rising real exchange rate—a product of the adjustments to the economic crisis and, especially of devaluation of the nominal exchange rate—raises the price of tradable goods (most of agriculture) relative to the price of nontradable goods (construction, services, and some perishable agricultural products). The terms of trade for agriculture benefit, in addition, from a reduction in industrial protectionism. Since the rate of interest and the prices of imported inputs rise, producers must switch their technologies and activities to those which are more labor and natural resource intensive. For price signals to induce an investment response, inflation must also be brought under control.

The second entry point is a rising productivity in agriculture through the diffusion of land-saving technological change backed by investments in irrigation, infrastructure, and public goods for the rural sector. Given the current condition of austerity in public expenditures (one of the basic components of structural adjustment policies), these investments require giving explicit priority to the rural sector in the intersectoral allocation of the national budget and increasing the efficiency of

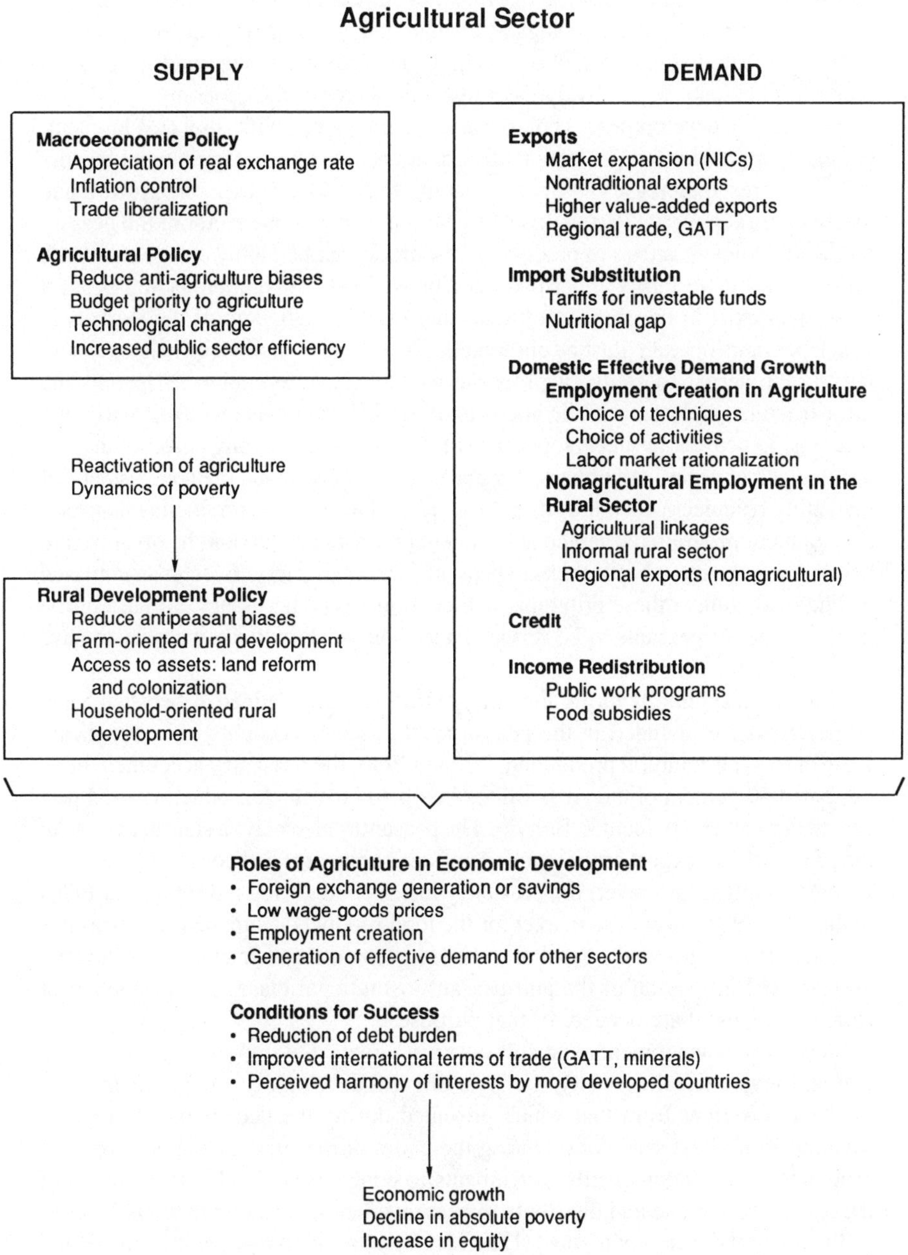

Agricultural Sector

SUPPLY	DEMAND

Macroeconomic Policy
  Appreciation of real exchange rate
  Inflation control
  Trade liberalization

Agricultural Policy
  Reduce anti-agriculture biases
  Budget priority to agriculture
  Technological change
  Increased public sector efficiency

Reactivation of agriculture
Dynamics of poverty

Rural Development Policy
  Reduce antipeasant biases
  Farm-oriented rural development
  Access to assets: land reform
    and colonization
  Household-oriented rural
    development

Exports
  Market expansion (NICs)
  Nontraditional exports
  Higher value-added exports
  Regional trade, GATT

Import Substitution
  Tariffs for investable funds
  Nutritional gap

Domestic Effective Demand Growth
  Employment Creation in Agriculture
    Choice of techniques
    Choice of activities
    Labor market rationalization
  **Nonagricultural Employment in the
  Rural Sector**
    Agricultural linkages
    Informal rural sector
    Regional exports (nonagricultural)

Credit

Income Redistribution
  Public work programs
  Food subsidies

Roles of Agriculture in Economic Development
- Foreign exchange generation or savings
- Low wage-goods prices
- Employment creation
- Generation of effective demand for other sectors

Conditions for Success
- Reduction of debt burden
- Improved international terms of trade (GATT, minerals)
- Perceived harmony of interests by more developed countries

Economic growth
Decline in absolute poverty
Increase in equity

Fig.1. Elements of a Strategy to Reduce Rural Poverty

management of public sector funds. Implementation of these two entry points—equilibrium prices and technological change and investment in public goods—induces a result that has been observed in the last five years: a lagging agricultural sector has become the relatively most dynamic sector of the economy.

Agricultural development is not, however, synonymous with rural development. On the supply side, reorganization of agriculture must be complemented by specific measures to increase peasant production, to accelerate economic growth, and to reduce rural poverty. Past experiences have shown that one sector of the peasantry (with sufficient access to productive resources) can be highly competitive with medium and large farms under two conditions. First, the numerous anti-peasant biases that exist in the rural institutions and in the functioning of the markets in which peasants operate must be eliminated. Strong biases do indeed exist, particularly in the access to credit, appropriate technology, information, irrigation and infrastructure, and other public goods and services. Markets are also clearly less favorable to peasant producers, because of their weak bargaining power with merchants, lack of access to public sector marketing facilities, and the nonexistence of marketing channels which they directly control. The second condition is that rural development programs, oriented at enhancing peasant production, be organized to help remove the main bottlenecks to peasant competitiveness. Even in an unbiased institutional context these programs will continue to be necessary, because of the large number of peasants to be serviced and their weak individual ability to have access to public services.

When both subfamily farms and family farms (usually defined as between 5 and 20 hectares) are included in the peasantry, that sector accounts for a significant share of total agricultural production. Around 1980, the peasantry accounted for an estimated 40 percent of the gross value of crop and livestock production—55 percent in Peru and 80 percent in Bolivia. The peasantry also plays a significant role in the production of export crops, such as coffee (41 percent) and cocoa (33 percent). In most countries, however, the peasantry lost ground during the 1960s and 1970s in the share of the domestic market for the food products it supplied. For peasants to benefit from a growing agriculture, they must maintain their share of the domestic market. Elimination of the anti-peasant institutional biases and promotion of rural development are needed for that purpose.

Since rural development must now occur in a context of improved real exchange rate and severe fiscal austerity, the style of rural development programs must be markedly different from that which prevailed during the decade of oil boom or accumulation of external debt. During the boom of the 1970s, rural development programs were fundamentally instruments to compensate for the depreciation of the real exchange rate and distribute to peasants their due share of the public rent.

Today, rural development must (1) be seen as a productive social investment and not as a compensatory social welfare program, (2) be directed at reallocating resources in the small farm sector toward the production of tradable goods for either import substitution or exports, (3) promote the use of technologies with a low import content and low capital intensity, and (4) increase the efficiency of the public sector and, specifically, seek cheaper and more resource-efficient ways of organizing rural development projects. Increased decentralization and participation are likely to be key for that purpose.

A rising agricultural supply must be accompanied by a simultaneous increase in effective demand (see figure 1). This is particularly essential for nontradable goods (which, consequently, have an inelastic demand) and for products with prices maintained above world market level with no further opportunity for import substitution. If in these cases income effects do not shift demand, technological change leads to a falling gross sectoral income and to asset depreciation in the first case and to an increase in the fiscal cost of agricultural subsidies in the second.

While some peasant production is aimed at the export market, the bulk of the surplus marketed by peasants is directed toward the domestic food market. Expansion of this market depends upon the growth of the whole economy and incomes generated in the rural sector, which still harbors 34 percent of the total population and where the nutritional gap is particularly large. Several programs for the rural sector have the capacity of contributing simultaneously to the generation of incomes for the rural poor and expansion of the domestic market for peasants' production. These programs include (1) the generation of employment in agriculture by eliminating the price distortions and the subsidies that induce the adoption of labor-saving machinery and the spread of livestock at the expense of more labor-intensive crops; (2) the generation of higher farm incomes through greater access to land and water by means of land reform, irrigation, and colonization programs; (3) the generation of self-employment in activities that are complementary to agriculture, such as raising small animals, processing agricultural products, handicrafts, and trade; and (4) the generation of nonagricultural employment in the rural areas in small industries tied to agriculture through backward, forward, and final-demand linkages.

ELEMENTS OF A RURAL DEVELOPMENT STRATEGY TO COMBAT RURAL POVERTY

The agriculture-led growth strategy outlined in figure 1 leads to the identification of five key elements to implement it.

FARM-ORIENTED RURAL DEVELOPMENT

These projects, the aim of which is to enhance production on peasant farms, are those for which the greatest experience has been accumulated, through the many integrated rural development initiatives in Latin America since the early 1970s (de Janvry 1981; and Lacroix 1985). Projects of this type include the Puebla project in Mexico and the Integrated Rural Development program in Colombia. These experiences indicate that such projects have the greatest chance of success when they are directed at that segment of the peasantry possessing enough productive resources to absorb the majority of family labor productively on the farm. The resources needed to stimulate production include credit, new technological alternatives, soil conservation, water control, infrastructure investments, extension, marketing, and the promotion of grassroots organizations. A realistic assessment of the potential of these programs to reduce rural poverty calls for explicitly confining them to the highest strata of peasant farms, that is, upper subfamily and family farms. For irrigated lands, the minimum viable farm size will generally be above 1 or 2 hectares; for those without irrigation, it is above 5 hectares.

Another commonly observed difficulty with these projects is the excessive number of activities they attempt simultaneously. This type of rural development project should be focused on the productive aspects of the peasant farm, and the constraints on the level of net income derived from production should be clearly identified and ranked. These constraints typically include lack of irrigation, lack of flexible access to credit, lack of appropriate technology for peasant farming systems, and the lack of farmer participation in the definition and management of projects to ensure sustainability.

While integrated rural development projects have sometimes proved effective, they have also met with considerable problems, because it is difficult to integrate the delivery of public services to peasant farms when these services originate in different branches of the public sector (Leonard 1984). The project approach also tends to isolate rural development initiatives from the mainstream of government initiatives and political life. If a careful ranking of limiting factors can be established, projects can be replaced by national or regional programs specifically aimed at removing a particular bottleneck. For the promotion of technological change, for instance, commodity programs have proved to be more effective than integrated rural development projects.

HOUSEHOLD-ORIENTED RURAL DEVELOPMENT

Rural households with little access to land must include a multiplicity of activities in their survival strategies. On subfamily farms of fewer than 1 or 2 irrigated hectares or 5 nonirrigated hectares, a majority of total household income is derived from nonagricultural activities. In these households, the division of labor implies that men work principally outside the farm and women are generally the main agricultural producers. In the Ecuadorian Sierra, for example, female labor represents 68 percent of total family labor applied to farms of less than 1 hectare. In much of the Altiplano, these women belong to ethnic communities and commonly do not speak Spanish; this situation requires specifically tailored ways of providing extension services to them.

Households on these small farms engage in a wide variety of activities complementary to agriculture that are also largely under the control of women. They include the raising of small animals and dairy cows, processing, handicrafts, and trade. It is clear that, in spite of the low percentage of total income derived from land, the farm production, however small, is an essential element of the household's income, security, and family survival. Since women are the main agriculturalists, there exist very specific constraints to raising labor productivity on these farms, particularly labor constraints and discrimination in access to institutions, as well as restrictions to raising the income derived from other activities within the family unit. For these reasons, rural development initiatives toward these small farms must take a household approach, as opposed to a farm approach.

Since little is as yet known about the effectiveness of such programs and because they serve a diverse clientele, it is important that these rural development programs be designed to experiment with diverse approaches (Korten 1980). This in turn will require careful monitoring and evaluation. Nongovernmental organizations have often been more successful than public sector agencies in this domain. Lessons learned from their most positive experiences should be shared and successful practices expanded, through public and international support.

LAND REFORM AND COLONIZATION

Any strategy directed at alleviating rural poverty must ensure that access to land is the major determinant of rural welfare. In spite of decades of land reform initiatives in most Latin American countries, access to land not only remains highly concentrated but has become increasingly so over time. Rural development programs initiated in the 1970s cannot be looked on as substitutes for redistributive land reform but should be seen as complements, to be implemented following resolution of the problem of access to land.

Colonization of the lowland tropics of Latin America has largely been spontaneous. This push toward the frontier is fundamentally the product of rural poverty in the areas of traditional peasant concentration—that is, of demographic explosion, soil erosion, paralysis of land reforms, investments insufficient to increase land productivity, loss of employment opportunities in commercial agriculture, and low labor absorption capacity in the urban-industrial sector. The current economic crisis, by increasing the levels of urban unemployment, is creating a new push toward the agricultural frontier. More often than not, this spontaneous colonization has created serious ecological problems and conflicts with indigenous populations. It is, consequently, urgent that colonization be carefully planned and the problems addressed through extension, credit, and infrastructure programs whenever it is deemed that ecological and ethnic problems can be resolved.

EMPLOYMENT CREATION AND LABOR MARKET REFORMS

Landless workers and marginal farmers rely heavily on agricultural wages as a major source of income. Yet this source of income is threatened by trends: labor displacement by mechanization and livestock, replacement of permanent workers by seasonal workers, substitution of semi-urbanized farm workers for workers of peasant origin on the temporary labor market, loss of power of labor unions, and the rising importance of largely unregulated labor contractors in mediating the relationship between labor supply and demand. It is, therefore, important that the price biases and subsidies that favor the diffusion of mechanical innovations and of labor-extensive activities be eliminated. Efforts must be made to rationalize the farm labor market in order to make the mechanisms of supply and demand more transparent. Short-run transition programs must also be organized, to protect the poorest rural households from the loss of rural employment and from the erosion of real wages created by rising food prices in the period of adjustment to the crisis; public works programs and use of World Food Program resources for community projects have proved to be effective for that purpose.

REINFORCING LINKAGES BETWEEN AGRICULTURE AND OTHER SECTORS

It is clear that agriculture cannot offer a solution to rural poverty for a significant fraction of the rural population. An extensive redistributive land reform and successful rural development projects would reduce this fraction but would still leave a significant quota of agricultural poverty to be solved outside of agriculture.

A development strategy that stimulates agricultural development through a rising real exchange rate and a rising productivity of labor will generate incomes in agriculture that can serve to activate other sectors of the economy through linkage effects. These include backward linkages (demand by agriculture for industrial inputs and services), forward linkages (adding value to agricultural output through its transformation), and final-demand or consumption linkages (the demand for goods and services originating in the expenditure of agricultural incomes). Many of these linkage effects can be located in the rural areas and organized in small decentralized firms with low capital intensity and low import content. This requires the identification of investment opportunities in small industries and the provision of technical assistance, training in management, and credit. Under conditions of surplus labor, if these constraints on supply are lifted, the level of activity of these small firms is fundamentally demand determined and can thus directly respond to the income effects created by successful agricultural reactivation.

Given the magnitude of the investments required in rural industries, it is essential that private capital from both national and international origins be attracted to these sectors. While it is difficult to attract private equity capital to agricultural production (basically for reasons of moral hazard and difficulty of supervision), this is not the case for rural industries. International loans should thus not be used to finance direct investment but to seek a multiplier effect by serving to attract private equity capital. This can be done in a variety of ways:

1. Provide information and legal and technical assistance to potential investors.
2. Develop the appropriate infrastructure and deliver the necessary other public goods to make private investment attractive.
3. Offer investment guarantee schemes of the type provided by the Investment Finance Corporation to foreign investors.
4. Provide investment standby guarantees to local banks that lend to rural industries. Under this scheme, public agencies would insure commercial banks against default on loans made to rural industries.
5. Implement debt-equity swaps, which can be used to give foreign investors, and nationals with foreign deposits, who want to invest in rural industries large discounts on access to local currency.

CONCLUSION

The current adjustments to the economic crisis, however disastrous for growth and welfare in the short run, offer a unique opportunity to use agriculture as a leading sector of future economic growth and to reduce rural poverty by pursuing an effective strategy of rural development. For this approach to be successful, explicit priority needs to be given to investment in agriculture, and structural adjustment programs (supported by international financing) must be continued. In this context, rural development is justified as an economically competitive social project and not as a welfare act, as seen in the past. Rural development must explicitly recognize the high degree of social differentiation that exists in the rural areas and deal simultaneously with the determinants of income for each social category, ranging from productivity enhancement to access to land, employment creation, and the promotion of decentralized nonagricultural activities tied to agriculture through production and consumption linkages.

NOTES

1. By appreciation of the real exchange rate we mean an increase in the ratio of the price of tradable goods to that of nontradable goods. Typically, a devaluation of the domestic currency, as occurred in most Latin American countries during the 1980s, will lead to an appreciation of the real exchange rate.

REFERENCES

Adelman, I. 1984. "Beyond Export-led Growth." *World Development* 12, no. 9, (September): 937–49.

Altimir, O. 1982. *The Extent of Poverty in Latin America.* World Bank Staff Working Paper, no. 522. Washington, D.C.: World Bank.

Corbo, V., and J. de Melo. 1987. "Lessons from the Southern Cone Policy Reforms." *The World Bank Research Observer* 2, no. 2 (July): 111–42.

de Janvry, A. 1981. *The Agrarian Question and Reformism in Latin America.* Baltimore: Johns Hopkins University Press.

de Janvry, A., and E. Sadoulet. 1988. "The Conditions for Compatibility between Aid and Trade in Agriculture." *Economic Development and Cultural Change.* 37, no. 1 (October): 1–30.

de Janvry, A., E. Sadoulet, and L. Wilcox. 1986. "Rural Labor in Latin America." ILO Working Paper 10-6/WP79. Geneva: International Labor Organization.

ECLA/FAO. 1986. *Peasant Agriculture in Latin America and the Caribbean.* Santiago: Economic Commission for Latin America.

Food and Agriculture Organization (FAO). 1988. *Potential for Agricultural and Rural Development in Latin America and the Caribbean,* 7 vols. Rome: United Nations Food and Agriculture Organization.

Hirschman, A. 1958. *The Strategy of Economic Development.* New Haven: Yale University Press.

Jorgenson, D. 1969. "The Role of Agriculture in Economic Development: Classical versus Neo-Classical Models of Growth." In *Subsistence Agriculture and Economic Development,* edited by C. Wharton. Chicago: Aldine.

Klein, E. 1984. "El Impacto Heterogeneo de la Modernizacion Agricola Sobre el Mercado de Travajo." *Socialismo y Participacion,* no. 30.

Korten, D. 1980. "Community Organization and Rural Development: A Learning Approach." *Public Administration Review* 40, no. 5 (September-October): 480–511.

Kouwenaar, A. 1986. "A Basic Needs Policy Model: A General Equilibrium Analysis with Special Reference to Ecuador." Ph.D. diss., The Hague.

Lacroix, R. 1985. "Integrated Rural Development in Latin America." World Bank Staff Working Paper, no. 716. Washington, D.C.: World Bank.

Lele, U., and J. Mellor. 1981. "Technological Change, Distributive Bias, and Labor Transfer in a Two-Sector Economy." *Oxford Economic Papers* 33, no. 3 (November): 426–41.

Leonard, D. 1984. "Disintegrating Agricultural Development." *Food Research Institute Studies* 19, no. 2: 177–86.

Scott, C. D. 1987. "Poverty and Inequality in the Rural Sector of Latin America and the Caribbean." Rome: United Nations Food and Agriculture Organization. Unpublished manuscript.

Twomey, M. 1987. "Latin American Agriculture and the Macroeconomy." Rome: United Nations Food and Agriculture Organization. Unpublished manuscript.

29

Agricultural Reform in the Soviet Union

KAREN BROOKS

Historians often consider the summer months of 1929 the eve of mass collectivization in the USSR. During the following three brutal years, ending with the famine of 1932–33, fifteen million peasant households became members of collective farms (see Lewin 1968; Volin 1970; Nove 1976; Davies 1980; Medvedev 1987). In the summer of 1989, the sixty-year experiment with a novel form of land tenure was drawing to a close. State and collective farms will remain, at least in the short run, but the rules that govern their functioning, both internally and in relation to the rest of the economy, will change. Precisely how they will change is the subject of current debate on agricultural policy in the USSR.

That debate is structured around an inescapable assessment of present-day collectivized agriculture in the USSR: it is very expensive. Collectivized agriculture emerged from the political, economic, and ideological turmoil of the Soviet Union in the 1920s. The decision to collectivize was most immediately a response to a marketing problem; peasants in the late 1920s reduced production and marketing of grain in response to poor relative prices and weakened incentives (Volin 1970; 189–202). The decline in grain procurements in 1927 and 1928 strengthened the positions of those who argued that markets, even regulated markets, could not produce the transfer of resources necessary to support rapid industrialization. Collectivization took decisions about production and marketing out of the hands of individual peasants and transferred them to the government and the party. The short-term control over marketed output came at a cost of progressively reduced efficiency in the agricultural sector. Low efficiency has brought high and rising costs of production, exacerbated by the growth in demand and factor substitutions that accompanied the transition of the USSR from a low-income to a middle-income country.

Many aspects of agricultural development in the USSR are particular to the geography and historical experience of its people and cannot be generalized to other countries. The brutality of forced collectivization should properly be laid to Stalin

KAREN BROOKS is assistant professor, Department of Agricultural and Applied Economics, University of Minnesota.

and the thousands of collaborators who implemented his orders. The extraordinary losses of the Red Army during World War II contributed to demographic problems of the postwar agricultural labor force. Yet the high costs of collectivized agriculture are embedded in the form of land tenure and resource management, rather than in particular Soviet experience.

By 1989, high costs of collectivized agriculture in the USSR had collided with decreased ability to pay the bill. Gorbachev's industrial modernization effort diverted resources from agriculture to heavy and light industry. Oil and gas had become more expensive in rubles to extract and earned fewer dollars on world markets. The debate over the new agricultural program announced in March of 1989 was about how much Soviet society could pay to retain some or all of the institutions of collectivized agriculture, and who should pay: consumers through high prices, producers through low earnings, or taxpayers through massive subsidies.

This essay on the Soviet experience is an inquiry into the causes and effects of the high costs of collectivized agriculture. The first section is a discussion of the sources of high cost on the supply side. The second covers the demand side and the contradictions between demand and supply policies. The third section presents the current farm financial crisis as the logical outcome of contradictory demand and supply policies and the catalyst for policy change. Finally, the fourth section presents the new agricultural program and some issues that will be important to the pace and extent of its implementation. I try to examine the functioning of collectivized agriculture in a large, middle-income, centrally planned economy and to call on names, dates, and particular Soviet policies only when necessary. (For a discussion of Soviet growth more generally, see Ofer 1987.)

Throughout this essay runs a division of Soviet experience into two periods: 1930–1953 under Stalin, when the institutions of collectivized agriculture were put in place, and 1965 to the present, when Brezhnev's modernization campaign dominated agricultural policy. It is simplistic but not entirely wrong to argue that in the earlier period the assigned role of agriculture was to contribute resources, mostly cheap food and labor, to the developing industrial economy and that collectivized agriculture was the institution adopted to facilitate the transfer. In the later period, agriculture should have assumed a new role: efficient user of the industrial inputs its earlier contribution helped to create, and generator and adopter of new biological and mechanical technology to bring food and fiber to an increasingly wealthy population at declining real costs.

The human toll of collectivized agriculture was appallingly evident in the early period; its economic cost was not unambiguously apparent until the second period. Most of the debate about the relative merits of collectivization has focused on the earlier period: Were resources transferred or simply destroyed? Did the reduction of political and economic rights of the rural work force hinder or promote growth? These are important moral and economic questions, but an understanding of the performance of collectivized agriculture in the second period is perhaps more important. A successful development strategy will hasten the transformation of an economy from a predominantly low-income rural economy to a middle-income one with a large proportion of the work force employed outside of agriculture. Agricultural institutions that perform poorly when development succeeds and yet prove very difficult to change will subvert growth in the longer run. This appears to be the major and unfortunate lesson of sixty years of Soviet collectivized agriculture.

SUPPLY SIDE: HIGH COSTS OF PRODUCTION

Land on collective and state farms is owned by the state and leased to the farms in perpetuity, free of charge. The average farm has about 6500 hectares of land (3500 of which are cultivated) and a work force of 450. People who work on collective and state farms also live there and have the right to farm a small plot of land adjacent to their homes. The private or household plot traditionally has not exceeded half a hectare, and livestock held on the private plot have been both strictly limited in number and intermittently taxed. The farm family can use the output of the household plot for their own consumption or for sale.

The sources of high costs of production on collective and state farms are diverse but can be grouped into three general areas: poor labor incentives, weak economic links among farms and between farms and the rest of the economy, and limited autonomy for farms in running their own economic affairs. Each of these sources of high cost can be linked to particular characteristics of collectivized agriculture (see Johnson and Brooks 1983).

LABOR MOBILITY AND LABOR INCENTIVES

In the 1930s most farms were collective farms; state farms existed but were few. People who lived and worked on collective farms were members of the farm, not employees of the state, and did not have rights to the social security, pensions, standardized wages, and occupational choice granted state employees. Collective farms were forbidden to hire the labor of nonmembers with the exception of trained specialists hired on contract. (Few trained agronomists or veterinarians would give up the status of state employee for that of collective farm member.) State employees carried internal passports, could change their legal place of residence and work, and could travel freely within the country. Collective farm members did not have the right to passports until 1974, and those who lacked passports needed special documents to leave the farm.

The special legal status of collective farm members raised the costs of leaving agriculture, despite working conditions and standards of living that lagged considerably behind opportunities in the growing industrial enterprises. Workers were not tied to the farm, but neither were they fully free to quit. For work on the collective fields they were paid according to a work point system used to divide residual farm profits after all obligations to the state and suppliers of nonlabor inputs had been met. Since procurement prices were low, residual profits were low, and work points were often worth little and paid in kind.

In 1939, 47 percent of the population within the Soviet borders were collective farm members or their minor children, and 3 percent of the population were un-collectivized peasants or craft workers. Many of these people, fully half of the Soviet population, supported themselves on the proceeds from their half-hectare private plots and were only tenuously linked into the monetary economy. The private plot was an essential and integral part of collectivized agriculture. It augmented the aggregate food supply, provided subsistence for the agricultural labor force, and its removal was the ultimate sanction against individuals who did not participate in collective labor.

By the time of Stalin's death, in 1953, it was apparent that labor productivity in agriculture was low. This was attributed in large part to the low pay, and a number of changes were made in the wage system under Khrushchev and Brezhnev. Khrushchev raised farm purchase prices in an effort to raise residual profits and the value of work points. Under Brezhnev, after 1966, the collective farm work point system was phased out and replaced with a standardized wage scale linked to wages on state farms. Thus, under Stalin and later Khrushchev, collective farm workers were paid a share of earnings, and under Brezhnev they were switched over to straight wage contracts. Both experiences offer instructive lessons about labor incentives under alternative forms of contracts in agriculture.

Labor incentives for teams whose members share output have been the subject of a large body of literature in economics. One of the conclusions of that literature is that teams can be an efficient form of organization if they are voluntary, if workers have alternatives to joining the team, and if each team member's contribution is observable at low cost (Alchian and Demsetz 1972; Sertel 1982).

The Soviet and Chinese experience with work point systems in agriculture provides an important empirical observation on this form of labor organization (see Lin 1988).[1] The costs of monitoring labor in agriculture are so high as to preclude all but the smallest teams or family units, chosen on a voluntary basis. With larger teams the costs of monitoring rise and individuals shirk, knowing that their own withdrawal of effort will be merged into the general poor performance of the team. The problem of shirking is present whether payment for work in the collective sector is high or low.

The switch-over to straight wage contracts after 1966 did not reduce shirking, although higher and guaranteed wages may have induced some workers to stay in agriculture who otherwise would have left. Team members carry at least a share of the cost of their own shirking; workers on straight wage contracts carry none at all. The move, under Brezhnev, to guaranteed wages thus raised wages without improving incentives for higher productivity, and so contributed to higher costs of production. Farms that could not pay the higher wages out of their own earnings were encouraged to take out loans to cover payrolls.

Under Khrushchev and Brezhnev and in the early Gorbachev years, the wage and payment system in agriculture was the object of constant tinkering in an effort to discover a successful formula to motivate people to work more responsibly. None of the changes succeeded in linking payment to an individual's economic performance, nor did any bring a noticeable improvement in labor productivity.

Collective farms are prohibited from hiring nonmembers as day laborers. This restriction kept the demand side of rural labor markets from developing while mandatory work days restricted the supply side. As a result, rural labor markets functioned poorly. Mobility of rural labor is particularly important when industrial growth is pulling workers from the countryside to the cities, as has been the case in the USSR in every decade since collectivization. The combination of inefficient distribution of agricultural workers and poor labor incentives explains much of the current concern about a labor shortage when 19 percent of the work force is still employed in agricultural production and a worker cultivates on average only eight hectares. Low labor productivity is an important source of high costs in agriculture, and one that a country with a declining birth rate and a high demand for labor in the industrial economy can ill afford.

LINKS BETWEEN AGRICULTURE AND THE REST OF THE ECONOMY

The economic function of collectivized agriculture in its early years was to facilitate extraction of resources from the sector, through taxation, low purchase prices, and reduced standards of living of agricultural workers. It served as well to assure political compliance, but political control would not have been as necessary had the economics not turned so against rural people.

The extent to which collectivization succeeded in transferring resources out of agriculture is a subject of debate (Millar 1970; Nove 1984). The loss of life and destruction of livestock and buildings plus the lower productivity of the resources that remained may have made the net transfer nil or negative. For example, because the number of horses and cattle on farms was halved between 1928 and 1933, many of the tractors produced in the 1930s were needed to replace slaughtered draft animals.

By the time of Stalin's death, in 1953, it was clear that Soviet agriculture was in a shambles, and the cause of that distress was seen to be the policy of taxation and disinvestment. Khrushchev increased the flow of resources to agriculture, and a full-fledged reinvestment campaign began under Brezhnev in 1965. For most of the period since 1965, agriculture has received 20 percent of annual total investment in the entire Soviet economy; only recently has the proportion fallen to 17 percent. This investment has been used for structures, land reclamation, machinery, animal inventories, and fertilizer and other chemicals. The use of fertilizer increased fourfold between 1965 and 1987, and both the number and the power of agricultural machines rose. Farms became more specialized. The proportion of the work force in agriculture declined from 54 percent in 1940 to 39 percent in 1960 and to 25 percent in 1970. With fewer people on farms, the farms' tasks of feeding its own work force through disbursements in kind diminished and of marketing output for the state retail network increased. Delivery quotas were changed to encourage specialization, and farms became dependent on off-farm suppliers for feed, fuel, fertilizer, and maintenance of machinery. The marketing function that linked farms to the rest of the economy on both the input and the output side became more important with specialization, yet the modernization campaign did not include institutional innovations to assure that investments went to the right places at the right times or were used well. Major and minor decisions about new projects and flows of current inputs reflected political jockeying of powerful local party officials. Without functioning markets or economic accountability, the return to resources played a small role in guiding their allocation.

Rural people chose to and were forced to buy more food in stores as farms became specialized and paid wages in money, rather than in kind. Urbanization and income growth increased demand for processed foods. Yet the investment under Brezhnev's modernization program, massive as it was, was concentrated on farms and input supply. "Downstream" capacity in transport, processing, and retailing did not grow to meet the increased demand. Losses of products after they left the farm—and sometimes even before—increased, and raised the costs of food and fiber actually delivered to consumers.

Funds that would have been better used for transport or processing went for irrigation or drainage of land that was poorly used or allowed to overgrow with weeds and scrub. Fertilizer, machinery, and capital investment often went not where the return was high, but, paradoxically, where it was low. Despite formal criteria to guide investment decisions, investment in agriculture has been marked by a conflict between investing to maximize return and investing to equalize productive conditions. The latter criterion gives the poorest and worst managed farms the best claim to investment, precisely because they are poor.

The input supply organizations through which much of the reinvestment has been channeled are state monopolies. Most input prices are centrally set, and these organizations have had little of the traditional monopolist's power to set prices. But they engage in a number of practices that increase the real prices farms pay, such as restricting availability of inexpensive items in high demand and forcing substitutions of more expensive models, inflating repair bills, and failing to make contracted deliveries. Farms denied alternative suppliers accept late shipments of fertilizer or feed and pay high prices for unnecessary repairs, but they do not reap benefits commensurate with the cost of these expenses.

The losses due to monopoly in the input supply industry have increased as more inputs have moved through these organizations during the modernization campaign. This source of high cost is external to the state or collective farm, but it is part of the economic structure in which farms are embedded. In the early years of collectivized agriculture, the state monopoly on marketing, of both inputs and output, was part of the mechanism through which agriculture was taxed. The monopoly was a good instrument for taxation, since farms could be forced to pay high prices for purchased inputs and to deliver output for low procurement prices. The state marketing monopoly, although external to the farms, was necessary for collectivized agriculture to function as intended in the 1930s.

The state monopoly in marketing is counterproductive when the goal of policy is to inject additional physical and financial resources into agriculture. Physical resources fail to give a high return and financial resources are siphoned out of the farm accounts and into those of the input suppliers. Retention of this inappropriate marketing institution throughout the reinvestment campaign greatly reduced the return to investment.

FARM AUTONOMY

An integral part of collectivized agriculture as it developed in the USSR was the removal of all effective economic decision making from the farm level. Decisions about what, when, and how to plant, when to hay and weed, and when to harvest and deliver have, from the earliest days, been made by people in the political departments of Machine Tractor Stations and later district and *oblast'* (similar to a state) party headquarters, who know about conditions on the farm because of telephone reports, if they know anything at all (see Miller 1970).

Now, in this period of reevaluation of sixty years of collectivized agriculture, the severance of decision making from implementation is a subject of anguished reflection. One expression of this is a populist sentiment that collectivization broke a mystical link between the peasant and the land and that Soviet agriculture has gone downhill ever since. Gorbachev does not fully espouse the populist view, but frequently argues that the agricultural worker must again become "master" (*khoziain*) of the land, that is, a manager who not only has incentive to work well but power to make responsible decisions.

The agricultural worker is twice removed from mastery of the land. The collective farm chairman (through the brigade leader) tells the worker what to do, but the farm chairman, in turn, receives orders from the local party apparatus. One reason costs are high in Soviet agriculture is that decisions about the use of expensive resources, such as fertilizer and labor, are made by people who have poorer information than those who are in the fields and barns.

The removal of farm autonomy during the early period of collectivization, like the state monopoly in marketing, was necessary for collectivized agriculture to function as the instrument of taxation it was designed to be. But lack of farm autonomy produced economic dysfunction when the general policy focus changed from extraction to reinvestment. Yet returning decision making to the farms and farm workers has proven to be very difficult.

Many of the most skilled producers were killed or exiled during the brutal period of forced collectivization (1929–32) and the campaign against prosperous peasants that preceded it. Those among the farming population who supported collectivization were usually poor peasants who had little managerial skill or experience. Prior to Khrushchev's amalgamation of farms in the 1950s, collective farms were smaller than they are now, but the task of managing even one hundred people producing a heterogeneous commodity mix is not trivial. Moreover, because wages were so low and resentment about collectivization was still high, one of the manager's main jobs was simply to persuade people to work in the collective fields. Many local people who had a decent skill for farming did not want to manage the collective farm, and those who did were suspected by the state of holding the interests of their neighbors and relatives higher than those of the state. Collective farm chairmen were appointed by the local party secretary and owed allegiance to him rather than to the farm members. The scarcity of trained agricultural specialists and rural party members meant that many farm chairmen in the early period were either politically suspect or professionally incompetent, or both. Political oversight and economic management were provided by the political department of the Machine Tractor Station, an instrument of the state monopoly on input supply. When the Machine Tractor Stations were dissolved, in 1958, and the machinery was sold (at high prices) to the farms, the stations' role in economic management went not to the farms but to the district party headquarters.

Cynthia Kaplan argues that the party has continued to meddle in the economic affairs of farms much more than in those of industry (Kaplan 1987). Party officials interfere with the decisions of industrial managers in exceptional, rather than normal, circumstances. Farm managers, on the contrary, receive a constant flow of telegrams, phone calls, reports to fill out, and summonses to headquarters. Kaplan attributes this special role of the party in agricultural management to educational policy during the postwar period, which created a much smaller cohort of ideologically acceptable agricultural specialists than industrial specialists. Moreover, the poor performance of agriculture in most years of the postwar period has created an atmosphere of continued crisis. Party officials are held responsible if the performance of agriculture in their jurisdictions deteriorates, and, as a consequence, few are willing to let decisions about farm management out of their hands.

By the 1970s collective farms were well staffed with trained agronomists and animal scientists. In 1987 there were approximately forty specialists and managers with specialized secondary or postsecondary education on the average state or collective farm. Indeed, now that small groups of workers are encouraged to become financially accountable, some are expressing reluctance to pay for the services of the huge army of specialists or to include them in independent production units. The farms are now probably overstaffed with specialists and clerical workers and certainly have the personnel and expertise to manage their own affairs. But they do not yet have the economic autonomy to do so.

Decisions about how to carry out assigned production or sales targets could be handled at the farm level now and would result in reduced costs. The assignment of targets, that is, decisions about what to produce, can also be taken at the farm or subfarm level. If the farm worker is to be "master" of the land, he or she must be able to decide what to produce. But privately made decisions about production can be consistent with societal needs only if prices reflect the social cost of resources and social valuation of products. Distorted prices provide a justification for retention of output targets and quotas, but they do not explain why farms cannot now be left alone to fulfill those assignments.

PROTECTIONISM

To these three sources of high costs of production (poor labor incentives, weak links to the rest of the economy, and limited farm autonomy) must be added the high costs of regional and national protectionism. The emphasis on regional self-sufficiency in food is less now than it has been at times in the past. Yet, paradoxically, regional self-sufficiency and attendant high costs of production appear to be on the rise with the current emphasis on greater economic independence and self-reliance at the republic level. Under the new rules, republics will not be required to deliver as much food to the national "all-union" fund as they did in the past, but neither can they count on central supply of commodities that they do not produce themselves. Interrepublican wholesale trade at negotiated prices is to replace commodities no longer readily available from the all-union fund, but marketing channels are not yet developed and guidelines to govern price negotiations are vague. The confusion is likely to result in increased self-sufficiency of food at the republic level over the next several years.

If interrepublican trade is reduced, high-cost producers will be protected from domestic competitors, as well as from low-cost producers in other countries. The state monopoly on foreign trade and nonconvertibility of the ruble have in the past offered domestic producers full protection against foreign competitors, despite the large net imports of food. Domestic prices have been fully insulated from developments on world markets. The protection and distorted exchange rate and domestic prices have made it virtually impossible to calculate domestic comparative advantage for the purpose of planning domestic production and purchases abroad.

A country as large as the USSR can trade within its own borders and realize substantial gains from regional specialization, but distorted prices and restrictions on internal trade limit even these gains. With no competition, the high costs engendered by poor labor incentives, weak linkages, and limited farm autonomy do not force producers out of business. Rather, they force producers to seek funds to cover the high costs. These funds have come from successive increases in state purchase prices and growing farm debt.

DEMAND SIDE: CONSTANT PRICES AND RISING INCOMES EXACERBATE SHORTAGES

Assurance of cheap food for the industrial working class was one of the primary economic objectives of collectivization.[2] Many developing countries pursue policies intended to supply cheap food to the urban working class. Most middle- and high-income countries protect their agricultural sectors. Many pass a portion of the cost on to consumers in the form of prices higher than those in international trade, although some also invest in productivity-enhancing research that ultimately reduces international prices. The Soviet Union is unusual in that it has kept the commitment to cheap food for urban people but has simultaneously committed itself to costly protection and subsidies for producers, an activity characteristic of countries with per capita incomes higher than those in the USSR.

Paradoxically, despite the enduring commitment to low and stable food prices, food absorbs a large share of family disposable income in the USSR, in comparison with middle- and high-income countries. Families with per capita earnings twice the official poverty level spend, on average, one-third of disposable income on food (*Narodnoe khoziaistvo 1987,* 404). Beef sells in state stores for 1.7–2 rubles per kilo (depending on location), or about $1.50 per pound at the current grossly over-valued official exchange rate. At a more realistic exchange rate, food prices would look much lower in international comparisons but would still absorb a high share of family budgets.

Official retail prices for most food items have not increased since 1962, when sporadic riots accompanied an attempt to increase meat prices. Nominal wages have more than doubled in the interval. Consumers are encouraged by distorted official prices to empty the shelves and then feel resentful that items they formally can afford (again at official prices) are not available. Most Soviet consumers, and many economists as well, view the ubiquitous shortages and lines as purely supply-side problems. Rising money incomes and constant nominal prices would keep the stores empty even if supply were growing well, which it is not.

Excess demand in the state retail sector spills over to the collective farm market, where products not owed to the state through the quota system can legally be sold at market-clearing prices. In 1987, prices on collective-farm markets were reported to average 2.72 times official state retail prices, although the price differential varied by location, season, and product. The market-clearing prices determined in the collective farm market rebound back to the state sector and permit state stores to charge real prices that are significantly higher than official prices. The difference is in the form of quality degradation, lack of service, lines, tied sales, and explicit bribes.

Consumers who buy food in state stores are thus paying real prices closer to market-clearing prices than to official prices. Many products are not available at all in state stores and are rationed and distributed at official prices through employers. Middle-class employees who can buy rationed quantities through the workplace probably pay close to the official price, but in the process, supply is diverted from the general retail network. People who are poor, retired, or live in the countryside have little access to food at state prices and pay the higher prices of the collective farm market or the cooperative stores. According to A. Komin, vice chairman of the State Committee on Prices, budget surveys indicate that families with per capita incomes less than 50 rubles per month pay prices 20 to 30 percent higher for meat than families with per capita incomes of 150 rubles per month, because the latter have privileged access to supplies at official state prices (*Izvestiia,* November 19, 1987, p. 2).

The most highly subsidized items are meat and dairy products. Since income elasticities for these foods are high and the distribution system channels the subsidy toward high-income consumers, the pricing system is both inefficient and regressive. Yet the beneficiaries of the subsidy are people whose political and economic support for *perestroika* (economic restructuring) is essential. The Soviet Union belongs to the growing group of countries that have found the economic imperative to change retail food subsidies thwarted by the political imperative not to.

Failure to raise retail prices and inject more diversity into the pricing structure is consistent with a general neglect of the demand side of the agricultural economy and preoccupation with supply. Until recently, in the USSR, there has been a poor understanding of the importance of activities between the producer and final consumer in middle-income and high-income economies. This is in part an inherited ideological bias against middlemen, who, it is argued, do not produce anything, but simply change a product in some way and then pass it on at a higher price. Modern Soviet consumers, particularly high-income urban residents, want and are able to pay for high-quality processed products, but instead must often stand in line for meat hacked up before their eyes with an axe.

The neglect of the demand side would seem to have little to do with collectivization, and yet, in fact, they are closely linked. Collectivization severed the many links between producer and consumer and reconnected them through state monopolies in procurement, processing, and retailing. Monopolists in an economy in chronic shortage have little need to inqure about consumer preferences. Experience with the state monopolies makes consumers wary of increases in official prices; they suspect that supply, quality, and service will be unchanged with higher prices.

The severity of disequilibrium in food markets and distortions evident on the demand side obscure the fact that the Soviet diet, on average, is adequate in calories and nutrients, reasonably diverse in the sources of these dietary components, fares rather well in international comparisons, and is slowly improving. For example, despite chronic shortages, Soviet consumers eat more meat than do Portuguese or Japanese, and do not lag too far behind British and Italian consumers. They lag considerably behind Americans in consumption of meat, but so do people in most countries of the world, including Western Europe. The Soviet diet is simply not one that Soviet consumers, with their current incomes and current prices, would choose to consume. The Soviet government has announced consumption norms that are to be met by specified deadlines, but unless prices are changed, consumers will not be satisfied even if the norms are met.

THE SUBSIDY: LARGE AND GROWING

Contradictions between supply and demand policies have caused a growing subsidy burden and farm debt problem, which together constitute a financial crisis of major proportions.

The state pays the difference between high producer prices and lower retail prices as a direct subsidy from the budget. The gap between retail prices and state costs is shown in table 1. The agroindustrial complex, including agricultural inputs, production, and processing, contributes about 12 percent of the traditional revenues of the Soviet state budget, but it absorbs about 25 percent, according to V. Semenov, vice minister of finance for the USSR and a noted expert on agricultural finance (Semenov 1987, 31).

The financial burden of agriculture on the state budget has been heavy and has been growing since the producer price increase of January 1, 1983. A further producer price increase, effective January 1990, was announced but was not implemented, for financial reasons. With declining sales of alcohol (a highly taxed item)

TABLE 1
RETAIL PRICES AND STATE COST PER KILOGRAM OF ANIMAL PRODUCTS
(IN 1985 RUBLES)

	Poultry	Beef	Lamb	Pork	Milk	Butter
Average retail prices	2.57	1.75	1.42	1.84	0.25	3.38
State cost	2.92	5.42	4.86	3.51	0.45	8.43
Excess of state costs over retail price	.35	3.67	3.44	1.67	0.20	5.05

SOURCE: V. Semenov, "Sovershenstvovanie finansovogo mekhanizma agropromyshlennogo kompleksa," *Ekonomika sel'skogo khoziaistva* 9 (1987): 34.

and rising food production, payments from the budget rise faster than contributions, and the subsidy grows. V. Pavlov, chairman of the State Committee on Prices, indicated in December 1987 that budgetary allocations to cover price subsidies for both inputs and output in 1988 were 73.4 billion rubles, suggesting that the growth in the subsidy is accelerating (*Sel'skaia zhizn'*, December 2, 1987). The figure for 1989 is 87.9 billion rubles (*Pravda*, October 28, 1988, pp. 4–5).

The large and growing food subsidy is a major contributor to macroeconomic imbalance. Food is not the only subsidized item; housing, public transportation, and most public services are offered at prices far below cost of delivery. The subsidies are offset by payments into the budget from enterprise profits and sales taxes. The budget deficit is now 100 billion rubles annually, or about 10 percent of GNP (Vanous 1988). Although other subsidies contribute to the deficit, the food subsidy, at 88 billion rubles, is clearly very large.

The agricultural budgetary subsidy is paid in several forms. The largest portion of the subsidy is used to cover the difference between costs of procuring, processing, and transporting agricultural products, and the receipts of state stores from retail trade in food. The state makes direct grants for investment and current expenses. Farms in the past have paid discounted prices for purchase of tractors, mineral fertilizer, and agricultural chemicals; and the budget has covered the difference between the farm price and the factory price. In the recent round of policy change the input price subsidy is being removed. In the future, farms will pay the manufacturing wholesale price for inputs and will be compensated with higher purchase prices.

Three-quarters of the expenditures on direct price subsidy are for meat and milk. The size of the price subsidy over time and its breakdown by commodity are shown in table 2.

The data on subsidies do not include farm indebtedness unless bad debts are written off the bank accounts by transfers from the budget. Much of the overdue farm debt has been used to pay current operating expenses, particularly payrolls. Since expectations that debts will be paid back are low, a large portion of farm debt should properly be considered subsidy. When the food program of 1982 went into effect in 1983, 9.7 billion rubles of bad debts were written off, and 11.1 billion rubles rescheduled for repayment to begin in 1991. Farm debt increased by 10 bil-

TABLE 2
STATE SUBSIDY TO COVER PRICE DIFFERENCES
(BILLIONS OF CURRENT RUBLES)

	1960	*1965*	*1970*	*1975*	*1980*	*1985*	*1986*
Meat and poultry	1.4	2.8	8.8	12.2	14.0	26.6	27.8
Fish	0.1	0.1	0.2	0.2	0.2	2.2	1.8
Milk	—	—	2.1	4.0	7.5	18.9	19.2
Grain		0.3	0.8	0.6	0.8	4.4	4.4
Potatoes, vegetables, and canned goods	—	—	0.2	0.7	1.4	3.0	3.7
Sugar	—	—	—	—	—	1.0	1.2
Total	1.5	3.2	12.1	19.7	23.9	56.0	57.9
As % payments of state budget	2.1	3.2	7.8	9.2	8.1	14.5	14.0

SOURCE: V. Semenov, "Sovershenstvovanie finansovogo mekhanizma agropromyshlennogo kompleksa," *Ekonomika sel'skogo khoziaistva* 9 (1987): 35.

lion rubles after the price increases of 1983. In 1988, fully half of the outstanding agricultural debt was rescheduled (72 billion rubles). In December 1989, the USSR Council of Ministers decided to write off 73.5 billion rubles of bad farm debt (Sovetskai Rossiia, December 7, 1989, p. 1).

In 1987, collective and state farms held 34 percent of the total bank indebtedness, compared to 15 percent in 1970. Farm debt in 1987, both short and long term, totaled 148 billion rubles, roughly twice the size of the direct subsidy. Inclusion of uncollectible debts would appreciably increase the already large subsidy.

Farm indebtedness and delayed repayment contribute to the financial constraints that agriculture places on the rest of the economy. The direct subsidy fuels inflation through its contribution to the budget deficit. The indirect subsidy, continued rescheduling of bad debt, also adds to inflation by permitting monetary flows in excess of real flows. The inflation seriously undercuts efforts to introduce better labor incentives throughout the economy; people are reluctant to work harder for rubles that are worth less.

ISSUES IN REFORMING THE SOVIET AGRICULTURAL SYSTEM

REMEDIES OF THE REFORM: FEW ON THE DEMAND SIDE

The remedy on the demand side is to increase food prices, but the quandary about how and how much, and how to compensate people for the increase, has stymied the general price reform to the enormous harm of the whole *perestroika* program. In January 1989, the general price reform scheduled for 1990/91 was postponed for several years, in large part because of the sensitivity of food price increases. Food prices cannot be excluded from price reform without introducing even greater distortions, and food prices cannot be touched now.

The severe disequilibrium in food pricing has spilled over to wreak havoc, not only on food marketing, but on the entire reform effort. Under the Law on the

Enterprise (the industrial reform legislation), managers of state enterprises are forced to take seriously estimates of profitability calculated with distorted prices. Much output is still produced and procured under quotas; only a small portion of the resources of industrial enterprises is allocated according to price signals. Yet the essence of the industrial reform is to increase that portion and enhance the allocative role of prices. Distorted prices will compound the difficulties of transition to the new system.

There is now widespread agreement that food prices cannot be increased until supplies improve significantly, to assure that products will be available at the new prices. In March 1989, Gorbachev announced that retail prices for most basic foods would be unchanged for two to three years.

The low level of food processing and packaging is to be remedied by investment of 77 billion rubles ($127 billion, at the current much overvalued official exchange rate) over five years in new processing equipment. Producers of military hardware have been given orders to reequip the food processing industry. Some of the equipment will be imported, and large credits negotiated in Western Europe in 1988 will be used in part to upgrade food processing.

Consumer and producer cooperatives could expand their activities greatly in food processing and retailing. An expanded cooperative sector would offer consumers in urban areas an alternative to the empty state stores and expensive collective farm markets. Cooperatives have somewhat greater flexibility in pricing than do state stores, although they will need more leeway still and legal and financial guarantees before they will become a significant presence in urban food markets.

Cooperatives dominate rural food retailing; in most villages that have a food store, it is a consumer cooperative. The rural cooperatives both buy and sell food. Since they are not part of the state retail system, they are not legally bound to sell at official state prices unless the product for sale came from the state procurement network.

Rural residents who buy food in their villages pay the higher prices of the cooperative network, unless they travel to cities and return laden with subsidized food. Much food is sold to the state under quota, transported to cities, offered in shops crowded with rural residents in for a day of shopping, and then carried on the train back to rural areas much like those from which it came. Higher prices in state stores and expansion of consumer cooperatives in both urban and rural areas would eliminate much uneconomical transport of food. A concerted effort to expand cooperative trade in food could be an interim demand-side component of the reform, but little increased activity is apparent yet in that area.

REFORM ON THE SUPPLY SIDE: FEWER BUREAUCRATS AND MORE LEASING

Since retail food prices will not be raised, the full burden of adjustment will fall on the supply side. The remedy here is to find a graceful formula for releasing producers from the constraints of farming on collective and state farms, without dismantling the farms. The formula proposed in summer of 1988 and again at the

March Plenum in 1989 is promotion of a lease contracting system similar to the household responsibility system in China.[3] Individuals or small groups of workers negotiate with the manager of a state or collective farm to use a portion of the farm's lands and working capital in exchange for delivery of output to the farm. Workers on lease contracts give up their guaranteed wages and earn either residual profits or a share of residual profits, depending on whether payment for use of the assets is a fixed or share rent. After the contract is signed, those with leases are to be left alone to make their own managerial decisions.

Some farm families are now taking out lease contracts, and attention is lavished upon them in the press. The exodus of people from poor regions of central and northern Russia now has a small counterflow of homesteaders returning to reclaim abandoned fields and buildings. Much attention to the leasing system is orchestrated propaganda, but the sense that finally, after sixty years, there are economic opportunities for ambitious people in the Soviet countryside is tremendously important.

Yet many people are not persuaded that the leasing system is either here to stay or in their interest. The reservations that many farm workers have about leasing are both legal and economic. Those entering into contracts need assurance that they are legal and that contract enforcement will be more effective than it has been in the past. New laws on leasing, ownership, and land tenure, adopted in fall of 1989 and spring of 1990, strengthen the legal rights of independent farm operators, but much ambiguity remains. The power of the parties entering into leasing agreements is very asymmetrical. Many are simply verbal agreements between a farm manager and workers and cannot be legally enforced.

Leaseholders earn residual profits and give up the right to guaranteed subsidized wages. Workers on poor and indebted farms are unlikely voluntarily to trade secure subsidized wages for earnings both riskier and, on average, lower. Higher productivity due to better labor incentives alone is not likely to compensate for the foregone wage subsidy. On the wealthier farms, where both earnings and capital stock are higher, many workers could earn more under the leasing system, but farm managers are reluctant to relinquish control over farm assets. Leasing, in this early stage, is promoted most as an option for poor farms, but workers on these farms may resist the loss of subsidy.

Where the interests of workers and managers make voluntary leasing feasible, problems remain in negotiation of the lease. Negotiations are a bilateral bargaining problem in which the manager can extract a large share of the economic rent associated with the contract. During both the contract negotiation and the growing season, the lessee faces a manager with monopoly power over allocation of assets, the marketing of output, and purchased inputs. Because the monopoly power remains and because contract enforcement is costly and uncertain, many producers will prefer share contracts to fixed rents.

Contracting in the Soviet context differs from Chinese experience in the early years of the household responsibility system. Soviet farms are specialized in their output and more dependent on purchased inputs, and the marketing function that the parent farm fulfills or does not fulfill for the lessee can make or break the contract independently of the diligence of the operator. This is true for Chinese lessees today and is a source of resentment and uncertainty, but it is even more critical for Soviet lessees, because of their greater specialization.

Although the contracting system may be more difficult to implement in the Soviet Union than in China, the Soviets may have some advantages, as well. The land/labor ratios in most parts of the USSR are much better than those in China, and individual leaseholds can be assigned that are not fragmented strips. Labor mobility in the USSR is very high, except in Central Asia, and able-bodied rural workers displaced by higher labor productivity in agriculture can readily find jobs in growing middle-sized cities and towns. The collective and state farms will remain, for the near future at least, and can oversee maintenance and expansion of rural infrastructure and input supply, if they withdraw in part or whole from production. The Soviet state does not have a clear political and social agenda for rural people like the Chinese emphasis on family planning and limitation of geographic mobility, with which to encumber the contract system. On the other hand, years of investment in the USSR in the technology of large scale production limit the divisibility of existing capital stock under contract.

The leasing system, if implemented, can address one major source of high costs of collectivized agriculture, that is, poor labor incentives. The leasing system will work best if monopoly in marketing, of both input and output, is reduced; but leasing does nothing directly to improve the economic linkages between constituent units in the agricultural economy. This source of high cost thus remains.

Farm managers will be more willing to delegate day-to-day management of farm assets to leaseholders if bureaucrats at the district and province level stop issuing orders about how and when to seed, weed, harvest, and hay. Despite repeated condemnations, from Khrushchev's time on, of bureaucratic interference in farm management, it has persisted. Gorbachev has tried two reorganizations in an effort to make the bureaucracy serve rather than impede food production. In 1982 he formed a new amalgam of committees at the district level. In 1985 he brought many of the fragmented and disconnected ministries with jurisdiction over food and fiber at the national, republic, province, and district level into one superministry called Gosagroprom.

In his speech at the Party Plenum in March 1989, Gorbachev acknowledged that neither the RAPO at the local level nor Gosagroprom had worked, and both were dissolved. Many of the functions of the national Gosagroprom will devolve to the republic level, and it is unclear what will happen to relations between farms and party bureaucrats at the local level.

The attempt to streamline the bureaucracy and give farm managers and workers more authority and better incentives is in direct conflict with increased emphasis on regional self-sufficiency in food. The trend toward self-sufficiency is also seen in the all-out campaign for urban workers to put in long hours on tiny garden plots outside the cities and for industrial enterprises to buy up bankrupt farms and supply meat, milk, and vegetables for their cafeterias and for employees to take home.

The party leader is ultimately responsible for adequate food supply in his region. If supply from the all-union fund is reduced and not replaced by a rapid expansion of interrepublican wholesale trade in food, party leaders will place their own procurement quotas on farms in an effort to generate adequate food supply from local sources. Relaxation of quotas at the national level combined with greater pressure for local self-sufficiency can thus worsen the regional allocation of food production and raise aggregate costs. If local consumption must come from local supply, farm autonomy is likely to decline, rather than increase. The rhetoric of regional self-sufficiency may be a short-run response to the budgetary crisis and worsening demand-induced shortages, but the short-run is long enough to stifle incentives for leasing and meaningful farm autonomy.

FINANCIAL REMEDIES: FEW OPTIONS

High costs of production and stable retail prices have created the large and growing subsidy. The subsidy, in turn, and concern about its growth, have increased reliance on indebtedness to keep poor farms in business, rather than giving them still higher prices or outright grants, since both of the latter would appear immediately in the subsidy accounts. Supply-side improvement that brings down costs of production will ease the financial crisis, as will the eventual and inevitable increase in retail food prices. These are both, however, medium- or long-term solutions to an immediate crisis. What can be done to improve finances at the farm and macro levels now?

Farms that are bankrupt are to be given two years grace in which to improve their finances. If they remain insolvent in 1991, they may be declared bankrupt and their assets offered on lease to anyone who will take them. Conservatives who seek to defend collectivized agriculture against reforms denounce bankruptcy as a violation of the social contract with the agricultural work force. The emphasis on regional self-sufficiency adds fuel to the controversy over bankruptcy; local leaders will fight to keep high-cost farms operating if the rhetoric of autarky prevails.

In his speech in March 1989, Gorbachev ruled out large-scale write-off of farm debt, arguing that a budget already in deficit could not afford it. The debt could not be collected, however, which explains the massive rescheduling that occurred in spring of 1989. In December of 1989 the government announced a massive 73.5 billion-ruble write-off of farm debt.

Changes in procurement prices will affect supply and finance at the farm and aggregate level. Prices and credit have been the instruments for delivering the subsidy to farms, and output prices have been so finely differentiated as to differ on a farm-by-farm basis. Farms have traditionally not paid land rent, and differentiated output prices were intended to incorporate a land tax or rent. With the deterioration of farm finances in the 1970s and 1980s, a number of special premiums were added on to the differentiated base prices. In the current reform, output prices are to be raised to compensate for removal of the input subsidies. Price zones are to be expanded, and uniform prices, reflecting marginal costs of production within zones, are to prevail. Farms will pay a land tax or land use fee differentiated according to the quality of land, but the tax rate and methodology for its calculation are not yet determined. Once prices are set in the procurement price revision, they will be adjusted over time with a parity price index incorporating changes in prices of a basket of inputs. The revised procurement prices will apply to commodities purchased by the state under quota. Sales outside of quota will flow through expanding wholesale trade at negotiated prices. If the reform is successful, quotas will be reduced and wholesale prices as well as state procurement prices will affect producers' decisions.

INTERNATIONAL TRADE IN FOOD

The maturation of collectivized agriculture in the USSR after 1965 had a number of profound effects on world trade in food. Rising incomes and stable retail prices stimulated demand for food. The postwar generation reached adulthood in the late 1960s, and they were less willing than their parents and grandparents to sacrifice current consumption for past calamities or future promises. Brezhnev and his colleagues embarked on the modernization campaign in recognition that growth in demand was outpacing that of supply.

The performance of the agricultural sector in the late 1960s was good, in part because the additional fertilizer, machinery, and higher wages boosted output, in part because weather was unusually favorable, and in part because Khrushchev's peripatetic campaigns gave way to steady and relentless investment. In 1971, Brezhnev and his colleagues decided to increase domestic herds and meat production, temporarily importing grain for feed until domestic grain production grew to match the new higher feed requirements. Large Soviet purchases in 1972 and 1973, when world supply was tight, marked the entry of the USSR into grain markets as a large net importer.

By the mid-1970s the modernization campaign had faltered, although investment continued. The Soviets were unable to exit from grain markets without abandoning the goal of higher domestic meat consumption, and they became regular purchasers of large and variable quantities of grain. Grain imports were followed by imports of sugar, oilseeds, dairy products, and meat, as domestic demand outgrew supply in these markets, as well. From a position of roughly balanced agricultural trade in the 1960s, the USSR in the 1970s and 1980s ranked among the world's largest net importers of agricultural products.

The trading behavior of the USSR was an outgrowth of the performance of collectivized agriculture in a middle-income economy. Demand for agricultural products grew rapidly with income growth and urbanization, but growth in supply was slow and expensive. The Soviets turned to world markets to cover part of the gap and paid for purchases with earnings from energy exports. The surge in energy prices allowed the USSR to retain institutional barriers to more efficient agriculture into the late 1980s.

The Soviet presence in world food markets during the 1970s and 1980s had a number of effects on developing countries. The increment in Soviet demand and the price umbrella provided by the high U.S. dollar and high U.S. support prices allowed exporters from the Third World to expand sales, whether directly to the USSR or to other trading partners. Importers from the Third World paid higher prices than they would have without the large Soviet purchases, but the expansion in supply allowed real prices to fall after their surge with the initial Soviet purchases. The variability of Soviet demand made prices more volatile for all market participants.

The emergence of the USSR as a major hard-currency food importer meant that countries in Eastern Europe and the developing world that had followed the Soviet model of agricultural development could not rely on the USSR for major shipments of food aid or soft-currency trade in food. Many of these countries, too, became net importers of commercial or concessionary food.

CONCLUSIONS

The maturation of collectivized agriculture in Eastern Europe, the USSR, China, and the developing world has significantly altered the geographic pattern of production, consumption, and trade in food. This is one of the more important developments in the world agricultural economy in the postwar period. Agricultural reform in the centrally planned economies, if successful, can be expected to have a correspondingly large impact on world agriculture. The effect will be a complex one, as flows of commodities, technology, and processing equipment and services adjust to changes in production and markets in these countries.

If the agricultural reform in the USSR is successful, the gains to Soviet citizens and to the world agricultural economy could be substantial. Improvement in agriculture will generate better consumption opportunities for Soviet people directly and will facilitate progress of the rest of the reform movement. The resulting income growth will sustain demand, not only for a better diet, but for one embodying more processing and services characteristic of high-income food economies. Imports of technology, for both processing and production, will substitute for some raw commodity imports. Imports of wheat would be likely to decline, but those of oilseeds and protein meals would probably increase.

Improvement of Soviet agriculture would change the volume and commodity composition of Soviet agricultural trade. Perhaps more importantly, it would contribute to the industrial reform and *perestroika's* explicit objective of integrating the USSR into the world economy in a more constructive way. In the postwar era, the Soviet Union has interacted with trading partners largely through purchase of food and manufactured items and sale of energy and weapons. This trading pattern is nothing short of bizarre for a country with the natural wealth and human and physical capital of the USSR. If agricultural reform can contribute to release of constraints on the rest of the economy and its fuller interaction with the world, the gains to people within and outside the USSR will be large.

If the agricultural reform is stymied by the conservative opposition or by its own internal contradictions, the entire *perestroika* program will fail economically. Success in agriculture cannot guarantee success in the industrial modernization effort, but failure in agriculture will inevitably sink the whole program. Standards of living will fall, and with them meat consumption and grain imports.

Polish per capita consumption of meat declined 20 percent in the 1980s with the near collapse of the economy. It is now, after the collapse, approximately at the same level as current Soviet consumption, 64 kilograms per person. Many people in poorer regions of the USSR consume 30 to 40 kilograms of meat per capita, compared to 70 to 80 in the Baltic republics and the best-provisioned major cities. Soviet consumers could reduce their meat intake even from current rather low levels while maintaining adequate calories, and the failure of *perestroika* would force that adjustment.

If the agricultural reform fails, the USSR will be left with a high-cost mature collectivized agriculture in an economy in which living standards are eroding while those of successful middle-income countries in the Third World rise. The erosion will come in part from the drag that a wasteful agricultural sector exerts on the rest of the economy. The years of *glasnost'* and critical examination of the economy have convinced many thoughtful Soviet citizens that their own institutions must change if the country is to maintain even a modest growth rate and look forward with optimism to the twenty-first century. They are unsure, mistrustful, and impatient with the general reform. They are also thoroughly disenchanted with collectivized agriculture as they have experienced it. Even before *glasnost'* made it acceptable to speak publicly, urban people knew the state of affairs in the countryside. Many have relatives still on farms and have been educated personally as drafted laborers sent from industrial enterprises to help bring in the harvest.

The record of collectivization, both in its first stage in the 1930s and in its mature period after 1965, continues to be evaluated in public. *Glasnost'*, and particularly Gorbachev's speech in March 1989, has had the salutary effect of inviting people to consider the shortcomings of rural institutions, rather than rural people, as they seek to understand their agrarian problem.

After sixty years of collectivized agriculture in the USSR, the country has begun a transition to a set of as yet unknown post-collectivist institutions. Their emergence is of considerable import, both to those who seek to understand how and why institutions change and to those who will live in the world shaped in part by post-collectivist agriculture.

Now that Soviet public officials and economists have joined the critique of collectivized agriculture, many idological barriers that had thwarted full evaluation of that experience have been removed, although severe restrictions on the availability of historical and current data remain. For most developing countries, the Soviet experience stands as a negative example of the high costs of a set of policies that those countries chose not to follow. For the smaller group of countries that followed the Soviet model, the Soviet experience has more profound implications. Some of these countries have already embarked upon reform, and are farther along than the USSR. Others, such as Ethiopia, Cuba, Vietnam, Laos, Rumania, Bulgaria, and Albania, have not.

For these countries, the lessons of the Soviet present and future, as well as the past, are particularly important as they near the challenges of difficult agricultural reforms. Those who delay are likely to find that collectivized agriculture imposes an increasing burden on economic growth.

NOTES

This work was supported by The Graduate School, University of Minnesota, and by the National Science Foundation.

1. See also Lin, Yao, and Wen, chapter 30 in this volume.—ED.
2. Whether collectivization delivered cheap food is still an open empirical question. Prices in the state stores were low, but quantities were limited and excess demand spilled over to the collective farm market, where peasants sold output from private plots at market prices that were much higher because of the poor supply in the collective sector.
3. See also Lin, Yao, and Wen, chapter 30 in this volume.—ED.

REFERENCES

Alchian, Armen A., and Harold Demsetz. 1972. "Production, Information Costs, and Economic Organization." *American Economic Review* 62:777–95.
Davies, R. W. 1980. *The Socialist Offensive*. Cambridge: Harvard University Press.
Johnson, D. Gale, and Karen McConnell Brooks. 1983. *Prospects for Soviet Agriculture in the 1980s*. Bloomington: Indiana University Press.
Kaplan, Cynthia S. 1987. *The Party and Agricultural Crisis Management in the USSR*. Ithaca: Cornell University Press.
Lewin, Moshe. 1968. *Russian Peasants and Soviet Power*. Evanston: Northwestern University Press.
Lin, Justin Yifu. 1988. "The Household Responsibility System in China's Agricultural Reform: A Theoretical and Empirical Study." *Economic Development and Cultural Change* 36, no. 3 (supplement): S199–224.
Medvedev, Zhores. 1987. *Soviet Agriculture*. New York: W. W. Norton.
Millar, James R. 1970. "Soviet Rapid Development and the Agricultural Surplus Hypothesis." *Soviet Studies* 22 (July).
Miller, Robert F. 1970. *100,000 Tractors*. Cambridge: Harvard University Press.
Narodnoe khoziaistvo, SSSR v 1987. 1988. Moscow: Finansy i Statistika, p. 404.
Nove, Alec. 1976. *An Economic History of the USSR*. New York: Penguin Books.
———. 1984. "The Contribution of Agriculture to Accumulation in the 1930s." Economic History Workshop Paper, no. 8384-15. Chicago: University of Chicago.
Ofer, Gur. 1987. "Soviet Economic Growth: 1928–1985." *Journal of Economic Literature* 25(4): 1767–1833.
Semenov, V. 1985. *Prodovol'stvennaia programma i finansy*. Moscow: Finansy i statistika.
———. 1987. "Sovershenstvovanie finansogo mekhanizma agropromyshlennogo kompleksa." *Ekonomika sel'skogo khoziaistva*, no. 9, pp. 31–39.
———. 1989. "Khozraschet i samofinansirovanie." *APK-Ekonomika, Upravlenie*. Issue no. 3.
Sertel, Murat. 1982. *Workers and Incentives*. Amsterdam: North-Holland.
Vanous, Jan, ed. 1988. *PlanEcon Report* 4, no. 41, November 4.
"Vokrug problemy potrebitel'skikh tsen." *Ekonomika i organizatsiia promyshlennogo proizvodstva* 12 (1986): 140.
Volin, Lazar. 1970. *A Century of Russian Agriculture*. Cambridge: Harvard University Press.

30

China's Agricultural Development: Recent Experience and Policy Issues

JUSTIN Y. LIN, XIANBIN YAO, AND G. JAMES WEN

Agriculture and the rural economy have always played key roles in the economic development strategy of the People's Republic of China. Providing the nation with sufficient food, improving the standard of living, especially in the rural areas, and modernizing the economy are among the most important considerations in the development of Chinese agricultural policy.

From 1978 to 1988, the Chinese government introduced several major policy changes that fundamentally altered the structure and organization of agriculture and the food system in the country.[1] The communal organization of agricultural production, upon which China had relied from 1958 through 1978, was replaced by a structure of individualized family farms, called the "household responsibility system." A more market-oriented system in farm produce marketing began emerging through a series of policy initiatives, such as raising the state purchase prices, reducing the scope of fixed state procurement, and encouraging open market exchanges. There is also evidence, as shown by Lin (1987b) and others, of increasing use of rural factor markets to allocate labor, land, and credit, as policy restrictions on the allocation of these resources were relaxed.

The purpose of this chapter is to describe the evolution of Chinese rural policy reforms since 1978 and to examine the effects of these changes on agricultural growth and rural development. The focus is on reforms in three areas: (1) the creation of the household responsibility system (HRS), (2) changes in the land tenure system, and (3) the development of new rural grain marketing policies. These areas

JUSTIN Y. LIN is professor of economics, Beijing University. XIANBIN YAO recently completed his Ph.D. in agricultural economics at Michigan State University. G. JAMES WEN is assistant professor of economics and finance, Baruch College.

Based in part on a paper presented by Justin Lin at the Twentieth International Conference of Agricultural Economics, Buenos Aires, 24–31 August 1988, and published in those proceedings by the International Association of Agricultural Economists.

form the core of the rural economic reforms over the 1978–88 period. Moreover, they encompass three fundamental debates that have preoccupied Chinese leaders since the creation of the People's Republic in 1949: the choice of the appropriate unit of production and accounting in agriculture, the appropriate land tenure system, and how agriculture should be linked to the rest of the economy through the input and output distribution systems. The issues are clearly interdependent. For example, while the household responsibility system improves the motivation of farmers to increase their short-term labor supply, it does not necessarily motivate them to increase their long-term land-specific investments. Furthermore, the HRS has not yet created a proper savings and investment mechanism to fill the vacuum left by the dismantling of the commune system and the shift to individual land tenure. In addition, the degree to which farmers can respond to the opportunities created by the HRS depends on how well the output marketing system works. With a reduction in the scope of fixed grain procurement under the recent reforms, open market channels have become increasingly important in coordinating the grain industry.

OVERVIEW OF AGRICULTURAL DEVELOPMENT IN CHINA, 1949–1978

In order to place the recent reforms in historical context, we first briefly describe the evolution of agricultural policy in China between 1949 and 1978. Soon after the creation of the People's Republic of China, in 1949, the Chinese leadership began transforming the economy into a system based on central planning, with the aim of fostering socialist development. In agriculture, this transformation went through several stages.[2] Between 1950 and 1952, the government undertook a thorough and sometimes violent land reform in order to redistribute land to poor peasants and break the political and economic power of the landlords and rich peasants. Once the land was redistributed, Mao Zedong and his supporters launched a series of actions that eventually led to the collectivization of Chinese agriculture.

During 1952–53, "mutual aid teams" were organized. These were teams of 6 to 15 households, which pooled their labor, draft animals, and other farm capital to cultivate their land jointly, although ownership of the land, farm tools, and animals remained in the hands of the individual households. During 1953–54, the mutual aid teams were merged into "elementary producers' cooperatives," consisting of 20 to 40 households. Ownership of land, tools, and animals remained private, but the allocation and management of all resources were centralized in a management committee. This centralization and pooling of resources allowed the cooperatives to undertake certain types of infrastructure development, such as building irrigation canals. Net income was distributed to members based upon the amount of land and labor they had contributed to the cooperative.

Beginning in 1956, elementary agricultural cooperatives were combined to form "advanced agricultural producers' cooperatives," which consisted of 100 to 300 households, the equivalent of a village. In these cooperatives, ownership of land

and capital goods was collective, and distribution of the cooperative's net income was based solely on the household's contribution of labor to the cooperative. Peasant households were still permitted to hold small private plots, amounting to between 2 and 5 percent of the arable land, with the amount varying over time. Private plots were devoted mainly to producing vegetables, fruit, and livestock for home use and for sale at rural periodic markets.

In 1958, the advanced agricultural producers' cooperatives were merged into a system of "people's communes." "A commune was an administrative unit, corresponding to a township of 4,000 to 5,000 households, within which farming, industrial production, commerce, and construction were carried out. The Commune Authority had the power to allocate labor and all other resources within its vast area. At first, the peasants' private plots were totally abolished as were rural free markets. The income distribution in a commune was based partly on work and partly on free supply of food." (Yeh 1985, 7). The commune system represented the basic organization of agricultural production in China for 20 years, until 1978, when the reforms described here began.

The various structures of farm production over the period 1950–78 were embedded within a broader economy-wide system of central planning. Through planning, the government guided resource allocation and income distribution by means of a vertically administered hierarchy. The marketing of most agricultural inputs and outputs was tightly controlled by the state. Staple foods were distributed through a mandatory procurement (quota) system linked to an urban rationing system, and rural factor markets were eliminated or strictly controlled. A lopsided policy emphasizing grain production was implemented, to achieve provincial and regional self-sufficiency in basic staples.

The Chinese model of agricultural development by central planning has been debated for decades. Three major aspects of the debate are worth mentioning. First, an important feature of central planning is its reliance on directives from the center to the grassroots level. The crucial factor for the success of this type of planning is the accuracy and timelinesss of information transmitted from the farm level to central planners and vice versa. But the generation and transmission of such timely and reliable information is difficult, if not impossible, to achieve in the agricultural sector because of the biological and spatial nature of the production process. Second, central planning often ignores material incentives, which are a key factor in motivating production and distribution in a socialist economy. The lesson from China's experience is that decentralization and material incentives are necessary to guide economic activities.

The third aspect of the debate concerning agricultural development under central planning is the appropriate role of agriculture in overall economic development. Many studies of Chinese agricultural policy from 1950 through the late 1970s argue that the agricultural sector in China was consistently taxed relative to the industrial sector through low product prices and mandatory procurement programs (e.g., Lardy 1983a; Tang 1984b; and Song and Luo, 1986). The aim was to extract resources from agriculture to finance the development of other sectors. But the level of resource extraction from agriculture was so high that it severely compromised agricultural growth and rural development. The poor performance of agriculture thus became a drag on the rest of the economy, hindering the development of the other sectors (Tang 1984a). Moreover, the policy of provincial and regional grain self-sufficiency led to uneconomic use of resources and a relative worsening of economic conditions in provinces not well endowed for grain production, further limiting both agricultural and nonagricultural growth (Lardy 1984).

Following the Cultural Revolution, in 1976, the Chinese government began to reconsider the role of agriculture and the rural economy in the context of national economic development. In the Third Plenary Session of the Eleventh Central Committee of the Communist Party of China, in December 1978, the Chinese leaders recommended some gradual changes in rural policies.[3] The policies adopted at the session encouraged the development of a diversified economy to replace the lopsided stress on grain production. Higher prices were set for the state purchases of farm produce, and production units were granted more freedom in making decisions about their own affairs. Between 1978 and 1988, the pace of reform accelerated rapidly, radically changing the organization of farm production, the rules governing land tenure, and the marketing system for agricultural products.

ORGANIZATION OF FARM PRODUCTION

THE COMMUNE SYSTEM, 1958–1978

The collective movement that was launched in the late 1950s was basically in operation for about 20 years, from 1958 to 1978. Communes were divided into brigades, and brigades into production teams. The production team, consisting of about 20–30 neighboring households, was generally the basic production and accounting unit. All resources were collectively owned and were allocated under the unified management of the team leader, with the exception of small plots reserved for the households' own use. Output from the team in excess of basic needs was procured by the government at prices lower than local market prices. Output from private plots was consumed by the households themselves or sold, either to the government or at rural periodic markets. Household sideline production (e.g., handicrafts) was sometimes encouraged, sometimes discouraged. Income from team production was the most important source of household income.[4]

Under the production team system, a peasant was awarded work points for each day's work. At the end of each year, the net team income, after deductions for taxes, the public welfare fund, and basic needs, was distributed according to the work points that each peasant had accumulated during the year. Work points were supposed to reflect the quantity and quality of effort that each member performed.[5]

THE HOUSEHOLD RESPONSIBILITY SYSTEM SINCE 1978

The commune, brigade, and production team system of production management, with its work point system of compensation, has been debated ever since its establishment in the late fifties. After the disaster of the Great Leap Forward of 1958, land was reallocated to individual families, and households were restored as the units of production in some parts of China, especially in Anhui Province in central China.[6] Production soon recovered in these areas. Nevertheless, this practice was soon prohibited and criticized as capitalistic. Although the reallocation of land to individual households was never totally extinguished and continued secretly, and sometimes openly, in some areas, a complete shift from the production team to individual household production was not possible until 1978, following the death of Chairman Mao, in 1976, and the beginning of recovery from the Cultural Revolution.[7]

Although it had been recognized in 1978 that solving the managerial problems within the production team system was the key to improving incentives, the household responsibility system was inconsistent with the socialist principle of collective farming and was prohibited in the document issued by the Fourth Plenary Session of the Eleventh Central Committee of the Communist Party of China, in September 1979 (Editorial Board of the China Agriculture Yearbook, 1980, 58). The official position in 1978 maintained that the production team was to remain the basic unit of production, income distribution, and accounting. Nevertheless, a small number of production teams, first secretly and later with the blessing of local authorities, began to try out the system of contracting land, other resources, and output quotas to individual households toward the end of 1978 in Feixi County and Anhui Province, areas frequently victimized by flood and drought. A year later these households achieved far higher yields than those of the production teams. The central authorities later acknowledged the existence of the household responsibility system but restricted its use to poor agricultural regions and poor teams, in which people had lost confidence in the commune system. But this restriction could not be implemented, because rich regions welcomed the household responsibility system as enthusiastically as the poor regions. The household responsibility system was officially recognized in late 1981, and by the end of 1983 almost all the rural households in China had adopted this new system.

It is worth emphasizing that the household responsibility system was worked out among farmers, initially without the knowledge and approval of the central government. It was generated through the efforts of peasants themselves and spread to other areas because of its merits. It was not imposed by the central authorities. In short, the shift evolved spontaneously in response to underlying economic forces.

The Economics of Team Production

Theoretically, the work point system is not inherently an inefficient incentive scheme.[8] If the monitoring of each peasant's work is perfect, the incentives to work will be excessive instead of suboptimal. This is because the return to a peasant's additional effort has two components. First, he will get a share of the increase in team output. Second, he will get a *larger share* of the total net team income, as now he contributes a larger share of total effort and thus has a larger share of work points. The former is itself insufficient to make him offer the optimal amount of effort, but the latter overcompensates as long as the average product per unit of effort is greater than the marginal product of effort. Since the relevant region of production, in general, is located at the point where the average product is greater than the marginal product, a peasant has an incentive to overwork. On the other hand, if there is no monitoring of effort, a peasant will not get more work points for his additional contribution of effort. In this case, the return to his increase in effort has only one component, namely a share of the increase in team output. The incentives to work are thus suboptimal. The size of the increase in the work point share for an additional unit of effort depends on the degree of monitoring. Therefore, the incentives to work in a production team are positively correlated with the degree of monitoring in the production process. The higher the degree of monitoring, the higher the incentives to work, and thus the more effort contributed.

But monitoring is not costless. The management of the production team needs to balance the gain in productivity due to the increase in incentives with the rise in the costs of monitoring. The monitoring of agricultural operations is particularly difficult because of the sequential nature and spatial dimensions of the agricultural production process. In agricultural production, the process typically spans several months over several hectares of land. Farming also requires peasants to shift tasks throughout the production season. In general, the quality of work provided by a peasant does not become apparent until harvest time. Furthermore, it is impossible to determine each individual's contribution by simply observing the outputs, because of the random impacts of nature on production. It is thus very costly to provide close monitoring of each peasant's effort contribution in agricultural production. Consequently, the optimal degree of monitoring in a team mainly engaged in agricultural production must be very low. The incremental income for an additional unit of effort will be only a small fraction of the marginal product of effort. Therefore, for peasants in a production team the incentives to work must also be low.[9]

In the household responsibility system, by definition, a peasant becomes the residual claimant. He does not need to divert resources to meter his own effort. The marginal return to his effort is the marginal product of effort. Although economies of scale are sacrificed in the HRS, it has been proved, assuming there is no monitoring in the team system and given some other simplifying assumptions, that the incentive structure in the HRS dominates that of the team system unless the coefficient of returns to scale is large, namely, higher than two (Lin 1988). Therefore, the incentives to work are improved by shifting from the production team system to the HRS. Peasants feel happier and contribute more effort to production in the HRS. Agricultural productivity thus jumps. The improvement in the incentive structure represents the major source of gain in this institutional change.

THE PRODUCTION IMPACT OF THE HOUSEHOLD RESPONSIBILITY SYSTEM

For the nation as a whole, the household responsibility system spread rapidly during the period 1980 to 1983, and by the end of 1983, almost all the production teams in China had been converted to the new system of farming (see table 1). At the same time, the gross value of agricultural output increased 25 percent between

TABLE 1
THE PROGRESS OF THE HOUSEHOLD RESPONSIBILITY SYSTEM AND THE
EVOLUTION OF AGRICULTURAL PRODUCTION

Year	Progress in HRS (%)	Gross Value of Crop Production (Million Yuan at 1980 Prices)	Percentage of Change in Real Value of Crop Production from Previous Year
1979	1.0	135,728	− 3.1
1980	14.4	137,815	1.5
1981	45.1	145,170	5.3
1982	80.4	161,718	11.4
1983	97.9	171,818	6.2
1984	98.9	186,800	8.7
1985	99.9	178,643	− 4.8
1986	99.9	183,989	3.0

Sources: The second column is the progress in the household responsibility system. The data for 1979–81 are from *Jinqjixue zhoubao (Economic Weekly)*, January 11, 1982. Figures for 1982–86 are from Editorial Board of China Agriculture Yearbook, *China Agriculture Yearbook*, various editions. Figures in the third and fourth columns are calculated from data in China State Statistics Bureau 1988.

1980 and 1983 at constant 1980 prices. Over the same period, the total horsepower of farm machinery increased 31 percent and the consumption of chemical fertilizer increased 22 percent. Also, a number of other policies were introduced in 1978 and 1979, whose impact was felt over the 1980–83 period when the HRS was growing rapidly. Therefore, without a careful statistical analysis of empirical data it is hard to determine how much of the growth in agricultural output between 1980 and 1983 should be credited purely to the shift from the production team system to the household responsibility system. The remainder of this section reports the attempt to use data at the provincial aggregate level to answer this question.

Although the effect of shifting from the production team system to the household responsibility system comes mainly from the increase in the supply of effort, total productivity is a better measure of its impact on agricultural production than a partial measure, such as labor productivity, would be, because effort has two components: quantity of effort and quality of effort. The quantity of effort, the brute force provided by a worker, is what enters into the traditional production function; and it is no different from the other factors of production, such as machinery, livestock, and fertilizer. The quality of effort is the allocative service provided by a worker in the production process. The efficient service flow provided by a given unit of land, machinery, fertilizer, or livestock depends on, among other things, how it is allocated. When allocative service provided by a worker increases, the efficient service flow derived from a given unit of input also increases. Consequently, the efficient service flow from given physical units of labor, land, tractors, and fertilizer, which are the inputs in a traditional production function, will all change when the incentives to work are improved by a change in the institution.

The approach used here to estimate the impact of the household responsibility system on productivity involves estimation of an aggregate agricultural production function of the unrestricted Cobb-Douglas type, using cross-sectional data from 29 provinces covering 1980, 1981, 1982, and 1983. To be specific, the production function that will be estimated is

$$\text{Log } Q = a_0 + a_1 \text{Log} L + a_2 \text{Log} S + a_3 \text{Log} T + a_4 \text{Log} F + a_5 PG + a_6 Y1$$
$$+ a_7 Y2 + a_8 Y3 + u.$$

Where Q is agricultural output, a_0 to a_8 are coefficients, L is labor, S is sown area, T is tractor power, F is fertilizer, PG is the rate of progress in the adoption of the household responsibility system, $Y1$ to $Y3$ are year dummies, and u is a residual term. Q, L, S, T, F are all normalized by the number of agricultural households in each province.[10]

PG, the rate of progress in the adoption of the HRS, is an endogenous variable. The adoption of the household responsibility system in each province can be interpreted as an induced institutional innovation process (Lin 1987c). If an area is more suitable for group farming because of its topology or other reasons, the adoption of the household responsibility system in that area will be slower. Such regional characteristics are included in the residual term of the regression equation; consequently, PG is correlated with the error term. Furthermore, the size of a cooperative farm and the technology adopted (i.e., the tractor power and the amount of fertilizer that are used in farming) also reflect regional characteristics; they are, thus, also correlated with the residual. Therefore, ordinary least squares will not produce unbiased estimates of the coefficients. To avoid these time-persistent, region-specific effects and obtain consistent estimates of the coefficients, the fixed-effects model was used in fitting the production function.

The result of fitting the Cobb-Douglas type production function to the data is reported for three alternative model specifications ($Q_1 - Q_3$) in table 2. As expected, the differences in the rate of shifting from the production team system to the household responsibility system across provinces has a positive significant ef-

TABLE 2
ESTIMATES OF THE INTERPROVINCE CROSS-SECTIONAL PRODUCTION FUNCTIONS
FOR AGRICULTURE, 1980–1983

	Q_1	Q_2	Q_3
Labor	.99 (3.33)	.78 (2.55)	.69 (2.26)
Sown area	.68 (1.44)	.55 (1.19)	.49 (1.34)
Tractor	.42 (2.06)	.47 (2.34)	.47 (3.04)
Fertilizer	− .03 (1.02)	− .04 (1.17)	− .03 (0.94)
Y_1	.05 (1.56)	− .01 (0.15)	—
Y_2	.14 (3.28)	.04 (0.68)	—
Y_3	.15 (2.45)	.02 (0.21)	—
PG	—	.12 (2.07)	.15 (3.75)
R^2	.543	.561	.557

NOTE: All variables are logarithms of original values, except for year dummies and PG (the rate of progress in the household responsibility system in each province). Units = average per household. Q_1–Q_3 are estimated with 28 province dummies. Numbers in parentheses are the t-statistics.

fect on the changes in the level of productivity, as reported in Q_2 and Q_3. The estimated value of 0.12 for the coefficient of *PG* in Q_2 is significant at the 5 percent level of confidence. Each of the values of the year dummies in Q_2 is not significantly different from zero.[11] Suppressing the year dummies in the regression for Q_3 changes the coefficients for the conventional variables very little, but the coefficient of the rate of progress in the household responsibility system increases to 0.15.

From table 1, we see that 30.7 percent of production teams in China switched to the household responsibility system during 1981, another 35.3 percent converted during 1982, and 17.5 percent of production teams changed in 1983. If .15 is accepted as the coefficient of the rate of progress in the household responsibility system, agricultural productivity should have grown by 4.5 percent for 1981 (0.15 times 30.7 percent), 5.3 percent for 1982, and 2.6 percent for 1983. These calculated growth rates are close to the estimated growth rates that are implied by the coefficients of the year dummies in Q_1. This suggests that almost all of the productivity growth that occurred between 1980 and 1983 was the result of the shift to the HRS.

LAND TENURE SYSTEM AND ITS IMPACT ON LONG-TERM PRODUCTION

Unlike the household responsibility system, the land tenure system and its long-term impact on farmers' behavior had not received much attention in China until the unexpected stagnation of crop production that began in 1985. Historically, the combination of mounting population pressure and limited amounts of cultivated land has not only provoked numerous peasant rebellions but has also stimulated various experiments in land ownership and tenure, in an effort to achieve both efficiency and equity. From public ownership to private ownership, from fixed rental to sharecropping, traditional China almost exhausted the possible alternatives in this field (Chao 1986).

Modern China has continued these experiments, launching a land reform program immediately after the 1949 revolution. But the Party soon became preoccupied with the prospect of polarization among peasants, and it denounced the private ownership of land and drove peasants toward collectivization, which culminated in the people's commune system in 1958. Under the commune system, the population pressure on China's limited land was disguised by collective ownership, by collective farming and by collective income distribution. The allocation of resources was left mainly to the commune authorities and their agents—the production brigades and the production teams. In addition to direct state investment in agriculture, the communes accumulated investment funds from their net revenues.

Under the communal system, farm members' income from the collectives was obtained after deducting investment funds and other public welfare funds. The level of these deductions was set by the commune authorities, under a command system of economic planning. Hence, there was little open debate among the commune members over how much should be used for these alternative public purposes. Furthermore, since the funds were deducted from the gross income of the commune before the residual was distributed to the members, individual households could not opt out of participating in this forced savings and investment program.

Under the household responsibility system, by contrast, collective land is leased to individual family farms, which can make their own decisions about how much to consume and save for long-term investment. However, few mechanisms to mobilize local resources have arisen to replace those used by the commune to finance infrastructure and other socially useful investments.

Land Tenure System since 1978

China's current land tenure system has been shaped largely by two factors: the egalitarianism in land allocation and population growth. The latter does not necessarily lead to the former if there are well-defined property rights; but under the HRS, the two are closely interrelated and interactive.

Under the HRS, the land of a typical Chinese village is still collectively owned. It is divided into two parts: food plots and duty plots. Food plots are distributed on a per capita basis for the purpose of feeding one's family, and are tax free. The remaining land is divided into duty plots, allocated contractually according to the number of laborers in each household, and is subject to the land tax. Egalitarianism is the main guide in allocating land among farm households.

To obtain duty land, the head of a household must sign a contract with the village authorities. The central government regulations state that a contract can be for up to fifteen years duration. Many contracts, however, are signed for only three to five years or less, because of pressures for land redistribution stemming from local population growth. The contract also stipulates the size of the in-kind land tax—in the form of grain or other crops. The amount of land tax is usually assessed on the basis of a farm's normal production.[12] In many areas, village land is allocated among households on a per capita basis regardless of the differences among households' labor endowments.

Population Growth and the Pressure for Land Redistribution

A delicate problem arises under the egalitarian land allocation rule when population continues to grow but land does not. The incremental demand for land can arise from two sources, population growth or labor growth.

Food Plots

Since land for food plots is allocated according to rural population, it would seem that as farmers move out of the farm sector, their demand for land will fall, but this is misleading. Under China's grain rationing system, only urban residents have the privilege of purchasing their food from the state-owned grain shops at a subsidized price; rural residents must feed their families by their own efforts. Yet, even since the restrictions on migration were eased in the early 1980s, rural migrants to the city have been refused access to state-supplied grain. These rural migrants have had to maintain access to land in their former villages even while living in the city. Village food plots remain the main source of food supply for these urban immigrants. Therefore, unless there are changes in the grain rationing system, the demand for rural food plots will expand in line with rural population growth, unaffected by the emigration rate or the speed of the rural industrialization. Because of the immense size of China's rural population, the increase in demand for rural food plots is considerable. In many densely populated places like the eastern coastal areas, there is not much land left for duty plots after the allocation of food plots.

Duty Plots

Only the demand for duty plots is affected by the speed of rural industrialization and rural emigration. In some coastal areas, emigrants from the farming sector retain rights to their village food plots and typically want to sublet some of their duty plots. However, the right to contract for a piece of village land is available to native villagers only, since the land is owned collectively. A land rental market does not exist to facilitate the transfer of land use rights. As a result, noncoastal farmers cannot benefit much from the increased availability of land in the coastal areas, and land in these areas is often not carefully farmed or is even left idle.

There is also no legal and institutional protection for land ownership and land use rights. Violations of property rights and use rights occur frequently. For instance, in Meitan County, Guizhou Province, 90 percent of civil disputes are related to land use rights or ownership. Most village authorities are under strong pressure (in the form of land disputes or tax refusal) to redistribute land after a certain period in order to accommodate the changes in population and labor and to equalize village quota burdens across households.

Thus, a rural household faces three sorts of uncertainty: uncertainty about the size and boundaries of its land area, uncertainty about its right to compensation if land is taken away, and uncertainty about recollectivization under ideological or population pressure (Wen, G. 1989).

DEBATE AND OPTIONS

Since the implementation of the HRS in the early 1980s, the following stylized facts have been observed across the country: (1) The amount of some current inputs, such as chemical fertilizers, consumed each year has increased dramatically, but the consumption of traditional organic fertilizers has fallen significantly. (2) Investments in tractors have increased, but investment in tractor-towed farm machines and other long-term investments in water conservation, land consolidation, and fertility improvement have stagnated. (3) Rural per capita income has increased significantly, and as a result, expenditures on housing have expanded across all income groups. Private ownership rights in housing, unlike those in land, are secure; hence, families have greater incentive to invest in housing than in land improvements. (4) The level of crop production was stagnant from 1985 through 1988. This stagnation occurred despite China's rapid population growth (15 million per annum), a doubling of per capita incomes between 1979 and 1988, and rapid industrial development. Thus, the stagnation of crop production was not induced by weak demand.

The leveling off of grain and other crop production since 1985, which is in marked contrast to the expansion of livestock production, has kindled a debate in China. Three arguments have been raised to explain the stagnation of land investment: unfavorable price parities for agricultural products, the fragmentation of land holdings, and lack of security in land use rights.

Unfavorable prices may explain the investment stagnation in recent years, when the high inflation rate may have made price parities unfavorable to farm products. However, they cannot explain why there was a fall in land investment during the late 1970s and early 1980s, when price parities were very favorable to agricultural products and crop production grew rapidly.

The proponents of the second argument (fragmentation of land holdings) and those of the third argument (insecurity of land use rights) suggest that the stagnation of crop production has something to do with the stagnation of land-specific investment. They also agree that the current land tenure system should be further reformed and that land ownership should be clearly defined and a legal system established to protect property rights. But they differ as to the nature of the distortion in land investment and how to solve it. Some Chinese analysts argue that land holdings under the HRS have become too fragmented to make investment in land profitable. Since land is still collectively owned, the proposed remedy is to concentrate land into preselected households known for their farming experience and willingness to remain farmers.

Shunyi County of Beijing, and Wuxi County, Changshu County, and Wu County of Jaingsu Province are all undergoing rapid industrialization. Experimental zones were established in these counties in late 1987 to pursue economies of scale in farming (Li 1988). The lack of sales or rental markets for land makes local government intervention in the allocation of land inevitable. Measures have been taken to encourage those who are now working in the nonfarm sector to return their land to village authorities. Sometimes pressure is reportedly exercised to force the return of land before the expiration of the HRS contract. But the big farms formed in these experimental zones are not performing well, and they cannot survive without substantial subsidies from the local authorities (*People's Daily,* Nov. 26, 1988).

Some proponents believe that the fall in land investment is largely related to the lack of security in land use rights as well as in property rights to investment (e.g., Zhou 1988). In a country like China—where land resources are limited, seasonally underused labor is common, and capital is relatively scarce—the scale of operation of a typical farm is expected to be small. For this reason, what is essential is not to help form big farms artificially but to define ownership clearly, establish a legal system to protect the various ownership and property rights, and open up sales or rental markets for factors of production that will allow the optimal scale of operation to be guided through open bidding and competition.

While realizing the importance of defining ownership and property rights clearly and of institutionalizing the protection of these rights, proponents within this group disagree on what kind of ownership should be adopted in the rural areas of China (Liu 1988). Four types of ownership have been put forward:

1. permanent tenancy system: land will be nationalized but leased to farmers permanently;
2. "tripartite" ownership: land will be owned by the state, collectives, and farmers jointly;
3. "double track" ownership: land will be owned by the state, but farmers will have rights to possess, operate, and inherit land under their names;
4. private ownership: farmers actually regain what they were allocated in the land reform program of early 1950s.

While debate is still under way on the advantages and shortcomings of various forms of land ownership, an experimental zone was established in Meitan County of Guizhou Privince in 1987 to reform land use rights (Li 1988). The essence of this reform is to sever the relation between population growth and land reallocation so that changes in family size among village households will not automatically be translated into pressure for land redistribution. This is reflected in a document endorsed by the Meitan County government in 1988 to abolish the egalitarian land allocation rule. Those households with a rising share of the village population are now supposed to support the newly added family population by themselves instead of imposing their burden on their neighbors. Accordingly, uncertainty about the use rights of one's land and about the property rights of one's land investment can be eliminated.

The main problem of the HRS lies in the difficulty for even the most successful farmers of securing larger land holdings under the current rules. Farm size is totally unrelated to the successful performance of the farm. Farmers cannot obtain extra land through bidding in land sales or rental markets, because no such markets exist in rural China. When population continues to grow, the land will be further fragmented under the egalitarian allocation rule. This will inhibit investment unless some other rule is adopted. In this sense, the experiment in Meitan County is very significant.

The only way to increase the scale of farming in a densely populated country, besides the collective farming system, which has proved to be a big failure, is to create enough nonfarm jobs to absorb underused rural labor. Land markets, at least land rental markets, can facilitate the efficient allocation of land resources, though they themselves are not a solution to fragmentation. However, without well-defined property rights, neither a sales market nor a rental market for land will work. The problem of land fragmentation is secondary to the lack of well-defined property rights and the lack of well-functioning factor markets.

Another relevant problem is how to finance public investment in agriculture. With the dismantling of the commune system, its public saving and investment mechanism has also ceased to function. But we should not conclude that the solution to the problem is to return to collectivization. Chinese history shows that as long as the government took care of the basic water conservancy system, the prosperity of the farming sector could be maintained under private ownership of land. One possible remedy might be to allow local governments more power to raise taxes and to organize large-scale public investment projects.

Observing how institutions are changed by economic forces is often enlightening. Recently, the Central Committee of the Chinese Communist Party suggested that the People's Congress amend the constitution to legalize compensated or uncompensated land transfer among organizations and individuals, although the selling and purchasing of land would still be illegal (*People's Daily,* overseas edition, March 7, 1988). This might be interpreted as a small but significant step towards establishing a land rental market.

China, with its huge population and limited arable land, is the last country on the earth that can afford to misuse its land resources. With population pressure and a tight budget, it is becoming more and more attractive to leave egalitarianism either to the past or to the remote future, when society might achieve the affluence to afford these values. There are many indications that the ideological barriers to efficiency will gradually be removed and that China's rural society may become open to various forms of contractual agreements, such as fixed rents, sharecropping, and hired labor. All of these once flourished in traditional China. Whether they will appear again and what forms they might take must be left to future study.

GRAIN MARKETING POLICY

Agricultural marketing and rural trade in China have long been dominated by central planning (Perkins 1966). Compulsory quota procurement programs were instituted in the early 1950s for major products such as grain, cotton, and oilseeds, and production teams were required to deliver quota targets to the state. Free market exchange was strictly controlled; only a limited number of agricultural commodities were allowed to be traded at local markets in the rural areas. Agricultural products were classified into three categories: (1) grain, cotton, and oilseeds; (2) sugar, tea, pork, poultry, eggs, and medicinal plants; and (3) "nonessential" products produced in relatively small quantities. Market exchange was permitted only for a small portion of production in the second category (beyond the state quota procurement) and for the third category. Urban residents obtained their basic supplies of grain, cooking oil, and cotton cloth at highly subsidized prices through a state-controlled rationing system.

The centralized marketing system was coordinated through a vertically administrated hierarchy. The central government computed the total grain requirements to be procured through the quota system and then allocated quotas to each province. The province in turn allocated quotas to each of its prefectures, and this process continued down to the production team, the basic unit of agricultural production and accounting. The Ministry of Food, and subsequently the Ministry of Commerce, and its subordinate grain departments handled grain procurement, processing, transportation, storage, and distribution.

Historically, the centrally controlled marketing system was used to transfer resources from the agricultural sector to the industrial sector. This transfer involved several steps. First, to ensure that the state could obtain the quantities of agricultural products it needed, the central and local governments instituted a production planning system, often setting targets in terms of the sown area for products subject to state procurement (Lardy 1983a). To further ensure that the desired quantities were actually delivered to the state procurement system, the quotas of individual production units were set so high that the units had to turn over their entire output to the state, after deductions for the consumption requirements of the production teams. These high quotas prevented a private market from developing to compete with the state procurement system. The transfer of resources out of agriculture was then completed by setting the quota procurement prices so low that they included an implicit tax on agriculture, the benefits of which flowed to the other sectors of the economy in terms of lower food and raw product prices.[13]

Between the mid-1950s and the late 1970s, the original state procurement system was gradually modified (Deng et al. 1988). The quotas of individual farm units were periodically reapportioned to take account of fluctuations in production and the changing size of farm units (families). In 1960, an "over-quota" purchase program at higher prices was introduced to stimulate production, and the basic quota purchase prices were raised several times over this period. While adjustments were made in the state procurement program in the 1960s and early 1970s, its central feature of compulsory deliveries and state monopoly remained unchanged. The base quota delivery was compulsory, and even the "over-quota" purchase later became involuntary (Lardy 1983b, 25).

Beginning in 1979, the central government introduced several important policy changes to boost production incentives, including a significant hike in farm purchase prices and a nationwide reduction in the volume of grain secured through quotas. To maintain the level of total state procurement, a "negotiated purchase" scheme was restored, in which the state trading agencies purchased farm products at market prices. These policy changes stimulated agricultural production, and the high state purchase prices induced farmers to sell more to the state. In fact, farmers in some areas even sold their on-farm grain stocks to take advantage of the high purchase prices (Zhou and Gao 1988). As a result of these policy shifts, total state grain procurement, including the base quota, over-quota, and negotiated purchases, more than doubled, from 50.7 million tons in 1978 to 107.5 million tons in 1984, with almost all the increase coming from over-quota purchases.[14]

But the dramatic supply response to these policy changes created new problems for the central government and for the state procurement system (Oi 1986). The dramatic rise in state purchases, especially over-quota procurement, increased the burden on the state budget, particularly since official retail food prices were kept low: The cost of the state price subsidy and marketing losses for agricultural products was 5.56 billion Yuan in 1978 and about 32.1 billion Yuan in 1984 (Wen, S. 1988, table 12). These costs represented 5 percent of the total state budget expenditure in 1978 and 21 percent in 1984 (China State Statistics Bureau, 1986).

The policy changes from 1978 to 1984 can be seen as a gradual shift from strict quantity planning to indicative price planning.[15] The use of price incentives to stimulate agricultural production and marketing turned out to be a mixed blessing. On the one hand, higher prices increased the marketed surplus. On the other hand, the state monopoly lacked the price flexibility needed to bring supply and demand into balance. For example, some regions and products were in surplus while others were in shortage (Zhou and Gao 1988, 103–4). Furthermore, high purchase prices and guaranteed procurement forced the state to assume most of the risks in marketing. Since consumers were protected by the government rationing system, most consumers did not share any of the market risks (Gao 1986). Because of these difficulties, attention has now turned to reestablishing a market-oriented production and distribution system.

THE EVOLUTION OF A DUAL MARKETING SYSTEM

When the rural reforms were started in 1978, Chinese policy makers stressed that markets were supplementary to the planned economy. In subsequent years, policy debate gradually shifted toward a more market-oriented approach. Since 1985, policy makers have articulated the view that the state regulates markets and markets guide enterprises.

In early 1985, the government of China announced a gradual phase-out of the state monopoly system for most farm commodities based on compulsory delivery quotas. For grain and cotton, mandatory quotas were to be replaced by a dual system of contract and market purchases. A fixed ceiling on the quantity of grain purchased under contract was to be negotiated by the state grain departments with farmers before the planting season. The new purchase prices for grain were set by blending 30 percent of the quota price and 70 percent of the over-quota price in the previous year. After meeting contract obligations, farmers were allowed to sell any remaining marketable surplus through other channels at market prices. A price floor, at the previous quota price level, was promised to prevent any sharp plunge in market prices.

Under the new contract procurement system, the decision of farmers to enter into a contract with the state may be influenced by such factors as the relative price advantage between the state and free market prices, access to different marketing channels, the farmers' perceptions about the stability of institutions governing the free-market and the contract systems, and the in-kind land tax policy (explained below). In theory, by forward contracting, farmers can be partially or completely protected from the risk in open market prices. This would generate a positive incentive for farmers to enter a contract with the state.

However, the new voluntary contract procurement system has been undermined by a number of factors. First, the state commitment to subsidizing urban grain consumers and other groups (e.g., the military) has been a major constraint on reforming the marketing system. While the procurement system was changed, the state food distribution system at the retail level remained unchanged. Rationing of food at subsidized prices acccounted for 80 percent of the total retail food sales in the late 1980s. To maintain this level of subsidized sales, the state was compelled to assure that it had access to a reliable supply of food. Second, the new contract purchase prices were not attractive enough to induce sufficient voluntary sales to the state. An immediate effect of the 1985 marketing policy was a 10 percent average reduction in marginal grain prices (Sicular 1988b). Although this reduction may have alleviated some of the burden of the price subsidy on the treasury, the combination of the lower marginal prices and several other factors resulted in a 7 percent decline in grain production from 1984 to 1985.

Third, since under the responsibility system the household is the basic farm production unit, the administrative cost to the state of implementing the contract purchase program with millions of farm households is very high. The lack of appropriate legal institutions, such as a commercial code, makes it difficult to put the contract program into operation. Fourth, in many grain producing areas, state fixed procurement is often interlocked with the in-kind land tax. Local officials and village leaders, who set the level of each farm's land tax (based either on the number of household members or on some measure of the farm's productivity), also allocate the fixed procurement contracts among farmers. These officials have an interest in assigning contracts widely among households, as this facilitates collection of the land tax. The tax payment is simply deducted from the amount paid the farmers for their grain upon delivery to the state. The farmers therefore perceive the contract as being closely linked with the tax system, which undermines the voluntary nature of the contract.

Changes in grain marketing policies since 1986 have included modest increases in the fixed procurement prices, a gradual reduction in the fixed procurement quantity, and a much greater reliance on the market to allocate grain.[16] In effect, rural grain marketing has become a two-tiered system, where the state procurement channel and free market channels coexist. For those households that sell to the market in addition to delivering their quotas, production and consumption decisions will depend on market prices, because the state procurement quantity is fixed.

A few recent studies (e.g., Watson 1988) have attempted to use national aggregate data to examine in more detail the organization and functioning of the free markets, the response of farm units to the dual marketing channels, and the types of supportive government interventions that are needed in addition to direct state participation in fixed grain procurement. It is difficult, however, to use such aggregate data to examine the details of how the new marketing institutions work in practice and how they affect farmer behavior. For more details on the micro-level impacts of the market reforms, we turn to a case study of grain marketing in Xin Xiang region in Henan Province of central China, based on research carried out in 1988. While the case study illustrates how some of the new market institutions are operating in practice, the pace of market reform in China differs greatly from region to region, and the observations of the study should not be generalized to the country as a whole.

A Case Study of the Dual Market Structure at the Farmgate Level

Farm households in Henan Province, central China are primarily engaged in agricultural production. The major crops grown include wheat, corn, rice, and cotton. Wheat is the main staple, accounting for about 70 percent of home grain consumption, with the remainder provided by maize and rice. In recent years, state procurement has become crop-specific in this area. By 1988, only wheat was under the state fixed purchase program. All other grain sales took place through free-market channels. Wheat remained under state fixed procurement because the area is a major surplus wheat producing region and hence is important in supplying grain to urban areas.[17]

The results of a 1988 survey of 150 farm households in the region reveal that an average of 23 percent of the 1987–88 wheat production went to the fixed procurement system, although the proportion per household varied from 6 percent to 65 percent.[18] Virtually all of the sample households met their contract obligations to deliver wheat to the state, because local officials and village leaders used different measures, varying from political persuasion to coercion (e.g., threatening to deny land-use rights), to ensure government wheat procurement.

Eighty of the 150 households also reported that they sold a portion of their remaining surplus through free-market channels. The total marketed surplus of wheat, including both the fixed procurement and the free-market sales, averaged 58 percent of total production. Of this, 40 percent moved through the fixed procurement system. In contrast, on a national level in 1987, approximately 50 percent of the marketed surplus of all grains moved through the fixed procurement system, down from 90 percent in 1978 (Yao 1990).

Further analysis indicated that the following factors had a significant impact on a household's level of sales through the free market: (1) Large farm households tended to sell less than small ones, mainly because of higher home consumption needs.[19] (2) Shortages of wheat for home consumption reduced the amount sold in the free markets. (3) The household's production variability, as measured by percentage deviations from normal yields, also had a negative effect on the level of free-market sales. These results suggest that maintaining household food security is an important factor in farmers' marketing decisions. (4) The amount of wheat left over for household use, after quota deliveries had been met, contributed positively to free-market sales. (5) The empirical results suggest that farmers responded positively to market prices, that is, higher market prices tended to induce more sales, although the interpretation should be made cautiously, as the price variables were measured in terms of the village-weighted averages for the whole season.[20] (6) Market access, measured in terms of the distance from villages to the nearest rural periodic markets and to the county town seat, did not have a significant impact on the free-market sales; but the condition of roads was correlated with sales.

One of the major findings of this research was that most of the free-market sales occurred at the village level. Since the free markets began operating in the area, private traders, in competition with each other, have been pushing local assembly markets closer to the farmgate. For example, 67 percent of the total free-market sales of wheat from the farm households took place at the village level, either directly to private traders or to local assemblers commissioned by buyers from more distant markets. The local periodic markets (usually located in the township seats), which traditionally had been the major assembly points for free-market sales, do not appear to have maintained that tradition. About 16 percent of the total free-market sales of wheat took place at the periodic markets and the remaining 17 percent was sold to state grain buying stations, which have been actively involved in the market purchases. The dispersed nature of the localized wheat assembly markets indicates the need to study such important issues as the price discovery process, the organizational structures of free marketing channels, and the characteristics of traders' behaviors.

The free markets in the study area in central China were subject to erratic governmental interventions and, at the same time, lacked necessary supportive institutional regulations. Local officials sometimes closed free markets for periods of time, especially when the state fixed procurement occurred. Although at least two official agencies, the Industrial Commerce and Market Business Administration and the Commodity Price Bureau, are in charge of regulating free markets in the area, these agencies find it difficult to regulate the dispersed local assembly markets. In addition, the neeeded support in terms of the credit, information dissemination, standardization, and so forth, is still lacking.

Moving from a centralized marketing arrangement to a more market-oriented system requires corresponding changes in institutions and regulations. One analyst observes that "the reforms and resurgence of markets in rural China have indeed given peasants more freedom, but at the same time, peasants face greater uncertainty. The abolition of the state monopoly over the purchase and sale of grain lifted the burden of forced quota, but it also removed the secure income offered by unified purchases." (Oi 1986, 289). These statements form a strong challenge to further policy reforms in the grain marketing system. If the market-oriented system is what is desired by the Chinese policy makers, policy consideration should focus on how to improve the functioning of the market, including the strengthening of supporting institutions.

SUMMARY

Dramatic institutional change is one of the constants of the four decades of modern Chinese agricultural development from 1949 through 1988. Looking particularly at the 1979–88 experience, the household responsibility system has improved farmers' incentives to produce and thus has corrected the problem of X-inefficiency in team production under the communal system. The new organization of farm production, along with other policy adjustments, contributed greatly to rapid agricultural growth from 1978 to 1984. A market-oriented rural economy was thus emerging in China at the end of the 1980s.

The Chinese experience shows that further reforms are needed to sustain agricultural growth in the 1990s. For example, the inherent uncertainty of property rights created by the current land allocation rules makes farmers hesitant to undertake long-term, land-specific investments. Opening up free markets without providing the necessary supportive institutions to regulate them also restrains farm supply response.

More fundamentally, the Chinese experience shows that during periods of economic reform, changes in one set of economic institutions, such as the land tenure system, typically lead to the need to change related institutions, such as the fiscal system and rural financial markets. Because the various institutions are likely to be evolving at different speeds, conflicts and contradictions between institutions will arise, calling forth the need for further reform. In such a situation, there is a high payoff to having in place a capacity to monitor developments in the economy and a willingness to experiment, as the Chinese have done, with alternative institutional arrangements in different parts of the country.

NOTES

The authors thank the editors of this volume for their help in improving the analysis and presentation of this chapter.

1. For a chronology of the agricultural policy changes between 1978 and 1988, see Walker and Kueh 1988, 1–3.

2. This section draws heavily on Yeh 1985. Other studies of Chinese agricultural policies from 1949 to 1978 include Perkins 1966; Lardy 1983a; Perkins and Yusuf 1984; Johnson 1985; and Song and Luo 1986.

3. The session adopted the "Decisions of the Central Committee of the Communist Party of China on Some Questions Concerning the Acceleration of Agricultural Development (Draft)." The draft was promulgated nine months later, in September 1979, by the Fourth Plenary Session of the CPC Central Committee. For the text of the decision, see Editorial Board of the China Agriculture Yearbook 1980, 56–62.

4. Fifty-nine percent of net per capita income was derived from the collective in 1957; it rose to 66.3 percent in 1978 (China State Statistics Bureau 1984, 471).

5. See also the description of the Soviet work point system in Brooks, chapter 29 in this volume.— ED.

6. The Great Leap Forward was an attempt to increase agricultural and industrial production extremely rapidly through the consolidation of advanced agricultural producers' cooperatives into people's communes; the establishment of rural industries, such as backyard furnaces to produce iron; and the free distribution of food. Party leaders called for the doubling of agricultural production in one year, clearly an impossible task. The disruption caused by the rapid collectivization of agriculture and changes in policy, combined with poor planning and poor weather, had disastrous consequences. Famine struck large areas of rural China, killing up to 30 million people (Johnson 1988, S226–27).

7. It was recently discovered that a village in Guizhou Province had adopted this practice secretly

more than ten years before the recent reform, but the villagers dared not admit it until the new policy was announced (Du 1985, 15).

8. For more details on the material presented in this section, see Lin 1987a, 1987c, 1988.

9. In a production team, the supply of effort also depends on the peer pressure, because of the team system's income-sharing property. For a formal model of the impacts of income-sharing on the incentives to work and the labor supply, see Lin 1987a.

10. Output of agricultural production in this study refers to crop production. Livestock, forestry, fishery, and sideline production are not included because of a lack of data. The output of agriculture is measured in constant prices of 1980. The value of crop output represented 63.7 percent of the total value of agricultural output in 1980 and 62.0 percent of that value in 1983. Labor in agricultural production includes those workers in farming, husbandry, fisheries, forestry, and household handicraft production. Workers in village-run industry are excluded. No deduction is made for the number of husbandry, forestry, and fishery workers, as these numbers are not available. As a consequence, the number of workers may be overestimated for areas with larger fishery and forestry industries. Sown area consists of the area for grain and cash crops. Tractor power refers to the total horsepower of big, medium-sized, and walking tractors. Fertilizer is measured in terms of the weights of efficient ingredients of N, P_2O_5, and K_2O contained in the gross weight of chemical fertilizer consumption. The rate of progress in the household responsibility system indicates the percentage of production teams in each province that had converted to the new system. Because only 14.4 percent of the production teams in China had adopted this new system by the end of 1980, it is assumed that the rate of progress was zero for each province in 1980. The rate of progress in 1981 refers to the percentage of teams converted to the household responsibility system in each province by August 1981, while rates for 1982 and 1983 indicate the progress by the end of each year. The data for 1981, 1982, and 1983 are provided by the Research Center for Rural Development of the State Council at Beijing. Data for 1983 can also be found in the *China Agriculture Yearbook 1983* (p. 69). All data, except for the the rates of progress in adopting the household responsibility system, are from the 1981 to 1984 volumes of the *China Agriculture Yearbook*.

11. The null hypothesis that the year dummies are jointly equal to zero has a computed F-statistic of 1.27. The critical value of this statistic, with 3 and 79 degrees of freedom, is 2.72 at the 5 percent significance level and 4.04 at the 1 percent level. Therefore, the null hypothesis cannot be rejected.

12. As explained below, in the case of grain producing farms, payment of the in-kind land tax is often interlocked with the family's grain quota delivery. Since the quota price is generally lower than the market price, farm households actually pay two taxes, the explicit land tax and the implicit tax embodied in the below-market quota prices.

13. The literature on the government's use of price policy to extract the agricultural surplus includes Stone 1988; Lardy 1983b; Wu 1984; and Song and Luo 1986.

14. The over-quota purchases were 16.6 million tons in 1978 and 69.3 million tons in 1984. During the same period, the level of base quota purchases remained practically unchanged, at 30.8 million tons in 1978 and 28.9 million tons in 1984 (Yao 1990).

15. For a detailed description of quantity and price planning in the Chinese agricultural sector, see Lardy 1983a.

16. Accordingly, the state distribution of foodgrain at the retail level has been cut, and some industrial grain purchases have been excluded from the subsidized distribution system.

17. The average wheat yield in 1986 for the entire Xin Xiang region was 3,345 kg per hectare, 900 kg higher than the provincial average and 600 kg above the national average. In 1986 close to half of the sown area in the region was devoted to wheat. Because of double-cropping in the region, wheat occupied all the arable land during the winter/spring season.

18. The 150 households surveyed were selected randomly among those considered to be grain producers. Households engaged in cotton production or whose main activities were not grain production were not included in the sample.

19. About one-fifth of the sample households registered a net inflow of grain, either from purchases or from nonmarket transactions.

20. Addressing the question of how farmers responded to the seasonal price patterns would require additional knowledge of farmers' storage decisions, which was not gathered in this case study.

REFERENCES

Chao, Kang. 1986. *The Man and Land in the Chinese History*, Stanford, Calif.: Stanford University Press.

China State Statistics Bureau. 1982, 1984, 1986, 1988. *China Statistical Yearbook*. Beijing: Statistical Press.

Deng, XueMing, et al. 1988. *DangDai ZhongGuo De LiangShi GongZuo (Contemporary China's Foodgrain Operations)*. Beijing: China Academy of Social Science Publishing House.

Du, Runsheng. 1985. *China's Rural Economic Reform*. Beijing: Social Science Press.

Editorial Board of China Agriculture Yearbook. 1980, 1981, 1982, 1983, 1984, 1985, 1986. *China Agriculture Yearbook*. Beijing: Agricultural Press.

Gao , XiaoMing. 1986. "LiangShi WenTi BeiWangLu" (A *Memo on Grain Problems*). Staff Paper. *FaShan YanJiu TongXun*, no. 21. Beijing: Research Center for Rural Development/Development Institute.

Jingjixue Zhoubao (Economic Weekly). January 11, 1982.

Johnson, D. Gale. 1985. "The Agriculture of the USSR and China: A Contrast in Reform." Office of Agricultural Economics Research Paper, no. 85:11. Chicago: University of Chicago.

———. 1988. "Economic Reforms in the People's Republic of China." *Economic Development and Cultural Change* 36, no. 3 (Supplement): S224–45.

Lardy, Nicholas R. 1983a. *Agriculture in China's Modern Economic Development*. London: Cambridge University Press.

———. 1983b. *Agricultural Prices in China*. World Bank Staff Working Paper, no. 606. Washington, D.C.: World Bank.

———. 1984. "Prices, Markets, and the Chinese Peasant." In *Agricultural Development in the Third World*, edited by Carl K. Eicher and John M. Staatz, 420–35. Baltimore: Johns Hopkins University Press.

Li, Shuzhong. 1988. "How is China's Rural Land System to be Reformed." *Liaowang* (overseas edition), December 19. Hong Kong.

Lin, Justin Y. 1987a. "Supervision, Incentives, and the Optimum Size of a Labor-Managed Firm." Economic Growth Center Discussion Paper, no. 525. New Haven: Yale University.

———. 1987b. "Rural Factor Markets in China after the Household Responsibility System Reform." Economic Growth Center Discussion Paper, no. 535. New Haven: Yale University.

———. 1987c. "The Household Responsibility System in China: A Peasant's Institutional Choice." *American Journal of Agricultural Economics*. 69(2): 410–15.

———. 1988. "The Household Responsibility System in China: A Theoretical and Empirical Study." *Economic Development and Cultural Change* 36(3) supplement: S199–S224.

Oi, Jean C. 1986. "Peasant Grain Marketing and State Procurement: China's Grain Contracting System." *The China Quarterly* 106:272–90.

Perkins, Dwight H. 1966. *Market Control and Planning in Communist China*. Cambridge: Harvard University Press.

Perkins, Dwight H., and Shahid Yusuf. 1984. *Rural Development in China*. Baltimore: Johns Hopkins University Press.

Sicular, Terry. 1988a. "Plan and Market in China's Agricultural Commerce." *Journal of Political Economy* 96(2): 283–307.

———. 1988b. "Agricultural Planning and Pricing in the Post-Mao Period." In *The China Quarterly* (special issue: "Food and Agriculture during the Post-Mao Era"), edited by K. R. Walker and Y. Y. Kueh, 116:671–705.

Song, Guoqing, and Xiaopeng Luo. 1986. *Jingji Jiegou yu Jingji Gaige (Economic Structure and Economic Reform)*. Beijing: China Rural Development Problems Research Group.

Stone, Bruce. 1988. "Relative Prices in the People's Republic of China: Rural Taxation through Public Monopsony." In *Agricultural Price Policy for Developing Countries*, edited by John W. Mellor and Raisuddin Ahmed, 103–24. Baltimore: Johns Hopkins University Press.

Tang, Anthony M. 1984a. "A Critical Appraisal of the Chinese Model of Development." In *Agricultural*

Development in the Third World, edited by Carl K. Eicher and John M. Staatz, 403–19. Baltimore: Johns Hopkins University Press.

———. 1984b. *An Analytical and Empirical Investigation of Agriculture in Mainland China, 1952–1980.* Seattle: University of Washington Press.

Walker, K. R., and Y. Y. Kueh, eds. 1988. *The China Quarterly* (special issue: "Food and Agriculture during the Post-Mao Era") no. 116.

Watson, Andrew. 1988. "The Reform of Agricultural Marketing in China since 1978." *The China Quarterly* 105:1–28.

Wen, G. James. 1989. "The Current Land Tenure System and Its Impact on Long-Term Performance of the Farming Sector: The Case of Modern China." Ph.D. dissertation, University of Chicago.

Wen, Simei. 1988. "The Role of Government Policy in Meeting the Challenge of Increased Food Demand: The Chinese Experience." Paper presented at the Asian Regional Seminar Proceedings of the Kellogg International Fellowship Program in Food Systems, Guangzhou, China, October. Guangzhou: Department of Agricultural Economics, South China Agricultural University.

Wu, Xiling. 1984. "Terms of Trade between Agriculture and Industry—Thirty Years of Experience in China." Master's thesis, Michigan State University, East Lansing.

Yao, Xianbin. 1990. "Market and Farm Household Level Impacts of Grain Marketing Reforms in China: A Case Study in Xinxiang." Ph.D. dissertation, Michigan State University, East Lansing.

Yeh, Martin H. 1985. "China's Agricultural Policies since 1949." Paper prepared for the 1984/85 seminar series, Department of Agricultural Economics and the Asia Studies Committee, University of Manitoba, Winnipeg. Mimeo.

Zhou, Qiren. 1988. "Land System: Valid Property Rights, Long-Term Tenancy, and Paid Transfer." *Jingji Cankao (Economic Information)*: November 2.

Zhou, Qiren, and XiaoMeng Gao. 1988. "ShiChang XingCheng: Zai MaoDun, ChongTu He MoCa Zhong FaZhan ShangPin HuoBi GuanXi." (Market Formation: To Develop Commodity and Monetary Relationships in the Midst of Contradictions, Conflicts, and Frictions). In *Gaige Mianlin Zidu Chuangxin (The Reform Confronts Institutional Innovations),* Qiren Zhou et al., 101–18. Shanghai: SanLian Publishing House.

31

Africa's Food Battles

CARL K. EICHER

Agriculture is the Achilles' heel of the economic development of sub-Saharan Africa.[1] But Africa's agrarian crisis is neither unique nor unexpected. In Latin America, industrialization ground to a halt during the Peron regime in Argentina in the 1950s because of a food crisis. The same pattern of events was repeated during India's food crisis of the mid-1960s and again in China in the late 1960s (Schultz 1965). With the benefit of hindsight, it is now understood that Africa's food crisis was quietly building up for two decades before it exploded onto television around the world when an estimated one million people died during the 1984–85 famine in Ethiopia.[2] When African nations presented their special appeal to the United Nations in May 1986 (OAU and ECA 1986), they were finally facing the day of reckoning and posing the strategic development question, What is to be done about African agriculture?

This chapter addresses three interrelated food battles in Africa: breaking the famine cycle, accelerating food production, and increasing consumption of food by the hungry and malnourished.[3] Without question, these battles represent the major challenge to social and technical scientists working on global agriculture in the 1990s.

THE CHANGING SOCIAL AND ECONOMIC CONTEXT

Africa's economic environment has been undergoing sweeping changes as a result of both internal and external shocks. These changes provide the context in which to examine Africa's three food battles in the 1990s.

STAGE OF SCIENTIFIC AND INSTITUTIONAL DEVELOPMENT

There is a growing awareness that many countries in Africa, after a third of a century of independence, may be generations behind Asia and Latin America in terms of their scientific and institutional development and the stock of high-level human capital. But, Africa's scientific and institutional gap should come as no surprise because of colonial underinvestment in training and Africa's 30 years of

CARL K. EICHER is professor of agricultural economics, Michigan State University.

A revised version of a plenary address presented at the Seventh World Congress of Rural Sociology, Bologna, June 1988.

503

independence compared with 150 years in Latin America. For example, in 1980 Africa had fewer than one-fifth the number of R&D scientists and engineers per million people as did Asia (Shapiro 1985; UNESCO 1988). Expatriates currently occupy about one-fourth of all scientific positions in national agricultural research services and colleges of agriculture in Africa. In Francophone countries, the percentage is much higher. For example, expatriates occupy 73 percent of all agricultural research and teaching positions in Côte d'Ivoire after 30 years of independence (Pardey and Roseboom 1989).

Both African states and donors are fumbling and generally confused on how to develop human capacity, strengthen agricultural institutions, and promote agricultural change at this early stage of development. In many countries there are few sound options to pursue in the short run, especially in those dominated by political instability. Somalia illustrates the complex nature of the development challenge in a dozen or more countries where the overarching problems are primarily social, political, and institutional. A recent United Nations/World Bank technical mission dug deeply into the mode of delivering aid to Somalia, a country riven with clan wars and generations behind most Asian countries in terms of its scientific, institutional, and administrative maturity. The team reported that donors were spending around US$100 million a year in the mid-1980s to support 1,200 expatriates on long-term technical assistance assignments in Somalia and to pay the cost of overseas training for Somali nationals (UNDP and IBRD 1985). But this revolving door approach is not achieving the ultimate objective, "the development of national capacity through the permanent transfer of skills and know-how to Somali nationals and national institutions" (UNDP and IBRD 1985).

NET FOOD BUYERS AND SELLERS

Surrounding the debate on how to tackle Africa's food production battle is the assumption that most smallholders are net food sellers and that higher producer prices will lead to increased farm output and rural welfare. But recent research has revealed the heterogeneity among smallholders and has illustrated the limitations of relying primarily on pricing policy to boost food production. For example, in recent years, between 15 and 73 percent of the rural households in the major grain-producing areas of Mali, Somalia, Senegal, Rwanda, and Zimbabwe were net food buyers and only 22 to 48 percent were net food sellers (Weber et al. 1988, 1046). Hence, raising official grain prices would, in the short run at least, hurt a large proportion of small farmers. Within countries, the regional impact of higher grain prices can also be strong. In Mali, for example, a farm level survey revealed that under normal rainfall conditions in 1985/86, 82 percent of the farm households producing grain in a semisubsistence area in the northern part of the country were net food buyers as compared with 18 percent of the farmers in southern Mali, an area with sufficient rainfall for smallholders to produce cotton, maize, millet, and sorghum (Staatz, Dione, and Dembele 1989).[4] In light of this new evidence, it follows that policy and institutional packages must be carefully honed to local food security profiles. Simple policy prescriptions of the past decade, such as raising farm prices, are inappropriate for the 1990s.

GROWING RURAL STRATIFICATION

When 17 colonies won their independence in 1960, Africa was a land surplus continent with three main types of farms: smallholders, middle farmers, and large-scale farms. During the 1960s, many African governments, with the encouragement of donors, gave priority to large-scale farms, including plantations, state farms, farm settlements, and ranches. However, because of the high failure rate of these schemes, donors threw their political voice and financial resources behind smallholders in the 1970s. The swing to smallholders was pursued with such fervor, however, that in many countries middle farmers were condemned. For example, President Nyerere of Tanzania condemned middle farmers because he assumed that they would exploit hired laborers and contribute to a widening of rural income disparities.

During the 1980s a new class of resource-poor farmers emerged in some countries as a result of rapid population growth and declining farm size. These resource-poor farm families generally had insufficient resources to employ the majority of their family labor on the farm. Resource-poor farmers also include a growing number of landless and bands of refugees who are victims of civil war, famine, and external aggression. Today there are four main types of farmers in Africa:

1. Resource poor farmers, usually net food buyers who sell some of their family labor to larger farmers and engage in a range of rural nonfarm activities to generate income to secure their family food needs.
2. Smallholders and herders, relying mainly on family labor to produce food, livestock, and export crops for domestic and international markets.
3. Middle "progressive" farmers, who own and operate their farms with the assistance of a pair of oxen and hired labor. Middle farmers can bear the risks of farm innovation, provide seasonal jobs to resource-poor farmers, and generate a marketable surplus.
4. Large-scale farmers. A new class of large-scale farmers is emerging from the ranks of soldiers, merchants, present and former civil servants, and the new professional class (Goheen 1988). In the Sudan, Kenya, Nigeria, and other countries, these absentee farmers are known as soldier or telephone farmers. They possess growing political power and they are skilled in extracting subsidies and services from the state under the banner of "getting agriculture moving."

Rural stratification is increasing throughout Africa, a process that has several important policy and research implications for the 1990s (Brokensha 1988; Nafziger 1988). The first implication is that diverse policies, technological packages, and institutional innovations are needed to deal with Africa's evolving agrarian structure. An agricultural development strategy that relies on new technology is simply too narrow to assist the four main groups of farmers in Africa in the 1990s. Different technologies and different institutional arrangements may be needed for each type of farmer.[5] In Malawi, for example, World Bank–assisted agricultural development projects are reaching only about 30 percent of the smallholders. These tend to be farms with more than one hectare of land and access to credit (Carr 1988). The second implication is that raising farm prices may not be in the best interest of resource-poor farmers who are net food buyers, except indirectly by increasing the demand for labor on middle-sized and larger farms. Third, the middle farmer should be "resurrected" and viewed as a positive force in getting agriculture moving in Africa.

Africa's capacity to deal with its food battles is severely constrained by its political instability, its early stage of scientific and institutional development, and a rapidly changing economic environment. Also, in many countries, there is a fundamental lack of political commitment to come to grips with poverty, malnutrition, and access to food. Because of these political and institutional barriers, traditional economics is a rather limited tool to understand food battles and their outcomes" (Sen 1984, 89). Hunger, malnutrition, and famine in Africa are just as much a function of political, macroeconomic, and institutional barriers as of a lack of technology. Illustrations from the agrarian chaos in Zambia, the Sudan, Ethiopia, Somalia, Chad, and Nigeria are too numerous to conclude otherwise.

THE FOOD SECURITY EQUATION: FOOD AVAILABILITY AND ACCESS TO FOOD

Over the past decade, there has been growing empirical support for two fundamental premises about the linkages between food availability, poverty, and access to food. These premises can be described as the two sides of the food security equation (Rukuni and Eicher 1988). The first is that increasing food production, storage, and trade can ensure national food availability, but food availability will not automatically end hunger and ensure that all people have enough to eat. The second is that because poverty is a central cause of hunger and malnutrition, special public and private efforts are needed to help resource-poor farmers and the landless increase their access to food through expanded home production, off-farm employment, new income streams, and targeted food transfer programs.

Today, specialists on both poles of the food security equation are advocating legitimate but partial solutions to dealing with Africa's three food battles. On one side, agricultural scientists such as Nobel laureate Norman Borlaug, the father of Asia's Green Revolution, argue that increasing food production is the priority issue in increasing food availability and ending hunger in Africa. Borlaug is optimistic about the stock of food crop technology on the shelf in Africa; he believes that the accelerated food production campaigns that fueled Asia's Green Revolution can significantly boost food production in Africa within five years (Borlaug 1988, 4). But numerous church and private voluntary agencies are critical of the Green Revolution approach of increasing food production through food monocropping, because of the resultant loss of genetic diversity and its alleged negative equity effects. For example, the Catholic Fund for Overseas Development (CAFOD) asserts that the net effect of the Green Revolution is "to reduce the number of people who work the land" (CAFOD 1984/85, 33), despite the impressive body of empirical evidence which refutes this argument.[6] An Oxfam report, *Cultivating Hunger,* asserts that Zimbabwe's hybrid maize seed "has tended to yield less than traditional varieties" (Twose 1984, 19) if it is planted without fertilizer, despite solid evidence to the contrary.[7]

On the food access or consumption side of the equation, economists such as Reutlinger (1977) and Sen (1981) have stressed the fundamental relationship between poverty and hunger and the need to increase access to or command over food (food entitlements) as the way to end hunger and famine. Others call for nutrition policy interventions (Berg 1987) and stress the positive role that food aid can play in emergency feeding programs, easing foreign exchange constraints and food-for-work programs.[8]

Sen's forceful advocacy of increasing food entitlements as the key to combating famine has revolutionized the study of famine and inspired a wide range of studies of famine and household food insecurity. Sen's analysis challenges the conventional wisdom of many agriculturalists who argue that famine is mainly caused by a precipitate decline in food production and that it can be cured by investments in food production and grain storage to ensure national food availability. Sen's work has helped contribute to a growing international awareness of the multiple causes of hunger and famine and the need for policy makers to devote more attention to the food access (demand) side of the hunger equation. But, in hammering home the fundamental relationship between poverty and famine, Sen's food entitlement approach can give the impression that food availability and food access are mutually exclusive rather than complementary approaches to combating hunger and famine.

A major challenge of the 1990s is to encourage African leaders, academics, and representatives from public and private voluntary organizations to search for common ground in dealing with famine, food production, and malnutrition in Africa. In practice, this means bringing representatives of both poles of the food security equation together in agreement that both the food availability and the food access views are legitimate though partial approaches to ending hunger and famine in Africa. Recently, Professor Sen has sought to strike such a balance by observing that, "given the number of people who derive their entitlements from food production in Africa, . . . the importance of expanding food production in Africa, among the strategies to combat hunger on that continent, cannot be denied. It is really more a question of the balance between the different elements in anti-hunger policy for Africa" (Sen 1988, 68–69).

THE FIRST BATTLE: BREAKING THE FAMINE CYCLE

Famine is a complex biological, technical, social, and political problem with a history since biblical times. Since the last famine in Asia occurred in 1979 (in Kampuchea), it is logical to examine why African countries have been unable to succeed, as Asian countries have, in breaking the famine cycle—especially when per capita aid flows to Africa have been two to four times higher than in most Asian countries. Since the publication of Sen's study of four famines in Asia and Africa

(Sen 1981), famine research has concentrated on food entitlement issues: access to food, poverty, household food insecurity, and the economic and administrative feasibility of food transfers through food for work, cash for work, and outright food gifts. Four issues surrounding the famine battle in Africa will be addressed: the incidence and severity of famine, civil war and famine, famine prevention under peacetime conditions, and lessons for Africa from Asia's famine prevention experience.

INCIDENCE AND SEVERITY OF FAMINE

The incidence of famine in Africa from 1945 to 1985 was lower than in the 1900–1940 period, the notable exception being Ethiopia. In addition, the severity of famine in the twentieth century has been less than in the nineteenth century, again with the exception of Ethiopia (Svedberg 1987). Major natural disasters in Africa are nearly all associated with drought. Famine has not occurred in the rain forest regions of Africa under peacetime conditions.

CIVIL WAR, EXTERNAL AGGRESSION, AND FAMINE

After three decades of independence, there is abundant evidence that civil war and political strife are the overarching constraints on the ability of many African states to end famine. For example, in spite of massive food aid to countries at war, such as Ethiopia, per capita calorie supplies are 10 percent higher in countries at peace than in those affected by war (Staatz 1988, B-2). Civil war has been the most underemphasized cause of famine in Africa since independence. Every major famine in Africa since 1960 has been directly or indirectly influenced by civil war and political conflict with the exception of the 1968–74 famine in the Sahel. The 1988/89 famines in Ethiopia, the Sudan, and Mozambique are, to a large degree, products of civil war and internal political struggles.[9] In Mozambique, external aggression and faulty economic policies have also shackled the economy and forced hundreds of thousands of people to flee to neighboring Malawi and Zimbabwe. Since the prognosis for ending civil war and political conflict in Africa is not promising, it follows that it will be difficult for Africa to emulate Asia and banish famine in the near future. To be sure, improvements in early warning systems and logistical support systems will improve Africa's capacity to cope with famine in the 1990s, but in the immediate future, Africa's battle with famine will be severely constrained by civil war. Some hope is on the horizon, however. One can make a case that détente among the superpowers may lead to less severe civil wars in Africa. The recent settlements in Angola and Namibia add support for this view.

FAMINE PREVENTION UNDER PEACETIME CONDITIONS: BOTSWANA'S EXPERIENCE

Instead of turning to Asia for guidance on famine prevention strategies, it would be prudent to draw on Africa's own experience in dealing with famine. Botswana's recent experience combating a five-year drought and breaking the famine cycle has several important lessons for other African states. The return of heavy rains to Botswana in 1987/88 ended the drought of 1981–86, the second drought in 65 years to last for five consecutive years. It is now appropriate to analyze why no one died from that drought. Because Botswana's semi-arid land base is ideally suited to livestock production, the nation normally produces 30 to 40 percent of its staple food requirements (mainly sorghum) and imports the balance in the form of food aid and commercial imports that are financed with foreign exchange earned from diamond, copper, and livestock exports. At the peak of the drought, in 1986, Botswana imported 95 percent of its staple food requirements.

During Botswana's 1979 drought, a consultant recommended that the government set up permanent machinery to deal with drought, because crop failures normally occur about four out of every ten years. The Parliament accepted the premise that recurring drought should be viewed as a normal course of events and voted to develop a permanent indigenous institutional capacity to deal with it. Subsequently, the government set up the Inter-Ministerial Drought Committee (IMDC) in the Ministry of Finance, chaired by the vice president, who is also the minister of finance. The IMDC is answerable to the Rural Development Council, which is composed of representatives of six ministries: Finance and Development Planning, Agriculture, Local Government and Lands, Education, Health, and Mineral Resources and Water Affairs.

Botswana's response to the 1981–86 drought concentrated on both sides of the food security equation and included (1) food availability programs, such as the drilling of wells, grants to crop farmers for replanting, and the preparation of feasibility studies for a major expansion of irrigation and (2) food consumption programs, including supplementary feeding and rural income and employment generation programs. In 1987, the supplementary feeding program assisted 613,056 beneficiaries, or about 60 percent of the total population; the Labor-Based Relief Program provided 45,207 jobs; the agricultural relief program assisted 20,000 farmers with a subsidy on animal traction and 120,000 farmers with free seed to plant up to three hectares of food crops.

During the 1981–86 drought the government demonstrated a high degree of political commitment and administrative capacity to prevent drought from leading to famine. Nevertheless, in drawing lessons from Botswana's famine prevention strategy for other African states, two caveats are in order. The first is the availability of internal resources to combat drought. Botswana had the fastest growing economy in the world from 1973–1985, when its inflation-adjusted rate of GNP grew at a brisk rate of 11.0 percent per year (World Bank 1987a). Botswana's growth has been propelled by diamond, mineral, and livestock exports, and its dynamic economy provides government revenue to finance food-for-work and school feeding programs during periods of drought, as well as foreign exchange to import food on commercial terms. Few other African nations, except perhaps oil-rich Gabon, have the government revenues and foreign exchange earnings to combat drought and famine. Second, Botswana is one of the few democratic governments in Africa, where both the ruling and opposition parties are committed to combating drought and hunger and helping rural people.

Despite these caveats, Botswana's experience in combating five consecutive years of drought and breaking the famine cycle has four strategic institutional lessons for the rest of Africa. First, countries with a high degree of crop and livestock production instability need to develop a cost-effective institutional capacity to deal with drought. Unless an indigenous capability is established to deal with drought and famine, short-term missions from international agencies will be brought in to take charge of famine management, and the development of a national capacity to deal with natural disasters will be postponed. Second, it is essential for every African country to maintain a public capacity to operate a strategic grain reserve and to distribute food aid during emergencies. The central questions are the size, costs, and benefits of public grain reserves. This lesson has important implications for current donor efforts to privatize government grain boards and grain trade.

The third lesson from Botswana is that famine prevention is too complex and multifaceted to be left to a single ministry, such as the ministry of agriculture or the ministry of health. For example, since epidemics are a major cause of death in famine situations, it is imperative for the ministries of agriculture and health to work together and play aggressive and complementary roles in combating drought and epidemics. The fourth lesson is that there is a poverty of technical solutions to low crop and livestock productivity and irrigation and water management problems in drought-prone countries such as Botswana, Somalia, Niger, and Mauritania. For example, the total cropped area under irrigation in Botswana in 1989 was about 3,000 hectares, a footnote in national crop statistics. Botswana and other drought-prone countries should accelerate long-term research on irrigation, water management, and food crops that subsistence families produce for themselves, such as sorghum, millet, cassava, and cowpeas.

ASIA'S FAMINE PREVENTION EXPERIENCE

Asia's success in boosting food production and conquering famine has spawned a large literature on the lessons of this experience for Africa (McAlpin 1987; Dreze 1988). Nevertheless, because of Africa's early stage of institutional development, great care must be exercised in drawing lessons from Asia for Africa. For example, many African governments, such as those in Chad, Malawi, Zimbabwe, and the Sudan, are swamped with refugees from neighboring countries, leaving them little time or resources for developing more permanent social security and employment protection programs like the famine codes introduced in India over 100 years ago, Sri Lanka's food stamp program, and the employment guarantee program in Maharashtra state in India.

THE FAMINE BATTLE: SYNTHESIS

The following insights can be drawn from Africa's experience in combating famine:

1. Famine in Africa must have multiple solutions, for it has multiple causes, including civil war, drought, poverty, disease, and ineffective national policies. Civil war, external aggression, and Africa's early stage of institutional development help explain why it is substantially more difficult to break the famine cycle in Africa than in Asia.

2. In countries at peace, there are known short-term measures to break the famine cycle in Africa.[10] Common anti-famine measures include:

    a) releasing national food reserves and importing food (on commercial terms or as food aid) to break the price spiral and hoarding;

    b) removing restrictions, to allow food to flow into the famine areas;

    c) quick disbursement of food- and cash-for-work programs, to inject purchasing power into local areas, and setting up of school feeding programs and local food kitchens to feed the destitute in local areas, rather than waiting for people to migrate in search of food and end up in refugee camps;

    d) public health distribution systems to combat epidemics; and

    e) seed grants to farmers to replant food crops.

3. Famine prevention cannot be left to the private sector and private voluntary organizations. African governments have a crucial role to play in combating drought and famine. For example, improved governmental capacity to deal with drought, food aid management, and epidemics is a major reason why the 1982–84 drought in the Sahel resulted in a minimal loss of life.

4. The most cost effective and reliable famine early warning system in Africa at this early stage of institutional development is a combination of monthly government reports on a few key statistical indicators, the involvement of opposition parties, a free press, and market signals to touch off alarm bells when staple food prices rise at the onset of a drought. Foreign aid–financed early warning schemes have a poor track record in Africa.

5. African states should resist the proclivity of donors to launch crash grain storage programs under the name of famine prevention and food security. The annual cost of storage should be compared with the cost of grain imports under alternative weather probabilities, projected world grain prices, and the political cost of increased food import dependency. The public sector has an important role to play in maintaining a national grain reserve.

6. Countries with a history of drought should develop a national research capacity in sorghum, millet, and cowpeas, the main rural food staples in semi-arid areas, and in cassava, an important staple in higher rainfall areas of savanna and rainforest ecologies.

7. Investment in irrigation should be conceptualized as a long-run anti-famine strategy in drought-prone countries such as Botswana, Malawi, Ethiopia, the Sudan, Chad, Senegal, and Niger. Reducing the dependency on rainfall through irrigation has been a proven element in famine prevention strategies in Asia. For example, as early as 1880, fifty percent of the rice under cultivation on Java and Madura in Indonesia was irrigated (Barker, Herdt, and Rose

1985, 98). Today, about 35 percent of the cropped area in India is under irrigation, as compared with 3 to 5 percent in Africa. But irrigation in Africa is in its infancy, because in almost all countries it has been cheaper to bring idle rainfed land under cultivation than to intensify production through irrigation. Moreover, the cost of irrigation is $5,000 to $15,000 per hectare in Africa, several times higher than in Asia (Moris 1987). Irrigation will expand slowly in Africa over the next 50 years.

THE SECOND BATTLE: FOOD PRODUCTION

In 1960, sub-Saharan Africa was a modest net exporter of food. Today, despite Africa's vast physical potential to produce food, Africa is importing around 8 million tons of food each year, and around 100 million people do not get enough to eat. To compound these problems, Africa's population of around 500 million is expected to reach a billion in 20 to 25 years. Accelerating food production is a long-term food battle—a battle that cannot be efficiently addressed through crash food production projects.

Two basic reasons underscore the urgency of doubling Africa's annual rate of growth of food production, from 1.7 percent (the average for 1961–80) to 3 to 5 percent. First, there is a need to meet the food demand accompanying Africa's rapid population growth rate (around 3.0 percent) and the growth in per capita income that will be spent on food. Second, there is a need to stabilize or reduce foodgrain imports, which are currently running at around 8 million metric tons per year. Table 1 presents a historical overview of the major trends in food production/consumption and trade for 1961–80. But the Africa-wide averages in table 1 should be taken with a grain of salt, because Africa's data base is extremely weak relative to Asia's and Latin America's.

Because the land area of the African continent is larger than the combined land area of Western Europe, the United States, and China, there is little to be gained by searching for a universal cause or solution for Africa's food production crisis. For

TABLE 1
AFRICA: GROWTH OF FOOD PRODUCTION, CONSUMPTION, AND TRADE

	Annual Growth Rates (%)
Production of all major food crops (1961–80)	+ 1.7
Cereals production (1961–80)	+ 1.8
Total human consumption of staple foods	+ 2.5
Population growth rate	+ 2.6
Staple food production per capita	− 0.9
Staple food consumption per capita	− 0.1
Food exports (1966/70–1976/80)	− 7.1
Food imports (1966/70–1976/80)	+ 9.2

Source: Staatz (1988), adapted from Paulino (1987).

example, during Zambia's food riots in late 1986, neighboring Zimbabwe was struggling to finance its national grain reserve that was equivalent to two years of domestic consumption. The disparity between Zimbabwe's "maize mountain" and Zambia's chronic food crises over the past decade cannot be blamed on colonialism, the weather, or other acts of God, because both countries are former British colonies producing the same staple food in the same agroecology and under the same general rainfall pattern (Rukuni and Eicher 1988). Zambia's empty harvest is basically the result of faulty governmental politics, flowing from Lusaka, not from London, Paris, or Washington. Zambia's obsession with copper over the past two decades has postponed the day of reckoning—the need to shift political priorities and economic policies in favor of agriculture and rural people. The striking contrast between the food situations in Zimbabwe and those in Zambia illustrates the need for country-specific food policies.

The second and third battles—increasing food production and combating malnutrition—are long-term problems that are inextricably linked and require joint conceptualization and planning. Country-specific food production strategies must be developed as an integral part of a long-run agricultural growth strategy. Mellor has forcefully argued that the food production and hunger battles should be tackled simultaneously through an agricultural strategy that links expanded crop and livestock production with other measures to generate jobs and income for rural people, so they can buy the expanded local food supplies.[11]

We shall examine the food production battle by analyzing Africa's empty harvest, from independence in 1960 to 1989. We then examine three contentious issues in the development of country-specific agricultural growth strategies: technology policy, size of farm, and favorable versus less favorable areas. We then examine the five prime movers of agricultural development and conclude with a case study of Zimbabwe's success in tripling smallholder maize production in six years.

AFRICA'S EMPTY HARVEST: 1960–1989

It is important to examine lagging food production in historical perspective. Since half to two-thirds of the social scientists working on Africa are focused on food and agricultural problems, there is a rich body of literature on the multiple causes of Africa's empty harvest in three decades of independence. The need to draw on this valuable experience is intensified by the frequent tendency of donors and African governments to ignore history and develop new projects. For example, natural resource projects are currently being given high priority in the Sahel, even though the results of some $15 billion dollars of donor assistance over the last 13 years have been disappointing (Club du Sahel and CILSS 1988). In livestock, the record of donor-financed projects has been so dismal that some donors have quietly folded their tents and withdrawn from the sector.[12]

Because Africa started independence in 1960 as a modest net food exporter (Paulino 1987), both African governments and donors devoted little attention to food production in the 1960s; it was assumed that favorable production trends would continue. But the death of an estimated 100,000 people in the 1968–74 drought in the Sahel set off alarm bells on the need to increase food production. This need to step up food production coincided with a concern by donors in the early 1970s to launch a direct attack on rural poverty. At the annual meeting of the World Bank in Nairobi in 1973, Robert McNamara urged African governments and donors to channel more resources to rural areas and the rural poor. McNamara's appeal coincided with the U.S. and U.K. initiatives of the early 1970s to help the rural poor, and it led to a dramatic expansion of foreign aid for Africa with emphasis on integrated rural development (IRD) and agricultural development projects (ADPs). But IRD in practice has proven to be administratively complex and costly. Even when individual IRD projects have been successful, it has frequently been difficult to replicate them on a subnational or national scale because of their high human resource intensity and recurrent costs requirements (Lele 1975).

The agricultural development projects (ADPs) promoted by the World Bank in Malawi in the mid-1970s and later in Nigeria and Sierra Leone are also being questioned because of their high recurrent and human capital intensities and the inability to sustain the projects after donor assistance is terminated. For example, the National Rural Development Program (NRDP) was launched in Malawi in the mid-1970s as a long-term (18-year) initiative to increase smallholder production. After a decade, the program had assisted about 30 percent of the smallholders with "above average land holdings who [had] gained access to credit, purchased input supplies, received extension advice and sold surplus produce" (Carr 1988, 2). But the program has had little impact on 70 percent of the farmers, the resource-poor farmers. The government is now attempting to determine how to broaden the NRDP to assist some of these farmers by the introduction of new export crops (e.g., tobacco), crop diversification, and the promotion of rural small-scale industry.

Beginning in the early 1980s donors sharply curtailed rural development projects because of the growing perception that there was a large gulf between dreams and deeds. For example, the World Bank evaluated its worldwide experience with rural development projects and concluded that "although lending targets were met, half of the audited rural development projects in Africa failed over the 1963 to 1986 period" (World Bank 1987b).

Nevertheless, the high failure of IRD and ADP projects since independence has not deterred new crash projects from being initiated by donors, many of whom are newcomers to Africa (Eicher 1989). An example of new crash approaches is the wave of natural resource projects being prepared for the Sahel under the banner of sustainability. Blinded by the determination to help Africa, especially after the 1984/85 famine, there is a danger that donors will not critically examine the food and livestock project failures in the Sahel over the past 15 years and incorporate this experience into the design of new natural resource projects in the 1990s. Also, in the rush to replace food and livestock projects in the Sahel with natural resource projects, there is a danger that the projects will be designed and implemented prematurely, that is, in the absence of a solid technical foundation. But this is not a problem restricted to the Sahel. It is a worldwide problem. For example, Vernon

Ruttan contends that "the sustainability movement is pressing for adoption of agricultural practices . . . before either the science has been done or the technology is available."[13]

Three lessons for the 1990s flow from Africa's empty harvest from 1960–1989. First, macro prices that discriminate against agriculture, such as overvalued exchange rates, and low official producer prices are a cancer on the best designed and implemented projects. Second, because of Africa's early stage of scientific and institutional development, many IRD and agricultural projects have been so overloaded with technical assistance and foreign aid subsidies (e.g., payment of recurrent costs) that even if the projects are successful, they cannot be replicated and sustained by national governments. Third, research and/or extension components in food, livestock, and area development projects have failed and have postponed the inevitable need to develop strong national research and extension services. Priority in the 1990s should be given to developing improved agricultural policies and strategic public investments to stimulate private capital formation and increased production by Africa's 50 million family farms. Under conditions of rapid population growth and an agricultural labor force that is projected to triple in size over the next 40 years, the challenge for African governments and donors is to reduce the emphasis on scattered projects and concentrate on the prime movers of agricultural development.

STOCK OF IMPROVED TECHNOLOGY: AFRICAN AND EXTERNAL VIEWS

There are two frequently asked questions about technology and agricultural development in Africa. The first is, Why can't Asia's Green Revolution be replicated in Africa? The second is, What is the stock of technology on the shelf, by commodity and by geographical area? The Green Revolution has achieved the impact of a "small footprint" on Africa's rural landscape. As of 1983 the total area of modern wheat and rice varieties under cultivation in sub-Saharan Africa was about 800,000 hectares (wheat 556,000 and rice 242,000) Dalrymple (1986a and 1986b), which is roughly equivalent to one-quarter of the annual cropped area in Zimbabwe, one of 45 countries in Africa. Since the Green Revolution has barely touched Africa, African leaders and the donor community must face up to the reality that the 13 International Agricultural Research Centers (IARCs) and French international research programs have not delivered the volume of new food crop technology that many experts had implicitly promised when the first CGIAR (Consultative Group on International Agricultural Research) center, the International Institute of Tropical Agriculture, was established in Nigeria some 20 years ago. In short, a wide variety of political, scientific, technical, and economic reasons explain why it is proving difficult to develop new Green Revolution food crop technology that is high yielding, biologically stable, and profitable for the smallholders of Africa. Three lessons can be drawn from the limited impact of the Green Revolution in Africa to date. The first is the need to strengthen the capacity of Africa's national agricultural research systems (NARS) to develop new technology and supplement the efforts of the CGIAR and the global research system. The second is to strengthen the capacity of Africa's NARS to become more efficient borrowers of technology from neighboring countries and the global research system. The third is the need for the CGIAR and the major donors to devote more attention to strengthening the scientific and managerial capacity of the NARS and faculties of agriculture in Africa.

Turning to the second question, available technology "on the shelf" is an opaque concept, especially for the wide range of commodities and 45 countries in sub-Saharan Africa. This explains why there are sharply opposing views on the stock of available improved technology. We shall examine this issue by comparing views from Africa with those of external observers. Dunstan Spencer, a Sierra Leonean authority on West African agriculture, reports that probably less than 2 percent of total sorghum, millet, and upland rice area in West Africa is sown with cultivars (varieties) developed through modern genetic research (Spencer 1986, 224). Turning to Nigeria, Professor Francis Idachaba reports that "almost a century after the introduction of formal agricultural research, there are still no sustained breakthroughs that could structurally transform Nigerian agriculture" (Idachaba 1985, 12).

More optimistic views about available technology come from external observers. First, the former Director General of the International Rice Research Institute (IRRI) in the Philippines recently asserted that the alley cropping technique, developed by the International Institute of Tropical Agriculture (IITA) of Nigeria, "in particular, merits large-scale adoption" (Swaminathan 1986, 23). But, in fact, several major hurdles remain before alley farming is ready for large-scale adoption, including the thorny problem of developing a suitable system for acid soils. Second, Borlaug is convinced that food crop technology is on the shelf and that accelerated food production campaigns can boost food production in Africa in three to five years (Borlaug 1988, 4). Third, the Food and Agriculture Organization recently asserted that, "except in arid and semi-arid areas without irrigation, food production [in Africa] can be roughly doubled with existing technology. Thus the immediate need is to provide adequate supplies of fertilizer, improved seeds, tools . . . " (FAO 1986, 61). The juxtaposition of the African and external views illustrates the need to focus the debate crop by crop and country by country. There is also a need to make a clear distinctions between improved technology in a technical sense—improved crop yields and/or increased livestock off-take rates—and technology that has been tested and found to be more *profitable* at the farm level.

In general, the largest stock of technology on the shelf is available for export crops, including cotton, tobacco, tea, coffee, and other commodities. Food crop technology is available for a few crops such as white maize, the staple food in eastern and southern Africa, soybeans and sorghum in Zimbabwe, hybrid sorghum in the Sudan (Ejeta 1988), sorghum in Zambia, maize in selected areas of West Africa, and cassava in Nigeria. For horticultural crops, improved technology is available for fruit, vegetables, and flowers in a few countries, such as Kenya and the Côte d'Ivoire, that have multinational firms engaged in production and marketing via established air freight routes to Europe.

In livestock production, the technical and social science research base for herders is seriously inadequate, especially for dry areas. For example, the International Livestock Center for Africa (ILCA) recently decided to abandon its ten-year research program on nomadic and seminomadic herding in dry Africa because of the lack of progress in developing improved technology for herders in these areas and the belief that research should be focused on the more favorable areas, where there is a potential for a bigger payoff.

Four generalizations emerge from this technology assessment. First, the stock of on-shelf food, horticultural, and livestock technology is inadequate in many countries in Africa. The lack of *profitable* on-shelf technology is a critical issue in countries such as Malawi and Rwanda, where most of the arable land has been brought under cultivation and future agricultural growth will have to come from increasing yields through the intensification of production. The second generalization is that on a geographical basis the technology gap is most acute in West Africa, where the stock of technology is inadequate for the big four: rice and wheat (the urban staples) and millet and sorghum (the rural staples). The third generalization is that even if improved technology is available it frequently will not be adopted by farmers, because it requires "higher prices, unavailable inputs, additional knowledge, lumpy capital, a non-existent marketing system or some other requirement beyond farmers' means" (Herdt, forthcoming). This illustrates the need to move beyond technological fundamentalism and examine technological development in relationship with the other prime movers of agricultural development. The fourth generalization is that, although a dozen or more African states have the size, resources, and capacity to produce new agricultural technology, intelligent borrowing of technology will be the single most important source of new technology for most African states in the foreseeable future, especially for the half of the countries in sub-Saharan Africa with fewer than five million people (Eicher 1989).

SIZE-OF-FARM DEBATE

The debate over what size farm can meet social, economic, and political criteria is alive after three decades of independence, even though smallholder agriculture is gaining support in policy circles in a growing number of countries. For example, in Kenya three-fourths of all farms are smallholders with less than two hectares of land and smallholders have increased their share of national production from 4 percent in 1965 to 49 percent in 1985 (Lele and Agarwal 1989). Among academics, there are still a few advocates of large farms. For example, Keith Hart supports large-scale river basin and irrigation development and contends that "the new states of West Africa need opportunities to prove to themselves, to their subjects and to the world that they, too, can harness the forces of nature on a grand scale" (Hart 1982, 95). Moreover, there is strong political support to maintain both small and large farms in Gabon, the Sudan, Zimbabwe, Zambia, Malawi, and Swaziland, and large ranches in Botswana. In Gabon, one large agribusiness firm with 2,550 hectares of land at Boumango produces enough maize and soy beans to feed 2.5 million chickens, enough to ensure national self-sufficiency in eggs and poultry meat for urban consumers. But many of these agribusiness firms are subsidized by overvalued exchange rates and special access to subsidized credit programs. The widespread failure of river basin schemes, state farms, plantations, and ranches in many African countries reinforces the position that smallholder farming should be the centerpiece of African farm policy in the 1990s.

However, farm policy in the 1990s should also aggressively support middle farmers in the 1990s. Farm size is a relative concept, however. In Africa, most middle-sized (crop) farms are around 5 to 15 hectares in size. Hence, a middle-sized farm in Africa would be an extremely small farm in the United States, Canada, or Australia. In Africa, middle farmers usually own a pair of oxen and a plow or have access to oxen and tractor hire services. They also rely mainly on family labor supplemented by hired labor at some peak times in the agricultural calendar (e.g., weeding and harvesting). There is abundant empirical evidence that middle farmers (1) can be a reliable source of innovation and agricultural growth, (2) play an "invisible" extension role by taking on the risk of new technology such as oxen or donkey traction, small tractors, tube wells, and (3) provide employment to local labor. African governments should adopt a pluralistic farm policy and support both smallholders and middle farmers in the 1990s.

FAVORABLE AND LESS FAVORABLE AREAS

One of the major debates on African agriculture in the 1990s is the degree to which countries should rely on favorable or less favorable natural resource areas to increase food and agricultural production. This issue was also debated in India in the 1960s; the debate was resolved by focusing Green Revolution food production campaigns (for wheat and rice) in favorable areas. In Africa in the 1960s public policy concentrated on export crops in favorable areas. When African policy makers and donors turned to food production and integrated rural development projects in the early 1970s, donors pressed for IRD projects in less favorable areas such as the Mandara mountains in northern Cameroon because it was assumed that these projects could both increase food production and help the rural poor. But the failure rate of the IRD projects in the 1970s and early 1980s was extremely high. Moreover, research in the 1980s has shown that the increase in marketable surplus of food is originating in the better endowed natural resource regions, even in countries where agriculture is assumed to have a unimodal agrarian structure dominated by smallholders. For example, the national campaign to increase smallholder maize production in Zimbabwe tripled maize output from 1979 to 1985, but 10 percent of the smallholders in higher rainfall zones accounted for 70 percent of the increase in the marketed surplus of maize (Rohrbach 1988). In Mali, around 70,000 smallholders are producing cotton and the bulk of the marketed surplus of sorghum, millet, and maize in the better-endowed region in southern Mali, whereas the future of food production is bleak in less favorable areas in northern Mali because of the lack of rainfall, technology, and supporting institutions such as credit (Dione 1989).

Country-specific research is urgently needed in Africa on the projected production, employment, and income distribution effects of crop and livestock production campaigns in favorable and less favorable areas in the 1990s. Africa can learn from Asia, where the debate over favorable and less favorable areas is also a major issue. For example, CIMMYT (International Center for Maize and Wheat Improvement) has achieved yield gains of wheat twice as high in favorable (1.0 percent per year) as in less favorable areas (0.5 percent or less per year). Looking ahead to possible food deficits in Asia in the 1990s, Byerlee recommends that foodgrain research and production in Asia be concentrated on favorable areas, because it is the most reliable source of increased output and it will also "benefit less favorable areas through technological spillovers, job creation, and lower food prices to the poor, including small farmers in less favorable areas who are usually net food buyers."[14]

The Prime Movers of Increasing Food and Agricultural Production

Africa's economic crisis of the 1980s has been countered with structural adjustment programs in some 30 countries, emphasizing the reform of macroeconomic policies. The immediate challenge in the early 1990s is to create an awareness that parallel action is needed to remove the technological, institutional, and human resource constraints on developing an efficient food and agriculture sector on a country by country basis. The concept of prime movers of agricultural development is useful in focusing policy debates on the big picture rather than on the minutiae of several thousand agricultural projects scattered across Africa's landscape. The prime movers can be defined as the strategic policies and complementary public investments that are required to stimulate farm production and restore the profitability of farming on a continuing basis.

The prime movers provide a simple framework for African states and donors to use in developing a country-specific agricultural growth strategy for the long pull. The challenge is to coordinate the sequencing of investments in the prime movers as a policy package. Since several of the prime movers are long-gestation investments, African governments and donors should make long-run commitments to human capital and institution building over the next 20 to 30 years, just as they did in Brazil and India in the 1950s and 1960s (Lele and Goldsmith 1989) and in Indonesia and Thailand in the 1970s and 1980s. Food aid can help fill the food gap for the coming 10 to 15 years, until the investments in the prime movers pay off in terms of increased food and agricultural production.

The five prime movers of African agricultural development are:

1. *The favorable economic environment* that flows from a political system that promotes, defends, and protects the economic interests of farmers and rural people.[15] The essence of food and agricultural policy is to assist Africa's 50 million family farms and traders in expanding rural production, generating rural jobs, raising rural incomes, and driving down the cost of supplying food to rural net food buyers and urban consumers. Two food policy preoccupations of the 1980s, food self-sufficiency and food self-reliance, should be quietly replaced with policies that promote food and export crop produc-

tion, rural employment generation (Eicher et al. 1970), and national and household food security (Eicher and Staatz 1986; Rukuni and Eicher 1988).

2. *Human capability* and managerial skills that are created through formal education, training, and on-the-job experience. Since Africa's stock of scientific and managerial capital per million people is roughly one-fifth of Asia's, human capital development must receive high priority by African states and by donors.

3. *New technology* that is secured by borrowing and through local technology generation. But a high level of scientific capacity is necessary for these nations to become "intelligent borrowers" of technology from neighboring countries, other parts of Africa, and the global research system.

4. *Rural capital formation*, such as physical capital (roads, irrigation, dams) and biological capital (improved livestock herds). The current emphasis on securing foreign aid to finance credit programs should be slowly replaced by policy reforms to encourage farm families to increase rural savings and mobilize family labor to improve land productivity, acquire draft animals, and improve the productivity of livestock herds.

5. *Rural institutions*, such as credit, seed multiplication, and marketing, to serve Africa's 50 million farmers and the millions of decision makers in the food system.

Which of the five prime movers is the most important? Empirical evidence shows that the prime movers should be promoted as a policy package, because they are complementary and they reinforce each other. Each by itself is limited. And given scarce resources, the sequencing of investments in the prime movers is a key issue.

Strengthening the Prime Movers as a Policy Package: Smallholder Maize Production in Zimbabwe

Zimbabwe's overflowing grain silos provide a textbook example of the payoff to strengthening the prime movers as a policy package (Muchena 1987; Rohrbach 1988). White maize contributes about 40 percent of the total calories in the average diet in Zimbabwe and it is the staple food in most of eastern and southern Africa. At independence in 1980, Zimbabwe inherited a dual agrarian structure of about 6,500 commercial farmers producing 90 percent of the marketed supply of maize and cotton and 99 percent of the tobacco, and 700,000 smallholders producing about 10 percent of the marketed surplus of maize and cotton and 1 percent of the tobacco. The new government introduced a comprehensive program to boost smallholder maize production, and in six years, 1979–85, smallholders tripled maize production by increasing the area under maize production by 90 percent and doubling maize yields. The smallholders sold 60 percent of the increase in maize output (Rohrbach 1988). Today, smallholders produce about 30 percent of the marketed surplus of maize, up from 10 percent at independence in 1980.

But Zimbabwe's smallholder maize revolution cannot be attributed to a single prime mover, such as higher prices or improved technology. The mainsprings of the revolution are the following:

1. Zimbabwe's maize revolution had its political origins in the Rhodesian Agricultural Union, which was established in Salisbury in 1905 to promote the political and economic interests of commercial farmers (Bratton 1987).[16]

2. Zimbabwe's smallholder maize revolution is rooted in public research on hybrid maize that was launched in 1932. It took 28 years of local research (1932–60) to develop the famous SR-52 hybrid variety, a long-season white variety produced primarily by commercial farmers (Eicher 1984). Research in the 1960s and 1970s produced short-season maize varieties for smallholders in low-rainfall areas. At independence in 1980, Zimbabwe had a backlog of maize varieties on the shelf ready for delivery to smallholders. Today, all of the commercial farmers plant hybrids and 80 percent of the maize area cultivated by smallholders is planted to hybrid varieties, the highest percentage in Africa (Rohrbach 1988).[17]

3. Maize seed is divisible and readily available to small, medium, and large farms. The Seed Co-op Company of Zimbabwe distributes hybrid maize seed in 2, 5, 10, 25, and 50 kilogram bags to farm supply centers and retail shops throughout the country.

4. Large public investments were made in feeder roads, extension, credit, and buying points for the government-operated Grain Marketing Board in areas where smallholders are concentrated.

   Maize prices to farmers were raised a number of times from 1980 to 1986, but inflation has outstripped price increases since 1984. The assured availability of fertilizer, hybrid maize seed, and buying points is probably as important as the farm level price of maize in influencing the rapid rate of smallholder adoption of hybrid maize.

5. The more favorable (better-watered) areas were the major source of increased production. In fact, 70 percent of the increase in marketable surplus of maize from smallholders came from 10 percent of the smallholders in the higher rainfall areas (Rohrbach 1988).

6. The research, extension, input delivery, and marketing organizations that have been promoted and nurtured by commercial farmers for decades have generated large "spillovers" or positive benefits for smallholders, particularly after the racial barriers limiting smallholders' access to these services were removed at independence in 1980.

Without question, no single prime mover, such as favorable producer prices or hybrid maize seed, was responsible for tripling smallholder maize production during the first six years of independence (Rohrbach 1988). Zimbabwe concentrated on the five prime movers as a policy package over a period of decades, including a 28-year research program on hybrid maize that led to the release of a high yielding hybrid variety (SR-52) for commercial farmers in 1960. Researchers then spent the

1960s and 1970s (the two decades before independence) developing shorter season (110–120–day) hybrid varieties for smallholders.

But a caveat is in order. Zimbabwe cannot serve as a food production model for all of Africa. The strategic lesson that emerges from Zimbabwe's first decade of independence is the need for African countries to focus on the prime movers of agricultural development as a policy package for the long pull. Zimbabwe's success during the first decade of independence, however, does not guarantee future success in food and agriculture. Zimbabwe faces some formidable problems in the 1990s, including rapid population growth, the loss of momentum in transforming its dual agrarian structure, the lack of technical packages for smallholders in low rainfall areas and the need to absorb three-fourths of its rural school leavers in the rural economy. It is an open question whether Zimbabwe will be able to maintain the agricultural momentum of its first decade of independence.

THE THIRD BATTLE: COMBATING MALNUTRITION AND HUNGER

Around 100 million people, or about one-fifth of Africa's population, do not get enough to eat. Twenty to thirty percent of Africa's children are malnourished. In a few areas, one-quarter or more of the children die before the age of five. This is the essence of Africa's long-term malnutrition and hunger battle. There is indisputable evidence that both rich and poor nations are unable to end hunger by simply producing more food and achieving national food self-sufficiency. The consumption side of the food security equation must be tackled at the same time that efforts are made to increase subsistence food production, rural employment, and rural purchasing power.

Poverty, a central cause of malnutrition, is deeply entrenched in Africa. Africa's poverty is captured by a single statistic: the total 1985 GNP of the 500 million people in the 45 countries of Africa was slightly less than the GNP of Spain, a nation of 40 million (World Bank 1987a). Because poverty is a central cause of hunger and malnutrition, it follows that raising rural incomes across the board is an important way of increasing food consumption and reducing hunger and malnutrition in Africa. Nevertheless, Behrman, Deolalikar, and Wolfe (1988) have cautioned their fellow economists not to overstate the importance of increasing income as a means of reducing malnutrition, because other factors, such as disease and the education of mothers, can also play a decisive role in determining the nutritional outcomes of families as well as of individual family members. Four aspects of the malnutrition and hunger battle will be addressed.

INCREASING FAMILY FOOD SECURITY OF RESOURCE-POOR FARMERS

In addressing rural hunger, the starting point is examining what can be done to help resource-poor farmers who produce much of what they consume. In these households, food availability and food access are fused in practice. Since the majority of the poor in rural Africa are engaged in producing at least some of their own food, it follows that in most food-deficit African countries, there is justification for improving the productivity of the staple food system of resource-poor farmers (Eicher and Staatz 1986). In theory, one of the most direct ways of increasing the real incomes of resource-poor farmers is to develop improved technology to increase the productivity of their main enterprise, staple food production. Increased staple food production may increase the per capita availability of home-produced foods, raise cash incomes by generating a marketable surplus of grain, or allow subsistence food needs to be produced with fewer resources, thus freeing land and labor to produce export crops like cotton and coffee.

But improving the productivity of staple foods is not promising in dry areas, where there is a paucity of irrigation, a lack of profitable technology for the staple foods sorghum and millet, and a lack of technical research on fruits and vegetables in order to broaden the food base for resource-poor farmers (Okigbo 1986). Moreover, even if improved technical packages are available for resource-poor farmers in dry areas, complementary investments are also necessary in farm and village processing, roads, transport, and marketing. Resource-poor farmers are also understandably reluctant to try to increase their income through specialization if there is not a reliable market for food. The case of millet and sorghum in Mali illustrates this basic point. The government of Mali has recently stopped making credit available to farmers producing only millet, because of the risky nature of the crop and the lack of a guaranteed market. By contrast, farmers producing cotton and sorghum in rotation have access to a government credit program, a guaranteed price for cotton at harvest time, and an assured market outlet for cotton through a special research and credit program for cotton farmers (Dione 1989). In short, increasing the food security of resource-poor farmers is a complex process that involves more than simply raising food prices or developing improved technology.

INCREASING FAMILY FOOD SECURITY THROUGH CASH CROPS AND LIVESTOCK

The second component of the long-term malnutrition battle is raising rural incomes and helping poor families increase their family food security by 1) increasing the production of established cash crops, such as cotton and oil palm; 2) developing *new* cash crops, such as natural rubber, fish, spices, cut flowers, and horticultural products for local and export markets; and 3) developing *new* markets such as the Middle East (Schapiro and Wainaina 1989). Although the global market prospects for primary products such as cocoa, cotton, and oil palm are not encouraging in the early 1990s, there are numerous opportunities for African countries to regain domestic markets now supplied by Asian countries. A prime example is oil palm in Nigeria. Once the world's largest oil palm producer, Nigeria currently produces about one-tenth the output of Malaysia. Nigeria routinely imports oil palm from Malaysia and cotton from other countries to meet its domestic needs. With a domestic market of 100 million people, increased production of oil palm, cowpeas, cotton, and other crops for domestic markets should be a central goal of Nigerian farm policy.

Turning to new export commodities, the starting point is to analyze potential "windows of opportunity" in regional and international markets and to work backwards to the national research, extension, and marketing systems. The next step is to decide whether the national agricultural research system can develop the capacity to borrow and/or develop new technology to exploit the window(s) of opportunity. This is followed by the development of formal or informal links with private banks and marketing firms to develop overseas markets. For example, New Zealand has pursued such a strategy to become the dominant exporter of kiwi fruit in the world. Thailand is pursuing a strategy to increase broiler exports in an attempt to move beyond its traditional role of supplying maize to the broiler industries of Taiwan and Japan. Thailand is now the third largest exporter of broilers in the world, following the United States and Brazil.

Kenya's success in expanding horticultural exports (fruits, vegetables, and cut flowers) is being closely studied in Africa. In 1967, Kenya created the Horticultural Crops Development Authority (HCDA) to develop its horticultural industry. The subsequent growth of local consumption and exports has been extraordinary, especially that of flowers. In fact, cut flowers increased from 458 tons in 1972 to 8,164 tons in 1986. Cut flowers are the leading foreign exchange earner among the airfreighted horticultural exports (Schapiro and Wainaina 1989). Around 100 large growers and 5,000 to 7,000 smallholders are currently producing horticultural products for some thirty countries. About 60 percent of the volume comes from smallholders, mostly on farms of less than 4 hectares in total size with about 1/4 to 1 hectare of land in export crops (Lele, Kinsey, and Obeya 1989). About 90 percent of Kenya's horticultural products are consumed locally, in urban areas and increasingly in rural areas.

Schapiro and Wainaina (1989) recently concluded that Kenya's horticultural export success is not attributable to any single factor, such as good weather or favorable market opportunities, but to a combination of public and private investment and government cooperation and restraint: "Government sponsored research, training, monitoring and other activities facilitated the expansion of the horticultural sector. However, it is what the government did not do—create a large bureaucratic structure and interfere to a significant extent with the market mechanism—that is most impressive. Without this combination of government's assistance and government restraint, it is highly unlikely that the expansion in horticultural exports would have been rapid or as large" (p. 93). In short there are no free lunches in African development. Zimbabwe's smallholder maize revolution and Kenya's horticultural boom cannot be traced to a single prime mover but to the efficient coordination of a complex array of public and private activities (Lee 1989).

RAISING RURAL INCOMES: RURAL SMALL-SCALE INDUSTRIES

Since in the 1990s most newcomers to the agricultural labor force in Africa will be unable to find jobs in industry or urban areas, there is a need to pursue an aggressive strategy of rural employment generation. For example, in Zimbabwe, the government estimates that only 20 percent of the newcomers to the rural labor force over the 1986–90 period will find jobs in rural areas. Based on the large research base on rural small-scale industry in Africa relative to a decade ago, there are a number of policies that can be used to step up income and employment generation in rural areas.[18] Since the main growth in demand for rural small-scale industries will come from income generated by crop and livestock production, the challenge is to develop macro policies and crop and livestock production campaigns to accelerate food and cash crop production at the same time to improve the policy environment to facilitiate the growth of rural small-scale industry.

DEVELOPING COST-EFFECTIVE NUTRITION INTERVENTIONS

The knowledge base on improving nutrition in Africa is woefully inadequate. Says Alan Berg (1987), "the prospects for mounting nutrition projects in Africa poses special problems . . . because of the [institutional, human, and financial] limitations to absorbing external assistance" (110). Which nutrition interventions are cost effective, administratively feasible, and institutionally sustainable at this stage of Africa's institutional maturity? We do not know the answer to this question. The pendulum among donors is now swinging from nutrition projects to food and nutrition policies, because many nutrition projects, as presently designed, are not sustainable after the life-of-project financing runs out, usually in four to six years. The research base on combating poverty and malnutrition in Africa is modest, because malnutrition is a politically sensitive research topic, especially in food surplus countries; it requires multidisciplinary cooperation. Finally, nutrition research requires continuity of scientific leadership, and it needs funding for 10 to 15 years—much like maize breeding research.

SUMMARY AND IMPLICATIONS

Africa is engaged in three food battles: breaking the famine cycle, increasing food production, and combating malnutrition and hunger. The food security equation provides a shorthand way of communicating the basic point that each of these battles can be legitimately approached from either the food production or the food consumption side. The challenge is to develop a balanced strategy that tackles both sides of the equation. Since there is no single path to national food security, one should expect many different approaches in a continent of 45 countries. For example, many countries will pursue national foodgrain self-sufficiency while others will export cocoa, livestock, and coffee to pay for food imports.

Famine, the first food battle, has been conquered in Asia but continues in Africa because of civil war, external aggression, political instability, and the lack of political commitment to ending famine. Without question, the Great African Famine of 1984–85 created a new international awareness of the multiple causes of famine. The advocates of combating famine by simply increasing food production are now on the defensive.

Developing an efficient food and agriculture sector is one of the cornerstones for the long-run solution to the second and third battles, lagging food production and malnutrition. While food aid, official development assistance, and private support from the NGO/PVO community can help meet Africa's food consumption needs in the short run, sustainable food and agricultural development must be built on mobilizing the energy of Africa's 50 million family farmers to increase both food and export crop production and on generating new income streams through rural small-scale industries. Because of explosive rates of population growth and rising food imports, there is a compelling need to lay out a long-term plan to increase food supplies as Africa's population doubles from 500 million to one billion over the next 20 to 25 years. The third battle, chronic hunger and malnutrition, is a long-run battle that should be tackled at the same time as the food production battle.

NOTES

I have benefited from comments by Sisay Asefa, Malcolm Blackie, Michael Lipton, Amartya Sen, Peter Svedberg, John Staatz, and Edouard Tapsoba. I am grateful to the following for support: The Twentieth Century Fund, The Rockefeller Foundation, ISNAR, and the Michigan State University's Food Security in Africa Cooperative Agreement, which is supported by the Bureau for Science and Technology and the Bureau for Africa, Agency for International Development, Washington, D.C.

1. Hereafter, Africa is used to refer to the 45 countries in sub-Saharan Africa, excluding North Africa and the Republic of South Africa.

2. The official government report in Ethiopia was 300,000 deaths, but there is evidence that the number was around a million.

3. For historical perspectives on the roots of the food crisis, see Eicher 1982; Spencer 1986; Lipumba 1988; Ndegwa 1985; Mellor, Delgado, and Blackie 1987; and Aboyade 1988.

4. The findings in Mali are reinforced by recent studies in Senegal, Rwanda, Somalia, and Zimbabwe (Weber et al. 1988).

5. For similar views on the need for multiple strategies to cope with rural stratification in Latin America and Asia, see de Janvry and Sadoulet, chapter 28, and Byerlee, chapter 27, in this volume.— ED.

6. See Hayami, chapter 26 in this volume.—ED.

7. Rohrbach's (1988) meticulous study of maize in Zimbabwe concludes that about 80 percent of the area under smallholder maize cultivation is planted with hybrid varieties because they consistently outyield the traditional open-pollinated varieties, even if the hybrids are planted without fertilizer.

8. See Singer, chapter 14 in this volume.—ED.

9. In Ethiopia, news of the 1972–74 famine was suppressed by Emperor Haile Selassie until the dramatic BBC newsreel by Johnathan Dimbleby was shown on U.K. television on 23 October 1974 (Jansson, Harris, and Penrose 1987). Ethiopians attribute the toppling of the dynasty of Haile Selassie to the BBC film. The role of civil war in Ethiopia's famines is discussed by Mariam (1986) and Kaplan (1988).

10. See Sen, chapter 11 in this volume.—ED.

11. See Mellor, chapter 6 in this volume.—ED.

12. Livestock projects have been plagued with technical, managerial, and financial problems. Most donors now admit that they plunged into financing livestock projects in the 1960s and 1970s without a clear conceptual understanding of the inner dynamics of nomadic and seminomadic pastoral systems. Also, with the benefit of hindsight, it is now obvious that the stock of technical knowledge for improving livestock productivity was woefully inadequate. The combined impact of the conceptual and technical problems is summarized by an anthropologist as follows: "As is often the case, where the World Bank led, other donors followed. . . . An estimated $625 million of international funds have

been invested in sub-Saharan African livestock development since the late 1960s. . . . More often than not the effect has been disappointing" (Dyson-Hudson 1985, 158).

13. See Ruttan, chapter 24 in this volume.—ED.

14. See Byerlee, chapter 27 in this volume.—ED.

15. But a favorable economic environment for farmers and rural people must go beyond the narrow concern over agricultural prices and include exchange rates, interest rates, wage policy, the domestic terms of trade between agriculture and industry, farm to market roads, seed and fertilizer delivery systems, and rural electrification.

16. The Rhodesian Agricultural Union was subsequently renamed the Commercial Farmers Union (CFU). Today there are three farm organizations: the CFU, representing 4,200 commercial farmers; the Zimbabwe National Farmers Union (ZNFU), representing 8,600 middle farmers or what are known as small-scale commercial farms, and the National Farmers Association of Zimbabwe (NFAZ) representing 800,000 smallholders or "communal farmers."

17. Echeverria (1988) reports that the percentages of maize area planted to hybrid varieties are: in industrial market economies, 100 percent; in Latin America, 49 percent; in Asia, 40 percent; and in Africa, 15 percent.

18. See Chuta and Liedholm, chapter 19 in this volume.—ED.

REFERENCES

Aboyade, Ojetunju. 1988. "Structural Adjustment and the African Economy." Keynote address presented at a seminar of the Kellogg International Fellowship Program in Food Systems, Harare, Zimbabwe, 8 February.

Barker, Randolph, Robert Herdt, with Beth Rose. 1985. *The Rice Economy of Asia.* Washington, D.C.: Resources for the Future.

Behrman, Jere, Anil B. Deolalikar, and Barbara L. Wolfe. 1988. "Nutrients: Impacts and Determinants." *World Bank Economic Review* 2 (September): 299–320.

Berg, Alan. 1987. *Malnutrition: What Can Be Done?* Baltimore: Johns Hopkins University Press.

Borlaug, Norman E. 1988. "History of the Sasakawa–Global 2000 Initiatives for Increasing Agricultural Production in Sub-Saharan Africa." Paper presented at the workshop "Reviewing the African Agricultural Projects," sponsored by the Global 2000 Project (Atlanta, Ga.), Nairobi, 18 March.

Bratton, Michael. 1987. "The Comrades and the Countryside: The Politics of Agricultural Policy in Zimbabwe." *World Politics* 39 (January): 174–202.

Brokensha, D. W. 1988. "Inequality in Rural Africa: Fallers Reconsidered." *Manchester Papers on Development* 3(2):1–21.

CAFOD (Catholic Fund for Overseas Development). 1984/85. *Just Food.* London: CAFOD.

Carr, S. J. 1988. "Modification and Extention of the National Rural Development Program." Paper presented at the Malawi Symposium on Agricultural Policies for Growth and Development, Lilongwe, October 31-November 4.

Club du Sahel and CILSS (Comité Inter-Etats de Luttre contre la Secheresse dans le Sahel). *The Sahel Facing the Future: Increasing Dependence or Structural Transformation.* Paris: Organization for Economic Cooperation and Development.

Dalrymple, Dana. 1986a. *Development and Spread of High Yielding Wheat Varieties in Developing Countries.* Washington, D.C.: United States Agency for International Development.

———. 1986b. *Development and Spread of High Yielding Rice Varieties in Developing Countries.* Washington, D.C.: United States Agency for International Development.

deLattre, Anne. 1988. "What Future for the Sahel?" *The OECD Observer* (August-September): 19–21.

Dioné, Josué. 1989. "Informing Food Security Policy in Mali: Interactions between Technology, Institutions, and Market Reforms." Ph.D. diss. Michigan State University.

Dreze, Jean. 1988. *Famine Prevention in India.* London: London School of Economics.

Dyson-Hudson, Neville. 1985. "Pastoral Production Systems and Livestock Development Projects: An

East African Perspective." In *Putting People First: Sociological Variables in Rural Development,* edited by M. Cernea, 155–86. New York: Oxford University Press.

Echeverria, Ruben. 1988. "Public and Private Sector Investments in Agricultural Research: The Case of Maize." Ph.D. diss. University of Minnesota.

Eicher, Carl K. 1982. "Facing up to Africa's Food Crisis." *Foreign Affairs* 61 (fall): 151–74.

———. 1984. "International Technology Transfer and the African Farmer: Theory and Practice." Working Paper 3/84. Harare: University of Zimbabwe, Department of Land Management.

———. 1989. *Sustainable Institutions for African Agricultural Development.* Working Paper, no. 19. The Hague: International Service for National Agricultural Research.

Eicher, Carl K., and John M. Staatz. 1986. "Food Security Policy in Sub-Saharan Africa." In *Agriculture in a Turbulent World Economy,* edited by A. Maunder and U. Renborg, 215–29. London: Gower.

Eicher, Carl K., T. Zalla, J. Kocher, and F. Winch. 1970. *Employment Generation in African Agriculture.* East Lansing: Michigan State University, Institute of International Agriculture.

Ejeta, Gebisa. 1988. "Development and Spread of Hageen Dura-1, the First Commerical Sorghum Hybrid in The Sudan." *Applied Agricultural Research* 3, no. 1: 29–35.

FAO (Food and Agriculture Organization). 1986. *African Agriculture: The Next 25 Years.* Vol. 5. Rome: FAO.

Goheen, Miriam. 1988. "Land Accumulation and Local Control: The Manipulation of Symbols and Power in NSO, Cameroon." In *Land and Society in Contemporary Africa,* edited by R. E. Downs and S. P. Reyna, 280–308. Hanover, N.H.: University Press of America.

Hart, Keith. 1982. *The Political Economy of West African Agriculture.* Cambridge: Cambridge University Press.

Herdt, Robert. Forthcoming. "Increased Crop Yields in Developing Countries: Sense and Nonsense." *Indian Journal of Agricultural Economics.* Golden jubilee edition.

Idachaba, F. S. 1985. "Priorities for Nigerian Agriculture in the Fifth National Development Plan, 1986–90." Ibadan, Nigeria: Nigerian Institute of Social and Economic Research.

Jansson, Kurt, Michael Harris, and Angela Penrose. 1987. *The Ethiopian Famine.* London: Zed Books.

Kaplan, Robert. 1988. *Surrender or Starve: The Wars behind the Famine.* Boulder, Colo.: Westview Press.

Lele, Uma. 1975. *The Design of Rural Development: Lessons from Africa.* Baltimore: Johns Hopkins University Press.

———. 1989. "Sources of Growth in East African Agriculture." *The World Bank Economic Review* 3, no. 1 (January): 119–44.

Lele, Uma, and M. Agarwal. 1989. *Smallholder and Large-Scale Agriculture in Africa: Are There Trade-Offs between Growth and Equity?* MADIA project. Washington, D.C.: World Bank.

Lele, Uma, and Arthur A. Goldsmith. 1989. "The Development of National Agricultural Research Capacity: India's Experience with the Rockefeller Foundation and Its Significance for Africa." *Economic Development and Cultural Change* 37 (January): 305–43.

Lele, Uma, Bill Kinsey, and Antonia Obeya. 1989. "Building Agricultural Research Capacity in Africa: Policy Lessons from the MADIA Countries." MADIA project, Washington, D.C.: World Bank.

Lipumba, Nguyuru. 1988. "Policy Reforms for Economic Development in Tanzania." In *Africa's Development Challenges and the World Bank: Hard Questions and Costly Choices,* edited by Stephen Cummins, 53–72. Boulder, Colo.: Lynne Rienner.

Mariam, Mesfin Wolde. 1986. *Rural Vulnerability to Famine in Ethiopia, 1958–77.* London: Intermediate Technology Publications.

McAlpin, Michelle. 1987. "Famine Relief Policy in India: Six Lessons for Africa." In *Drought and Hunger in Africa: Denying Famine a Future,* edited by Michael H. Glantz, 393–413. Cambridge: Cambridge University Press.

Mellor, John, Christopher Delgado, and Malcolm Blackie, eds. 1987. *Accelerating Food Production in Sub-Saharan Africa.* Baltimore: Johns Hopkins University Press.

Moris, John. 1987. "Irrigation as a Privileged Solution in African Development." *Development Policy Review* 5, no. 2 (June): 99–123.

Muchena, S. M. 1987. "Agricultural Development in Zimbabwe." In *Improving Food Crop Production on Small Farms in Africa*, 1–5. Rome: U.N. Food and Agriculture Organization.

Nafziger, E. Wayne. 1988. *Inequality in Africa: Political Elites, Proletariat, Peasants and the Poor.* Cambridge: Cambridge University Press.

Ndegwa, Philip. 1985. *Africa's Development Crisis and Related International Issues*. Nairobi: Heinemann.

OAU (Organization of African Unity) and ECA (Economic Commission for Africa). 1986. *Africa's Submission to the Special Session of the United Nations General Assembly on Africa's Economic and Social Crisis*. Addis Ababa: OAU.

Okigbo, Bede. 1986. "Broadening the Food Base in Africa: The Potential of Traditional Food Plants." *Food and Nutrition* 12, no. 1: 4–17.

Pardey, Philip, and Johannes Roseboom. 1989. *ISNAR Agricultural Research Indicator Series: A Global Data Base on National Agricultural Research Systems*. Cambridge: Cambridge University Press for ISNAR.

Paulino, Leonardo. 1987. "The Evolving Food Situation." In Mellor, Delgado, and Blackie, 23–38.

Reutlinger, Shlomo. 1977. "Malnutrition: A Poverty or Food Problem?" *World Development* 5 (August): 715–24.

Rohrbach, David. 1988. "The Growth of Smallholder Maize Production in Zimbabwe (1979–1985): Implications for Food Security." In Rukuni and Bernsten, 307–28.

Rukuni, Mandivamba, and Richard Bernsten, eds. 1988. *Southern Africa: Food Security Policy Options*. Harare, Zimbabwe: University of Zimbabwe/Michigan State University Food Security Project.

Rukuni, Mandivamba and Carl K. Eicher. 1988. "The Food Security Equation in Southern Africa." In *Poverty, Policy and Food Security in Southern Africa*, edited by Coralie Bryant, 133–57. Boulder, Colo.: Lynne Rienner.

Schultz, T. W. 1965. *Economic Crises in World Agriculture*. Ann Arbor: University of Michigan Press.

Sen, Amartya. 1981. *Poverty and Famines*. Oxford: Clarendon Press.

———. 1984. "Food Battles: Conflicts in the Access to Food." *Food and Nutrition* 10, no. 1: 81–90.

———. 1988. "Food Entitlements and Economic Chains." In *Science, Ethics and Food*, edited by Brian W. J. LeMay, 58–76. Washington, D.C.: Smithsonian Institution Press.

Schapiro, Martin, and Stephen Wainaina. 1989. "Kenya: A Case Study of the Production and Export of Horticultural Commodities." In *Successful Development in Africa: Case Studies of Projects, Programs and Policies*, EDI 79–94. Washington, D.C.: World Bank.

Shapiro, Kenneth. 1985. "Strengthening Agricultural Research and Educational Institutions in Africa." Hearings before the Subcommittee on Foreign Operations of the Senate Committee on Appropriations, U.S. Senate, March 26, Washington, D.C.

Spencer, Dunstan. 1986. "Agricultural Research: Lessons of the Past, Strategies for the Future." In *Strategies for African Development*, edited by Robert J. Berg and Jennifer Whitaker, 182–214. Berkeley: University of California Press.

Staatz, John. 1988. "Food Supply and Demand in Sub-Saharan Africa." In *Global Food Security: Focus on Africa*. Washington, D.C.: National Committee for World Food Day.

Staatz, John M., Josue Dione, and N. Nango Dembele. 1989. "Cereals Market Liberalization in Mali." *World Development* 7, no. 5: 703–18.

Svedberg, Peter. 1987. "Explaining Famine in Sub-Saharan Africa." Helsinki: WIDER. June, (Mimeo).

Swaminathan, M. S. 1986. *Sustainable Nutrition Security for Africa: Lessons from India*. San Francisco: The Hunger Project.

Twose, Nigel. 1984. *Cultivating Hunger: An Oxfam Study of Food, Power and Poverty.* Oxford: Oxfam.

UNDP (United Nations Development Program) and IBRD (International Bank for Reconstruction and Development). 1985. *Somalia: Report of a Joint Technical Cooperation Assessment Mission*. New York and Washington: UNDP and IBRD.

UNESCO. 1988. *UNESCO Statistical Yearbook, 1988*. New York: United Nations Educational, Scientific and Cultural Organization.

530 *Carl K. Eicher*

Weber, Michael, John M. Staatz, John S. Holtzman, Eric W. Crawford, and Richard H. Bernsten. 1988. "Informing Food Security Decisions in Africa: Empirical Analysis and Policy Dialogue." *American Journal of Agricultural Economics* 70, no. 5 (December): 1045–54.

World Bank. 1987a. *The World Bank Atlas, 1987*. Washington, D.C.: World Bank.

World Bank. 1987b. *Rural Development: World Bank Experience, 1965–86*. Washington, D.C.: World Bank.

32

Managing Agricultural Development in Africa

UMA J. LELE

Throughout most of sub-Saharan Africa, agriculture is in crisis. Frequent droughts, growing expenditures on food imports, and falling export earnings have been cutting into living standards and growth prospects. The effects have been pervasive, not only on incomes of agricultural producers, who include most of Africa's poor, but also on supplies of food and raw materials for industry, on employment, savings, and government revenues, and on the demand for goods and services produced outside agriculture. Yet policy changes and planning for the resumption of growth in agriculture are hampered by a pervasive lack of country-specific information. Reform efforts all too often try to apply general remedies to Africa's diverse problems.

Prompted by these concerns, the World Bank in 1985 launched a cross-country comparative study, Managing Agricultural Development in Africa (MADIA). The study analyzed developments in agriculture in Kenya, Malawi, and Tanzania in East Africa, and Cameroon, Nigeria, and Senegal in West Africa, since independence, and drew lessons for future policies and programs. This article draws on the findings of that study.

EAST AFRICA

The three East African countries studied inherited broadly similar production possibilities at independence. However, Kenya's agriculture, formerly the preserve of one of the largest European settlements in sub-Saharan Africa, was much more advanced than Malawi's or Tanzania's. In both Kenya and Malawi, population growth has put intense pressure on agricultural land; and the structure of land holding has been dualistic, with a few large and many very small farms. In Tanzania, land has been abundant in most areas and the possibilities for agricultural production more diverse.

UMA J. LELE is an agricultural economist with the World Bank, Washington, D.C.

Reprinted from *Finance and Development*, March 1989:45–48, by permission of the World Bank and the author.

Since independence, the three countries have followed different policy paths with very different outcomes for agriculture. Kenya, which has achieved the fastest growth of agricultural output, has given smallholders a leading role in its development strategy. It has thereby achieved the greatest success in reconciling growth with equity, and in developing both foodcrops (especially maize) and export crops (tea, coffee, and horticultural crops). Malawi achieved substantial growth in high-value agricultural exports (especially tobacco, tea, and sugar) until 1983, but largely from estates; smallholder production grew little or not at all in per capita terms. Tanzania, as is well known, has given precedence in its development strategy to equity over growth. In the 1970s, heavy investments in industry and social welfare programs led to a severe overextension of government resources and neglect of agriculture.

These differences in countries' performance reflect their differing macroeconomic policy environments and agricultural policies. Both Kenya and Malawi have maintained a macroeconomic policy environment that broadly favors agriculture and allows them to adjust better than Tanzania to the severe external shocks all three East African countries have faced. These shocks have included substantial terms-of-trade losses on agricultural exports. Unlike Tanzania, Kenya and Malawi have avoided prolonged overvaluation of their currencies, and thus implicit taxation of agriculture, and their budgetary deficits and inflation rates have been smaller and more stable than Tanzania's. Their shares of government expenditures in GDP have been smaller than Tanzania's, but they have devoted larger shares of their government budgets to agriculture and infrastructure.

As to agricultural policies, Kenya avoided explicit taxation of its smallholders by passing on international price changes to tea and coffee producers. Malawi, by contrast, responded to new opportunities for exporting tobacco in the mid-1960s and 1970s by promoting a rapid expansion of burley and flue-cured tobacco production on estates, because it was thought that only large farms could achieve the rapid growth necessary. Malawian smallholders retreated increasingly into subsistence farming, and the distribution of agricultural income and assets became increasingly skewed. The differences in the policies the two countries pursued in the 1970s, combined with differences in initial institutional endowments, left Kenyan small farmers better able than their Malawian counterparts to adopt improved maize and other technology in the 1980s and created stronger growth linkages with the rest of the economy.

In Tanzania the government heavily taxed the major export, coffee. Though other exports were taxed less heavily and later even subsidized, producer prices have not compensated adequately for the implicit taxation caused by increasing overvaluation of the currency. Export crops have stagnated in both the large-scale and smallholder sectors, and smallholders have moved out of these crops into foodcrops. The difficulties created for smallholders by price and tax policies compounded the effects of institutional instability through such policies as involuntary resettlement in Ujamaa villages and successive official experiments with cooperative and public sector production and distribution arrangements.

WEST AFRICA

The presence of oil in Nigeria and Cameroon and phosphates in Senegal has meant that agriculture plays a smaller role in these economies than in the three East African countries studied. Nigeria inherited better infrastructure and institutional endowments than Cameroon or Senegal. Cameroon has more abundant and diverse agricultural land than Nigeria, where population pressure is higher. Senegal's variable and declining rainfall and poor natural resources for agriculture make it the least well endowed for agriculture of the three.

Unlike their East African counterparts, all three economies benefited in the 1970s from changes in their international terms of trade. The boom in the extractive sector, however, had adverse consequences for agriculture. It inflated incomes and expenditures, swelled the movement of population into cities, reducing labor availability in agriculture, and encouraged a shift in consumption away from traditional domestic foods toward imported rice and wheat.

Agricultural performance has been best in Cameroon. Like Kenya, Cameroon has followed relatively stable and predictable macroeconomic and sectoral policies. It has expanded its output of robusta coffee, cotton, and oil palm and achieved the highest cotton yields in Africa (1,300 kilograms per hectare). Taxation encouraged a fall in the quality and profitability of arabica coffee, however, leading to a switch to food and horticultural crops. In response to growing urban demand, the government has encouraged production of relatively high-cost "new" crops such as rice and sugar over traditional foodcrops such as cassava, yams, and sorghum.

Nigeria's agriculture declined rapidly in the wake of the oil boom, in part because of the implicit taxation of export crops through overvaluation of the currency, but also because of ever-changing thrusts in policy initiatives, neglect of technology, and erosion of the capacity of state and local governments to provide services.

Senegal's difficult natural conditions for agriculture have been exacerbated by poor policies. The loss of French protection for groundnuts, its main export, encouraged it to diversify out of agriculture into industry and, within agriculture, into irrigated rice. Its economic diversification and import substitution of rice have turned out to be costly, as is discussed below.

PRODUCTIVITY

Agricultural output in all the countries studied has grown more from expansion in area, and changes in cropping patterns, than from increases in yields per hectare. Yields on estates have risen impressively in Kenya and Malawi. But, except for coffee in Kenya, cotton in Cameroon and Senegal, and maize in areas of assured rainfall, together with occasional irrigated rice schemes, average crop yields per hectare have not risen significantly on smallholdings. (Though productivity may have risen on original land holdings, in many areas population pressure has brought increasingly marginal land into cultivation, perhaps affecting statistics on average yields per hectare.) The need to increase land—and labor—productivity is becoming urgent.

All the countries studied have had major institutional problems in generating new agricultural technology, but Kenya has been quite successful in promoting technological change in maize, as well as in tea and coffee, pineapples, vegetables, potatoes, wheat, and pyrethrum. Over 60 percent of Kenya's small farms cultivate hybrid maize, compared to less than 10 percent in Malawi or Tanzania. In the West African countries, the most promising and cost-effective technical improvement has been the expansion of maize production under diverse conditions and, in the Francophone countries, of cotton; productivity in traditional crops has not increased.

ADJUSTMENT

Thus far, the main efforts of adjustment programs in agriculture in the six countries studied have been to rationalize prices and reduce the role of government in marketing. Many of the price reforms have sought to remove subsidies and to reduce the taxation of agriculture by adjusting exchange rates and bringing domestic producer prices into line with international prices. In East Africa, programs have also concentrated on governments' intervention in markets and better allocation of resources to agriculture. Nigeria's program includes the removal of price distortions in the export crop sector; its export marketing boards were abolished in 1986. Senegal has abolished marketing boards, removed input subsidies, and revised producer prices.

The changes in relative prices have changed the mixture of crops being grown, but have not changed the low levels of productivity. This has brought home the need to address issues other than prices—such as land tenure arrangements, the generation and adoption of new technologies, and the institutional development necessary to broaden access to credit, extension services, and markets.

The studies undertaken for MADIA have stressed the paucity of information on the very diverse microeconomic and institutional factors that determine producers' decisions. These factors need to be better understood on a specific basis so that price reforms can be complemented by the technological and institutional changes that specific countries and regions need if they are to achieve productivity growth.[1]

ROLE OF AID

Aid flows to MADIA countries have been large and have had a profound effect on the scale, direction, and quality of recipients' development efforts. Excluding Nigeria, which received little concessional assistance in the 1970s, concessional foreign assistance supplied 20 to 60 percent of government expenditures in 1970–85 and was equivalent to between 5 and 20 percent of GDP. Just as important as financial assistance has been the donors' role in the formulation of policy and investment strategies. Success in development depends less on the size of aid flows than on the quality of assistance.

The development of smallholder tea and coffee in Kenya, cotton in Cameroon, and maize in northern Nigeria and elsewhere provides outstanding examples of the catalytic role that well-conceived assistance can play in agriculture. Overall, however, aid has made a relatively small contribution to the agricultural growth that has occurred.

In many instances, the swinging pendulum of donor's concerns has tended to divert attention from basic long-run problems. Development strategies in the 1970s tended to concentrate on "quick" poverty alleviation, which gave priority to helping low-income regions and populations and to raising food crop production, mainly to meet growing urban demand. The results of these poverty-oriented strategies, and of efforts to replace imported food with domestic production, were mixed. In the 1980s, the emphasis switched to equally "quick" solutions, based on the correction of price incentives and liberalization of markets, designed to raise production, particularly of exports. Most recently, interest has revived in food security.

FIVE PREREQUISITES FOR AGRICULTURAL GROWTH

Too little attention has been paid to five prerequisites for achieving broadly based, sustainable agricultural growth.

BALANCING FOOD AND EXPORT CROPS

In the 1970s governments, often encouraged by donors, shifted investments away from traditional export and foodcrops into new, high-cost, production of rice, wheat, and sugar for the urban sector. Reasons included export pessimism; humanitarian concerns about food security and poverty, especially in light of the 1973–74 food crisis and severe African drought; the likelihood of Africa's increased exports competing with those of some aid-giving countries; rising domestic demand for food from growing populations; and expections of rising world food prices. Efforts to ensure food security are obviously essential on welfare as well as economic grounds, but priority was in practice given to diversifying out of traditional foodcrops into new, high-cost production of rice and wheat for the urban sector.

The first lesson of the 1970s is the need to interpret the food security mandate broadly: it is often more efficient for a country to import certain foods (especially those consumed by urban dwellers), using revenues earned from thriving agricultural exports, than to grow all its own. Unfortunately, production of traditional foodcrops stagnated and agricultural export earnings fell; as a result, food import bills grew while the capacity to meet them shrank.

The second lesson is that whether at the household or at the national level, food security requires high and stable agricultural incomes. These can best be achieved by a balanced production strategy for food and export crops that draws on the productive capacity developed over a long period. Donors' advice and financial support for diversification out of traditional export crops, in which recipient countries had a strong comparative advantage, into new activities was unfortunate. Such advice confused comparative advantage, based on the costs of the alternative production possibilities *within* a country, with the separate issue of the country's domestic costs relative to those of *other*, competitor, countries. In so doing, it failed to recognize the fundamental importance of cost-reducing technologies for maintaining competitiveness in traditional food and export activities. There was also a good deal of optimism about how quickly diversification could be achieved.

In Senegal, for example, economic analysis undertaken in the 1970s suggested that the country had lost its comparative advantage in its main export, groundnuts. This, combined with high projected rice prices in the mid-1970s, reinforced the government's desire to shift its own and donor support out of groundnuts into irrigated rice. Senegal lost shares of world trade in groundnuts and related products. Though it is true that Senegal's groundnut exports are less competitive than they once were, the MADIA results suggest that a more cautious approach to moving out of groundnut exports, together with a more purposive emphasis on cost-reducing technology, would have maintained Senegal's competitiveness in a growing edible-oil market.

In Kenya after 1973–74, donors shifted their emphasis away from development of traditional export crops, warning of poor export prospects and the need for diversification. Notwithstanding, Kenya pushed ahead on the basis of its comparative advantage through very supportive government policies toward tea and coffee. Kenya's exports of these crops have grown rapidly, supplying increasing shares of world trade in these crops and 50–60 percent of the country's export earnings.

In their support for adjustment in the 1980s, donors have again turned toward exports, and particularly toward correcting price distortions. Such price reforms have been easier than expected. But they now need to be followed by efforts to tackle long-term problems, such as the decline in research capacity in export crops and the need to develop new export markets. Unfortunately, the long-term attrition that has taken place in the export crop expertise of Britain and France has not been offset by growth of such expertise within Africa or from other sources that assist Africa.

RECONCILING GROWTH WITH EQUITY

Donors' pervasive pessimism about export markets in the 1970s, together with a heightened concern for poverty alleviation, led them to reorient their approach to development away from growth and toward equity concerns. This change coincided with African governments' goals of expanding access to public services. Much progress was made in broadening participation in rural development and laying some of the foundations of long-term growth—for example through improving health and extending access to education. However, a large number of donor-funded projects inspired by concern for the poor depended on raising farm production in marginal areas and areas where there were no suitable technologies for raising agricultural productivity; most such projects have had low economic rates of return.[2] A more balanced strategy would give priority to areas of known potential in the medium run while methodically seeking long-term solutions for resource-poor areas, including consideration of investment in human resources and of appropriate subsidies for certain groups in the short run and promotion of emigration, to areas of more potential or to pursue activities other than agriculture, in the long run.

SHORT-TERM MACRO-POLICY ADJUSTMENTS VERSUS LONG-TERM CAPACITY BUILDING

There is good reason for donors' emphasis, in the 1980s, on relatively short-run policy reform. Nevertheless, it has left many donors with a need to rebuild their own capacity to assist with badly needed longer-term development investments. This is increasingly being recognized in the donor community.

HUMAN CAPITAL AND INSTITUTIONAL DEVELOPMENT

By and large, relations between donors and governments still place much more emphasis on transfers of finance and technical assistance than on the development and use of African institutional and human capacity. Donors have often fallen back on technological and organizational solutions arising from their own backgrounds and expectations, which may have little to do with recipients' needs or their organizational and personnel endowments.

The successful cases of smallholder development cited earlier in tea, coffee, cotton, and maize expansion have all involved complex packages of public policy measures, designed on the basis of detailed local knowledge, together with strong field-level services that have responded to the grassroots needs of local producers, who have themselves developed a stake in the success of such efforts. In future, much will depend on how well African governments explain and donors understand the constraints on growth in individual projects and subsectors, and on the emphasis placed on training and relying on people with local knowledge. Governments themselves need to place greater emphasis on using external assistance to develop their own capacity.

PUBLIC SECTOR

The MADIA study emphasizes the strategic role the public sector has played wherever growth has occurred, by promoting a macroeconomic environment that is conducive to growth, an investment pattern that expands the supply of human and physical infrastructure, and an institutional strategy that supports agricultural research and extension and broadens factor and product markets.

In countries at early stages of development, the public sector plays a vital role in developing markets and broadening opportunities by investing in public goods. Where privatization is to be attempted, its speed, timing, and extent are all crucial to its success, especially at early stages of development. Unless the public sector has already helped to put in place transport and information networks that allow markets to function, and arrangements that ensure adequate supplies of credit to crop traders, and unless regulations exist that promote competition in the private sector, public monopolies may be replaced by private monopolies. The private sector may choose only to operate where profits are quick and high—as has been shown by experience with the liberalization of several African markets for grain and for fertilizer.

CONCLUSIONS

To sum up, the key issues identified by the MADIA study include the following:

1. High and rising pressure on land, and the urgent need to raise factor productivity. In much of sub-Saharan Africa, technology development in agriculture is only now beginning to receive high priority. As yet, there are not strong enough links between the nature of resource endowments, the substance of development strategy, and the content of technology policy. Research and extension efforts in many cases need to be broadened, beyond plant breeding and toward, for example, soil management techniques and the integration of cropping with livestock and forestry.
2. Mounting evidence that adjustment based on macroeconomic reforms and "getting prices right" cannot alone put African agriculture back onto a growth path. The study highlights the diversity of country circumstances and the importance of understanding individual countries' specific endowments, long-term processes of development, and needs, to which reform and investment packages must be tailored if they are to have sustainable positive effects. Unless the growing tendency of Africa's multilateral donors to "call the shots" on recipients' policies is accompanied by better and more consistent help with building indigenous capacity for development planning and implementation, the gains made under structural adjustment will not be maintained. In this context it will be necessary to reinstate aid at the level of projects and subsectors in its essential role as a catalyst of development, within the context of appropriately funded and targeted sector and macroeconomic policies.
3. The desirability of reviving production of traditional food and export crops in which African countries still have a clear comparative advantage. More research is needed on export crops, as a complement to, for example, the currently exclusive focus on foodcrops of the Consultative Group for International Agricultural Research.
4. The danger of relying on privatization to solve fiscal imbalances, and the need for effective actions by the public sector, especially in research, infrastructure, and information networks, to provide the preconditions for successful privatization and for smallholder agricultural growth.

NOTES

1. See Ajay Chhibber, "Raising Agricultural Output: Price and Nonprice Factors," *Finance and Development,* June 1988.

2. See Julian Blackwood, "World Bank Experience with Rural Development," *Finance and Development*, December 1988.

Name Index

Subject Index

Afghanistan, 329

Africa, 131, 132, 402, 440–41, 503–530, 531–39; agricultural development management in, 531–39; agricultural development strategies for, 85–86, 440, 511–27, 531–38; agricultural research in, 394–95, 504, 515–16, 538; donors of developmental aid in, 534–37; export crops in, 523–24, 532, 535–36, 538; food battles in, 440, 503–30; food production in, 142, 202–3, 533–34; food security policies in, 113, 119, 120, 133–34, 522–25; foreign aid flows to, 534–35; Green Revolution in, 10, 259 n. 11, 505, 515; favorable and marginal areas in, 518, 536–37; farming systems research in, 386; irrigation in, 511–12; malnutrition and poverty in, 506, 522; prime movers of agricultural development in, 519–22, 535–39; research needs of, 510, 511, 516–17; resource-poor farmers in, 504–6, 522–23; rural stratification in, 505; scientific and institutional development in, 503–4; smallholder production in, 120, 254, 532, 533, 534; stock of improved technology in, 515–17, 534; structural adjustment policies in, 25, 437, 534; structure of landholdings in, 531–32; urban consumers in, 156, 157. *See also* West Africa

Agricultural development, 3–30, 41–45, 47–67, 70–86, 97–111; and access to food, 127–29; in China, 480–502; conservation model of, 90–91; diffusion model of, 7, 8, 9, 92–93; dual-sector models of, 4, 6, 12, 27, 41, 50; on food prices, effects of, 73; employment effects of, 72, 77–81; frontier model of, 89–90; and Green Revolution, 416–23; high-payoff input model of, 44, 93, 94, 104; in historical perspective, 3–37; induced innovation model of, 44–45, 97–112; "jump strategy" of, 51, 53–54; models of, 15–20, 89–96; and price policy, 160–67; prime movers of, 440, 519–22; and rural women, 290–308; strategies, 16, 21, 28, 63–67, 77–86, 127–29, 449–57; strategies for Africa, 85–86, 440, 511–27, 531–38; supply-side factors, 450–53; target rates of

growth in, 45; urban-industrial impact model of, 91–92

Agricultural development programs: basic need projects, 75; community development projects, 7–8, 20–21, 44; failings of, 72–73; integrated rural development (IRD) projects, 20, 75, 453–54, 514, 518; for women, 301–6

Agricultural policy: components of successful, 28; designing, 206–21; new macroeconomics of, 140–53; political framework for, 154–58; reforms, in China, 480–502; reforms, in the Soviet Union, 459–79

Agricultural production: choice of technique in, 215–16; in developing countries, 60–63; growth in, 262–65, 270, 272; of relative price changes, effect on, 177–85

Agricultural research: in Africa, 394–95, 504, 515–16, 538; and agricultural productivity, 372–74; in Asia, 429–30; beneficiaries of, 376, 377; and decentralization, 271–72, 273, 275, 276–77; in developing countries, 287–88, 377; economics of, 371–83; entrepreneurship in, 283–84, 380–81; expenditures on, 372–73; and farming systems research, 19, 256, 385, 390–92, 395; and incentives for researchers, 379; investment in, 9, 94, 95; in Latin America, 372, 375, 378, 379; organization of, 107, 377–80, 381, 382 n. 16; paying for, 374–77; and price distortions, 380; private-sector role in, 109, 375, 376, 430; public-sector role in, 377, 430; rate of return to investment in, 164, 255, 263, 373, 410; in small countries, 277; socialization of, 102, 105, 107; and sustainable agriculture, 401–3; and technological change, 102–4; timeframe for results of, 255, 521; in the United States, 103, 264, 267, 270–73, 274, 275–76, 377

Agricultural transformation, 47–69; policy approaches to, 50, 62–67; and population growth, 42–43; stages of, 41–43, 50–60

Algeria, 202, 342–43, 346, 352

Asia, 22, 42–43, 424–33; agricultural research in, 429–30; agriculture in, 22, 78, 424–33; and diminishing returns in agriculture,

544